EJB 3 in Action

EJB 3 in Action

DEBU PANDA
REZA RAHMAN
DEREK LANE

MANNING

Greenwich
(74° w. long.)

For online information and ordering of this and other Manning books, please go to www.manning.com. The publisher offers discounts on this book when ordered in quantity. For more information, please contact:

Special Sales Department
Manning Publications Co.
Sound View Court 3B   Fax: (609) 877-8256
Greenwich, CT 06830   Email: orders@manning.com

Manning Publications Co.   Copyeditor: Liz Welch
Sound View Court 3B   Typesetter: Denis Dalinnik
Greenwich, CT 06830   Cover designer: Leslie Haimes

ISBN 1-933988-34-7

Second, corrected printing, June 2007

Printed in the United States of America
 2 3 4 5 6 7 8 9 10 – MAL – 11 10 09 08 07

To my wife Renuka, without whose encouragement and support
this book would not have seen light
and to Nistha and Nisheet, who sacrificed more than a year
of their childhood while I worked on the book

—D.P.

To my loving wife Nicole, for her enduring patience and unwavering support

—R.R.

To my Dad, for always helping me keep things in perspective

—D.L.

brief contents

vii

contents

preface

In its early days, EJB was inspired by the distributed computing ideas of technologies such as CORBA and was intended to add scalability to server-side applications. EJB and J2EE enjoyed some of the greatest buzz in the industry during the dot.com boom.

The initial goal for EJB was to provide a simpler alternative to CORBA through components and framework benefits—but the component benefits were oversold. By the time EJB 2 was released, it became apparent that EJB could be used as a framework to make server-side development easier—but it was complicated. It became a heavy framework that provided features such as remoting, transaction management, security, state maintenance, persistence, and web services. It was loaded with more features with each release, and while the development tools matured, its inventors failed to address the growing complexity.

As the community became disenchanted with the limitations of EJB 2, innovative open source tools like Spring and Hibernate emerged. They, along with the creeping dominance of Microsoft.NET and the rise of scripting frameworks like Ruby on Rails, were signs of the increasing discontent with the complexities of Java. It was time for JCP and expert groups to work on the simplification of Java development. That was the sole motivation behind Java EE 5 and the goal of the EJB 3 Expert through Group.

For a technology with a wide deployment base, the changes to EJB 3 are nothing short of stunning. EJB 3 successfully melds innovative techniques to make component development as easy as possible. These techniques include Java 5 annotations, metadata programming, dependency injection, AspectJ-like interceptors, as well as intelligent defaulting. The heavyweight inheritance-based programming model was abandoned in favor of POJO programming and the verbose XML descriptor was now out of the developer's way.

The changes to the persistence model were particularly dramatic. EJB 3 leaves behind the flawed Entity Beans model in favor of the lightweight Java Persistence API (JPA). Unlike Entity Beans, JPA is not container-based. It has more in common with Object Relational Mapping tools such as Hibernate, Oracle TopLink, and JDO than it does with EJB2 CMP Entity Beans. It can be used either inside or outside the container and aims to become the de-facto persistence standard for Java. Its Java Persistence Query Language (JPQL) standardizes object relational queries and supports native SQL queries.

We liked the changes made in EJB 3. The simplification of the EJB 3 specification has been well received in the Java community. Even the competing Spring framework has integrated with JPA and is implementing some features of EJB 3.

Since EJB is POJO-based, every Java developer can easily become an EJB developer! We felt the need for an EJB 3 book that presents the technology with a fresh approach without too much legacy EJB 2. Together, the three of us have significant experience using EJB 3, ORM, and lightweight frameworks like Spring. We have strived to keep our book different from other books on EJB 2 and EJB 3 by providing practical examples, best practices, and tips for performance tuning. We do not overlook the case made for competing frameworks such as Spring and do not hesitate to recommend them when these frameworks make sense. In fact, we have dedicated a complete chapter on the interoperability of Spring with EJB 3.

We hope that you can use this book to quickly learn how to use EJB 3 effectively in your next enterprise applications.

acknowledgments

Authoring a book requires great effort and it is difficult to list everyone who helped us during this project. First and foremost we would like to thank everyone at Manning, especially publisher Marjan Bace and development editor Jackie Carter, for their encouragement and support during the past year. We would also like to thank others at Manning who worked on different stages of the project: editors Lianna Wlasiuk and Betsey Henkels, review editor Karen Tegtmayer, and project editor Mary Piergies. Our sincere thanks also to King Wang of Oracle who performed the technical review of the book before it went to press, to Liz Welch who copyedited our prose, and to typesetter Denis Dalinnik who converted our Word documents into a real book!

Many reviewers spent their valuable time reading the manuscript at various stages of development and their feedback greatly improved the quality of the book. They are Glenn Stokol, Deiveehan Nallazhagappan, Peter George, Berndt Hamboeck, Pat Dennis, Vincent Yin, Thomas Scheuchzer, Chuk Munn, TVS Murthy, Norman Richards, Eric Raymond, Rob Abbe, Bas Vodde, Awais Bajwa, Kunal Mittal, Riccardo Audano, Dan Dobrin, King Wang, Alan Mackenzie, Deren Ebdon, Andrus Adamchik, Matt Payne, Vinny Carpenter, Alex Pantaleev, and Chris Richardson. Finally we would like to thank Micah Silverman who initiated this project but could not stay involved due to lack of time.

DEBU PANDA

I would like to thank my wife, Renuka, for her immense support and continuous encouragement and for her patience with all the late-night, early-morning, and weekend hours I spent on the book in the past 16 months. I would also like to thank my kids, Nistha and Nisheet, who had to share their *bapa* with the computer.

I would like to thank my in-laws, Hari Shankar Mishra and Premsila Mishra, who took care of the children, helping me to focus on the book. Thanks also to my parents, Ganga Narayan and Ratnamani Panda, for developing my interest in writing.

Many thanks to Mike Lehmann, Director of Product Management and Steve G. Harris, Vice President of Oracle Application Server Development for allowing me to fit this book into my busy schedule, and for their constant encouragement. Thanks to Robert Campbell, Jason Haley, and the entire EJB Container and TopLink development team at Oracle for quickly addressing product issues that helped me to build code samples before the EJB 3 specification was finalized. I would also like to thank King Wang for agreeing to be the technical editor of the book and for his help in fixing the errors in our code examples.

My special thanks to my previous manger Rob Clark who encouraged me to venture into the world of blogging and evangelizing that helped me gain recognition in the Java community.

Finally, I would like to thank my coauthors Reza Rahman and Derek Lane for their hard work and dedication in transforming my drafts into a great book.

REZA RAHMAN

I am grateful to my family, friends, and colleagues for supporting me throughout the arduous task of writing this book. I am thankful to my mentors Jason Hughes at Fry Communications, Narayan Natarajan at Accenture, and Rob Collier at Accenture for their guidance and encouragement. It is your hard work over the past few years that inspired me to take on this project. Words cannot do justice to the spirited help provided by Ray Case on chapters 6 and 7. Thank you my friend, and I hope your family works through the turbulent waters you are navigating right now.

Editor Betsey Henkels deserves special thanks for giving us leeway to experiment in the early stages and to distill our ideas. I am grateful to Debu Panda for his leadership, humility, and foresight. Thanks to Derek Lane for his sincere and much needed efforts. Last but not least, I am grateful to Marjan Bace, Jackie Carter, and the entire team at Manning for seeing the value in this book, for all the back-breaking work on their part, for demanding nothing short of the best from us, and for being patient through the tough moments.

DEREK LANE

I would like to thank the Manning team and Jackie Carter for asking me to be a part of this project. Thanks also to Debu Panda and Reza Rahman for the tremendous amount of work they put into the book.

I am amazed and grateful for the work done by the reviewers of our book, whose names are listed above. Many of them read the manuscript several times at different stages of development and offered detailed suggestions and guidance. A special word of thanks goes to Craig Walls, who took precious time away from working on the second edition of *Spring in Action*, to provide a much needed sounding board for some of the more advanced sections of this book. Reviewers rarely get the full credit they deserve, yet they represent the interests of you, our readers, during the writing process. Having been a reviewer on numerous works myself, I fully appreciate their remarkable efforts.

about this book

EJB 3 is meant to recast Java server-side development into a mold you might not expect. And so have we tried to make this an EJB book you might not anticipate.

Most server-side Java books tend to be serious affairs—heavy on theory, slightly preachy, and geared toward the advanced developer. Nine out of ten EJB 2.x books follow this pattern. While we easily fit the stereotype of geeks and aren't the funniest comedians or entertainers, we have tried to add some color to our writing to keep this book as lighthearted and down-to-earth as possible. The tone is intended to be friendly, conversational, and informal. We made a conscious effort to drive the chapter content with examples that are close to the real world problems you deal with every day. In most cases, we introduce a problem that needs to be solved, show you the code to solve it using EJB 3, and explore features of the technology using the code as a crutch.

We do cover theory when it is unavoidable and we don't assume that you have a Ph.D. in computer science. We try to avoid theory for theory's sake and try to make the discussion as lively, and short, as we can make it. The goal of this book is to help you learn EJB 3 quickly and effectively, not to be a comprehensive reference book. We don't cover features you are unlikely to use. Instead, we provide deep coverage of the most useful EJB 3 features, discuss various options so you can make educated choices, warn you about common pitfalls, and tell you about battle-hardened best practices.

If you've picked up this book, it is unlikely you are a complete newcomer to Java. We assume you've done some work in Java, perhaps in the form of web development using a presentation tier technology like JSF, Struts, JSP, or Servlets. If you come from the client-side end of the spectrum using technologies like Swing and AWT, don't worry. A web development background isn't a requirement for EJB. We do assume you are familiar with database technologies such as JDBC, and have at least a casual familiarity with SQL. We don't assume you are familiar with middleware-centric technologies like Spring, Hibernate, TopLink, JDO, iBA-TIS, or AspectJ. You don't need to be an EJB 2.x expert to pick up this book. We don't even assume you know any of the Java EE technologies that EJB is dependent on, such as the Java Naming and Directory Interface (JNDI), Java Remote Method Invocation (RMI), or the Java Messaging Service (JMS). In fact, we assume you are not familiar with middleware concepts like remoting, pooling, concurrent programming, security, or distributed transactions. This book is ideally suited for a Java developer with a couple of years' experience who is curious about EJB 3. By the same token, there is enough depth here to keep an EJB 2.x or Spring/Hibernate veteran engaged. Familiar material is placed in a logical sequence so that it can easily be skipped.

You might find this book different from others in one more important way. EJB is a server-side middleware technology. This means that it doesn't live in a vacuum and must be integrated with other technologies to fulfill its mission. Throughout the book, we talk about how EJB 3 integrates with technologies like JSF, JSP, Servlets, Ajax, and even Swing-based Java SE clients. We also talk about how EJB 3 aligns with complementary technologies like Spring.

This book is about EJB 3 as a standard, not a specific application server technology. For this reason, we will avoid tying our discussion around any specific application server implementation. Instead, the code samples in this book are designed to run with any EJB 3 container or persistence provider. The website accompanying this book at www.manning.com/panda will tell you how you can get the code up and running in GlassFish and Oracle Application Server 10g. Maintaining the application server-specific instructions on the publisher's website instead of in the book will allow us to keep the instructions up-to-date with the newest implementation details.

Roadmap

This book is divided into five parts.

Part 1 provides an overview of EJB. Chapter 1 introduces EJB 3 and EJB types and makes the case for EJB 3. Chapter 2 explores core concepts such as metadata annotations, dependency injection, and provides code examples of each EJB type.

Part 2 covers the building of business logic with session beans and MDB. Chapter 3 dives into the details of session beans and outlines best practices. Chapter 4 gives a quick introduction to messaging, JMS, and covers MDB in detail. Chapter 5 covers advanced topics such as dependency injection, interceptors, and timers. Chapter 6 discusses transaction and security.

Part 3 provides in-depth coverage of the EJB 3 Java Persistence API. Chapter 7 introduces concepts on domain modeling and describes implementing domain models with JPA. Chapter 8 covers object-relational mapping with JPA. Chapter 9 provides in-depth coverage manipulating entities using EntityManager API. Chapter 10 covers querying entities using Query API and JPQL.

Part 4 provides guidelines for effectively using EJB 3 in your enterprise applications. Chapter 11 discusses packaging of EJBs and entities. It introduces all XML descriptors. Chapter 12 covers using EJB 3 design patterns and JPA from other application tiers. Chapter 13 turns to advanced topics such as entity locking and performance tuning of EJB 3 applications.

Part 5 looks at interoperability and integration issues with EJB 3 and other frameworks. Chapter 14 covers interoperability with EJB 2 and migration of EJB 2 applications to EJB 3. Chapter 15 introduces web services and discusses web services applications with EJB 3 and JAX WS 2.0. Chapter 16 uncovers how you can integrate EJB 3 with the Spring framework to build great enterprise applications.

The book has five appendixes. Appendix A is a tutorial on JNDI and RMI and appendix B provides a primer to databases. Appendixes C and D cover references to annotations and XML descriptors. We also provide instructions on how to install and configure Java EE RI (Glassfish) and how to deploy the code samples in appendix E.

Source Code Downloads

In addition to the setup instructions for the Java EE 5 Reference Implementation server based on Glassfish and the Oracle Application Server, the publisher's website houses all of the source code presented in this book. The source code for each chapter is downloadable as a separate zip file, each one containing instructions on how to deploy the code to an application server and get it running. You can download the code from the book's web page: www.manning.com/panda or www.manning.com/EJB3inAction.

Source Code Conventions

Because of the example-driven style of this book, the source code was given a great deal of attention. Larger sections of code in the chapters are presented as their own listings. All code is formatted using the fixed-width `Courier` font for visibility. All inside code, such as XML element names, method names, Java type names, package names, variable names, and so on are also formatted using the `Courier` font. Some code is formatted as **`Courier Bold`** to highlight important sections. In some cases, we've abbreviated the code to keep it short and simple. In all cases, the full version of the abbreviated code is contained in the downloadable zip files. We encourage you to set up your development environment for each chapter before you begin reading it. The setup instructions for the development environment are also included on the website.

Author Online

Purchase of *EJB 3 in Action* includes free access to a private web forum run by Manning Publications where you can make comments about the book, ask technical questions, and receive help from the authors and from other users. To access the forum and subscribe to it, point your web browser to www.manning.com/panda. This page provides information on how to get on the forum once you are registered, what kind of help is available, and the rules of conduct on the forum.

Manning's commitment to our readers is to provide a venue where a meaningful dialog between individual readers and between readers and the author can take place. It is not a commitment to any specific amount of participation on the part of the authors, whose contribution to the AO remains voluntary (and unpaid). We suggest you try asking the authors some challenging questions, lest their interest stray!

The Author Online forum and the archives of previous discussions will be accessible from the publisher's website as long as the book is in print.

About the Authors

DEBU PANDA is a Lead Product Manager of the Oracle Application Server development team where he drives development of the Java EE container. He has more than 15 years of experience in the IT industry and has published numerous articles on enterprise Java technologies in several magazines and has presented at many conferences. His J2EE-focused weblog can be found at debupanda.com.

REZA RAHMAN is an architect at Tripod Technologies. Reza has been working with Java EE since its inception in the mid-nineties. He has developed enterprise systems in the publishing, financial, telecommunications, and manufacturing industries and has worked with Enterprise Java Beans, Spring, and Hibernate.

DEREK LANE is the CTO for Semantra, Inc. He has over 20 years' experience in the IT arena. He is the founder of both the Dallas/Fort Worth, Texas MicroJava User Group and the Oklahoma City Java User Groups, and is active in numerous technology groups in the southwestern United States.

About the Title

By combining introductions, overviews, and how-to examples, the *In Action* books are designed to help learning *and* remembering. According to research in cognitive science, the things people remember are things they discover during self-motivated exploration.

Although no one at Manning is a cognitive scientist, we are convinced that for learning to become permanent it must pass through stages of exploration, play, and, interestingly, re-telling of what is being learned. People understand and remember new things, which is to say they master them, only after actively exploring them. Humans learn *in action*. An essential part of an *In Action* guide is that it is example-driven. It encourages the reader to try things out, to play with new code, and explore new ideas.

There is another, more mundane, reason for the title of this book: our readers are busy. They use books to do a job or solve a problem. They need books that allow them to jump in and jump out easily and learn just what they want just when they want it. They need books that aid them *in action*. The books in this series are designed for such readers.

About the Cover Illustration

The figure on the cover of *EJB 3 in Action* is a "Russian Girl with Fur," taken from a French travel book, *Encyclopedie des Voyages* by J. G. St. Saveur, published in 1796. Travel for pleasure was a relatively new phenomenon at the time and travel guides such as this one were popular, introducing both the tourist as well as the armchair traveler to the inhabitants of other regions of France and abroad.

The diversity of the drawings in the *Encyclopedie des Voyages* speaks vividly of the uniqueness and individuality of the world's towns and provinces just 200 years ago. This was a time when the dress codes of two regions separated by a few dozen miles identified people uniquely as belonging to one or the other. The travel guide brings to life a sense of isolation and distance of that period and of every other historic period except our own hyperkinetic present.

Dress codes have changed since then and the diversity by region, so rich at the time, has faded away. It is now often hard to tell the inhabitant of one continent from another. Perhaps, trying to view it optimistically, we have traded a cultural and visual diversity for a more varied personal life. Or a more varied and interesting intellectual and technical life.

We at Manning celebrate the inventiveness, the initiative, and the fun of the computer business with book covers based on the rich diversity of regional life two centuries ago brought back to life by the pictures from this travel guide.

Part 1

Overview of the EJB landscape

This book is about EJB 3, the shiny new version of the Enterprise Java-Beans standard. The timely rebirth of EJB is made possible through innovations introduced in Java SE 5, such as metadata annotations as well as the adoption of ideas like dependency injection and object-relational mapping (ORM)-based persistence.

Chapter 1 introduces EJB as a technology. The chapter also touches on the unique strengths EJB has as a development platform and the great new features that promote productivity and ease of use. Chapter 2 provides realistic code samples and presents the ActionBazaar application, the imaginary enterprise system developed throughout the book. Chapter 2 is easily the most code-intensive chapter in the book. Our goal is to give you a feel for how EJB 3 looks as quickly and as easily as possible.

This part presents EJB 3 as a powerful and highly usable platform worth its place as the de facto standard for mission-critical enterprise development. We also offer a first glimpse into the impressive Java Persistence API, a promising technology that aims to standardize Java ORM and expand EJB 3 beyond the traditional boundaries of web-based client-server applications managed by containers.

What's what in EJB 3

This chapter covers

- EJB as component and framework
- Types of EJBs
- EJB containers and persistence provider
- Reasons for choosing EJB 3

One day, when God was looking over his creatures, he noticed a boy named Sadhu whose humor and cleverness pleased him. God felt generous that day and granted Sadhu three wishes. Sadhu asked for three reincarnations—one as a ladybug, one as an elephant, and the last as a cow. Surprised by these wishes, God asked Sadhu to explain himself. The boy replied, "I want to be a ladybug so that everyone in the world will admire me for my beauty and forgive the fact that I do no work. Being an elephant will be fun because I can gobble down enormous amounts of food without being ridiculed. I will like being a cow the best because I will be loved by all and useful to mankind." God was charmed by these answers and allowed Sadhu to live through the three incarnations. He then made Sadhu a morning star for his service to humankind as a cow.

EJB too has lived through three incarnations. When it was first released, the industry was dazzled by its innovations. But like the ladybug, EJB 1 had limited functionality. The second EJB incarnation was just about as heavy as the largest of our beloved pachyderms. The brave souls who could not do without its elephant power had to tame the awesome complexity of EJB 2. And finally, in its third incarnation, EJB has become much more useful to the huddled masses, just like the gentle bovine that is sacred for Hindus and respected as a mother whose milk feeds us well.

Many people have put in a lot of hard work to make EJB 3 as simple and lightweight as possible without sacrificing enterprise-ready power. EJB components are now little more than plain old Java objects (POJOs) that look a lot like code in a Hello World program. We hope you agree with us as you read through the next chapters that EJB 3 has all the makings of a star.

We've strived to keep this book as practical as possible without skimping on content. The book is designed to help you learn EJB 3 as quickly and easily as possible. At the same time, we won't neglect the basics where needed. We'll also dive into deep waters with you where we can, share with you all the amazing sights we've discovered, and warn you about any lurking dangers.

This book is about the radical transformation of an important and uniquely influential technology in the Java world. We suspect you are not picking this book up to learn too much about EJB 2. You probably either already know EJB or are completely new to the world of EJB. In either case, spending too much time on previous versions is a waste of your time—you won't be surprised to learn that EJB 3 and EJB 2 have very little in common. If you are curious about the journey that brought us to the current point, we encourage you to pick up one of the many good books on the previous versions of EJB.

Our goal in this chapter is to tell you what's what in EJB 3, explain why you should consider using it, and, for EJB 2 veterans, outline the significant improvements the newest version offers. We'll then jump right into code in the next chapter to build on the momentum of this one. With these goals in mind, let's now start with a broad overview of EJB.

1.1 EJB overview

In very straightforward terms, Enterprise JavaBeans (EJB) is a platform for building portable, reusable, and scalable business applications using the Java programming language. Since its initial incarnation, EJB has been touted as a component model or framework that lets you build enterprise Java applications without having to reinvent services such as transactions, security, automated persistence, and so on that you may need for building an application. EJB allows application developers to focus on building business logic without having to spend time on building infrastructure code.

From a developer's point of view, an EJB is a piece of Java code that executes in a specialized runtime environment called the *EJB container*, which provides a number of component services. The persistence services are provided by a specialized framework called the *persistence provider*. We'll talk more about the EJB container, persistence provider, and services in section 1.3.

In this section, you'll learn how EJB functions as both a component and a framework. We'll also examine how EJB lends itself to building layered applications. We'll round off this section by listing a few reasons why EJB might be right for you.

1.1.1 EJB as a component

In this book, when we talk about EJBs, we are referring to the server-side *components* that you can use to build parts of your application, such as the business logic or persistence code. Many of us tend to associate the term *component* with developing complex and heavyweight CORBA, Microsoft COM+ code. In the brave new world of EJB 3, a component is what it ought to be—nothing more than a POJO with some special powers. More importantly, these powers remain invisible until they are needed and don't distract from the real purpose of the component. You will see this firsthand throughout this book, especially starting with chapter 2.

The real idea behind a component is that it should effectively encapsulate application behavior. The users of a component aren't required to know its inner workings. All they need to know is what to pass in and what to expect back.

There are three types of EJB components: session beans, message-driven beans, and entities. Session beans and message-driven beans are used to implement business logic in an EJB application, and entities are used for persistence.

Components can be reusable. For instance, suppose you're in charge of building a website for an online merchant that sells technology books. You implement a module to charge the credit card as part of a regular Java object. Your company does fairly well, and you move on to greener pastures. The company then decides to diversify and begins developing a website for selling CDs and DVDs. Since the deployment environment for the new site is different, it can't be located on the same server as your module. The person building the new site is forced to duplicate your credit card module in the new website because there's no easy way to access your module. If you had instead implemented the credit card–charging module as an EJB component as shown in figure 1.1 (or as a web service), it would have been much easier for the new person to access it by simply making a call to it when she needed that functionality. She could have reused it without having to understand its implementation.

Given that, building a reusable component requires careful planning because, across enterprise applications within an organization, very little of the business logic may be reusable. Therefore, you may not care about the reusability of EJB components, but EJB still has much to offer as a framework, as you'll discover in the next section.

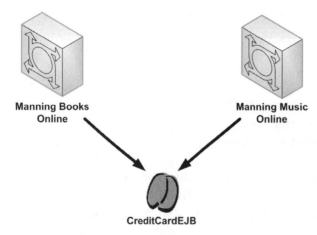

Manning Books
Online

Manning Music
Online

CreditCardEJB

Figure 1.1
EJB allows development of reusable components. For example, you can implement the credit card–charging module as an EJB component that may be accessed by multiple applications.

1.1.2 *EJB as a framework*

As we mentioned, EJB components live in a container. Together, the components, or EJBs, and the container can be viewed as a framework that provides valuable services for enterprise application development.

Although many people think EJBs are overkill for developing relatively simple web applications of moderate size, nothing could be further from the truth. When you build a house, you don't build everything from scratch. Instead, you buy materials or even the services of a contractor as you need it. It isn't too practical to build an enterprise application from scratch either. Most server-side applications have a lot in common, including churning business logic, managing application state, storing and retrieving information from a relational database, managing transactions, implementing security, performing asynchronous processing, integrating systems, and so on.

As a framework, the EJB container provides these kinds of common functionality as out-of-the-box *services* so that your EJB components can use them in your applications without reinventing the wheel. For instance, let's say that when you built the credit card module in your web application, you wrote a lot of complex and error-prone code to manage transactions and security access control. You could have avoided that by using the declarative transaction and security services provided by the EJB container. These services, as well as many others you'll learn about in section 1.3, are available to the EJB components when they are deployed in the EJB container, as you can see in figure 1.2. This means writing high-quality, feature-rich applications much faster than you might think.

The container provides the services to the EJB components in a rather elegant new way: metadata annotations are used to preconfigure the EJBs by specifying the type of services to add when the container deploys the EJBs. Java 5 introduced

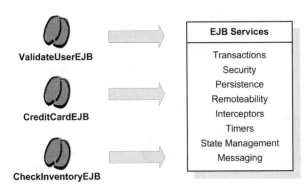

ValidateUserEJB

CreditCardEJB

CheckInventoryEJB

EJB Services

Transactions
Security
Persistence
Remoteability
Interceptors
Timers
State Management
Messaging

Figure 1.2
EJB as a framework provides services to EJB components.

metadata annotations, which are property settings that mark a piece of code, such as a class or method, as having particular attributes. This is a declarative style of programming, in which the developer specifies what should be done and the system adds the code to do it.

In EJB, metadata annotations dramatically simplify development and testing of applications, without having to depend on an external XML configuration file. It allows developers to declaratively add services to EJB components as and when they need. As figure 1.3 depicts, an annotation transforms a simple POJO into an EJB.

As you'll learn, annotations are used extensively throughout EJB, and not only to specify services. For example, an annotation can be used to specify the type of the EJB component.

Although it's sometimes easy to forget, enterprise applications have one more thing in common with a house. Both are meant to last, often much longer than anyone expects. Being able to support high-performance, fault-tolerant, scalable applications is an up-front concern for the EJB platform instead of being an afterthought. Not only will you be writing good server-side applications faster, but also you can expect your platform to grow with the success of your application. When the need to support a larger number of users becomes a reality, you won't have to rewrite your code. Thankfully these concerns are taken care of by EJB container vendors. You'll be able to count on moving your application to a distributed, clustered server farm by doing nothing more than a bit of configuration.

Last, but certainly not least, with a world that's crazy about service-oriented architecture (SOA) and interoperability, EJB lets you turn your application into a web services powerhouse with ease when you need to.

The EJB framework is a standard Java technology with an open specification. If it catches your fancy, you can check out the real deal on the Java Community Process (JCP) website at www.jcp.org/en/jsr/detail?id=220. EJB is supported by a large number of companies and open source groups with competing but compatible implementations. On the one hand, this indicates that a large group of people will work hard to keep EJB competitive. On the other hand, the ease of portability

POJO　　　　　Annotation　　　　　EJB

Figure 1.3
EJBs are regular Java objects that may be configured using metadata annotations.

means that you get to choose what implementation suits you best, making your application portable across EJB containers from different vendors.

Now that we've provided a high-level introduction to EJB, let's turn our attention to how EJB can be used to build layered applications.

1.1.3 Layered architectures and EJB

Most enterprise applications contain a large number of components. Enterprise applications are designed to solve a unique type of customer problem, but they share many common characteristics. For example, most enterprise applications have some kind of user interface and they implement business processes, model a problem domain, and save data into a database. Because of these commonalities, you can a follow a common architecture or design principle for building enterprise applications known as *patterns*.

For server-side development, the dominant pattern is *layered architectures*. In a layered architecture, components are grouped into tiers. Each tier in the application has a well-defined purpose, sort of like a profession but more like a section of a factory assembly line. Each section of the assembly line performs its designated task and passes the remaining work down the line. In layered architectures, each layer delegates work to a layer underneath it.

EJB allows you to build applications using two different layered architectures: the traditional four-tier architecture and domain-driven design (DDD). Let's take a brief look at each of these architectures.

Traditional four-tier layered architecture

Figure 1.4 shows the traditional four-tier server architecture. This architecture is pretty intuitive and enjoys a wide popularity. In this architecture, the *presentation layer* is responsible for rendering the graphical user interface (GUI) and handling user input. The presentation layer passes down each request for application functionality to the business logic layer. The *business logic layer* is the heart of the application and contains workflow and processing logic. In other words, business logic layer components model distinct actions or processes the application can perform, such as billing, searching, ordering, and user account maintenance. The business logic layer retrieves data from and saves data into the database by utilizing the persistence tier. The *persistence layer* provides a high-level object-oriented (OO) abstraction over the database layer. The *database layer* typically consists of a relational database management system (RDBMS) like Oracle, DB2, or SQL Server.

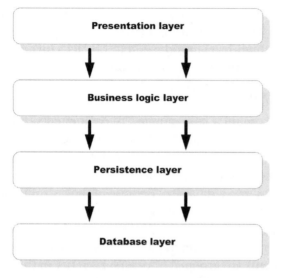

Figure 1.4
Most traditional enterprise applications have at least four layers. 1) The presentation layer is the actual user interface and can either be a browser or a desktop application. 2) The business logic layer defines the business rules. 3) The persistence layer deals with interactions with the database. 4) The database layer consists of a relational database such as Oracle that stores the persistent objects.

EJB is obviously not a presentation layer technology. EJB is all about robust support for implementing the business logic and persistence layers. Figure 1.5 shows how EJB supports these layers via its services.

In section 1.3 we'll go into more detail on EJB services. And in section 1.2 we'll explore EJB bean types. For now, just note that the bean types called session beans and message-driven beans (MDBs) reside in and use the services in the

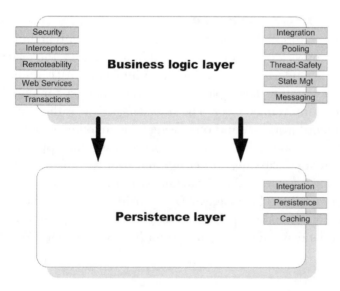

Figure 1.5
The component services offered by EJB 3 at each supported application layer. Note that each service is independent of the other, so you are for the most part free to pick the features important for your application. You'll learn more about services in section 1.3.

business logic tier, and the bean types called entities reside in and use services in the persistence tier.

The traditional four-tier layered architecture is not perfect. One of the most common criticisms is that it undermines the OO ideal of modeling the business domain as objects that encapsulate both data and behavior. Because the traditional architecture focuses on modeling business processes instead of the domain, the business logic tier tends to look more like a database-driven procedural application than an OO one. Since persistence-tier components are simple data holders, they look a lot like database record definitions rather than first-class citizens of the OO world. As you'll see in the next section, DDD proposes an alternative architecture that attempts to solve these perceived problems.

Domain-driven design

The term *domain-driven design* (DDD) may be relatively new but the concept is not (see *Domain-Driven Design: Tackling Complexity in the Heart of Software*, by Eric Evans [Addison-Wesley Professional, 2003]). DDD emphasizes that domain *objects* should contain business logic and should not just be a dumb replica of database records. Domain objects are known as entities in EJB 3 (see section 1.2 for a discussion on entities). With DDD, the `Catalog` and `Customer` objects in a trading application are typical examples of entities, and they may contain business logic.

In his excellent book *POJOs in Action* (Manning, 2006), author Chris Richardson points out the problem in using domain objects just as a data holder.

> Some developers still view persistent objects simply as a means to get data in and out of the database and write procedural business logic. They develop what Fowler calls an "anemic domain model".... Just as anemic blood lacks vitality, anemic object models only superficially model the problem and consist of classes that implement little or no behavior.

Yet, even though its value is clear, until this release of EJB, it was difficult to implement DDD. Chris goes on to explain how EJB 2 encouraged procedural code:

> ... J2EE developers write procedural-style code [because] it is encouraged by the EJB architecture, literature, and culture, which place great emphasis on EJB components. EJB 2 components are not suitable for implementing an object model.

Admittedly, implementing a real domain model was almost impossible with EJB 2 because beans were not POJOs and did not support many OO features. such as inheritance and polymorphism. Chris specifically targets entity beans as the problem:

EJB 2 entity beans, which are intended to represent business objects, have numerous limitations that make it extremely difficult to use them to implement a persistent object model.

The good news is that EJB 3 enables you to easily follow good object-oriented design or DDD. The entities defined by EJB 3 Java Persistence API (JPA) support OO features, such as inheritance or polymorphism. It's easy to implement a persistence object model with the EJB 3 JPA. More importantly, you can easily add business logic to your entities, so that implementing a rich domain model with EJB 3 is a trivial task.

Note, though, that many people don't like adding complex business logic in the domain object itself and prefer creating a layer for procedural logic referred to as the *service layer* or *application layer* (see *Patterns of Enterprise Application Architecture*, by Martin Fowler [Addison-Wesley Professional, 2002]). The application layer is similar to the business logic layer of the traditional four-tier architecture, but is much thinner. Not surprisingly, you can use session beans to build the service layer. Whether you use the traditional four-tier architecture or a layered architecture with DDD, you can use entities to model domain objects, including modeling state and behavior. We'll discuss domain modeling with JPA entities in chapter 7.

Despite its impressive services and vision, EJB 3 is not the only act in town. You can combine various technologies to more or less match EJB services and infrastructure. For example, you could use Spring with other open source technologies such as Hibernate and AspectJ to build your application, so why choose EJB 3? Glad you asked...

1.1.4 Why choose EJB 3?

At the beginning of this chapter, we hinted at EJB's status as a pioneering technology. EJB is a groundbreaking technology that has raised the standards of server-side development. Just like Java itself, EJB has changed things in ways that are here to stay and inspired many innovations. In fact, up until a few years ago the only serious competition to EJB came from the Microsoft .NET framework.

In this section, we'll point out a few of the compelling EJB 3 features that we feel certain will have this latest version at the top of your short list.

Ease of use

Thanks to the unwavering focus on ease of use, EJB 3 is probably the simplest server-side development platform around. The features that shine the brightest are POJO programming, annotations in favor of verbose XML, heavy use of sensible defaults, and JPA, all of which you will be learning about in this book. Although the number of EJB services is significant, you'll find them very intuitive. For the most part, EJB 3 has a practical outlook and doesn't demand that you understand the theoretical intricacies. In fact, most EJB services are designed to give you a break from this mode of thinking so you can focus on getting the job done and go home at the end of the day knowing you accomplished something.

Integrated solution stack

EJB 3 offers a complete stack of server solutions, including persistence, messaging, lightweight scheduling, remoting, web services, dependency injection (DI), and interceptors. This means that you won't have to spend a lot of time looking for third-party tools to integrate into your application. In addition, EJB 3 provides seamless integration with other Java EE technologies, such as JDBC, JavaMail, Java Transaction API JTA (JTA), Java Messaging Service (JMS), Java Authentication and Authorization Service (JAAS), Java Naming and Directory Interface (JNDI), Java Remote Method Invocation (RMI), and so on. EJB is also guaranteed to seamlessly integrate with presentation-tier technologies like JavaServer Pages (JSP), servlets, JavaServer Faces (JSF), and Swing.

Open Java EE standard

EJB is a critical part of the Java EE standard. This is an extremely important concept to grasp if you are to adopt EJB 3. EJB 3 has an open, public API specification, which organizations are encouraged to use to create a container or persistence provider implementation. The EJB 3 standard is developed by the Java Community Process (JCP), consisting of a nonexclusive group of individuals driving the Java standard. The open standard leads to broader vendor support for EJB 3, which means you don't have to depend on a proprietary solution.

Broad vendor support

EJB is supported by a large and diverse variety of independent organizations. This includes the technology world's largest, most respected, and most financially strong names, such as Oracle and IBM, as well as passionate and energetic open source groups like JBoss and Geronimo.

Wide vendor support translates to three important advantages for you. First, you are not at the mercy of the ups and downs of a particular company or group of people. Second, a lot of people have concrete long-term interests to keep the technology as competitive as possible. You can essentially count on being able to take advantage of the best-of-breed technologies both in and outside the Java world in a competitive timeframe. Third, vendors have historically competed against one another by providing value-added nonstandard features. All of these factors help keep EJB on the track of continuous healthy evolution.

Stable, high-quality code base

Although EJB 3 is a groundbreaking step, most application server implementations will still benefit from a relatively stable code base that has lived through some of the most demanding enterprise environments over a prolonged period of time. Most persistence provider solutions like JDO, Hibernate, and TopLink are also stable products that are being used in many mission-critical production environments. This means that although EJB 3 is very new, you can expect stable implementations relatively quickly. Also, because of the very nature of standards-based development, the quality of EJB 3 container implementations is generally not taken lightly by vendors. To some degree, this helps ensure a healthy level of inherent implementation quality.

Clustering, load balancing, and failover

Features historically added by most application server vendors are robust support for clustering, load balancing, and failover. EJB application servers have a proven track record of supporting some of the largest high-performance computing (HPC)-enabled server farm environments. More importantly, you can leverage such support with no changes to code, no third-party tool integration, and relatively simple configuration (beyond the inherent work in setting up a hardware cluster). This means that you can rely on hardware clustering to scale up your application with EJB 3 if you need to.

EJB 3 is a compelling option for building enterprise applications. In the following sections, we explain more about EJB types and how to use them. We also discuss containers and persistence providers and explore the services they provide. By the time you finish reading sections 1.2 and 1.3, you'll have a good idea of what EJBs are and where they run, and what services they offer. So let's get started!

1.2   Understanding EJB types

If you're like most developers, you always have a tight deadline to meet. Most of us try to beg, borrow, or steal reusable code to make our lives easier. Gone are those days when developers had the luxury to create their own infrastructure when building a commercial application. While several commercial and open source frameworks are available that can simplify application development, EJB is a compelling framework that has a lot to offer.

We expect that by now you're getting excited about EJB and you're eager to learn more. So let's jump right in and see how you can use EJB as a framework to build your business logic and persistence tier of your applications, starting with the beans.

In EJB-speak, a component is a "bean." If your manager doesn't find the Java-"coffee bean" play on words cute either, blame Sun's marketing department. Hey, at least we get to hear people in suits use the words "enterprise" and "bean" in close sequence as if it were perfectly normal...

As we mentioned, EJB classifies beans into three types, based on what they are used for:

- Session beans
- Message-driven beans
- Entities

Each bean type serves a purpose and can use a specific subset of EJB services. The real purpose of bean types is to safeguard against overloading them with services that cross wires. This is akin to making sure the accountant in the horn-rimmed glasses doesn't get too curious about what happens when you touch both ends of a car battery terminal at the same time. Bean classification also helps you understand and organize an application in a sensible way; for example, bean types help you develop applications based on a layered architecture.

As we've briefly mentioned, session beans and message-driven beans (MDBs) are used to build business logic, and they live in the *container*, which manages these beans and provides services to them. Entities are used to model the persistence part of an application. Like the container, it is the *persistence provider* that manages entities. A persistence provider is pluggable within the container and is abstracted behind the Java Persistence API (JPA). This organization of the EJB 3 API is shown in figure 1.6.

We'll discuss the container and the persistence provider in section 1.3. For the time being, all you need to know is that these are separate parts of an EJB implementation, each of which provide support for different EJB component types.

Let's start digging a little deeper into the various EJB component types, starting with session beans.

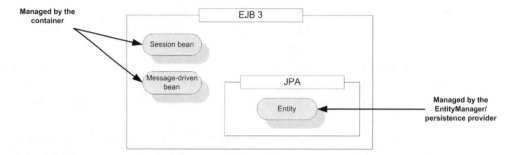

Figure 1.6   Overall organization of the EJB 3 API. The Java persistence API is completely separable from the EJB 3 container. The business logic processing is carried out by through two component types: session beans and message-driven beans. Both components are managed by the container. Persistence objects are called entities, which are managed by the persistent provider through the EntityManager interface.

1.2.1 *Session beans*

A session bean is invoked by a client for the purpose of performing a specific business operation, such as checking the credit history for a customer. The name *session* implies that a bean instance is available for the duration of a "unit of work" and does not survive a server crash or shutdown. A session bean can model any application logic functionality. There are two types of session beans: *stateful* and *stateless*.

A stateful session bean automatically saves bean state between client invocations without your having to write any additional code. A typical example of a state-aware process is the shopping cart for a web merchant like Amazon. In contrast, stateless session beans do not maintain any state and model application services that can be completed in a single client invocation. You could build stateless session beans for implementing business processes such as charging a credit card or checking customer credit history.

A session bean can be invoked either locally or remotely using Java RMI. A stateless session bean can be exposed as a web service.

1.2.2 *Message-driven beans*

Like session beans, MDBs process business logic. However, MDBs are different in one important way: clients never invoke MDB methods directly. Instead, MDBs are triggered by messages sent to a messaging server, which enables sending asynchronous messages between system components. Some typical examples of messaging servers are IBM WebSphere MQ, SonicMQ, Oracle Advanced Queueing, and TIBCO. MDBs are typically used for robust system integration or asynchronous processing. An example of messaging is sending an inventory-restocking request from an automated retail system to a supply-chain management system. Don't worry too much about messaging right now; we'll get to the details later in this book.

Next we'll explain the concept of persistence and describe how object-relational frameworks help enable automated persistence.

1.2.3 *Entities and the Java Persistence API*

One of the exciting new features of EJB 3 is the way it handles persistence. We briefly mentioned persistence providers and the JPA earlier, but now let's delve into the details.

Persistence is the ability to have data contained in Java objects automatically stored into a relational database like Oracle, SQL Server, and DB2. Persistence in EJB 3 is managed by the JPA. It automatically persists the Java objects using a technique called object-relational mapping (ORM). ORM is essentially the process of mapping data held in Java objects to database tables using configuration. It relieves you of the task of writing low-level, boring, and complex JDBC code to persist objects into a database.

The frameworks that provide ORM capability to perform automated persistence are known as ORM frameworks. As the name implies, an ORM framework performs transparent persistence by making use of object-relational mapping metadata that defines how objects are mapped to database tables. ORM is not a new concept and has been around for a while. Oracle TopLink is probably the oldest ORM framework in the market; open source framework JBoss Hibernate popularized ORM concepts among the mainstream developer community.

In EJB 3 terms, a persistence provider is essentially an ORM framework that supports the EJB 3 Java Persistence API (JPA). The JPA defines a standard for

- The creation of ORM configuration metadata for mapping entities to relational tables
- The EntityManager API—a standard API for performing CRUD (create, read, update, and delete)/persistence operations for entities
- The *Java Persistence Query Language* (JPQL), for searching and retrieving persisted application data

Since JPA standardizes ORM frameworks for the Java platform, you can plug in ORM products like JBoss Hibernate, Oracle TopLink, or BEA Kodo as the underlying JPA "persistence provider" for your application.

It may occur to you that automated persistence is something you'll find useful for all kinds of applications, not just server-side applications such as those built with EJB. After all, JDBC, the grandfather of JPA, is used in everything from large-scale real-time systems to desktop-based hacked-up prototypes. This is exactly why JPA is completely separate from the rest of EJB 3 and usable in plain Java SE environments.

Entities are the session bean and MDB equivalent in the JPA world. Let's take a quick glance at them next, as well as the `EntityManager` API and the Java Persistence Query Language (JPQL).

Entities

If you're using JPA to build persistence logic of your applications, then you have to use entities. Entities are the Java objects that are persisted into the database. Just as session beans model processes, entities model lower-level application concepts that high-level business processes manipulate. While session beans are the "verbs" of a system, entities are the "nouns." Examples include an `Employee` entity, a `User` entity, an `Item` entity, and so on. Here's another perfectly valid (and often simpler-to-understand) way of looking at entities: they are the OO representations of the application data stored in the database. In this sense, entities survive container crashes and shutdown. You must be wondering how the persistence provider knows where the entity will be stored. The real magic lies in the ORM metadata; an entity contains the data that specifies how it is mapped to the database. You'll see an example of this in the next chapter. JPA entities support a full range of relational and OO capabilities, including relationships between entities, inheritance, and polymorphism.

The EntityManager

The JPA `EntityManager` interface manages entities in terms of actually providing persistence services. While entities tell a JPA provider how they map to the database, they do not persist themselves. The `EntityManager` interface reads the ORM metadata for an entity and performs persistence operations. The `Entity-Manager` knows how to add entities to the database, update stored entities, and delete and retrieve entities from the database. In addition, the JPA provides the ability to handle lifecycle management, performance tuning, caching, and transaction management.

The Java Persistence Query Language

JPA provides a specialized SQL-like query language called the Java Persistence Query Language (JPQL) to search for entities saved into the database. With a robust and flexible API such as JPQL, you won't lose anything by choosing automated persistence instead of handwritten JDBC. In addition, JPA supports native, database-specific SQL, in the rare cases where it is worth using.

At this point, you should have a decent high-level view of the various parts of EJB. You also know that you need an EJB container to execute session beans and MDBs as well as a persistence provider to run your entities, so that these components can access the services EJB 3 provides. The container, the persistence provider, and the services are the central concepts in EJB 3, and we'll address them next.

1.3 *Getting inside EJB*

When you build a simple Java class, you need a Java Virtual Machine (JVM) to execute it. In a similar way (as you learned in the previous section) to execute session beans and MDBs you need an EJB container, and to run your entities you need a persistence provider. In this section we give you a bird's-eye view of containers and persistence providers and explain how they are related.

In the Java world, containers aren't just limited to the realm of EJB 3. You're probably familiar with a web container, which allows you to run web-based applications using Java technologies such as servlets, JSP, or JSF. A *Java EE container* is an application server solution that supports EJB 3, a web container, and other Java EE APIs and services. BEA WebLogic Server, Sun Microsystems's GlassFish, IBM WebSphere, JBoss Application Server, and Oracle Application Server 10*g* are examples of Java EE containers. The relationship between the Java EE container, web container, EJB container, and JPA persistence provider is shown in figure 1.7.

If you install a Java EE–compliant application server such as GlassFish, it will contain a preconfigured web container, EJB container, and a JPA provider. However, some vendors and open source projects may provide only a web container such as Tomcat or an EJB 3–compliant persistence provider such as Hibernate. These containers provide limited functionality compared to what you get with a complete Java EE 5 container.

In this section, we'll focus on how the EJB container and the persistence provider work, and we'll finish with a more complete discussion of EJB services. First, let's tackle the EJB container.

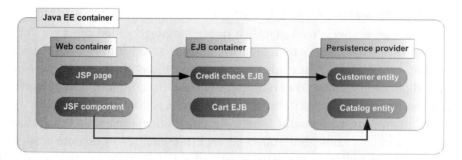

Figure 1.7   Java EE container typically contains web and EJB containers and a persistence provider. The stateless session bean (Credit Check EJB) and stateful session bean (Cart EJB) are deployed and run in the EJB container. Entities (Customer and Catalog) are deployed and run within an EJB persistence provider and can be accessed by either web or EJB container components.

1.3.1 *Accessing EJB services: the EJB container*

Think of the container as simply an extension of the basic idea of a JVM. Just as the JVM transparently manages memory on your behalf, the container transparently provides EJB component services such as transactions, security management, remoting, and web services support. As a matter of fact, you might even think of the container as a JVM on steroids, whose purpose is to execute EJBs. In EJB 3, the container provides services applicable to session beans and MDBs only. The task of putting an EJB 3 component inside a container is called *deployment*. Once an EJB is successfully deployed in a container, it can be used in your applications.

The persistence provider is the container counterpart in JPA. We'll briefly talk about it next.

1.3.2 *Accessing JPA services: the persistence provider*

In section 1.2.3, we mentioned that the persistence provider's job is to provide standardized JPA services. Let's explore how it does that. Instead of following the JVM-like container model, JPA follows a model similar to APIs, like JDBC. JPA provides persistence services such as retrieving, adding, modifying, and deleting JPA entities when you explicitly ask for them by invoking EntityManager API methods.

The "provider" terminology comes from APIs such as JDBC and JNDI too. If you've worked with JDBC, you know that a "provider" is essentially the vendor implementation that the JDBC API uses under the covers. Products that provide JPA implementation are *persistence providers* or *persistence engines*. JBoss Hibernate and Oracle TopLink are two popular JPA providers.

Since JPA is completely pluggable and separable, the persistence provider and container in an EJB 3 solution need not come from the same vendor. For example, you could use Hibernate inside a BEA WebLogic container if it suits you better, instead of the Kodo implementation WebLogic ships with.

But without services, what good are containers? In the next section, we explore the services concept critical to EJB.

1.3.3 *Gaining functionality with EJB services*

The first thing that should cross your mind while evaluating any technology is what it really gives you. What's so special about EJB? Beyond a presentation-layer technology like JSP, JSF, or Struts, couldn't you create your web application using just the Java language and maybe some APIs like JDBC for database access? The plain answer is that you could—if deadlines and cutthroat competition were not realities. Indeed, before anyone dreamed up EJB this is exactly what people did. What the resulting long hours proved is that you tend to spend a lot of time solving very common system-level problems instead of focusing on the real business solution. These bitter experiences emphasized the fact that there are common solutions that can be reused to solve common development problems. This is exactly what EJB brings to the table.

EJB is a collection of "canned" solutions to common server application development problems as well as a roadmap to common server component patterns. These "canned" solutions, or *services*, are provided by either the EJB container or the persistence provider. To access those services, you build the application components and deploy them into the container. Most of this book will be spent explaining how you can exploit EJB services.

In this section, we briefly introduce some of the services EJB offers. Obviously, we can't explain the implementation details of each service in this section. Neither is it necessary to cover every service EJB offers right now. Instead, we briefly list the major EJB 3 services in table 1.1 and explain what they mean to you from a practical perspective. This book shows you how to use each of the services shown in table 1.1 in your application.

Despite its robust features, one of the biggest beefs people had with EJB 2 was that it was too complex. It was clear that EJB 3 had to make development as simple as possible instead of just continuing to add additional features or services. If you have worked with EJB 2 or have simply heard or read that it is complex, you should be curious as to what makes EJB 3 different. Let's take a closer look.

Table 1.1   Major EJB 3 component services and why they are important to you. The persistence services are provided by the JPA provider.

Service	Applies To	What It Means for You
Integration	Session beans and MDBs	Helps glue together components, ideally through simple configuration instead of code. In EJB 3, this is done through dependency injection (DI) as well as lookup.
Pooling	Stateless session beans, MDBs	For each EJB component, the EJB platform creates a pool of component instances that are shared by clients. At any point in time, each pooled instance is only allowed to be used by a single client. As soon as an instance is finished servicing a client, it is returned to the pool for reuse instead of being frivolously discarded for the garbage collector to reclaim.
Thread-safety	Session beans and MDBs	EJB makes all components thread-safe and highly performant in ways that are completely invisible. This means that you can write your server components as if you were developing a single-threaded desktop application. It doesn't matter how complex the component itself is; EJB will make sure it is thread-safe.
State management	Stateful session beans	The EJB container manages state transparently for stateful components instead of having you write verbose and error-prone code for state management. This means that you can maintain state in instance variables as if you were developing a desktop application. EJB takes care of all the details of session maintenance behind the scenes.
Messaging	MDBs	EJB 3 allows you to write messaging-aware components without having to deal with a lot of the mechanical details of the Java Messaging Service (JMS) API.
Transactions	Session beans and MDB	EJB supports declarative transaction management that helps you add transactional behavior to components using simple configuration instead of code. In effect, you can designate any component method to be transactional. If the method completes normally, EJB commits the transaction and makes the data changes made by the method permanent. Otherwise the transaction is rolled back.
Security	Session beans	EJB supports integration with the Java Authentication and Authorization Service (JAAS) API, so it is very easy to completely externalize security and secure an application using simple configuration instead of cluttering up your application with security code.
Interceptors	Session beans and MDBs	EJB 3 introduces AOP in a very lightweight, accessible manner using *interceptors*. This allows you to easily separate out crosscutting concerns such as logging, auditing, and so on in a configurable way.
Remote access	Session beans	In EJB 3, you can make components remotely accessible without writing any code. In addition, EJB 3 enables client code to access remote components as if they were local components using DI.

continued on next page

Table 1.1   **Major EJB 3 component services and why they are important to you. The persistence services are provided by the JPA provider.** *(continued)*

Service	Applies To	What It Means for You
Web services	Stateless session beans	EJB 3 can transparently turn business components into robust web services with minimal code change.
Persistence	Entities	Providing standards-based, 100 percent configurable automated persistence as an alternative to verbose and error-prone JDBC/SQL code is a principal goal of the EJB 3 platform.
Caching and performance	Entities	In addition to automating persistence, JPA transparently provides a number of services geared toward data caching, performance optimization, and application tuning. These services are invaluable in supporting medium to large-scale systems.

1.4 *Renaissance of EJB*

Software is organic. Much like carbon-based life forms, software grows and evolves. Features die. New features are born. Release numbers keep adding up like the rings of a healthy tree. EJB is no exception to the rule of software evolution. In fact, as far as technologies go, the saga of EJB is more about change than it is about stagnation. Only a handful of other technologies can boast the robust metamorphosis and continuous improvements EJB has pulled off.

It's time to catch a glimpse of the new incarnation of EJB, starting with an example of a simple stateless session bean and then revealing the features changes that make EJB an easy-to-use development tool.

To explore the new features of EJB 3, we'll be pointing out some of the problems associated with EJB 2. If you are not familiar with EJB 2, don't worry—the important thing to remember is how the problems have been resolved in EJB 3.

The problems associated with EJB 2 have been widely discussed. In fact, there have been entire books, such as *Bitter EJB* (Manning Publications, 2003) written about this topic. Chris Richardson in *POJOs in Action* rightfully identified the amount of sheer code you had to write to build an EJB:

> You must write a lot of code to implement an EJB—You must write a home interface, a component interface, the bean class, and a deployment descriptor, which for an entity bean can be quite complex. In addition, you must write a number of boilerplate bean class methods that are never actually called but that are required by the interface the bean class implements. This code isn't conceptually difficult, but it is busywork that you must endure.

In this section, we'd like to walk through some of those points and show you how they have been resolved in EJB 3. As you will see, EJB 3 specifically targets the thorniest issues in EJB 2 and solves them primarily through bold adoption and clever adaptation of the techniques widely available in popular open source solutions such as Hibernate and Spring. Both of which have passed the "market incubation test" without getting too battered. In many ways, this release primes EJB for even further innovations by solving the most immediate problems and creating a buffer zone for the next metamorphosis.

But first, let's look at a bit of code. You will probably never use EJB 2 for building simple applications such as Hello World. However, we want to show you a simple EJB implementation of the ubiquitous Hello World developed using EJB 3. We want you to see this code for a couple reasons: first, to demonstrate how simple developing with EJB 3 really is, and second, because this will provide context for the discussions in the following sections and make them more concrete.

1.4.1 *HelloUser Example*

Hello World examples have ruled the world since they first appeared in *The C Programming Language* by Brian Kernighan and Dennis Ritchie (Prentice Hall PTR, 1988). Hello World caught on and held ground for good reason. It is very well suited to introducing a technology as simply and plainly as possible. While almost every technology book starts with a Hello World example, to keep things lively and relevant we plan to deviate from that rule and provide a slightly different example.

In 2004, one of the authors, Debu, wrote an article for the TheServerSide.com in which he stated that when EJB 3 was released, it would be so simple you could write a Hello World in it using only a few lines of code. Any experienced EJB 2 developer knows that this couldn't be accomplished easily in EJB 2. You had to write a home interface, a component interface, a bean class, and a deployment descriptor. Well, now that EJB 3 has been finalized, let's see if Debu was right in his prediction (listing 1.1).

Listing 1.1 HelloUser Session bean

```
   package ejb3inaction.example;
public interface HelloUser {        <--❶ HelloUser POJI
      public void sayHello(String name);
   }

   package ejb3inaction.example;
   import javax.ejb.Stateless;
```

```
@Stateless      <--●❷  Stateless annotation
public class HelloUserBean implements HelloUser {  <--●❸  HelloUserBean POJO
    public void sayHello(String name) {
        System.out.println("Hello " + name + " welcome to EJB 3!");
    }
}
```

Listing 1.1 is indeed a complete and self-contained example of a working EJB! Note that for simplicity we have kept both the interface and class as part of the same listing. As you can see, the EJB does not look much more complex than your first Java program. The interface is a plain old Java interface (POJI) ❶ and the bean class is a plain old Java object (POJO) ❸. The funny @Stateless symbol in listing 1.1 is a metadata annotation ❷ that converts the POJO to a full-powered stateless EJB. If you are not familiar with metadata annotations, we explore them in chapter 2. In effect, they are "comment-like" configuration information that can be added to Java code.

To execute this EJB, you have to deploy it to the EJB container. If you want to execute this sample, download the zip containing code examples from www.manning.com/panda and follow the online instructions to deploy and run it in your favorite EJB container.

However, don't worry too much about the details of this code right now; it's just a simple illustration. We'll dive into coding details in the next chapter. Our intent for the Hello World example is to use it as a basis for discussing how EJB 3 addresses the thorniest issues that branded EJB 2 as ponderous.

Let's move on now and take a look at what has transformed the EJB elephant into the EJB cow.

1.4.2 *Simplified programming model*

We heartily agree with Chris Richardson's quote: one of the biggest problems with EJB 2 was the sheer amount of code you needed to write in order to implement an EJB.

If we had attempted to produce listing 1.1 as an EJB 2 example, we would have had to work with several classes and interfaces just to produce the simple one-line output. All of these classes and interfaces had to either implement or extend EJB API interfaces with rigid and unintuitive constraints such as throwing java.rmi.RemoteException for all methods. Implementing interfaces like javax.ejb.SessionBean for the bean implementation class was particularly time consuming since you had to provide an implementation for lifecycle callback methods like `ejbCreate`, `ejbRemove`, `ejbActivate`, `ejbPassivate`, and `setSession-Context`, whether or not you actually used them. In effect, you were forced to deal with several mechanical steps to accomplish very little. IDE tools like JBuilder, JDeveloper, and WebSphere Studio helped matters a bit by automating some of these steps. However, in general, decent tools with robust support were extremely expensive and clunky.

As you saw in listing 1.1, EJB 3 enables you to develop an EJB component using POJOs and POJIs that know nothing about platform services. You can then apply configuration metadata, using annotations, to these POJOs and POJIs to add platform services such as remoteability, web services support, and lifecycle callbacks only as needed.

The largely redundant step of creating home interfaces has been done away with altogether. In short, EJB service definitions have been moved out of the type-safe world of interfaces into deploy and runtime configurations where they are suited best. A number of mechanical steps that were hardly ever used have now been automated by the platform itself. In other words, *you do not* have to write a lot of code to implement an EJB!

1.4.3 *Annotations instead of deployment descriptors*

In addition to having to write a lot of boilerplate code, a significant hurdle in managing EJB 2 was the fact that you still had to do a lot of XML configuration for each component. Although XML is a great mechanism, the truth is that not everyone is a big fan of its verbosity, poor readability, and fragility.

Before the arrival of Java 5 metadata annotations, we had no choice but to use XML for configuration. EJB 3 allows us to use metadata annotations to configure a component instead of using XML deployment descriptors. As you might be able to guess from listing 1.1, besides eliminating verbosity, annotations help avoid the monolithic nature of XML configuration files and localize configuration to the code that is being affected by it. Note, though, you can still use XML deployment descriptors if they suit you better or simply to supplement annotations. We'll talk more about this in chapter 2.

In addition to making the task of configuration easier, EJB 3 reduces the total amount of configuration altogether by using sensible defaults wherever possible. This is especially important when you're dealing with automated persistence using ORM, as you'll see in chapters 7, 8, 9, and 10.

1.4.4 *Dependency injection vs. JNDI lookup*

One of the most tedious parts of EJB 2 development was writing the same few lines of boilerplate code many times to do a JNDI lookup whenever you needed to access an EJB or a container-managed resource, such as a pooled database connection handle. In *POJOs in Action*, Chris Richardson sums it up well:

> A traditional J2EE application uses JNDI as the mechanism that one component uses to access another. For example, the presentation tier uses a JNDI lookup to obtain a reference to a session bean home interface. Similarly, an EJB uses JNDI to access the resources that it needs, such as a JDBC DataSource. The trouble with JNDI is that it couples application code to the application server, which makes development and testing more difficult.

In EJB 3, JNDI lookups have been turned into simple configuration using metadata-based dependency injection (DI). For example, if you want to access the HelloUser EJB that we saw in listing 1.1 from another EJB or servlet, you could use code like this:

```
...
@EJB
private HelloUser helloUser;

void hello(){
    helloUser.sayHello("Curious George");
}
...
```

Isn't that great? The @EJB annotation transparently "injects" the HelloUser EJB into the annotated variable. EJB 3 dependency injection essentially gives you a simple abstraction over a full-scale enterprise JNDI tree. Note you can still use JNDI lookups where they are unavoidable.

1.4.5 *Simplified persistence API*

A lot of the problems with the EJB 2 persistence model were due to the fact that it was applying the container paradigm to a problem for which it was ill suited. This made the EJB 2 entity bean programming model extremely complex and unintuitive. Enabling remote access was one of the prime motivators behind making entity beans container-managed. In reality, very few clients made use of this feature because of performance issues, opting to use session beans as the remote access point.

Undoubtedly entity beans were easily the worst part of EJB 2. EJB 3 solves the problem by using a more natural API paradigm centered on manipulating metadata-based POJOs through the `EntityManager` interface. Moreover, EJB 3 entities do not carry the unnecessary burden of remote access.

Another limitation with EJB 2 was that you couldn't send an EJB 2 entity bean across the wire in different tiers. EJB developers discovered an anti-pattern for this problem: adding another layer of objects—the data transfer objects (DTOs). Chris sums it up nicely:

> *You have to write data transfer objects*—A data transfer object (DTO) is a dumb data object that is returned by the EJB to its caller and contains the data the presentation tier will display to the user. It is often just a copy of the data from one or more entity beans, which cannot be passed to the presentation tier because they are permanently attached to the database. Implementing the DTOs and the code that creates them is one of the most tedious aspects of implementing an EJB.

Because they are POJOs, entities can be transferred between different tiers without having to resort to anti-patterns such as data transfer objects.

The simplification of the persistence API leads to several other benefits, such as standardization of persistence frameworks, a separable persistence API that can be used outside EJB container, and better support of object-oriented features such as inheritance and polymorphism. We'll see EJB 3 persistence in action in chapter 2, but now let's take a close look at some of the main features of the persistence API.

Standardized persistence

One of the major problems with EJB 2 entity beans was that ORM was never standardized. EJB 2 entity beans left the details of database mapping configuration to the provider. This resulted in entity beans that were not portable across container implementations. The EJB 2 query mechanism, EJB-QL, had a similar unfinished feel to it. These standardization gaps have in effect given rise to highly divergent alternative ORM paradigms like Hibernate, Oracle TopLink, and JDO.

A major goal of JPA is to close the standardization gaps left by EJB 2. EJB 3 solidifies automated persistence with JPA in three distinct ways. First, it provides a robust ORM configuration set capable of handling most automated persistence complexities. Second, the Java Persistence Query Language (JPQL) significantly improves upon EJB-QL, standardizing divergent OR query technologies. Third, the `EntityManager` API standardizes ORM CRUD operations. But standardization isn't the only benefit of the simplified API: another great feature is that it can run outside the container.

The cleanly separated Java Persistence API

As we touched on in section 1.2.3, API persistence isn't just a solution for server-side applications. Persistence is a problem that even a standalone Swing-based desktop application has to solve. This is the realization that drove the decision to make JPA a cleanly separated API in its own right, that can be run outside an EJB 3 container. Much like JDBC, JPA is intended to be a general-purpose persistence solution for any Java application. This is a remarkably positive step in expanding the scope of EJB 3 outside the traditional realm of server applications.

Better persistence-tier OO support

Because EJB 2 entity beans were record oriented, they didn't support rich OO features like inheritance and polymorphism, and they didn't permit the mixing of persistent state and domain logic. As you saw in section 1.1.3, this made it impossible to model the domain layer in DDD architecture.

EJB 3 entities have robust OO support, not just because they are POJOs but also because the JPA ORM mapping scheme is designed with OO in mind. JPQL has robust support for OO as well. Getting impatient to learn more about JPA? Stick with us and we'll have many discussions on JPA throughout the book; part 3 is devoted to discussions on JPA.

Test-driven development has become quite popular because it can dramatically improve performance of software applications. Let's see how EJB 3 improves the testability of applications.

1.4.6 *Unit-testable POJO components*

Being able to unit-test component state or logic in response to simulated input is a critical technique in increasing code quality. In EJB 2, only functional testing of components was possible since components had to be deployed to the container to be executed. While functional testing simulating user interactions with the system is invaluable, it is not a good substitute for lower-level unit testing.

Because all EJB 3 components are POJOs, they can easily be executed outside the container. This means that it is possible to unit-test all component business logic using testing frameworks such as JUnit or TestNG.

These are just the primary changes to EJB 3; there are many more that we'll cover throughout the book.

Just in case you thought you had to choose between Spring and EJB 3, we thought we'd mention why they don't necessarily need to be regarded as competing technologies.

1.4.7 EJB 3 and Spring

As we mentioned earlier, EJB 3 and Spring are often seen as competitors; however, if you look more closely, you can see that they can also be complementary. Spring has some particularly strong points: support for inversion of control (IoC) for components with simple lifecycles such as singletons; feature-heavy (but slightly more complex) aspect-oriented programming (AOP) support; a number of simple interfaces such as `JdbcTemplate` and `JmsTemplate` utilizing common usage patterns of low-level Java EE APIs; and so on.

EJB 3, on the other hand, provides better support for transparent state management with stateful session beans, pooling, thread-safety, robust messaging support with MDBs, integrated support for distributed transaction management, standardized automated persistence through JPA, and so on.

From a levelheaded, neutral point of view, EJB 3 and Spring can be complementary technologies. The good news is that parts of both the Spring and Java EE communities are working diligently to make Spring/EJB 3 integration a reality. This is particularly good news if you have a significant investment in Spring but want to utilize the benefits of EJB 3. We'll talk about Spring/EJB 3 integration in more detail in chapter 16. However, we'd like to list the possibilities now.

Treating EJB 3 business-tier components as Spring beans

It is possible to treat EJB 3 business-tier components as Spring beans. This translates into an architecture shown in figure 1.8. In this architecture, Spring is used for gluing together the application that contains EJB 3 business-tier components.

The Spring Pitchfork project, part of Spring 2, is meant to make such an integration scenario completely transparent. The Spring framework plans to

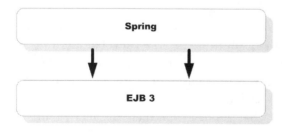

Figure 1.8
Spring/EJB 3 integration strategy. It is possible to use EJB 3 business-tier components as if they were Spring beans. This allows you to use the complementary strengths of both technologies in a "hybrid" fashion.

support EJB 3 annotation metadata specifying stateless session beans, interceptors, resource injection, and so on.

Integrating the JPA into Spring

Suppose that you find Spring is a good fit for your business-tier needs and you simply want to standardize your persistence layer. In this case, it is easy to integrate JPA directly into Spring, much like Spring/Hibernate or Spring/JDO integration. This scheme is shown in figure 1.9.

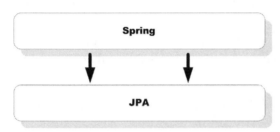

Figure 1.9
Spring/JPA integration. Because JPA is a cleanly separable API, you can integrate Spring with JPA just as you would integrate Hibernate.

In addition to using Spring with JPA, you may find yourself in a situation where you would like to use both Spring and EJB 3 session beans together. Let's examine the possibilities of such integration.

Using Spring interfaces inside EJB 3 components

Yet another interesting idea is to use some of the Spring interfaces like Jdbc-Template and JmsTemplate or even Spring beans inside EJB 3 components. You can do this either through direct instantiation or access through the Spring application context. Container vendors like JBoss, Oracle, and BEA are working to provide seamless support for integrating Spring beans into session beans and MDBs. This kind of integration is visualized in figure 1.10. We'll discuss combining the power of EJB 3 and Spring in chapter 16.

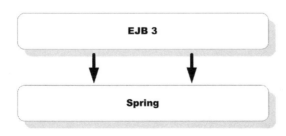

Figure 1.10
In certain cases, it might be a good idea to use Spring from EJB 3. Although it is possible to do so today, such support is likely to be much better in the future.

1.5 *Summary*

You should now have a good idea of what EJB 3 is, what it brings to the table, and why you should consider using it to build server-side applications. We gave you an overview of the new features in EJB 3, including these important points:

- EJB 3 components are POJOs configurable through simplified meta-data annotations.
- Accessing EJBs from client applications has become very simple using dependency injection.
- EJB 3 standardizes the persistence with the Java Persistence API, which defines POJO entities that can be used both inside and outside the container.

We also provided a taste of code to show how EJB 3 addresses development pain points that were inherent with EJB 2, and we took a brief look at how EJB 3 can be used with Spring.

Armed with this essential background, you are probably eager to look at more code. We aim to satisfy this desire, at least in part, in the next chapter. Get ready for a whirlwind tour of the entire EJB 3 API that shows just how easy the code really is.

A first taste of EJB

2

This chapter covers

- Metadata annotations
- Dependency injection
- The ActionBazaar application
- Code examples of session beans, MDBs, and entities

In this age of hyper-competitiveness, learning a new technology by balancing a book on your lap while hacking away at a business problem on the keyboard has become the norm. Let's face it—somewhere deep down you probably prefer this "baptism by fire" to trudging the same old roads over and over again. This chapter is for the brave pioneer in all of us, eager to peek over the horizon into the new world of EJB 3.

The first chapter gave you a 20,000-foot view of the EJB 3 landscape from on board a hypersonic jet. We defined EJB, described the services it offers as well as the EJB 3 architectural vision, and listed the different parts of EJB 3. This chapter is a low-altitude fly-over with a reconnaissance airplane. Here, we'll take a quick look at the code for solving a realistic problem using EJB 3. The example solution will use all of the EJB 3 components types, a layered architecture, and some of the services we discussed in chapter 1.

EJB 3 offers a wide range of features and services. To keep things sane, the examples in this chapter are designed to show you the high-level features and services of EJB 3, and to introduce you to the major players: the beans and clients. Thanks to the almost invisible way most EJB 3 services are delivered, this is pretty easy to do. You'll see exactly how easy and useful EJB 3 is and how quickly you could pick it up.

We start by covering some basic concepts necessary for understanding the examples, and then we introduce the application that runs throughout the book: ActionBazaar. In the rest of the chapter, we illustrate each EJB type with an example from the ActionBazaar application. We implement business logic with session beans and then we add the power of asynchronous messaging by adding a message-driven bean (MDB). Finally you'll discover the most powerful innovation of EJB 3 by looking at a simple example of a Java Persistence API (JPA) entity.

If you aren't a big fan of views from heights, don't worry too much. Think of this chapter as that first day at a new workplace, shaking hands with the stranger in the next cubicle. In the chapters that follow, you'll get to know more about your new coworkers' likes, dislikes, and eccentricities; and you'll learn how to work around these foibles. All you are expected to do right now is put names to faces.

> **NOTE**   In the examples in this chapter, we won't explore the solutions beyond what is necessary for discussing the EJB 3 component types but will leave some of it for you as a brainteaser. If you want to, you can peek at the entire solution by downloading the zip containing code examples file from www.manning.com/panda. In fact, we highly recommend that you follow

the tutorial on the site to set up your development environment using the code. That way, you can follow along with us and even tinker with the code on your own—including running it inside a container.

EJB 3 is a fundamental paradigm shift from previous versions. A number of innovations, some familiar and some unfamiliar, make this paradigm shift possible. A good place to start this chapter is with an exploration of three of the most important innovations.

2.1 New features: simplifying EJB

There are three primary sources of complexities in EJB 2: the heavyweight programming model, direct use of the Java Naming Directory Interface (JNDI), and a verbose XML deployment descriptor. Three primary techniques in EJB 3 eliminate these sources of complexity: metadata annotations, minimal deployment descriptors, and dependency injection. In the following sections, we introduce all three of these major innovations that make developing EJB 3 as quick and easy as possible. Let's begin by looking at how annotations and deployment descriptors work.

2.1.1 Replacing deployment descriptors with annotations

Service configuration using Java metadata annotations is easily the most important change in EJB 3. As you'll see throughout the book, annotations simplify the EJB programming model, remove the need for detailed deployment descriptors, and act as an effective delivery mechanism for dependency injection.

In the next few years, it's likely that annotations will play a greater role in improving Java Standard Edition (SE) and Java Enterprise Edition (EE) usability by leaps and bounds. In case you aren't familiar with the metadata annotation facility added in Java SE 5.0, let's review it first.

Java metadata annotations: a brief primer

Annotations essentially allow us to "attach" additional information (officially called *attributes*) to a Java class, interface, method, or variable. The additional information conveyed by annotations can be used by a development environment like Eclipse, the Java compiler, a deployment tool, a persistence provider like Hibernate, or a runtime environment like the Java EE container. Another way to think about annotations is that they are "custom" Java modifiers (in addition to `private`, `public`, `static`, `final`, and so on) that can be used by anything handling Java source or byte code. This is how annotations look:

```
import mypackage.Author;

@Author("Debu Panda, Reza Rahman and Derek Lane")
public class EJB3InAction implements ManningBook
```

The `@Author` symbol is the annotation. It essentially tells whoever is using the `EJB3InAction` Java class that the authors are Debu Panda, Reza Rahman, and Derek Lane. More interestingly, it adds this bit of extra information about the class without forcing us to implement an interface, extend a class, or add a member variable or method. Since an annotation is a special kind of interface, it must be imported from where it is defined. In our case, the `@Author` annotation is defined in the `mypackage.Author.class` file. This is all there is to making the compiler happy. The runtime environment decides how the `@Author` annotation should be used. For example, it could be used by the Manning website engine to display the author names for this book.

Like many of the Java EE 5.0 innovations, annotations have humble beginnings. The `@` character is a dead giveaway to the grandparent of annotations—JavaDoc tags. The next step in the evolution of the annotation from the lumbering caveman JavaDoc tag was the XDoclet tool. If you've done a significant amount of work with EJB 2, you are likely already familiar with XDoclet. XDoclet acted as a source code preprocessor that allowed to you to process custom JavaDoc tags and do whatever you needed to do with the tagged source code, such as generate PDF documentation, additional source code, or even EJB 2 deployment descriptors. XDoclet referred to this paradigm as *attribute-oriented programming*. In case you're curious, you can find out more about XDoclet at http://xdoclet.source-forge.net/xdoclet/index.html.

The sleek new annotation facility essentially makes attribute-oriented programming a core part of the Java language. Although this is entirely possible, it is probably unlikely you'll be creating your own annotations. If your inner geek just won't leave you alone, feel free to explore Jason Hunter's article, *Making the Most of Java's Metadata* (www.oracle.com/technology/pub/articles/hunter_meta.html). You can find out more about annotations in general at http://java.sun.com/j2se/1.5.0/docs/guide/language/annotations.html.

Note that, just like anything else, annotations and attribute-oriented programming have a few weaknesses. Specifically, it isn't always a good idea to mix and match configuration with source code such as annotations. This means that you would have to change source code each time you made a configuration change to something like a database connection resource or deployment environment entry.

EJB 3 solves this problem by allowing you to override annotations with XML deployment descriptors where appropriate.

Know your deployment descriptor

A *deployment descriptor* is simply an XML file that contains application configuration information. Every deployment unit in Java EE can have a deployment descriptor that describes its contents and environment. Some typical examples of deployment units are the Enterprise Archive (EAR), Web Application Archive (WAR), and the EJB (ejb-jar) module. If you have ever used EJB 2, you know how verbose the XML (ejb-jar.xml) descriptor was. Most elements were required even if they were trivial. This added to the complexity of using EJB. For example, you could have had the following deployment descriptor for the HelloUserBean that we saw in chapter 1:

```
<enterprise-beans>
    <session>
        <ejb-name>HelloUserBean</ejb-name>
        <local>ejb3inaction.example.HelloUser</local>
        <ejb-class>ejb3inaction.example.HelloUserBean</ejb-class>
        <session-type>Stateless</session-type>
        <transaction-type>Container</transaction-type>
    </session>
</enterprise-beans>
```

We'll discuss deployment descriptors in greater detail when we talk about EJB packaging in chapter 11. The good news is that EJB 3 makes deployment descriptors completely optional. You can now use metadata annotations instead of descriptor entries, thus making the development experience much simpler. Note that we'll primarily use annotations throughout this book. This is not because we think deployment descriptors are unimportant or outdated, but because concepts are more easily explained using annotations. As a matter of fact, although deployment descriptors involve dealing with often confusing and verbose XML, we think they can be an excellent mechanism for separating coding concerns from deployment and configuration concerns. With this fact in mind, we present the deployment descriptor counterparts for each of the annotations described in the chapter (and more) in appendix D.

You can use deployment descriptor entries only for corner cases where you need them. (A *corner case* is a problem or situation that occurs only outside normal operating parameters.)

Mixing annotations and deployment descriptors

Annotations and descriptors are not mutually exclusive. In fact, in EJB 3 they're designed for harmonious coexistence. Deployment descriptor entries override configuration values hard-coded into EJB components. As an example, we could override the `@Author` annotation we just introduced with the following imaginary deployment descriptor:

```
<ManningBooks>
    <ManningBook>
        <BookClass>EJB3InAction</BookClass>
        <Author>Larry, Moe and Curly</Author>
    </ManningBook>
</ManningBooks>
```

At runtime, the Manning website engine would detect that the authors of the `EJB3InAction` book really are Larry, Moe, and Curly, and not Debu Panda, Reza Rahman, and Derek Lane.

This is an invaluable feature if you develop enterprise applications that can be deployed to a variety of environments. In the simplest case, the differing environments could be a test and a production server. In the most complex case, you could be selling shrink-wrapped enterprise applications deployed to an unknown customer environment. The most obvious way of mixing and matching annotation and XML metadata is to use XML for deployment environment–specific configurations while using annotations for everything else. If you really don't like annotations, that's fine too. You can avoid using them completely in favor of XML deployment descriptors. We'll primarily focus on annotations rather than deployment descriptors in this book simply because they are so much more intuitive to look at and explain.

Common metadata annotations

Obviously, EJB defines its own set of standard annotations. We'll be discussing these annotations throughout this book.

During the course of developing Java EE 5.0, it became apparent that the Java EE container as a whole could use some of the annotations geared toward EJB 3. In particular, these annotations are extremely useful in integrating EJB with the web/servlet tier. Some of these annotations were separated out of the EJB 3 spec and christened *common metadata annotations*. These annotations are a core part of what makes EJB 3 development, including dependency injection, easy. Table 2.1 lists some of the major common metadata annotations. We'll discuss them throughout this part of the book, starting with some of the most fundamental ones in this chapter.

Table 2.1 Major metadata annotations introduced in Java EE. Although primarily geared toward EJB, these annotations apply to Java EE components such as servlets and JSF managed beans as well as application clients. Annotations defined in the `javax.annotation.*` package are defined by the Common Metadata Annotations API (JSR-250).

Annotations	Usage	Components That Can Use Them
`javax.annotation.Resource`	Dependency injection of resources such as `Data-Source`, JMS objects, etc.	EJB, web, application client
`javax.ejb.EJB`	Dependency injection of session beans	EJB, web, application client
`javax.jws.WebServiceRef`	Dependency injection of web services	EJB, web, application client
`javax.persistence.PersistenceContext`	Dependency injection of container-managed `EntityManager`	EJB, web
`javax.persistence.PersistenceUnit`	Dependency injection of `EntityManagerFactory`	EJB, web
`javax.annotation.PostConstruct`	Lifecycle method	EJB, web
`javax.annotation.PreDestroy`	Lifecycle method	EJB, web
`javax.annotation.security.RunAs`	Security	EJB, web
`javax.annotation.security.RolesAllowed`	Security	EJB
`javax.annotation.security.PermitAll`	Security	EJB
`javax.annotation.security.DenyAll`	Security	EJB
`javax.annotation.security.DeclareRoles`	Security	EJB, web

As you can see, dependency injection is front and center of the common metadata annotations, including the `@Resource`, `@EJB`, `@WebServiceRef`, `@Persistence-Context`, and `@PersistenceUnit` annotations. Just as metadata annotations take the ugliness of descriptors away from the developer's view, dependency injection solves the complexities surrounding manual JNDI lookups. Let's take a look at this concept next.

2.1.2 *Introducing dependency injection*

Almost every component uses another component or resource to implement functionality. The primary goal of dependency injection (DI) is to make component interdependencies as loosely coupled as possible. In real terms, this means that one component should call another component or resource only through an interface and that components and resources should be glued together using configuration instead of code. As a result, component implementations can easily be swapped out as necessary simply by reconfiguring the application.

If you've used JNDI extensively in EJB 2, you'll appreciate how much this means. We won't talk about JNDI very much here since in most cases you can get away without knowing anything about it. If you don't know about JNDI and are curious to learn more, we discuss it in some length in appendix A. Figure 2.1 shows the difference between manual JNDI lookups and DI.

In a sense, injection is lookup *reversed*. As you can see, in the manual JNDI lookup model, the bean explicitly retrieves the resources and components it needs. As a result, component and resource names are hard-coded in the bean. With DI, on the other hand, the container reads target bean configuration, figures out what beans and resources the target bean needs, and injects them into the

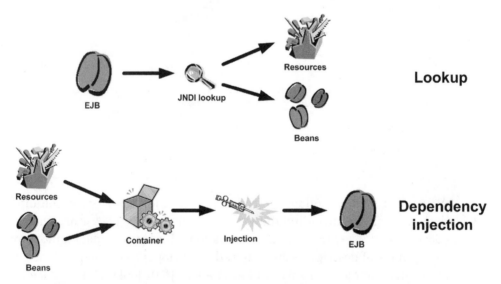

Figure 2.1   When you're using JNDI, it's the responsibility of the client to do a lookup and obtain a reference to the object. In EJB 3, you may think dependency injection is the opposite of JNDI. It is the responsibility of the container to inject an object based on the dependency declaration.

bean at runtime. In the end, you write no lookup code and can easily change configuration to swap out beans and resources as needed.

In essence, DI allows you to declare component dependencies and lets the container deal with the complexities of service or resource instantiation, initialization, sequencing, and supplies the service or resource references to the clients as required. As we work our way through the examples in this chapter, you'll see several places where we use DI, including @EJB to inject EJBs in section 2.3, @Resource to inject JMS resources in section 2.4, and @PersistenceContext to inject container-managed EntityManager in section 2.5.

> **NOTE** Lightweight application containers like the Spring Framework and Pico-Container popularized the idea of DI. To learn more about the roots of DI itself, visit www.martinfowler.com/articles/injection.html. This article, by Martin Fowler, faithfully examines the pros and cons of DI over JNDI-style manual lookups. Since the article was written before EJB 3 was conceived, you might find the discussion of EJB 2 cool as well!

Now that we've covered some of the most fundamental concepts of EJB 3, it is time to warm up to code. The problem we solve in this chapter utilizes an essential element of this book—*ActionBazaar*. ActionBazaar is an imaginary enterprise system around which we'll weave most of the material in this book. In a sense, this book is a case study of developing the ActionBazaar application using EJB 3.

Let's take a quick stroll around the bazaar to see what it is all about.

2.2 *Introducing the ActionBazaar application*

ActionBazaar is a simple online auctioning system like eBay. Sellers dust off the treasures hidden away in basement corners, take a few out-of-focus pictures, and post their item listings on ActionBazaar. Eager buyers get in the competitive spirit and put exorbitant bids against each other on the hidden treasures with the blurry pictures and misspelled descriptions. Winning bidders pay for the items. Sellers ship sold items. Everyone is happy, or so the story goes.

As much as we would like to take credit for it, the idea of ActionBazaar was first introduced in *Hibernate in Action* by Christian Bauer and Gavin King (Manning, 2004) as the *CaveatEmptor* application. *Hibernate in Action* primary dealt with developing the persistence layer using the Hibernate object-relational mapping (ORM) framework. The idea was later used by Patrick Lightbody and Jason Carreira in *WebWork in Action* (Manning, 2005) to discuss the open source presentation-tier framework. We thought this was a pretty good idea to adopt for EJB 3.

The next two parts of this book roughly follow the course of developing each layer of the ActionBazaar application as it relates to EJB 3. We'll use EJB 3 to develop the business logic tier in part 2, and then the persistence tier in part 3. We'll deal with the presentation layer as necessary as well.

This section will introduce you to the ActionBazaar application. We start with a subset of the architecture of ActionBazaar, and then we'll design a solution based on EJB 3 and JPA. After this section, the rest of the chapter explores some of the important features of EJB 3, using examples from the ActionBazaar application to introduce you to the various bean types and show how they are used.

Let's begin by taking a look at the requirements and design of our example.

2.2.1 *Starting with the architecture*

For the purposes of introducing all three EJB 3 component types across the business logic and persistence layers, let's focus on a small subset of ActionBazaar functionality in this chapter—starting from bidding on an item and ending with ordering the item won. This set of application functionality is shown in figure 2.2.

The functionality represented in figure 2.2 encompasses the "essentials" of ActionBazaar. The major functionalities not covered are: posting an item for sale, browsing items, and searching for items. We'll save these pieces of functionality for parts 2 and 3. This includes presenting the entire domain model, which we'll

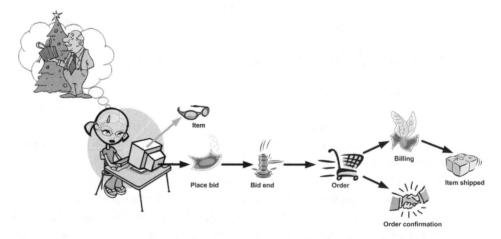

Figure 2.2   A chain of representative ActionBazaar functionality used to quickly examine a cross section of EJB 3. The bidder bids on a desired item, wins the item, orders it, and instantaneously receives confirmation. Parallel with order confirmation, the user is billed for the item. Upon successful receipt of payment, the seller ships the item.

discuss in chapter 7 when we start talking about domain modeling and persistence using JPA.

The chain of actions in figure 2.2 starts with the user deciding to place a bid on an item. Our user, Jenny, spots the perfect Christmas gift for Grandpa and quickly puts down a starting bid of $5.00. After the timed auction ends, the highest bidder wins the item. Jenny gets lucky and no one else bids on the item, so she wins it for the grand sum of $5.00. As the winning bidder, Jenny is allowed to order the item from the seller, Joe. An order includes all the items we've come to expect from online merchants—shipping information, billing details, a total bill with calculated shipping and handling costs, and so on. Persuasive Jenny gets Mom to foot the bill with her credit card and has the order shipped directly to Grandpa's address. Not unlike many e-businesses such as Amazon.com and eBay, ActionBazaar does not make the user wait for the billing process to finish before confirming an order. Instead, the order is confirmed as soon as it is reasonably validated and the billing process is started in parallel in the background. Jenny gets an order confirmation number back as soon as she clicks the Order button. Although Jenny doesn't realize it, the process to charge Mom's credit card starts in the background as she is receiving the confirmation. After the billing process is finished, both Jenny and the seller, Joe, are sent e-mail notifications. Having been notified of the receipt of the money for the order, Joe ships the item, just in time for Grandpa to get it before Christmas!

In the next section, you'll see how the business logic and persistence components for this set of actions can be implemented using EJB 3. Before peeking at the solution diagram in the next section, you should try to visualize how the components might look with respect to an EJB-based layered architecture. How do you think session beans, MDBs, entities, and the JPA API fit into the picture, given our discussion? Chances are, with the probable exception of the messaging components, your design will closely match ours.

2.2.2 An EJB 3–based solution

Figure 2.2 shows how the ActionBazaar scenario in the previous section can be implemented using EJB 3 in a traditional four-tier layering scheme. For our purposes, the presentation tier is essentially an amorphous blob that generates business-tier requests in response to user actions. If you examine the scenario in figure 2.2, you'll see that only two processes are triggered by the user—adding a bid to an item and ordering items won. One more process might be apparent: the background billing process to charge the order, triggered by order confirmation. If you guessed that the billing process is triggered through a message, you guessed right. As you can see in figure 2.3, the bidding and ordering processes are implemented as session beans (`PlaceBidBean` and `PlaceOrderBean`) in the business logic tier. On the other hand, the billing process is implemented as an MDB (`OrderBillingMDB`) since it is triggered by a message sent from the `PlaceOrderBean` instead of a direct user request.

All three of the processes persist data. The `PlaceBidBean` needs to add a bid record to the database. Similarly, the `PlaceOrderBean` must add an order record. Alternatively, the `OrderBillingMDB` updates the order record to reflect the results of the billing process. These database changes are performed through two entities in the JPA-managed persistence tier—the `Bid` and `Order` entities. While the `PlaceBidBean` uses the `Bid` entity, the `PlaceOrderBean` and `OrderBillingMDB` use the `Order` entity.

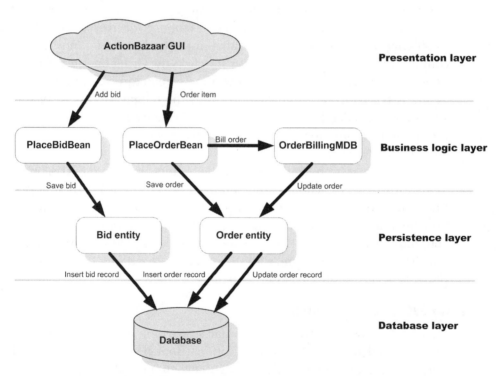

Figure 2.3 The ActionBazaar scenario implemented using EJB 3. From the EJB 3 perspective, the presentation layer is an amorphous blob that generates business-tier requests. The business-logic tier components match up with the distinct processes in the scenario—putting a bid on an item, ordering the item won, and billing the user. The billing MDB is triggered by a message sent by the order confirmation process. The business-tier components use JPA entities to persist application state into the database.

Recall that although JPA entities contain ORM configuration, they do not persist themselves. As you'll see in the actual code solutions, the business-tier components have to use the JPA `EntityManager` API to add, delete, update, and retrieve entities as needed.

If your mental picture matches up with figure 2.3 pretty closely, it is likely the code we are going to present next will seem intuitive too, even though you don't know EJB 3.

In the following sections, we explore each of the EJB 3 component types using our scenario. Without further ado, we can now begin our whirlwind tour of EJB 3 component types, starting with the session beans in the business-logic tier.

2.3 *Building business logic with session beans*

Session beans are meant to model business processes or actions, especially as perceived by the system user. This is why they are ideal for modeling the bidding and ordering processes in our scenario. Session beans are the easiest but most versatile part of EJB.

Recall that session beans come in two flavors: stateful and stateless. We'll take on stateless session beans first, primarily because they are simpler. You'll then discover how you can add statefulness to the ActionBazaar application by using a stateful session bean. Along the way, we introduce you to an example of a session bean client in a web tier, and then build a standalone Java client for a session bean.

2.3.1 *Using stateless beans*

Stateless session beans are used to model actions or processes that can be done in one shot, such as placing a bid on an item in our ActionBazaar scenario. The `addBid` bean method in listing 2.1 is called from the ActionBazaar web tier when a user decides to place a bid. The parameter to the method, the `Bid` object, represents the bid to be placed. The `Bid` object contains the ID of the bidder placing the bid, the ID of the item being bid on, and the bid amount. As we know, all the method needs to do is save the passed-in `Bid` data to the database. In a real application, you would see more validation and error-handling code in the `addBid` method. Since the point is to show you what a session bean looks like and not to demonstrate the über geek principles of right and proper enterprise development, we've conveniently decided to be slackers. Also, as you'll see toward the end of the chapter, the `Bid` object is really a JPA entity.

Listing 2.1 PlaceBid stateless session bean code

```
package ejb3inaction.example.buslogic;

import javax.ejb.Stateless;
import ejb3inaction.example.persistence.Bid;
                                                    Marks POJO as stateless
@Stateless                                          session bean
public class PlaceBidBean implements PlaceBid {
    ...
    public PlaceBidBean() {}

    public Bid addBid(Bid bid) {
        System.out.println("Adding bid, bidder ID=" +
                                      bid.getBidderID()
                + ", item ID=" + bid.getItemID() + ",
                                          bid amount="
                + bid.getBidAmount() + ".");

        return save(bid);
    }
    ...
}
...
package ejb3inaction.example.buslogic;

import javax.ejb.Local;
import ejb3inaction.example.persistence.Bid;

@Local                              Marks EJB business
public interface PlaceBid {         interface as local
    Bid addBid(Bid bid);
}
```

The first thing that you have probably noticed is how plain this code looks. The
PlaceBidBean class is just a plain old Java object (POJO) and the PlaceBid interface
is a plain old Java interface (POJI). There is no cryptic EJB interface to implement,
class to extend, or confusing naming convention to follow. In fact, the only notable features in listing 2.1 are the two EJB 3 annotations: @Stateless and @Local:

- @Stateless—The @Stateless annotation tells the EJB container that Place-
  BidBean is a stateless session bean. This means that the container automatically provides such services to the bean as automatic concurrency control,
  thread safety, pooling, and transaction management. In addition, you can
  add other services for which stateless beans are eligible, such as transparent
  security and interceptors.

- `@Local`—The `@Local` annotation on the `PlaceBid` interface tells the container that the `PlaceBid` EJB can be accessed locally through the interface. Since EJB and servlets are typically collocated in the same application, this is probably perfect. Alternatively, we could have marked the interface with the `@Remote` annotation. Remote access through the `@Remote` annotation is provided under the hood by Java Remote Method Invocation (RMI), so this is the ideal means of remote access from Java clients.

If the EJB needs to be accessed by non-Java clients like Microsoft .NET applications, web services–based remote access can be enabled using the `@WebService` annotation applied either on the interface or the bean class.

That's pretty much all we're going to say about stateless session beans for now. Let's now turn our attention to the client code for using the `PlaceBid` EJB.

2.3.2 *The stateless bean client*

Virtually any client can use the `PlaceBid` EJB in listing 2.1. However, the most likely scenario for EJB usage is from a Java-based web tier. In the ActionBazaar scenario, the `PlaceBid` EJB is probably called from a JavaServer Page (JSP) or servlet. For simplicity, let's assume that the `PlaceBid` EJB is used by a servlet named `PlaceBidServlet`. Listing 2.2 shows how the code might look. The servlet's `service` method is invoked when the user wants to place a bid. The bidder's ID, item ID, and the bid amount are passed in as HTTP request parameters. The servlet creates a new `Bid` object, sets it up, and passes it to the EJB `addBid` method.

Listing 2.2   A simple servlet client for the PlaceBid EJB

```
package ejb3inaction.example.buslogic;

import javax.ejb.EJB;
import javax.servlet.*;
import javax.servlet.http.*;
import java.io.*;
import ejb3inaction.example.persistence.Bid;

public class PlaceBidServlet extends HttpServlet {
    @EJB
    private PlaceBid placeBid;           Injects instance
                                         of PlaceBid EJB

    public void service(HttpServletRequest request,
        HttpServletResponse response) throws ServletException,
            IOException {
        int bidderID = Integer.parseInt(
            request.getParameter("bidder_id"));
```

```
        int itemID = Integer.parseInt(
            request.getParameter("item_id"));
        double bidAmount = Double.parseDouble(
            request.getParameter("bid_amount"));

        Bid bid = new Bid();
        bid.setBidderID(bidderID);
        bid.setItemID(itemID);
        bid.setBidAmount(bidAmount);

        placeBid.addBid(bid);
        ...
    }
    ...
}
```

As you can see in listing 2.2, EJB from the client side looks even simpler than developing the component code. Other than the @EJB annotation on the place-Bid private variable, the code is no different than using a local POJO.

> **NOTE** When the servlet container sees the @EJB annotation as the servlet is first loaded, it looks up the PlaceBid EJB behind the scenes and sets the placeBid variable to the retrieved EJB reference. If necessary, the container will look up the EJB remotely over RMI.

The @EJB annotation works in any component that is registered with the Java EE container, such as a servlet or JavaServer Faces (JSF) backing bean. As long as you are using the standard Java EE stack, this is probably more than sufficient.

There are a couple other interesting items in this code that illustrate concepts we introduced earlier. Let's take a closer look.

EJB 3 dependency injection

Although we mentioned DI in the beginning of the chapter, if you are not familiar with it you may think that what the @EJB annotation is doing is a little unusual—in a nifty, "black-magic" kind of way. In fact, if we didn't tell you anything about the code, you might have been wondering if the placeBid private variable is even usable in the servlet's service method since it is never set! If fact, if the container didn't intervene we'd get the infamous java.lang.NullPointerException when we tried to call the addBid method in listing 2.2 since the placeBid variable would still be null. One interesting way to understand DI is to think of it as "custom" Java variable instantiation. The @EJB annotation in listing 2.2 makes the container "instantiate" the `placeBid` variable with the EJB named `PlaceBid` before the variable is available for use.

Recall our discussion in section 2.1.2 that DI can be viewed as the opposite of JNDI lookup. Recall also that JNDI is the container registry that holds references to all container-managed resources such as EJBs. Clients gain access to session beans like our `PlaceBid` EJB directly or indirectly through JNDI. In EJB 2, you would have to manually populate the `placeBid` variable using JNDI lookup code that looks like the following:

```
Object ejbHome = new InitialContext().lookup("java:comp/env/PlaceBid");
PlaceBidHome placeBidHome = (PlaceBidHome)
    PortableRemoteObject.narrow(ejbHome, PlaceBidHome.class);
PlaceBid placeBid = placeBidHome.create();
```

It isn't easy to fully appreciate DI until you see code like this. EJB 3 DI using the `@EJB` annotation reduces all this mechanical JNDI lookup code to a single statement! In a nontrivial application, this can easily translate to eliminating hundreds of lines of redundant, boring, error-prone code. You can think of EJB 3 DI as a high-level abstraction over JNDI lookups.

Understanding statelessness

An interesting point about the `PlaceBid` stateless bean is that as long as calling the `addBid` method results in the creation of a new bid record each time, the client doesn't care about the internal state of the bean. There is absolutely no need for the stateless bean to guarantee that the value of any of its instance variables will be the same across any two invocations. This property is what statelessness means in terms of server-side programming.

The `PlaceBid` session bean can afford to be stateless because the action of placing a bid is simple enough to be accomplished in a single step. The problem is that not all business processes are that simple. Breaking a process down into multiple steps and maintaining internal state to "glue together" the steps is a common technique to present complex processes to the user in a simple way. Statefulness is particularly useful if what the user does in a given step in a process determines what the next step is. Think of a questionnaire-based setup wizard. The user's input for each step of the wizard is stored behind the scenes and is used to determine what to ask the user next. Stateful session beans make maintaining server-side application state as easy as possible.

2.3.3 Using stateful beans

Unlike stateless session beans, stateful session beans guarantee that a client can expect to set the internal state of a bean and count on the state being maintained between any number of method calls. The container makes sure this happens by doing two important things behind the scenes.

Maintaining the session

First, the container ensures that a client can reach a bean dedicated to it across more than one method invocation. Think of this as a phone switchboard that makes sure it routes you to the same customer service agent if you call a technical support line more than once in a given period of time (the period of time is the "session").

Second, the container ensures that bean instance variable values are maintained for the duration of a session without your having to write any session maintenance code. In the customer service example, the container makes sure that your account information and call history in a given period of time automatically appear on your agent's screen when you call technical support. This "automagic" maintenance of session state is a huge leap from having to fiddle with the HTTP session, browser cookies, or hidden HTML form variables to try to accomplish the same thing. As we'll see in the coming code samples, you can develop stateful beans as if you are developing in a "Hello World" application, not a web application with verbose code to maintain session state. The ActionBazaar ordering process is a great example for stateful session beans since it is broken up into four steps, each of which correspond to a screen presented to the user:

1 Adding items to the order. If the user started the ordering process by clicking the Order Item button on the page displaying an item won, the item is automatically added to the order. The user can still add additional items in this step.

2 Specifying shipping information, including the shipping method, shipping address, insurance, and so on.

3 Adding billing information, such as credit card data and the billing address.

4 Confirming the order after reviewing the complete order, including total cost.

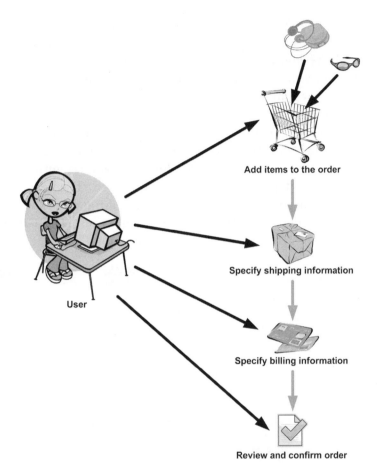

Add items to the order

Specify shipping information

Specify billing information

Review and confirm order

User

Figure 2.4 To make an otherwise overwhelming process manageable, the ActionBazaar ordering process is broken down into several steps. The first of these steps is to add one or more item to the order. The second step is to specify shipping information for the order. The third is to specify the billing information. Reviewing and confirming the order finishes the ordering process.

Figure 2.4 depicts these ordering steps. With a stateful bean, the data the user enters at each step can be cached into bean variables until the ordering workflow completes, when the user confirms the order.

Now that we know what we want, let's see how we can implement it.

Implementing the solution

Listing 2.3 shows a possible implementation of the ActionBazaar ordering workflow using a bean named `PlaceOrderBean`. As you can see, each of the ordering steps maps to a method in the `PlaceOrderBean` implementation. The `addItem`, `set-ShippingInfo`, `setBillingInfo`, and `confirmOrder` methods are called in sequence from the web tier in response to user actions in each step. The `setBidderID` method essentially represents an implicit workflow setup step. It is called at the beginning of the workflow behind the scenes by the web application to identify the currently logged-in user as the bidder placing the order. Except for the `confirm-Order` method, the remaining methods do little more than simply save user input into stateful instance variables. In a real application, of course, these methods would be doing a lot more, such as error handling, validation, figuring out the user's options for a given step, calculating costs, and so on. The `confirmOrder` method does several things using the data accumulated throughout the session: the complete order is saved into the database, the billing process is started in parallel, and an order ID is returned to the user as confirmation.

Listing 2.3   PlaceOrderBean stateful session bean

```
package ejb3inaction.example.buslogic;

import javax.ejb.*;
import java.util.ArrayList;
import java.util.List;                    ❶ Marks POJO
                                            as stateful

@Stateful
public class PlaceOrderBean implements PlaceOrder {
    private Long bidderID;
    private List<Long> items;             ❷ Defines stateful
    private ShippingInfo shippingInfo;      instance
    private BillingInfo billingInfo;        variables

    public PlaceOrderBean () {
        items = new ArrayList<Long>();
    }

    public void setBidderID(Long bidderId) {
        this.bidderId = bidderId;
    }

    public void addItem(Long itemId) {
        items.add(itemId);
    }

    public void setShippingInfo(ShippingInfo shippingInfo) {
        this.shippingInfo = shippingInfo;
    }
```

```
public void setBillingInfo(BillingInfo billingInfo) {
    this.billingInfo = billingInfo;
}
```

❸ **Contains remove method**

```
@Remove
public Long confirmOrder() {
    Order order = new Order();
    order.setBidderId(bidderId);
    order.setItems(items);
    order.setShippingInfo(shippingInfo);
    order.setBillingInfo(billingInfo);

    saveOrder(order);
    billOrder(order);

    return order.getOrderId();
}
...
}
...
package ejb3inaction.example.buslogic;
import javax.ejb.Remote;
@Remove
public interface PlaceOrder {
    void setBidderId(Long bidderId);
    void addItem(Long itemId);
    void setShippingInfo(ShippingInfo shippingInfo);
    void setBillingInfo(BillingInfo billingInfo);
    Long confirmOrder();
}
```

❹ **Defines remote business interface**

As you can see, overall there is no big difference between developing a stateless and a stateful bean. In fact, from a developer's perspective, the only difference is that the PlaceOrderBean class is marked with the @Stateful annotation instead of the @Stateless annotation ❶. As we know, though, under the hood this makes a huge difference in how the container handles the bean's relationship to a client and the values stored in the bean instance variables ❷. The @Stateful annotation also serves to tell the client-side developer what to expect from the bean if behavior is not obvious from the bean's API and documentation.

It is also important to note the @Remove annotation ❸ placed on the confirm-Order method. Although this annotation is optional, it is critical from a server performance standpoint.

NOTE The `@Remove` annotation marks the end of the workflow modeled by a stateful bean. In our case, we are telling the container that there is no longer a need to maintain the bean's session with the client after the `confirmOrder` method is invoked. If we didn't tell the container what method invocation marks the end of the workflow, the container could wait for a long time until it could safely time-out the session. Since stateful beans are guaranteed to be dedicated to a client for the duration of a session, this could mean a lot of "orphaned" state data consuming precious server resources for long periods of time!

There is virtually no difference between the bean interfaces for our stateless and stateful bean examples. Both are POJIs marked with the `@Remote` annotation to enable remote client access ❹.

Let's now take a quick look at stateful beans from the client perspective. As you might expect, compared to stateless beans there are no major semantic differences.

2.3.4 A stateful bean client

It is clear that the `PlaceOrder` EJB is called from the ActionBazaar web tier. However, to give a slightly more colorful perspective on things, we'll deliberately stay out of web-tier client examples this time. We'll use a thick Java application that functions as a test script to run through the entire workflow of the `PlaceOrder` EJB using some dummy data. This test script could have just as easily been part of a very high-level regression test suite using a framework like JUnit or NUnit.

NOTE If you have management buy-in to invest in extensive unit testing, you might also note the fact that because of the POJO-centric nature of EJB 3, our example application could be easily modified to a full-scale unit test using dummy data sources and the like. We'll leave this for you as an exercise in case you are interested in exploring further by tweaking the source code available for download from www.manning.com/ panda. If unit testing and code coverage are not viable topics to bring up in your work environment, don't worry; we don't assume you do a ton of unit testing.

Listing 2.4 shows the code for the stateful session bean client.

Listing 2.4 Stateful session bean client

```
package ejb3inaction.example.buslogic;

import javax.ejb.EJB;
```

```
public class PlaceOrderTestClient {
    @EJB                                    ⤶ Injects an instance of EJB
    private static PlaceOrder placeOrder;

    public static void main(String [] args) throws Exception {
        System.out.println("Exercising PlaceOrder EJB...");
        placeOrder.setBidderId(new Long(100));
        placeOrder.addItem(new Long(200));
        placeOrder.addItem(new Long(201));
        placeOrder.setShippingInfo(
          new ShippingInfo("123 My Sweet Home",
          "MyCity","MyState"));
        placeOrder.setBillingInfo(
          new BillingInfo("123456789","VISA","0708"));
        Long orderId = placeOrder.confirmOrder();
        System.out.println("Order confirmation number: " + orderId);


    }
}
```

There is nothing special you need to do from the client side to use stateful beans. As a matter of fact, there is virtually no difference in the client code between using a stateless and a stateful bean, other than the fact that the client can safely assume that the EJB is maintaining state even if it is sitting on a remote application server. The other remarkable thing to note about listing 2.4 is the fact that the @EJB annotation is injecting a remote EJB into a standalone client. This is accomplished by running the client in the application client container (ACC).

NOTE   The application client container is a mini Java EE container that can be run from the command line. Think of it as a souped-up Java Virtual Machine (JVM) with some Java EE juice added. You can run any Java SE client such as a Swing application inside the ACC as if you were using a regular old JVM. The beauty of it is that the ACC will recognize and process most Java EE annotations such as the @EJB DI annotation. Among other things, the client container can look up and inject EJBs on remote servers, communicate with remote EJBs using RMI, provide authentication, perform authorization, and so forth. The application client really shines if you need to use EJBs in an SE application or would like to inject real resources into your POJO during unit testing.

Any Java class with a `main` method can be run inside the ACC. Typically, though, an application client is packaged in a JAR file that must contain a `Main-Class` in the `Manifest` file. Optionally, the JAR may contain a deployment descriptor (application-client.xml) and a jndi.properties file that contains the environment properties for connecting to a remote EJB container. Let's assume you packaged up your application client classes in a JAR file named chapter2-client.jar. Using Sun Microsystems's GlassFish application server, you could launch your application client inside the ACC as follows:

```
appclient -client  chapter2-client.jar
```

This finishes our brief introduction to session beans using our ActionBazaar scenario. We are now ready to move on to the next business-tier EJB component: message-driven beans.

2.4 Messaging with message-driven beans

Just as session beans process direct business requests from the client, MDBs process indirect *messages*. In enterprise systems, messaging has numerous uses, including system integration, asynchronous processing, and distributed system communication. If you've been working on enterprise development for some time, you're probably familiar with at least the idea of messaging. In the most basic terms, messaging involves communicating between two separate processes, usually across different machines. Java EE messaging follows this same idea—just on steroids. Most significantly, Java EE makes messaging robust by adding a reliable middleman between the message sender and receiver. This idea is illustrated in figure 2.5.

In Java EE terms, the reliable middleman is called a messaging *destination*, powered by message-oriented middleware (MOM) servers like IBM's MQSeries or Progress Software's SonicMQ. Java EE standardizes messaging through a well-known API, Java Messaging Service (JMS), upon which MDBs are heavily dependent.

Figure 2.5   The Java EE "pony express" messaging model. Java EE adds reliability to messaging by adding a middleman that guarantees the delivery of messages despite network outages, even if the receiver is not present on the other end when the message is sent. In this sense, Java EE messaging has much more in common with the postal service than it does with common RPC protocols like RMI. We'll discuss this model in much greater detail in chapter 4.

We'll discuss messaging, JMS, and MDBs in much greater detail in chapter 4. For the moment, this is all you really need to know.

Next, we'll build a simple example of message producer and an MBD. In our ActionBazaar example, we enable asynchronous order billing through messaging. To see how this is done, let's revisit the parts of the `PlaceOrderBean` introduced in listing 2.3 that we deliberately left hidden, namely the implementation of the `billOrder` method.

2.4.1 *Producing a billing message*

As we discussed in our high-level solution schematic in section 2.2, the `Place-OrderBean` accomplishes asynchronous or "out-of-process" order billing by generating a message in the `confirmOrder` method to request that the order billing be started in parallel. As soon as this billing request message is sent to the messaging middleman, the `confirmOrder` method returns with the order confirmation to the user. We'll now take a look at exactly how this piece is implemented. As you can see in listing 2.5, the billing request message is sent to a messaging destination named `jms/OrderBillingQueue`. Since you have already seen most of the implementation of the `PlaceOrder` bean, we won't repeat a lot of the code shown in listing 2.3 here.

Listing 2.5 PlaceOrderBean that produces the JMS message

```
package ejb3inaction.example.buslogic;

...
import javax.annotation.Resource;
import javax.ejb.Remove;
import javax.ejb.Stateful;
import javax.jms.*;
...

@Stateful
public class PlaceOrderBean implements PlaceOrder {
    @Resource(name="jms/QueueConnectionFactory")
    private ConnectionFactory connectionFactory;          ❶ Injects JMS
                                                             resources
    @Resource(name="jms/OrderBillingQueue")
    private Destination billingQueue;
    ...
    @Remove
    public Long confirmOrder() {
        Order order = new Order();
        order.setBidderId(bidderId);
        order.setItems(items);
```

```
            order.setShippingInfo(shippingInfo);
            order.setBillingInfo(billingInfo);

            saveOrder(order);
            billOrder(order);

            return order.getOrderId();
        }
        ...
    private void billOrder(Order order) {
        try {
            Connection connection =
                connectionFactory.createConnection();
            Session session =
                connection.createSession(false,
                    Session.AUTO_ACKNOWLEDGE);
            MessageProducer producer =
                session.createProducer(billingQueue);
            ObjectMessage message =
                session.createObjectMessage();
            message.setObject(order);
            producer.send(message);
            producer.close();
            session.close();
            connection.close();
        } catch(Exception e){
            e.printStackTrace();
        }
    }
}
```

❷ **Contains JMS setup code**

❸ **Creates and sends the message**

❹ **Releases JMS resources**

Not surprisingly, the code to send the message in listing 2.5 is heavily dependent on the JMS API. In fact, that's all that the code in the `billOrder` method consists of. If you're familiar with JDBC, the flavor of the code in the method might seem familiar. The end result of the code is that the newly created `Order` object is sent as a message to a JMS destination named `jms/OrderBillingQueue`. We won't deal with the intricacies of JMS immediately, but we'll save a detailed discussion of this essential messaging API for chapter 4. It is important to note a few things right now, though.

The first thing is that two JMS resources, including the message destination, are *injected* using the `@Resource` annotation ❶ instead of being looked up.

NOTE   As we stated earlier, in addition to the `@EJB` annotation the `@Resource` annotation provides DI functionality in EJB 3. While the `@EJB` annotation is limited to injecting EJBs, the `@Resource` annotation is much more general purpose and can be used to inject anything that the container knows about.

As shown in listing 2.5, the container looks up the JMS resources specified through the name parameter and injects them into the connectionFactory and billingQueue instance variables. The name parameter values specify what resources are bound to the EJB's environment naming context. Then the PlaceOrderBean establishes a connection to the JMS provider, and creates a session and a message producer ❷. Secondly, it is important to realize that the MessageProducer.send method ❸ doesn't wait for a receiver to receive the message on the other end. Because the messaging server guarantees that the message will be delivered to anyone interested in the message, this is just fine. In fact, this is exactly what enables the billing process to start in parallel to the ordering process, which continues on its merry way as soon as the message is sent. You should also note how loosely coupled the ordering and billing processes are. The ordering bean doesn't even know who picks up and processes its message; it simply knows the message destination! Finally, PlaceOrderBean cleans up all resources used by it ❹.

As we know from our solution schematic in section 2.2, the OrderBillingMDB processes the request to bill the order. It continuously listens for messages sent to the jms/OrderBillingQueue messaging destination, picks up the messages from the queue, inspects the Order object embedded in the message, and attempts to bill the user. We'll depict this scheme in figure 2.6 to reinforce the concept.

Figure 2.6 Asynchronously billing orders using MDBs. The stateful session bean processing the order sends a message to the order-billing queue. The billing MDB picks up this message and processes it asynchronously.

Let's take a look now at how the OrderBillingMDB is implemented.

2.4.2 Using the order billing message processor MDB

The OrderBillingMDB's sole purpose is to attempt to bill the bidder for the total cost of an order, including the price of the items in the order, shipping, handling, insurance costs, and the like. Listing 2.6 shows the abbreviated code for the order billing MDB. Recall that the Order object passed inside the message sent by the PlaceOrder EJB contains a BillingInfo object. The BillingInfo object tells OrderBillingMDB how to bill the customer—perhaps by charging a credit card or crediting against an online bank account. However the user is supposed to be charged, after attempting to bill the user the MDB notifies both the bidder and seller of the results of the billing attempt. If billing is successful, the seller ships to the address specified in the order. If the billing attempt fails, the bidder must correct and resubmit the billing information attached to the order.

Last but not least, the MDB must also update the order record to reflect what happened during the billing attempt. Feel free to explore the complete code sample and deployment descriptor entries containing the JMS resource configuration in the zip containing code examples.

Listing 2.6 OrderBillingMDB

```java
package ejb3inaction.example.buslogic;

import javax.ejb.MessageDriven;
import javax.ejb.ActivationConfigProperty;
import javax.jms.Message;
import javax.jms.MessageListener;
import javax.jms.ObjectMessage;
import ejb3inaction.example.persistence.Order;
import ejb3inaction.example.persistence.OrderStatus;

@MessageDriven(               ← Marks POJO as MDB
    activationConfig = {
        @ActivationConfigProperty(
            propertyName="destinationName",           Specifies JMS
            propertyValue="jms/OrderBillingQueue")     destination to get
    }                                                  messages from
)
public class OrderBillingMDB implements MessageListener {
    ...                            Implements javax.jms.
    public void onMessage(Message message) {   MessageListener interface
        try {
            ObjectMessage objectMessage = (ObjectMessage) message;
            Order order = (Order) objectMessage.getObject();

            try {
                bill(order);
                notifyBillingSuccess(order);
                order.setStatus(OrderStatus.COMPLETE);
            } catch (BillingException be) {
                notifyBillingFailure(be, order);
                order.setStatus(OrderStatus.BILLING_FAILED);
            } finally {
                update(order);
            }
```

```
        } catch (Exception e) {
            e.printStackTrace();
        }
    }
    ...
}
```

As you might have noticed from the code, MDBs are really session beans in JMS disguise. Like stateless beans, MDBs are not guaranteed to maintain state. The `@MessageDriven` annotation is the MDB counterpart of the `@Stateless` and `@Stateful` annotations—it makes the container transparently provide messaging and other EJB services into a POJO. The activation configuration properties nested inside the `@MessageDriven` annotation tells the container what JMS destination the MDB wants to receive messages from.

> **NOTE**   Behind the scenes, the container takes care of several mechanical details to start listening for messages sent to the destination specified by the activation configuration properties. As soon as a message arrives at the destination, the container forwards it to an instance of the MDB.

Instead of implementing a remote or local business interface, MDBs implement the `javax.jms.MessageListener` interface. The container uses this well-known JMS interface to invoke an MDB. The `onMessage` method defined by the interface has a single `javax.jms.Message` parameter that the container uses to pass a received message to the MDB. Believe it or not, this is more or less all you need to know to get by when using MDBs, as long as you have a decent understanding of messaging and JMS.

This wraps up this chapter's discussion of the EJB 3 business-tier components. As we mentioned earlier, we'll devote the entirety of the next part of the book to this vital part of the EJB platform. For now, let's move on to the other major part of EJB, the Persistence API.

2.5   *Persisting data with EJB 3 JPA*

The Java Persistence API (JPA) is the persistence-tier solution for the Java EE platform. Although a lot has changed in EJB 3 for session beans and MDBs, the changes in the persistence tier have truly been phenomenal. In fact, other than some naming patterns and concepts, JPA has very little in common with the EJB 2 entity bean model. JPA does not follow the container model (which is just not very

well suited to the problem of persistence);
instead, it follows an API paradigm similar
to JDBC, JavaMail, or JMS. As you'll soon
see, the JPA `EntityManager` interface defines
the API for persistence while JPA entities
specify how application data is mapped to
a relational database. Although JPA takes a
serious bite out of the complexity in saving enterprise data, ORM-based persistence is still a nontrivial topic. We'll devote
the entire third part of this book to JPA,
namely chapters 7 through 10.

In almost every step of our ActionBazaar scenario, data is saved into the database using JPA. We won't bore you by going
over all of the persistence code for the scenario. Instead, we'll introduce JPA using a
representative example and leave you to
explore the complete code on your own.
You'll see what EJB 3 persistence looks like
by revisiting the `PlaceBid` stateless session
bean. As a reminder to how the bidding
process is implemented, figure 2.7 depicts
the various components that interact with
one another when a bidder creates a bid in
ActionBazaar.

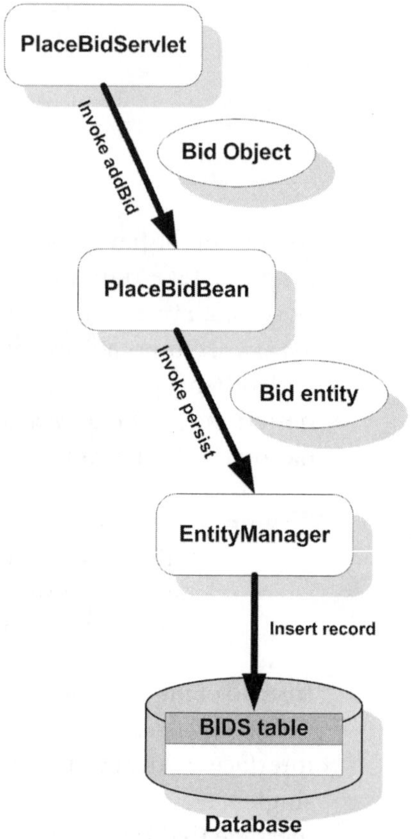

Recall that the `PlaceBidServlet` calls
the `PlaceBidBean`'s `addBid` method to add a
`Bid` entity into the database. The `Place-
BidBean` uses the JPA `EntityManager`'s per-
sist method to save the bid. Let's first

Figure 2.7   **PlaceBidServlet invokes the
addBid method of PlaceBid EJB and passes
a Bid object. The PlaceBidEJB invokes the
persist method of EntityManager to save
the Bid entity into the database. When the
transaction commits, you'll see that a
corresponding database record in the BIDS
table will be stored.**

take a look at the JPA, and then we'll see the `EntityManager` in action.

2.5.1   *Working with the Java Persistence API*

You might have noticed in listing 2.1 that we kept the code to save a bid into the
database conveniently out of sight. The `PlaceBid` EJB's `addBid` method references
the hidden save method to persist the `Bid` object to the database. Listing 2.8 will
fill in this gap by showing you what the save method actually does. The save

method uses the JPA `EntityManager` to save the `Bid` object. But first let's take a quick look at the fourth and final kind of EJB—the JPA entity. Listing 2.7 shows how the `Bid` entity looks.

Listing 2.7   Bid entity

```
package ejb3inaction.example.persistence;

import java.io.Serializable;
import java.sql.Date;
import javax.persistence.Column;
import javax.persistence.Entity;
import javax.persistence.Id;
import javax.persistence.Table;
import javax.persistence.GenerationType;
import javax.persistence.GeneratedValue;

@Entity          ◁━❶ Marks POJO as entity
@Table(name="BIDS")                    ◁━❷ Specifies table mapping
public class Bid implements Serializable {
    private Long bidID;
    private Long itemID;
    private Long bidderID;
    private Double bidAmount;
    private Date bidDate;

              ❸  Contains entity ID
    @Id    ◁┘
    @GeneratedValue(strategy=GenerationType.AUTO)    ◁━❹ Generates ID value
    @Column(name="BID_ID")                      ◁┐
    public Long getBidID() {
        return bidID;
    }

    public void setBidID(Long bidID) {
        this.bidID = bidID;
    }

    @Column(name="ITEM_ID")                     ◁━❺ Specifies
    public Long getItemID() {                        column
        return itemID;                               mappings
    }

    public void setItemID(Long itemID) {
        this.itemID = itemID;
    }

    @Column(name="BIDDER_ID")                   ◁┘
    public Long getBidderID() {
        return bidderID;
    }
```

```
    public void setBidderID(Long bidderID) {
        this.bidderID = bidderID;
    }

    @Column(name="BID_AMOUNT")
    public Double getBidAmount() {
        return bidAmount;
    }

    public void setBidAmount(Double bidAmount) {
        this.bidAmount = bidAmount;
    }

    @Column(name="BID_DATE")
    public Date getBidDate() {
        return bidDate;
    }

    public void setBidDate(Date bidDate) {
        this.bidDate = bidDate;
    }
}
```

❺ Specifies column mappings

You probably have a good idea of exactly how object-relational mapping in JPA works just by glancing at listing 2.7, even if you have no familiarity with ORM tools such as Hibernate. Think about the annotations that mirror relational concepts such as tables, columns, and primary keys.

The @Entity annotation signifies the fact that the Bid class is a JPA entity ❶. Note that Bid is a POJO that does not require a business interface, unlike session and message-driven beans. The @Table annotation tells JPA that the Bid entity is mapped to the BIDS table ❷. Similarly, the @Column annotations ❺ indicate which Bid properties map to which BIDS table fields. Note that entities need not use getter- and setter-based properties. Instead, the field mappings could have been placed directly onto member variables exposed through nonprivate access modifiers. (You'll learn more about access via entity properties and fields in chapter 7.) The @Id annotation is somewhat special. It marks the bidID property as the primary key for the Bid entity ❸. Just like a database record, a primary key uniquely identifies an entity instance. We have used the @GeneratedValue annotation with strategy set to GenerationType.AUTO ❹ to indicate that the persistence provider should automatically generate the primary key when the entity is saved into the database.

> **NOTE** If you have used EJB 2 you may remember that it was almost rocket science to generate primary key values with container-managed persistence (CMP) entity beans. With EJB 3 JPA, the generation of primary keys is a snap; you have several options, such as table, sequence, identity key, and so on. We'll discuss primary-key generation in chapter 8.

The `Bid` entity could have been related to a number of other JPA entities by holding direct object references (such the `Bidder` and `Item` entities). EJB 3 JPA allows such object reference–based implicit relationships to be elegantly mapped to the database. We've decided to keep things simple for now and not dive into this topic quite so early; we'll discuss entity relationship mapping in chapter 8.

Having looked at the `Bid` entity, let's now turn our attention to how the entity winds up in the database through the `PlaceBid` bean.

2.5.2 *Using the EntityManager*

You've probably noticed that the `Bid` entity doesn't have a method to save itself into the database. The JPA `EntityManager` performs this bit of heavy lifting by reading ORM configuration and providing entity persistence services through an API-based interface.

> **NOTE** The `EntityManager` knows how to store a POJO entity into the database as a relational record, read relational data from a database, and turn it into an entity; update entity data stored in the database; and delete data mapped to an entity instance from the database. As you'll see in chapters 9 and 10, the `EntityManager` has methods corresponding to each of these CRUD (Create, Read, Update, Delete) operations, in addition to support for the robust Java Persistence Query Language (JPQL).

As promised earlier, listing 2.8 shows how the `PlaceBid` EJB uses `EntityManager` API to persist the `Bid` entity.

Listing 2.8 Saving a bid record using the EJB 3 JPA

```
package ejb3inaction.example.buslogic;

...
import javax.persistence.PersistenceContext;
import javax.persistence.EntityManager;
...

@Stateless
```

```
public class PlaceBidBean implements PlaceBid {
    @PersistenceContext(unitName="actionBazaar")
    private EntityManager entityManager;                    Injects instance of
                                                      ❶    EntityManager
    ...
    public Bid addBid(Bid bid) {
        System.out.println("Adding bid, bidder ID=" + bid.getBidderID()
            + ", item ID=" + bid.getItemID() + ", bid amount="
                + bid.getBidAmount() + ".");

        return save(bid);
    }

    private Bid save(Bid bid) {
        entityManager.persist(bid);      ◁── ❷ Persists entity instance
         return bid;
    }
}
```

The true magic of the code in listing 2.8 lies in the `EntityManager` interface. One interesting way to think about the `EntityManager` interface is as an "interpreter" between the object-oriented and relational worlds. The manager reads the ORM mapping annotations like `@Table` and `@Column` on the `Bid` entity and figures out how to save the entity into the database. The `EntityManager` is injected into the `Place-Bid` bean through the `@PersistenceContext` annotation ❶. Similar to the `name` parameter of the `@Resource` annotation in listing 2.5, the `unitName` parameter of the `@PersistenceContext` annotation points to the persistence unit specific to ActionBazaar. A *persistence unit* is a group of entities packaged together in an application module. You'll learn more about persistence units in chapters 9 and 11.

In the `save` method, the `EntityManager persist` method is called to save the `Bid` data into the database ❷. After the `persist` method returns, a SQL statement much like the following is issued against the database to insert a record corresponding to the bid:

```
INSERT INTO BIDS (BID_ID, BID_DATE, BIDDER_ID, BID_AMOUNT, ITEM_ID)
VALUES (52, NULL, 60, 20000.50, 100)
```

It might be instructive to look back at listing 2.7 now to see how the `EntityManager` figures out the SQL to generate by looking at the object-relational mapping annotations on the `Bid` entity. Recall that the `@Table` annotation specifies that the bid record should be saved in the `BIDS` table while each of the `@Column` annotations in listing 2.7 tells JPA which `Bid` entity field maps to which column in the `BIDS` table. For example, the `bidId` property maps to the `BIDS.BID_ID` column, the `bidAmount` property maps to the `BIDS.BID_AMOUNT` column, and so on. As we discussed earlier, the `@Id` and `@GeneratedValue` value annotations specify that the `BID_ID` column is the primary key of the `BIDS` table and that the JPA provider should automatically generate a value for the column before the `INSERT` statement is issued (the 52 value in the SQL sample). This process of translating an entity to columns in the database is exactly what object-relational mapping and JPA is all about.

This brings us to the end of this brief introduction to the EJB 3 Java Persistence API—and to the end of this whirlwind chapter. At this point, it should be clear to you how simple, effective, and robust EJB 3 is, even from a bird's-eye view.

2.6 Summary

As we stated in the introduction, the goal of this chapter was not to feed you the "guru pill" for EJB 3, but rather to show you what to expect from this new version of the Java enterprise platform.

This chapter introduced the ActionBazaar application, a central theme to this book. Using a scenario from the ActionBazaar application, we showed you a cross section of EJB 3 functionality, including stateless session beans, stateful session beans, message-driven beans, and the EJB 3 Java Persistence API. You also learned some basic concepts such as deployment descriptors, metadata annotations, and dependency injection.

We used a stateless session bean (`PlaceBidBean`) to implement the business logic for placing a bid for an item in an auctioning system. To access the bean, we built a very simple servlet client that used dependency injection. We then saw a stateful session bean (`PlaceOrderBean`) that encapsulated the logic for ordering an item, and we built an application client that accesses the `PlaceOrderBean`. We saw an example of an MDB, `OrderBillingMDB`, that processes a billing request when a message arrives on a JMS queue. Finally, we built an entity for storing bids and used the `EntityManager` API to persist the entity to the database.

Most of the rest of this book roughly follows the outline of this chapter. Chapter 3 revisits session beans; chapter 4 discusses messaging, JMS and MDBs; chapter 5 expands on dependency injection and discusses such topics as interceptors and timers; and chapter 6 explores transactions and security management in EJB. Chapters 7 through 10 are devoted to a detailed exploration of the Persistence API. Finally, chapters 11 through 16 cover advanced topics in EJB.

In the next chapter, we'll shift to a lower gear and dive into the details of session beans.

Part 2

Building business logic with EJB 3

Part 2 of this book covers how you can use EJB 3 components (session beans and message-driven beans) to build business logic for your enterprise Java applications. Chapter 3 covers session beans in detail and describes the development of both stateless and stateful beans and their clients. The chapter provides guidelines to help you decide whether to use stateless or stateful session beans. Asynchronous communication is accomplished by messaging, and chapter 4 explores messaging and message-driven beans. You can use several advanced features, such as dependency injection, interceptors, and timers; these topics are examined in chapter 5. Chapter 6 covers enterprise applications development concerns, such as transaction and security.

Building business
logic with session beans

3

This chapter covers

- Development of stateless and stateful session beans
- Session bean lifecycle
- Session bean clients
- Session bean performance considerations and best practices

At the heart of any enterprise application lies its business logic. In an ideal world, application developers should only be concerned with defining and implementing the business logic, while concerns like presentation, persistence, or integration should largely be window dressing. From this perspective, session beans are the most important part of the EJB technology because their purpose in life is to model high-level business processes.

If you think of a business system as a horse-drawn chariot with a driver carrying the Greco-Roman champion to battle, session beans are the driver. Session beans utilize data and system resources (the chariot and the horses) to implement the goals of the user (the champion) using business logic (the skills and judgment of the driver). For this and other reasons, sessions beans, particularly stateless session beans, have been popular, even despite the problems of EJB 2. EJB 3 makes this vital bean type a lot easier to use.

In chapter 1 we briefly introduced session beans. In chapter 2 we saw simple examples of these beans in action. In this chapter, we'll discuss session beans in much greater detail, focusing on their purpose, the different types of session beans, how to develop them, and some of the advanced session bean features available to you.

We start this chapter by exploring some basic session bean concepts, and then discuss some fundamental characteristics of session beans. We then cover each type—stateful and stateless—in detail before introducing bean client code. Finally, we examine session bean best practices at the end of the chapter.

3.1 *Getting to know session beans*

A typical enterprise application will have numerous business activities or processes. For example, our ActionBazaar application has processes such as creating a user, adding an item for auctioning, bidding for an item, ordering an item, and many more. Session beans can be used to encapsulate the business logic for all such processes.

The theory behind session beans centers on the idea that each request by a client to complete a distinct business process is completed in a *session*. So what is a session? If you have used a Unix server you may have used Telnet to connect to the server from a PC client. Telnet allows you to establish a login session with the Unix server for a finite amount of time. During this session you may execute several commands in the server. Simply put, a *session* is a connection between a client and a server that lasts for a finite period of time.

A session may either be very short-lived, like an HTTP request, or span a long time, like a login session when you Telnet or FTP into a Unix server. Similar to a typical Telnet session, a bean may maintain its state between calls, in which case it is stateful, or it may be a one-time call, in which case it's stateless. A typical example of a stateful application is the module that a bidder uses to register himself in the ActionBazaar application. That process takes place in multiple steps. An example of a stateless business module is the application code that is used to place a bid for an item. Information, such as user ID, item number, and amount, is passed in and success or failure is returned. This happens all in one step. We'll examine the differences between stateless and stateful session beans more closely in section 3.1.4.

As you might recall, session beans are the only EJB components that are invoked directly by clients. A client can be anything, such as a web application component (servlet, JSP, JSF, and so on), a command-line application, or a Swing GUI desktop application. A client can even be a Microsoft .NET application using web services access.

At this point you might be wondering what makes session beans special. After all, why use a session bean simply to act as a business logic holder? Glad that you asked. Before you invest more of your time, let's address this question first. Then we'll show you the basic anatomy of a session bean and explore the rules that govern it before examining the differences between stateless and stateful session beans.

3.1.1 Why use session beans?

Session beans are a lot more than just business logic holders. Remember the EJB services we briefly mentioned in chapter 1? The majority of those services are specifically geared toward session beans. They make developing a robust, feature-rich, impressive business logic tier remarkably easy (and maybe even a little fun). Let's take a look at some of the most important of these services.

Concurrency and thread safety

The whole point of building server-side applications is that they can be shared by a large number of remote clients at the same time. Because session beans are specifically meant to handle client requests, they must support a high degree of concurrency safely and robustly. In our ActionBazaar example, it is likely thousands of concurrent users will be using the `PlaceBid` session bean we introduced in chapter 2. The container employs a number of techniques to "automagically" make sure you don't have to worry about concurrency or thread safety. This means that we can develop session beans as though we were writing a standalone desktop application used by a single user. You'll learn more about these "automagic" techniques, including pooling, session management, and passivation, later in this chapter.

Remoting and web services

Session beans support both Java Remote Method Invocation (RMI)-based native and Simple Object Access Protocol (SOAP)-based web services remote access. Other than some minor configuration, no work is required to make session bean business logic accessible remotely using either method. This goes a long way toward enabling distributed computing and interoperability. You'll see session bean remoteability in action in just a few sections.

Transaction and security management

Transactions and security management are two enterprise-computing mainstays. Session beans, with their pure configuration-based transactions, authorization, and authentication, make supporting these requirements all but a nonissue. We won't discuss these services in this chapter, but chapter 6 is devoted to EJB transaction management and security.

Timer services and interceptors

Interceptors are EJB's version of lightweight aspect-oriented programming (AOP). Recall that AOP is the ability to isolate "crosscutting" concerns into their own modules and apply them across the application through configuration. Crosscutting concerns include things like auditing and logging that are repeated across an application but are not directly related to business logic. We'll discuss interceptors in great detail in chapter 5.

Timer services are EJB's version of lightweight application schedulers. In most medium- to large-scale applications, you'll find that you need some kind of scheduling services. In ActionBazaar, scheduled tasks could be used to monitor when the bidding for a particular item ends and determine who won an auction. Timer services allow us to easily turn a session bean into a recurring or nonrecurring scheduled task. We'll save the discussion of timer services for chapter 5 as well.

Now that you are convinced you should use session beans, let's look at some of their basic characteristics.

A session bean alternative: Spring

Clearly, EJB 3 session beans are not your only option in developing your application's business tier. POJOs managed by lightweight containers such as Spring could also be used to build the business logic tier. Before jumping on either the EJB 3 session bean or Spring bandwagon, think about what your needs are.

If your application needs robust support for accessing remote components or the ability to seamlessly expose your business logic as web services, EJB 3 is the clear choice. Spring also lacks good equivalents of instance pooling, automated session state maintenance, and passivation/activation. Because of heavy use of annotations, you can pretty much avoid "XML Hell" using EJB 3; the same cannot be said of Spring. Moreover, because it is an integral part of the Java EE standard, the EJB container is natively integrated with components such as JSF, JSP, servlets, the JTA transaction manager, JMS providers, and Java Authentication and Authorization Service (JAAS) security providers of your application server. With Spring, you have to worry whether your application server fully supports the framework with these native components and other high-performance features like clustering, load balancing, and failover.

If you aren't worried about such things, then Spring is not a bad choice at all and even offers a few strengths of its own. The framework provides numerous simple, elegant utilities for performing many common tasks such as the `JdbcTemplate` and `JmsTemplate`. If you plan to use dependency injection with regular Java classes, Spring is great since DI only works for container components in EJB 3. Also, Spring AOP or AspectJ is a much more feature-rich (albeit slightly more complex) choice than EJB 3 interceptors.

Nevertheless, if portability, standardization, and vendor support are important to you, EJB 3 may be the way to go. EJB 3 is a mature product that is the organic (though imperfect) result of the incremental effort, pooled resources, shared ownership, and measured consensus of numerous groups of people. This includes the grassroots Java Community Process (JCP); some of the world's most revered commercial technology powerhouses like IBM, Sun, Oracle, and BEA; and spirited open-source organizations like Apache and JBoss.

3.1.2 *Session beans: the basics*

Although we briefly touched on session beans in the previous chapter, we didn't go into great detail about developing them. Before we dive in, let's revisit the code in chapter 2 to closely examine some basic traits shared by all session beans.

The anatomy of a session bean

Each session bean implementation has two distinct parts—one or more bean interfaces and a bean implementation class. In the `PlaceBid` bean example from chapter 2, the bean implementation consisted of the `PlaceBid` interface and the `PlaceBidBean` class, as shown in figure 3.1.

All session beans must be divided into these two parts. This is because clients cannot have access to the bean implementation class directly. Instead, they must use session beans through a business interface. None-theless, *interface-based programming* is a sound idea any-way, especially when using dependency injection.

Interface-based programming is the practice of not using implementation classes directly whenever possible. This approach promotes loose coupling since implementation classes can easily be swapped out without a lot of code changes. EJB has been a major catalyst in the popularization of interface-based programming; even the earliest versions of EJB followed this paradigm, later to form the basis of DI.

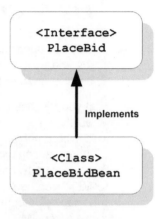

Figure 3.1   Parts of the PlaceBid session bean. Each session bean has one or more interfaces and one implementation class.

The session bean business interface

An interface through which a client invokes the bean is called a *business interface*. This interface essentially defines the bean methods appropriate for access through a specific access mechanism. For example, let's revisit the `PlaceBid` interface in chapter 2:

```
@Local
public interface PlaceBid {
    Bid addBid(Bid bid);
}
```

Since all EJB interfaces are POJIs, there isn't anything too remarkable in this code other than the `@Local` annotation specifying that it's a local interface. Recall that a business interface can be remote or even web service-accessible instead. We'll talk more about the three types of interfaces in section 3.2.3. The interesting thing to note right now is the fact that a single EJB can have multiple interfaces. In other words, EJB implementation classes can be *polymorphic*, meaning that different clients using different interfaces could use them in completely different ways.

The EJB bean class

Just like typical OO programming, each interface that the bean intends to support must be explicitly included in the bean implementation class's `implements` clause. We can see this in the code for the `PlaceBidBean` from chapter 2:

```
@Stateless
public class PlaceBidBean implements PlaceBid {
    ...
    public PlaceBidBean() {}

    public Bid addBid(Bid bid) {
        System.out.println("Adding bid, bidder ID=" + bid.getBidderID()
            + ", item ID=" + bid.getItemID() + ", bid amount="
                + bid.getBidAmount() + ".");

        return save(bid);
    }
    ...
}
```

The `PlaceBidBean` class provides the concrete implementation of the `addBid` method required by the `PlaceBid` interface. Session bean implementation classes can never be abstract, which means that all methods mandated by declared business interfaces must be implemented in the class.

Note that EJB implementation classes can have nonprivate methods that are not accessible through any interface. Such methods can be useful for creating clever unit-testing frameworks and while implementing lifecycle callback, as you'll learn in section 3.2.5. Also, an EJB bean class can make use of OO inheritance. You could use this strategy to support a custom framework for your application. For example, you could put commonly used logic in a parent POJO class that a set of beans inherits from.

Unit-testing your session beans

It is clear that session beans are POJOs. Since EJB annotations are ignored by the JVM, session beans can be unit-tested using a framework like JUnit or TestNG without having to deploy them into an EJB container. For more information on JUnit, browse www.junit.org.

On the other hand, since several container-provided services such as dependency injection cannot be used outside the container, you cannot perform functional testing of applications using EJBs outside the container—at least not easily.

Now that we've looked at the basic structure of session beans, we'll outline relatively simple programming rules for a session bean.

3.1.3 Understanding the programming rules

Like all EJB 3 beans, session beans are POJOs that follow a small set of rules. The following summarizes the rules that apply to all types of session beans:

- As we discussed earlier in section 3.1.2, a session bean must have at least one business interface.

- The session bean class must be concrete. You cannot define a session bean class as either final or abstract since the container needs to manipulate it.

- You must have a no-argument constructor in the bean class. As we saw, this is because the container invokes this constructor to create a bean instance when a client invokes an EJB. Note that the compiler inserts a default no-argument constructor if there is no constructor in a Java class.

- A session bean class can subclass another session bean or any other POJO. For example, a stateless session bean named `BidManager` can extend another session bean `PlaceBidBean` in the following way:

```
@Stateless
public BidManagerBean extends PlaceBidBean implements BidManager {
    ...
}
```

- The business methods and lifecycle callback methods may be defined either in the bean class or in a superclass. It's worth mentioning here that annotation inheritance is supported with several limitations with EJB 3 session beans. For example, the bean type annotation `@Stateless` or `@Stateful` specified in the `PlaceBidBean` superclass will be ignored when you deploy the `BidManagerBean`. However, any annotations in the superclasses used to define lifecycle callback methods (more about that later in this section) and resource injections will be inherited by the bean class.

- Business method names must not start with "ejb." For example, avoid a method name like `ejbCreate` or `ejbAddBid` because it may interfere with EJB infrastructure processing. You must define all business methods as public, but not final or static. If you are exposing a method in a remote business interface of the EJB, then make sure that the arguments and the return type of the method implement the `java.io.Serializable` interface.

You'll see these rules applied when we explore concrete examples of stateless and stateful session beans in sections 3.2 and 3.3, respectively.

Now that we've looked at the basic programming rules for the session beans, let's discuss the fundamental reasons behind splitting them into two groups.

3.1.4 *Conversational state and session bean types*

Earlier, we talked about stateful and stateless session beans. However, we have so far avoided the real differences between them. This grouping of bean types centers on the concept of the *conversational state*.

A particular business process may involve more than one session bean method call. During these method calls, the session bean may or may not maintain a *conversational state*. This terminology will make more sense if you think of each session bean method call as a "conversation," or "exchange of information," between the client and the bean. A bean that maintains conversational state "remembers" the results of previous exchanges, and is a *stateful session bean*. In Java terms, this means that the bean will store data from a method call into instance variables and use the cached data to process the next method call. *Stateless session beans* don't maintain any state. In general, stateful session beans tend to model multistep workflows, while stateless session beans tend to model general-purpose, utility services used by the client.

The classic example of maintaining conversational state is the e-commerce website shopping cart. When the client adds, removes, modifies, or checks out items from the shopping cart, the shopping cart is expected to store all the items that were put into it while the client was shopping. As you can imagine, except for the most complex business processes in an application, most session bean interactions don't require a conversational state. Putting in a bid at ActionBazaar, leaving buyer or seller feedback, and viewing a particular item for bid are all examples of *stateless* business processes.

As you'll soon see, however, this does not mean that stateless session beans cannot have instance variables. Even before we explore any code, common sense should tell us that session beans must cache *some* resources, like database connections, for performance reasons. The critical distinction here is *client expectations*. As long as the client does not need to depend on the fact that a session bean uses instance variables to maintain conversational state, there is no need to use a stateful session bean.

3.1.5 *Bean lifecycle callbacks*

A session bean has a lifecycle. This mean that beans go through a predefined set of state transitions. If you've used Spring or EJB 2, this should come as no surprise. If you haven't, the concept can be a little tricky to grasp.

To understand the bean lifecycle, it is important to revisit the concept of *managed resources*. Recall that the container manages almost every aspect of session beans. This means that neither the client nor the bean is responsible for determining when bean instances are created, when dependencies are injected, when bean instances are destroyed, or when to take optimization measures. Managing these actions enables the container to provide the abstractions that constitute some of the real value of using EJBs, including DI, automated transaction management, AOP, transparent security management, and so on.

The lifecycle events

The lifecycle of a session bean may be categorized into several phases or events. The most obvious two events of a bean lifecycle are *creation* and *destruction*. All EJBs go through these two phases. In addition, stateful session beans go through the *passivation/activation* cycle, which we discuss in depth in section 3.3.5. Here, we take a close look at the phases shared by all session beans: creation and destruction.

The lifecycle for a session bean starts when a bean instance is created. This typically happens when a client receives a reference to the bean either by doing a JNDI lookup or by using dependency injection. The following steps occur when a bean is initialized:

1 The container invokes the `newInstance` method on the bean object. This essentially translates to a constructor invocation on the bean implementation class.

2 If the bean uses DI, all dependencies on resources, other beans, and environment components are injected into the newly created bean instance.

Figure 3.2 depicts this series of events.

After the container determines that an instance is no longer needed, the instance is destroyed. This sounds just fine until you realize that the bean might need to know when some of its lifecycle transitions happen. For example, suppose that the resource being injected into a bean is a JDBC data source. That means that it would be nice to be able to know when it is injected so you can open the JDBC database connection to be used in the next business method invocation. In a similar way, the bean would also need to be notified before it is destroyed so that the open database connection can be properly closed.

This is where callbacks come in.

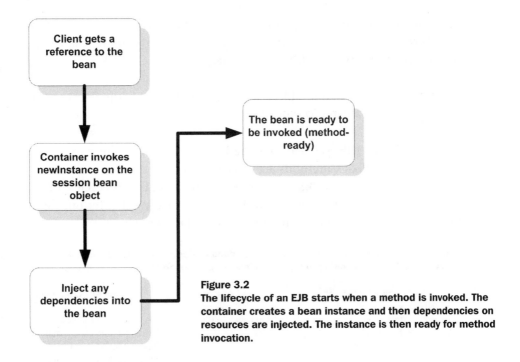

Figure 3.2
The lifecycle of an EJB starts when a method is invoked. The container creates a bean instance and then dependencies on resources are injected. The instance is then ready for method invocation.

Understanding lifecycle callbacks

Lifecycle callbacks are bean methods (not exposed by a business interface) that the container calls to notify the bean about a lifecycle transition, or event. When the event occurs, the container invokes the corresponding callback method, and you can use these methods to perform business logic or operations such as initialization and cleanup of resources.

Callback methods are bean methods that are marked with metadata annotations such as @PostContruct and @PreDestroy. They can be public, private, protected, or package-protected. As you might have already guessed, a Post-Construct callback is invoked just after a bean instance is created and dependencies are injected. A PreDestroy callback is invoked just before the bean is destroyed and is helpful for cleaning up resources used by the bean.

While all session beans have PostConstruct and PreDestroy lifecycle events, stateful session beans have two additional ones: PrePassivate and PostActivate. Since stateful session beans maintain state, there is a stateful session bean instance for each client, and there could be many instances of a stateful session bean in the container. If this happens, the container may decide to deactivate a stateful bean instance temporarily when not in use; this process is called *passivation*. The container activates the bean instance again when the client needs it; this process is called *activation*. The `@PrePassivate` and `@PostActivate` annotations apply to the passivation and activation lifecycle events.

NOTE You can define a lifecycle callback method either in the bean class or in a separate interceptor class.

Table 3.1 lists the lifecycle callback method annotations, where they are applied, and what the callback methods are typically used for.

In sections 3.2.4 and 3.3.4, you'll learn how to define lifecycle callback methods in the bean class for stateless and stateful beans. We'll defer our discussion of lifecycle callback methods in the interceptor classes to chapter 5.

Table 3.1 Lifecycle callbacks are created to handle lifecycle events for an EJB. You can create these callback methods either in the bean class or in an external interceptor class.

Callback Annotation	Type of EJB	Typically Used For...
`javax.annotation.` `PostConstruct`	Stateless, stateful, MDB	This annotated method is invoked after a bean instance is created and dependency injection is complete. Generally this callback is used to initialize resources (for example, opening database connections).
`javax.annotation.` `PreDestroy`	Stateless, stateful, MDB	This annotated method is invoked prior to a bean instance being destroyed. Generally this callback is used to clean up resources (for example, closing database connections).
`javax.ejb.PrePassivate`	Stateful	This annotated method is invoked prior to a bean instance being passivated. Generally this callback is used to clean up resources, such as database connections, TCP/IP sockets, or any resources that cannot be serialized during passivation.
`javax.ejb.PostActivate`	Stateful	This annotated method is invoked after a bean instance is activated. Generally this callback is used to restore resources, such as database connections that you cleaned up in the `PrePassivate` method.

At this point, let's launch our detailed exploration with the simpler stateless session bean model and save stateful session beans for later.

3.2 *Stateless session beans*

As noted earlier, stateless session beans model tasks don't maintain conversational state. This means that session beans model tasks can be completed in a single method call, such as placing a bid. However, this does not mean that all stateless session beans contain a single method, as is the case for the `PlaceBid-Bean` in chapter 2. In fact, real-world stateless session beans often contain several closely related business methods, like the `BidManager` bean we'll introduce soon. By and large, stateless session beans are the most popular kind of session beans. They are also the most performance efficient. To understand why, take a look at figure 3.3, which shows a high-level schematic of how stateless session beans are typically used by clients.

As you'll learn in section 3.2.4, stateless beans are *pooled*. This means that for each managed bean, the container keeps a certain number of instances handy in a pool. For each client request, an instance from the pool is quickly assigned to the client. When the client request finishes, the instance is returned to the pool for reuse. This means that a small number of bean instances can service a relatively large number of clients.

In this section you'll learn more about developing stateless session beans. We'll develop part of the business logic of our ActionBazaar system using a stateless session to illustrate its use. You'll learn how to use `@Stateless` annotations as well as various types of business interfaces and lifecycle callbacks supported with stateless session beans.

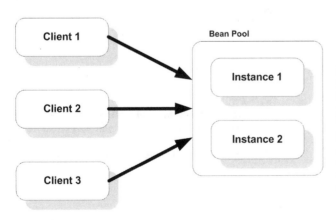

Figure 3.3
Stateless session bean instances can be pooled and may be shared between clients. When a client invokes a method in a stateless session bean, the container either creates a new instance in the bean pool for the client or assigns one from the bean pool. The instance is returned to the pool after use.

Before we jump into analyzing code, let's briefly discuss the ActionBazaar business logic that we'll implement as a stateless session bean.

3.2.1 *The BidManagerBean example*

Bidding is a critical part of the ActionBazaar functionality. Users can bid on an item and view the current bids, while ActionBazaar administrators and customer service representatives can remove bids under certain circumstances. Figure 3.4 depicts these bid-related actions.

Because all of these bid-related functions are simple, single-step processes, a stateless session bean can be used to model all of them. The BidManagerBean presented in listing 3.1 contains methods for adding, viewing, and canceling (or removing) bids. This is essentially an enhanced, more realistic version of the basic PlaceBid EJB we saw earlier. The complete code is available for download from www.manning.com/panda in the zip containing code examples.

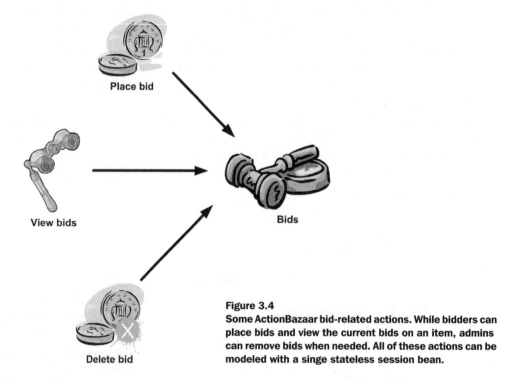

Figure 3.4
Some ActionBazaar bid-related actions. While bidders can place bids and view the current bids on an item, admins can remove bids when needed. All of these actions can be modeled with a singe stateless session bean.

NOTE   We are using JDBC for simplicity only because we have not introduced the EJB 3 Java Persistence API (JPA) in any detail quite yet, and we don't assume you already understand ORM. Using JDBC also happens to demonstrate the usage of dependency injection of resources and the stateless bean lifecycle callbacks pretty nicely! In general, you should avoid using JDBC in favor of JPA once you are comfortable with it.

Listing 3.1 Stateless session bean example

```
@Stateless(name="BidManager")                          ←─➊  Marks as stateless bean
public class BidManagerBean implements BidManager {
    @Resource(name="jdbc/ActionBazaarDS")   ←┐
    private DataSource dataSource;               ➋  Injects data source
    private Connection connection;
    ...
    public BidManagerBean() {}
                                      ➌  Receives PostConstruct
                                          callback
    @PostConstruct                ←┘
    public void initialize() {
        try {
          connection = dataSource.getConnection();
        } catch (SQLException sqle) {
            sqle.printStackTrace();
        }
    }

    public void addBid(Bid bid){
        try {
            Long bidId = getBidId();
            Statement statement = connection.createStatement();
            statement.execute(
                "INSERT INTO BIDS ("
                  + "BID_ID, "
                  + "BID_AMOUNT, "
                  + "BID_BIDDER_ID, "
                  + "BID_ITEM_ID) "
                  + "VALUES ("
                  + bidId + ", "
                  + bid.getAmount() + ", "
                  + bid.getBidder().getUserId() + ", "
                  + bid.getItem().getItemId()+ ")");

        } catch (Exception e) {
            e.printStackTrace();
        }
    }
                            ➍  Receives PreDestroy callback
    @PreDestroy     ←┘
    public void cleanup() {
```

```
            try {
               connection.close();
            } catch (SQLException sqle) {
               sqle.printStackTrace();
            }
         }


         private Long getBidId() { ... }

         public void cancelBid(Bid bid) {...}

         public List<Bid> getBids(Item item) {...}
         ...
      }
      ...                  ❺   Designates remote
      @Remote   ◁─┘            business interface
      public interface BidManager {
         void addBid(Bid bid);
         void cancelBid(Bid bid);
         List<Bid> getBids(Item item);
      }
```

As you've seen before, the @Stateless annotation marks the POJO as a stateless
session bean ❶. The BidManagerBean class implements the BidManager interface,
which is marked @Remote ❺. We use the @Resource annotation to perform injection of a JDBC data source ❷. The BidManagerBean has a no-argument constructor that the container will use to create instances of BidManagerBean EJB object.
The PostConstruct ❸ and PreDestroy ❹ callbacks are used to manage a JDBC
database connection derived from the injected data source. Finally, the addBid
business method adds a bid into the database.

   We'll start exploring the features of EJB 3 stateless session beans by analyzing
this code next, starting with the @Stateless annotation.

3.2.2 Using the @Stateless annotation

The @Stateless annotation marks the BidManagerBean POJO as a stateless session
bean. Believe it or not, other than marking a POJO for the purposes of making
the container aware of its purpose, the annotation does not do much else. The
specification of the @Stateless annotation is as follows:

```
@Target(TYPE) @Retention(RUNTIME)
public @interface Stateless {
    String name() default "";
```

```
String mappedName() default "";
String description() default "";

}
```

The single parameter, `name`, specifies the name of the bean. Some containers use this parameter to bind the EJB to the global JNDI tree. Recall that JNDI is essentially the application server's managed resource registry. All EJBs automatically get bound to JNDI as soon as they catch the container's watchful eye. You'll see the `name` parameter in use again in chapter 11 when we discuss deployment descriptors. In listing 3.1, the bean name is specified as `BidManager`. As the annotation definition shows, the `name` parameter is optional since it is defaulted to an empty `String`. We could easily omit it as follows:

```
@Stateless
public class BidManagerBean implements BidManager {
```

If the `name` parameter is omitted, the container assigns the name of the class to the bean. In this case, the container assumes the bean name is `BidManager-Bean`. `mappedName` is a vendor-specific name that you can assign to your EJB; some containers, such as the GlassFish application server, use this name to assign the global JNDI name for the EJB. As we noted, the `BidManagerBean` implements a business interface named `BidManager`. Although we've touched on the idea of a business interface, we haven't dug very deeply into the concept. This is a great time to do exactly that.

3.2.3 *Specifying bean business interfaces*

In section 3.1, we introduced you to EJB interfaces. Now let's explore a bit more how they work with stateless session beans. Client applications can invoke a stateless session bean in three different ways. In addition to local invocation within the same JVM and remote invocation through RMI, stateless beans can be invoked remotely as web services.

Three types of business interfaces correspond to the different access types; each is identified through a distinct annotation. Let's take a detailed look at these annotations.

Local interface

A *local interface* is designed for clients of stateless session beans collocated in the same container (JVM) instance. You designate an interface as a local business interface by using the `@Local` annotation. The following could be a local interface for the `BidManagerBean` class in listing 3.1:

```
@Local
public interface BidManagerLocal {
    void addBid(Bid bid);
    void cancelBid(Bid bid);
    List<Bid> getBids(Item item);
}
```

Local interfaces don't require any special measures in terms of either defining or implementing them.

Remote interface

Clients residing outside the EJB container's JVM instance must use some kind of *remote interface*. If the client is also written in Java, the most logical and resource-efficient choice for remote EJB access is Java Remote Method Invocation (RMI). In case you are unfamiliar with RMI, we provide a brief introduction to RMI in appendix A. For now, all you need to know is that it is a highly efficient, TCP/IP-based remote communication API that automates most of the work needed for calling a method on a Java object across a network. EJB 3 enables a stateless bean to be made accessible via RMI through the @Remote annotation. The Bid-Manager business interface in our example uses the annotation to make the bean remotely accessible:

```
@Remote
public interface BidManager extends Remote {
    ...
}
```

A remote business interface may extend java.rmi.Remote as we've done here, although this is optional. Typically the container will perform byte-code enhancements during deployment to extend java.rmi.Remote if your bean interface does not extend it. Remote business interface methods are not required to throw java.rmi.RemoteException unless the business interface extends the java.rmi. Remote interface. Remote business interfaces do have *one* special requirement: all parameters and return types of interface methods *must* be Serializable. This is because only Serializable objects can be sent across the network using RMI.

Web service endpoint interface

The third type of interface is specific to stateless session beans that you haven't seen yet: the *web service endpoint interface* (also known as SEI). The ability to expose a stateless session bean as a SOAP-based web service is one of the most powerful features of EJB 3. All you need to do to make a bean SOAP accessible is mark a business interface with the `@javax.jws.WebService` annotation. The following defines a simple web service endpoint interface for the `BidManagerBean`:

```
@WebService
public interface BidManagerWS {
    void addBid(Bid bid);
    List<Bid> getBids(Item item);
}
```

Note we have omitted the `cancelBid` bean method from the interface; we don't want this functionality to be accessible via a web service, although it is accessible locally as well as remotely through RMI. The `@WebService` annotation doesn't place any special restrictions on either the interface or the implementing bean. We discuss EJB web services in greater detail in chapter 15.

Working with multiple business interfaces

Although it is tempting, you *cannot* mark the same interface with more than one access type annotation. For example, you cannot mark the `BidManager` interface in listing 3.1 with both the `@Local` and `@Remote` annotations instead of creating separate `BidManagerLocal` (local) and `BidManager` (remote) interfaces, although both interfaces expose the exact same bean methods.

However, a business interface can extend another interface, and you can remove code duplication by creating a business interface that has common methods and business interfaces that extend the common "parent" interface. For example, you can create a set of interfaces utilizing OO inheritance as follows:

```
public interface BidManager{
    void addBid(Bid bid);
    List<Bid> getBids(Item item);
}

@Local
public interface BidManagerLocal extends BidManager {
    void cancelBid(Bid bid);
}

@Remote
public interface BidManagerRemote extends BidManagerLocal {
}

@WebService
public interface BidManagerWS extends BidManager {
}
```

If you want, you can apply the `@Local`, `@Remote`, or `@WebService` annotation in the bean class without having to implement the business interface as follows:

```
@Remote(BidManager.class)
@Stateless
public class BidManagerBean {
    ...
}
```

The preceding code marks the `BidManager` interface as remote through the bean class itself. This way, if you change your mind later, all you'd have to do is change the access type specification in the bean class without ever touching the interface.

Next, we move on to discussing the EJB lifecycle in our example.

3.2.4 *Using bean lifecycle callbacks*

We introduced you to lifecycle callback methods, or callbacks, earlier in the chapter; now let's take a deeper look at how they are used with stateless session beans. As far as EJB lifecycles go, stateless session beans have a simple one, as depicted in figure 3.5. In effect, the container does the following:

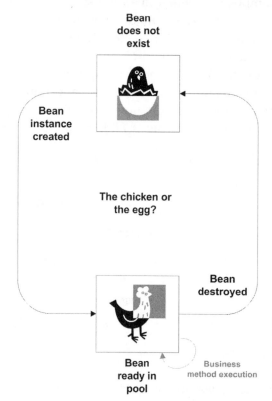

Figure 3.5
The chicken or the egg—the stateless session bean lifecycle has three states: does not exist, idle, or busy. As a result, there are only two lifecycle callbacks corresponding to bean creation and destruction.

1   Creates bean instances using the default constructor as needed.

2   Injects resources such as database connections.

3   Puts instances in a managed pool.

4   Pulls an idle bean out of the pool when an invocation request is received from the client (the container may have to increase the pool size at this point).

5   Executes the requested business method invoked through the business interface by the client.

6   When the business method finishes executing, pushes the bean back into the "method-ready" pool.

7   As needed, retires (a.k.a. destroys) beans from the pool.

An important point to note from the stateless session bean lifecycle is that since beans are allocated from and returned to the pool on a per-invocation basis, stateless session beans are extremely performance friendly and a relatively small number of bean instances can handle a large number of virtually concurrent clients.

As you know, there are two types of stateless session bean lifecycle callback methods: (1) callbacks that are invoked when the `PostConstruct` event occurs immediately after a bean instance is created and set up, and all the resources are injected; and (2) callbacks that are invoked when the `PreDestroy` event occurs, right before the bean instance is retired and removed from the pool. Note that you can have multiple `PostConstruct` and `PreDestroy` callbacks for a given bean (although this is seldom used) in a class or in a separate interceptor class (discussed in chapter 5).

In listing 3.1, the lifecycle callback methods embedded in the bean are `initialize` and `cleanup`. Callbacks must follow the pattern of void `<METHOD>()`. Unlike business methods, callbacks cannot throw checked exceptions (any exception that doesn't have `java.lang.RuntimeException` as a parent).

Typically, these callbacks are used for allocating and releasing injected resources that are used by the business methods, which is exactly what we do in our example of `BidManagerBean` in listing 3.1. In listing 3.1 we open and close connections to the database using an injected JDBC data source.

Recall that the `addBid` method in listing 3.1 inserted the new bid submitted by the user. The method created a `java.sql.Statement` from an open JDBC connection and used the statement to insert a record into the `BIDS` table. The JDBC connection object used to create the statement is a classic heavy-duty resource. It is expensive to open and should be shared across calls whenever possible. It can hold a number of native resources, so it is important to close the JDBC connection when it is no longer needed. We accomplish both these goals using callbacks as well as resource injection.

In listing 3.1, the JDBC data source from which the connection is created is injected using the `@Resource` annotation. We explore injecting resources using the `@Resource` annotation in chapter 5; for now, this is all that you need to know.

Let's take a closer look at how we used the callbacks in listing 3.1.

PostConstruct callback

The `setDataSource` method saves the injected data source in an instance variable. After injecting all resources, the container checks whether there are any designated `PostConstruct` methods that need to be invoked before the bean instance is put into the pool. In our case, we mark the `initialize` method in listing 3.1 with the `@PostConstruct` annotation:

```
@PostConstruct
public void initialize() {
    ...
    connection = dataSource.getConnection();
    ...
}
```

In the `initialize` method, we create a `java.sql.Connection` from the injected data source and save it into the `connection` instance variable used in `addBid` each time the client invokes the method.

PreDestroy callback

At some point the container decides that our bean should be removed from the pool and destroyed (perhaps at server shutdown). The `PreDestroy` callback gives us a chance to cleanly tear down bean resources before this is done. In the `cleanup` method marked with the `@PreDestroy` annotation in listing 3.1, we tear down the open database connection resource before the container retires our bean:

```
@PreDestroy
public void cleanup() {
    ...
    connection.close();
    connection = null;
    ...
}
```

Since bean instances from the pool are assigned randomly for each method invocation, trying to store client-specific state across method invocations is useless since the same bean instance may not be used for subsequent calls by the same client. On the other hand, stateful session beans, which we'll discuss next, are ideally suited for this situation.

3.3 *Stateful session beans*

Stateful session beans are guaranteed to maintain conversational state. They are not programmatically very different from their stateless cousins: as a matter of fact, the only real difference between stateless and stateful beans is how the container manages their lifecycle. Unlike with stateless beans, the container makes sure that subsequent method invocations by the same client are handled by the same stateful bean instance. Figure 3.6 shows the one-to-one mapping between a bean instance and a client enforced behind the scenes by the container. As far as you are concerned, this one-to-one relation management happens "automagically."

The one-to-one mapping between a client and a bean instance makes saving bean conversational state in a useful manner possible. However, this one-to-one correlation comes at a price. Bean instances cannot be readily returned to the pool and reused while a client session is still active. Instead, a bean instance must be squirreled away in memory to wait for the next request from the client owning the session. As a result, stateful session bean instances held by a large number of concurrent clients can have a significant memory footprint. An optimization technique called *passivation*, which we'll discuss soon, is used to alleviate this problem. Stateful session beans are ideal for multistep, workflow-oriented business processes. In this section, we explore stateful beans by using the ActionBazaar bidder account creation workflow as an example.

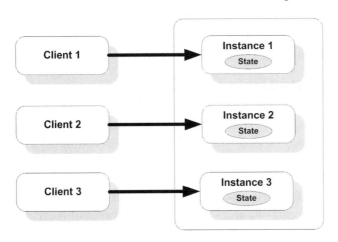

Figure 3.6
Stateful bean session maintenance. There is a bean instance reserved for a client and each instance stores the client's state information. The bean instance exists until either removed by the client or timed out.

We describe a use case of our ActionBazaar application and implement it using a stateful session bean. We show you additional programming rules for stateful session beans, and then we examine stateful bean lifecycle callback methods and the `@Remove` annotation. Finally, we summarize differences between stateless and stateful session beans.

However, before we jump into code, let's briefly examine the rules specific to developing a stateful session bean.

3.3.1 Additional programming rules

In section 3.1.3, we discussed the programming rules that apply to all session beans. Stateful session beans have a few minor twists on these rules:

- Stateful bean instance variables used to store conversational state must be Java primitives or `Serializable` objects. We'll talk more about this requirement when we cover passivation.

- Since stateful session beans cannot be pooled and reused like stateless beans, there is a real danger of accumulating too many of them if we don't have a way to destroy them. Therefore, we have to define a business method for removing the bean instance by the client using the `@Remove` annotation. We'll talk more about this annotation soon.

- In addition to the `PostConstruct` and `PreDestroy` lifecycle callback methods, stateful session beans have the `PrePassivate` and `PostActivate` lifecycle callback methods. A `PrePassivate` method is invoked before a stateful bean instance is passivated and `PostActivate` is invoked after a bean instance is brought back into the memory and is method ready.

You'll see these rules applied when we explore a concrete stateful session beans example next. As we did for stateless beans, we'll utilize the example as a jumping-off point to detail stateful features.

3.3.2 The BidderAccountCreatorBean example

The process to create an ActionBazaar bidder account is too involved to be implemented as a single-step action. As a result, account creation is implemented as a multistep process. At each step of the workflow, the would-be bidder enters digestible units of data. For example, the bidder may enter username/password information first; then biographical information such as name, address, and contact information; then billing information such as credit card and bank account data; and so forth. At the end of a workflow, the bidder account is created or the entire task is abandoned. This workflow is depicted in figure 3.7.

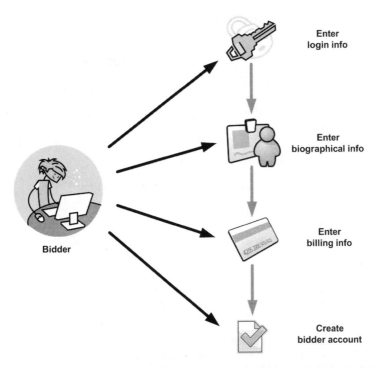

Figure 3.7 The ActionBazaar bidder account creation process is broken up into multiple steps: entering username/password, entering biographical information, entering billing information, and finally creating the account. This workflow could be implemented as a stateful session bean.

Each step of the workflow is implemented as a method of the `BidderAccountCreatorBean` presented in listing 3.2. Data gathered in each step is incrementally cached into the stateful session bean as instance variable values. Calling either the `cancelAccountCreation` or `createAccount` method ends the workflow. The `createAccount` method creates the bidder account in the database and is supposed to be the last "normal" step of the workflow. The `cancelAccountCreation` method, on the other hand, prematurely terminates the process when called by the client at any point in the workflow and nothing is saved into the database. The full version of the code is available for download in the zip containing code examples from this book's website.

Listing 3.2 Stateful session bean example

```
@Stateful(name="BidderAccountCreator")          ◁─❶  Marks POJO stateful
public class BidderAccountCreatorBean
        implements BidderAccountCreator {
```

```
@Resource(name="jdbc/ActionBazaarDS")
private DataSource dataSource;

private LoginInfo loginInfo;
private BiographicalInfo biographicalInfo;
private BillingInfo billingInfo;

private Connection connection;

public BidderAccountCreatorBean () {}

@PostConstruct
@PostActivate
public void openConnection() {
    try {
        connection = dataSource.getConnection();
    } catch (SQLException sqle) {
        sqle.printStackTrace();
    }
}

public void addLoginInfo(LoginInfo loginInfo) {
    this.loginInfo = loginInfo;
}

public void addBiographicalInfo(
        BiographicalInfo biographicalInfo) {
    this.biographicalInfo = biographicalInfo;
}

public void addBillingInfo(BillingInfo billingInfo) {
    this.billingInfo = billingInfo;
}

@PrePassivate
@PreDestroy
public void cleanup() {
    try {
        connection.close();
        connection = null;
    } catch (SQLException sqle) {
        sqle.printStackTrace();
    }
}

@Remove
public void cancelAccountCreation() {
    loginInfo = null;
    biographicalInfo = null;
    billingInfo = null;
}

@Remove
```

2 Contains stateful instance variables

3 Receives PostConstruct callback

4 Receives PostActivate callback

5 Receives PrePassivate callback

6 Receives PreDestroy callback

7 Designates remove methods

```
public void createAccount() {
    try {
        Statement statement = connection.createStatement();
        statement.execute(
            "INSERT INTO BIDDERS(" +
                "username, " +
                ...
                "first_name, " +
                ...
                "credit_card_type, " +
                ...
                ") VALUES (" +
                "'" + loginInfo.getUsername() + "', " +
                ...
                "'" + biographicalInfo.getFirstName() + "', " +
                ...
                "'" + billingInfo.getCreditCardType() + "', " +
                ...

                ")");
        statement.close();
    } catch (SQLException sqle) {
        sqle.printStackTrace();
    }
}
}
...
@Remote
public interface BidderAccountCreator extends Remote {
    void addLoginInfo(LoginInfo loginInfo);
    void addBiographicalInfo(BiographicalInfo biographicalInfo);
    void addBillingInfo(BillingInfo billingInfo);
    void cancelAccountCreation();
    void createAccount();
}
```

As we mentioned earlier, it should not surprise you that the code has a lot in common with the stateless session bean code in listing 3.1.

NOTE   As before, we are using JDBC for simplicity in this example because we want you to focus on the session bean code right now and not JPA. We'll cover JPA in the part 3 of this book. An interesting exercise for you is to refactor this code using JPA and notice the radical improvement over JDBC!

We are using the @Stateful annotation to mark the BidderAccountCreatorBean POJO ❶. Other than the annotation name, this annotation behaves exactly like the @Stateless annotation, so we won't mention it any further. The bean implements the BidderAccountCreator remote business interface. As per stateful bean programming rules, the BidderAccountCreatorBean has a no-argument constructor.

Just like in listing 3.1, a JDBC data source is injected using the @Resource annotation. Both the PostConstruct ❸ and PostPassivate ❹ callbacks prepare the bean for use by opening a database connection from the injected data source. On the other hand, both the PrePassivate ❺ and PreDestroy ❻ callbacks close the cached connection.

The loginInfo, biographicalInfo, and billingInfo instance variables are used to store client conversational state across business method calls ❷. Each of the business methods models a step in the account creation workflow and incrementally populates the state instance variables. The workflow is terminated when the client invokes either of the @Remove annotated methods ❼.

There is no point to repeating our discussion of the features that are identical to the ones for stateless session beans, so we'll avoid doing so. However, let's explore the features unique to stateful session beans next, starting with the stateful bean business interfaces.

3.3.3 *Business interfaces for stateful beans*

Specifying stateful bean business interfaces works in almost exactly the same way as it does for stateless beans—with a couple of exceptions. Stateful session beans support local and remote invocation through the @Local and @Remote annotations. However, a stateful session bean *cannot* have a web service endpoint interface. This is because SOAP-based web services are inherently stateless in nature. Also, you should always include at least one @Remove annotated method in your stateful bean's business interface. The reason for this will become clear as we discuss the stateful bean lifecycle next.

3.3.4 *Stateful bean lifecycle callbacks*

As we mentioned in section 3.1, the lifecycle of the stateful session bean is very different from that of a stateless session bean because of passivation. In this section, we explain this concept in more depth. Let's start by looking at the lifecycle of a stateful bean, as shown in figure 3.8. The container follows these steps:

1   Always creates new bean instances using the default constructor whenever a new client session is started.

2 Injects resources.

3 Stores the instance in memory.

4 Executes the requested business method invoked through the business interface by the client.

5 Waits for and executes subsequent client requests.

6 If the client remains idle for a period of time, the container *passivates* the bean instance. Essentially, passivation means that the bean is moved out of active memory, serialized, and stored in temporary storage.

7 If the client invokes a passivated bean, it is activated (brought back into memory from temporary storage).

8 If the client does not invoke a passivated bean instance for a period of time, it is destroyed.

9 If the client requests the removal of a bean instance, it is first activated if necessary and then destroyed.

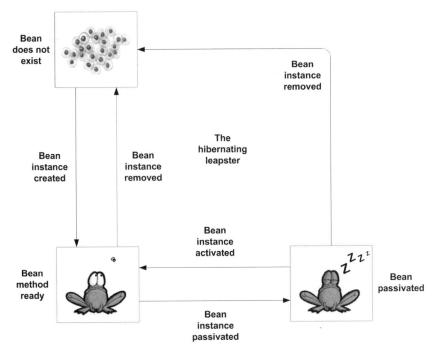

Figure 3.8   The lifecycle of a stateful session bean. A stateful bean maintains client state and cannot be pooled. It may be passivated when the client is not using it and must be activated when the client needs it again.

Like a stateless session bean, the stateful session bean has lifecycle callback methods, or callbacks, that are invoked when the PostConstruct event occurs (as an instance is created) and when the PreDestroy event occurs (before the instance is destroyed). But now we have two new callback events for which we can have callbacks: PrePassivate and PostActivate, which are part of the passivation process. We'll discuss them next.

Just as in listing 3.1, we use a PostConstruct callback in listing 3.2 to open a database connection from the injected data source so that it can be used by business methods. Also as in listing 3.1, we close the cached connection in preparation for bean destruction in a PreDestroy callback. However, you should note that we invoke the very same method for both the PreDestroy and PrePassivate callbacks:

```
@PrePassivate
@PreDestroy
public void cleanup() {
    ...
}
```

Similarly, the exact same action is taken for both the PostConstruct and PostActivate callbacks:

```
@PostConstruct
@PostActivate
public void openConnection() {
    ...
}
```

To see why this is the case, let's discuss activation and passivation in a little more detail.

Passivation and activation

If clients don't invoke a bean for a long enough time, it is not a good idea to continue keeping it in memory. For a large number of beans, this could easily make the machine run out of memory. The container employs the technique of *passivation* to save memory when possible.

> **NOTE** *Passivation* essentially means saving a bean instance into disk instead of holding it in memory. The container accomplishes this task by serializing the entire bean instance and moving it into permanent storage like a file or the database. *Activation* is the opposite of passivation and is done when the bean instance is needed again. The container activates a bean instance by retrieving it from permanent storage, deserializing it, and moving it back into memory. This means that all bean instance

variables that you care about and should be saved into permanent storage must either be a Java primitive or implement the `java.io.Serializable` interface.

The point of the `PrePassivate` callback is to give the bean a chance to prepare for serialization. This may include copying nonserializable variable values into `Serializable` variables and clearing unneeded data out of those variables to save total disk space needed to store the bean. Most often the prepassivation step consists of releasing heavy-duty resources such as open database, messaging server, and socket connections that cannot be serialized. A well-behaved bean should ensure that heavy-duty resources are both closed *and* explicitly set to null before passivation takes place.

From the perspective of a bean instance, there isn't much of a difference between being passivated and being destroyed. In both cases, the current instance in memory would cease to exist. As a result, in most cases you'll find that the same actions are performed for both the `PreDestroy` and `PrePassivate` callbacks, as we do in listing 3.2. Pretty much the same applies for the `PostConstruct`–`PostActivate` pair. For both callbacks, the bean needs to do whatever is necessary to make itself ready to service the next incoming request. Nine times out of ten, this means getting hold of resources that either are not instantiated or were lost during the serialization/deserialization process. Again, listing 3.2 is a good example since the `java.sql.Connection` object cannot be serialized and must be reinstantiated during activation.

Destroying a stateful session bean

In listing 3.2, the `cancelAccountCreation` and `createAccount` methods are marked with the `@Remove` annotation. Beyond the obvious importance of these methods in implementing vital workflow logic, they play an important role in maintaining application server performance. Calling business methods marked with the `@Remove` annotation signifies a desire by the client to end the session. As a result, invoking these methods triggers immediate bean destruction.

To gain an appreciation for this feature, consider what would happen if it did not exist. If `remove` methods were not an option, the client would have no way of telling the container when a session should be ended. As a result, every stateful bean instance ever created would always have to be timed out to be passivated (if the container implementation supports passivation) and timed out again to be finally destroyed. In a highly concurrent system, this could have a drastic performance impact. The memory footprint for the server would constantly be artificially high, not to mention how there would be wasted CPU cycles and disk space used in the unnecessary activation/passivation process. This is why it is critical that you remove stateful bean instances when the client is finished with its work instead of relying on the container to destroy them when they time out.

Believe it or not, these are the only few stateful bean–specific features that we needed to talk about! Before concluding this section on stateful beans, we'll briefly summarize the differences between stateful and stateless session beans as a handy reference in table 3.2.

Table 3.2 The main differences between stateless and stateful session beans

Features	Stateless	Stateful
Conversational state	No	Yes
Pooling	Yes	No
Performance problems	Unlikely	Possible
Lifecycle events	`PostConstruct`, `PreDestroy`	`PostConstruct`, `PreDestroy`, `PrePassivate`, `PostActivate`
Timer (discussed in chapter 5)	Yes	No
`SessionSynchronization` for transactions (discussed in chapter 6)	No	Yes
Web services	Yes	No
Extended `PersistenceContext` (discussed in chapter 9)	No	Yes

Thus far we have explored how to develop session beans. In the next section, we discuss how session beans are actually accessed and used by clients.

3.4 Session bean clients

A session bean works for a client and may either be invoked by local clients collocated in the same JVM or by a remote client outside the JVM. In this section we first discuss how a client accesses a session bean and then see how the @EJB annotation is used to inject session bean references.

Almost any Java component can be a session bean client. POJOs, servlets, JSPs, or other EJBs can access session beans. In fact, stateless session beans exposed through web services endpoints can even be accessed by non-Java clients such as .NET applications. However, in this section we concentrate on clients that access session beans either locally or remotely through RMI. In chapter 15 you'll see how EJB web service clients look.

Fortunately, in EJB 3 accessing a remote or local session bean looks exactly the same. As a matter of fact, other than method invocation patterns, stateless and stateful session beans pretty much look alike from a client's perspective too. In all of these cases, a session bean client follows these general steps to use a session bean:

1 The client obtains a reference to the beans directly or indirectly from JNDI.

2 All session bean invocations are made through an interface appropriate for the access type.

3 The client makes as many method calls as are necessary to complete the business task at hand.

4 In case of a stateful session bean, the last client invocation should be a remove method.

To keep things as simple as possible, let's explore a client that uses the BidManagerBean stateless session bean to add a bid to the ActionBazaar site. We'll leave it as an exercise for you to extend the client code to use the BidderAccountCreatorBean stateful session bean. For starters, let's see how the code to use the BidManagerBean from another EJB might look:

```
@Stateless
public class GoldBidderManagerBean implements GoldBidderManager {
    @EJB
    private BidManager bidManager;

    public void addMassBids(List<Bid> bids) {
        for (Bid bid : bids) {
            bidManager.addBid(bid);
        }
    }
}
```

This code uses dependency injection through the @javax.ejb.EJB annotation to obtain a reference to the BidManagerBean. This is by far the easiest method of procuring a reference to a session bean. Depending on your client environment, you might have to use one of the two other options available for obtaining EJB references: using EJB context lookup or using JNDI lookup. Since neither of these options is used often in real life, we'll focus on DI for right now. However, we'll discuss both EJB context lookup and JNDI lookup in greater detail in coming chapters, as well as in appendix A.

3.4.1 *Using the @EJB annotation*

Recall from our discussion on DI in chapter 2 that the @EJB annotation is specifically intended for injecting session beans into client code. Also recall that since injection is only possible within managed environments, this annotation only works inside another EJB, in code running inside an application-client container (ACC), or in components registered with the web container (such as a servlet or JSF backing bean). However, some application servers will support injection of EJB references into POJOs as a vendor-specific extension. Here is the specification for the @EJB annotation:

```
@Target({TYPE, METHOD, FIELD}) @Retention(RUNTIME)
public @interface EJB {
    String name() default "";
    Class beanInterface() default Object.class;
    String beanName() default "";
}
```

All three of the parameters for the @EJB annotation are optional. The name element suggests the JNDI name that is used to bind the injected EJB in the environment-naming context. The beanInterface specifies the business interface to be used to access the EJB. The beanName element allows us to distinguish among EJBs if multiple EJBs implement the same business interface. In our GoldBidManagerBean code, we chose to use the remote interface of the BidManagerBean. If we want to use the local interface of the BidManagerBean EJB instead, we can use the following:

```
@EJB
private BidManagerLocal bidManager;
```

We have not specified the name parameter for the @EJB annotation in this code and the JNDI name is derived from the interface name (BidManagerLocal in our case). If we want to inject an EJB bound to a different JNDI name, we can use the @EJB annotation as follows:

```
@EJB(name="BidManagerRemote")
private BidManager bidManager;
```

3.4.2 *Injection and stateful session beans*

For the most part, using DI is a no-brainer. There are a few nuances to keep an eye on while using DI with stateful beans, though. You can inject a stateful session into another stateful session bean instance if you need to. For example, you can inject the `BidderAccountCreator` stateful EJB from `UserAccountRegistration` EJB that is another stateful session bean as follows:

```
@Stateful
public class UserAccountRegistrationBean
        implements UserAccountRegistration {
    @EJB
    private BidderAccountCreator bidderAccountCreator;
    ...
}
```

This code will create an instance of `BidderAccountCreatorBean` which will be specifically meant for the client accessing the instance of the `UserAccount-RegistrationBean`. If the client removes the instance of `UserAccountRegistra-tionBean`, the associated instance of `BidderAccountCreatorBean` will also be automatically removed.

Keep in mind that you must not inject a stateful session bean into a stateless object, such as a stateless session bean or servlet that may be shared by multiple concurrent clients (you should use JNDI in such cases instead). However, injecting an instance of a stateless session bean into a stateful session bean is perfectly legal. Chapter 12 discusses in much greater detail how you can use EJB from other tiers.

This concludes our brief discussion on accessing session beans. Next, we'll briefly explore potential performance issues of stateful session beans.

3.5 Performance considerations for stateful beans

Whether or not they deserve it, stateful session beans have received a bad rap as performance bottlenecks. There is truth behind this perception, quite possibly due to poor initial implementations for most popular application servers. In recent years, these problems have been greatly alleviated with effective under-the-hood optimizations as well as better JVM implementations. However, you still have to keep a few things in mind in order to use session beans effectively. More or less, these techniques are essential for using any stateful technology, so pay attention even if you decide against using stateful beans. In this section you'll learn techniques to effectively use stateful session beans and other alternatives for building stateful applications.

3.5.1 Using stateful session beans effectively

There is little doubt that stateful session beans provide extremely robust business logic processing functionality if maintaining conversational state is an essential application requirement. In addition, EJB 3 adds extended persistence contexts specifically geared toward stateful session beans (discussed in chapters 9 and 13), significantly increasing their capability. Most popular application servers such as WebSphere, WebLogic, Oracle, and JBoss provide high availability by clustering EJB containers running the same stateful bean. A clustered EJB container replicates session state across container instances. If a clustered container instance crashes for any reason, the client is routed to another container instance seamlessly without losing state. Such reliability is hard to match without using stateful session beans. Nonetheless, there are a few things to watch out for while using stateful session beans.

Choosing session data appropriately

Stateful session beans can become resource hogs and cause performance problems if not used properly. Since the container stores session information in memory, if you have thousands of concurrent clients for your stateful session bean you may run out of memory or cause a lot of *disk thrashing* by the container as it passivates and activates instances to try to conserve memory. Consequently, you have to closely examine what kind of data you are storing in the conversation state and make sure the total memory footprint for the stateful bean is as small as possible. For example, it may be a lot more efficient to store just the `itemId` for an `Item` instead of storing the complete `Item` object in an instance variable.

If you cluster stateful beans, the conversational state is replicated between different instances of the EJB container. State replication uses network bandwidth. Storing a large object in the bean state may have a significant impact on the performance of your application because the containers will spend time replicating objects to other container instances to ensure high availability. We'll discuss more about EJB clustering in chapter 13.

Passivating and removing beans

The rules for passivation are generally implementation specific. Improper use of passivation policies (when passivation configuration is an option) may cause performance problems. For example, the Oracle Application Server passivates bean instances when the idle time for a bean instance expires, when the maximum number of active bean instances allowed for a stateful session bean is reached, or when the threshold for JVM memory is reached. You have to check the documentation for your EJB container and appropriately set passivation rules. For example, if we set the maximum number of active instances allowed for a stateful bean instance to 100 and we usually have 150 active clients, the container will continue to passivate and activate bean instances, thus causing performance problems.

You can go a long way toward solving potential memory problems by explicitly removing the no longer required bean instances rather than depending on the container to time them out. As discussed earlier, you can annotate a method with the @Remove annotation that signals the container to remove the bean instance.

Given the fact that stateful session beans can become performance bottlenecks whether through improper usage or under certain circumstances, it is worth inspecting the alternatives to using them.

3.5.2 *Stateful session bean alternatives*

This section examines a few alternative strategies to implementing stateful business processing, as well as some issues you may need to consider when using them.

The first alternative to stateful beans is replacing them with a combination of persistence and stateless processing. In this scheme, we essentially move state information from memory to the database on every request.

You should carefully examine whether you want to maintain state between conversations in memory. Base your decision completely based on your application requirements and how much tolerance of failure you have. For example, in the BidderAccountCreator EJB you can probably avoid the use of conversational state by not maintaining instance variables to store the user information in memory and save data in the database on each method call.

Second, you may choose to build some mechanism at the client side to maintain state. This requires additional coding, such as storing the state as an object in client memory or in a file.

The downside of these two approaches is that it is difficult to guarantee high availability and they may not be viable options for your application. In fact, you would lose all of the advantages that the container provides by hand-coding proprietary solutions such as the ones outlined here, including automated passivation and robust, transparent state maintenance.

Third, you may choose to maintain session state in the web container if you're building a web application. Although HTTP is a stateless protocol, the Java Servlet API provides the ability to maintain state by using the HttpSession object. The servlet container does not have to do heavy lifting like passivation and activation, and may perform better in certain situations. Be aware that too much data in the HttpSession could decrease performance of the servlet container as well, so this is not a silver bullet either. Moreover, you cannot use this option with thick or Java SE clients.

So when you need to maintain state in your applications and your clients are Java SE clients, then the first two options we discussed earlier may be more difficult to implement. Hence, stateful session beans are probably the only viable option as long as you carefully weigh the performance considerations we outlined earlier.

We'll close our discussion on session beans by outlining some best practices for session beans that you can use to build your application's business logic.

3.6 *Session bean best practices*

In this section we outline some of the best practices for session beans that you can use while building the business logic tier for your application.

Choose your bean type carefully. Stateless session beans will be suitable most of the time. Carefully examine whether your application needs stateful session beans, because it comes with a price. If the EJB client lies in the web tier, then using `HttpSession` may be a better choice than stateful session beans under some circumstances.

Carefully examine interface types for session beans. Remote interfaces involve network access and may slow down your applications. If the client will always be used within the same JVM as the bean, then use a local interface.

If you are using DI, make sure you don't inject a stateful session bean into a stateless session bean or servlet. Injected EJB instances are stored in an instance variable and are available globally for subsequent clients even if a stateless bean instance is returned to the pool, and an injected stateful bean instance may contain inaccurate state information that will be available to a different client. It's legal to inject a stateful bean instance to another stateful session bean or an application client.

Separate crosscutting concerns such as logging and auditing using business interceptors (which we discuss in chapter 5) instead of spreading them all over the business logic.

Closely examine what kind of data you are storing in the conversation state. Try to use small, primitive instance variables in a stateful bean whenever possible as opposed to large nested composite objects.

Don't forget to define remove methods in a stateful session bean.

Tune passivation and timeout configurations to find the optimal values for your application.

3.7 Summary

In this chapter, we examined the various session bean types and how stateless session beans and stateful session beans differ. We looked at the programming rules for both stateless and stateful session beans, and you saw comprehensive examples of both bean types. As you learned, stateless session beans have a simple life-cycle and can be pooled. Stateful beans require instances for each client, and for that reason they can consume a lot of resources. In addition, passivation and activation of stateful beans can impact performance if used inappropriately.

You learned about alternatives for using stateful session beans, and that session bean clients can be either local or remote. We showed you that dependency injection simplifies the use of EJB and saves you from having to perform complex JNDI lookups. Finally, we provided some best practices for developing session beans.

At this point you have all the ammunition necessary to build the business logic of your application using stateless and stateful session beans. In the next chapter we'll discuss how you can build messaging applications with message-driven beans.

Messaging and developing MDBs

In this chapter we'll take a closer look at developing message-driven beans (MDBs) as well as provide you with an overview of the concepts and technologies these powerful EJB 3 components build on. First we'll introduce you to basic messaging concepts, and then we'll explore the Java Messaging Service (JMS) by creating a message producer. Finally, we'll take a look at MDBs, the EJB 3 answer to messaging.

You should gain an understanding of messaging and JMS before diving into MDB for two reasons. First, most MDBs you'll encounter are glorified JMS message consumers implementing JMS interfaces (such as `javax.jms.MessageListener`) and using JMS components (such as `javax.jms.Message`). Second, for most solutions with MDB your messaging will involve much more than simply consuming messages. For the simplest of these tasks, such as sending messages, you'll have to understand JMS. This chapter assumes a basic familiarity with JMS and we offer only a brief description of it.

If you're comfortable with messaging and JMS, feel free to skip to the sections on MDBs. It is good to reinforce what you know from time to time, though, so you just might want to quickly jog through the first few sections with us anyway.

4.1 *Messaging concepts*

When we talk about messaging in the Java EE context, what we really mean is the process of *loosely coupled, asynchronous communication* between system components. Most communication between components is synchronous, such as simple method invocation or Java RMI. In both cases, the invoker and the invocation target have to be present for the communication to succeed. Synchronous communication also means that the invoker must wait for the target to complete the request for service before proceeding.

As an analogy, you're communicating synchronously when you (the invoker) call and talk to someone over the phone. But what if the person (the invocation target) isn't available? If possible, you leave a voicemail message. The voicemail service makes the communication asynchronous by storing your message so that the receiver can listen to it later and respond. Message-oriented middleware (MOM) enables messaging in much the same way that a voicemail service does—by acting as the middleman between a message sender and the receiver so that they don't have to be available simultaneously. In this section, we briefly introduce MOM, show how messaging is used in our ActionBazaar application, and examine popular messaging models.

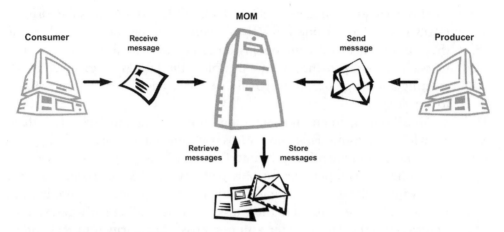

Figure 4.1 Basic MOM message flow. When the producer sends a message to the software, it is stored immediately and later collected by the consumer. Looks a lot like e-mail, doesn't it?

4.1.1 Message-oriented middleware

Message-oriented middleware is software that enables asynchronous messages between system components. When a message is sent, the software stores the message in a location specified by the sender and acknowledges receipt immediately. The message sender is called a *producer*, and the location where the message is stored is called a *destination*. At a later point in time, any software component interested in messages at that particular destination can retrieve currently stored messages. The software components receiving the messages are called the message *consumers*. Figure 4.1 depicts the various components of MOM.

MOM is not a new concept by any means. MOM products include IBM WebSphere MQ, TIBCO Rendezvous, SonicMQ, ActiveMQ, and Oracle Advanced Queuing.

To flesh out messaging concepts a bit more, let's explore a problem in the ActionBazaar application. We'll continue working on this problem as we progress through the chapter.

4.1.2 Messaging in ActionBazaar

As an additional source of revenue, ActionBazaar will list items for bid when the company is able to find good bulk deals through its extensive purchasing network. These items, displayed on the site as "ActionBazaar Specials," come with "complete satisfaction" guarantees. ActionBazaar automatically ships these items from their warehouse to winning bidders as soon as they order them. When

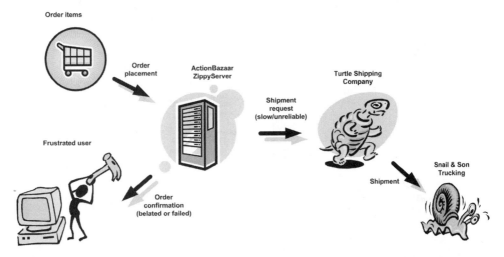

Figure 4.2   ActionBazaar ordering before MOM is introduced. Slow B2B processing is causing customer dissatisfaction.

ActionBazaar started as a two-person Internet operation, Joe and John, the two founders, made a sweet deal with Turtle Shipping Company's founder Dave Turtle. As a part of the deal, Joe and John agreed to ship with Turtle for a few years.

As soon as a user places an order for an "ActionBazaar Special," a shipping request is sent to the Turtle system via a business-to-business (B2B) connection, as shown in figure 4.2. The order confirmation page loads only after Turtle confirms receipt. Now that the number of ActionBazaar customers has gone through the roof, the slow Turtle servers and B2B connection simply cannot keep up and completing a shipping order takes what seems like forever. To make matters worse, the Turtle server occasionally goes down, causing orders to fail altogether.

Taking a closer look at things, we see that we could make the forwarding process of the shipping request asynchronous and solve this problem. Instead of communicating directly with the Turtle server, the ActionBazaar ordering process could send a message containing the shipping request to MOM, as depicted in figure 4.3. As soon as the message is stored in MOM, the order can be confirmed without making the user wait. At a later point in time, the Turtle server could request pending shipping request messages from MOM and process them at its own pace.

In this case, the most obvious advantage MOM is offering is an increase in reliability. The reliability stems from not insisting that both the ActionBazaar and Turtle servers be up and running at the same time. Also, the servers are not expected to function at the same processing rate. In the most extreme case, even

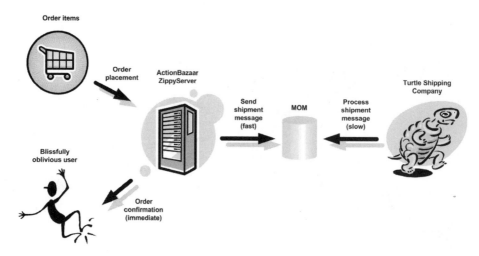

Figure 4.3   ActionBazaar ordering after MOM is introduced. Messaging enables both fast customer response times and reliable processing.

if the Turtle server is down at any given time the shipping request is not lost and is simply delivered later. Another significant advantage of messaging is loosely coupled system integration. We could, if we wanted to, easily switch from the Turtle Shipping Company to O'Hare Logistics once our current contract runs out. Note how different this is from having to know the exact interface details of the Turtle servers for synchronous communication technologies like RMI or even remote session beans.

So far we've described a particular form of messaging known as *point-to-point* to explain basic messaging concepts. This is a good time to move away from this simplification and fully discuss messaging models.

4.1.3 Messaging models

A *messaging model* is simply a way of messaging when a number of senders and consumers are involved. It will be more obvious what this means as we describe each model. Two popular messaging models are standardized in Java EE: point-to-point (PTP) messaging and publish-subscribe messaging. We'll discuss each of these messaging models next.

Point-to-point

You can probably guess from the names of the messaging models how they function. In the PTP scheme, a single message travels from a single producer (point A)

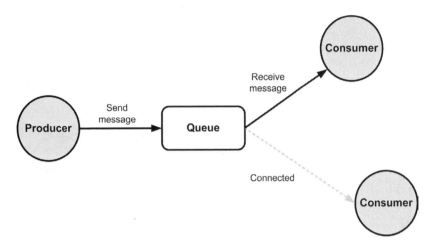

Figure 4.4   The PTP messaging model with one producer and two consumers

to a single consumer (point B). PTP message destinations are called *queues*. Note that PTP doesn't guarantee that messages are delivered in any particular order—the term *queue* is more symbolic than anything else. Also, if more than one potential receiver exists for a message, a random receiver is chosen, as figure 4.4 shows. The classic message-in-a-bottle story is a good analogy of PTP messaging. The message in a bottle is set afloat by the lonely castaway (the producer). The ocean (the queue) carries the message to an anonymous beach dweller (the consumer) and the message can only be "found" once.

The ActionBazaar shipping request forwarding problem is an excellent candidate for the PTP model, as we want to be guaranteed that the message is received once and only once.

Publish-subscribe (pub-sub)

Publish-subscribe messaging is much like posting to an Internet newsgroup. As shown in figure 4.5, a single producer produces a message that is received by any number of consumers who happen to be connected to the destination at the time. Much like Internet postings, the message destination in this model is called a *topic* and a consumer is called a *subscriber*.

Pub-sub messaging works particularly well in broadcasting information across systems. For example, it could be used to broadcast a system maintenance notification several hours before an outage to all premium sellers whose systems are directly integrated with ActionBazaar and who are listening at the moment.

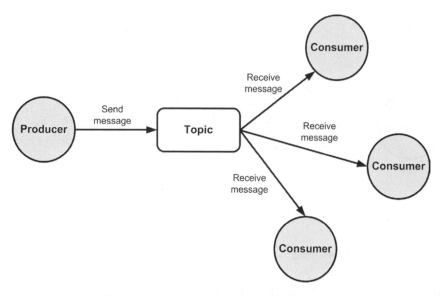

Figure 4.5   The publish-subscribe messaging model with one producer and three consumers. Each topic subscriber receives a copy of the message.

At this point, you should have a good conceptual foundation of messaging and are perhaps eager to get a taste of some code. Next, we take a brief look at JMS and implement the ActionBazaar message producer for sending the message.

The request-reply model

In the ActionBazaar example, you might want a receipt confirmation from Turtle once they have the shipping request you sent to the queue.

A third kind of model called request-reply comes in handy in these kinds of situations. In this model, we give the message receiver enough information so that they might "call us back." This is known as an overlay model because it is typically implemented on top of either the PTP or pub-sub models.

For example, in the PTP model the sender specifies a queue to be used to send a reply to (in JMS, this is called the *reply to* queue) as well as a unique ID shared by both the outgoing and incoming messages (known as the *correlation ID* in JMS). The receiver receives the message and sends a reply to the reply queue, copying the correlation ID. The sender receives the message in the reply queue and determines which message received a reply by matching the correlation ID.

4.2 *Introducing Java Messaging Service*

In this section we provide an overview to JMS API by building a basic message producer. JMS is a deceptively simple and small API to a very powerful technology. The JMS API is to messaging what the Java Database Connectivity (JDBC) API is to database access. JMS provides a uniform, standard way of accessing MOM in Java and is therefore an alternative to using product-specific APIs. With the exception of Microsoft Message Queuing (MSMQ), most major MOM products support JMS.

The easiest way to learn JMS might be by looking at code in action. We're going to explore JMS by first developing the ActionBazaar code that sends out the shipping request. We develop a message producer using JMS and learn about structure of the message interface; then in the next section, we develop the message consumer using MDBs.

4.2.1 *Developing the JMS message producer*

As we described in our scenario in section 4.1.2, when a user places an order for an "ActionBazaar Special," a shipping request is sent to a queue shared between ActionBazaar and Turtle. The code in listing 4.1 sends the message out and could be part of a method in a simple Java object invoked by the ActionBazaar application. All relevant shipping information—such as the item number, shipping address, shipping method, and insurance amount—is packed into a message and sent out to `ShippingRequestQueue`.

Listing 4.1 JMS code that sends out shipping requests from ActionBazaar

```
@Resource(name="jms/QueueConnectionFactory")
  private ConnectionFactory connectionFactory;          ⟵  Injects connection
                                                            factory and
@Resource(name="jms/ShippingRequestQueue")                  destination
  private Destination destination;

Connection connection = connectionFactory.createConnection();
Session session = connection.createSession(true,          ⟶ Connects,
    Session.AUTO_ACKNOWLEDGE);                              creates
                                                           session,
MessageProducer producer = session.createProducer(destination); ⊔  producer

ObjectMessage message = session.createObjectMessage();   ⟵ Creates message
ShippingRequest shippingRequest = new ShippingRequest();
shippingRequest.setItem(item);
shippingRequest.setShippingAddress(address);             Creates
shippingRequest.setShippingMethod(method);               payload
shippingRequest.setInsuranceAmount(amount);
```

```
message.setObject(shippingRequest);        Sets payload

producer.send(message);        Sends message

session.close();
connection.close();
```

As we explain each logical step of this code in the following sections, we'll go through a large subset of the JMS API components and see usage patterns. Note that for simplicity we have removed the code for exception handling.

Retrieving the connection factory and destination

In JMS, *administrative objects* are similar to JDBC `javax.sql.DataSource` objects. These are resources that are created and configured outside the code and stored in JNDI. JMS has two administrative objects: `javax.jms.ConnectionFactory` and `javax.jms.Destination`, both of which we use in listing 4.1. We then retrieve the connection factory using dependency injection with the `@Resource` annotation, and the connection factory encapsulates all the configuration information needed to connect to MOM. We also inject the queue to forward the shipping request to, aptly named, `ShippingRequestQueue`. With EJB 3, using resources is much easier; you don't have to deal with the complexity of JNDI or configure resource references in deployment descriptors. Chapter 5 discusses dependency injection in greater detail.

The next step in listing 4.1 is creating a connection to MOM and getting a new JMS session.

Opening the connection and session

The `javax.jms.Connection` object represents a live MOM connection, which we create using the `createConnection` method of the connection factory. Connections are thread-safe and designed to be sharable because opening a new connection is resource intensive. A JMS session (`javax.jms.Session`), on the other hand, provides a single-threaded, task-oriented context for sending and receiving messages. We create a session from the connection using the `createSession` method. The first parameter of the method specifies whether the session is transactional. We've decided that our session should be transactional and therefore set the parameter to `true`. This means that the requests for messages to be sent won't be realized until either the session's `commit` method is called or the session is closed. (If the session isn't transactional, messages will be sent as soon as the `send` method is invoked.) The second parameter of the `createSession` method specifies the acknowledge mode and only has an effect for nontransactional sessions receiving messages, which we'll discuss later. Having set up the session, we are now ready to take on the meat of the matter: sending the message.

Preparing and sending the message

The session is not directly used for sending or receiving messages (we could argue that having it do so would simplify the JMS API). Instead, a javax.jms.Message-Producer needed to send messages to the shipping request queue is constructed using the session's createProducer method. Then we create and populate the javax.jms.Message to be sent. In our example, we send the Serializable Java object ShippingRequest to Turtle, so the most appropriate message type for us is javax.jms.ObjectMessage (which we create using the createObjectMessage method). We then create an instance of the ShippingRequest object and set the item number, shipping address, shipping method, and insurance amount fields. Once ShippingRequest is set up, we set it as the payload of the message using set-Object. Finally, we instruct the message producer to send the message out using the send method.

Releasing resources

A large number of resources are allocated under the hood for both the session and connection objects, so it is important to explicitly close both once we've finished with them, as we do with

```
session.close();
connection.close();
```

This step is even more important in our case since no messages are sent out until our transactional session is committed when we close the session.

If all goes well, a message containing the shipping request winds up in the queue. Before we look at the message consumer code that receives this message, let's discuss the javax.jms.Message object in a little more detail.

4.2.2 The JMS message interface

The Message interface standardizes what is exchanged across JMS and is an extremely robust data encapsulation mechanism. As figure 4.6 shows, a JMS message has the following parts: the message header, message properties, and the message body, each of which is detailed in the sections that follow.

A good analogy for JMS messages is mailing envelopes. Let's see how this analogy fits next.

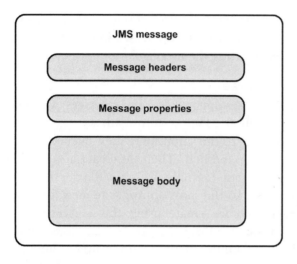

Figure 4.6
Anatomy of a message. A
JMS message has a header,
properties, and a body.

Message headers

Headers are name-value pairs common to all messages. In our envelope analogy, the message header is the information on an envelope that is pretty standard: the to and from addresses, postage, and postmark. For example, the JMS message version of a postmark is the `JMSTimestamp` header. MOM sets this header to the current time when the message is sent.

Here are some other commonly used JMS headers:

- `JMSCorrelationID`
- `JMSReplyTo`
- `JMSMessageID`

Message properties

Message properties are just like headers, but are explicitly created by the application instead of being standard across messages. In the envelope analogy, if you decide to write "Happy Holidays" on the envelope to let the receiver know the envelope contains a gift or note, the text is a property instead of a header. In the ActionBazaar example, one way to mark a shipping request as fragile would be to add a boolean property called `Fragile` and set it to true. The code to do this would look like this:

```
message.setBooleanProperty("Fragile", true);
```

A property can be a boolean, byte, double, float, int, long, short, `String`, or `Object`.

Message body

The *message body* contains the contents of the envelope; it is the payload of the message. What you're trying to send in the body determines what message type you should use. In listing 4.1, we chose `javax.jms.ObjectMessage` because we were sending out the `ShippingRequest` Java object. Alternatively, we could have chosen to send `BytesMessage`, `MapMessage`, `StreamMessage`, or `TextMessage`. Each of these message types has a slightly different interface and usage pattern. There are no hard-and-fast rules dictating the choice of message types. Explore all the choices before making a decision for your application.

> **The Spring JmsTemplate**
>
> Spring's `JmsTemplate` greatly simplifies common JMS tasks like sending messages by automating generic code. Using `JmsTemplate`, our entire message producer code could be reduced to a few lines. This is a great way to take care of tasks, as long as you aren't doing anything too complicated such as using temporary queues, JMS headers, and properties.
>
> At the time of this writing, Spring doesn't have very robust asynchronous message-processing capabilities when compared to MDB. Any future MDB-like features in Spring are likely to utilize the relatively arcane JCA container, which leaves room for a great Spring/EJB 3 integration case.

We just finished reviewing most of the major parts of JMS that you need to send and use with MDB. While full coverage of JMS is beyond the scope of this chapter, we encourage you to fully explore the fascinating JMS API by visiting http://java.sun.com/products/jms/docs.html. In particular, you should explore how JMS message consumers work.

Having taken a closer look at JMS messages, the time is right to look at the Turtle server message consumer, which we'll build using an MDB.

4.3 Working with message-driven beans

We'll now build on our brief coverage of MDBs in chapters 1 and 2 and explore MDBs in detail, why you should consider using them, and how to develop them. We'll also discuss some best practices as well as pitfalls to avoid when developing MDBs.

Message-driven beans are EJB components designed to consume the asynchronous messages we've been discussing. Although MDBs are intended to handle many different kinds of messages (see the sidebar "JCA Connectors and Messaging"), we'll primarily focus on MDBs that process JMS messages because most enterprise applications use JMS. From this perspective, you might ask why we'd need to employ EJBs to handle the task of consuming messages at all when we could use the code we just developed for the JMS message consumer. We'll address this question next. We'll develop a simple message consumer application using MDBs and show you how to use the `@MessageDriven` annotation. You'll also learn more about the `MessageListener` interface, activation configuration properties, and the MDB lifecycle.

JCA connectors and messaging

Although by far JMS is the primary messaging provider for MDBs, as of EJB 2.1 it is not the only one. Thanks to the Java EE Connector Architecture (JCA), MDBs can receive messages from any enterprise information system (EIS), such as PeopleSoft HR or Oracle Manufacturing, not just MOMs that support JMS.

Suppose you have a legacy application that needs to send messages to an MDB. You can do this by implementing a JCA-compliant adapter/connector that includes support for *message inflow contract*. Once your JCA resource adapter or connector is deployed to a Java EE container, you can use the message inflow contract to have an asynchronous message delivered to an endpoint inside the container. A JCA endpoint is essentially the same as a JMS destination—it acts as a server proxy to an MDB (a message consumer/listener in JMS terms). As soon as a message arrives at the endpoint, the container triggers any registered MDBs listening to the endpoint and delivers the message to it.

For its part, the MDB implements a listener interface that is appropriate to the JCA connector/message type and passes activation configuration parameters to the JCA connector and registers as a listener to the JCA connector (we'll discuss message listeners and activation configuration parameters shortly). JCA also enables MOM providers to integrate with Java EE containers in a standardized manner using a JCA-compliant connector or resource adapter.

For more information on JCA, visit http://java.sun.com/j2ee/connector/index.jsp.

4.3.1 Why use MDBs?

Given the less-than-stellar reputation of EJB 2, you might question the value of EJB 3 MDBs. The truth is, MDBs have enjoyed a reasonable degree of success even in the darkest hours of EJB. In this section, we'll explain why you should take a serious look at MDBs.

Multithreading

Your business application may require multithreaded message consumers that can process messages concurrently. MDBs help you avoid complexity because they handle multithreading right out of the box, without any additional code. They manage incoming messages among multiple instances of beans (in a pool) that have no special multithreading code themselves. As soon as a new message reaches the destination, an MDB instance is retrieved from the pool to handle the message, as figure 4.7 shows. This is popularly known as MDB pooling, which you'll learn about when we discuss the MDB lifecycle later in this chapter.

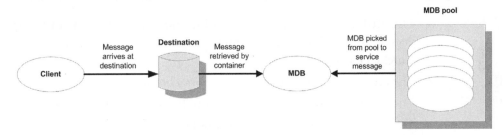

Figure 4.7   As soon as a message arrives at its destination, the container retrieves it and assigns a servicing MDB instance from the pool.

Simplified messaging code

In addition, MDBs relieve you from coding the mechanical aspects of processing messages—tasks such as looking up connection factories or destinations, creating connections, opening sessions, creating consumers, and attaching listeners. As you'll see when we build the Turtle message consumer MDB, all these tasks are handled behind the scenes for you. In EJB 3, using sensible defaults for common circumstances eliminates most of the configuration. In the worst-case scenario, you'll have to supply configuration information using simple annotations or through the deployment descriptor.

Starting message consumption

To start picking up messages from the shipping request queue, someone needs to invoke the appropriate method in your code. In a production environment, it is not clear how this will be accomplished. Starting message consumption through a user-driven manual process obviously is not desirable. In a server environment, almost every means of executing the method on server startup is highly system dependent, not to mention awkward. The same is true about stopping message receipt manually. On the other hand, registered MDBs would be bootstrapped or torn down gracefully by the container when the server is started or stopped.

We'll continue consolidating these three points as we start investigating a real example of developing MDBs soon. Before we do that, though, let's list the simple rules for developing an MDB.

4.3.2 *Programming rules*

Like all EJBs, MDBs are plain Java objects that follow a simple set of rules and sometimes have annotations. Don't take these rules too seriously yet; simply note them in preparation for going through the code-intensive sections that follow.

- The MDB class must directly (by using the `implements` keyword in the class declaration) or indirectly (through annotations or descriptors) implement a message listener interface.

- The MDB class must be concrete. It cannot be either a final or an abstract class.

- The MDB must be a POJO class and not a subclass of another MDB.

- The MDB class must be declared public.

- The bean class must have a no-argument constructor. If you don't have any constructors in your Java class, the compiler will create a default constructor. The container uses this constructor to create a bean instance.

- You cannot define a finalize method in the bean class. If any cleanup code is necessary, it should be defined in a method designated as `PreDestroy`.

- You must implement the methods defined in the message listener interface. These methods must be public and cannot be static or final.

- You must not throw the `javax.rmi.RemoteException` or any runtime exceptions. If a `RuntimeException` is thrown, the MDB instance is terminated.

We'll apply these rules next in developing our example MDB.

4.3.3 *Developing a message consumer with MDB*

Let's now explore developing an MDB by reworking the Turtle server JMS message consumer as an MDB. To make the code a bit more interesting, we'll actually implement the `processShippingRequest` method mentioned in the JMS code. Listing 4.2 shows the MDB code that first retrieves shipping requests sent to the queue and then saves each request in the Turtle database table named `SHIPPING_REQUEST`. Note that we're using JDBC for simplicity's sake and because it lets us demonstrate the MDB lifecycle methods for opening and closing JDBC connections. We recommend that you consider EJB 3 Java Persistence API (discussed in part 3) for persisting your data instead of using straight JDBC.

Listing 4.2   Turtle server shipping request processor MDB

```
package ejb3inaction.example.buslogic;

import javax.ejb.MessageDriven;
import javax.ejb.ActivationConfigProperty;
import javax.annotation.PostConstruct;
import javax.annotation.PreDestroy;
import javax.annotation.Resource;
import javax.jms.JMSException;
import javax.jms.Message;
import javax.jms.MessageListener;
import java.sql.*;
import javax.sql.*;

@MessageDriven(
    name="ShippingRequestProcessor",
    activationConfig = {
        @ActivationConfigProperty(
            propertyName="destinationType",
            propertyValue="javax.jms.Queue"),
        @ActivationConfigProperty(
            propertyName="destinationName",
            propertyValue="jms/ShippingRequestQueue")
    }
)
public class ShippingRequestProcessorMDB
        implements MessageListener {
    private java.sql.Connection connection;
    private DataSource dataSource;

    @Resource
    private MessageDrivenContext context;

    @Resource(name="jdbc/TurtleDS")
    public void setDataSource(DataSource dataSource) {
        this.dataSource = dataSource;
    }

    @PostConstruct
    public void initialize() {
        try {
            connection = dataSource.getConnection();
        } catch (SQLException sqle) {
            sqle.printStackTrace();
        }
    }

    @PreDestroy
```

1 Defines @MessageDriven annotation

2 Implements message listener

3 Injects MessageDrivenContext

4 Uses resource injection

5 Defines lifecycle callbacks

```
public void cleanup() {
    try {
        connection.close();
        connection = null;
    } catch (SQLException sqle) {
        sqle.printStackTrace();
    }
}
```

```
public void onMessage(Message message) {          ⑥  Implements
    try {                                             onMessage method
        ObjectMessage objectMessage = (ObjectMessage)message;
        ShippingRequest shippingRequest =
            (ShippingRequest)objectMessage.getObject();
        processShippingRequest(shippingRequest);
    } catch (JMSException jmse) {
        jmse.printStackTrace();
        context.setRollbackOnly();
    } catch (SQLException sqle) {
        sqle.printStackTrace();
        context.setRollbackOnly();
    }
}
```

```
                                    Processes business logic  ⑦
private void processShippingRequest(ShippingRequest request)
        throws SQLException {
    Statement statement = connection.createStatement();
    statement.execute(
        "INSERT INTO "
            + "SHIPPING_REQUEST ("
            + "ITEM, "
            + "SHIPPING_ADDRESS, "
            + "SHIPPING_METHOD, "
            + "INSURANCE_AMOUNT ) "
            + "VALUES ( "
            + request.getItem() + ", "
            + "\'" + request.getShippingAddress() + "\', "
            + "\' " + request.getShippingMethod() + "\', "
            + request.getInsuranceAmount() + " )");
    }
}
```

The @MessageDriven annotation ① identifies this object as an MDB and specifies
the MDB configuration, including the fact that we are listening on the shipping
request queue. Our code then marks this MDB as a JMS message listener ②. The
onMessage method implements the message listener interface ⑥ and processes
incoming messages. A message-driven context is injected ③ and used inside the

onMessage method ❻ to roll back transactions as needed. A database resource is injected ❹. The lifecycle callbacks ❺ open and close a connection derived from the database resource. Finally, the shared JDBC connection is used by the business logic ❼ called in onMessage to save each shipping request into the database.

Next, we'll examine the major MDB features by analyzing this code in greater detail, starting with the @MessageDriven annotation.

4.3.4 *Using the @MessageDriven annotation*

MDBs are one of the simplest kinds of EJBs to develop, and they support the smallest number of annotations. In fact, the @MessageDriven annotation and the @ActivationConfigProperty annotation nested inside it are the only MDB-specific annotations. The @MessageDriven annotation in our example represents what you'll typically use most of the time. The annotation is defined as follows:

```
@Target(TYPE)
@Retention(RUNTIME)
public @interface MessageDriven {
    String name() default "";
    Class messageListenerInterface default Object.class;
    ActivationConfigProperty[] activationConfig() default {};
        String mappedName();
    String description();

}
```

Notice that all three of the annotation's arguments are optional. If you are a minimalist, you can keep the annotation as simple as this:

```
@MessageDriven
public class ShippingRequestProcessorMDB
```

and leave any details to be added elsewhere, such as in the deployment descriptor.

The first element, name, specifies the name of the MDB—in our case, Shipping-RequestProcessor. If the name element is omitted, the code uses the name of the class, ShippingRequestProcessorMDB, in our example. The second parameter, messageListenerInterface, specifies which message listener the MDB implements. The last parameter, activationConfig, is used to specify listener-specific configuration properties. Let's take a closer look at the two last parameters.

4.3.5 *Implementing the MessageListener*

An MDB implements a message listener interface for the very same reason our plain JMS consumer implemented the javax.jms.MessageListener interface. The container uses the listener interface to register the MDB with the message provider and to pass incoming messages by invoking implemented message listener methods. Using the `messageListenerInterface` parameter of the `@MessageDriven` annotation is just one way to specify a message listener; we could have done the following instead:

```
@MessageDriven(
    name="ShippingRequestJMSProcessor",
    messageListenerInterface="javax.jms.MessageListener")
public class ShippingRequestProcessorMDB {
```

However, we chose to omit this parameter and specified the interface using the `implements` keyword:

```
public class ShippingRequestProcessorMDB implements MessageListener {
```

Yet another option is to specify the listener interface through the deployment descriptor and leave this detail out of our code altogether. The approach you choose is largely a matter of taste. We prefer the second approach because it resembles our JMS example.

MDBs let you specify a message listener with relative flexibility, which is especially cool if you consider the following scenario: suppose that we decide to switch messaging technologies and use Java API for XML Messaging (JAXM) to send shipping requests instead of JMS. (JAXM is essentially a SOAP-based XML messaging API. For more information, visit http://java.sun.com/webservices/jaxm/.) Thanks to JCA support, we can use still use MDBs to receive shipping requests (see the sidebar "JCA Connectors and Messaging" to learn how this might be done). All we have to do is switch to the JAXM message listener interface, `javax.jaxm.OneWayMessageListener`, instead of using `javax.jms.MessageListener`. We can reuse most of the MDB code and configuration:

```
public class ShippingRequestProcessorMDB implements
    javax.jaxm.OneWayMessageListener {
```

However you choose to specify the message listener, make sure you provide a valid implementation of all methods required by your message listener—especially when using the deployment descriptor approach, where there are no compile-time checks to watch your back. Next, let's take a look at the last (but definitely not least) parameter of the `@MessageDriven` annotation: `activationConfig`.

4.3.6 Using ActivationConfigProperty

The `activationConfig` property of the `@MessageDriven` annotation allows you to provide messaging system–specific configuration information through an array of `ActivationConfigProperty` instances. `ActivationConfigProperty` is defined as follows:

```
public @interface ActivationConfigProperty {
    String propertyName();
    String propertyValue();
}
```

Each activation property is essentially a name-value pair that the underlying messaging provider understands and uses to set up the MDB. The best way to grasp how this works is through example. Here, we provide three of the most common JMS activation configuration properties: `destinationType`, `connectionFactory-JndiName`, and `destinationName`:

```
@MessageDriven(
    name="ShippingRequestProcessor",
    activationConfig = {
        @ActivationConfigProperty(
            propertyName="destinationType",
            propertyValue="javax.jms.Queue"),
        @ActivationConfigProperty(
            propertyName="connectionFactoryJndiName",
            propertyValue="jms/QueueConnectionFactory"
        ),
        @ActivationConfigProperty(
            propertyName="destinationName",
            propertyValue="jms/ShippingRequestQueue")
    }
)
```

First, the `destinationType` property tells the container this JMS MDB is listening to a queue. If we were listening to a topic instead, the value could be specified as `javax.jms.Topic`. Next, `connectionFactoryJndiName` specifies the JNDI name of the connection factory that should be used to create JMS connections for the MDB. Finally, the `destinationName` parameter specifies that we are listening for messages arriving at a destination with the JNDI name of `jms/ShippingRequestQueue`.

There are a few other configuration properties for JMS that we'll describe in the sections that follow. Visualizing what happens behind the scenes can help you remember these configuration properties. The container does something similar to our JMS message consumer setup steps (as shown in listing 4.2) to bootstrap the MDB. Most of the method parameters that we specify during those steps are made available as configuration properties in the MDB world.

acknowledgeMode

Messages are not actually removed from the queue until the consumer acknowledges them. There are many "modes" through which messages can be acknowledged. By default, the acknowledge mode for the underlying JMS session is assumed to be Auto-acknowledge, which means that the session acknowledged messages on our behalf in the background. This is the case for our example (since we omitted this property). All of the acknowledgment modes supported by JMS are listed in table 4.1. We could change the acknowledge mode to Dups-ok-acknowledge (or any other acknowledge mode we discuss in table 4.1) using the following:

```
@ActivationConfigProperty(
    propertyName="acknowledgeMode",
    propertyValue="Dups-ok-acknowledge")
```

Table 4.1 JMS session acknowledge modes. For nontransacted sessions, you should choose the mode most appropriate for your project. In general, Auto-acknowledge is the most common and convenient. The only other mode supported with MDB is Dups-ok-acknowledge.

Acknowledgment Mode	Description	Supported with MDB
Auto-acknowledge	The session automatically acknowledges receipt after a message has been received or is successfully processed.	YES
Client-acknowledge	You have to manually acknowledge the receipt of the message by calling the `acknowledge` method on the message.	NO
Dups-ok-acknowledge	The session can lazily acknowledge receipt of the message. This is similar to Auto-acknowledge but useful when the application can handle delivery of duplicate messages and rigorous acknowledgment is not a requirement.	YES
SESSION_TRANSACTED	This is returned for transacted sessions if the `Session.getAcknowledgeMode` method is invoked.	NO

subscriptionDurability

If our MDB is listening on a topic, we can specify whether the topic subscription is durable or nondurable.

Recall that in the pub-sub domain, a message is distributed to all currently subscribed consumers. In general, this is much like a broadcast message in that anyone who is not connected to the topic at the time does not receive a copy of the message. The exception to this rule is what is known as a *durable subscription*.

Once a consumer obtains a durable subscription on a topic, all messages sent to the topic are guaranteed to be delivered to that consumer. If the *durable subscriber* is not connected to a topic when a message is received, MOM retains a copy of the message until the subscriber connects and delivers the message. The following shows how to create a durable subscriber:

```
MessageConsumer playBoySubscriber = session.createDurableSubscriber(
    playBoyTopic, "JoeOgler");
```

Here, we are creating a durable subscription message consumer to the `javax.jms.Topic` playBoyTopic with a subscription ID of JoeOgler. From now on, all messages to the topic will be held until a consumer with the subscription ID JoeOgler receives them. You can remove this subscription with the following code:

```
session.unsubscribe("JoeOgler");
```

If you want the MDB to be a durable subscriber, then `ActivationConfigProperty` would look like this:

```
@ActivationConfigProperty(
    propertyName="destinationType",
    propertyValue="javax.jms.Topic"),
@ActivationConfigProperty(
    propertyName="subscriptionDurability",
    propertyValue="Durable")
```

For nondurable subscriptions, explicitly set the value of the `subscriptionDurability` property to `NonDurable`, which is also the default.

messageSelector

The `messageSelector` property is the MDB parallel to applying a selector for a JMS consumer. Our current code consumes all messages at the destination. If we prefer, we could filter the messages we retrieve by using a *message selector*— a criterion applied to the headers and properties of messages specifying which messages the consumer wants to receive. For example, if we want to receive all shipping requests whose `Fragile` property is set to `true`, we use the following code:

```
MessageConsumer consumer = session.createConsumer(destination,
    "Fragile IS TRUE");
```

As you might have noticed, the selector syntax is almost identical to the WHERE clause in SQL 92, but the selector syntax uses message header and property names instead of column names. Selector expressions can be as complex and expressive as you need them to be. They can include literals, identifiers, whitespace, expressions, standard brackets, logical and comparison operators, arithmetic operators, and null comparisons.

Using our JMS message selector example, we could specify in our MDB that we want to handle only fragile shipping requests as follows:

```
@ActivationConfigProperty(
    propertyName="messageSelector",
    propertyValue="Fragile IS TRUE")
```

Table 4.2 summarizes some common message selector types.

Table 4.2 Commonly used message selector types. The selector syntax is almost identical to the SQL WHERE clause.

Type	Description	Example

Literals	Can be strings, exact or approximate numeric values, or booleans.	`BidManagerMDB`
		`100`
		`TRUE`

Identifiers	Can be a message property or header name; case sensitive.	`RECIPIENT`
		`NumOfBids`
		`Fragile`
		`JMSTimestamp`

Whitespace	Same as defined in the Java language specification: space, tab, form feed, and line terminator.	
Comparison operators	Comparison operators, such as =, >, >=, <=, <>.	`RECIPIENT='BidManagerMDB'` `NumOfBids>=100`
Logical operators	All three types of logical operators—NOT, AND, OR—are supported.	`RECIPIENT='BidManagerMDB'` `AND NumOfBids>=100`
Null comparison	IS NULL and IS NOT NULL comparisons.	`FirstName IS NOT NULL`
True/false comparison	IS [NOT] TRUE and IS [NOT] FALSE comparisons.	`Fragile IS TRUE` `Fragile IS FALSE`

We're now ready to examine lifecycle callbacks in MDBs.

4.3.7 Using bean lifecycle callbacks

As you recall from chapter 3, similar to stateless session beans, MDBs have a simple lifecycle (see figure 4.8 for a refresher). The container is responsible for the following:

- Creates MDB instances and sets them up
- Injects resources, including the message-driven context (discussed in the next chapter in detail)
- Places instances in a managed pool
- Pulls an idle bean out of the pool when a message arrives (the container may have to increase the pool size at this point)
- Executes the message listener method; e.g., the `onMessage` method
- When the `onMessage` method finishes executing, pushes the idle bean back into the "method-ready" pool
- As needed, retires (or destroys) beans out of the pool

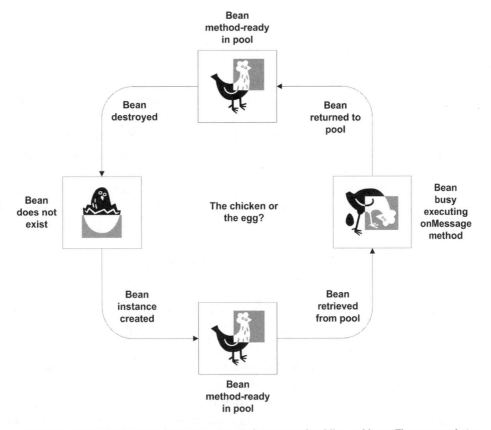

Figure 4.8 The MDB lifecycle has three states: does not exist, idle, and busy. There are only two lifecycle callbacks corresponding to bean creation and destruction; you can use PostConstruct and PreDestroy methods to receive these callbacks.

The MDB's two lifecycle callbacks are (1) `PostConstruct`, which is called immediately after an MDB is created and set up and all the resources are injected, and (2) `PreDestroy`, which is called right before the bean instance is retired and removed from the pool. These callbacks are typically used for allocating and releasing injected resources that are used by the `onMessage` method, which is exactly what we do in our example.

The `processShippingRequest` method saves shipping requests that the `onMessage` method extracts from the incoming JMS message:

```
private void processShippingRequest(ShippingRequest request)
        throws SQLException {
    Statement statement = connection.createStatement();
    statement.execute(
        "INSERT INTO "
            + "SHIPPING_REQUEST ("
          ...
            + request.getInsuranceAmount() + " )");
}
```

The method creates a statement from an open JDBC connection and uses it to save a record into the `SHIPPING_REQUEST` table containing all the fields from the `ShippingRequest` object. The JDBC connection object used to create the statement is a classic heavy-duty resource. It is expensive to open and should be shared whenever possible. On the other hand, it can hold a number of native resources, so it is important to close the connection when it is no longer needed. We accomplish both these goals using callback methods as well as resource injection.

First, the JDBC data source that the connection is created from is injected using the `@Resource` annotation:

```
@Resource(name="jdbc/TurtleDS")
public void setDataSource(DataSource dataSource) {
    this.dataSource = dataSource;
}
```

The `@Resource` annotation tells the EJB container that it should look up a `java.sql.DataSource` named `jdbc/TurtleDS` from JNDI and pass it to the `setDataSource` method after creating a new instance of the bean. The `setDataSource` method, in turn, saves the data source in an instance variable. After injecting resources, the container checks whether there are any designated `PostConstruct` methods that need to be invoked before the MDB is put into the pool. In our case, we mark the `initialize` method with the `@PostConstruct` annotation:

```
@PostConstruct
public void initialize() {
```

```
    ...
    connection = dataSource.getConnection();
    ...
}
```

In the `initialize` method, we are obtaining a `java.sql.Connection` from the injected data source and saving it into the `connection` instance variable used in `processShippingRequest`. At some point, the container decides that our bean should be removed from the pool and destroyed (perhaps at server shutdown). The `PreDestroy` callback gives us a chance to cleanly tear down bean resources before this is done. In the `cleanup` method marked with the `@PreDestroy` annotation, we tear down the database connection resource before the container retires our bean:

```
@PreDestroy
public void cleanup() {
    ...
    connection.close();
    connection = null;
    ...
}
```

Although database resources and their management are the primary uses of resource injection and lifecycle methods in MDBs, another important resource being used in the JMS sections are also important for MDB. We're referring to the JMS destination and connection factory administrative objects, as well as the JMS connections. Let's explore how these are utilized in MDBs.

4.3.8 *Sending JMS messages from MDBs*

Somewhat ironically, a task you'll find yourself performing time and again in an MDB is sending JMS messages. As a simple example, suppose that we have an incomplete shipping request and we need to communicate that to Action-Bazaar from `ShippingRequestProcessorMDB`. The easiest way to handle this notification is via JMS messages sent to an error queue that ActionBazaar listens to. Fortunately, you've already seen how to send a JMS message in listing 4.1. This task is even simpler and more robust in MDBs. We can inject the queue named `jms/ShippingErrorQueue` and the connection factory named `jms/QueueConnectionFactory` by using the `@Resource` annotation:

```
@Resource(name="jms/ShippingErrorQueue")
private javax.jms.Destination errorQueue;
@Resource(name="jms/QueueConnectionFactory")
private javax.jms.ConnectionFactory connectionFactory;
```

We can then create and destroy a shared `javax.jms.Connection` instance using life-cycle callbacks, just as we managed the JDBC connection in the previous section:

```
@PostConstruct
public void initialize() {
    ...
    jmsConnection = connectionFactory.createConnection();
    ...
}
@PreDestroy
public void cleanup() {
    ...
    jmsConnection.close();
    ...
}
```

Finally, the business method that sends the error message looks much like the rest of the JMS session code in listing 4.1:

```
private void sendErrorMessage(ShippingError error) {
    Session session = jmsConnection.createSession(true,
        Session.AUTO_ACKNOWLEDGE);
    MessageProducer producer = session.createProducer(errorQueue);
    ...
    producer.send(message);
    session.close();
}
```

Although we didn't explicitly show it in our example, there is one more MDB feature you should know about: MDB transaction management. We'll discuss EJB transactions in general in much more detail in the next chapter, so here we'll give you the "bargain basement" version.

4.3.9 Managing MDB transactions

In our plain JMS examples, we specified whether the JMS session would be transactional when we created it. On the other hand, if you look closely at the MDB example it doesn't indicate anything about transactions. Instead, we're letting the container use the default transactional behavior for MDBs. By default, the container will start a transaction before the `onMessage` method is invoked and will commit the transaction when the method returns, unless the transaction was marked as `rollback` through the message-driven context. You'll learn more about transactions in chapter 6.

This brief discussion of transaction management concludes our analysis of the basic features that MDBs offer. We've discussed how you can use MDBs to leverage the power of messaging without dealing with the low-level details of the messaging API. As you've seen, MDBs provide a host of EJB features for free, such as multithreading, resource injection, lifecycle management, and container-managed transactions. We've formulated our code samples so that you can use them as templates for solving real business problems. At this point, we'll give you tips for dealing with the nuances of MDBs.

4.4 *MDB best practices*

Like all technologies, MDBs have some pitfalls to watch for and some best practices that you should keep in mind. This is particularly true in demanding environments where messaging is typically deployed.

Choose your messaging models carefully. Before you wade knee deep in code, consider your choice of messaging model carefully. You might find that PTP will solve your problem nine times out of ten. In some cases, though, the pub-sub approach is better, especially if you find yourself broadcasting the same message to more than one receiver (such as our system outage notification example). Luckily, most messaging code is domain independent, and you should strive to keep it that way. For the most part, switching domains should be just a matter of configuration.

Remember modularization. Because MDBs are so similar to session beans, it is natural to start putting business logic right into message listener methods. Business logic should be decoupled and modularized away from messaging-specific concerns. We followed this principle by coding the `processShippingRequest` method and invoking it from `onMessage`. An excellent practice (but one that would have made this chapter unnecessarily complicated) is to put business logic in session beans and invoke them from the `onMessage` method.

Make good use of message filters. There are some valid reasons for using a single messaging destination for multiple purposes. Message selectors come in handy in these circumstances. For example, if you're using the same queue for both shipping requests and order cancellation notices, you can have the client set a message property identifying the type of request. You can then use message selectors on two separate MDBs to isolate and handle each kind of request.

Conversely, in some cases, you might dramatically improve performance and keep your code simple by using separate destinations instead of using selectors. In our example, using separate queues and MDBs for shipping requests and cancellation orders could make message delivery much faster. In this case, the client would have to send each request type to the appropriate queue.

Choose message types carefully. The choice of message type is not always as obvious as it seems. For example, it is a compelling idea to use XML strings for messaging. Among other things, this tends to promote loose coupling between systems. In our example, the Turtle server would know about the format of the XML message and not the ShippingRequest object itself.

The problem is that XML tends to bloat the size of the message, significantly degrading MOM performance. In certain circumstances, it might even be the right choice to use binary streams in the message payload, which puts the least amount of demand on MOM processing as well as memory consumption.

Be wary of poison messages. Imagine that a message is handed to you that your MDB was not able to consume. Using our example, let's assume that we receive a message that's not an ObjectMessage. As you can see from this code snippet, if this happens the cast in onMessage will throw a java.lang.ClassCastException:

```
try {
    ObjectMessage objectMessage = (ObjectMessage)message;      ⟵  Wrong
    ShippingRequest shippingRequest =                              message type
            (ShippingRequest)objectMessage.getObject();           fails cast
        processShippingRequest(shippingRequest);
} catch (JMSException jmse) {
    jmse.printStackTrace();
    context.setRollBackOnly();
}
```

Since onMessage will not complete normally, the container will be forced to roll back the transaction and put the message back on the queue instead of acknowledging it (in fact, since a runtime exception is thrown, the bean instance will be removed from the pool). The problem is, since we are still listening on the queue, the same message will be delivered to us again and we will be stuck in the accept/die loop indefinitely! Messages that cause this all-too-common scenario are called *poison messages*.

The good news is that many MOMs and EJB containers provide mechanisms that deal with poison messages, including "redelivery" counts and "dead message" queues. If you set up the redelivery count and dead message queue for the shipping request destination, the message delivery will be attempted for the specified number of times. After the redelivery count is exceeded, the message will be moved to a specially designated queue for poison messages called the "dead message" queue. The bad news is that these mechanisms are not standardized and are vendor specific.

Configure MDB pool size. Most EJB containers let you specify the maximum number of instances of a particular MDB the container can create. In effect, this controls the level of concurrency. If there are five concurrent messages to process and the pool size is set to three, the container will wait until the first three messages are processed before assigning any more instances. This is a double-edged sword and requires careful handling. If you set your MDB pool size too small, messages will be processed slowly. At the same time, it is desirable to place *reasonable* limits on the MDB pool size so that many concurrent MDB instances do not choke the machine. Unfortunately, at the time of this writing, setting MDB pool sizes is not standardized and is provider specific.

4.5 *Summary*

In this chapter, we covered basic messaging concepts, JMS, and MDBs. Messaging is an extremely powerful technology for the enterprise, and it helps build loosely coupled systems. JMS allows you to use message-oriented middleware (MOM) from enterprise Java applications. Using the JMS API to build a message consumer application can be time consuming, and MDBs make using MOM in a standardized manner through Java EE extremely easy.

Note, however, that messaging and MDBs are not right for all circumstances and can be overused. One such case is using the request/reply model (discussed in the sidebar "The request-reply model"), which entails a lot of extra complexity compared to simple PTP or pub-sub messaging. If you find yourself using this model extensively and in ways very close to synchronous messaging, it might be worth thinking about switching to a synchronous technology such as RMI, SOAP, or remote session bean calls.

A few major EJB features we touched on in this chapter are dependency injection, interceptors, timers, transaction, and security. As you've seen, EJB 3 largely relieves us from these system-level concerns while providing extremely robust and flexible functionality. We'll discuss dependency injection, timers, and interceptors in the next chapter.

Learning advanced EJB concepts

In the previous two chapters we focused on developing session beans and message-driven beans (MDBs). Although we discussed a few bean type-specific features in detail, we generally avoided covering topics not closely related to introducing the basics. In this chapter we build on the material in the previous chapters and introduce advanced concepts applicable to MDBs and session beans. It is very likely that you'll find these EJB 3 features extremely helpful while using EJB in the real world.

We begin by discussing the how containers provide the services behind the scenes and how to access environment information. We then move on to advanced use of dependency injection, JNDI lookups, EJB interceptors, and the EJB timer service. As you'll learn, EJB 3 largely relieves you from these system-level concerns while providing extremely robust and flexible functionality.

As a foundation for the rest of the chapter, we briefly examine these EJB internals first.

5.1 EJB internals

Although we've talked about the role of the container and the concept of managed services, we haven't explained how most containers go about providing managed services. The secret to understanding these and the other EJB services is knowing how the container provides them. Without going into too much detail, we'll discuss EJB objects—which perform the magic of providing the service—and then examine the EJB context—which a bean can use to access runtime environment and use container services.

5.1.1 EJB behind the scenes

EJB centers on the idea of managed objects. As we saw in the previous chapters, EJB 3 beans are just annotated POJOs themselves. When a client invokes an EJB method using the bean interface, it doesn't work directly on the bean instance. The container makes beans "special" by acting as a *proxy* between the client and the actual bean instance. This enables the container to provide EJB services to the client on behalf of the bean instance.

NOTE　For each bean instance, the container automatically generates a proxy called an *EJB object*. The EJB object has access to all the functionality of the container, including the JNDI registry, security, transaction management, thread pools, session management, and pretty much anything else that is necessary to provide EJB services. The EJB object is aware of the bean configuration and what services the POJO is supposed to provide.

Since all requests to the EJB instance are passed through the EJB object proxy, the EJB object can "insert" container services to client requests as needed, including managing all aspects of the bean lifecycle. Figure 5.1 is a typical representation of this technique.

As you've seen in the previous chapters, the beauty of this technique is that all the service details are completely transparent to bean clients and even to bean developers. In fact, a container implementation is free to implement the services in the most effective way possible and at the same time provide vendor-specific feature and performance enhancements. This is fundamentally all there is to the "magic" parts of EJB. For session beans, the client interacts with the EJB object through the business interface. For MDBs, however, the EJB object or message endpoint sits between the message provider and the bean instance.

Let's now take a look at how EJBs access the container environment in which the EJB object itself resides.

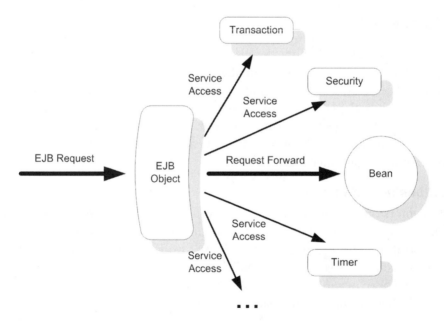

Figure 5.1 The "magic" of EJB. The container-generated EJB object receives all EJB client requests as the proxy, and reads configuration and inserts container services as required before forwarding client requests to the bean instance.

5.1.2 *EJB context: accessing the runtime environment*

EJB components are generally meant to be agnostic of the container. This means that in the ideal case, EJB components should merely hold business logic and never access the container or use container services directly. As you'll recall, services like transaction management, security, dependency injection, and so forth are meant to be "overlaid" on the bean through configuration.

However, in the real world, it is sometimes necessary for the bean to explicitly use container services in code. These are the situations the EJB context is designed to handle. The `javax.ejb.EJBContext` interface is essentially your backdoor into the mystic world of the container. In this section, we define `EJBContext`, explain its use, and show you how to use dependency injection to retrieve `EJBContext`.

Defining the EJBContext Interface

As you can see in listing 5.1, the `EJBContext` interface allows direct programmatic access to services such as transaction and security, which are typically specified through configuration and completely managed by the container.

> **Listing 5.1   javax.ejb.EJBContext interface**

```
public interface EJBContext {
    public Principal getCallerPrincipal();              Bean-managed
    public boolean isCallerInRole(String roleName);     security
    public EJBHome getEJBHome();

    public EJBLocalHome getEJBLocalHome();
    public boolean getRollbackOnly();                   transaction
    public UserTransaction getUserTransaction();        management
    public void setRollbackOnly();
    public TimerService getTimerService();          ◁─  Access to timer service

    public Object lookup(String name);              ◁─  JNDI lookup
}
```

Let's look briefly at what each of these methods do (table 5.1). We'll save a detailed analysis for later, when we discuss the services that each of the methods is related to. For now, you should note the array of services offered through the EJB context as well as the method patterns.

Table 5.1   You can use javax.ejb.EJBContext to access runtime services.

Methods	Description
`getCallerPrincipal` `isCallerInRole`	These methods are useful when using in bean-managed security. We discuss these two methods further in chapter 6 when we discuss programmatic security.
`getEJBHome getEJBLocalHome`	These methods are used to obtain the bean's "remote home" and "local home" interfaces, respectively. Both are optional for EJB 3 and are hardly used beyond legacy EJB 2.1 beans. We won't discuss these methods beyond this basic introduction. They are mainly provided for backward compatibility.
`getRollbackOnly,` `setRollbackOnly`	These methods are used for EJB transaction management in the case of *container-managed transactions*. We discuss container-managed transactions in greater detail in chapter 6.
`getUserTransaction`	This method is used for EJB transaction management in the case of *bean-managed transactions*. We discuss bean-managed transactions in greater detail in chapter 6.
`getTimerService`	This method is used to get access to the EJB timer service. We discuss EJB timers later in this chapter.
`lookup`	This method is used to get references to objects stored in the JNDI registry. With the introduction of DI in EJB 3, direct JNDI lookup has been rendered largely unnecessary. However, there are some edge cases that DI cannot handle, or perhaps DI is simply not available. This method proves handy in such circumstances. We discuss this topic later in this section.

Both session and message-driven beans have their own subclasses of the `javax.ejb.EJBContext` interface. As shown in figure 5.2, the session bean–specific subclass is `javax.ejb.SessionContext`, and the MDB-specific subclass is `javax.ejb.MessageDrivenContext`.

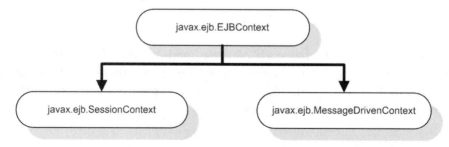

Figure 5.2   The EJB context interface has a subclass for each session and message-driven bean type.

Each subclass is designed to suit the particular runtime environment of each bean type. As a result, they either add methods to the superclass or invalidate methods not suited for the bean type. For example, it doesn't make sense to call the `isCallerInRole` method from an MDB because the MDB is not invoked directly by a user.

Using EJBContext

As we discussed earlier, you can gain access to several container services such as transaction or security by using `EJBContext`. Interestingly, you can access `EJB-Context` through DI. For example, a `SessionContext` could be injected into a bean as follows:

```
@Stateless
public class PlaceBidBean implements PlaceBid {
            @Resource
    SessionContext context;
    . . .
  }
```

In this code snippet, the container detects the `@Resource` annotation on the context variable and figures out that the bean wants an instance of its session context. The `SessionContext` adds a number of methods specific to the session bean environment, including `getBusinessObject`, `getEJBLocalObject`, `getEJBObject`, `getInvokedBusinessInterface`, and `getMessageContext`. All of these are fairly advanced methods that are rarely used. Note that the `getEJBLocalObject` and `getEJBObject` methods are meant for EJB 2 beans and will generate exceptions if used with EJB 3 beans. We won't discuss these methods further and will leave them for you to explore on your own.

MessageDrivenContext adds no methods specific to MDB. Rather, it throws exceptions if the `isCallerInRole`, `getEJBHome`, or `getEJBLocalHome` methods are called since they make no sense in a messaging-based environment (recall that a message-driven bean has no business interface and is never invoked directly by the client). Much like a session context, a `MessageDrivenContext` can be injected as follows:

```
@MessageDriven
public class OrderBillingMDB {
            @Resource MessageDrivenContext context;
    . . .
  }
```

> **NOTE**   It is illegal to inject a `MessageDrivenContext` into a session bean or a
> `SessionContext` into an MDB.

This is about as much time as we need to spend on the EJB context right now. Rest assured that you'll see more of it in chapter 6. In the meantime, let's turn our attention back to a vital part of EJB 3—dependency injection. We provided a brief overview of DI in chapter 2 and have been seeing EJB DI in action in the last few chapters. We just saw an intriguing use case in injecting EJB contexts. In reality, EJB DI is a like a Swiss army knife: it is an all-in-one tool that can be used in unexpected ways. Let's take a look at some of these advanced uses next.

5.2 Accessing resources using DI and JNDI

We've seen EJB 3 DI in its primary incarnations already—the `@javax.ejb.EJB` and `@javax.annotation.Resource` annotations. EJB 3 DI comes in two more forms—the `@javax.persistence.PersistenceContext` and `@javax.persistence.Persistence-Unit` annotations. We'll see these two annotations in action in part 3 of this book.

We've also witnessed only a small part of the power of the `@Resource` annotation. So far, we've used the `@Resource` annotation to inject JDBC data sources, JMS connection factories, and JMS destinations. Unlike some lightweight containers such as Spring, EJB 3 does not permit injection of POJOs that aren't beans. However, the `@Resource` annotation allows for a variety of other uses, some of which we cover in the coming section. In this section we'll show you how to use the `@Resource` annotation and its parameters. You'll learn the difference between setter and field injection, and you'll see the `@Resource` annotation in action when we inject a variety of resources such as e-mail, environment entries, and the timer service. Finally, you'll learn how to look up resources using JNDI and the lookup method in `EJBContext`.

5.2.1 Resource injection using @Resource

The `@Resource` annotation is by far the most versatile mechanism for DI in EJB 3. As we noted, in most cases the annotation is used to inject JDBC data sources, JMS resources, and EJB contexts. However, the annotation can also be used for e-mail server resources, environment entries, ORB reference, or even EJB references. Let's take a brief look at each of these cases. For convenience, we'll use the familiar JDBC data source example to explain the basic features of the `@Resource` annotation before moving on to the more involved cases. The following code injects a data source into the `PlaceBid` bean from chapter 2:

```
@Stateless
public class PlaceBidBean implements PlaceBid {
    ...
    @Resource(name="jdbc/actionBazaarDB")
    private javax.sql.DataSource dataSource;
```

In this case, the container would not have to work very hard to figure out what resource to inject because the name parameter is explicitly specified. As we know, this parameter specifies the JNDI name of the resource to be injected, which in our case is specified as jdbc/actionBazaarDB. Although we didn't mention this little detail before, the value specified by the name parameter is actually interpreted further by the container similar to a value specified in the res-ref-name in the <resource-ref> tag in the deployment descriptor, as in the following example:

```
<resource-ref>
    <res-ref-name>jdbc/actionBazaarDB</res-ref-name>
    <res-type>javax.sql.DataSource</res-type>
</resource-ref>
```

The value of the name parameter in @Resource (or res-ref-name) is translated to a fully qualified JNDI mapping in the form java:comp/env/[value of the name parameter] (see the accompanying sidebar). In our example, the complete JNDI path for the resource will be java:comp/env/jdbc/actionBazaarDB. If you don't specify the name element in the @Resource annotation, the JNDI name for the resource will be of the form java:comp/env/ [bean class name including package]/ [name of the annotated field/property]. If we didn't specify the name element in the @Resource annotation, the container would use java:comp/env/action-bazaar.buslogic.PlaceBidBean/dataSource as the JNDI name.

The environment naming context and resolving global JNDI names

If you know how JNDI references worked in EJB 2, you're familiar with the environment naming context (ENC). ENC allows portability of the application without having to depend on global JNDI names. Global JNDI names for resources differ between application server implementations, and ENC allows you to use a JNDI location that starts with java:comp/env/ instead of hard-coding the actual global JNDI name. EJB 3 essentially assumes that all JNDI names used in code are local references and automatically prepends names with the java:comp/env/ prefix.

This automatic interpretation of EJB 3 JNDI names into local references is a nice alternative to mentioning the local ENC (`java:comp/env`) prefix over and over again. However, this convenience does come at a price. Since you cannot use global names with the `name` parameter, you have to make sure that you perform the mapping between the ENC and global JNDI names in all cases. Fortunately, many application servers will automatically resolve the ENC name to the global JNDI name if a resource with the same global JNDI name exists. For example, if you are using the Sun GlassFish or Oracle Application Server and you define a data source as shown here, the application server will automatically map the data source to the global JNDI resource bound to `jdbc/ActionBazaarDS`, even if you didn't explicitly map the resource:

```
@Resource(name="jdbc/ActionBazaarDS")
private javax.jdbc.DataSource myDB;
```

Moreover, application servers allow you to explicitly specify a global JNDI name using the `mappedName` parameter of the `@Resource` annotation. For example, if you're using the JBoss Application Server and you have a data source with a global JNDI name of `java:/DefaultDS`, you can specify the resource mapping as follows:

```
@Resource(name="jdbc/ActionBazaarDS", mappedName="java:/DefaultDS")
private javax.jdbc.DataSource myDB;
```

In this case, the container will look up the data source with the global JNDI name of `java:/DefaultDS` when the ENC `java:comp/env/jdbc/ActionBazaarDS` is resolved.

However, remember that using the `mappedName` parameter makes code less portable. Therefore, we recommend you use deployment descriptors for mapping global JNDI names instead.

Note that, similar to the `@Resource` annotation, the `@EJB` annotation has a `mappedName` parameter as well.

Behind the scenes, the container resolves the JNDI references to the resources and binds the resource to the ENC during deployment. If the resource is not found during injection, the container throws a runtime exception and the bean becomes unusable.

Beyond JNDI name mapping, the `@Resource` annotation is meant to be a lot more flexible when it needs to be than what is apparent in our deliberately straightforward data source injection example. To illustrate some of these robust features, let's take a look at the definition for the annotation:

```
@Target({TYPE, METHOD, FIELD})
@Retention(RUNTIME)
public @interface Resource {
    public enum AuthenticationType {
        CONTAINER,
        APPLICATION
    }
    String name() default "";
    Class type() default Object.class;
    AuthenticationType authenticationType() default
AuthenticationType.CONTAINER;
    boolean shareable() default true;
    String mappedName() default "";
description() default "";
}
```

The first point you should note from the definition of the @Resource annotation is that it is not limited to being applied to instance variables. As the @Target value indicates, it can be applied to *setter methods,* and even classes.

Setter vs. field injection

Other than field injection, setter injection is the most commonly used option for injection. To see how it works, let's transform our data source example to use setter injection:

```
@Stateless
public class PlaceBidBean implements PlaceBid {
    ...
    private DataSource dataSource;
    ...
    @Resource(name="jdbc/actionBazaarDB")
    public void setDataSource(DataSource dataSource) {
        this.dataSource = dataSource;
    }
```

As you can see, setter injection relies on JavaBeans property-naming conventions. In case you are unfamiliar with them, the conventions dictate that the instance variables of an object should always be private so that they cannot be externally accessible. Instead, an instance variable named *XX* should have corresponding nonprivate methods named *getXX* and *setXX* that allow it to be accessed and set externally. We've seen how the *setter* for the PlaceBidBean dataSource variable looks. The *getter* could look like this:

```
public DataSource getDataSource() {
    return dataSource;
}
```

Just as in instance variable injection, the container inspects the `@Resource` annotation on the `setDataSource` method before a bean instance becomes usable,
looks up the data source from JNDI using the `name` parameter value, and calls the
`setDataSource` method using the retrieved data source as parameter.

> **NOTE**   Whether or not to use setter injection is largely a matter of taste.
> Although setter injection might seem like a little more work, it provides
> a couple of distinct advantages. First, it is easier to unit-test by invoking
> the public setter method from a testing framework like JUnit. Second, it
> is easier to put initialization code in the setter if you need it.

In our case, we can open a database connection in the `setDataSource` method as
soon as injection happens:

```
private DataSource dataSource;
private Connection connection;
...
@Resource(name="jdbc/actionBazaarDB")
public void setDataSource(DataSource dataSource) {
    this.dataSource = dataSource;
    this.connection = dataSource.getConnection();
}
```

The optional `type` parameter of the `@Resource` annotation can be used to explicitly set the type of the injected resource. For example, we could have chosen to tell
the container that the injected resource is of type `javax.sql.DataSource`:

```
@Resource(name="jdbc/actionBazaarDB",
          type=javax.sql.DataSource.class)
private DataSource dataSource;
```

If omitted, the type of the injected resource is assumed to be the same as the type
of the instance variable or property.

The `type` element is mandatory when the `@Resource` annotation is used at
the class level and uses JNDI to obtain a reference to the resource. Let's take a
closer look.

Using @Resource at the class level

You may recall from our earlier discussion that DI is supported only in the managed classes and that you cannot use injection in helper or utility classes. In most
applications, you can use helper classes, and you have to use JNDI to look up a
resource. (If you aren't familiar with JNDI, refer to appendix A for a brief discussion.) To look up a resource from the helper class, you have to reference the
resource in the EJB class as follows:

```
@Resource(name="jdbc/actionBazaarDB",mappedName="jdbc/actionBazaarDS",
        type=javax.sql.DataSource.class)
@Stateless
public class PlaceBidBean implements PlaceBid
```

You can look up the resource either from the EJB or the helper class as follows:

```
Context ctx = new InitialContext();
DataSource ds = (DataSource) ctx.lookup("java:comp/env/jdbc/ActionBazaarDB")
```

Before we conclude this section, let's look at some remaining parameters of the @Resource annotation (table 5.2). The other parameters—authenticationType, shareable, description, and mappedName—are not used often and we won't cover them in great detail.

Table 5.2   The @Resource annotation can be used to inject resources. The parameters in the table are not used regularly and are included for your reference in case you need them.

Parameter	Type	Description	Default
authentication-Type	enum Authentication-Type {CONTAINER, APPLICATION}	The type of authentication required for accessing the resource. The CONTAINER value means that the container's security context is used for the resource. The APPLICATION value means that authentication for the resource must be provided by the application. We discuss EJB security at greater length in chapter 6.	CONTAINER
shareable	boolean	Specifies whether the resource can be shared.	true
description	String	The description of the resource.	" "
mappedName	String	A vendor-specific name that the resource may be mapped to, as opposed to the JNDI name. See the sidebar "The environment naming context and resolving global JNDI names" for details on this parameter.	" "

Using injection for JDBC data sources is just the tip of the iceberg. We'll look at the other uses of EJB DI next. In general, we avoid talking about how the resources are defined in the deployment descriptor for now; we'll discuss that in much greater detail when we examine application packaging and deployment descriptor tags in chapter 11.

5.2.2 *The @Resource annotation in action*

In the previous sections we discussed the various parameters of the `@Resource` annotation, and you learned how to use field or setter injection with `@Resource` to inject JDBC data sources. Next you'll see how to use the `@Resource` annotation to inject resources such as JMS objects, mail resources, `EJBContext`, environment entries, and the timer service.

Injecting JMS resources

Recall the discussion on messaging and MDBs in chapter 4. If your application has anything to do with messaging, it is going to need to use JMS resources such as `javax.jms.Queue`, `javax.jms.Topic`, `javax.jms.QueueConnectionFactory`, or `javax.jms.TopicConnectionFactory`. Just like JDBC data sources, these resources are stored in the application server's JNDI context and can be injected through the `@Resource` annotation. As an example, the following code injects a `Queue` bound to the name `jms/actionBazaarQueue` to the `queue` field:

```
@Resource(name="jms/actionBazaarQueue")
private Queue queue;
```

EJBContext

Earlier (section 5.2) we discussed the `EJBContext`, `SessionContext`, and `MessageDrivenContext` interfaces. One of the most common uses of injection is to gain access to EJB contexts. The following code, used in the `PlaceBid` session bean, injects the EJB type specific context into the `context` instance variable:

```
@Resource SessionContext context;
```

Note that the injected session context is not stored in JNDI. In fact, it would be incorrect to try to specify the `name` parameters in this case at all and servers will probably ignore the element if specified. Instead, when the container detects the `@Resource` annotation on the `context` variable, it figures out that the EJB context specific to the current bean instance must be injected by looking at the variable data type, `javax.ejb.SessionContext`. Since `PlaceBid` is a session bean, the result of the injection would be the same if the variable were specified to be the parent class, `EJBContext`. In the following code, an underlying instance of `javax.ejb.SessionContext` is still injected into the context variable, even if the variable data type is `javax.ejb.EJBContext`:

```
@Resource EJBContext context;
```

Using this code in a session bean would make a lot of sense if you did not plan to use any of the bean-type specific methods available through the `SessionContext` interface anyway.

Accessing environment entries

If you have been working with enterprise applications for any length of time, it is likely you have encountered situations where some parameters of your application change from one deployment to another (customer site information, product version, and so on). It is overkill to save this kind of "semi-static" information in the database. This is exactly the situation environment entry values are designed to solve.

For example, in the ActionBazaar application, suppose we want to set the censorship flag for certain countries. If this flag is on, the ActionBazaar application checks items posted against a censorship list specific to the country the application deployment instance is geared toward. We can inject an instance of an environment entry as follows:

```
@Resource
private boolean censorship;
```

Environment entries are specified in the deployment descriptor and are accessible via JNDI. The ActionBazaar censorship flag could be specified like this:

```
<env-entry>
    <env-entry-name>censorship</env-entry-name>
    <env-entry-type>java.lang.Boolean</env-entry-type>
    <env-entry-value>true</env-entry-value>
</env-entry>
```

Environment entries are essentially meant to be robust application constants and support a relatively small range of data types. Specifically, the values of the `<env-entry-type>` tag are limited to these Java types: `String`, `Character`, `Byte`, `Short`, `Integer`, `Long`, `Boolean`, `Double`, and `Float`. Because environment entries are accessible via JNDI they can be injected by name. We could inject the censorship flag environment entry into any EJB by explicitly specifying the JNDI name as follows:

```
@Resource(name="censorship")
private boolean censorship;
```

As you might gather, the data types of the environment entry and the injected variable must be compatible. Otherwise, the container throws a runtime exception while attempting DI.

Accessing e-mail resources

In addition to JDBC data sources and JMS resources, the other heavy-duty resource that enterprise applications often use is the JavaMail API, `javax.mail.Session`. JavaMail `Session`s that abstract e-mail server configuration can be stored in the application server JNDI registry. The `Session` can then be injected into an EJB (with the `@Resource` annotation) and used to send e-mail. In the ActionBazaar application, this is useful for sending the winning bidder a notification after bidding on an item is over. The DI code to inject the mail `Session` looks like this:

```
@Resource(name="mail/ActionBazaar")
private javax.mail.Session mailSession;
```

We'll leave configuring a mail session using the deployment descriptor as an exercise for you, the reader. You can find the one-to-one mapping between annotations and deployment descriptors in appendix D.

Accessing the timer service

The container-managed timer service gives EJBs the ability to schedule tasks in a simple way. (You'll learn more about timers in section 5.4.) We inject the container timer service into an EJB using the `@Resource` annotation:

```
@Resource
javax.ejb.TimerService timerService;
```

Just as with the EJB context, the timer service is not saved in JNDI, but the container resolves the resource by looking at the data type of the injection target.

The `@Resource` annotation may be used for injecting EJB references accessible via JNDI into other EJBs. However, the `@EJB` annotation is intended specifically for this purpose and should be used in these circumstances instead. Refer to the discussion in chapter 3 for details about this annotation.

EJB 3 and POJO injection

As you might have noted, the one DI feature glaringly missing is the ability to inject resources into POJOs and to inject POJOs that are not EJBs. You can still indirectly accomplish this by storing POJOs in the JNDI context (not a particularly easy thing to do) or using proprietary extension of your container vendor. We hope that a future version of EJB 3 will provide expanded support for POJO injection similar to other lightweight DI-capable frameworks like Spring.

You can also use POJO injection with Spring-enabled EJB 3 beans if you really need POJO injection in your EJB applications. We'll save the topic of EJB 3 and Spring for chapter 16. We have provided a workaround for POJO injection in chapter 12.

@Resource and annotation inheritance

In chapter 3, you learned that an EJB bean class may inherit from another EJB class or a POJO. If the superclass defines any dependencies on resources using the @Resource annotation, they are inherited by the subclass. For example, Bid-ManagerBean extends another stateless EJB, PlaceBidBean, where PlaceBidBean defines a resource, as in this example:

```
@Stateless
public class PlaceBidBean implements PlaceBid{
@Resource(name="censorship")
    private boolean censorship;
  ..
}


@Stateless
public class BidManagerBean extends PlaceBidBean implements BidManager{
  ..
  }
```

The environment entry defined in the PlaceBidBean will be inherited by the BidManagerBean and dependency injection will occur when an instance of Bid-ManagerBean is created.

As useful as DI is, it cannot solve every problem. There are some cases where you must programmatically look up resources from a JNDI registry yourself. We'll talk about some of these cases next, as well as show you how to perform programmatic lookups.

5.2.3 *Looking up resources and EJBs*

Although you can use the @EJB or @Resource annotation to inject resource instances, you may still need to look up items from JNDI in several advanced cases (if you are unfamiliar with JNDI itself, check out the brief tutorial in appendix A). You can use the @EJB or @Resource annotation at the EJB class level to define dependency on an EJB or a resource. There are two ways of using programmatic lookups—using either the EJB context or a JNDI initial context. We'll look at both methods.

Recall from our earlier discussion that you can look up any object stored in JNDI using the EJBContext.lookup method (including session bean references). This technique can be used to accomplish one extremely powerful feature that DI cannot accomplish: using lookups instead of DI allows you to determine which resource to use dynamically at runtime instead of being constrained to using static configuration that cannot be changed programmatically. All you have to do is specify a different name in the lookup method to retrieve a different resource. As a result, program logic driven by data and/or user input can determine dependencies instead of deploy-time configuration.

The following code shows the EJB context lookup method in action:

```
@EJB(name="ejb/BidderAccountCreator", beanInterface =
    BidderAccountCreator.class)
@Stateless
public class GoldBidderManagerBean implements GoldBidderManager {
@Resource SessionContext sessionContext;
...
BidderAccountCreator accountCreator
    = (BidderAccountCreator)
        sessionContext.lookup(
            "ejb/BidderAccountCreator");
...
accountCreator.addLoginInfo(loginInfo);
...
accountCreator.createAccount();
```

Note that while using the class-level reference annotation you must explicitly specify the reference name as the complete JNDI pathname. Also note that once an EJB context is injected (as in the sample lookup code), it could be passed into any non-bean POJO to perform the actual lookup.

While both DI and lookup using the EJB context are relatively convenient, the problem is that they are only available inside the Java EE container (or an application client container). For POJOs outside a container, you are limited to the most basic method of looking up JNDI references—using a JNDI initial context. The code to do this is a little mechanical, but it isn't too complex:

```
Context context = new InitialContext();
BidderAccountCreator accountCreator
    = (BidderAccountCreator)
        context.lookup("java:comp/env/ejb/BidderAccountCreator");
...
accountCreator.addLoginInfo(loginInfo);
...
accountCreator.createAccount();
```

The `InitialContext` object can be created by any code that has access to the JNDI API. Also, the object can be used to connect to a remote JNDI server, not just a local one.

Although this code probably looks harmless enough, you should avoid it if at all possible. Mechanical JNDI lookup code was one of the major pieces of avoidable complexity in EJB 2, particularly when these same bits of code are repeated hundreds of times across an application.

In the next section, we cover one of the most exciting new features in EJB 3: interceptors.

5.3 AOP in the EJB world: interceptors

Have you ever been in a situation in which your requirements changed toward the end of the project and you were asked to add some common missing feature, such as logging or auditing, for EJBs in your application? Adding logging code in each of your EJB classes would be time consuming, and this common type of code also causes maintainability issues and requires you to modify a number of Java classes. Well, EJB 3 interceptors solve this problem. In our example you simply create a logging interceptor that does the logging, and you can make it the default interceptor for your application. The logging interceptor will be executed when any bean method is executed. If the requirement for logging changes, then you have to change only one class. In this section, you'll learn how interceptors work.

5.3.1 What is AOP?

It is very likely you have come across the term *aspect-oriented programming (AOP)*. The essential idea behind AOP is that for most applications, common application code repeated across modules not necessarily for solving the core business problem are considered as infrastructure concerns.

The most commonly cited example of this is logging, especially at the basic debugging level. To use our ActionBazaar example, let's assume that we log the entry into every method in the system. Without AOP, this would mean adding logging statements at the beginning of every single method in the system to log the action of "entering method XX"! Some other common examples where AOP applies are auditing, profiling, and statistics.

The common term used to describe these cases is *crosscutting concerns*—concerns that cut across application logic. An AOP system allows the separation of crosscutting concerns into their own modules. These modules are then applied across the relevant cross section of application code, such as the beginning of every method call. Tools like AspectJ have made AOP relatively popular. For great coverage of AOP, read *AspectJ in Action* by Ramnivas Laddad (Manning, 2003).

EJB 3 supports AOP-like functionality by providing the ability to intercept business methods and lifecycle callbacks. Now buckle up and get ready to jump into the world of EJB 3 interceptors, where you'll learn what interceptors are and how to build business method and lifecycle callback interceptors.

5.3.2 *What are interceptors?*

Essentially the EJB rendition of AOP, *interceptors* are objects that are automatically triggered when an EJB method is invoked (interceptors are *not* new concepts and date back to technologies like CORBA). While EJB 3 interceptors provide sufficient functionality to handle most common crosscutting concerns (such as in our logging example), they do not try to provide the level of functionality that a full-scale AOP package such as AspectJ offers. On the flip side, EJB 3 interceptors are also generally a lot easier to use.

Recall our discussion in section 5.1 on how the EJB object provides services such as transactions and security. In essence, the EJB object is essentially a sophisticated built-in interceptor that makes available a whole host of functionality. If you wanted to, you could create your own EJB-esque services using interceptors.

In the pure AOP world, interception takes place at various points (called *point cuts*) including at the beginning of a method, at the end of a method, and when an exception is triggered. If you are familiar with AOP, an EJB interceptor is the most general form of interception—it is an *around invoke advice*. EJB 3 interceptors are triggered at the beginning of a method and are around when the method returns; they can inspect the method return value or any exceptions thrown by the method. Interceptors can be applied to both session and message-driven beans.

Let's examine business method interceptors further by implementing basic logging on the `PlaceBid` session bean from chapter 2. Once you understand how this works, applying it to an MDB should be a snap. Figure 5.3 shows a

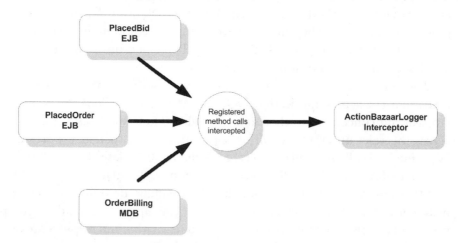

Figure 5.3 Business interceptors are typically used to implement common code. The Action-BazaarLogger implements common logging code used by all EJBs in the ActionBazaar system.

business method interceptor that implements common logging code in the ActionBazaar application.

Listing 5.2 contains the code for our interceptors. The interceptor attached to the addBid method will print a log message to the console each time the method is invoked. In a real-world application, this could be used as debugging information (and perhaps printed out using java.util.logging or Log4J).

Listing 5.2 EJB business method interceptors

```
@Stateless
public class PlaceBidBean implements PlaceBid {
    ...
    @Interceptors(ActionBazaarLogger.class)     ◁─❶ Attaching interceptor
    public void addBid(Bid bid) {
        ...
    }
}

public class ActionBazaarLogger {
    @AroundInvoke                    ◁─❷ Specifying interceptor method
    public Object logMethodEntry(
        InvocationContext invocationContext)
            throws Exception {
        System.out.println("Entering method: "
            + invocationContext.getMethod().getName());
        return invocationContext.proceed();
    }
}
```

Let's take a bird's-eye view of this code before analyzing each feature in detail in the coming sections. The interceptor class, ActionBazaarLogger, is attached to the addBid method of the PlaceBid stateless session bean using the @javax. interceptor.Interceptors annotation ❶. The ActionBazaarLogger object's log-MethodEntry method is annotated with @javax.interceptor.AroundInvoke and will be invoked when the addBid method is called ❷. The logMethodEntry method prints a log message to the system console, including the method name entered using the javax.interceptor.InvocationContext. Finally, the invocation context's proceed method is invoked to signal to the container that the addBid invocation can proceed normally.

We will now start a detailed analysis of the code, starting with attaching the interceptor using the @Interceptors annotation.

5.3.3 *Specifying interceptors*

The @Interceptors annotation allows you to specify one or more interceptor classes for a method or class. In listing 5.2 we attach a single interceptor to the addBid method:

```
@Interceptors(ActionBazaarLogger.class)
public void addBid (...
```

You can also apply the @Interceptors annotation to an entire class. When you do, the interceptor is triggered if any of the target class's methods are invoked. For example, if the ActionBazaarLogger is applied at the class level as in the following code, our logMethodEntry method will be invoked when the PlaceBid class's addBid or addTimeDelayedBid method is called by the client (imagine that the addTimeDelayedBid method adds a bid after a specified interval of time):

```
@Interceptors(ActionBazaarLogger.class)
@Stateless
public class PlaceBidBean implements PlaceBid {
    public void addBid (...
    public void addTimeDelayedBid (...
}
```

As we explained, the @Interceptors annotation is fully capable of attaching more than one interceptor either at a class or method level. All you have to do is provide a comma-separated list as a parameter to the annotation. For example, a generic logger and a bidding statistics tracker could be added to the PlaceBid session bean as follows:

```
@Interceptors({ActionBazaarLogger.class, BidStatisticsTracker.class})
public class PlaceBidBean { ... }
```

Besides specifying method- and class-level interceptors, you can create what is called a *default interceptor*. A default interceptor is essentially a catchall mechanism that attaches to all the methods of every bean in the EJB module. Unfortunately, you cannot specify these kinds of interceptors by using annotations and must use deployment descriptor settings instead. We won't discuss deployment descriptors in any great detail at this point, but we'll show you how setting the ActionBazaarLogger class as a default interceptor for the ActionBazaar application might look:

```
<assembly-descriptor>
    <interceptor-binding>
        <ejb-name>*</ejb-name>
        <interceptor-class>
            actionbazaar.buslogic.ActionBazaarLogger
```

```
          </interceptor-class>
        </interceptor-binding>
    </assembly-descriptor>
```

An interesting question that might have already crossed your mind is what would happen if you specified default, class-, and method-level interceptors for a specific target method (yes, this is perfectly legal). In which order do you think the interceptors would be triggered?

Somewhat counterintuitive to how Java scoping typically works, the interceptors are called from the larger scope to the smaller scope. That is, the default interceptor is triggered first, then the class-level interceptor, and finally the method-level interceptor. Figure 5.4 shows this behavior.

If more than one interceptor is applied at any given level, they are executed in the order in which they are specified. In our `ActionBazaar-Logger` and `BidStatisticsTracker` example, the `ActionBazaarLogger` is executed first since it appears first in the comma-separated list in the `@Interceptors` annotation:

```
@Interceptors({ActionBazaarLogger.class,
    BidStatisticsTracker.class})
```

Unfortunately, the only way to alter this execution order is to use the `interceptor-order` element in the deployment descriptor; there are no annotations for changing interceptor order. However, you can disable interceptors at the

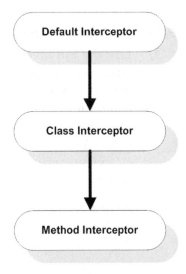

Figure 5.4   The order in which business method interceptors are invoked. Default interceptors apply to all methods of all EJBs in an ejb-jar package. Class-level interceptors apply to all methods of a specific class. Method-level interceptors apply to one specific method in a class. Default application-level interceptors are invoked first, then class-level interceptors, then method-level interceptors.

default or class levels if you need to. Applying the `@javax.interceptor.Exclude-DefaultInterceptors` annotation on either a class or a method disables all default interceptors on the class or method. Similarly the `@javax.interceptor.Exclude-ClassInterceptors` annotation disables class-level interceptors for a method. For example, both default and class-level interceptors may be disabled for the `addBid` method using the following code:

```
@Interceptors(ActionBazaarLogger.class)
@ExcludeDefaultInterceptors
```

```
@ExcludeClassInterceptors
public void addBid (...
```

Next we'll take a detailed look at the interceptor classes themselves.

5.3.4 *Implementing business interceptors*

Like the EJB lifecycle callback methods that we discussed in chapters 3 and 4, business interceptors can be implemented either in the bean class itself or in separate classes. However, we recommend that you create interceptor methods external to the bean class, because that approach allows you to separate crosscutting concerns from business logic and you can share the methods among multiple beans. After all, isn't that the whole point of AOP?

As you can see in listing 5.2, following the general EJB 3 philosophy, an interceptor class is simply a POJO that may have a few annotations.

Around invoke methods

It's important to realize that an interceptor must always have only one method that is designated as the *around invoke* (AroundInvoke) *method*. Around invoke methods must not be business methods, which means that they should not be public methods in the bean's business interface(s).

An around invoke method is automatically triggered by the container when a client invokes a method that has designated it to be its interceptor. In listing 5.2, the triggered method is marked with the @AroundInvoke annotation:

```
@AroundInvoke
public Object logMethodEntry(
    InvocationContext invocationContext)
        throws Exception {
    System.out.println("Entering method: "
            + invocationContext.getMethod().getName());
    return invocationContext.proceed();
}
```

In effect, this means that the logMethodEntry method will be executed whenever the ActionBazaarLogger interceptor is triggered. As you might gather from this code, any method designated AroundInvoke must follow this pattern:

```
Object <METHOD>(InvocationContext) throws Exception
```

The InvocationContext interface passed in as the single parameter to the method provides a number of features that makes the AOP mechanism extremely flexible. The logMethodEntry method uses just two of the methods included in the interface. The getMethod().getName() call returns the name of the method being intercepted—addBid in our case.

The call to the `proceed` method is extremely critical to the functioning of the interceptor. In our case, we always return the object returned by `Invocation-Context.proceed` in the `logMethodEntry` method. This tells the container that it should proceed to the next interceptor in the execution chain or call the intercepted business method. On the other hand, not calling the `proceed` method will bring processing to a halt and avoid the business method (and any other interceptor down the execution chain) from being called.

This feature can be extremely useful for procedures like security validation. For example, the following interceptor method prevents the intercepted business method from being executed if security validation fails:

```
@AroundInvoke
public Object validateSecurity(InvocationContext invocationContext)
    throws Exception {
    if (!validate(...)) {
        throw new SecurityException("Security cannot be validated. " +
            "The method invocation is being blocked.");
    }

    return invocationContext.proceed();
}
```

The InvocationContext interface

The `InvocationContext` interface has a number of other useful methods. Here is the definition of the interface:

```
public interface InvocationContext {
    public Object getTarget();
    public Method getMethod();
    public Object[] getParameters();
    public void setParameters(Object[]);
    public java.util.Map<String,Object> getContextData();
    public Object proceed() throws Exception;
}
```

The `getTarget` method retrieves the bean instance that the intercepted method belongs to. This method is particularly valuable for checking the current state of the bean through its instance variables or accessor methods.

The `getMethod` method returns the method of the bean class for which the interceptor was invoked. For `AroundInvoke` methods, this is the business method on the bean class; for lifecycle callback interceptor methods, `getMethod` returns null.

The `getParameters` method returns the parameters passed to the intercepted method as an array of objects. The `setParameters` method, on the other hand, allows us to change these values at runtime before they are passed to the method.

These two methods are helpful for interceptors that manipulate bean parameters to change behavior at runtime.

An interceptor in ActionBazaar that transparently rounds off all monetary values to two decimal places for all methods across the application could use the getParameters and setParameters methods to accomplish its task.

The key to understanding the need for the InvocationContext.getContext-Data method is the fact that contexts are shared across the interceptor chain for a given method. As a result, data attached to an InvocationContext can be used to communicate between interceptors. For example, assume that our security validation interceptor stores the member status into invocation context data after the user is validated:

```
invocationContext.getContextData().put("MemberStatus", "Gold");
```

As you can see, the invocation context data is simply a Map used to store name-value pairs. Another interceptor in the invocation chain can now retrieve this data and take specific actions based on the member status. For example, a discount calculator interceptor can reduce the ActionBazaar item listing charges for a Gold member. The code to retrieve the member status would look like this:

```
String memberStatus =
    (String) invocationContext.getContextData().get("MemberStatus");
```

The following is the AroundInvoke method of the DiscountVerifierInterceptor that actually uses the invocation context as well as most of the methods we discussed earlier:

```
@AroundInvoke
public Object giveDiscount(InvocationContext context)
    throws Exception {
    System.out.println("*** DiscountVerifier Interceptor"
        + " invoked for " + context.getMethod().getName() + " ***");

    if (context.getMethod().getName().equals("chargePostingFee")
        && (((String)(context.getContextData().get("MemberStatus")))
        .equals("Gold"))) {
        Object[] parameters = context.getParameters();
        parameters[2] = new Double ((Double) parameters[2] * 0.99);
        System.out.println (
            "*** DiscountVerifier Reducing Price by 1 percent ***");
        context.setParameters(parameters);
    }

    return context.proceed();
}
```

You can throw or handle a runtime or checked exception in a business method interceptor. If a business method interceptor throws an exception before invoking the `proceed` method, the processing of other interceptors in the invocation chain and the target business method will be terminated.

Recall our discussion on lifecycle callback methods in chapters 3 and 4. This isn't readily obvious, but lifecycle callbacks are a form of interception as well. While method interceptors are triggered when a business method is invoked, lifecycle callbacks are triggered when a bean transitions from one lifecycle state to another. Although this was not the case in our previous lifecycle examples, in some cases such methods can be used for crosscutting concerns (e.g., logging and profiling) that can be shared across beans. For this reason, you can define lifecycle callbacks in interceptor classes in addition to business method interceptors. Let's take a look at how to do this next.

5.3.5 *Lifecycle callback methods in the interceptor class*

Recall that the `@PostConstruct`, `@PrePassivate`, `@PostActivate`, and `@PreDestroy` annotations can be applied to bean methods to receive lifecycle callbacks. When applied to interceptor class methods, lifecycle callbacks work in exactly the same way. Lifecycle callbacks defined in an interceptor class are known as *lifecycle callback interceptors* or *lifecycle callback listeners*. When the target bean transitions lifecycles, annotated methods in the interceptor class are triggered.

The following interceptor class logs when ActionBazaar beans allocate and release resources when beans instances are constructed and destroyed:

```
public class ActionBazaarResourceLogger {
    @PostConstruct
    public void initialize (InvocationContext context) {
        System.out.println ("Allocating resources for bean: "
            + context.getTarget());
        context.proceed();
    }

    @PreDestroy
    public void cleanup (InvocationContext context) {
        System.out.println ("Releasing resources for bean: "
            + context.getTarget());
        context.proceed();
    }
}
```

As the code sample shows, lifecycle interceptor methods cannot throw checked exceptions (it doesn't make sense since there is no client for lifecycle callbacks to bubble a problem up to).

Note that a bean can have the same lifecycle callbacks both in the bean itself as well as in one or more interceptors. That is the whole point of calling the `InvocationContext.proceed` method in lifecycle interceptor methods as in the resource logger code. This ensures that the next lifecycle interceptor method in the invocation chain or the bean lifecycle method is triggered. There is absolutely no difference between applying an interceptor class with or without lifecycle callbacks. The resource logger, for example, is applied as follows:

```
@Interceptors({ActionBazaarResourceLogger.class})
public class PlaceBidBean { ... }
```

You might find that you will use lifecycle callbacks as bean methods to manage resources a lot more often than you use interceptor lifecycle callbacks to encapsulate crosscutting concerns such as logging, auditing, and profiling. However, interceptor callbacks are extremely useful when you need them.

As a recap, table 5.3 contains a summary of both business method interceptors and lifecycle callbacks.

Table 5.3 Differences between lifecycle and business method interceptors. Lifecycle interceptors are created to handle EJB lifecycle callbacks. Business method interceptors are associated with business methods, and are automatically invoked when a user invokes the business method.

Supported Feature	Lifecycle Callback Methods	Business Method Interceptor
Invocation	Gets invoked when a certain lifecycle event occurs.	Gets invoked when a business method is called by a client.
Location	In a separate Interceptor class or in the bean class.	In the class or an interceptor class.
Method signature	`void <METHOD>(InvocationContext)`–in a separate interceptor class. `void <METHOD>()`–in the bean class.	`Object <METHOD>(InvocationContext)` throws `Exception`
Annotation	`@PreDestroy, @PostConstruct, @PrePassivate, @PostActivate`	`@AroundInvoke`
Exception handling	May throw runtime exceptions but must not throw checked exceptions. May catch and swallow exceptions. No other lifecycle callback methods are called if an exception is thrown.	May throw application or runtime exception. May catch and swallow runtime exceptions. No other business interceptor methods or the business method itself are called if an exception is thrown before calling the `proceed` method.

continued on next page

Table 5.3   Differences between lifecycle and business method interceptors. Lifecycle interceptors are created to handle EJB lifecycle callbacks. Business method interceptors are associated with business methods, and are automatically invoked when a user invokes the business method. *(continued)*

Supported Feature	Lifecycle Callback Methods	Business Method Interceptor
Transaction and security context	No security and transaction context. Transaction and security are discussed in chapter 6.	Share the same security and transaction context within which the original business method was invoked.

This is all we want to say about interceptors right now. Clearly, interceptors are an extremely important addition to EJB. It is likely that the AOP features in future releases of EJB will grow more and more robust. Interceptors certainly have the potential to evolve into a robust way of extending the EJB platform itself, with vendors offering new out-of-the-box interceptor-based services.

Let's move on to the final vital EJB 3 feature we'll cover in this chapter: the timer service. Timers can be used only by stateless session beans and MDBs.

5.4   *Scheduling: the EJB 3 timer service*

Scheduled tasks are a reality for most nontrivial applications. For example, your business application may have to run a daily report to determine inventory levels and automatically send out restocking requests. For most legacy applications, it is typical to have a batch job to clean up temporary tables at the start or end of each day. If fact, it is fair to say schedulers are an essential holdover from the mainframe days of batch computing. As a result, scheduling tools, utilities, and frameworks have been a development mainstay for a long time. The Unix cron utility is probably the most popular and well-loved scheduling utility. The System Task Scheduler, generally lesser known, is the Microsoft Windows counterpart of cron.

In the Java EE world, you have a few options for scheduling tasks and activities. Most Java EE application servers come with a scheduling utility that is sufficiently useful. There are also a number of feature-rich, full-scale scheduling packages available for enterprise applications. Flux is an excellent commercial scheduling package, while Quartz is a good-quality open source implementation. EJB timer services are the standard Java EE answer to scheduling. As you'll soon learn, while it does not try to compete with full-scale scheduling products, the EJB 3 timer service is probably sufficient for most day-to-day application development requirements. Because it is so lightweight, the service is also extremely easy to use.

In the next few sections, we'll build a scheduling service using EJB 3 timers and show you how to use the @Timeout annotation.

5.4.1 *What are timers?*

In a sense, the EJB 3 timer service is based on the idea of time-delayed callbacks. In other words, the service allows you to specify a method (appropriately called the *timeout method*) that is automatically invoked after a specified interval of time. The container invokes the timeout method on your behalf when the time interval you specify elapses. As you'll see, you can use the timer service to register for callbacks triggered once at a specific time or at regular intervals.

We can only use timers in stateless session beans and MDBs because of their asynchronous, stateless nature. However, unlike stateless session beans and MDBs, timers are persistent and can survive a container crash or restart. Timers are also *transactional*, that is, a transaction failure in a timeout method rolls back the actions taken by the timer. Figure 5.5 illustrates how timers work.

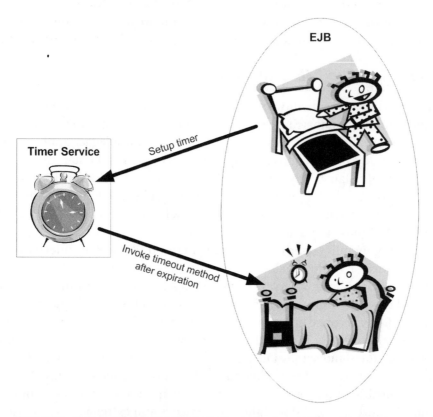

Figure 5.5   How an EJB timer works. A client may invoke an EJB method which creates a timer that registers a callback in the EJB timer service. The EJB container invokes the timeout method in the bean instance when the timer expires.

As the figure demonstrates, an EJB method can register a time-driven callback with the container timer service. When the time interval specified by the EJB expires, the timer service invokes the timeout method pointed to by the EJB. We'll show you how this works with a simple example next.

5.4.2 *Using the timer service*

Let's explore the features of the EJB 3 timer service by adding a timer to the PlaceBid EJB we introduced in chapter 2. We'll add a timer in the addBid method to check the status of the newly placed bid every 15 minutes. Although we won't code it, another compelling use case is to create a timer when an item is added for bidding. Such a timer could be triggered when the auction time expired and would determine the winning bidder. We'll leave the implementation of this timer as an exercise for you.

Among other things, the timer we'll implement will notify the bidder via e-mail if they have been outbid. We have omitted most of the code that is not absolutely necessary to explain timer functionality in listing 5.3. The complete code is included in the downloadable code samples if you are interested in exploring further.

Listing 5.3 Using the EJB 3 timer service

```
public class PlaceBidBean implements PlaceBid {
    ...
    @Resource TimerService timerService;      ←❶ Timer service injected
    ...
    public void addBid(Bid bid) {
        ... Code to add the bid ...
        timerService.createTimer(15*60*1000, 15*60*1000, bid);   ←┐
        ...                                               Timer created ❷
    }
    ...                    ❸  Timeout method
    @Timeout   ←┘
    public void monitorBid(Timer timer) {
        Bid bid = (Bid) timer.getInfo();
        ... Code to monitor the bid ...
    }
}
```

We use EJB 3 resource injection to gain access to the timer service ❶. In the addBid method, after we add the bid we schedule a timer service callback to occur every 15 minutes ❷. The newly added Bid is attached as timer information when the timer is registered. At regular intervals, the monitorBid method is called by the timer service, which is designated with the `@Timeout` annotation ❸. The `monitorBid` method retrieves the `Bid` instance attached as timer information and monitors the bid.

We'll explore EJB timer services details using listing 5.3 as a jumping-off point in the next few sections, starting with ways to get access to the EJB 3 timer service.

Accessing the timer service

As you just saw in listing 5.3, the EJB timer service can be injected into a Java EE component using the `@Resource` annotation. Alternatively, you can get access to the container timer service through the EJB context:

```
@Resource SessionContext context;
...
TimerService timerService = context.getTimerService();
```

Which method you choose is largely a matter of taste. In general, if you are already injecting an EJB context, you should avoid injecting the timer service as well, in order to avoid redundant code. Instead, you should use the `getTimer-Service` method as in the previous code. However, if you aren't using the EJB context for anything else, it makes perfect sense to simply inject the `TimerService` as we did in listing 5.3.

Next let's take a closer look at the injected timer service.

Using the TimerService interface

In listing 5.3, we use the `TimerService` interface to register a `Timer`. As you'll soon see, a `Timer` is simply a Java EE representation of a scheduled task. The `createTimer` method used in listing 5.3 is one of four overloaded methods provided in the `TimerService` interface to add `Timer`s. The one we used specified that the `Timer` should initially trigger in 15*60*1000 milliseconds (15 minutes), repeat every 15*60*1000 milliseconds (15 minutes), and added a `Bid` instance as `Timer` information:

```
timerService.createTimer(15*60*1000, 15*60*1000, bid);
```

Let's take a look at the complete definition of the `TimerService` interface to get a clearer picture of the range of options available (listing 5.4).

> **Listing 5.4 Specification for the TimerService interface is used to create either single-event or recurring timers**

```
public interface javax.ejb.TimerService {
    public Timer createTimer(long duration,
        java.io.Serializable info);
```

```
        public Timer createTimer(long initialDuration,
            long intervalDuration, java.io.Serializable info);
        public Timer createTimer(java.util.Date expiration,
            java.io.Serializable info);
        public Timer createTimer(java.util.Date initialExpiration,
            long intervalDuration, java.io.Serializable info);
        public Collection getTimers();
}
```

The first version of the createTimer method ❶ allows us to create a single-event timer that is fired only once and not repeated. The first parameter, duration, specifies the time in milliseconds, after which the timeout method should be invoked. The second parameter, info, allows us to attach an arbitrary piece of information to the timer. Note that timer info objects must always be Serializable, as is the Bid object we used in listing 5.3. Note also that the info parameter can be left null if it is not really needed.

You've already seen the second version of the createTimer method ❷ in action in listing 5.3. It allows us to create recurring timers with initial timeout and interval durations set in milliseconds. The third version ❸ is similar to the first in that it allows us to create a timer that fires once and only once. However, this version allows us to specify the expiration value as a specific instant in time represented by a java.util.Date instead of a long time offset. The fourth ❹ and second versions of the createTimer method differ from each other in the same way. Using a concrete date instead of an offset from the current time generally makes sense for events that should be fired at a later time. However, this is largely a matter of taste. All of these methods return a generated Timer reference. In general, this returned value is not used very often. Behind the scenes, all of the TimerService methods associate the current EJB as the callback receiver for the generated Timers. The final method of the TimerService interface, getTimers ❺, retrieves all of the active Timers associated with the current EJB. This method is rarely used, and we won't discuss it further.

Having looked at the TimerService interface and how to create timers, let's now take a closer look at how to implement timeout methods.

Implementing timeout methods

In listing 5.3, we mark monitorBid to be the timeout method using the @Timeout annotation:

```
@Timeout
public void monitorBid(Timer timer) {
```

When the timer or timers created for the PlaceBid EJB expire, the container invokes the designated timeout method—monitorBid. Using the @Timeout annotation is by far the simplest, but not the only way to specify timeout methods. As you might have guessed, methods marked with the @Timeout annotation are expected to follow this convention:

```
void <METHOD>(Timer timer)
```

A bean can have at most one timeout method, which can be specified (through annotation @Timeout or deployment descriptor timeout-method) either on the bean class or on a superclass. If the bean class implements the javax.ejb.Timed-Object interface, the ejbTimeout method is the bean's timeout method.

The Timer for which the callback was invoked is passed in as a parameter for the method as processing context. This is because multiple Timers, especially in the case of repeating intervals, may invoke the same timeout method. Also, as you saw in listing 5.3, it is often necessary to use the TimerService interface to pass around data to the timeout methods as Timer information.

We'll finish our analysis of the EJB 3 timer service code by taking a closer look at the Timer interface next.

Using the Timer interface

As we mentioned, the container passes us back the Timer instance that triggered the timeout method. In the monitorBid method, we use the interface to retrieve the Bid instance stored as timer information through the getInfo method:

```
@Timeout
public void monitorBid(Timer timer) {
    Bid bid = (Bid) timer.getInfo();
    ... Code to monitor the bid ...
}
```

A number of other useful methods are defined in the Timer interface. We'll explore them through the definition of the Timer interface (listing 5.5).

Listing 5.5   The javax.ejb.Timer interface

```
public interface javax.ejb.Timer {
    public void cancel();

    public long getTimeRemaining();

    public java.util.Date getNextTimeout();

    public javax.ejb.TimerHandle getHandle();
```

```
        public java.io.Serializable getInfo();
}
```

The `cancel` method is particularly useful in canceling a timer prior to its expiration. You can use this method to stop timers prematurely. In our bid-monitoring example, we can use this method to stop the chain of recurring callbacks when bidding on the item is over.

It is vital to invoke the `cancel` method for recurring `Timers` when they are no longer needed. Otherwise, the EJB will spin in an infinite loop unnecessarily. This is a subtle, common, and easy mistake to make.

The `getTimeRemaining` method can be used on either a single-use or interval timer. The return value of this method indicates the remaining time for the timer to expire, in milliseconds. You might find that this method is rarely used. The `getNextTimeout` method indicates the next time a recurring `Timer` will time out, as a `java.util.Date` instead of a `long` time offset. Similar to the `getTimeRemaining` method, this method is useful in the rare instance that you might need to determine whether to cancel a `Timer` based on when it will fire next.

The `getHandle` method returns a `Timer` handle. `javax.ejb.TimerHandle` is a serialized object that you can store and then use to obtain information about the `Timer` (by using the `getTimer` method available through `TimerHandle`). This is a relatively obscure method that we'll leave for you to explore on your own if you want to. You have already seen the `getInfo` method in action. This method is extremely useful in writing nontrivial timeout functions and accessing extra processing information attached to the `Timer` by the bean method creating the `Timer`.

Let's now discuss situations where EJB `Timers` are an appropriate fit.

EJB timers and transactions

EJB `Timers` are transactional objects. If the transaction that a timer is triggered under rolls back for some reason (e.g., as a result of a runtime exception in the timeout method), the timer creation is undone. In addition, the timeout method can be executed in a transactional context. You can specify a transactional attribute for the timeout method—`Required` or `RequiresNew`—and the container `will` start a transaction before invoking the timeout method. If the transaction fails, the container will make sure the changes made by the failed method do not take effect and will retry the timeout method.

We'll talk about EJB transactions in much greater detail in the next chapter.

5.4.3 *When to use EJB timers*

Clearly, although EJB timers are relatively feature-rich, they are not intended to go toe-to-toe against full-fledged scheduling solutions like Flux or Quartz. However, under some circumstances they are sufficient if not ideal. Like almost all other technology choices, this decision comes down to weighing features against needs for your specific situation and environment.

Merits of timers

Here are some of the merits of using EJB 3 timers:

- Timers are part of the EJB specification. Hence, applications using EJB timers will remain portable across containers instead of being locked into the nonstandard APIs of job schedulers like Quartz.

- Since the EJB timer service comes as a standard part of a Java EE application server, using it incurs no additional cost in terms of time or money. No extra installation or configuration is required as would be the case for an external job scheduler, and you won't need to worry about integration and support.

- The timer is a container-managed service. No separate thread pools or user threads are required for it, as would be the case with an external scheduler. For the same reasons, the EJB timer service is likely to have better out-of-the-box performance than third-party products.

- Transactions are fully supported with timers (see the sidebar titled "EJB timers and transactions"), unlike external job schedulers, in which you may need to do extra setup for supporting JTA.

- By default, EJB timers are persisted and survive EJB lifecycles and container restarts. The same cannot be said of all third-party schedulers.

Limitations for timers

The following are the primary limitations of EJB timers:

- EJB timers are meant for long-running business processes and not real-time applications where precision timing is absolutely critical. Commercial schedulers may provide much better guarantees in terms of precision than the EJB 3 timer service.

- EJB timers lack support for extremely flexible cron-type timers, blackout dates, workflow modeling for jobs, and so on. These advanced features are commonly available with external job schedulers.

- There is no robust GUI admin tool to create, manage, and monitor EJB 3 timers. Such tools are generally available for third-party job schedulers.

This concludes our analysis of EJB 3 timers and marks the end of this chapter. In general, you should attempt to use EJB 3 timers first. Resort to third-party schedulers only if you run into serious limitations that cannot be easily overcome.

Although robust schedulers are a compelling idea, in general they are complex and should not be used frivolously. However, there are many complex, scheduling-intensive applications where robust schedulers are a must, especially in industries like banking and finance.

5.5 *Summary*

In this chapter, we covered a few advanced concepts common to all EJB types:

- The EJB object acts as a proxy between clients and container where you can use `EJBContext` to access container runtime information and services.
- Interceptors are lightweight AOP features in EJB 3 for dealing with cross-cutting concerns such as logging and auditing. You can use interceptors at the EJB module level, class level, or method level.
- EJB timers provide a lightweight scheduling service that you can use in your applications.

You'll find these advanced features useful in moderate-sized, real-life applications.

The only two features common to session and MDBs that we did not cover in this chapter are transaction and security management. You'll learn more about these features in the next chapter.

6

Transactions and security

Transaction and security management are important aspects of any serious enterprise development effort. By the same token, both are system-level concerns rather than true business application development concerns, which is why they often become an afterthought. In the worst-case scenario, these critical aspects of application development are overlooked altogether. Given these facts, you'll be glad to know that EJB 3 provides functionality in both realms that is robust enough for the most demanding environments, and yet simple enough for those who prefer to focus on developing business logic. Although we have briefly mentioned these features in previous chapters, we haven't dealt with them in any detail until this chapter.

The first part of this chapter is devoted to exploring the rich transaction management features of EJB 3. We'll briefly discuss transactions and explore container-managed and bean-managed transactions support in EJB. The remainder of the chapter deals with EJB security features, and you'll learn about declarative and programmatic security support.

6.1 *Understanding transactions*

We engage in transactions almost every day—when withdrawing money from an ATM or paying a phone bill, for example. Transactions in computing are a closely related concept but differ slightly and are a little harder to define. In the most basic terms, a *transaction* is a grouping of tasks that must be processed as an inseparable unit. This means every task that is part of the transaction must succeed in order for the transaction to succeed. If any of the tasks fail, the transaction fails as well. You can think of a transaction as a three-legged wooden stool. All three legs must hold for the stool to stand. If any of them break, the stool collapses. In addition to this *all-or-nothing* value proposition, transactions must guarantee a degree of reliability and robustness. We will come back to what this last statement means when we describe what are called the ACID (atomicity, consistency, isolation, and durability) properties of transactions. A successful transaction is *committed*, meaning its results are made permanent, whereas a failed transaction is *rolled back*, as if it never happened.

To explore transaction concepts further, let's take a look at a sample problem in the ActionBazaar application. Before exploring transaction support in EJB, we'll briefly discuss ACID properties, transaction management concepts such as resource and transaction managers, and two-phase commits.

6.1.1 *A transactional solution in ActionBazaar*

Some items on ActionBazaar have a "Snag-It" ordering option. This option allows a user to purchase an item on bid at a set price before anyone else bids on it. As soon as the first bid is placed on an item, the Snag-It option disappears. This feature has become popular because neither the buyer nor the seller needs to wait for bidding to finish as long as they both like the initial Snag-It price tag. As soon as the user clicks the Snag-It button, the ActionBazaar application makes sure no bids have been placed on the item, validates the buyer's credit card, charges the buyer, and removes the item from bidding. Imagine what would happen if one of these four actions failed due to a system error, but the rest of the actions were allowed to succeed. For example, assume that we validate and charge the customer's credit card successfully. However, the order itself fails because the operation to remove the item from bid fails due to a sudden network outage and the user receives an error message. Since the credit card charge was already finalized, the customer is billed for a failed order! To make matters worse, the item remains available for bidding. Another user can put a bid on the item before anyone can fix the problem, creating an interesting situation for the poor customer support folks to sort out. We can see this situation in figure 6.1.

While creating ad hoc application logic to automatically credit the customer back in case of an error is a Band-Aid for the problem, transactions are ideally suited to handle such situations. A transaction covering all of the ordering steps ensures that no actual ordering operation changes are finalized until the entire operation finishes successfully. If any errors occur, all pending data changes, including the credit card charge, are aborted. On the other hand, if all the operations succeed the transaction is marked successful and all ordering changes are made permanent.

Although this all-or-nothing value proposition is a central theme of transactional systems, it is not the only attribute. A number of properties apply to transactional systems; we'll discuss them next.

6.1.2 *ACID properties*

The curious acronym ACID stands for *atomicity, consistency, isolation, and durability*. All transactional systems are said to exhibit these four characteristics. Let's take a look at each of these characteristics.

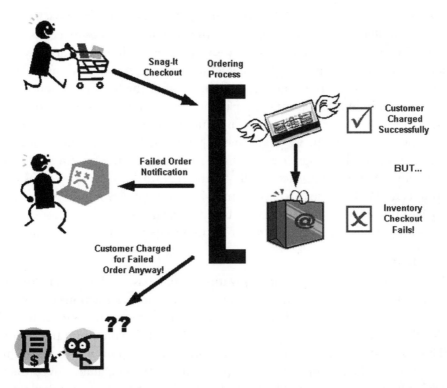

Figure 6.1 Because the ordering process is not covered by a transaction, ActionBazaar reaches a strange state when a Snag-It order fails halfway through. The customer is essentially billed for a failed order.

Atomicity

As we've seen in our ActionBazaar scenario, transactions are atomic in nature; they either commit or roll back together. In coding terms, you band together an arbitrary body of code under the umbrella of a transaction. If something unexpected and irrecoverable happens during the execution of the code, the result of the attempted execution is completely undone so that it has no effect on the system. Otherwise, the results of a successful execution are allowed to become permanent.

Consistency

This is the trickiest of the four properties because it involves more than writing code. This is the most common way of describing the consistency property: if the system is in a state consistent with the business rules before a transaction begins, it must remain in a consistent state after the transaction is rolled back or committed. A corollary to this statement is that the system *need not be* in a consistent state *during* the transaction. Think of a transaction as a sandbox or sanctuary—you are temporarily protected from the rules while inside it. As long as you make sure all the business rules in the system remain intact after the last line of code in a transaction is executed, it doesn't matter if you are in an inconsistent state at an arbitrary point in the transaction. Using our example, it is fine if we charge the customer even though we really haven't removed the item from bidding yet, because the results of our code will have no impact on the system *until* and *unless* our transaction finishes successfully. In the real world, setting up rules and constraints in the database (such as primary keys, foreign key relationships, and field constraints) ensures consistency so that transactions encountering error conditions are rejected and the system is returned to its pretransactional state.

Isolation

If you understand thread synchronization or database locking, you already know what isolation is. The isolation property makes sure transactions do not step on one another's toes. Essentially, the transaction manager (a concept we'll define shortly) ensures that nobody touches your data while you are in the transaction. This concept is especially important in concurrent systems where any number of processes can be attempting to manipulate the same data at any given time. Usually isolation is guaranteed by using low-level database locks hidden away from the developer. The transaction manager places some kind of lock on the data accessed by a transaction so that no other processes can modify them until the transaction is finished.

In terms of our example, the transaction isolation property is what guarantees that no bids can be placed on the item while we are in the middle of executing the Snag-It ordering steps since our "snagged" item record would be locked in the database.

Durability

The last of the four ACID properties is durability. Transaction durability means that a transaction, once committed, is guaranteed to become permanent. This is usually implemented by using transaction logs in the database server. (The application server can also maintain a transaction log. However, we'll ignore this fact for the time being.) Essentially, the database keeps a running record of all data changes made by a transaction before it commits. This means that even if a sudden server error occurs during a commit, once the database recovers from the

---

Isolation levels

The concept of isolation as it pertains to databases is not as cut and dried as we just suggested. As you might imagine, making transactions wait for one another's data locks limits the number of concurrent transactions that can run on a system. However, different isolation strategies allow for a balance between concurrency and locking, primarily by sacrificing lock acquisition strictness. Each isolation strategy corresponds to an *isolation level*. Here are the four most common isolation levels, from the highest level of concurrency to the lowest:

- *Read uncommitted*—At this isolation level, your transaction can read the uncommitted data of other transactions, also known as a "dirty" read. You should *not* use this level in a multithreaded environment.

- *Read committed*—Your transaction will never read uncommitted changes from another transaction. This is the default level for most databases.

- *Repeatable read*—The transaction is guaranteed to get the same data on multiple reads of the same rows until the transaction ends.

- *Serializable*—This is the highest isolation level and guarantees that none of the tables you touch will change during the transaction, including adding new rows. This isolation level is *very* likely to cause performance bottlenecks.

A good rule of thumb is to use the highest isolation level that yields an acceptable performance level. Generally, you do not directly control isolation levels from EJBs—the isolation level is set at the database resource level instead.

---

error changes can be reverted to be properly reapplied (think of untangling a cassette tape and rewinding it to where the tape started tangling). Changes made during the transaction are applied again by executing the appropriate entries from the transaction log (replaying the rewound tape to finish). This property is the muscle behind transactions ensuring that *commit* really does mean commit.

In the next section, we'll examine the internals of transaction management and define such concepts as distributed transactions, transaction managers, and resource managers.

6.1.3 *Transaction management internals*

As you have probably already guessed, application servers and enterprise resources like the database management system do most of the heavy lifting in transaction management. Ultimately, everything that you do in code translates into low-level database operations such as locking and unlocking rows or tables in a database, beginning a transaction log, committing a transaction by applying log entries, or rolling back a transaction by abandoning the transaction log. In enterprise transaction management, the component that takes care of transactions for *a particular resource* is called a *resource manager*. Remember that a *resource* need not just be a database like Oracle. It could be a message server like IBM MQSeries or an enterprise information system (EIS) like PeopleSoft CRM.

Most enterprise applications involve only a single resource. A transaction that uses a single resource is called a *local transaction*. However, many enterprise applications use more than one resource. If you look carefully at our Snag-It order example, you'll see that it most definitely involves more than one database: the credit card provider's database used to charge the customer, as well as the Action-Bazaar database to manage bids, items, and ordering. It is fairly apparent that for sane business application development some kind of abstraction is needed to manage multiple resources in a single transaction. This is exactly what the *transaction manager* is—a component that, under the hood, coordinates a transaction over multiple distributed resources.

From an application's view, the transaction manager is the application server or some other external component that provides simplified transaction services. As figure 6.2 shows, the application program (ActionBazaar) asks the *transaction*

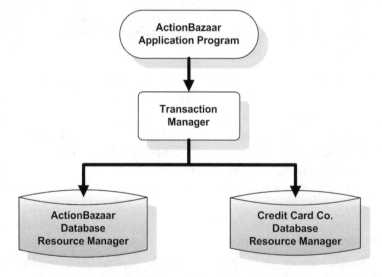

Figure 6.2 Distributed transaction management. The application program delegates transaction operations to the transaction manager, which coordinates between resource managers.

manager to start, commit, and roll back transactions. The transaction manager coordinates these requests among multiple resource managers, and each transaction phase may translate to numerous low-level resource commands issued by the *resource managers*.

Next, we'll discuss how transactions are managed across multiple resources. In EJB, this is done with two-phase commits.

6.1.4 Two-phase commit

How transactions are managed in a distributed environment involving more than one resource is extremely interesting. The protocol commonly used to achieve this is called the *two-phase commit*.

Imagine what would happen if no special precautions were taken while attempting to commit a transaction involving more than one database. Suppose that the first database commits successfully, but the second fails. It would be difficult to go back and "undo" the finalized changes to the first database. To avoid this problem, the two-phase commit protocol performs an additional preparatory step before the final commit. During this step, each resource manager involved is asked if the current transaction can be successfully committed. If any of the resource managers indicate that the transaction cannot be committed if attempted, the entire transaction is abandoned (rolled back). Otherwise, the transaction is allowed to proceed and all resource managers are asked to commit. As table 6.1 shows, only distributed transactions use the two-phase commit protocol.

We have just reviewed how transactions work and what makes them reliable; now let's take a look at how EJB provides these services for the application developer.

Table 6.1 A transaction may be either local or global. A local transaction involves one resource and a global transaction involves multiple resources.

Property	Local	Global Transaction
Number of resources	One	Multiple
Coordinator	Resource Manager	Transaction manager
Commit protocol	Single-Phase	Two-phase

> ### The XA protocol
>
> To coordinate the two-phase commit across many different kinds of resources, the transaction manager and each of the resource managers must "talk the same tongue," or use a common protocol. In the absence of such a protocol, imagine how sophisticated even a reasonably effective transaction manager would have to be. The transaction manager would have to be developed with the proprietary communication protocol of every supported resource.
>
> The most popular distributed transaction protocol used today is the XA protocol, which was developed by the X/Open group. Java EE uses this protocol for implementing distributed transaction services.

6.1.5 Transaction management in EJB

Transaction management support in EJB is provided through the Java Transaction API (JTA). JTA is a small, high-level API exposing functionality at the distributed transaction manager layer, typically provided by the application server. As a matter of fact, for the most part, as an EJB developer you will probably need to know about only one JTA interface: `javax.transaction.UserTransaction`. This is because the container takes care of most transaction management details behind the scenes. As an EJB developer, you simply tell the container where the transaction begins and ends (called *transaction demarcation* or establishing *transaction boundaries*) and whether to roll back or commit.

There are two ways of using transactions in EJB. Both provide abstractions over JTA, one to a lesser and one to a greater degree. The first is to declaratively manage transactions through container-managed transaction (CMT); this can be done through annotations or the deployment descriptor. On the other hand, bean-managed transaction (BMT) requires you to explicitly manage transactions programmatically. It is important to note that in this version of EJB, only session beans and MDBs support BMT and CMT. The EJB 3 Java Persistence API is not directly dependent on either CMT or BMT but can transparently plug into any transactional environment while used inside a Java EE container. We'll cover this functionality when we discuss persistence in upcoming chapters. In this chapter, we'll explore CMT and BMT as they pertain to the two bean types we discussed in chapter 3 (session beans) and chapter 4 (MDBs).

> **JTS vs. JTA**
>
> These like-sounding acronyms are both related to Java EE transaction management. JTA defines application transaction services as well as the interactions among the application server, the transaction manager, and resource managers. Java Transaction Service (JTS) deals with how a transaction manager is implemented. A JTS transaction manager supports JTA as its high-level interface and implements the Java mapping of the OMG Object Transaction Service (OTS) specification as its low-level interface.
>
> As an EJB developer, there really is no need for you to deal with JTS.

Container-managed transactions are by far the simplest and most flexible way of managing EJB transactions. We'll take a look at them first.

6.2 *Container-managed transactions*

In a CMT, the container starts, commits, and rolls back a transaction on our behalf. Transaction boundaries in declarative transactions are always marked by the start and end of EJB business methods. More precisely, the container starts a JTA transaction before a method is invoked, invokes the method, and depending on what happened during the method call, either commits or rolls back the managed transaction. All we have to do is tell the container how to manage the transaction by using either annotations or deployment descriptors and ask it to roll back the transaction when needed. By default, the container assumes that you will be using CMT on all business methods. This section describes CMT in action. We'll build the Snag-It ordering system using CMT and you'll learn how to use the @TransactionManagement and @TransactionAttribute annotations. Also, you'll learn both how to roll back a transaction using methods of EJBContext and when an application exception is raised.

6.2.1 *Snag-It ordering using CMT*

Listing 6.1 implements the Snag-It ordering scenario as the method of a stateless session bean using CMT. This is fine since the user can order only one item at a time using the Snag-It feature and no state information has to be saved between calls to the OrderManagerBean. The bean first checks to see if there are any bids on the item, and if there are none, it validates the customer's credit card, charges the customer, and removes the item from bidding. To keep the code sample as simple as possible, we've omitted all details that are not directly necessary for our explanation of CMT.

Listing 6.1   Implementing Snag-It using CMT

```
@Stateless
@TransactionManagement(TransactionManagementType.CONTAINER)  ◄─┐
public class OrderManagerBean {                            ① Uses CMT
    @Resource                              ② Injects EJB context
    private SessionContext context;
...
    @TransactionAttribute(TransactionAttributeType.REQUIRED)  ◄─┐
    public void placeSnagItOrder(Item item, Customer customer){
        try {                                  Defines Transaction
            if (!bidsExisting(item)){          attribute for method ③
                validateCredit(customer);
                chargeCustomer(customer, item);
                removeItemFromBidding(item);
            }
        } catch (CreditValidationException cve) {
            context.setRollbackOnly();
        } catch (CreditProcessingException cpe){
            context.setRollbackOnly();          ④ Rolls back on
        } catch (DatabaseException de) {           exception
            context.setRollbackOnly();
        }
    }
}
```

First we tell the container that it should manage the transactions for this bean ①. If we do not specify the @TransactionManagement annotation or the transaction-type element in the deployment descriptor, the container assumes that we intend to use a CMT. The EJB context is injected into the bean ②. A transaction is required for the placeSnagItOrder method ③ and one should be started by the container when needed. If an exception stops us from completing the Snag-It order, we ask the container to roll back the transaction using the injected EJB-Context object's setRollbackOnly method ④.

Let's take a closer look at the TransactionManagement annotation ①.

6.2.2   The @TransactionManagement annotation

The @TransactionManagement annotation specifies whether CMT or BMT is to be used for a particular bean. In our case, we specify the value TransactionManagementType.CONTAINER—meaning the container should manage transactions on the bean's behalf. If we wanted to manage transactions programmatically instead, we'd specify `TransactionManagementType.BEAN` for the `TransactionManagement` value. Notably, although we have explicitly included the annotation in our example, if we leave it out the container will assume CMT anyway. When we explore BMT, it will be more obvious why a CMT is the default and most commonly used choice.

Next, we'll look at the second transaction-related annotation in listing 6.1: `@TransactionAttribute`.

6.2.3 *The @TransactionAttribute annotation*

Although the container does most of the heavy lifting in CMT, you still need to tell the container how it should manage transactions. To understand what this means, consider the fact that the transaction which wraps around your bean's method could be started by the container specifically when calling your method, or it could be inherited from a client calling your method (otherwise called *joining* a transaction). Let's explore this idea a little more using our example. The `place-SnagItOrder` method in listing 6.1 calls a number of methods such as `bidsExisting`, `validateCredit`, `chargeCustomer`, and `removeItemFromBidding`. As figure 6.3 shows, these method calls could simply be forwarded to other session bean invocations, such as `BidManagerBean.bidsExist`, `BillingManagerBean.validateCredit`, `BillingManagerBean.chargeCustomer`, and `ItemManagerBean.removeFromBidding`.

We already know that the `placeSnagItOrder` method is managed by a transaction. What if all the session beans we are invoking are also managed by CMT? Should the container reuse the transaction created for our method to invoke the other methods? Should our existing transaction be independent of the other session beans' transactions? What happens if any of the methods cannot support transactions? The `@TransactionAttribute` annotation tells the container how to handle all these situations. The annotation can be applied either to individual CMT bean methods or to the entire bean. If the annotation is applied at the bean

Figure 6.3 The method invocations from the CMT session bean is actually forwarded to other session beans that may be using various transaction attributes.

level, all business methods in the bean inherit the transaction attribute value specified by it. In listing 6.1, we specify that the value of the @TransactionAttribute annotation for the placeSnagItOrder method should be TransactionAttribute-Type.REQUIRED. There are six choices for this annotation defined by the enumerated type TransactionAttributeType. Table 6.2 summarizes their behavior.

Table 6.2 Effects of transaction attributes on EJB methods

Transaction Attribute	Caller Transaction Exists?	Effect
REQUIRED	No	Container creates a new transaction.
	Yes	Method joins the caller's transaction.
REQUIRES_NEW	No	Container creates a new transaction.
	Yes	Container creates a new transaction and the caller's transaction is suspended.
SUPPORTS	No	No transaction is used.
	Yes	Method joins the caller's transaction.
MANDATORY	No	javax.ejb.EJBTransactionRequired-Exception is thrown.
	Yes	Method joins the caller's transaction.
NOT_SUPPORTED	No	No transaction is used.
	Yes	The caller's transaction is suspended and the method is called without a transaction.
NEVER	No	No transaction is used.
	Yes	javax.ejb.EJBException is thrown.

Let's take a look at what each value means and where each is applicable.

REQUIRED

REQUIRED is the default and most commonly applicable transaction attribute value. This value specifies that the EJB method must always be invoked within a transaction. If the method is invoked from a nontransactional client, the container will start a transaction before the method is called and finish it when the method returns. On the other hand, if the caller invokes the method from a transactional context, the method will *join* the existing transaction. In case of transactions propagated from the client, if our method indicates that the transaction should be rolled back, the container will not only roll back the whole transaction but will also throw a `javax.transaction.RollbackException` back to the client. This lets the client know that the transaction it started has been rolled back by another method. Our `placeSnagItOrder` method is most likely invoked from a nontransactional web tier. Hence, the `REQUIRED` value in the `@TransactionAttribute` annotation will cause the container to create a brand-new transaction for us when the method is executed. If all the other session bean methods we invoke from our bean are also marked `REQUIRED`, when we invoke them they will join the transaction created for us. This is just fine, since we want the entire ordering action to be covered by a single "umbrella" transaction. In general, you should use the `REQUIRED` value if you are modifying any data in your EJB method and you aren't sure whether the client will start a transaction of its own before calling your method.

REQUIRES_NEW

The `REQUIRES_NEW` value indicates that the container must always create a new transaction to invoke the EJB method. If the client already has a transaction, it is temporarily *suspended* until our method returns. This means that the success or failure of our new transaction has no effect on the existing client transaction. From the client's perspective:

1 Its transaction is paused.

2 Our method is invoked.

3 Our method either commits or rolls back its own transaction.

4 The client's transaction is resumed as soon as our method returns.

The `REQUIRES_NEW` attribute has limited uses in the real world. You should use it if you need a transaction but don't want a rollback to affect the client. Also use this value when you don't want the client's rollback to affect *you*. Logging is a great example. Even if the parent transaction rolls back, you want to be able to record the failure in your logs. On the other hand, failing to log a minor debugging message should not roll back your entire transaction and the problem should be localized to the logging component.

SUPPORTS

The `SUPPORTS` attribute essentially means the EJB method will inherit whatever the transactional environment of the caller is. If the caller does not have a transaction, the EJB method will be called without a transaction. On the other hand, if the caller is transactional, the EJB method will join the existing transaction and won't cause the exiting transaction to be suspended. This approach avoids any needless overhead in suspending or resuming the client transaction. The SUPPORTS attribute is typically useful for methods that perform read-only operations such as retrieving a record from a database table. In our Snag-It example, the session bean method for checking whether a bid exists on the item about to be ordered can probably have a SUPPORTS attribute since it modifies no data.

MANDATORY

MANDATORY really means *requires existing*—that is, the caller must have a transaction before calling an EJB method and the container should never create a transaction on behalf of the client. If the EJB method using the MANDATORY attribute is invoked from a nontransactional client, the container throws an EJBTransaction-RequiredException. This value is also very rarely used. You should use this value if you want to make sure the client fails if you request a rollback. We can make a reasonable case to require a MANDATORY transaction on a session bean method that charges the customer. After all, we want to make sure nothing is accidentally given away for free if the client neglects to detect a failure in the method charging the customer, and the invoker's transaction can be forcibly rolled back by us when necessary.

NOT_SUPPORTED

If we assign NOT_SUPPORTED as the transaction attribute, the EJB method cannot be invoked in a transactional context. If a caller with an associated transaction invokes the method, the container will suspend the transaction, invoke the method, and then resume the transaction when the method returns. This attribute is typically useful only for an MDB supporting a JMS provider in nontransactional, auto-acknowledge mode. To recap from chapter 5, in such cases the message is acknowledged as soon as it is successfully delivered and the MDB has no capability or apparent need to support rolling back message delivery.

NEVER

In a CMT, NEVER really means *never*. In other words, this attribute means that the EJB method can never be invoked from a transactional client. If such an attempt is made, a javax.ejb.EJBException is thrown. This is probably the least-used transaction attribute value. It could be used if your method is changing a nontransactional resource (such as a text file) and you want to make sure the client knows about the nontransactional nature of the method.

Transaction attributes and MDBs

As we mentioned in chapter 4, MDBs don't support all of the six transaction attributes we just discussed. Although you can apply any of the attributes to a stateful or stateless session bean, MDBs only support the REQUIRED and NOT_SUPPORTED attributes. This relates to the fact that no client ever invokes MDB methods directly; it is the *container* that invokes MDB methods when it receives an incoming message. Since there is no existing client transaction to suspend or join, REQUIRES_NEW, SUPPORTS, and MANDATORY make no sense (refer to table 6.2). NEVER makes no sense either, since we don't need that strong a guard against the container. In effect, depending on message acknowledgment on method return, we need only tell the container of two conditions: we need a transaction (REQUIRED) that encapsulates the message listener method, or we do not need transaction support (NOT_SUPPORTED).

So far, we've taken a detailed look at how transactions are created and managed by the container. We know that the successful return of a CMT method causes the container to commit a method or at least not roll it back if it is a joined transaction. We've explained how a CMT method can mark an available transaction as rolled back, but we've not yet discussed the actual mechanics. Let's dig into the underpinnings next.

6.2.4 *Marking a CMT for rollback*

If the appropriate business conditions arise, a CMT method can ask the container to roll back a transaction as soon as possible. The important thing to note here is that the transaction is not rolled back immediately, but a flag is set for the container to do the actual rollback when it is time to end the transaction. Let's go back to a snippet of our scenario in listing 6.1 to see exactly how this is done:

```
@Resource
private SessionContext context;
...
public void placeSnagItOrder(Item item, Customer customer){
    try {
        ...
        validateCredit(customer);
        ...
    } catch (CreditValidationException cve) {
        context.setRollbackOnly();
        ...
```

As this snippet shows, the setRollbackOnly method of the injected javax.ejb. EJBContext marks the transaction to be rolled back when we are unable to validate the user's credit card, a CreditValidationException is thrown, and we cannot allow the order to complete. If you go back and look at the complete listing, we do the same thing to head off other serious problems, such as the database server goes down or if we have trouble charging the credit card.

To keep things simple, assume that the container starts a new transaction because the `placeSnagItOrder` method is invoked from a nontransactional web tier. This means that after the method returns, the container will check to see if it can commit the transaction. Since we set the rollback flag for the underlying transaction through the `setRollbackOnly` method, the container will roll back instead. Because the EJB context in this case is really a proxy to the underlying transaction, you should never call the `setRollbackOnly` method unless you are sure there is an underlying transaction to flag. Typically, you can only be sure of this fact if your method has a REQUIRED, REQUIRES_NEW, or MANDATORY transaction attribute. If your method is not invoked in a transaction context, calling this method will throw `java.lang.IllegalStateException`.

Another `EJBContext` method you should know about is `getRollbackOnly`. The method returns a `boolean` telling you whether the underlying CMT transaction has already been marked for rollback.

> **NOTE**   The `setRollbackOnly` and `getRollbackOnly` methods can only be invoked in an EJB using CMT with these transaction attributes: REQUIRED, REQUIRES_NEW, or MANDATORY. Otherwise, the container will throw an `IllegalStateException`.

If you suspect that this method is used very infrequently, you are right. There is one case in particular when it is useful to check the status of the transaction you are participating in: before engaging in a very long, resource-intense operation. After all, why expend all that effort for something that is already going to be rolled back? For example, let's assume that ActionBazaar checks a potential Power Seller's creditworthiness before approving an account. Since this calculation involves a large set of data collection and business intelligence algorithms that potentially involve third parties, it is undertaken only if the current transaction has not already been rolled back. The code could look like this:

```
@Resource
private SessionContext context;
... checkCreditWorthiness(Seller seller) { ...
    if (!context.getRollbackOnly()) {
        DataSet data = getDataFromCreditBureauRobberBarons(seller);
        runLongAndConvolutedBusinessAnalysis(seller, data);
        ...
    } ...
```

If the model of catching exceptions just to call the `setRollbackOnly` method seems a little cumbersome, you're in luck. EJB 3 makes the job of translating exceptions into transaction rollback almost transparent using the `Application-Exception` paradigm. We'll examine the role of exception handling in transaction management next.

6.2.5 *Transaction and exception handling*

The subject of transactions and exception handling in EJB 3 is intricate and often confusing. However, properly used, exceptions used to manage transactions can be extremely elegant and intuitive.

To see how exceptions and transactions work together, let's revisit the exception-handling code in the `placeSnagItOrder` method:

```
try {
    // Ordering code throwing exceptions.
    if (!bidsExisting(item)){
        validateCredit(customer);
        chargeCustomer(customer, item);
        removeItemFromBidding(item);
    }
} catch (CreditValidationException cve) {
    context.setRollbackOnly();
} catch (CreditProcessingException cpe){
    context.setRollbackOnly();
} catch (DatabaseException de) {
    context.setRollbackOnly();
}
```

As you can see, the `CreditValidationException`, `CreditProcessingException`, and `DatabaseException` exceptions being thrown are essentially the equivalent of the managed transaction being rolled back. To avoid this all-too-common mechanical code, EJB 3 introduces the idea of controlling transactional outcome through the `@javax.ejb.ApplicationException` annotation. The best way to see how this works is through an example. Listing 6.2 reimplements the `placeSnagItOrder` method using the `@ApplicationException` mechanism to roll back CMTs.

Listing 6.2 Using @ApplicationException to roll back CMTs

```
public void placeSnagItOrder(Item item, Customer customer)
    throws CreditValidationException,                              ❶ Declares
        CreditProcessingException, DatabaseException {                exceptions on
                                                                      throws clause
    if (!bidsExisting(item)){
        validateCredit(customer);             ❷ Throws exceptions
        chargeCustomer(customer, item);          from method body
```

```
        removeItemFromBidding(item);
    }
}
...
@ApplicationException(rollback=true)
public class CreditValidationException extends Exception {
...
@ApplicationException(rollback=true)
public class CreditProcessingException extends Exception {
...
@ApplicationException(rollback=false)
public class DatabaseException extends
    RuntimeException {
...
```

❷ **Throws exceptions from method body**

❸ **Specifies Application-Exception**

❹ **Marks RuntimeException as ApplicationException**

The first change from listing 6.1 you'll notice is the fact that the try-catch blocks have disappeared and have been replaced by a throws clause in the method declaration ❶. However, it's a good idea for you to gracefully handle the application exceptions in the client and generate appropriate error messages. The various nested method invocations still throw the three exceptions listed in the throws clause ❷. The most important thing to note, however, is the three @Application-Exception specifications on the custom exceptions. The @ApplicationException annotation ❸ identifies a Java checked or unchecked exception as an *application exception*.

NOTE   In EJB, an application exception is an exception that the client is expected to handle. When thrown, such exceptions are passed directly to the method invoker. By default, all checked exceptions except for java.rmi.RemoteException are assumed to be application exceptions. On the other hand, all exceptions that inherit from either java.rmi.RemoteExceptions or java.lang.RuntimeException are assumed to be *system exceptions* (as you might already know, all exceptions that inherit from java.lang.RuntimeException are unchecked). In EJB, it is not assumed that system exceptions are expected by the client. When encountered, such exceptions are *not* passed to the client as is but are wrapped in a javax.ejb.EJBException instead.

In listing 6.2, the @ApplicationException annotations on CreditValidation-Exception and CreditProcessingException do not change this default behavior since both would have been assumed to be application exceptions anyway. However, by default, DatabaseException ❹ would have been assumed to be a system

Session synchronization

Although using CMT doesn't give you full control over when a transaction is started, committed, or rolled back, you can be notified about the transaction's lifecycle events. This is done simply by having your CMT bean implement the `javax.ejb.SessionSynchronization` interface. This interface defines three methods:

- `void afterBegin()`—Called right after the container creates a new transaction and before the business method is invoked.

- `void beforeCompletion()`—Invoked after a business method returns but right before the container ends a transaction.

- `void afterCompletion(boolean committed)`—Called after the transaction finishes. The boolean `committed` flag indicates whether a method was committed or rolled back.

Implementing this interface in a stateful session bean can be considered close to having a poor man's persistence mechanism, because data can be loaded into the bean when the transaction starts and unloaded right before the transaction finishes, while the `afterCompletion` callback can be used to reset default values. However, you can make a valid argument that since session beans are supposed to model processes, if it makes sense to cache some data and synchronize with the database as a natural part of a process, then this practice is just fine, if not fairly elegant.

Note this facility doesn't make much sense in a stateless session bean or MDB where data should not be cached anyway; therefore, the interface is not supported for those bean types.

exception. Applying the `@ApplicationException` annotation to it causes it to be treated as an application exception instead.

More than the `@ApplicationException` annotation itself, the `rollback` element changes default behavior in profound ways. By default, application exceptions do not cause an automatic CMT rollback since the `rollback` element is defaulted to `false`. However, setting the element to `true` tells the container that it should roll back the transaction before the exception is passed on to the client. In listing 6.2, this means that whenever a `CreditValidationException`, `CreditProcessingException`, or `DatabaseException` is thrown, the transaction will be rolled back and the client will receive an exception indicating the cause for failure, accomplishing exactly the same thing as the more verbose code in listing 6.1 aims to do. If the container detects a system exception, such as an

ArrayIndexOutOfBounds or NullPointerException that you didn't plan for, it will still roll back the CMT. However, in such cases the container will also assume that the bean is in inconsistent state and will destroy the instance. Because unnecessarily destroying bean instances is costly, you should never deliberately use system exceptions.

Although the simplified code is very tempting, we recommend that you use application exceptions for CMT rollback carefully. Using the setRollbackOnly method, however verbose, removes the guesswork from automated transaction management, especially for junior developers who might have a hard time understanding the intricacies of exception handling in EJB. However, don't interpret this to mean you should avoid using custom application exceptions in general. In fact, we encourage the use of this powerful and intuitive errror-handling mechanism widely used in the Java realm.

As you can clearly see, CMT relieves you from all but the most unavoidable details of EJB transaction management. However, for certain circumstances, CMT may not give you the level of control you need. BMT gives you this additional control while still providing a powerful, high-level API, as you'll see next.

6.3 *Bean-managed transactions*

The greatest strength of CMT is also its greatest weakness. Using CMT, you are limited to having the transaction boundaries set at the beginning and end of business methods and relying on the container to determine when a transaction starts, commits, or rolls back. BMT, on the other hand, allows you to specify exactly these details programmatically, using semantics similar to the JDBC transaction model with which you might already be familiar. However, even in this case, the container helps you by actually creating the physical transaction as well as taking care of a few low-level details. With BMT, you must be much more aware of the underlying JTA transaction API, primarily the javax.transaction.UserTransaction interface, which we'll introduce shortly. But first, we'll redevelop the Snag-It ordering code in BMT so that we can use it in the next few sections. You'll learn more about the javax.transaction.UserTransaction interface and how to use it. We'll also discuss the pros and cons of using BMT over CMT.

6.3.1 *Snag-It ordering using BMT*

Listing 6.3 reimplements the code in listing 6.1 using BMT. It checks if there are any bids on the item ordered, validates the user's credit card, charges the customer, and removes the item from bidding. Note that the import statements are omitted and error handling trivialized to keep the code sample short.

Listing 6.3   Implementing Snag-It using BMT

```
@Stateless)
@TransactionManagement(TransactionManagementType.BEAN)    ←━❶ Uses BMT
public class OrderManagerBean {
    @Resource                                         ❷ Injects UserTransaction
    private UserTransaction userTransaction;

    public void placeSnagItOrder(Item item, Customer customer){
        try {
            userTransaction.begin();    ←━❸ Starts transaction
            if (!bidsExisting(item)){
                validateCredit(customer);
                chargeCustomer(customer, item);
                removeItemFromBidding(item);
            }                                      ❹ Commits
            userTransaction.commit();       ←┘      transaction
        } catch (CreditValidationException cve) {
            userTransaction.rollback();
        } catch (CreditProcessingException cpe){      ❺ Rolls back
            userTransaction.rollback();                  transaction on
        } catch (DatabaseException de) {                 exception
            userTransaction.rollback();
        } catch (Exception e) {
            e.printStackTrace();
        }
    }
}
```

Briefly scanning the code, you'll note that the @TransactionManagement annotation specifies the value TransactionManagementType.BEAN as opposed to TransactionManagementType.CONTAINER, indicating that we are using BMT this time ❶. The TransactionAttribute annotation is missing altogether since it is applicable only for CMT. A UserTransaction, the JTA representation of a BMT, is injected ❷ and used explicitly to begin ❸, commit ❹, or roll back ❺ a transaction. The transaction boundary is much smaller than the entire method and includes only calls that really need to be atomic. The sections that follow discuss the code in greater detail, starting with getting a reference to the javax.transaction.UserTransaction.

6.3.2 Getting a UserTransaction

The UserTransaction interface encapsulates the basic functionality provided by a Java EE transaction manager. JTA has a few other interfaces used under different circumstances. We won't cover them, as most of the time you'll be dealing with UserTransaction. (For full coverage of JTA, check out http://java.sun.com/products/jta/.) As you might expect, the UserTransaction interface is too intricate under the hood to be instantiated directly and must be obtained from the container. In listing 6.3, we used the simplest way of getting a UserTransaction: injecting it through the @Resource annotation. There are a couple of other ways to do this: using JNDI lookup or through the EJBContext.

JNDI lookup

The application server binds the UserTransaction to the JNDI name java:comp/UserTransaction. You can look it up directly using JNDI with this code:

```
Context context = new InitialContext();
UserTransaction userTransaction =
    (UserTransaction) context.lookup("java:comp/UserTransaction");
userTransaction.begin();
// Perform transacted tasks.
userTransaction.commit();
```

This method is typically used outside of EJBs—for example, if you need to use a transaction in a helper or a nonmanaged class in the EJB or web tier where dependency injection is not supported. If you find yourself in this situation, you might want to think long and hard about moving the transactional code to an EJB where you have access to greater abstractions.

EJBContext

You can also get a UserTransaction by invoking the getUserTransaction method of the EJBContext. This approach is useful if you're using a SessionContext or MessageDrivenContext for some other purpose anyway, and a separate injection just to get a transaction instance would be redundant. Note that you can only use the getUserTransaction method if you're using BMT. Calling this in a CMT environment will cause the context to throw an IllegalStateException. The following code shows the getUserTransaction method in action:

```
@Resource
private SessionContext context;
...
UserTransaction userTransaction = context.getUserTransaction();
userTransaction.begin();
```

```
// Perform transacted tasks.
userTransaction.commit();
```

On a related but relevant note, you cannot use the EJBContext getRollbackOnly and setRollbackOnly methods in BMT, and the container will throw an Illegal-StateException if accessed. Next, let's see how the obtained UserTransaction interface is actually used.

6.3.3 *Using UserTransaction*

You've already seen the UserTransaction interface's most frequently used methods: begin, commit, and rollback. The UserTransaction interface has a few other useful methods we should take a look at as well. The definition of the entire interface looks like this:

```
public interface UserTransaction {
void begin() throws NotSupportedException, SystemException;
void commit() throws RollbackException,
HeuristicMixedException, HeuristicRollbackException, SecurityException,
    IllegalStateException, SystemException;

void rollback()
      throws IllegalStateException,
          SecurityException, SystemException;

void setRollbackOnly() throws IllegalStateException,
SystemException;

int getStatus() throws SystemException;
void setTransactionTimeout(int seconds) throws SystemException;
}
```

The begin method creates a new low-level transaction behind the scenes and associates it with the current thread. You might be wondering what would happen if you called the begin method twice before calling rollback or commit. You might think this is possible if you want to create a nested transaction, a paradigm supported by some transactional systems. In reality, the second invocation of begin would throw a NotSupportedException since Java EE doesn't support nested transactions. The commit and rollback methods, on the other hand, remove the transaction attached to the current thread by using the begin method. While commit sends a "success" signal to the underlying transaction manager, rollback abandons the current transaction. The setRollbackOnly method on this interface might be slightly counterintuitive as well. After all, why bother marking a transaction as rolled back when you can roll it back yourself?

To understand why, consider the fact that we could call a CMT method from our BMT bean that contains a lengthy calculation and checks the transactional flag before proceeding (like our Power Seller credit validation example in section 6.2.4). Since our BMT transaction would be propagated to the CMT method, it might be programmatically simpler, especially in a long method, to mark the transaction rolled back using the `setRollbackOnly` method instead of writing an involved `if-else` block avoiding such conditions. The `getStatus` method is a more robust version of `getRollbackOnly` in the CMT world. Instead of returning a `boolean`, this method returns an integer-based status of the current transactions, indicating a more fine-tuned set of states a transaction could possibly be in. The `javax.transaction.Status` interface defines exactly what these states are, and we list them in table 6.3.

The `setTransactionTimeout` method specifies the time, in seconds, in which a transaction must finish. The default transaction timeout value is set to different values for different application servers. For example, JBoss has a default

Table 6.3 The possible values of the javax.transaction.Status interface. These are the status values returned by the UserTransaction.getStatus method.

Status	Description
STATUS_ACTIVE	The associated transaction is in an active state.
STATUS_MARKED_ROLLBACK	The associated transaction is marked for rollback, possibly due to invocation of the `setRollbackOnly` method.
STATUS_PREPARED	The associated transaction is in the prepared state because all resources have agreed to commit (refer to the two-phase commit discussion in section 6.1.4).
STATUS_COMMITTED	The associated transaction has been committed.
STATUS_ROLLEDBACK	The associated transaction has been rolled back.
STATUS_UNKNOWN	The status for associated transaction is not known (very clever, don't you agree?).
STATUS_NO_TRANSACTION	There is no associated transaction in the current thread.
STATUS_PREPARING	The associated transaction is preparing to be committed and awaiting response from subordinate resources (refer to the two-phase commit discussion in section 6.1.4).
STATUS_COMMITTING	The transaction is in the process of committing.
STATUS_ROLLING_BACK	The transaction is in the process of rolling back.

transaction timeout value of 300 seconds whereas Oracle Application Server 10*g* has a default transaction timeout value of 30 seconds. You might want to use this method if you're using a very long-running transaction. Typically, it is better to simply set the application server-wide defaults using vendor-specific interfaces, however. At this point, you are probably wondering how to set a transaction timeout when using CMT instead. This is only supported by containers using either an attribute in the vendor-specific deployment descriptor or vendor-specific annotations.

Comparing listings 6.1 and 6.3, you might ask if the additional complexity and verbosity associated with BMT is really worth it. Let's explore this issue in detail next.

6.3.4 *The pros and cons of BMT*

CMT is the default transaction type for EJB transactions. In general, BMT should be used sparingly because it is verbose, complex, and difficult to maintain. There are some concrete reasons to use BMT, however. BMT transactions need not begin and end in the confines of a single method call. If you are using a stateful session bean and need to maintain a transaction across method calls, BMT is your only option. Be warned, however, that this technique is complicated and error prone and you might be better off rewriting your application rather than attempting this. Can you spot a bug in listing 6.3? The last catch block did not roll back the transaction as all the other catch blocks did. But even that is not enough; what if the code throws an error (rather than an exception)? Whichever way you do it, it is error prone and we recommend using CMT instead.

Another argument for BMT is that you can fine-tune your transaction boundaries so that the data held by your code is isolated for the shortest time possible. Our opinion is that this idea indulges in premature optimization, and again, you are probably better off refactoring your methods to be smaller and more specific anyway. Another drawback for BMT is the fact that it can never join an existing transaction. Existing transactions are always suspended when calling a BMT method, significantly limiting flexible component reuse.

This wraps up our discussion of EJB transaction management. It is now time to turn our attention to another critical aspect of enterprise Java development: security.

6.4 *Exploring EJB security*

Securing enterprise data has always been a primary application development concern. This is especially true today in the age of sophisticated cyber-world hackers, phishers, and identity/data thieves. Consequently, security is a major concern in developing robust Java EE solutions. EJB has a security model that is elegant, flexible, and portable across heterogeneous systems.

In the remainder of this chapter, we'll explore some basic security concepts such as authentication and authorization, users, and groups, and we'll investigate the Java EE/EJB security framework. We'll also take a look at both declarative and programmatic security in EJB 3.

Let's start with two of the most basic ideas in security: authentication and authorization.

6.4.1 *Authentication vs. authorization*

Securing an application involves two primary functions: authentication and authorization. Authentication must be done before authorization can be performed, but as you'll see, both are necessary aspects of application security. Let's explore both of these concepts.

Authentication

Authentication is the process of verifying user identity. By authenticating yourself, you prove that you are who you say you are. In the real world, this is usually accomplished through visual inspection/identity cards, signature/handwriting, fingerprint checks, and even DNA tests. In the computer world, the most common method of authentication is by checking username and password. All security is meaningless if someone can log onto a system with a false identity.

Authorization

Authorization is the process of determining whether a user has access to a particular resource or task, and it comes into play once a user is authenticated. In an open system, an authenticated user can access any resource. In a realistic security environment, this all-or-nothing approach would be highly ineffective. Therefore, most systems must restrict access to resources based on user identity. Although there might be some resources in a system that are accessible to all, most resources should be accessed only by a limited group of people.

Both authentication and authorization, but especially authorization, are closely tied to other security concepts, namely *users*, *groups*, and *roles*, which we'll look at next.

6.4.2 *Users, groups, and roles*

To perform efficient and maintainable authorization, it is best if you can organize users into some kind of grouping. Otherwise, each resource must have an associated list of all the users that can access it. In a nontrivial system, this would easily become an administrator's nightmare. To avoid this problem, users are organized into *groups* and groups as a whole are assigned access to resources, making the access list for an individual resource much more manageable.

The concept of *role* is closely related to the concept of *group*, but is a bit tricky to understand. For an EJB application, roles are much more critical than users and groups. To understand the distinction, consider the fact that you might not be building an in-house solution but a packaged Java EE application. Consequently, you might not know the exact operational environment your application will be deployed in once it is purchased by the customer. As a result, it's impossible for you to code for the specific group names a customer's system administrator will choose. Neither should you care about groups. What you do care about is what *role* a particular user in a group plays for your application. In the customer system, user Joe might belong to the system group called *peons*. Now assume that an ActionBazaar integrated B2B Enterprise Purchasing System is installed on the customer's site. Among other things, this type of B2B installation transparently logs in all existing users from the customer system into the ActionBazaar site through a custom desktop shortcut. Once logged in, from ActionBazaar's perspective, Joe could simply be a *buyer* who buys items online on behalf of the B2B customer company. To another small application in the operational environment, user Joe might be an *administrator* who changes system-wide settings. For each deployed application in the operational environment, it is the responsibility of the system administrator to determine what *system group* should be mapped to what *application role*. In the Java EE world, this is typically done through vendor-specific administrative interfaces. As a developer, you simply need to define what roles your application's users have and leave the rest to the assembler or deployer. For ActionBazaar, roles can be buyers, sellers, administrators, and so on.

Let's solidify our understanding of application security in EJB using an ActionBazaar example.

6.4.3 *A security problem in ActionBazaar*

At ActionBazaar, customer service representatives (CSRs) are allowed to cancel a user's bid under certain circumstances (for example, if the seller discloses something in answer to an e-mail question from the bidder that should have been mentioned on the item description). However, the cancel bid operation doesn't check if the user is actually a CSR as long as the user can locate the functionality on the ActionBazaar site—for example, by typing in the correct URL. Figure 6.4 illustrates the security problem in ActionBazaar.

A clever hacker breaks into the ActionBazaar web server logs and figures out the URL used by CSRs to cancel bids. Using this knowledge, he devises an even cleverer "shill bidding" scheme to incite users to overpay for otherwise cheap items. The hacker posts items on sale and uses a friend's account to incite a bidding war with genuine bidders. If at any point genuine bidders give up bidding and a fake bid becomes the highest bid, the hacker avoids actually having to pay for the item and losing money in posting fees by canceling his highest fake bid through the stolen URL. No one is any wiser as the genuine bidders as well as the ActionBazaar system think the highest bid was canceled for legitimate reasons. The end result is that an honest bidder is fooled into overpaying for otherwise cheap items.

After a while, ActionBazaar customer service finally catches onto the scheme thanks to a few observant users and makes sure the bid canceling action is authorized for CSRs only. Now if a hacker tries to access the functionality, the system simply denies access, even if the hacker has a registered ActionBazaar account

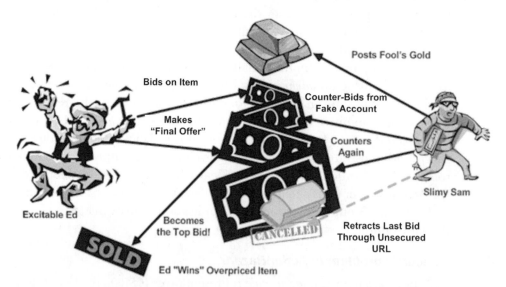

Figure 6.4 A security breach in ActionBazaar allows a hacker to shill bids by posting an item, starting a bidding war from a fake account and then at the last minute canceling the highest fake bid. The end result is that an unsuspecting bidder winds up with an overpriced item.

and accesses the functionality through the URL or otherwise. As we discuss how security is managed by EJB in the next section, you will begin to see what an actual solution looks like.

6.4.4 *EJB 3 and Java EE security*

Java EE security is largely based on the Java Authentication and Authorization Service (JAAS) API. JAAS essentially separates the authentication system from the Java EE application by using a well-defined, pluggable API. In other words, the Java EE application need only know how to talk to the JAAS API. The JAAS API, in contrast, knows how to talk to underlying authentication systems like Lightweight Directory Access Protocol (LDAP), such as Microsoft Active Directory or Oracle Internet Directory (OID) using a vendor plug-in. As a result, you can easily swap between authentication systems simply by swapping JAAS plug-ins without changing any code. In addition to authentication, the application server internally uses JAAS to perform authorization for both the web and EJB tiers. When we look at programmatic EJB security management, we'll directly deal with JAAS very briefly when we discuss the JAAS `javax.security.Principal` interface. Feel free to explore JAAS at http://java.sun.com/products/jaas/ since our discussion is limited to what is needed for understanding EJB security.

JAAS is designed so that both the authentication and authorization steps can be performed at any Java EE tier, including the web and EJB tiers. Realistically, however, most Java EE applications are web accessible and share an authentication system across tiers, if not across the application server. JAAS fully leverages this reality and once a user (or entity, to use a fancy security term) is authenticated at any Java EE tier, the authentication context is passed through tiers whenever possible, instead of repeating the authentication step. The `Principal` object we already mentioned represents this sharable, validated authentication context. Figure 6.5 depicts this common Java EE security management scenario.

As shown in figure 6.5, a user enters the application through the web tier. The web tier gathers authentication information from the user and authenticates the supplied credentials using JAAS against an underlying security system. A successful authentication results in a valid user `Principal`. At this point, the `Principal` is associated with one or more roles. For each secured web/EJB tier resource, the application server checks if the principal/role is authorized to access the resource. The `Principal` is transparently passed from the web tier to the EJB tier as needed.

A detailed discussion of web tier authentication and authorization is beyond the scope of this book, as is the extremely rare scenario of standalone EJB authentication using JAAS. However, we'll give you a basic outline of web tier security to

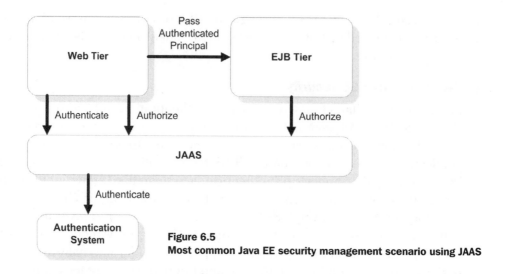

Figure 6.5
Most common Java EE security management scenario using JAAS

serve as a starting point for further investigation before diving into authorization management in EJB 3.

Web tier authentication and authorization

The web tier servlet specification (http://java.sun.com/products/servlet/) successfully hides a great many low-level details for both authentication and authorization. As a developer, you simply need to tell the servlet container what resources you want secured, how they are secured, how authentication credentials are gathered, and what roles have access to secured resources. The servlet container, for the most part, takes care of the rest. Web tier security is mainly configured using the `login-config` and `security-constraint` elements of the `web.xml` file. Listing 6.4 shows how securing the administrative module of ActionBazaar might look using these elements.

Listing 6.4   Sample web.xml elements to secure order canceling and other ActionBazaar admin functionality

```
<login-config>
    <auth-method>BASIC</auth-method>           ◁─❶
    <realm-name>ActionBazaarRealm</realm-name>   ◁─❷
</login-config>

...
<security-constraint>
    <web-resource-collection>
        <web-resource-name>
```

```
         ActionBazaar Administrative Component
      </web-resource-name>
      <url-pattern>/admin/*</url-pattern>      ←❸
   </web-resource-collection>
   <auth-constraint>
      <role-name>CSR</role-name>       ←❹
   </auth-constraint>
</security-constraint>
```

Listing 6.4 specifies how the web container should gather and validate authentication ❶. In our case, we have chosen the simplest authentication mechanism, BASIC. BASIC authentication uses an HTTP header–based authentication scheme that usually causes the web browser to gather username/password information using a built-in prompt. Other popular authentication mechanisms include FORM and CLIENT-CERT. FORM is essentially the same as BASIC except for the fact that the prompt used is an HTML form that you create. CLIENT-CERT, on the other hand, is an advanced form of authentication that bypasses username/password prompts altogether. In this scheme, the client sends a public key certificate stored in the client browser to the web server using Secured Socket Layer (SSL) and the server authenticates the contents of the certificate instead of a username/password. The credentials are then validated by the JAAS provider.

Next we specify the realm the container should authenticate against ❷. A *realm* is essentially a container-specific abstraction over a JAAS-driven authentication system. We then specify that all URLs that match the pattern /admin/* should be secured ❸. Finally, we specify that only validated principals with the CSR role can access the secured pages ❹. In general, this is all there really is to securing a web application using JAAS, unless you choose to use programmatic security, which essentially follows the same pattern used in programmatic EJB security.

EJB authentication and authorization

At the time of writing, authenticating and accessing EJBs from a standalone client without any help from the servlet container is still a daunting task that requires you to thoroughly understand JAAS. In effect, you'd have to implement all of the authentication steps that the servlet container nicely abstracts away from you. Thankfully, this task is not undertaken very often and most application servers provide a JAAS login module that can be used by applications.

On the other hand, the authorization model in EJB 3 is simple yet powerful. Much like authorization in the web tier, it centers on the idea of checking whether the authenticated `Principal` is allowed to access an EJB resource based on the

`Principal`'s role. Like transaction management, authentication can be either declarative or programmatic, each of which provides a different level of control over the authentication process. In addition, like the transaction management features discussed in this chapter, security applies to session beans and MDBs, and not the JPA entities.

We'll first explore declarative security management by coding our bid-canceling scenario presented in 6.4.3 and then move on to exploring programmatic security management.

6.4.5 Declarative security

Listing 6.5 applies authentication rules to the `BidManagerBean` that includes the `cancelBid` method our clever hacker used for his shill-bidding scheme. Now, only CSRs are allowed to use this method. Note that we have omitted method implementation since this is not relevant to our discussion.

Listing 6.5 Securing bid cancellation using declarative security management

```
@DeclareRoles({"BIDDER", "CSR", "ADMIN"})      ← ❶ Declares roles for bean
@Stateless
public class BidManagerBean implements BidManager {
    @RolesAllowed({"CSR", "ADMIN"})
    public void cancelBid(Bid bid, Item item) {...}      ❷ Specifies roles with
                                                            access to method

    @PermitAll
    public List<Bid> getBids(Item item) {...}      ❸ Permits all system roles
}                                                     access to method
```

Listing 6.5 features some of the most commonly used security annotations defined by common metadata annotations for Java Platform Specification JSR-250, `javax.annotation.security.DeclareRoles`, `javax.annotation.security.RolesAllowed`, and `javax.annotation.security.PermitAll`. Two other annotations that we have not used but will discuss are `javax.annotation.security.DenyAll` and `javax.annotation.security.RunAs`. Let's start our analysis of the code and security annotations with the `@DeclareRoles` annotation.

Declaring roles

We highly recommend that you declare the security roles to be employed in your application, EJB module, EJB, or business methods. There are a few ways of declaring roles, one of which is through the `@DeclareRoles` annotation, which we use in listing 6.5 ❶. This annotation applies at either the method or the class level and consists of an array of role names. We are specifying that the `BidManagerBean` use the roles of BIDDER, CSR, and ADMIN. Alternatively, we could have specified roles for the entire enterprise application or EJB module through deployment descriptors. The ActionBazaar application could use the roles of guests, bidders, sellers, Power Sellers, CSRs, admins, and so on. If we never declare roles, the container will automatically build a list of roles by inspecting the @RolesAllowed annotation. Remember, when the application is deployed, the local system administrator must map each role to groups defined in the runtime security environment.

Specifying authenticated roles

The @RolesAllowed annotation is the crux of declarative security management. This annotation can be applied to either an EJB business method or an entire class. When applied to an entire EJB, it tells the container which roles are allowed to access any EJB method. On the other hand, we can use this annotation on a method to specify the authentication list for that particular method. The tremendous flexibility offered by this annotation becomes evident when you consider the fact that you can override class-level settings by reapplying the annotation at the method level (for example, to restrict access further for certain methods). However, we discourage such usage because at best it is convoluted and at worst it can cause subtle mistakes that are hard to discern. In listing 6.5, we specify that only CSR and ADMIN roles be allowed to cancel bids through the cancelBid method ❷. The @PermitAll and @DenyAll annotations are conveniences that perform essentially the same function as the @RolesAllowed annotation.

@PermitAll and @DenyAll

We can use the @PermitAll annotation to mark an EJB class or a method to be invoked by any role. We use this annotation in listing 6.5 ❸ to instruct the container that any user can retrieve the current bids for a given item. You should use this annotation sparingly, especially at the class level, as it is possible to inadvertently leave security holes if it is used carelessly. The @DenyAll annotation does exactly the opposite of @PermitAll. That is, when used at either the class or the method level, it renders functionality inaccessible by any role. You might be wondering why you would ever use this annotation. Well, the annotation makes sense when you consider the fact that your application may be deployed in wide-ranging environments that you did not envision. You can essentially invalidate methods or classes that might be inappropriate for a particular environment without changing code by using the @DenyAll annotation. Just as with the @RolesAllowed annotation, when applied at the method level these annotations will override bean-level authorization settings.

NOTE The three security annotations, @PermitAll, @DenyAll, and @Role-Allowed, cannot simultaneously be applied to the same class or the same method.

Let's now wrap up our discussion of declarative security management by discussing our final annotation, @RunAs.

@RunAs

The @RunAs annotation comes in handy if you need to dynamically assign a new role to the existing Principal in the scope of an EJB method invocation. You might need to do this, for example, if you're invoking another EJB within your method but the other EJB requires a role that is different from the current Principal's role. Depending on the situation, the new "assumed" role might be either more restrictive, lax, or neither. For example, the cancelBid method in listing 6.5 might need to invoke a statistics-tracking EJB that manages historical records in order to delete the statistical record of the canceled bid taking place. However, the method for deleting a historical record might require an ADMIN role. Using the @RunAs annotation, we can temporarily assign a CSR an ADMIN role so that the statistics-tracking EJB thinks an admin is invoking the method:

```
@RunAS("ADMIN")
@RolesAllowed("CSR")
public class BidManagerBean implements BidManager{
public void cancelBid(Bid bid, Item item) {...}
}
```

You should use this annotation sparingly since like the @PermitAll annotation, it can open up security holes you might not have foreseen.

As you can see, declarative security gives you access to a powerful authentication framework while staying mostly out of the way. The flexibility available to you through the relatively small number of relevant annotations should be apparent as well. If you have ever rolled out your own security or authentication system, one weakness might have crossed your mind already. The problem is that although you can authenticate a role using declarative security, what if you need to provide security settings specific to individuals, or even simple changes in method behavior based on the current Principal's role? This is where programmatic EJB security steps onto the stage.

6.4.6 Using EJB programmatic security

In effect, programmatic security provides direct access to the Principal as well as a convenient means to check the Principal's role in the code. Both of these functions are made available through the EJB context. We'll begin exploring programmatic security by redeveloping the bid-canceling scenario as a starting point. Listing 6.6 implements the scenario.

Listing 6.6 Securing bid cancellation using programmatic security

```
@Stateless
public class BidManagerBean implements BidManager {        ❶ Injects EJB context
    @Resource SessionContext context;
    ...
    public void cancelBid(Bid bid, Item item) {            ❷ Checks authorization
        if (!context.isCallerInRole("CSR")) {
            throw new SecurityException(                   ❸ Throws exception
                "No permissions to cancel bid");              on violation
        }
        ...
    }
    ...
}
```

Listing 6.6 first injects the EJB context ❶. We use the isCallerInRole method of the EJBContext to see if the underlying authenticated principal has the CSR role ❷. If it does not, we throw a java.lang.SecurityException notifying the user about the authorization violation ❸. Otherwise, the bid cancellation method is allowed to proceed normally. We discuss both the security management related methods provided in the EJB context next, namely isCaller-InRole and getCallerPrincipal.

isCallerInRole and getCallerPrincipal

Programmatic security is made up solely of the two previously mentioned security-related methods. The methods are defined in the javax.ejb.EJBContext interface as follows:

```
public interface EJBContext {
    ...
    public java.security.Principal getCallerPrincipal();
    public boolean isCallerInRole(java.lang.String roleName);
    ...
}
```

You've already seen the isCallerInRole method in action; it is fairly self-explanatory. Behind the scenes, the EJB context retrieves the Principal associated with the current thread and checks if any of its roles match the name you provided. The getCallerPrincipal method gives you direct access to the java.

security.Principal representing the current authentication context. The only method of interest in the Principal interface is getName, which returns the name of the Principal. Most of the time, the name of the Principal is the login name of the validated user. This means that just as in the case of a homemade security framework, you could validate the individual user if you needed to.

For example, let's assume that we had a change of heart and decided that in addition to the CSRs, bidders can cancel their own bids as long as the cancellation is done within a minute of putting in the bid. We could implement this using the getCallerPrincipal method as follows:

```
public void cancelBid(Bid bid, Item item) {
    if (!context.isCallerInRole("CSR")
        && !(context.getCallerPrincipal().getName().equals(
            bid.getBidder().getUsername()) && (bid.getTimestamp() >=
                (getCurrentTime() - 60*1000))))) {
        throw new SecurityException(
            "No permissions to cancel bid");
    }
    ...
}
```

Note, though, that there is no guarantee exactly what the Principal name might return. In some environments, it can return the role name, group name, or any other arbitrary String that makes sense for the authentication system. Before you use the Principal.getName method, you should check the documentation of your particular security environment. As you can see, the one great drawback of programmatic security management is the intermixing of security code with business logic as well as the potential hard-coding of role and Principal names. In previous versions of EJB, there was no way of getting around these shortfalls. However, in EJB 3 you can alleviate this problem somewhat by using interceptors. Let's see how to accomplish this next.

Using interceptors for programmatic security

As you know, in EJB 3 you can set up interceptors that are invoked before and after (around) any EJB business method. This facility is ideal for crosscutting concerns that should not be duplicated in every method, such as programmatic security (discussed in chapter 5) . We could reimplement listing 6.6 using interceptors instead of hard-coding security in the business method (see listing 6.7).

Listing 6.7 Using interceptors with programmatic security

```
public class SecurityInterceptor {       ❶   Marks intercepted invocation
    @AroundInvoke
```

```
    public Object checkUserRole(InvocationContext context)
        throws Exception {
        if (!context.getEJBContext().isCallerInRole("CSR")) {
            throw new SecurityException(
                "No permissions to cancel bid");
        }

        return context.proceed();
    }
}

@Stateless
public class BidManagerBean implements BidManager {
    @Interceptors(actionbazaar.security.SecurityInterceptor.class)
    public void cancelBid(Bid bid, Item item) { ... }
```

Accesses EJBContext from InvocationContext ❷

Specifies interceptor for method ❸

The `SecurityInterceptor` class method `checkUserRole` is designated as `Around-Invoke`, meaning it would be invoked whenever a method is intercepted ❶. In the method, we check to see if the `Principal` is a CSR ❷. If the role is not correct, we throw a `SecurityException`. Our `BidManagerBean`, on the other hand, specifies the `SecurityInterceptor` class as the interceptor for the `cancelBid` method ❸.

Note that although using interceptors helps matters a bit in terms of removing hard-coding from business logic, there is no escaping the fact that there is still a lot of hard-coding going on in the interceptors themselves. Moreover, unless you're using a simple security scheme where most EJB methods have similar authorization rules and you can reuse a small number of interceptors across the application, things could become complicated very quickly. In effect, you'd have to resort to writing ad hoc interceptors for method-specific authentication combinations (just admin, CSR and admin, everyone, no one, and so on). Contrast this to the relatively simple approach of using the declarative security management annotations or deployment descriptors. All in all, declarative security management is the scheme you should stick with, unless you have an absolutely unavoidable reason not to do so.

6.5 *Summary*

In this chapter, we discussed the basic theory of transactions, transaction management using CMT and BMT, basic security concepts, as well as programmatic and declarative security management. Both transactions and security are crosscutting concerns that ideally should not be interleaved with business logic. The EJB 3 take on security and transaction management tries to reflect exactly this belief, fairly successfully in our opinion, while allowing some flexibility.

An important point to consider is the fact that even if you specify nothing for transaction management in your EJB, the container still assumes default transactional behavior. However, the container applies no default security settings if you leave it out. The assumption is that at a minimum, an application server would be authenticated and authorized at a level higher than EJB (for example, the web tier). Nevertheless, we definitely recommend that you not leave yourself vulnerable by ignoring security at the mission-critical EJB layer where most of your code and data is likely to reside. Security vulnerabilities are insidious and you are better safe than sorry. Most importantly, the security features of EJB 3 are so easy to use that there is no reason to risk the worst by ignoring them.

The discussion on security and transactions wraps up our coverage of session and message-driven beans. Neither feature is directly applied to the EJB Persistence API as they were for entity beans in EJB 2. You'll see why this is the case as we explore the persistence API in the next few chapters.

Part 3

Diving into the Java Persistence API (JPA)

The goal of this part is to provide deep and broad coverage of JPA in a digestible manner. After reading this part of the book, you will have all the knowledge necessary to start developing robust business applications using JPA.

Chapter 7, "Implementing domain models," covers domain modeling, a central concept in ORM. The chapter describes how a conceptual business application domain model is translated to JPA entities, embedded objects, and entity relationships.

Chapter 8, "Object-relational mapping," takes on the most complicated aspects of ORM: mapping entities, embedded objects, and entity relationships to databases. The chapter covers the annotations you can use for mapping objects to tables and fields to table columns. It also explores mapping various data types, primary keys, relationships, and OO inheritance to databases.

Chapter 9, "Manipulating entities with EntityManager," describes the JPA `EntityManager`, a central interface that defines persistence operations. You'll learn how the `EntityManager` interface is used to create, update, delete, and retrieve entities persisted in the database. The chapter also deals with the entity lifecycle as it relates to ORM persistence operations.

Chapter 10, "Using the query API and JPQL to retrieve entities," covers object-relational queries. The chapter explores the use of the JPA query interface in detail. In addition, the chapter outlines how the Java Persistence Query Language (JPQL) is used to retrieve entities from the database in an extremely flexible and robust manner.

7
Implementing domain models

This chapter covers

- Domain modeling concepts
- Entities and entity identity
- Relationships between entities

Most of today's enterprise systems save their data into a relational database of some kind. This is why persistence—the process of saving and retrieving data from permanent storage—has been a major application development concern for many decades. As a matter of fact, some authoritative sources claim that a great majority of enterprise development efforts concentrate on the problem of persistence.

Arguably, after JDBC, EJB 2 entity beans have been the most significant groundbreaking solution to the problem of persistence in Java. Unfortunately, many of us who developed entity beans experienced an API that felt overcomplicated, cumbersome, and unpolished. It is pretty fair to say entity beans were the most weakly conceived part of EJB 2. In the past few years, lightweight persistence solutions like Hibernate and TopLink successfully filled the gap left open by entity beans. The EJB 3 Java Persistence API (JPA) brings the innovative ideas created by these popular solutions into the Java EE standard and leaves behind the entity beans paradigm.

Domain modeling is a concept inseparably linked with persistence. In fact, it is often the domain model that is persisted. As a result, it makes good sense to present JPA by breaking things down into four chapters that might mirror the iterative process of developing the domain model and persistence layer of the Action-Bazaar application. We have decided on four convenient development phases: defining, persisting, manipulating, and querying the domain model. In this chapter, we briefly introduce domain modeling, present the ActionBazaar domain model, and implement part of the domain model using the EJB 3 JPA. In chapter 8 we explain how entities in our domain model are persisted into a database by using object-relational mapping. In chapter 9, we manipulate the entities using the `EntityManager` API. Finally, in chapter 10, we query the persisted entities using the EJB 3 query API.

7.1 *Domain modeling and the JPA*

Often the first step to developing an enterprise application is creating the domain model—that is, listing the entities in the domain and defining the relationships between them.

In this section we'll first present a primer on domain modeling. Then we'll explore the ActionBazaar problem domain and identify actors in a domain model, such as objects, relationships, and cardinality. We'll provide a brief overview of how domain modeling is supported with the EJB 3 Java Persistence API and then build a simple domain object as a Java class.

7.1.1 *Introducing domain models*

Although you may have been warned that domain modeling is complex, the idea behind it is pretty simple. In effect, a *domain model* is a conceptual image of the problem your system is trying to solve. Literally, it is made up of the objects in the "system universe" and the relationships or associations between them. As you can guess, an *object* in a domain model need not be a physical object but just a concept used by your system. A *relationship*, on the other hand, is an imaginary link between objects that need to "know" about one another. The critical thing to remember is that the domain model describes the objects and how the objects might relate to one another, but not how a system acts on the objects.

We like to think of a domain model as a set of interlocking toy blocks. Each uniquely shaped block in the set is an *object*. The shape of each block determines how they fit with one another. Each such "fit" is a *relationship*. In the end, though, you put together the blocks into whatever configuration sparks your imagination. The master plan for putting together the final results forms the *business rules* of the application. The business rules are implemented by the session beans and MDBs we discussed in previous chapters, while the persistence API implements the domain model that the business rules act on.

We won't talk about domain modeling much further than what is needed for explaining the concepts we just introduced. However, we encourage you to explore the topic further by checking out the excellent books written on the subject of domain modeling, most notably *Patterns of Enterprise Applications Architecture* by Martin Fowler (Addison-Wesley, 2002). UML class diagrams are the most popular method of creating the initial domain model. However, we are going to avoid using formal class diagrams throughout this chapter and in the rest of the book. Instead, we'll use the simplest diagrams possible, which might have a shallow resemblance to UML.

7.1.2 *The ActionBazaar problem domain*

Modeling the entire ActionBazaar domain will introduce complexity that we don't need in order to explain JPA. To avoid this unnecessary complexity, we are going to develop the core functionality of the ActionBazaar application that is directly related to buying and selling items on bid online.

> **NOTE** Admittedly, this is a slightly unoriginal example. We considered using an example tangential to the central theme of ActionBazaar but decided against it and remained true to the ActionBazaar core concept.

As figure 7.1 shows, at the heart of it ActionBazaar centers on the following activities:

- Sellers post an item on ActionBazaar.
- Items are organized into searchable and navigable categories.
- Bidders place bids on items.
- The highest bidder wins.

NOTE   If you are familiar with use cases and the list looks a lot like use cases, they really are.

In our artificially simplistic scenario, we can pick out the domain *objects* by scanning the list of activities and looking for nouns: seller, item, category, bidder, bid, and order. Our goal is to identify the domain objects or entities that we want to persist in the database. In the real world, finding domain objects usually involves hours of work and many iterations spent analyzing the business problem. We'll make our initial diagram by randomly throwing together our objects into figure 7.2.

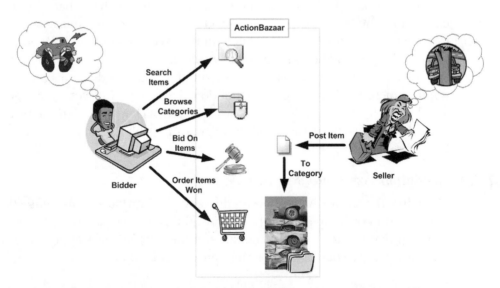

Figure 7.1   The core functionality of ActionBazaar. Sellers post items into searchable and navigable categories. Bidders bid on items and the highest bid wins.

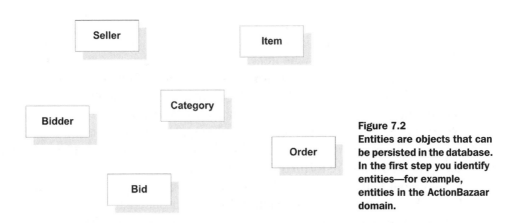

Figure 7.2
Entities are objects that can be persisted in the database. In the first step you identify entities—for example, entities in the ActionBazaar domain.

Putting in the links between objects that should know about each other (these are the infamously complex domain *relationships*) will complete our domain model. We encourage you to spend some time looking at figure 7.2 guessing how the objects might be related before peeking at the finished result in figure 7.3.

We won't spell out every relationship in figure 7.3, since most are pretty intuitive even with the slightly cryptic arrows and numbers. We'll explain what is going on with the arrows and numbers in just a bit when we talk about direction and

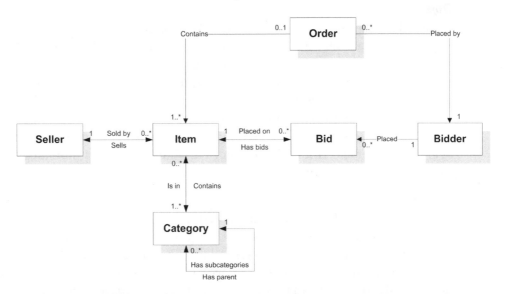

Figure 7.3   The ActionBazaar domain model complete with entities and relationships. Entities are related to one another and the relationship can be one-to-one, one-to-many, many-to-one, or many-to-many. Relationships can be either uni- or bidirectional.

multiplicity of relationships. For now, all you need to note is the text describing how objects are related to one another. For example, an item is sold by a seller, a seller may sell more than one item, the item is in one or more categories, each category may have a parent category, a bidder places a bid on an item, and so on. You should also note that although the domain model describes the possibilities for cobbling objects together, it does not actually describe the way in which the objects are manipulated. For instance, although you can see that an order consists of one or more items and is placed by a bidder, you are not told how or when these relationships are formed. But by applying a bit of common sense, it is easy to figure out that an item won through a winning bid is put into an order placed by the highest bidder. These relationships are probably formed by the business rules after the bidding is over and the winner checks out the item won.

We'll clarify the concepts behind domain model objects, relationships, and multiplicity next before moving on to the JPA.

7.1.3 *Domain model actors*

Domain modeling theory identifies four domain model "actors": objects, relationships, the multiplicity of relationships, and the optionality of relationships. Let's fill in the details that we have left out so far about all four actors.

Objects

From a Java developer perspective, domain objects are closely related to Java objects. Like Java objects, domain objects can have both behavior (*methods* in Java terms) and state (*instance variables* in Java). For example, the category domain object probably has the name, creation date, and modification date as attributes. Similarly, a category probably also has the behavior of being renamed and the modification date updated. There are likely hundreds of instances of category domain objects in the ActionBazaar, such as "Junkyard Cars for Teenagers," "Psychedelic Home Décor from the Sixties," "Cheesy Romantic Novels for the Bored," and so on.

Relationships

In Java terms, a *relationship* is manifested as one object having a reference to another. If the `Bidder` and `BillingInfo` objects are related, there is probably a `BillingInfo` instance variable in `Bidder`, a `Bidder` instance variable in `BillingInfo`, or both. Where the object reference resides determines the direction of the arrows in figure 7.3. If `Bidder` has a reference to `BillingInfo`, the arrow should point from `Bidder` to `BillingInfo`. Or suppose `Item` and `Bid` have references to each other; an `Item` *has* `Bids` on it and `Bids` are *placed on* `Items`. Signifying this fact,

Rich vs. anemic domain models

As we mentioned, domain models are eventually persisted into the database. It might already be obvious that it is easy to make the domain model objects look exactly like database tables. As a matter of fact, this is exactly why data modeling is often synonymous to domain modeling and DBAs (or data analysts) are often the domain experts. In this mode of thinking, domain objects contain attributes (mapping to database table columns) but no behavior. This type of model is referred to as the *anemic model*.

A *rich domain model*, on the other hand, encapsulates both object attributes and behavior and utilizes objected-oriented design such as inheritance, polymorphism, and encapsulation.

An anemic domain model may not necessarily be a bad thing for some applications. For one thing, it is painless to map objects to the database. As a rule of thumb, the richer the domain model is, the harder it is to map it to the database, particularly while using inheritance.

the arrow connecting `Bid` and `Item` points in both directions in figure 7.3. This is what is meant by a *bidirectional* relationship or association between `Bid` and `Item` as opposed to a *unidirectional* relationship or association between `Seller` and `BillingInfo`. Typically, objects are nouns and relationships are verbs such as *has, is part of, is member of, belongs to*, and so on.

Multiplicity, or cardinality

As you can probably infer from figure 7.3, not all relationships are one-to-one. That is, there may be more than one object on either side of a relationship. For example, a `Category` can have more than one `Item`. Multiplicity or cardinality refers to this multifaceted nature of relationships. The multiplicity of a relationship can be:

- *One-to-one*—Each side of the relationship may have at most only one object. An `Employee` object can have only one ID card and an ID card can only be assigned to one employee.

- *One-to-many*—A particular object instance may be related to multiple instances of another. For example, an `Item` can have more than one `Bid`. Note that, taken from the point of view of a `Bid`, the relationship is said to be *many-to-one*. For example, many `Bids` can be placed by a `Bidder` in figure 7.3.

- *Many-to-many*—If both sides of the relationship can have more than one object, the relationship is many-to-many. For example, an `Item` can be in more than one `Category` and a `Category` can have multiple `Items`.

Ordinality, or optionality

Ordinality, or optionality, of a relationship determines whether an associated entity exists. For example, we have a bidirectional one-to-one association between `User` and `BillingInfo`, and every user need not always have billing information, so the relationship is *optional*. However, `BillingInfo` always belongs to a `User` and hence the optionality for the `BillingInfo`-`User` association is false.

Having established the basic concepts of domain modeling, we can now start discussing how the domain model is persisted using the EJB 3 Java Persistence API and actually begin implementing our domain model.

7.1.4 *The EJB 3 Java Persistence API*

In contrast to EJB 2 entity beans, the EJB 3 Java Persistence API (JPA) is a metadata-driven POJO technology. That is, to save data held in Java objects into a database, our objects are not required to implement an interface, extend a class, or fit into a framework pattern. In fact, persisted objects need not contain a single inline statement of JPA. All we have to do is code our domain model as plain Java objects and use annotations or the XML to give the persistence provider the following information:

- What our domain objects are (for example, using the `@Entity` and `@Embedded` annotations)

- How to uniquely identify a persisted domain object (for example, using the `@Id` annotation)

- What the relations between objects are (for example, using the `@OneToOne`, `@OneToMany`, and `@ManyToMany` annotations)

- How the domain object is mapped to database tables (for example, using various object-relational mapping annotations like `@Table`, `@Column`, or `@JoinColumn`)

As you can see, although O/R mapping using the JPA (or any other O/R frameworks like Hibernate) is a great improvement over entity beans or JDBC, automated persistence is still an inherently complex activity. The large number of persistence-related annotations and wide array of possible arrangements is a result of this fact. To make it all as digestible as possible, we'll only cover the first three items in this

> ## SQL-centric persistence: Spring JdbcTemplate and iBATIS
>
> Like many of us, if you are comfortable with SQL and JDBC and like the control and flexibility offered by do-it-yourself, hands-on approaches, O/R in its full-blown, black magic, automated form may not be for you. As a matter of fact, O/R tools like Hibernate and the EJB 3 Java Persistence API (JPA) might seem like overkill, even despite the long-term benefits offered by a higher-level API.
>
> If this is the case, you should give tools like Spring `JdbcTemplate` and iBATIS a very close look. Both of these tools do an excellent job abstracting out really low-level, verbose JDBC mechanics while keeping the SQL/database-centric feel of persistence intact.
>
> However, you should give O/R frameworks and JPA a fair chance. You just might find that these options make your life a lot easier and OO-centric, freeing you to use your neuron cycles to solve business problems instead.

chapter, leaving the fourth (how the domain object is mapped to database tables) to chapter 8. Moreover, we'll stray from our pattern of presenting and then analyzing a complete example, since the wide breadth of the persistence API would not yield to the pattern nicely. Instead, we are going to explore the persistence API by visiting each step in our list using specific cases from the ActionBazaar example, analyzing features and intricacies along the way. Not straying from previous chapters, however, we'll still focus on using annotations, leaving the description of deployment descriptor equivalents for a brief discussion in chapter 11.

7.1.5 *Domain objects as Java classes*

Let's now get our feet wet by examining some code for JPA. We'll pick a representatively complex domain object, Category, and see what it might look like in Java code. The Category class in listing 7.1 is a simple POJO class that is a domain object built using Java. This is a candidate for becoming an entity and being persisted to the database. As we mentioned earlier, the Category domain object may have the category name and modification date as attributes. In addition, there are a number of instance variables in the POJO class that express domain relationships instead of simple attributes of a category. The id attribute also does more than simply serving as a data holder for business logic and identifies an instance of the Category object. You'll learn about identity in the next section.

Listing 7.1   Category domain object in Java

```
package ejb3inaction.actionbazaar.model;
import java.sql.Date;
                                          ❶  Plain Java object
public class Category {          ◁┐
    protected Long id;           ◁─❷  Instance variable uniquely identifying object

                                         ❸  Object attribute
    protected String name;              instance variable
    protected Date modificationDate;

    protected Set<Item> items;                    ❹  Instance
    protected Category parentCategory;               variables for
    protected Set<Category> subCategories;           relationships

    public Category() {}

    public Long getId() {
        return this.id;
    }

    public void setId(Long id) {
        this.id = id;
    }

    public String getName() {
        return this.name;
    }

    public void setName(String name) {
        this.name = name;
    }
                                        Getters and setters  ❺
    public Date getModificationDate() {    for each instance
        return this.modificationDate;            variable
    }

    public void setModificationDate(Date modificationDate) {
        this.modificationDate = modificationDate;
    }

    public Set<Item> getItems() {
        return this.items;
    }

    public void setItems(Set<Item> items) {
        this.items = items;
    }

    public Set<Category> getSubCategories() {
        return this.subCategories;
    }
```

```
    public void setSubCategories(Set<Category> subCategories) {
        this.subCategories = subCategories;
    }

    public Category getParentCategory() {
        return this.parentCategory;
    }

    public void setParentCategory(Category parentCategory) {
        this.parentCategory = parentCategory;
    }
}
```

Getters and setters for each instance variable ❺

The `Category` POJO ❶ has a number of protected instance fields ❸ ❹, each with corresponding setters and getters that conform to JavaBeans naming conventions ❺. In case you are unfamiliar with them, JavaBeans rules state that all instance variables should be nonpublic and made accessible via methods that follow the *getXX* and *setXX* pattern used in listing 7.1, where *XX* is the name of the property (instance variable). Other than `name` and `modificationDate`, all the other properties have a specific role in domain modeling and persistence. The `id` field is used to store a unique number that identifies the category ❷. The `items` property stores all the items stored under a category and represents a many-to-many relationship between items and categories. The `parentCategory` property represents a self-referential many-to-one relationship between parent and child categories. The `subCategories` property maintains a one-to-many relationship between a category and its subcategories.

The `Category` class as it stands in listing 7.1 is a perfectly acceptable Java implementation of a domain object. The problem is that the EJB 3 persistence provider has no way of distinguishing the fact that the `Category` class is a domain object instead of just another random Java object used for business logic, presentation, or some other purpose. Moreover, note that the properties representing relationships do not make direction or multiplicity clear. Lastly, the persistence provider also needs to be told about the special purpose of the `id` property. We'll start solving some of these problems by using JPA annotations next, starting with identifying the `Category` class as a domain object.

7.2 Implementing domain objects with JPA

In the previous few sections you learned about domain modeling concepts and identified part of the ActionBazaar domain model. Also, we briefly introduced some commonly used metadata annotations supported by JPA. In this section, you'll see some of the JPA annotations in action as we implement part of the domain model using the EJB 3 JPA. We'll start with the @Entity annotation that converts a POJO to an entity. Then you'll learn about field- and property-based persistence and entity identity. Finally, we'll discuss embedded objects.

7.2.1 *The @Entity annotation*

The @Entity annotation marks a POJO as a domain object that can be uniquely identified. You may think of the annotation as the persistence counterpart of the @Stateless, @Stateful, and @MessageDriven annotations. Mark the Category class as an entity as follows:

```
@Entity
public class Category {
    ...
    public Category() { ... }
    public Category(String name) { ... }
    ...
}
```

As the code snippet demonstrates, all nonabstract entities must have either a public or a protected no-argument constructor. The constructor is used to create a new entity instance by using the new operator as follows:

```
Category category = new Category();
```

One of the coolest features of JPA is that since entities are POJOs, they support a full range of OO features like inheritance and polymorphism, with a few persistence-related nuances thrown in. You can have an entity extend either another entity or even a nonentity class. For example, it would be good design to extend both the Seller and Bidder domain object classes from a common User class, as shown in figure 7.4.

As the code snippet that follows shows, this class could store information common to all users like the user ID, username, and email address:

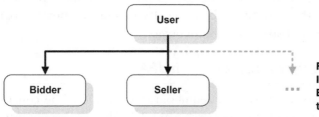

Figure 7.4
Inheritance support with entities.
Bidder and Seller entities extend
the User entity class.

```
@Entity
public class User {      ◁⏌  Parent entity class
    ...
    String userId;
    String username;
    String email;
    ...
}

@Entity
public class Seller extends User { ...     ◁⏋
                                            ┃  Entity
                                            ┃  subclasses
@Entity
public class Bidder extends User { ...     ◁⏌
```

Because the parent User class is declared an entity, all the inherited fields like username and email are persisted when either the Seller or Bidder entity is saved. A slightly counterintuitive nuance you should note is that this would not be the case if the User class were not an entity itself. Rather, the value of the inherited properties would be discarded when either Seller or Bidder is persisted. The preceding code snippet also demonstrates an interesting weakness—the User class could be persisted on its own, which is not necessarily desirable or appropriate application behavior. One way to avoid this problem is to declare the User class abstract, since abstract entities are allowed but cannot be directly instantiated or saved. In any case, this is probably better OO design anyway. Since JPA supports entity inheritance, the relationship between entities and queries may be polymorphic. We discuss handling polymorphic queries in chapter 10.

Obviously the ultimate goal of persistence is to save the properties of the entity into the database (such as the name and modification date for the Category entity in listing 7.1). However, things are not as simple as they seem, and there are a few twists regarding entity data persistence that you need to have a good grasp of.

7.2.2 *Persisting entity data*

An entity, because it is a persistent object, has some state that is stored into the database. In this section we discuss access types, how to define a transient field, and data types supported by JPA.

Field- vs. property-based persistence

An entity maintains its state by using either fields or properties (via setter and getter methods). Although JavaBeans object property-naming conventions have been widely used in the Java platform for a good number of years, some developers consider these conventions to be overkill and would rather access instance variables directly. The good news is that JPA supports this paradigm (whether it should is an open question—we'll express our viewpoint in a moment). Defining O/R mapping using fields or instance variables of entity is known as *field-based access*, and using O/R mapping with properties is known as *property-based access*.

If you want to use *field-based access*, you can declare all your POJO persisted data fields public or protected and ask the persistence provider to ignore getters/setters altogether. You would only have to provide some indication on at least one of the instance variables that they are to be used for persistence directly. You can do this by using the @Id annotation that we'll discuss next that applies to either a property or a field. Depending on your inclination, this transparent flexibility may or may not seem a little counterintuitive. In the early releases of the EJB 3 specification, the @Entity annotation had an element named accessType for explicitly specifying the persistence data storage type as either FIELD or PROPERTY. As you'll see, O/R mapping using XML provides an element named access to specify the access type. However, many developers do not like this element and want the additional flexibility of having the JPA provider dynamically determine the access type based on entity field usage patterns.

The following snippet shows what field-based persistence might look like:

```
@Entity
public class Category {
    @Id
    public Long id;

    public String name;
    public Date modificationDate;

    public Category() {}
}
```

Here, the persistence provider would infer that the id, name, and modification-Date public fields should be persisted since the @Id annotation is used on the id field. The annotations would have been applied to getters if we did not intend to use fields for persistence instead of properties.

> **NOTE** Annotations used with a setter method are ignored by the persistence provider for property-based access.

One caveat in choosing between field- and property-based persistence is that both are one-way streets; you cannot mix and match access types in the same entity or in any entity in the POJO hierarchy. Field-based persistence is a one-way street in another important way: you give up the OO benefits of encapsulation/ data hiding that you get from getters and setters if you expose the persistence fields to be directly manipulated by clients. Even if you used field-based access, we recommend that you make the fields private and expose the fields to be modified by getter/setter method.

For example, property setters are often used in nontrivial applications to validate the new data being set or to standardize POJO data in some fashion. In our example, we could automatically convert `Category` names to uppercase in the `setName` method:

```
public void setName(String name) {
    this.name = name.toUpperCase();
}
```

In general, we highly recommend that you use field-based access with accessor methods or property-based access. It is much easier to have it and not need it than to find out that you need it later on and have to engage in a large-scale, painful refactoring effort in the face of deadlines.

By default, the persistence provider saves all entity fields or properties that have JavaBeans-style public or protected setters and getters (for example, `get-Name` and `setName` in listing 7.1). In addition, persisted setters and getters cannot be declared `final`, as the persistence provider may need to override them.

Defining a transient field

If necessary, you can stop an entity property from being persisted by marking the getter with the `@Transient` annotation. A transient field is typically useful for caching some data that you do not want to save in the database. For example, the `Category` entity could have a property named `activeUserCount` that stores the number of active users currently browsing items under the directory or a `generatedName` field that is generated by concatenating the category ID and name. However, saving this runtime information into the database would not make much sense. You could avoid saving the property by using `@Transient` as follows:

```
@Entity
public class Category {
    ...
    @Transient
    protected Long activeUserCount;
    transient public String generatedName

    ...
```

```
        public Long getActiveUserCount() {
        return activeUserCount;
    }


    public void setActiveUserCount(Long activeUserCount) {
        this.activeUserCount = activeUserCount;
    }
    ...
}
```

You could achieve the same effect by using the `@Transient` tag on the getter when using property-based access.

Note that defining a field with the `transient` modifier as we've done with `generatedName` has the same effect as the `@Transient` annotation.

Persistent data types

Before we move on from the topic of persisted POJO data and start exploring identity and relations, we need to discuss exactly what field data can be persisted. Ultimately, persisted fields/properties wind up in a relational database table and have to go through an extremely powerful, high-level API to get there. Because of this fact, there are some restrictions on what data types can be used in a persisted field/property. In general, these restrictions are not very limiting, but you should be aware of them nonetheless. Table 7.1 lists the data types that can be used in a persisted field/property.

Table 7.1   Data types allowable for a persisted field/property

Types	Examples
Java primitives	`int, double, long`
Java primitives wrappers	`java.lang.Integer, java.lang.Double`
String type	`java.lang.String`
Java API `Serializable` types	`java.math.BigInteger, java.sql.Date`
User-defined `Serializable` types	Class that implements `java.io.Serializable`
Array types	`byte[], char[]`
Enumerated type	`{SELLER, BIDDER, CSR, ADMIN}`
Collection of entity types	Set<Category>
Embeddable class	Classes that are defined `@Embeddable`

We'll discuss the @Embeddable annotation after we discuss entity identities. For now, think of an embeddable object as a custom data type for an entity that encapsulates persisted data.

We have already touched on the issue of identity when we talked about uniquely identifying the Category domain object through the id property. Let's now take up the topic of entity identity in greater detail.

7.2.3 *Specifying entity identity*

Every entity of the domain model must be uniquely identifiable. This requirement is due partly to the fact that at some point entities must be persisted into a uniquely identifiable row in a database table (or set of rows in multiple tables). If you are familiar with the concept of database table primary keys, this should come as no surprise. Without primary keys, you would never be able to uniquely identify and retrieve the data you put into a record since you would not know which row it went into after performing the save! The concept of being able to distinguish different instances of the same object holding a different set of data is not completely alien to object-oriented programming either. Consider the equals method in java.lang.Object, meant to be overridden by subclasses as necessary. This method is the OO equivalent of comparing the primary keys of two distinct database records. In most cases, the equals method is implemented by comparing the data that uniquely identifies instances of the same object from one another. In the case of the Category object, you might imagine that the equals method would look like this:

```
public boolean equals (Object other) {
    if (other instanceof Category) {
        return this.name.equals(((Category)other).name)
    } else {
        return false;
    }
}
```

In this case, we would be assuming that the name instance variable uniquely identifies a Category. The name field therefore is the *identity* for the Category object. In listing 7.1, however, we choose the id field as the identity for Category. This choice will be more obvious when we talk about mapping the Category object into a database table. As you'll see, in effect, we choose this instance variable because we get it free from the database as a unique Category identifier, and it is less resource intensive than comparing the java.lang.String name field since it is a numeric java.lang.Long. Another benefit of using the numeric type key is automatic generation. There are several ways of telling the persistence provider where the identity of an entity is stored. Starting with the simplest and ending with the most complex, these are as follows:

- Using the `@Id` annotation
- Using the `@IdClass` annotation
- Using the `@EmbeddedId` annotation

Let's look at each of these mechanisms next.

The @Id annotation

Using the `javax.persistence.Id` annotation is the simplest way of telling the persistence provider where the entity identity is stored. The `@Id` annotation marks a field or property as identity for an entity. Since we are using property-based persistence for the `Category` entity, we could let the API know that we are using the `id` property as the identity by applying the `@Id` annotation to the `getId` method as in the following code snippet. In the case of field-based persistence, the `@Id` annotation would have been applied directly to an instance variable instead.

```
@Entity
public class Category {
    ...
    protected Long id;
    ...

    @Id
    public Long getId() {
        return this.id;
    }

    public void setId(Long id) {
        this.id = id;
    }
    ...
}
```

Because the identity we specify will end up in a database primary key column, there are limitations to what data types an identity might have. EJB 3 supports primitives, primitive wrappers, and `Serializable` types like `java.lang.String`, `java.util.Date`, and `java.sql.Date` as identities. In addition, when choosing numeric types you should avoid types such as `float`, `Float`, `double`, and so forth because of the indeterminate nature of type precision. For example, let's assume that we are using float data as the identity, and specify 103.789 and 103.787 as the identity values for two separate entity instances. If the database rounds these values to two-digit decimal precision before storing the record, both of these values would map to 103.79 and we would have a primary key violation! Another type you should avoid choosing as identifier is TimeStamp.

An important consideration to note is that using the `@Id` annotation on its own works only for identities with just one field or property. In reality, you'll often have to use more than one property or field (known as composite key) to uniquely identify an entity. For sake of illustration, assume that we changed our minds and decided that a `Category` is uniquely identified by its name and creation date. There are two ways we can accomplish this: by using either the `@IdClass` or `@EmbeddedId` annotation.

The @IdClass annotation

In effect, the `@IdClass` annotation enables you to use more than one `@Id` annotation in a sensible way. This is the basic problem with using more than one `@Id` field or property in an entity class: it is not obvious how to compare two instances in an automated fashion. This is especially true since in cases where composite keys are necessary, one or more of the fields that constitute the primary key are often relationship or association fields (or foreign keys in database terminology). For example, although this is not the case for us, the `Bid` domain object might have an identity consisting of the `item` to bid on, the `bidder`, as well as a bid amount:

```
public class Bid {
    private Item item;
    private Bidder bidder;
    private Double amount;
    ...
}
```

In this snippet, both the `item` and `bidder` instance variables represent relationship references to other entities. You could be tempted to combine `item`, `bidder`, and `amount` as a composite key for `Bid`, but remember that it might be the case that neither of the references is simple enough to compare instances using the `equals` method, as it would be for a `java.lang.String` or `java.lang.Long`. This is where a designated `IdClass` comes in. The best way to understand how this works is through an example.

For simplicity, we'll return to our `Category` object with the name and creation date identity. Listing 7.2 shows how the solution might look.

Listing 7.2 Specifying category identity using IdClass

```
public class CategoryPK implements Serializable {
    String name;
    Date createDate;
```
❶ Stored identity fields

```
public CategoryPK() {}     ←─❷ Empty constructor

                                            ❸  equals method
public boolean equals(Object other) {     ←─   comparing identity
    if (other instanceof CategoryPK) {
        final CategoryPK otherCategoryPK = (CategoryPK)other;
        return (otherCategoryPK.name.equals(name) &&
            otherCategoryPK.createDate.equals(createDate));
    }

    return false;
}

public int hashCode() {     ←─❹ Hashcode implementation
    return super.hashCode();
}
}

@Entity
@IdClass(CategoryPK.class)     ←─❺ IdClass specification
public class Category {
    public Category() {}

    @Id
    protected String name;
                                ❻  Identity
    @Id                             fields
    protected Date createDate;
    ...
}
```

As shown in listing 7.2, the `CategoryPK` class is designated as the `IdClass` for `Category` ❻. The `Category` class has two identity fields marked by the `@Id` annotation: `name` and `creationDate` ❻. These two identity fields are mirrored in the `CategoryPK` class ❶. The constructor ❷ is used to create an instance of the primary key object. The `equals` method implemented in `CategoryPK` compares the two mirrored identity fields to determine if two given identities are equal ❸. The magic here is that at runtime, the persistence provider determines if two `Category` objects are equal by copying the marked `@Id` fields into the corresponding fields of the `CategoryPK` object and using `CategoryPK.equals`. Note that any `IdClass` must be `Serializable` and must provide a valid `hashCode` implementation ❹. In effect, all that is happening here is that we are specifying exactly how to compare multiple identity fields using an external `IdClass` ❺. The disadvantage to using `@IdClass` is the slight redundancy and associated maintainability problems in repeating the definition of identity fields in the entity and the `IdClass`. In our case the `name` and createDate fields are defined in both the Category and CategoryPK classes. However, the IdClass approach keeps your domain model clutter free, especially as opposed to the slightly awkward object model proposed by the third approach, which uses the @EmbeddedId annotation.

The @EmbeddedId annotation

Using the @EmbeddedId annotation is like moving the IdClass right into your entity and using the identity fields nested inside it to store entity data. Take a look at what we mean in listing 7.3, which rewrites listing 7.2 using @EmbeddedId.

Listing 7.3   Specifying category identity using EmbeddedId

```
@Embeddable    ←──❶
public class CategoryPK {
    String name;
    Date createDate;

    public CategoryPK() {}

    public boolean equals(Object other) {                          ←─┐
        if (other instanceof CategoryPK) {                           │
            final CategoryPK otherCategoryPK = (CategoryPK)other;    │
            return (otherCategoryPK.name.equals(name) &&             │
                otherCategoryPK.createDate.equals(createDate));      │
        }                                                          ❷ │
                                                                     │
        return false;                                                │
    }                                                                │
                                                                     │
    public int hashCode() {                                        ←─┘
        return super.hashCode();
    }
}

@Entity
public class Category {
    public Category() {}

    @EmbeddedId    ←──❸
    protected CategoryPK categoryPK;
    ...
}
```

In listing 7.3, notice that the identity fields, name and createDate, are absent altogether from the Category class. Instead, an Embeddable object instance, categoryPK ❶, is designated as the identity using the @EmbeddedId annotation ❸. The

CategoryPK object itself is almost identical to the IdClass used in listing 7.1 and contains the name and createDate fields. We still need to implement the equals and hashCode methods ❷. The only difference is that the @Embedded object need not be Serializable. In effect, the object designated as @EmbeddedId is expected to be a simple data holder encapsulating only the identity fields. Note that the @Id annotation is missing altogether since it is redundant. As a matter of fact, you are not allowed to use Id or IdClass in conjunction with EmbeddedId. As you can see, although this approach saves typing, it is a little awkward to justify in terms of object modeling (even the variable name, categoryPK, is more reminiscent of relational databases than OO). It is a little unwieldy too. Imagine having to write category.categoryPK.name to use the name field for any other purpose than as a primary key, as opposed to using category.name. However, whatever method you choose is ultimately a matter of personal taste.

Unless you really need a composite primary key because you are stuck with a legacy database, we don't recommend using it and instead recommend a simple generated key (also known as surrogate key) that you'll learn about in chapter 8.

One concept is critical: identities can only be defined *once* in an entire entity hierarchy. Having had a sufficient introduction to the idea of entities and identities, you are now ready to explore the @Embeddable annotation in greater detail.

7.2.4 *The @Embeddable annotation*

Let's step back a second from the idea of identities into the world of pure OO domain modeling. Are all domain objects always identifiable on their own? How about objects that are simply used as convenient data holders/groupings inside other objects? An easy example would be an Address object used inside a User object as an elegant OO alternative to listing street address, city, zip, and so forth directly as fields of the User object. It would be overkill for the Address object to have an identity since it is not likely to be used outside a User object. This is exactly the kind of scenario for which the @Embeddable annotation was designed. The @Embeddable annotation is used to designate persistent objects that need not have an identity of their own. This is because Embeddable objects are identified by the entity objects they are nested inside and never persisted or accessed on their own. Put another way, Embeddable objects share their identities with the enclosing entity. An extreme case of this is the @EmbeddedId situation where the Embeddable object *is* the identity. Listing 7.4 contains a user/address example to help you gain a better understanding of the most commonly used Embeddable object semantic patterns.

Listing 7.4   Using embedded objects

```
@Embeddable                    ◁━❶ Embeddable address
public class Address {
    protected String streetLine1;
    protected String streetLine2;
    protected String city;
    protected String state;
    protected String zipCode;
    protected String country;
    ...
}

@Entity
public class User {
    @Id
    protected Long id;             ◁━❷ Shared identity
    protected String username;
    protected String firstName;
    protected String lastName;
    @Embedded
    protected Address address;     ◁━❸ Embedded address
    protected String email;
    protected String phone;
    ...
}
```

In listing 7.4, the embeddable `Address` object ❶ is embedded inside a `User` entity ❸ and shares the identity marked with the `@Id` annotation ❷. It is illegal for an `@Embeddable` object to have an identity. Also, the EJB 3 API does not support nested embedded objects. In most cases, embedded objects are stored in the same database record as the entity and are only materialized in the OO world. We'll show you how this works in chapter 8.

Our discussion of embedded objects rounds out our coverage of domain objects. We'll take a look at domain object relationships next.

7.3 *Entity relationships*

Earlier in the chapter, we explored the concepts of domain relationships, direction, and multiplicity. As a review, we'll summarize those concepts here before diving into the details of how to specify domain relationships using JPA. As you might have noted in our domain object code samples, a relationship essentially means that one entity holds an object reference to another. For example, the `Bid` object holds a reference to the Item object the bid was placed on. Therefore, a relationship exists between the Bid and Item domain objects. Recall that relationships can be either unidirectional or bidirectional. The relationship between Bidder and Bid in figure 7.3 is unidirectional, since the Bidder object has a reference to Bid but the Bid object has no reference to the Bidder. The Bid-Item relationship, on the other hand, is bidirectional, meaning both the Bidder and Item objects have references to each other. Relationships can be one-to-one, one-to-many, many-to-one, or many-to-many. Each of these relationship types is expressed in JPA through an annotation. Table 7.2 lists the relationship annotations we'll discuss in the following sections.

Table 7.2 Domain relation types and corresponding annotations

Type of relationship	Annotation
One-to-one	@OneToOne
One-to-many	@OneToMany
Many-to-one	@ManyToOne
Many-to-many	@ManyToMany

We explore each annotation using examples next.

7.3.1 @OneToOne

The @OneToOne annotation is used to mark uni- and bidirectional one-to-one relationships. Although in most systems one-to-one relationships are rare, they make perfect sense for domain modeling. In fact, our ActionBazaar example in figure 7.3 has no one-to-one relationship. However, we can imagine that the User domain object parent to both Seller and Bidder has a one-to-one relationship with a BillingInfo object. The BillingInfo object might contain billing data on a user's credit card, bank account, and so on. Let's start by seeing what a unidirectional relationship would look like.

Unidirectional one-to-one

For the time, being, let's assume that the User object has a reference to the BillingInfo but not vice versa. In other words, the relationship is unidirectional, as shown in figure 7.5.

Figure 7.5   A one-to-one relationship between the User and BillingInfo entities. A User may have at most one instance of the BillingInfo object and the BillingInfo object cannot exist without a User.

Listing 7.5 illustrates this relationship.

Listing 7.5   Unidirectional one-to-one relationship

```
@Entity
public class User {
    @Id
    protected String userId;
    protected String email;               ❶ One-to-one relationship between
    @OneToOne                                User and BillingInfo
    protected BillingInfo billingInfo;
}

@Entity
public class BillingInfo {
    @Id
    protected Long billingId;
    protected String creditCardType;
    protected String creditCardNumber;
    protected String nameOnCreditCard;
    protected Date creditCardExpiration;
    protected String bankAccountNumber;
    protected String bankName;
    protected String routingNumber;
}
```

In listing 7.5, the User class holds a BillingInfo reference in the persisted billingInfo field. Since the billingInfo variable holds only one instance of the BillingInfo class, the relationship is one-to-one. The @OneToOne annotation indicates that the persistence provider should maintain this relationship in the database ❶. Let's take a closer look at the definition of the @OneToOne annotation to better understand its features:

```
@Target({METHOD, FIELD}) @Retention(RUNTIME)
public @interface OneToOne {
    Class targetEntity() default void.class;
    CascadeType[] cascade() default {};
    FetchType fetch() default EAGER;
```

```
        boolean optional() default true;
        String mappedBy() default "";
    }
```

First, note that this annotation can be applied to either fields or properties since the `Target` is specified to be `METHOD`, `FIELD`. We are using field-based persistence for the examples to keep things simple. The `targetEntity` element tells the persistence provider what the related entity class is. In most cases, this is redundant since the container can infer the class from the class of the field or the return type of the property getter and setter. However, you can specify it explicitly anyway if you prefer. You'll see a case in which this element is indispensable when we explore one-to-many relations. The `cascade` and `fetch` parameters are best discussed after we introduce object-relational mapping in the next chapter. For now, suffice it to say that `cascade` controls what happens to related data when the relationship is altered or deleted and `fetch` specifies when and how the related fields are populated from database tables.

Listing 7.6 shows an example of how the `@OneToOne` annotation might be applied to a property instead of a field.

Listing 7.6 Property-based unidirectional one-to-one relationship

```
@Entity
public class User {
    private Long userId;
    private String email;
    private BillingInfo billing;
    ...                                        One-to-one relationship
    @OneToOne                              ◁─┘ using properties
    public BillingInfo getBilling() {
        this.billing;
    }

    public void setBilling(BillingInfo billing) {
        this.billing = billing;
    }
}

@Entity
public class BillingInfo {
    private Long billingId;
    private String creditCardType;
    ...
}
```

The `optional` element tells the persistence provider if the related object must always be present. By default, this is set to `true`, which means that a corresponding related object need not exist for the entity to exist. In our case, not every user always has billing information (for example if the user just signed up), so the relationship is *optional* and the `billing` field can sometimes be `null`. If the `optional` parameter is set to `false`, the entity cannot exist if the relationship or association does not hold. In other words, no `User` without `BillingInfo` could ever exist. You'll see the `mappedBy` parameter in action in the next section when we discuss bidirectional associations.

Bidirectional one-to-one

The real point of having domain relationships between entities is to be able to reach one entity from another. In our previous example, we can easily reach the billing information through the `billingInfo` reference when we have an instance of a `User`. In some cases, you need to be able to access related entities from either side of the relationship (admittedly, this is rare for one-to-one relationships). For example, the ActionBazaar application may periodically check for credit card expiration dates and notify users of imminently expiring credit cards. As a result, the application should be able to access user information from a given `Billing-Info` entity and the `User`-`BillingInfo` relationship should really be bidirectional. In effect, bidirectional one-to-one relationships are implemented using two `@One-ToOne` annotations pointing to each other on either side of the bidirectional relationship. Let's see how this works in listing 7.7 by refactoring the code from listing 7.5.

Listing 7.7 Bidirectional one-to-one relationship

```
@Entity
public class User {
    @Id
    protected String userId;
    protected String email;                    ❶ One-to-one
    @OneToOne                                     relationship
    protected BillingInfo billingInfo;
}

@Entity
public class BillingInfo {
    @Id
    protected Long billingId;
    protected String creditCardType;
    ..
```

```
    protected String routingNumber;
    @OneToOne(mappedBy="billingInfo", optional="false");
    protected User user;
}
```

2 Reciprocal relationship to User

In listing 7.7, the User class still has a relationship to the BillingInfo class through the billingInfo variable **1**. However, in this case the relationship is bidirectional because the BillingInfo class also has a reference to the User class through the user field **2**. The @OneToOne annotation on the user field has two more interesting things going on. The first is the mappedBy="billingInfo" specification **2**. This tells the container that the "owning" side of the relationship exists in the User class's billingInfo instance variable. The concept of a *relationship owner* doesn't originate from domain modeling. It exists as a convenience to define the database mapping for a relationship only once instead of repeating the same mapping for both directions of a relationship. You'll see this concept in action in chapter 8 when we describe O/R mapping. For now, simply note the role of the mappedBy attribute.

The second interesting feature of the @OneToOne annotation on the user field is that the optional parameter is set to false this time. This means that a Billing-Info object cannot exist without a related User object. After all, why bother storing credit card or bank account information that is not related to an existing user?

7.3.2 *@OneToMany and @ManyToOne*

As you might have gathered from the ActionBazaar domain model in figure 7.3, one-to-many and many-to-one relationships are the most common in enterprise systems. In this type of relationship, one entity will have two or more references of another. In the Java world, this usually means that an entity has a collection-type field such as java.util.Set or java.util.List storing multiple instances of another entity. Also, if the association between two entities is bidirectional, one side of the association is one-to-many and the opposite side of the association is many-to-one.

In figure 7.6, the relationship between Bid and Item is one-to-many from the perspective of the Item object, while it is many-to-one from the perspective of

Figure 7.6   Every Item has one or more Bids where more than one Bid may be placed on an Item. Therefore, the relationship between Item and Bid is one-to-many whereas the relationship between Bid and Item is many-to-one.

the Bid. Similar to the one-to-one case, we can mark the owning side of the relationship by using the mappedBy column on the entity that is not the owner of the relationship. We'll analyze these relationships further by actually coding the Bid-Item relationship (see listing 7.8).

Listing 7.8   One-to-many bidirectional relationship

```
@Entity
public class Item {
    @Id
    protected Long itemId;
    protected String title;
    protected String description;
    protected Date postdate;
    ...
    @OneToMany(mappedBy="item")         ◁── One-to-many
    protected Set<Bid> bids;                 relationship
    ...
}

@Entity
public class Bid {
    @Id
    protected Long bidId;
    protected Double amount;
    protected Date timestamp;            Corresponding
    ...                                  many-to-one
    @ManyToOne                       ◁── relationship
    protected Item item;
    ...
}
```

One-to-many relationship

Listing 7.8 shows that the Item domain object has a Set of Bid objects that it has references to. To signify this domain relationship, the bids field is marked with a @OneToMany annotation. There are a few nuances about the @OneToMany annotation we should talk about. To explore them, take a quick look at the definition of the annotation:

```
@Target({METHOD, FIELD}) @Retention(RUNTIME)
public @interface OneToMany {
    Class targetEntity() default void.class;
    CascadeType[] cascade() default {};
    FetchType fetch() default LAZY;
    String mappedBy() default "";
}
```

As you'll notice, this is literally identical to the definition of the `@OneToOne` annotation, including the `mappedBy` element. As a matter of fact, the only element we need to discuss further is `targetEntity`. Remember that this element is used to specify the class of the related entity if it is not immediately obvious. In the `@OneToMany` annotation used in listing 7.8, this parameter is omitted since we are using Java generics to specify the fact that the `bids` variable stores a `Set` of `Bid` objects:

```
@OneToMany(mappedBy="item")
protected Set<Bid> bids;
```

Imagine, however, what would happen if we did not use generics on the `Set`. In this case, it would be impossible for the persistence provider to determine what entity the `Item` object has a relation to. This is exactly the situation the `targetEntity` parameter is designed for. We would use it to specify the entity at the other end of the one-to-many relationship as follows:

```
@OneToMany(targetEntity=Bid.class,mappedBy="item")
protected Set bids;
```

Many-to-one as owning-side of relationship

Also, note the `mappedBy="item"` value on the `@OneToMany` annotation. This value specifies the owning side of the bidirectional relationship as the `items` field of the `Bid` entity.

Because the relationship is bidirectional, the `Bid` domain object has a reference to an `Item` through the `item` variable. The `@ManyToOne` annotation on the `item` variable tells the persistence provider that more than one `Bid` entity could hold references to the same `Item` instance. For bidirectional one-to-many relationships, `ManyToOne` is always the owning side of the relationship. Because of this fact, the `mappedBy` element does not exist in the definition of the `@ManyToOne` annotation:

```
@Target({METHOD, FIELD}) @Retention(RUNTIME)
public @interface ManyToOne {
    Class targetEntity() default void.class;
    CascadeType[] cascade() default {};
    FetchType fetch() default EAGER;
    boolean optional() default true;
}
```

Other than this minor difference, all the other elements of the `@ManyToOne` annotation have the same purpose and functionality as the elements in the `@OneToOne` and `@OneToMany` annotations.

The last type of domain relationship is many-to-many, which we'll discuss next.

7.3.3 *@ManyToMany*

While not as common as one-to-many, many-to-many relationships occur quite frequently in enterprise applications. In this type of relationship, both sides might have multiple references to related entities. In our ActionBazaar example, the relationship between `Category` and `Item` is many-to-many, as shown in figure 7.7.

Figure 7.7   The relationship between Category and Item is many-to-many because every category may have one or more items, whereas each item may belong to more than one category.

That is, a category can contain multiple items and an item can belong to multiple categories. For example, a category named "Sixties Fashion" could contain items like "Bellbottom Pants" and "Platform Shoes." "Bellbottom Pants" and "Platform Shoes" could also be listed under "Uncomfortable and Outdated Clothing." Although many-to-many relationships can be unidirectional, they are often bidirectional because of their crossconnecting, mutually independent nature. Not too surprisingly, a bidirectional many-to-many relationship is often represented by `@ManyToMany` annotations on opposite sides of the relationship. As with the one-to-one and one-many relationships, you can identify the owning side of the relationship by specifying `mappedBy` on the "subordinate" entity; you may have to use the `targetEntity` attribute if you're not using Java generics.

The definition for `@ManyToMany` is identical to `OneToMany` and holds no special intricacies beyond those already discussed:

```
@Target({METHOD, FIELD}) @Retention(RUNTIME)
public @interface ManyToMany {
    Class targetEntity() default void.class;
    CascadeType[] cascade() default {};
    FetchType fetch() default LAZY;
    String mappedBy() default "";
}
```

To round off our discussion of many-to-many relationships, listing 7.9 shows how the `Item`-`Category` relationship might look.

Listing 7.9   Many-to-many relationship between Category and Items

```
@Entity
public class Category {
```

```
    @Id
    protected Long categoryId;
    protected String name;            Owning
    ...                               many-to-many
    @ManyToMany                  ◁┘   relationship
    protected Set<Item> items;
    ...
}

@Entity
public class Item {
    @Id
    protected Long itemId;
    protected String title;           Subordinate
    ...                               many-to-many
    @ManyToMany(mappedBy="items")  ◁┘ relationship
    protected Set<Category> categories;
    ...
}
```

In listing 7.9, the `Category` object's `items` variable is marked by the `@ManyToMany` annotation and is the owning side of the bidirectional association. In contrast, the `Item` object's `categories` variable signifies the subordinate bidirectional many-to-many association. As in the case of one-to-many relationships, the `@ManyToMany` annotation is missing the `optional` attribute. This is because an empty `Set` or `List` implicitly means an optional relationship, meaning that the entity can exist even if no associations do.

As a handy reference, we summarize the various elements available in the `@OneToOne`, `@OneToMany`, `@ManyToOne`, and `@ManyToMany` annotations in table 7.3.

Table 7.3 Elements available in the @OneToOne, @OneToMany, @ManyToOne, and @ManyToMany annotations

Element	@OneToOne	@OneToMany	@ManyToOne	@ManyToMany
targetEntity	Yes	Yes	Yes	Yes
cascade	Yes	Yes	Yes	Yes
fetch	Yes	Yes	Yes	Yes
optional	Yes	No	Yes	No
mappedBy	Yes	Yes	No	Yes

> ### RIP: container-managed relationships
>
> If you have used EJB 2, you might be familiar with the container-managed relationship (CMR) feature of entity beans with bidirectional relationships. This feature monitored changes on either side of the relationship and updated the other side automatically. CMR is not supported in this version because entities can possibly be used outside of containers. However, mimicking this feature is not too hard using a few extra lines of code. Let us take the `User-BillingInfo` one-to-one relationship, for example. The code for changing the `BillingInfo` object for a `User` and making sure both sides of the relationship are still accurate would look like this:
>
> ```
> user.setBilling(billing);
> billing.setUser(user);
> ```

7.4 *Summary*

In this chapter, we discussed basic domain modeling concepts: entities, relationships, and how to define them using JPA. The lightweight API makes creating rich, elegant, object-oriented domain models a simple matter of applying annotations or deployment descriptor settings to plain Java objects. The even greater departure from the heavyweight, framework code–laden approach of EJB 2 is the fact that the new persistence API can be separated altogether from the container, as you'll see in upcoming chapters.

It is interesting to note that the API doesn't directly control relationship multiplicity. In the case of one-to-one and many-to-one relationships, the `optional` element somewhat specifies the multiplicity of the relationship. However, in the case of one-to-many and many-to-many relationships, the API does not enforce multiplicity at all. It is instead the responsibility of the programmer to control the size of the collection holding entity references (`java.util.Set` objects in our examples) and therefore control multiplicity.

In chapter 8 we move on to the next step in building the ActionBazaar persistence layer and show you how to map the entities and relationships we created to the database using object-relational mapping.

Object-relational
mapping

In the previous chapter, we used EJB 3 JPA features to create a POJO domain model that supported a full range of OO features, including inheritance. We discussed entities, embedded objects, and the relationships between them using EJB 3 annotations. In this chapter, you'll learn how to persist our domain model into a relational database using object-relational mapping (ORM), which is the basis for JPA. In effect, ORM specifies how sets of Java objects, including references between them, are mapped to rows and columns in database tables. The first part of this chapter briefly discusses the difference between the object-oriented and relational world, also known as "impedance mismatch." Later sections of the chapter explore the ORM features of the EJB 3 JPA.

If you are a seasoned enterprise developer, you are probably comfortable with relational databases. If this is not the case, then refer to appendix B for a primer on some relatively obscure relational database concepts such as normalization and sequence columns that you must grasp to have a clear understanding of the intricacies of O/R mapping.

We start our discussion by taking a look at the basic motivation behind O/R mapping, the so-called impedance mismatch. Then we'll begin our analysis by mapping domain objects, and move on to mapping relations. Finally we'll examine the concept of map inheritance and you'll learn about the inheritance strategies supported by JPA.

8.1 *The impedance mismatch*

The term *impedance mismatch* refers to the differences in the OO and relational paradigms and difficulties in application development that arise from these differences. The persistence layer where the domain model resides is where the impedance mismatch is usually the most apparent. The root of the problem lies in the differing fundamental objectives of both technologies.

Recall that when a Java object holds a reference to another, the actual referred object is not copied over into the referring object. In other words, Java accesses objects by reference and not by value. For example, two different `Item` objects containing the same `category` instance variable value really point to the same `Category` object in the JVM. This fact frees us from space efficiency concerns in implementing domain models with a high degree of conceptual abstraction. If this were not the case, we'd probably store the identity of the referred `Category` object (perhaps in an `int` variable) inside the `Item` and materialize the link when necessary. This is in fact almost exactly what is done in the relational world.

The JVM also offers the luxury of inheritance and polymorphism (by means that are very similar to the object reference feature) that does not exist in the relational world. Lastly, as we mentioned in the previous chapter, a rich domain model object includes behavior (methods) in addition to attributes (data in instance variables). Databases tables, on the other hand, inherently encapsulate only rows, columns, and constraints, and not business logic. These differences mean that the relational and OO model of the same conceptual problem look very different, especially for an appropriately normalized database created by an experienced DBA. Table 8.1 summarizes some of the overt mismatches between the object and relational worlds.

Table 8.1   The impedance mismatch: obvious differences between the object and relational worlds

OO Model (Java)	Relational Model
Object, classes	Table, rows
Attributes, properties	Columns
Identity	Primary key
Relationship/reference to other entity	Foreign key
Inheritance/polymorphism	Not supported
Methods	Indirect parallel to SQL logic, stored procedures, triggers.
Code is portable	Not necessarily portable, depending on vendor

In the following sections, we'll crystallize the object-relational mismatch a little more by looking at a few corner cases while saving a persistence layer domain model into the database. (As you'll recall from chapter 2, a *corner case* is a problem or situation that occurs only outside normal operating parameters.) We'll also discuss problems in mapping objects to database tables and provide a brief overview of ORM.

8.1.1   *Mapping objects to databases*

The most basic persistence layer for a Java application could consist of saving and retrieving domain objects using the JDBC API directly. To flush out the particularly rough spots in the object-relational mismatch, we'll assume automated ORM does not exist and that we are following the direct JDBC route to persistence. Later we'll see that the EJB 3 Persistence API irons out these rough spots through simple configuration. Scott Ambler has written an interesting article that discusses the problem of mapping objects to a relational database (www.agiledata.org/essays/mappingObjects.html).

One-to-one mapping

As we discussed in the previous chapter, one-to-one relationships between entities, though rare in applications, make a great deal of sense in the domain-modeling world. For example, the User and BillingInfo objects represent two logically separate concepts in the real world (we assume) that are bound by a one-to-one relationship. Moreover, we also know that it does not make very much sense for a BillingInfo object to exist without an associated User. The relationship could be unidirectional from User to BillingInfo. Figure 8.1 shows this relationship, and listing 8.1 implements it.

Listing 8.1   One-to-one relationship between User and BillingInfo

```java
public class User {
    protected String userId;
    protected String email;
    protected BillingInfo billing;        ◁⎯  Object reference for
}                                          ❶  one-to-one relationship

public class BillingInfo {
    protected String creditCardType;
    protected String creditCardNumber;
    protected String nameOnCreditCard;
    protected Date creditCardExpiration;
    protected String bankAccountNumber;
    protected String bankName;
    protected String routingNumber;
}
```

From an OO perspective, it would make sense for the database tables storing this data to mirror the Java implementation in listing 8.1. In this scheme, two different tables, USERS and BILLING_INFO, would have to be created, with the billing object reference in the User object ❶ translated into a foreign key to the BILLING_INFO table's key in the USERS table (perhaps called BILLING_ID). The problem is

Figure 8.1   A unidirectional one-to-one (optional) relationship between User and BillingInfo

that this scheme does not make complete sense in the relational world. As a matter of fact, since the objects are merely expressing a one-to-one relationship, normalization would dictate that the USERS and BILLING_INFO tables be merged into one. This would eliminate the almost pointless BILLING_INFO table and the redundant foreign key in the USERS table. The extended USERS table could look like this:

```
USER_ID                  NOT NULL, PRIMARY KEY  NUMBER
EMAIL                    NOT NULL               VARCHAR2(255)
CREDIT_CARD_TYPE                                VARCHAR2(255)
CREDIT_CARD_NUMBER                              VARCHAR2(255)
NAME_ON_CREDIT_CARD                             VARCHAR2(255)
CREDIT_CARD_EXPIRATION                          DATE
BANK_ACCOUNT_NUMBER                             VARCHAR2(255)
BANK_NAME                                       VARCHAR2(255)
ROUTING_NUMBER                                  VARCHAR2(255)
```

In effect, our persistence layer mapping code would have to resolve this difference by pulling field data out of both the USERS and related BILLING_INFO tables and storing it into the columns of the combined USERS table. A bad approach, but an all-too-common one, would be to compromise your domain model to make it fit the relational data model (get rid of the separate BillingInfo object). While this would certainly make the mapping code simpler, you would lose out on a sensible domain model. In addition, you would write awkward code for the parts of your application that deal only with the BillingInfo object and not the User object. If you remember our discussion in chapter 7, then you probably realize that BillingInfo may make sense as an embedded object since you do not want to have a separate identity, and want to store the data in the USERS table.

One-to-many relationships

The relational primary-key/foreign-key mechanism is ideally suited for a parent-child one-to-many relationship between tables. Let's take the probable relationship between the ITEMS and BIDS tables, for example. The tables will probably look like those shown in listing 8.2.

Listing 8.2   One-to-many relationship between ITEMS and BIDS tables

```
ITEMS
ITEM_ID        NOT NULL, PRIMARY KEY    NUMBER
TITLE          NOT NULL                 VARCHAR2(255)
DESCRIPTION    NOT NULL                 CLOB
INITIAL_PRICE  NOT NULL                 NUMBER
BID_START_DATE NOT NULL                 TIMESTAMP
BID_END_DATE   NOT NULL                 TIMESTAMP
```

```
ITEM_SELLER_ID   NOT NULL,                    NUMBER
                 FOREIGN KEY (USERS(USER_ID))

BIDS
BID_ID           NOT NULL, PRIMARY KEY   NUMBER
AMOUNT           NOT NULL                NUMBER
BID_DATE         NOT NULL                TIMESTAMP
BID_BIDDER_ID    NOT NULL,               NUMBER
                 FOREIGN KEY (USER(USER_ID))
BID_ITEM_ID      NOT NULL,               NUMBER
                 FOREIGN KEY (ITEMS(ITEM_ID))
```

Foreign key signifying one-to-many relationship

The ITEM_ID foreign key into the ITEMS table from the BIDS table means that multiple BIDS table rows can refer to the same record in the ITEMS table. This implements a many-to-one relationship going from the BIDS table to the ITEMS table, and it is simple to retrieve an item given a bid record. On the other hand, retrieval from ITEMS to BIDS will require a little more effort in looking for BIDS rows that match a given ITEM_ID key. As we mentioned in the previous chapter, however, the relationship between the Item and Bid domain objects is one-many *bidirectional*. This means that the Item object has a reference to a set of Bid objects while the Bid object holds a reference to an Item object. As a Java developer, you might have expected the ITEMS table to contain some kind of reference to the BIDS table in addition to the ITEM_ID foreign key in the BIDS table. The problem is that such a table structure simply does not make sense in the relational world. Instead, our ORM layer must translate the parent-child unidirectional database relationship into a bidirectional one-to-many relationship in the OO world by using a lookup scheme instead of simple, directional references.

Many-to-many

Many-to-many relationships are common in enterprise development. In our ActionBazaar domain model presented in chapter 7, the relationship between the Item and Category domain objects is many-to-many. That is, an item can belong in multiple categories while a category can contain more than one item. This is fairly easy to implement in the OO world with a set of references on either side of the relationship. In the database world, on the other hand, the only way to implement a relationship is through a foreign key, which is inherently one-to-many. As a result, the only real way to implement many-to-many relationships is by breaking them down into two one-to-many relationships. Let's see how this works by taking a look at the database table representation of the item-category relationship in listing 8.3.

Listing 8.3   Many-to-many relationship between ITEMS and CATEGORIES tables

```
ITEMS
ITEM_ID          NOT NULL, PRIMARY KEY       NUMBER      ◁──┘ ITEMS table primary key
TITLE            NOT NULL                    VARCHAR2(255)
...


CATEGORIES                                               CATEGORIES table
CATEGORY_ID      NOT NULL, PRIMARY KEY       NUMBER      ◁──┘ primary key
NAME             NOT NULL                    VARCHAR2(255)
...                              Table linking
                                 CATEGORIES and ITEMS              ITEMS table
CATEGORIES_ITEMS        ◁──┘                                      foreign key        CATEGORIES
ITEM_ID          NOT NULL, PRIMARY KEY    NUMBER  ◁──┘                               table foreign
                 FOREIGN KEY(ITEMS(ITEM_ID))                                         key
CATEGORY_ID      NOT NULL, PRIMARY KEY    NUMBER                            ◁──┘
                 FOREIGN KEY(CATEGORIES(CATEGORY_ID))
```

The CATEGORIES_ITEMS table is called an *association* or *intersection table* and accomplishes a pretty neat trick. The only two columns it contains are foreign key references to the ITEMS and CATEGORIES tables (ironically the two foreign keys combined are the primary key for the table). In effect, it makes it possible to match up arbitrary rows of the two related tables, making it possible to implement many-to-many relationships. Since neither related table contains a foreign key, relationship direction is completely irrelevant. To get to the records on the other side of the relationship from either side, we must perform a join in the ORM layer involving the association layer. For example, to get all the items under a category, we must retrieve the CATEGORY_ID, join the CATEGORIES_ITEMS table with the ITEMS table, and retrieve all item data for rows that match the CATEGORY_ID foreign key. Saving the relationship into the database would involve saving a row CATEGORIES_ITEMS table that links rows stored in CATEGORIES and ITEM tables. Clearly, the many-to-many relationships are modeled differently in the relational world than they are in the OO world.

Inheritance

Unlike the three previous cases (one-to-one, one-to-many, and many-to-many), *inheritance* is probably the most severe case of the object-relational mismatch. Inheritance therefore calls for solutions that are not elegant fits to relational theory at all. The OO concept of inheritance has no direct equivalent in the relational world. However, there are a few creative ways that O/R solutions bridge this gap, including:

- Storing each object in the inheritance hierarchy in completely separated tables
- Mapping all classes into a single table
- Storing superclass/subclasses in related tables

Because none of these strategies is simple, we'll save a detailed discussion for later in the chapter (section 8.4).

8.1.2 *Introducing O/R mapping*

In the most general sense, the term *object-relational mapping* means any process that can save an object (in our case a Java `Object`) into a relational database. As we mentioned, for all intents and purposes you could write home-brewed JDBC code to do that. In the realm of automated persistence, ORM means using primarily configuration metadata to tell an extremely high-level API which tables a set of Java `Object`s are going to be saved into. It involves the hopefully simple act of figuring out what table row an `Object` instance should be saved into and what field/property data belongs in what column. In EJB 3, the configuration metadata obviously consists either of annotations or deployment descriptor elements, or both. As our impedance mismatch discussion points out, there are a few wrinkles in the idealistic view of automated persistence. Because of the inherent complexity of the problem, EJB 3 cannot make the solution absolutely effortless, but it goes a long way in making it less painful. In the next section, we start our discussion of EJB 3 ORM by covering the simple case of saving an entity without regard to domain relations or inheritance.

ORM portability in EJB 2

One of the greatest weaknesses of EJB 2 container-managed persistence (CMP) entity beans was that EJB 2 never standardized the process of ORM. Instead, mapping strategies were left up to the individual vendors, whose approaches varied widely. As a result, porting entity beans from one application server to another more or less meant redoing O/R mapping all over again. This meant that the portability that EJB 2 promised meant little more than empty words.

EJB 3 firmly standardizes O/R mapping and gets us much closer to the goal of portability. As a matter of fact, as long as you are careful to steer clear of application server-specific features, you can likely achieve portability.

Other than smoothing out the impedance problems by applying generalized strategies behind the scenes, there are a few other benefits to using O/R. Even disregarding the edge cases discussed earlier, if you have spent any time writing application persistence layers using JDBC, you know that substantial work is required. This is largely because of the repetitive "plumbing" code of JDBC and the large volume of complicated handwritten SQL involved. As you'll soon see, using ORM frees you from this burden and the task of persistence largely becomes an exercise in simple configuration. The fact that the EJB 3 persistence provider generates JDBC and SQL code on your behalf has another very nice effect: because the persistence provider is capable of automatically generating code optimized to your database platform from your database-neutral configuration data, switching databases becomes a snap. Accomplishing the same using handwritten SQL is tedious work at best and impossible at worst. Database portability is one of the most appealing features of the EJB 3 Java Persistence API that fits nicely with the Java philosophy, but has been elusive for some time.

Now that we've looked at the reasons for O/R mapping, let's see how EJB 3 implements it.

8.2 *Mapping entities*

This section explores some of the fundamental features of EJB 3 O/R mapping by taking a look at the implementation of the ActionBazaar User entity. You'll see how to use several ORM annotations such as @Table, @Column, @Enumerated, @Lob, @Temporal, and @Embeddable.

> **NOTE** If you remember from our discussion in chapter 7, User is the superclass to both the Seller and Bidder domain objects. To keep this example simple, we'll ignore the inheritance and use a persistence field to identify the user type in the table USERS. We will use the same example to demonstrate inheritance mapping in section 8.4.

The User entity contains fields that are common to all user types in ActionBazaar, such as the user ID, username (used for login and authentication), first name, last name, user type (bidder, seller, admin, etc.), user-uploaded picture, and user account creation date. All fields are mapped and persisted into the database for the User entity in listing 8.4. We have used field-based persistence for the entity to keep the code sample short.

Listing 8.4 Mapping an entity

```
@Entity
@Table(name="USERS")
@SecondaryTable(name="USER_PICTURES",
    pkJoinColumns=@PrimaryKeyJoinColumn(name="USER_ID"))
public class User implements Serializable {

    @Id
    @Column(name="USER_ID", nullable=false)
    protected Long userId;

    @Column(name="USER_NAME", nullable=false)
    protected String username;

    @Column(name="FIRST_NAME", nullable=false, length=1)
    protected String firstName;

    @Column(name="LAST_NAME", nullable=false)
    protected String lastName;

    @Enumerated(EnumType.ORDINAL)
    @Column(name="USER_TYPE", nullable=false)
    protected UserType userType;

    @Column(name="PICTURE", table="USER_PICTURES")
    @Lob
    @Basic(fetch=FetchType.LAZY)
    protected byte[] picture;

    @Column(name="CREATION_DATE", nullable=false)
    @Temporal(TemporalType.DATE)
    protected Date creationDate;

    @Embedded
    protected Address address;

    public User() {}
}

@Embeddable
public class Address implements Serializable {
    @Column(name="STREET", nullable=false)
    protected String street;

    @Column(name="CITY", nullable=false)
    protected String city;

    @Column(name="STATE", nullable=false)
    protected String state;
```

❶ Column mappings

❷ Enumerated column

❸ BLOB field

❹ Lazy loading

❺ Temporal field

❻ Embedded field

❼ Embeddable class with column mapping

```
@Column(name="ZIP_CODE", nullable=false)
protected String zipCode;

@Column(name="COUNTRY", nullable=false)
protected String country;
}
```

Briefly scanning listing 8.4, you see that the User entity is mapped to the USERS table joined with the USER_PICTURES table using the USER_ID primary key. Each of the fields is mapped to a database column using the @Column annotation ❶. We deliberately made the listing feature-rich, and quite a few interesting things are going on with the columns. The userType field is restricted to be an ordinal enumeration ❷. The picture field is marked as a binary large object (BLOB) ❸ that is lazily loaded ❹. The creationDate field is marked as a temporal type ❺. The address field is an embedded object ❻. The column mapping for Address object is defined in the object ❼ using the @Column annotation. All in all, the @Table, @SecondaryTable, @Column, @Enumerated, @Lob, @Basic, @Temporal, @Embedded, and @Embeddable ORM annotations are used. Let's start our analysis of O/R with the @Table annotation.

Annotations vs. XML in O/R mapping

The difficulty of choosing between annotations and XML deployment descriptors manifests itself most strikingly in the arena of EJB 3 O/R mapping. XML descriptors are verbose and hard to manage, and most developers find them to be a pain-point for Java EE. While O/R mapping with annotations makes life simpler, you should keep in mind that you are hard-coding your database schema in your code in a way similar to using JDBC. This means that the slightest schema change will result in a recompilation and redeployment cycle as opposed to simple configuration. If you have a stable database design that rarely changes or you are comfortable using JDBC data access objects (DAOs), then there is no issue here. But if you have an environment where the database schema is less stable (subject to change more often), you're probably better off using descriptors. Luckily, you can use XML descriptors to override ORM annotations after deploying to a production environment. As a result, changing your mind in response to the reality on the ground may not be a big deal.

8.2.1 *Specifying the table*

@Table specifies the table containing the columns to which the entity is mapped. In listing 8.4, the @Table annotation makes the USERS table's columns available for ORM. In fact, by default all the persistent data for the entity is mapped to the table specified by the annotation's name parameter. As you can see from the annotation's definition here, it contains a few other parameters:

```
@Target(TYPE)
@Retention(RUNTIME)
public @interface Table {
    String name() default "";
    String catalog() default "";
    String schema() default "";
    UniqueConstraint[] uniqueConstraints() default {};
}
```

The @Table annotation itself is optional. If it's omitted, the entity is assumed to be mapped to a table in the default schema with the same name as the entity class. If the name parameter is omitted, the table name is assumed to be the same as the name of the entity. This will be just fine if we are mapping to the USER table.

> **NOTE** Most persistence providers include a great developer-friendly feature known as *automatic schema generation*. The persistence provider will automatically create database objects for your entities when they do not exist in the database. This behavior is not mandated by specification and is configured using vendor-specific properties. Most of our code examples rely on automatic schema generation. In chapter 11, we'll provide an example configuration to enable automatic schema generation.

We won't discuss the catalog and schema parameters in depth since they are hardly ever used. In effect, they allow you to fully qualify the mapped table. For example, we could have explicitly specified that the USERS table belongs in the ACTIONBAZAAR schema like so:

```
@Table(name="USERS", schema="ACTIONBAZAAR")
public class User
```

> **NOTE** We've already discussed what a *schema* is. For all intents and purposes, you can think of a *catalog* as a "meta-schema" or a higher-level abstraction for organizing schemas. Often, a database will only have one common system catalog.

By default, it is assumed that the table belongs in the schema of the data source used. You'll learn how to specify a data source for a persistence module in chapter 11 when we discuss entity packaging. The uniqueConstraints parameter is not used that often either. It specifies unique constraints on table columns and is only used when table autocreation is enabled. Here's an example:

```
@Table(name="CATEGORIES",
       uniqueConstraints=
           {@UniqueConstraint(columnNames={"CATEGORY_ID"})})
```

If it does not exist and autogeneration is enabled, the code puts a unique constraint on the CATEGORY_ID column of the CATEGORIES table when it is created during deployment time. The uniqueConstraints parameter supports specifying constraints on more than one column. It is important to keep mind, however, that EJB 3 implementations are not mandated to support generation of tables, and it is a bad idea to use automatic table generation beyond simple development databases. Most entities will typically be mapped to a single table. The User object happens to be mapped to two tables, as you might have guessed from the @SecondaryTable annotation used in listing 8.4. We'll come back to this later after we take a look at mapping entity data using the @Column annotation.

8.2.2 Mapping the columns

The @Column annotation maps a persisted field or property to a table column. All of the fields used in listing 8.3 are annotated with @Column. For example, the userId field is mapped to the USER_ID column:

```
@Column(name="USER_ID")
protected Long userId;
```

It is assumed that the USER_ID column belongs to the USERS table specified by the @Table annotation. Most often, this is as simple as your @Column annotation will look. At best, you might need to explicitly specify which table the persisted column belongs to (when you map your entity to multiple tables using the @SecondaryTable annotation) as we do for the picture field in listing 8.4:

```
@Column(name="PICTURE", table="USER_PICTURES")
...
protected byte[] picture;
```

As you can see from the definition in listing 8.5, a number of other parameters exist for the annotation.

Listing 8.5   The @Column annotation

```
@Target({METHOD, FIELD})
@Retention(RUNTIME)
public @interface Column {
    String name() default "";              ❶  Specifies unique constraint
    boolean unique() default false;
    boolean nullable() default true;          Specifies if column
    boolean insertable() default true;     ❷  allows nulls
    boolean updatable() default true;
    String columnDefinition() default "";
    String table() default "";             ❸  Length of column
    int length() default 255;
    int precision() default 0;      ❹  Decimal precision of column
    int scale() default 0;
}
                                        ❺  Decimal scale of column
```

The insertable and updatable parameters are used to control persistence behavior. If the insertable parameter is set to false, the field or property will not be included in the INSERT statement generated by the persistence provider to create a new record corresponding to the entity. Likewise, setting the updatable parameter to false excludes the field or property from being updated when the entity is saved. These two parameters are usually helpful in dealing with read-only data, like primary keys generated by the database. They could be applied to the userId field as follows:

```
@Column(name="USER_ID", insertable=false, updatable=false)
protected Long userId;
```

When a User entity is first created in the database, the persistence provider does not include the USER_ID as part of the generated INSERT statement. Instead, we could be populating the USER_ID column through an INSERT-induced trigger on the database server side. Similarly, since it does not make much sense to update a generated key, it is not included in the UPDATE statement for the entity either. The rest of the parameters of the @Column annotation are only used for automatic table generation and specify column creation data. The nullable parameter specifies whether the column supports null values ❷, the unique parameter ❶ indicates if the column has a unique constraint, the length parameter ❸ specifies the size of the database column, the precision parameter ❹ specifies the precision of a decimal field, and the scale parameter ❺ specifies the scale of a decimal column. Finally, the columnDefinition parameter allows you to specify the exact SQL to create the column.

We won't cover these parameters much further than this basic information since we do not encourage automatic table creation. Note that the @Column annotation is optional. If omitted, a persistent field or property is saved to the table column matching the field or property name. For example, a property specified by the getName and setName methods will be saved into the NAME column of the table for the entity.

Next, let's take a look at a few more annotations applied to entity data, starting with @Enumerated.

8.2.3 *Using @Enumerated*

Languages like C and Pascal have had enumerated data types for decades. Enumerations were finally introduced in Java 5. In case you are unfamiliar with them, we'll start with the basics. In listing 8.4, the user type field has a type of UserType. UserType is a Java enumeration that is defined as follows:

```
public enum UserType {SELLER, BIDDER, CSR, ADMIN};
```

This effectively means that any data type defined as UserType (like our persistent field in the User object) can only have the four values listed in the enumeration. Like an array, each element of the enumeration is associated with an index called the *ordinal*. For example, the UserType.SELLER value has an ordinal of 0, the User-Type.BIDDER value has an ordinal of 1, and so on. The problem is determining how to store the value of enumerated data into the column. The Java Persistence API supports two options through the @Enumerated annotation. In our case, we specify that the ordinal value should be saved into the database:

```
@Enumerated(EnumType.ORDINAL)
...
protected UserType userType;
```

This means that if the value of the field is set to UserType.SELLER, the value 0 will be stored into the database. Alternatively, you can specify that the enumeration value name should be stored as a String:

```
@Enumerated(EnumType.STRING)
...
protected UserType userType;
```

In this case a UserType.ADMIN value would be saved into the database as "ADMIN". By default an enumerated field or property is saved as an ordinal. This would be the case if the @Enumerated annotation is omitted altogether, or no parameter to the annotation is specified.

8.2.4 *Mapping CLOBs and BLOBs*

An extremely powerful feature of relational databases is the ability to store very large data as binary large object (BLOB) and character large object (CLOB) types. These correspond to the JDBC `java.sql.Blob` and `java.sql.Clob` objects. The `@Lob` annotation designates a property of field as a CLOB or BLOB. For example, we designate the picture field as a BLOB in listing 8.4:

```
@Lob
@Basic(fetch=FetchType.LAZY)
protected byte[] picture;
```

Whether a field or property designated `@Lob` is a CLOB or a BLOB is determined by its type. If the data is of type `char[]` or `String`, the persistence provider maps the data to a CLOB column. Otherwise, the column is mapped as a BLOB. An extremely useful annotation to use in conjunction with `@Lob` is `@Basic`. `@Basic` can be marked on any attribute with direct-to-field mapping. Just as we have done for the `picture` field, the `@Basic(fetch=FetchType.LAZY)` specification causes the BLOB or CLOB data to be loaded from the database only when it is first accessed. Postponing of loading of entity data from the database is known as lazy loading. (You will learn more about lazy loading in chapter 9.) This is a great feature since LOB data is usually very memory intensive and should only be loaded if needed. Unfortunately, lazy loading of LOB types is left as optional for vendors by the EJB 3 specification and there is no guarantee that the column will actually be lazily loaded.

8.2.5 *Mapping temporal types*

Most databases support a few different temporal data types with different granularity levels corresponding to DATE (storing day, month, and year), TIME (storing just time and not day, month, or year) and TIMESTAMP (storing time, day, month, and year). The `@Temporal` annotation specifies which of these data types we want to map a `java.util.Date` or `java.util.Calendar` persistent data type to. In listing 8.3, we save the `creationDate` field into the database as a DATE:

```
@Temporal(TemporalType.DATE)
protected Date creationDate;
```

Note this explicit mapping is redundant while using the `java.sql.Date`, `java.sql.Time` or `java.sql.Timestamp` Java types. If we do not specify a parameter for `@Temporal` annotation or omit it altogether, the persistence provider will assume the data type mapping to be TIMESTAMP (the smallest possible data granularity).

8.2.6 *Mapping an entity to multiple tables*

This is not often the case for nonlegacy databases, but sometimes an entity's data must come from two different tables. In fact, in some rare situations, this is a very sensible strategy. For example, the User entity in listing 8.4 is stored across the USERS and USER_PICTURES tables, as shown in figure 8.2.

This makes excellent sense because the USER_PICTURES table stores large binary images that could significantly slow down queries using the table. However, this approach is rarely used. Isolating the binary images into a separate table in conjunction with the *lazy loading* technique discussed in section 8.2.4 to deal with the picture field mapped to the USER_PICTURE table can result in a significant boost in application performance. The @SecondaryTable annotation enables us to derive entity data from more than one table and is defined as follows:

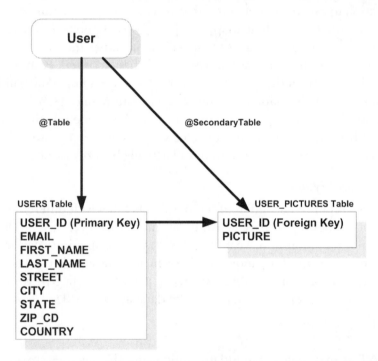

Figure 8.2   An entity can be mapped to more than one table; for example, the User entity spans more than one table: USERS and USER_PICTURES. The primary table is mapped using @Table and the secondary table is mapped using @SecondaryTable. The primary and secondary tables must have the same primary key.

```
@Target({TYPE}) @Retention(RUNTIME)
public @interface SecondaryTable {
    String name();
    String catalog() default "";
    String schema() default "";
    PrimaryKeyJoinColumn[] pkJoinColumns() default {};
    UniqueConstraint[] uniqueConstraints() default {};
}
```

Notice that other than the pkJoinColumns element, the definition of the annotation is identical to the definition of the @Table annotation. This element is the key to how annotation works. To see what we mean, examine the following code implementing the User entity mapped to two tables:

```
@Entity
@Table(name="USERS")
@SecondaryTable(name="USER_PICTURES",
    pkJoinColumns=@PrimaryKeyJoinColumn(name="USER_ID"))
public class User implements Serializable {
..}
```

Obviously, the two tables in @Table and @SecondaryTable are related somehow and are joined to create the entity. This kind of relationship is implemented by creating a foreign key in the secondary table referencing the primary key in the first table. In this case, the foreign key also happens to be the primary key of the secondary table. To be precise, USER_ID is the primary key of the USER_PICTURES table and it references the primary key of the USERS table. The pkJoinColumns=@PrimaryKey-JoinColumn(name="USER_ID") specification assumes this relationship. The name element points to the USER_ID foreign key in the USER_PICTURES secondary table. The persistence provider is left to figure out what the primary key of the USERS table is, which also happens to be named USER_ID. The provider performs a join using the detected primary key in order to fetch the data for the User entity. In the extremely unlikely case that an entity consists of columns from more than two tables, we may use the @SecondaryTables annotation more than once for the same entity. We won't cover this case here, but encourage you to explore it if needed.

Before we conclude the section on mapping entities, let's discuss a vital feature of JPA: primary key generation.

8.2.7 *Generating primary keys*

When we identify a column or set of columns as the *primary key*, we essentially ask the database to enforce uniqueness. Primary keys that consist of business data are called *natural keys*. The classic example of this is SSN as the primary key for an EMPLOYEE table. CATEGORY_ID or EMPLOYEE_ID, on the other hand, are examples of *surrogate keys*. Essentially, surrogate keys are columns created explicitly to function as primary keys. Surrogate keys are popular and we highly recommend them, especially over compound keys.

There are three popular ways of generating primary key values: identities, sequences, and tables. Fortunately, all three strategies are supported via the @GeneratedValue annotation and switching is as easy as changing the configuration. Let's start our analysis with the simplest case: using identities.

Identity columns as generators

Many databases such as Microsoft SQL Server support the identity column. You can use an identity constraint to manage the primary key for the User entity as follows:

```
@Id
@GeneratedValue(strategy=GenerationType.IDENTITY)
@Column(name="USER_ID")
protected Long userId;
```

This code assumes that an identity constraint exists on the USERS.USER_ID column. Note that when using IDENTITY as the generator type, the value for the identity field may not be available before the entity data is saved in the database because typically it is generated when a record is committed.

The two other strategies, SEQUENCE and TABLE, both require the use of an externally defined generator: a SequenceGenerator or TableGenerator must be created and set for the GeneratedValue. You'll see how this works by first taking a look at the sequence generation strategy.

Database sequences as generators

To use sequence generators, first define a sequence in the database. The following is a sample sequence for the USER_ID column in an Oracle database:

```
CREATE SEQUENCE USER_SEQUENCE START WITH 1 INCREMENT BY 10;
```

We are now ready to create a sequence generator in EJB 3:

```
@SequenceGenerator(name="USER_SEQUENCE_GENERATOR",
    sequenceName="USER_SEQUENCE",
            initialValue=1, allocationSize=10)
```

The @SequenceGenerator annotation creates a sequence generator named USER_SEQUENCE_GENERATOR referencing the Oracle sequence we created and matching its setup. Naming the sequence is critical since it is referred to by the @GeneratedValue annotation. The initialValue element is pretty self-explanatory: allocationSize specifies by how much the sequence is incremented each time a value is generated.

The default values for `initialValue` and `allocationSize` are 0 and 50, respectively. It's handy that the sequence generator need not be created in the same entity in which it is used. As a matter of fact, any generator is shared among all entities in the persistence module and therefore each generator must be uniquely named in a persistence module. Finally, we can reimplement the generated key for the USER_ID column as follows:

```
@Id
@GeneratedValue(strategy=GenerationType.SEQUENCE,
    generator="USER_SEQUENCE_GENERATOR")
@Column(name="USER_ID")
protected Long userId;
```

Sequence tables as generators

Using table generators is just as simple as with a sequence generator. The first step is creating a table to use for generating values. The table must follow a general format like the following one created for Oracle:

```
CREATE TABLE SEQUENCE_GENERATOR_TABLE
    (SEQUENCE_NAME VARCHAR2(80) NOT NULL,
     SEQUENCE_VALUE NUMBER(15) NOT NULL,
     PRIMARY KEY (SEQUENCE_NAME));
```

The SEQUENCE_NAME column is meant to store the name of a sequence, and the SEQUENCE_VALUE column is meant to store the current value of the sequence. The next step is to prepare the table for use by inserting the initial value manually as follows:

```
INSERT INTO
    SEQUENCE_GENERATOR_TABLE (SEQUENCE_NAME, SEQUENCE_VALUE)
VALUES ('USER_SEQUENCE', 1);
```

In a sense, these two steps combined are the equivalent of creating the Oracle sequence in the second strategy. Despite the obvious complexity of this approach, one advantage is that the same sequence table can be used for multiple sequences in the application. We are now prepared to create the `TableGenerator` utilizing the table:

```
@TableGenerator (name="USER_TABLE_GENERATOR",
    table="SEQUENCE_GENERATOR_TABLE",
    pkColumnName="SEQUENCE_NAME",
    valueColumnName="SEQUENCE_VALUE",
    pkColumnValue="USER_SEQUENCE")
```

If you need to, you can specify the values for `initialValue` and `allocationSize` as well. Finally, we can use the table generator for USER_ID key generation:

```
@Id
@GeneratedValue(strategy=GenerationType.TABLE,
    generator="USER_TABLE_GENERATOR")
@Column(name="USER_ID")
protected Long userId;
```

Default primary key generation strategy

The last option for key generation is to let the provider decide the best strategy for the underlying database by using the AUTO specification as follows:

```
@Id
@GeneratedValue(strategy=GenerationType.AUTO)
@Column(name="USER_ID")
protected Long userId;
```

This is a perfect match for automatic table creation because the underlying database objects required will be created by the JPA provider.

> **NOTE** You'd assume that if Oracle were the underlying database, the persistence provider probably would choose SEQUENCE as the strategy; if SQL Server were the underlying database, IDENTITY would likely be chosen on your behalf. However, this may not be true, and we recommend that you check the documentation of your persistence provider. For example, TopLink Essentials uses a table generator as the default autogenerator for all databases.

Keep in mind that although generated values are often used for surrogate keys, you could use the feature for any persistence field or property. Before we move on to discussing entity relations, we'll tackle the most complicated case of mapping basic entity data next—mapping embeddable objects.

Standardization of key generation

Just as EJB 3 standardizes O/R mapping, it standardizes key generation as well. This is a substantial leap from EJB 2, where you had to resort to various sequence generator patterns to accomplish the same for CMP entity beans. Using sequences, identity constraints, or tables was a significant effort, a far cry from simple configuration, not to mention a nonportable approach.

8.2.8 *Mapping embeddable classes*

When discussing embeddable objects in chapter 7, we explained that an embeddable object acts primarily as a convenient data holder for entities and has no

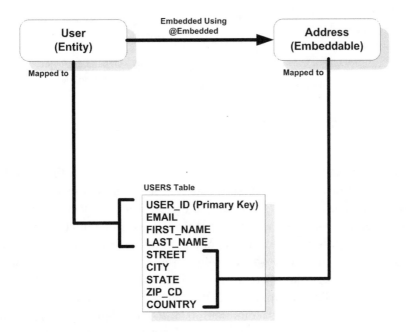

Figure 8.3 Embeddable objects act as convenient data holders for entities and have no identity of their own. Address is an embeddable object that is stored as a part of the User entity that is mapped to the USERS table.

identity of its own. Rather, it shares the identity of the entity class it belongs to. Let's now discuss how embeddable objects are mapped to the database (figure 8.3).

In listing 8.4, we included the Address embedded object introduced in chapter 7 in the User entity as a data field. The relevant parts of listing 8.4 are repeated in listing 8.6 for easy reference.

Listing 8.6 Using embeddable objects

```
@Table(name="USERS")        ←❶  Table stores both entity and embeddable object
...
public class User implements Serializable {
                                    ❷  Shared identity
    @Id                         ←┘
    @Column(name="USER_ID", nullable=false)
    protected Long userId;
    ...                    ❸  Embedded field
    @Embedded              ←┘
    protected Address address;
    ...
}
...
```

```
@Embeddable                                          ◁──④  Embeddable object
public class Address implements Serializable {
    @Column(name="STREET", nullable=false)      ◁─┐
    protected String street;                       │  ⑤  Embeddable object
    ...                                            │      field mappings
    @Column(name="ZIP_CODE", nullable=false)    ◁─┘
    protected String zipCode;
    ...
}
```

The User entity defines the address field as an embedded object ③. Notice that unlike the User entity, the embeddable Address object ④ is missing an @Table annotation. This is because EJB 3 does not allow embedded objects to be mapped to a table different from the enclosing entity, at least not directly through the @Table annotation. Instead, the Address object's data is stored in the USERS table that stores the enclosing entity ①. Therefore, the @Column mappings applied to the fields of the Address object ⑤ really refer to the columns in the USERS table. For example, the street field is mapped to the USERS.STREET column, the zipCode field is mapped to the USERS.ZIP_CODE column, and so on. This also means that the Address data is stored in the same database row as the User data, and both objects share the USER_ID identity column ②. Other than this minor nuance, all data mapping annotations used in entities are available for you in embedded objects and behave in exactly the same manner. In general, this is the norm and embedded objects are often stored in the same table as the enclosing entity. However, if this does not suit you, it is possible to store the embeddable object's data in a separate table and use the @SecondaryTable annotation to retrieve its data into the main entity using a join. We won't detail this solution, as it is fairly easy to figure out and we'll leave it for you to experiment with instead.

Sharing embeddable classes between entities

One of the most useful features of embeddable classes is that they can be shared between entities. For example, our Address object could be embedded inside a BillingInfo object to store billing addresses while still being used by the User entity. The important thing to keep in mind is that the embeddable class definition is shared in the OO world and *not* the actual data in the underlying relational tables. As we noted, the embedded data is created/populated using the table mapping of the entity class. However, this means that all the embeddable data must be mapped to both the USERS and BILLING_INFO tables. In other words, both tables must contain some mappable street, city, or zip columns.

An interesting wrinkle to consider is the fact that the same embedded data could be mapped to columns with different names in two separate tables. For example, the "state" data column in BILLING_INFO could be called STATE_CODE instead of STATE. Since the @Column annotation in Address maps to a column named STATE, how will this column be resolved? The solution to the answer is overriding the column mapping in the enclosing entity using the AttributeOverride annotation as follows:

```
@Embedded
@AttributeOverrides({@AttributeOverride(
    name="state",
    column=@Column(name="STATE_CODE"))})
protected Address address;
```

In effect, the AttributeOverride annotation is telling the provider to resolve the embedded "state" field to the STATE_CODE table for the enclosing entity.

We have now finished looking at all the annotations required for mapping entities except for mapping OO inheritance. Let's now move on to looking at EJB 3 features for mapping entity relations.

8.3 *Mapping entity relationships*

In the previous chapter we explored implementing domain relationships between entities. In section 8.1.1 we briefly discussed the problems translating relationships from the OO world to the database world. In this section, you'll see how these solutions are actually implemented in EJB 3 using annotations, starting with one-to-one relationships. We'll explore mapping of all types of relationships: one-to-one, one-to-many, many-to-one, and many-to-many.

8.3.1 *Mapping one-to-one relationships*

As you know, one-to-one relationships are mapped using primary/foreign key associations. It should be pretty obvious that a parent-child relationship usually exists between the entities of a one-to-one relationship. For example, in the User-BillingInfo relationship mentioned earlier, the User entity could be characterized as the parent. Depending on where the foreign key resides, the relationship could be implemented in two different ways: using the @JoinColumn or the @Primary-KeyJoinColumn annotation.

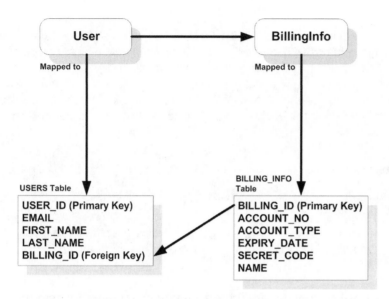

Figure 8.4 User has a one-to-one unidirectional relationship with BillingInfo. The User and BillingInfo entities are mapped to the USERS and BILLING_INFO tables, respectively, and the USERS table has a foreign key reference to the BILLING_INFO table. Such associations are mapped using @JoinColumn.

Using @JoinColumn

If the underlying table for the referencing entity is the one containing the foreign key to the table to which the referenced "child" entity is mapped, you can map the relationship using the @JoinColumn annotation (figure 8.4).

In our User-BillingInfo example shown in figure 8.4, the USERS table contains a foreign key named USER_BILLING_ID that refers to the BILLING_INFO table's BILLING_ID primary key. This relationship would be mapped as shown in listing 8.7.

> **Listing 8.7** Mapping a one-to-one unidirectional relationship using @JoinColumn

```
@Entity
@Table(name="USERS")
public class User {
    @Id
    @Column(name="USER_ID")
    protected String userId;
    ...
    @OneToOne
    @JoinColumn(name="USER_BILLING_ID",                    Foreign key ❶
        referencedColumnName="BILLING_ID", updatable=false)
```

```
    protected BillingInfo billingInfo;
}

@Entity
@Table(name="BILLING_INFO")
public class BillingInfo {
    @Id
    @Column(name="BILLING_ID")        ◁──❷  Primary key
    protected Long billingId;
    ...
}
```

The `@JoinColumn` annotation's `name` element refers to the name of the foreign key in the USERS table ❶. If this parameter is omitted, it is assumed to follow this form:

```
<relationship field/property name>_<name of referenced primary key column>
```

In our example, the foreign key name would be assumed to be `BILLINGINFO_ BILLING_ID` in the USERS table. The `referencedColumnName` element specifies the name of the primary key or a unique key the foreign key refers to. If you don't specify the `referencedColumnName` value, it is assumed to be the column containing the identity of the referenced entity. Incidentally, this would have been fine in our case as `BILLING_ID` is the primary key for the `BILLING_INFO` table ❷.

Like the `@Column` annotation, the `@JoinColumn` annotation contains the `updatable`, `insertable`, `table`, and `unique` elements. The elements serve the same purpose as the elements of the `@Column` annotation. In our case, `updatable` is set to false, which means that the persistence provider would not update the foreign key even if the `billingInfo` reference were changed. If you have more than one column in the foreign key, you can use the `JoinColumns` annotation instead. We won't cover this annotation since this situation is very unlikely, if not bad design.

If you have a bidirectional one-to-one relationship, then the entity in the inverse side of the relationship will contain the `mappedBy` element, as we discussed in chapter 7. If the `User` and `BillingInfo` entities have a bidirectional relationship, we must modify the `BillingInfo` entity to have the one-to-one relationship definition pointing to the `User` entity as follows:

```
@Entity
public class BillingInfo {
    @OneToOne(mappedBy="billingInfo")
    protected User user;
 ..
}
```

As you can see, the mappedBy element identifies the name of the association field in the owning side of the relationship. In a bidirectional relationship, the *owning* side is the entity that stores the relationship in its underlying table. In our example, the USERS table stores the relationship in the USER_BILLING_ID field and thus is the relationship owner. The one-to-one relationship in BillingInfo has the mappedBy element specified as billingInfo, which is the relationship field defined in the User entity that contains the definition for @JoinColumn.

Note that you do not have to define @JoinColumn in the entities of both sides of one-to-one relationships.

Next we'll discuss how you define the one-to-one relationship when the foreign key is in the table to which the child entity is mapped.

Using @PrimaryKeyJoinColumn

In the more likely case that the foreign key reference exists in the table to which the referenced entity is mapped, the @PrimaryKeyJoinColumn would be used instead (figure 8.5).

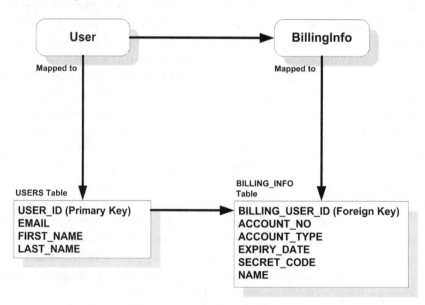

Figure 8.5 User has a one-to-one unidirectional relationship with BillingInfo. The User and BillingInfo entities are mapped to the USERS and BILLING_INFO tables, respectively, and the BILLING_INFO and USERS tables share the same primary key; the primary key of the BILLING_INFO table is also a foreign key referencing the primary key of the USERS table. Such associations are mapped using @PrimaryKeyJoinColumn.

Typically, @PrimaryKeyJoinColumn is used in one-to-one relationships when both the referenced and referencing tables share the primary key of the referencing table. In our example, as shown in figure 8.5, the BILLING_INFO table would contain a foreign key reference named BILLING_USER_ID pointing to the USER_ID primary key of the USERS table. In addition, BILLING_USER_ID would be the primary key of the BILLING_INFO table. The relationship would be implemented as shown in listing 8.8.

Listing 8.8 Mapping a one-to-one relationship using @PrimaryKeyJoinColumn

```
@Entity
@Table(name="USERS")
public class User {
    @Id
    @Column(name="USER_ID")
    protected Long userId;
    ...
    @OneToOne
    @PrimaryKeyJoinColumn(name="USER_ID",               Parent primary
        referencedColumnName="BILLING_USER_ID")          key join
    protected BillingInfo billingInfo;
}

@Entity
@Table(name="BILLING_INFO")
public class BillingInfo {
    @Id
    @Column(name="BILLING_USER_ID")
    protected Long userId;
    ...
}
```

The @PrimaryKeyJoinColumn annotation's name element refers to the primary key column of the table storing the current entity. On the other hand, the referencedColumnName element refers to the foreign key in the table holding the referenced entity. In our case, the foreign key is the BILLING_INFO table's BILLING_USER_ID column, and it points to the USERS.USER_ID primary key. If the names of both the primary key and foreign key columns are the same, you may omit the referencedColumnName element since this is what the JPA provider will assume by default. In our example, if we rename the foreign key in the BILLING_INFO table from BILLING_USER_ID to USER_ID to match the name of the primary key in the USERS table, we may omit the referencedColumnName value so that the provider can default it correctly.

If you have a composite primary key in the parent table (which is rare if you are using surrogate keys), you should use the `@PrimaryKeyJoinColumns` annotation instead. We encourage you to explore this annotation on your own.

You'll learn how to map one-to-many and many-to-one relationships next.

8.3.2 *One-to-many and many-to-one*

As we mentioned in the previous chapter, one-to-many and many-to-one relationships are the most common in enterprise systems and are implemented using the `@OneToMany` and `@ManyToOne` annotations. For example, the `Item`-`Bid` relationship in the ActionBazaar system is one-to-many, since an `Item` holds references to a collection of `Bids` placed on it and a `Bid` holds a reference to the `Item` it was placed on. The beauty of EJB 3 persistence mapping is that the same two annotations we used for mapping one-to-one relationships are also used for one-to-many relationships. This is because both relation types are implemented as a primary-key/foreign-key association in the underlying database. Let's see how to do this by implementing the `Item`-`Bid` relationship shown in listing 8.9.

Listing 8.9   One-to-many bidirectional relationship mapping

```
@Entity
@Table(name="ITEMS")
public class Item {
    @Id
    @Column(name="ITEM_ID")
    protected Long itemId;
    ...
    @OneToMany(mappedBy="item")      ◁—❶  One-to-many
    protected Set<Bid> bids;
    ...
}

@Entity
@Table(name="BIDS")
public class Bid {
    @Id
    @Column(name="BID_ID")
    protected Long bidId;
    ...
    @ManyToOne
    @JoinColumn(name="BID_ITEM_ID",           ❷  Many-to-one
        referencedColumnName="ITEM_ID")
    protected Item item;
    ...
}
```

Since multiple instances of BIDS records would refer to the same record in the ITEMS table, the BIDS table will hold a foreign key reference to the primary key of the ITEMS table. In our example, this foreign key is BID_ITEM_ID, and it refers to the ITEM_ID primary key of the ITEMS table. This database relationship between the tables is shown in figure 8.6. In listing 8.9 the many-to-one relationship is expressed in ORM using @JoinColumn annotations. In effect, a @Join-Column annotation's job is to specify a primary/foreign key relationship in the underlying data model. Note that the exact @JoinColumn specification could have been repeated for both the Bid.item and Item.bids persistent fields on either side of the relationship. In @ManyToOne ❷, the name element specifies the foreign key, BID_ITEM_ID, and the referencedColumnName element specifies the primary key, ITEM_ID. From the Item entity's perspective, this means the persistence provider would figure out what Bid instances to put in the bids set by retrieving the matching BID_ITEM_ID in the BIDS table.

After performing the join, the JPA provider will see what BIDS records are retrieved by the join and populate them into the bids set. Similarly, when it is time to form the item reference in the Bid entity, the persistence provider would populate the @JoinColumn-defined join with the available BID_ITEM_ID foreign key, retrieve the matched ITEMS record, and put it into the item field.

Instead of repeating the same @JoinColumn annotation, we have used the mappedBy element ❶ we mentioned but did not describe in chapter 7.

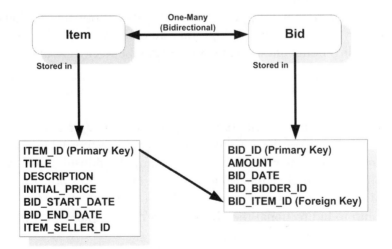

Figure 8.6 The one-to-many relationship between the Item and Bid entities is formed through a foreign key in the BIDS table referring to the primary key of the ITEMS table.

> **NOTE**   The persistence provider will generate deployment-time errors if you specify `@JoinColumn` on both sides of a bidirectional one-to-many relationship.

You can specify this element in the `OneToMany` element on the `Item.bids` variable as follows:

```
public class Item {
    ...
    @OneToMany(mappedBy="item")
    protected Set<Bid> bids;
    ...
}
```

The `mappedBy` element is essentially pointing to the previous relationship field `Bid.item` with the `@JoinColumn` definition. In a bidirectional one-to-many relationship, the owner of the relationship is the entity side that stores the foreign key—that is, the *many* side of the relationship.

The persistence provider will know to look it up appropriately when resolving `Bid` entities. In general, you have to use the `mappedBy` element wherever a bidirectional relationship is required. If you do not specify the `mappedBy` element with the `@OneToOne` annotation, the persistence provider will treat the relationship as a unidirectional relationship. Obviously, this would not be possible if the one-to-many relationship reference were unidirectional since there would be no owner of the relationship to refer to.

Unfortunately, JPA does not support unidirectional one-to-many relationships using a foreign key on the target table and you cannot use the following mapping if you have a unidirectional one-to-many relationship between `Item` and `Bid`:

```
@OneToMany(cascade=CascadeType.ALL)
@JoinColumn(name="ITEM_ID", referencedColumnName="BID_ITEM_ID")
    protected Set<Bid> bids;
```

Although many persistence providers will support this mapping, this support is not standardized and you have to use a join or intersection table using the `@JoinTable` annotation similar to the many-to-many relationship that we discuss in section 8.3.3. Unidirectional one-to-many relationships are scarce, and we'll leave this you to explore on your own. We recommend that you convert your relationship to bidirectional thereby avoiding the complexities involved in maintaining another table.

Also, the `@ManyToOne` annotation does not support the `mappedBy` element since it is always on the side of the relationship that holds the foreign key, and the inverse side can never be the relationship owner.

A final point to remember is that foreign keys can refer back to the primary key of the same table it resides in. There is nothing stopping a `@JoinColumn` annotation from specifying such a relationship. For example, the many-to-one relationship between subcategories and parent categories could be expressed as shown in listing 8.10.

Listing 8.10   Many-to-one self-referencing relationship mapping

```
@Entity
@Table(name="CATEGORIES")
public class Category implements Serializable {
    @Id
    @Column(name="CATEGORY_ID")
    protected Long categoryId;
    ...
    @ManyToOne
    @JoinColumn(name="PARENT_ID",                    ❶
        referencedColumnName="CATEGORY_ID")
    Category parentCategory;    ...
```

In listing 8.10, the `Category` entity refers to its parent through the `PARENT_ID` foreign key pointing to the primary key value of another record in the `CATEGORY` table. Since multiple subcategories can exist under a single parent, the `@Join-Column` annotation specifies a many-one relationship ❶.

We'll conclude this section on mapping domain relationships by dealing with the most complex relationship mapping: many-to-many.

8.3.3   *Many-to-many*

As we mentioned in section 8.1.1, a many-to-many relationship in the database world is implemented by breaking it down into two one-to-many relationships stored in an association or join table. In other words, an association or join table allows you to indirectly match up primary keys from either side of the relationship by storing arbitrary pairs of foreign keys in a row. This scheme is shown in figure 8.7.

The `@JoinTable` mapping in EJB 3 models this technique. To see how this is done, take a look at the code in listing 8.11 for mapping the many-to-many relationship between the `Item` and `Category` entities. Recall that a `Category` can contain multiple `Items` and an `Item` can belong to multiple `Category` entities.

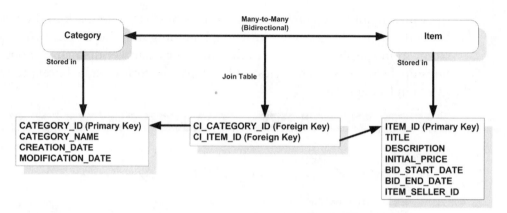

Figure 8.7 Many-to-many relationships are modeled in the database world using join tables. A join table essentially pairs foreign keys pointing to primary keys on either side of the relationship.

Listing 8.11 Many-to-many relationship mapping

```
@Entity
@Table(name="CATEGORIES")
public class Category implements Serializable {
    @Id
    @Column(name="CATEGORY_ID")
    protected Long categoryId;

    @ManyToMany
    @JoinTable(name="CATEGORIES_ITEMS",
        joinColumns=
            @JoinColumn(name="CI_CATEGORY_ID",
                referencedColumnName="CATEGORY_ID"),
        inverseJoinColumns=
            @JoinColumn(name="CI_ITEM_ID",
                referencedColumnName="ITEM_ID"))
    protected Set<Item> items;
    ...
}

@Entity
@Table(name="ITEMS")
public class Item implements Serializable {
    @Id
    @Column(name="ITEM_ID")
    protected Long itemId;
    ...
    @ManyToMany(mappedBy="items")
```

❶ Owning many-to-many

◁─**❷ Subordinate many-to-many**

```
        protected Set<Category> categories;
        ...
    }
```

The `@JoinTable` annotation's `name` element specifies the association or join table, which is named `CATEGORIES_ITEMS` in our case ❶. The `CATEGORIES_ITEMS` table contains only two columns: `CI_CATEGORY_ID` and `CI_ITEMS_ID`. The `CI_CATEGORY_ID` column is a foreign key reference to the primary key of the `CATEGORIES` table, while the `CI_ITEM_ID` column is a foreign key reference to the primary key of the `ITEMS` table. The `joinColumns` and `inverseJoinColumns` elements indicate this. Each of the two elements describes a join condition on either side of the many-to-many relationship. The `joinColumns` element describes the "owning" relationship between the `Category` and `Item` entities, and the `inverseJoinColumns` element describes the "subordinate" relationship between them. Note the distinction of the owning side of the relationship is purely arbitrary.

Just as we used the `mappedBy` element to reduce redundant mapping for one-to-many relationships, we are using the `mappedBy` element on the `Item.categories` field ❷ to point to the `@JoinTable` definition in `Category.items`. We can specify more than one join column with the `@JoinColumns` annotation if we have more than one column that constitutes the foreign key (again, this is an unlikely situation that should be avoided in a clean design). From the perspective of the `Category` entity, the persistence provider will determine what `Item` entities go in the `items` collection by setting the available `CATEGORY_ID` primary key against the combined joins defined in the `@JoinTable` annotation, figuring out what `CI_ITEM_ID` foreign keys match, and retrieving the matching records from the `ITEMS` table.

The flow of logic is essentially reversed for populating `Item.categories`. While saving the relationship into the database, the persistence provider might need to update all three of the `ITEMS`, `CATEGORIES`, and `CATEGORIES_ITEMS` tables as necessary. For a typical change in relational data, the `ITEMS` and `CATEGORIES` tables will remain unchanged while the foreign key references in the `CATEGORIES_ITEMS` table will change. This might be the case if we move an item from one category to the other, for example. Because of the inherent complexity of many-to-many mappings, the `mappedBy` element of the `@ManyToMany` annotation shines in terms of reducing redundancy.

If you have a unidirectional many-to-many relationship, then the only difference is that the inverse side of the relationship does not contain the `mappedBy` element.

We have now finished discussing entity relational mapping and will tackle mapping OO inheritance next before concluding the chapter.

8.4 Mapping inheritance

In section 8.1.1 we mentioned the difficulties in mapping OO inheritance into relational databases. We also alluded to the three strategies used to solve this problem: putting all classes in the OO hierarchy in the same table, using joined tables for the super- and subclasses, or using completely separate tables for each class. We'll explore how each strategy is actually implemented in this section.

Recall from section 8.2.7 that we could easily utilize different strategies for generating sequences more or less by changing configuration parameters for the @GeneratedValue annotation. The @Inheritance annotation used to map OO inheritance tries to follow the same philosophy of isolating strategy-specific settings into the configuration. We'll explore inheritance mapping using the three strategies offered through the @Inheritance annotation by implementing a familiar example.

As we mentioned earlier, the ActionBazaar system has several user types, including sellers and bidders. We have also introduced the idea of creating a User superclass common to all user types. In this scheme of things, the User entity would hold data and behavior common to all users, while subclasses like Bidder and Seller would hold data and behavior specific to user types. Figure 8.8 shows a simplified class diagram for this OO hierarchy.

In this section you'll learn how all the entities in the hierarchy in figure 8.8 can be mapped to database tables using different types of inheritance mapping strategies supported by JPA:

- Single table
- Joined tables
- Table per class

You'll also learn about polymorphic relationships.

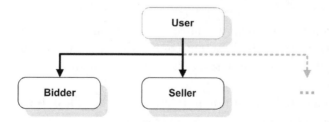

Figure 8.8
The ActionBazaar user hierarchy. Each user type like Bidder and Seller inherit from the common User superclass. The empty arrow signifies there may be some other subclasses of the User class.

8.4.1 *Single-table strategy*

In the single-table strategy, all classes in the inheritance hierarchy are mapped to a single table. This means that the single table will contain a superset of all data stored in the class hierarchy. Different objects in the OO hierarchy are identified using a special column called a *discriminator* column. In effect, the discriminator column contains a value unique to the object type in a given row. The best way to understand this scheme is to see it implemented. For the ActionBazaar schema, assume that all user types, including `Bidders` and `Sellers`, are mapped into the `USERS` table. Figure 8.9 shows how the table might look.

	USER_ID	USERNAME		USER_TYPE	CREDIT_WORTH		BID_FREQUENCY
Bidder records	1	eccentric-collector	...	B	NULL	...	5.70
	2	packrat	...	B	NULL	...	0.01
Seller record	3	snake-oil-salesman	...	S	$10,000.00	...	NULL

Figure 8.9 Storing all ActionBazaar user types using a single table

As figure 8.9 depicts, the `USERS` table contains data common to all users (such as `USER_ID` and `USERNAME`), `Bidder`-specific data (such as `BID_FREQUENCY`) and `Seller`-specific data (such as `CREDIT_WORTH`). Records 1 and 2 contain `Bidder` records while record 3 contains a `Seller` record. This is indicated by the B and S values in the `USER_TYPE` column. As you can imagine, the `USER_TYPE` discriminator column can contain values corresponding to other user types, such as A for admin or C for CSR. The persistence provider maps each user type to the table by storing persistent data into relevant mapped columns, setting the `USER_TYPE` value correctly and leaving the rest of the values NULL.

The next step to understanding the single-table strategy is to analyze the actual mapping implementation. Listing 8.12 shows the mapping for the `User`, `Bidder`, and `Seller` entities.

Listing 8.12 Inheritance mapping using a single table

```
@Entity
@Table(name="USERS")
@Inheritance(strategy=InheritanceType.SINGLE_TABLE)       ❶ Inheritance
                                                             strategy
@DiscriminatorColumn(name="USER_TYPE",
    discriminatorType=DiscriminatorType.STRING, length=1)  ❷ Discriminator
public abstract class User ...                               column
```

```
@Entity
@DiscriminatorValue(value="S")        ◄─❸  Seller discriminator
public class Seller extends User ...

@Entity
@DiscriminatorValue(value="B")        ◄─❹  Bidder discriminator
public class Bidder extends User
```

The inheritance strategy and discriminator column has to be specified on the root entity of the OO hierarchy. In listing 8.12, we specify the strategy to be Inheritance-Type.SINGLE_TABLE in the @Inheritance annotation on the User entity ❶. The @Table annotation on the User entity specifies the name of the single table used for inheritance mapping, USERS. The @DiscriminatorColumn annotation ❷ specifies the details of the discriminator column. The name element specifies the name of the discriminator, USER_TYPE. The discriminatorType element specifies the data type of the discriminator column, which is String, and the length element specifies the size of the column, 1. Both subclasses of User, Bidder, and Seller specify a discriminator value using the @DiscriminatorValue annotation. The Seller class specifies its discriminator value to be S ❸. This means that when the persistence provider saves a Seller object into the USERS table, it will set the value of the USER_TYPE column to S. Similarly, Seller entities would only be reconstituted from rows with a discriminator value of S. Likewise, the Bidder subclass specifies its discriminator value to be B ❹. Every subclass of User is expected to specify an appropriate discriminator value that doesn't conflict with other subclasses. If you don't specify a discriminator value for a subclass, the value is assumed to be the name of the subclass (such as Seller for the Seller entity).

Single table is the default inheritance strategy for EJB 3. Although this strategy is simple to use, it has one great disadvantage that might be apparent from figure 8.5. It does not fully utilize the power of the relational database in terms of using primary/foreign keys and results in a large number of NULL column values.

To understand why, consider the Seller record (number 3) in figure 8.9. The BID_FREQUENCY value is set to NULL for this record since it is not a Bidder record and the Seller entity does not map this column. Conversely, none of the Bidder records ever populate the CREDIT_WORTH column. It is not that hard to imagine the quantity of redundant NULL-valued columns in the USERS table if there are a significant numbers of users (such as a few thousand).

NOTE   For the very same reason, the strategy also limits the ability to enforce data integrity constraints. For example, if you want to enforce a column constraint that `BID_FREQUENCY` cannot be `NULL` for a `Bidder`, you would not be able to enforce the constraint since the same column will contain `Seller` records for which the value may be `NULL`. Typically, such constraints are enforced through alternative mechanisms such as database triggers for the single-table strategy.

The second inheritance strategy avoids the pitfalls we've described and fully utilizes database relationships.

8.4.2 Joined-tables strategy

The joined-tables inheritance strategy uses one-to-one relationships to model OO inheritance. In effect, the joined-tables strategy involves creating separate tables for each entity in the OO hierarchy and relating direct descendants in the hierarchy with one-to-one relationships. For a better grasp, let's see how the data in figure 8.10 might look using this strategy.

In the joined-tables strategy, the parent of the hierarchy contains only columns common to its children. In our example, the `USERS` table contains columns common to all ActionBazaar user types (such as `USERNAME`). The child table in the hierarchy contains columns specific to the entity subtype. Here, both the `BIDDERS` and `SELLERS` tables contain columns specific to the `Bidder` and `Seller` entities, respectively (for example, the `SELLERS` table contains the `CREDIT_WORTH` column). The parent-child OO hierarchy chain is implemented using one-to-one relationships. For example, the `USERS` and `SELLERS` tables are related through the `USER_ID` foreign key in the `SELLERS` table pointing to the primary key of the `USERS` table. A similar relationship exists between the `BIDDERS` and `USERS` tables. The discriminator column in the `USERS` table is still used, primarily as a way of easily differentiating

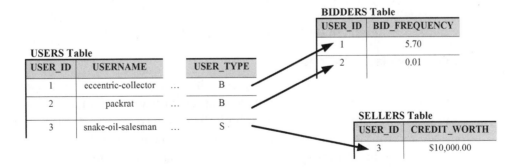

Figure 8.10 Modeling inheritance using joined tables. Each entity in the OO hierarchy corresponds to a separate table and parent-child relationships are modeled using one-to-one mapping.

data types in the hierarchy. Listing 8.13 shows how the mapping strategy is implemented in EJB 3.

Listing 8.13   Inheritance mapping using joined tables

```
@Entity
@Table(name="USERS")
@Inheritance(strategy=InheritanceType.JOINED)        ←┘ Inheritance strategy
@DiscriminatorColumn(name="USER_TYPE",
    discriminatorType=STRING, length=1)
public abstract class User ...

@Entity
@Table(name="SELLERS")
@DiscriminatorValue(value="S")
@PrimaryKeyJoinColumn(name="USER_ID")       ←┘ Primary key join
public class Seller extends User ...

@Entity
@Table(name="BIDDERS")
@DiscriminatorValue(value="B")
@PrimaryKeyJoinColumn(name="USER_ID")       ←┘ Primary key join
public class Bidder extends User ...
```

Listing 8.13 uses the @DiscriminatorColumn and @DiscriminatorValue annotations in exactly the same way as the single-table strategy. The @Inheritance annotation's strategy element is specified as JOINED, however. In addition, the one-to-one relationships between parent and child tables are implemented through the @PrimaryKeyJoinColumn annotations in both the Seller and Bidder entities. In both cases, the name element specifies the USER_ID foreign key. The joined-tables strategy is probably the best mapping choice from a design perspective. From a performance perspective, it is worse than the single-table strategy because it requires the joining of multiple tables for polymorphic queries.

8.4.3   Table-per-class strategy

Table-per-class is probably the simplest inheritance strategy for a layperson to understand. However, this inheritance strategy is the worst from both a relational and OO standpoint. In this strategy, both the superclass (concrete class) and subclasses are stored in their own table and no relationship exists between any of the tables. To see how this works, take a look at the tables in figure 8.11.

As figure 8.11 shows, entity data are stored in their own tables even if they are inherited from the superclass. This is true even for the USER_ID primary key. As a

USERS Table

USER_ID	USERNAME
0	super-user

SELLERS Table

USER_ID	USERNAME	CREDIT_WORTH
3	snake-oil-salesman	

BIDDERS Table

USER_ID	USERNAME	BID_FREQUENCY
1	eccentric-collector	5.70
2	packrat	0.01

Figure 8.11
The table-per-class inheritance strategy. Super- and subclasses are stored in their own, entirely unrelated tables.

result, primary keys in all tables *must* be mutually exclusive for this scheme to work. In addition, inherited columns are duplicated across tables, such as the USERNAME column. Using this inheritance strategy, we define the strategy in the superclass and map tables for all the classes. Listing 8.14 shows how the code might look.

Listing 8.14   Inheritance mapping using the table-per-class strategy

```
@Entity
@Table(name="USERS")
@Inheritance(strategy=InheritanceType.TABLE_PER_CLASS)
public class User {
...
@Entity
@Table(name="SELLERS")
public class Seller extends User {
...
@Entity
@Table(name="BIDDERS")
public class Bidder extends User {
```

Inheritance strategy ❷

Table mappings ❶

As you can see, the inheritance strategy ❷ is specified in the superclass entity, User. However, all of the concrete entities in the OO hierarchy are mapped to separate tables and each have a @Table specification ❶. The greatest disadvantage of using this mapping type is that it does not have good support for polymorphic relations or queries because each subclass is mapped to its own table.

The limitation is that when you want to retrieve entities over the persistence provider, you must use SQL UNION or retrieve each entity with separate SQL for each subclass in the hierarchy.

Besides being awkward, this strategy is the hardest for an EJB 3 provider to implement reliably. As a result, implementing this strategy has been made optional for the provider by the EJB 3 specification. We recommend that you avoid this strategy altogether.

This completes our analysis of the three strategies for mapping OO inheritance. Choosing the right strategy is not as straightforward as you might think. Table 8.2 compares each strategy.

The single-table strategy is relatively simple and is fairly performance friendly since it avoids joins under the hood. Even inserts and updates in the single-table strategy perform better when compared to the joined-tables strategy. This is because in the joined-tables strategy, both the parent and child tables need to be modified for a given entity subclass. However, as we mentioned, the single-table

Table 8.2   The EJB 3 JPA supports three different inheritance strategies. The table-per-class choice is optional and the worst of these strategies.

Feature	Single Table	Joined Tables	Table per Class
Table support	One table for all classes in the entity hierarchy: ■ Mandatory columns may be nullable. ■ The table grows when more subclasses are added.	One for the parent class, and each subclass has a separate table to store polymorphic properties Mapped tables are normalized.	One table for each concrete class in the entity hierarchy
Uses discriminator column?	Yes	Yes	No
SQL generated for retrieval of entity hierarchy	Simple SELECT	SELECT clause joining multiple tables	One SELECT for each subclass or UNION of SELECT
SQL for insert and update	Single INSERT or UPDATE for all entities in the hierarchy	Multiple INSERT, UPDATE: one for the root class and one for each involved subclass	One INSERT or UPDATE for every subclass
Polymorphic relationship	Good	Good	Poor
Polymorphic queries	Good	Good	Poor
Support in EJB 3 JPA	Required	Required	Optional

strategy results in a large number of NULL-valued columns. Moreover, adding a new subclass essentially means updating the unified table each time.

In the joined-tables strategy, adding a subclass means adding a new child table as opposed to altering the parent table (which may or may not be easier to do). By and large, we recommend the joined-tables strategy since it best utilizes the strengths of the relational database, including the ability to use normalization techniques to avoid redundancy. In our opinion, the performance cost associated with joins is relatively insignificant, especially with surrogate keys and proper database indexing.

The table-per-class strategy is probably the worst choice of the three. It is relatively counterintuitive, uses almost no relational database features, and practically magnifies the object relational impedance instead of attempting to bridge it. The most important reason to avoid this strategy, however, is that EJB 3 makes it optional for a provider to implement it. As a result, choosing this strategy might make your solution nonportable across implementations.

Beside these inheritance strategies, the EJB 3 JPA allows an entity to inherit from a nonentity class. Such a class is annotated with `@MappedSuperClass`. Like an embeddable object, a mapped superclass does not have an associated table.

Eclipse ORM tool

As we mentioned earlier, EJB 3 makes O/R mapping a lot easier, but not quite painless. This is largely because of the inherent complexity of ORM and the large number of possible combinations to handle. The good news is that a project to create an Eclipse-based EJB 3 mapping tool code-named Dali is under way (www.eclipse.org/dali/). The project is led by Oracle and supported by JBoss and BEA. It will be a part of Eclipse web tool project (WTP) and will support creating and editing EJB 3 O/R mappings using either annotations or XML. Also, two commercial products, Oracle JDeveloper and BEA Workshop, support development of EJB 3 applications.

8.4.4 *Mapping polymorphic relationships*

In chapter 7 we explained that JPA fully supports inheritance and polymorphism. Now that we have completed our examination of mapping relationships and inheritance, you are probably anxious to learn about polymorphic associations. A relationship between two entities is said to be *polymorphic* when the actual relationship may refer to instances of a subclass of the associated entity. Assume that there is a bidirectional many-to-one relationship between the `ContactInfo` and

User entities. We discussed earlier that User is an abstract entity and entities such as Bidder, Seller, and so forth inherit from the User class. When we retrieve the relationship field from the ContactInfo entity, the retrieved instance of the User entity will be an instance of its subclass, either Bidder or Seller. The greatest benefit of JPA is that you don't have to do any extra work to map polymorphic associations; you just define the relationship mapping between the superclass and the associated entity and the association becomes polymorphic.

8.5 Summary

In this chapter, we explored basic database concepts and introduced the object-relational impedance problem. We reviewed ORM annotations such as @Table and @Column, and mapped some of the entities into database tables.

We also reviewed the various types of primary key generation strategies as well as the mapping of composite primary keys.

In addition, we examined the different types of relationships introduced in the previous chapter and showed you how to use JPA annotations such as @JoinColumn and @PrimaryKeyColumn to map those into database tables. You learned that many-to-many and unidirectional one-to-many relationships require association tables. We hope that the limitation to support unidirectional relationships using a target foreign key constraint will be addressed in a future release.

We showed you the robust OO inheritance mapping features supported by JPA and compared their advantages and disadvantages. Of the three inheritance mapping strategies, using joined tables is the best from a design perspective.

You should note, however, that we avoided some complexities in this chapter. First, we used field-based persistence in all of our code samples to keep them as short and simple as possible. Second, we only mentioned the most commonly used elements for the annotations featured in the chapter. We felt justified in doing so as most of the annotation elements we avoided are rarely used. We do encourage you to check out the full definition of all the annotations in this chapter available online at http://java.sun.com/products/persistence/javadoc-1_0-fr/javax/persistence/package-tree.html.

In the next chapter, you'll learn how to manipulate the entity and relationships we mapped in this chapter using the EntityManager API.

Manipulating entities
with EntityManager

This chapter covers

- Persistence context and its scope
- Container- and application-managed entity managers
- Entity lifecycle and CRUD operations
- Detachment and merge operations
- Entity lifecycle listeners

In chapter 7 you learned how to develop the application domain model using JPA. In chapter 8 you saw how domain objects and relationships are mapped to the database. While the ORM annotations we explored in chapter 8 indicate how an entity is persisted, the annotations don't do the actual persisting. This is performed by applications using the `EntityManager` interface, the topic of this chapter.

To use an analogy, the domain model annotated with ORM configuration is like a children's toy that needs assembly. The domain model consists of the parts of the toy. The ORM configuration is the assembly instructions. While the assembly instructions tell you how the toy parts are put together, you do the actual assembly. The `EntityManager` is the toy assembler of the persistence world. It figures out how to persist the domain by looking at the ORM configuration. More specifically, the `EntityManager` performs CRUD (Create, Read, Update, Delete) operations on domain objects. The *Read* part includes extremely robust search and retrieval of domain objects from the database. This chapter covers each of the CRUD operations that the `EntityManager` provides, with the exception of the *search* part of search and retrieval. In addition to simple primary key–based domain object retrieval, JPA provides SQL SELECT–like search capabilities through the EJB 3 query API. The query API is so extensive and powerful that we'll dedicate chapter 10 to it while briefly touching on it in this one.

Before we dive down into the persistence operations, you'll learn about the `EntityManager` interface, the lifecycle of entities, the concept of persistence context, and how to obtain an instance of `EntityManager`. We'll discuss entity lifecycle callback listeners before concluding with best practices.

Before we get into too much code, we're going to gently introduce the `Entity-Manager` and briefly cover some concepts useful in understanding the nuances behind this critical part of JPA.

9.1 Introducing the EntityManager

The `EntityManager` API is probably the most important and interesting part of the Java Persistence API. It manages the lifecycle of entities. In this section you'll learn about the `EntityManager` interface and its methods. We'll explore the entity lifecycle, and you'll also learn about persistence contexts and their types.

9.1.1 The EntityManager interface

In a sense, the `EntityManager` is the bridge between the OO and relational worlds, as depicted in figure 9.1. When you request that a domain entity be created, the `EntityManager` translates the entity into a new database record. When you request

Figure 9.1 The EntityManager acts as a bridge between the OO and relational worlds. It interprets the O/R mapping specified for an entity and saves the entity in the database.

that an entity be updated, it tracks down the relational data that corresponds to the entity and updates it. Likewise, the EntityManager removes the relational data when you request that an entity be deleted. From the other side of the translation bridge, when you request that an entity be "saved" in the database, the Entity-Manager creates the Entity object, populates it with relational data, and "returns" the Entity back to the OO world.

Besides providing these explicit SQL-like CRUD operations, the EntityManager also quietly tries to keep entities synched with the database automatically as long as they are *within the EntityManager's reach* (this behind-the-scenes synchronization is what we mean when we talk about "managed" entities in the next section). The EntityManager is easily the most important interface in JPA and is responsible for most of the ORM black magic in the API.

Despite all this under-the-hood power, the EntityManager is a small, simple, and intuitive interface, especially compared to the mapping steps we discussed in the previous chapter and the query API (which we explore in chapter 10). In fact, once we go over some basic concepts in the next few sections, the interface might seem almost trivial. You might already agree if you take a quick look at table 9.1. The table lists some of the most commonly used methods defined in the Entity-Manager interface.

Table 9.1 The EntityManager is used to perform CRUD operations. Here are the most commonly used methods of the EntityManager interface.

Method Signature	Description
`public void persist(Object entity);`	Saves (persists) an entity into the database, and also makes the entity managed.
`public <T> T merge(T entity);`	Merges an entity to the EntityManager's persistence context and returns the merged entity.

continued on next page

Table 9.1 The EntityManager is used to perform CRUD operations. Here are the most commonly used methods of the EntityManager interface. *(continued)*

Method Signature	Description
`public void remove(Object entity);`	Removes an entity from the database.
`public <T> T find(Class<T> entityClass, Object primaryKey);`	Finds an entity instance by its primary key.
`public void flush();`	Synchronizes the state of entities in the `EntityManager`'s persistence context with the database.
`public void setFlushMode(FlushModeType flushMode);`	Changes the flush mode of the `EntityManager`'s persistent context. The flush mode may either be AUTO or COMMIT. The default flush mode is AUTO, meaning that the `EntityManager` tries to automatically synch the entities with the database.
`public FlushModeType getFlushMode();`	Retrieves the current flush mode.
`public void refresh(Object entity);`	Refreshes (resets) the entity from the database.
`public Query createQuery(String jpqlString);`	Creates a dynamic query using a JPQL statement.
`public Query createNamedQuery(String name);`	Creates a query instance based on a named query on the entity instance.

`public Query createNativeQuery(String sqlString);`
 	
`public Query createNativeQuery(String sqlString, Class result Class);`
 	
`public Query createNativeQuery(String sqlString, String resultSetMapping);`
	Creates a dynamic query using a native SQL statement.

`public void close();`	Closes an application-managed `EntityManager`.
`public boolean isOpen();`	Checks whether an `EntityManager` is open.
`public EntityTransaction getTransaction();`	Retrieves a transaction object that can be used to manually start or end a transaction.
`public void joinTransaction();`	Asks an `EntityManager` to join an existing JTA transaction.

Don't worry too much if the methods are not immediately obvious. Except for the methods related to the query API (`createQuery`, `createNamedQuery`, and `create-NativeQuery`), we'll discuss them in detail in the coming sections. The few `Entity-Manager` interface methods that we didn't just cover are rarely ever used, so we won't spend time discussing them. Once you've read and understood the material in this chapter, though, we encourage you to explore them on your own. The EJB 3 Java Persistence API final specification is available at http://jcp.org/en/jsr/detail?id=220.

The JPA entity: a set of trade-offs

Nothing in life is free...

As we mentioned (and will explore further in this and future chapters), the reworked EJB 3 JPA entity model brings a whole host of features to the table: simplicity, OO support, and unit testability, to name a few. However, the JPA entity loses some that were available in the EJB 2 model because of its separation from the container. Because the `EntityManager` and not the container manages entities, they cannot directly use container services such as dependency injection, the ability to define method-level transaction and declarative security, remoteability, and so on.

However, the truth of the matter is that most layered applications designed using the EJB 2 CMP entity bean model never utilized container services directly anyway. This is because entity beans were almost always used through a session bean façade. This means that entity beans "piggybacked" over container services configured at the session bean level. The same is true for JPA entities. In real terms, the JPA model loses very little functionality.

Incidentally, losing the magic word "bean" means that JPA entities are no longer EJB components managed by the container. So if you catch someone calling JPA entities "beans," feel free to gently correct them!

Even though JPA is not container-centric like session beans or MDBs, entities still have a lifecycle. This is because they are "managed" by JPA in the sense that the persistence provider keeps track of them under the hood and even automatically synchronizes entity state with the database when possible. We'll explore exactly how the entity lifecycle looks in the following section.

9.1.2 *The lifecycle of an entity*

An entity has a pretty simple lifecycle. Making sense of the lifecycle is easy once you grasp a straightforward concept: the `EntityManager` knows nothing about a POJO regardless of how it is annotated, until you tell the manager to start treating the POJO like a JPA entity. This is the exact opposite of POJOs annotated to be session beans or MDBs, which are loaded and managed by the container as soon as the application starts. Moreover, the default behavior of the EntityManager is to manage an entity for as short a time as possible. Again, this is the opposite of container-managed beans, which remain managed until the application is shut down.

An entity that the EntityManager is keeping track of is considered *attached* or *managed*. On the other hand, when an EntityManager stops managing an entity, the entity is said to be *detached*. An entity that was never managed at any point is called *transient* or *new*.

Figure 9.2 summarizes the entity lifecycle.

Let's take a close look at the managed and detached states.

Managed entities

When we talk about *managing an entity's state*, what we mean is that the Entity-Manager makes sure that the entity's data is synchronized with the database. The EntityManager ensures this by doing two things. First, as soon as we ask an Entity-Manager to start managing an entity, it synchronizes the entity's state with the database. Second, until the entity is no longer managed, the EntityManager ensures that changes to the entity's data (caused by entity method invocations, for example) are reflected in the database. The EntityManager accomplishes this feat by holding an object reference to the managed entity and periodically checking for data

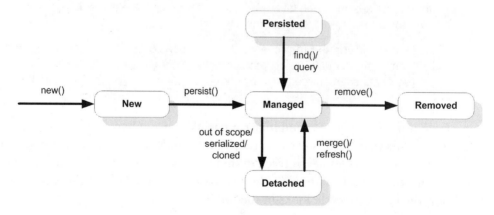

Figure 9.2   An entity becomes managed when you persist, merge, refresh, or retrieve an entity. It may also be attached when we retrieve it. A managed entity becomes detached when it is out of scope, removed, serialized, or cloned.

freshness. If the `EntityManager` finds that any of the entity's data has changed, it automatically synchronizes the changes with the database. The `EntityManager` stops managing the entity when the entity is either deleted or moves out of persistence provider's reach.

An entity can become attached to the `EntityManager`'s context when you pass the entity to the `persist`, `merge`, or `refresh` method. Also an entity becomes attached when you retrieve using the `find` method or a query within a transaction. The state of the entity determines which method you will use.

When an entity is first instantiated as in the following snippet, it is in the *new* or *transient* state since the `EntityManager` doesn't know it exists yet:

```
Bid bid = new Bid();
```

Hence the entity instance is not managed yet. It will become managed if the `EntityManager`'s `persist` method creates a new record in the database corresponding to the entity. This would be the most natural way to attach the `Bid` entity in the previous snippet to the `EntityManager`'s context:

```
manager.persist(bid);
```

A managed entity becomes detached when it is out of scope, removed, serialized, or cloned. For example, the instance of the `Bid` entity will become detached when the underlying transaction commits.

Unlike entities explicitly created using the `new` operator, an entity retrieved from the database using the `EntityManager`'s `find` method or a query is attached if retrieved within a transactional context. A retrieved instance of the entity becomes detached immediately if there is no associated transaction.

The `merge` and `refresh` methods are intended for entities that have been retrieved from the database and are in the detached state. Either of these methods attaches entities to the entity manager. `EntityManager.merge` updates the database with the data held in the entity, and `refresh` does the opposite—it resets the entity's state with data from the database. We'll discuss these methods in much greater detail in section 9.3.

Detached entities

A detached entity is an entity that is no longer managed by the `EntityManager` and there is no guarantee that the state of the entity is in synch with the database. Detachment and merge operations become handy when you want to pass an entity across application tiers. For example, you can detach an entity and pass it to the web tier, then update it and send it back to the EJB tier, where you can merge the detached entity to the persistence context.

The usual way entities become detached is a little subtler. Essentially, an attached entity becomes detached as soon as it goes out of the EntityManager context's scope. Think of this as the expiration of the invisible link between an entity and the EntityManager at the end of a logical unit of work or a session. An Entity-Manager session could be limited to a single method call or span an arbitrary length of time. (Reminds you of session beans, doesn't it? As you'll soon see, this is not entirely an accident.) For an EntityManager whose session is limited to a method call, all entities attached to it become detached as soon as a method returns, even if the entity objects are used outside the method. If this is not absolutely crystal clear right now, it will be once we talk about the EntityManager persistence context in the next section.

Entity instances also become detached through cloning or serialization. This is because the EntityManager quite literally keeps track of entities through Java object references. Since cloned or serialized instances don't have the same object references as the original managed entity, the EntityManager has no way of knowing they exist. This scenario occurs most often in situations where entities are sent across the network for session bean remote method calls.

In addition, if you call the clear method of EntityManager, it forces all entities in the persistence context to be detached. Calling the EntityManager's remove method will also detach an entity. This makes perfect sense since this method removes the data associated with the entity from the database. As far as the Entity-Manager is concerned, the entity no longer exists, so there is no need to continue managing it. For our Bid entity, this would be an "apt demise":

```
manager.remove(bid);
```

We'll return to this discussion on detachment and merge operations in section 9.3.3.

A good way to remember the entity lifecycle is through a convenient analogy. Think of an entity as an aircraft and the EntityManager as the air traffic controller. While the aircraft is outside the range of the airport (detached or new), it is not guided by the air traffic controller. However, when it does come into range (managed), the traffic controller manages the aircraft's movement (state synchronized with database). Eventually, a grounded aircraft is guided into takeoff and goes out of airport range again (detached), at which point the pilot is free to follow her own flight plan (modifying a detached entity without state being managed).

The *persistence context scope* is the equivalent of airport radar range. It is critical to understand how the persistence context works to use managed entities effectively. We'll examine the relationship between the persistence context, its scope, and the `EntityManager` in the next section.

9.1.3 *Persistence contexts, scope, and the EntityManager*

The persistence context plays a vital role in the internal functionality of the `Entity-Manager`. Although we perform persistence operations by invoking methods on the `EntityManager`, the `EntityManager` itself does not directly keep track of the lifecycle of an individual entity. In reality, the `EntityManager` delegates the task of managing entity state to the currently available persistence context.

In a very simple sense, a persistence context is a self-contained collection of entities managed by an `EntityManager` during a given persistence scope. The persistence scope is the duration of time a given set of entities remains managed.

The best way to understand this is to start by examining what the various persistence scopes are and what they do and then backtracking to the meaning of the term. We'll explain how the persistence context and persistence scope relates to the `EntityManager` by first exploring what the persistence context is.

There are two different types of persistence scopes: *transaction* and *extended*.

Transaction-scoped EntityManager

An `EntityManager` associated with a transaction-scoped persistence context is known as a *transaction-scoped* `EntityManager`. If a persistence context is under transaction scope, entities attached during a transaction are automatically detached when the transaction ends. (All persistence operations that may result in data changes must be performed inside a transaction, no matter what the persistence scope is.) In other words, the persistence context keeps managing entities while the transaction it is enclosed by is active. Once the persistence context detects that a transaction has either been rolled back or committed, it will detach all managed entities after making sure that all data changes until that point are synchronized with the database. Figure 9.3 depicts this relationship between entities, the transaction persistence scope, and persistence contexts.

Extended EntityManager

The life span of the extended `EntityManager` lasts across multiple transactions. An extended `EntityManager` can only be used with stateful session beans and lasts as long as the bean instance is alive. Therefore, in persistence contexts with extended scope, how long entities remain managed has nothing to do with transaction

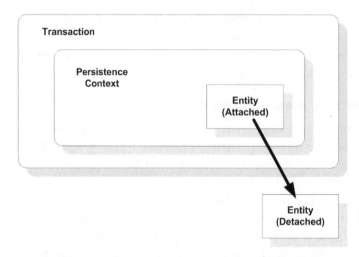

Figure 9.3
Transaction-scoped
persistence contexts only
keep entities attached
within the boundaries of
the enclosing transaction.

boundaries. In fact, once attached, entities pretty much stay managed as long as the EntityManager instance is around. As an example, for a stateful session bean, an EntityManager with extended scope will keep managing all attached entities until the EntityManager is closed as the bean itself is destroyed. As figure 9.4 shows, this means that unless explicitly detached through a remove method to end the life of the stateful bean instance, entities attached to an extended persistence context will remain managed across multiple transactions.

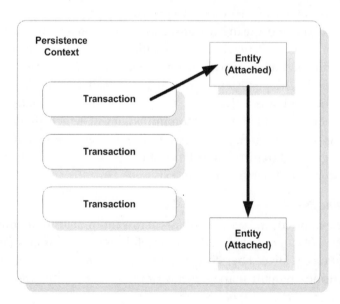

Figure 9.4
For an extended persistence
context, once an entity is
attached in any given
transaction, it is managed for
all transactions in the lifetime
of the persistence context.

The term *scope* is used for persistence contexts in the same manner that it is used for Java variable scoping. It describes how long a particular persistence context remains active. Transaction-scoped persistence contexts can be compared to method local variables, in the sense that they are only in effect within the boundaries of a transaction. On the other hand, persistence contexts with extended scope are more like instance variables that are active for the lifetime of an object—they hang around as long as the EntityManager is around.

At this point, we've covered the basic concepts needed to understand the functionality of the EntityManager. We are now ready to see the EntityManager itself in action.

9.1.4 Using the EntityManager in ActionBazaar

We'll explore the EJB 3 EntityManager interface by implementing an Action-Bazaar component. We'll implement the ItemManagerBean stateless session bean used to provide the operations to manipulate items. As listing 9.1 demonstrates, the session bean provides methods for adding, updating, and removing Item entities using the JPA EntityManager.

Listing 9.1 ItemManagerBean using the container-managed, transaction-scoped entity manager

```java
@Stateless
public class ItemManagerBean implements ItemManager {
    @PersistenceContext(unitName="actionBazaar")
    private EntityManager entityManager;          ◁──❶ Injects EntityManager
                                                         instance
    public ItemManagerBean() {}

    public Item addItem(String title, String description,
            byte[] picture, double initialPrice, long sellerId) {
        Item item = new Item();
        item.setTitle(title);
        item.setDescription(description);                 Retrieves entity ❷
        item.setPicture(picture);                         using primary key
        item.setInitialPrice(initialPrice);
        Seller seller = entityManager.find(Seller.class, sellerId);  ◁─┘
        item.setSeller(seller);
        entityManager.persist(item);      ◁──❸ Persists entity instance

        return item;
    }

    public Item updateItem(Item item) {
        entityManager.merge(item);        ◁──❹ Merges changes to database
        return item;
    }
```

```
public Item undoItemChanges(Item item) {
    entityManager.refresh(entityManager.merge(item));
    return item;
}
```
**Refreshes entity
from database** ❺

```
public void deleteItem(Item item) {
    entityManager.remove(entityManager.merge(item));
}
}
```
**Removes
entity from** ❻ **database**

`ItemManagerBean` is a pretty good representation of the most common ways the `EntityManager` API is used. First, an instance of the `EntityManager` is injected using the `@PersistenceContext` annotation ❶ and is used in all the session bean methods that manipulate entities. As you might imagine, the `addItem` method is used by the presentation layer to add an item posted by the seller to the database. The `persist` method is used by `addItem` to add a new `Item` entity to the database ❸. The `addItem` method also uses the `EntityManager`'s `find` method to retrieve the `Seller` of the `Item` using the entity's primary key ❷. The retrieved `Seller` entity is set as an association field of the newly instantiated `Item` entity along with all other item data.

The `updateItem` method updates the `Item` entity data in the database using the `merge` method ❹. This method could be invoked from an administrative interface that allows a seller to update a listing after an item is posted. The `EntityManager`'s `refresh` method is used in the `undoItemChanges` method to discard any changes made to an `Item` entity and to reload it with the data stored in the database ❺. The `undoItemChanges` method could be used by the same administrative interface that uses the `updateItem` method to allow the user to start over with modifying a listing (think of an HTTP form's "reset" button).

Lastly, an `Item` entity is removed from the database using the `remove` method ❻. This method could be used by an ActionBazaar administrator to remove an offending listing.

Now that we've "surface-scanned" the code in listing 9.1, we're ready to start our in-depth analysis of the `EntityManager` API. We'll start from the most logical point: making an `EntityManager` instance available to the application.

9.2 Creating EntityManager instances

`EntityManager` is like the conductor of an orchestra who manages the show. Say you'd like to bring the orchestra to your town for a performance. You first get in touch with and attempt to hire the conductor. Similarly, the first obvious step to performing any persistence operation is obtaining an instance of an `EntityManager`.

In listing 9.1, we do this by injecting an instance using the `@Persistence-Context` annotation. If you are using a container, this is more or less all you will need to know about getting an instance of an `EntityManager`.

All `EntityManager` instances injected using the `@PersistenceContext` annotation are container managed. This means that the container takes care of the mundane task of looking up, opening, and closing the `EntityManager` behind the scenes. In addition, unless otherwise specified, injected `EntityManagers` have transaction scope. Just as you aren't limited to using the transaction scope, you are not limited to using a container-managed `EntityManager` either.

JPA fully supports creating application-managed `EntityManagers` that you explicitly create, use, and release, including controlling how the `EntityManager` handles transactions. This capability is particularly important for using JPA outside the container.

In this section we'll explore how to create and use both container- and application-managed `EntityManagers`.

9.2.1 *Container-managed EntityManagers*

As you saw earlier, container-managed `EntityManagers` are injected using the `@PersistenceContext` annotation. Let's take a look at the definition of the annotation to start exploring its features:

```
@Target({TYPE, METHOD, FIELD})
@Retention(RUNTIME)
public @interface PersistenceContext {
    String name() default "";
    String unitName() default "";
    PersistenceContextType type default TRANSACTION;
    PersistenceProperty[] properties() default {};
}
```

The first element of the annotation, `name`, specifies the JNDI name of the persistence context. This element is used in the unlikely case you have to explicitly mention the JNDI name for a given container implementation to be able to look up an `EntityManager`. In most situations, leaving this element empty is fine, except when you use `@PersistenceContext` at the class level to establish reference to the persistence context.

The `unitName` element specifies the name of the *persistence unit*. A *persistence unit* is essentially a grouping of entities used in an application. This idea is useful when you have a large Java EE application and would like to separate it into several logical areas (think Java packages). For example, ActionBazaar entities could be grouped into *general* and *admin* units.

Persistence units cannot be set up using code, and you must configure them through the `persistence.xml` deployment descriptor. We'll return to the topic of configuring persistence units in chapter 11; for now, all you need to understand is that you can get an `EntityManager` for the *admin* unit using the `unitName` element as follows:

```
@PersistenceContext(unitName="admin")
EntityManager entityManager;
```

In the typical case that a Java EE module has a single persistence unit, specifying the `unitName` might seem redundant. In fact, most persistence providers will resolve the unit correctly if you don't specify a `unitName`. However, we recommend specifying a persistence unit name even if you only have one unit. This ensures that you are not dependent on container-specific functionality since the specification doesn't state what the persistence provider must do if the `unitName` is not specified.

EntityManager scoping

The element `type` specifies the `EntityManager` scope. As we noted, for a container-managed `EntityManager`, scope can either be `TRANSACTION` or `EXTENDED`. If the `type` element is left empty, the scope is assumed to be `TRANSACTION`. Not surprisingly, the typical use of the `type` element is to specify `EXTENDED` for an `EntityManager`. The code would look like this:

```
@PersistenceContext(type=PersistenceContextType.EXTENDED)
EntityManager entityManager;
```

You are not allowed to use extended persistence scope for stateless session beans or MDBs. If you stop and think for second, the reason should be pretty obvious. The real reason for using extended scope in a bean would be to manage entity state across multiple method calls, even if each method call is a separate transaction. Since neither sessions nor message-driven beans are supposed to implement such functionality, it makes no sense to support extended scope for these bean types. On the other hand, extended persistence scope is ideal for stateful session beans. An underlying `EntityManager` with extended scope could be used to cache and maintain the application domain across an arbitrary number of method calls from a client. More importantly, you could do this and still not have to give up method-level transaction granularity (most likely using CMT). We'll return to our discussion of how you can use an extended persistence context for stateful session beans as an effective caching mechanism in chapter 13.

NOTE The real power of container-managed `EntityManager`s lies in the high degree of abstraction they offer. Behind the scenes, the container instantiates `EntityManager`s, binds them to JNDI, injects them into beans on demand, and closes them when they are no longer needed (typically when a bean is destroyed).

It is difficult to appreciate the amount of menial code the container takes care of until you see the alternative. Keep this in mind when looking at application-managed `EntityManager`s in the coming section. Note that container-managed `EntityManager`s are available to all components in a Java EE container, including JSF-backing beans and servlets. However, be aware of the fact that `Entity-Manager`s are not thread-safe; thus, injecting them frivolously into presentation-layer components can readily land you in some trouble. We'll discuss this nuance in the sidebar "EntityManagers and thread safety."

EntityManagers and thread safety

It is very easy to forget the fact that web-tier components are meant to be used by multiple concurrent threads. Servlet-based components like JSPs are deliberately designed this way because they are intended to achieve high throughput through statelessness.

However, this fact means that you cannot use resources that are not thread-safe as servlet instance variables. The `EntityManager` falls under this category, so injecting it into a web component is a big no-no. One way around this problem is to use the `SingleThreadModel` interface to make a servlet thread-safe. In practice, this technique severely degrades application performance and is almost always a bad idea.

Some vendors might try to solve this problem. If you are extremely comfortable with your container vendor, you could count on this. Remember, though, one very important benefit of using EJB 3 is portability across container implementations. You shouldn't give up this advantage frivolously.

If you must use container-managed `EntityManager`s from your servlet, the best option is to look up an instance of the `EntityManager` inside your method as follows:

```
@PersistenceContext(name="pu/actionBazaar",
                    unitName="ActionBazaar")
public class ItemServlet extends HttpServlet {
    @Resource private UserTransaction ut;
    public void service (HttpServletRequest req,
                    HttpServletResponse resp)
            throws ServletException, IOException {
```

```
            Context ctx = new InitialContext();
            EntityManager em =(EntityManager)
                      ctx.lookup(
                 "java:comp/env/pu/actionBazaar");

            ...
            ut.begin();
            em.persist(item);
            ut.commit();
            ...
        }
        ...
    }
```

The other alternative is to use an application-managed EntityManager with a JTA transaction. It is worth noting that EntityManagerFactory is thread-safe.

Now that you are familiar with working with EntityManager inside the container, let's move on to the application-managed EntityManager.

9.2.2 Application-managed EntityManager

An application-managed EntityManager wants nothing to do with a Java EE container. This means that you must write code to control every aspect of the Entity-Manager's lifecycle. By and large, application-managed EntityManagers are most appropriate for environments where a container is not available, such as Java SE or a lightweight web container like Tomcat.

However, a justification to use application-managed EntityManagers inside a Java EE container is to maintain fine-grained control over the EntityManager life-cycle or transaction management. For this reason, as well as to maintain flexibility, the EJB 3 API provides a few conveniences for using application-managed EntityManagers inside a container. This happens to suit us well too, because it provides an effective approach to exploring application-managed Entity-Managers (see listing 9.2) by reusing the code in listing 9.1.

Listing 9.2   ItemManagerBean using an application-managed EntityManager

```
@Stateless
public class ItemManagerBean implements ItemManager {
    @PersistenceUnit
    private EntityManagerFactory entityManagerFactory;         Injects Entity-
    private EntityManager entityManager;                  ❶   ManagerFactory
                                                               instance
    public ItemManagerBean() {}

    @PostConstruct
```

```
public void initialize() {
    entityManager = entityManagerFactory.createEntityManager();
}
...
public Item updateItem(Item item) {
    entityManager.joinTransaction();
    entityManager.merge(item);
    return item;
}
...
@PreDestroy
public void cleanup() {
    if (entityManager.isOpen()) {
        entityManager.close();
    }
}
...
}
```

Creates EntityManager ❷

❸ **Explicitly joins JTA transaction**

❹ **Closes EntityManager**

It should be fairly obvious that we are more or less explicitly doing what the container did for us behind the scenes in listing 9.1. First we inject an instance of `EntityManagerFactory` ❶. We create an `EntityManager` using the injected entity manager factory after the bean is constructed ❷ and close it ❹ before the bean is destroyed, mirroring what the container does automatically. The same is true when we explicitly join a container-managed JTA transaction ❸ before performing an `EntityManager` operation.

EntityManagerFactory

As you can see in listing 9.2, we get an instance of an application-managed `Entity-Manager` using the `EntityManagerFactory` interface. If you have used JDBC, this is essentially the same idea as creating a `Connection` from a `DriverManager` factory. In a Java EE environment, you have the luxury of using the `@PersistenceUnit` annotation to inject an instance of an `EntityManagerFactory`, just as we do in listing 9.2. This useful annotation is defined as follows:

```
@Target({TYPE, METHOD, FIELD})
@Retention(RUNTIME)
public @interface PersistenceUnit {
    String name() default "";
    String unitName() default "";
}
```

The `name` and `unitName` elements serve exactly the same purpose as they do for the `@PersistenceContext` annotation. While the `name` element can be used to point to

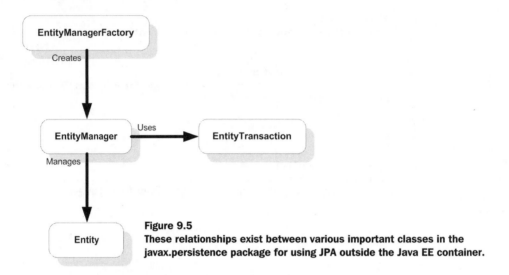

Figure 9.5
These relationships exist between various important classes in the javax.persistence package for using JPA outside the Java EE container.

the JNDI name of the `EntityManagerFactory`, the `unitName` element is used to specify the name of the underlying persistence unit.

Figure 9.5 shows the relationships between important interfaces made available by JPA outside the container.

The `EntityManagerFactory`'s `createEntityManager` method creates an application-managed `EntityManager`. This is probably the most commonly used method in the interface, in addition to the `close` method. We don't explicitly close the factory in listing 9.2 since the container takes care of cleaning up all resources it injects (unlike the `EntityManager`, which is created programmatically and is explicitly closed). Table 9.2 lists all the methods in the `EntityManagerFactory` interface. As you can see, most of them are fairly self-explanatory.

Table 9.2   The EntityManager factory is used to create an instance of an application-managed EntityManager.

Method	Purpose
`EntityManager createEntityManager()`	Creates an application-managed `EntityManager`.
`EntityManager createEntityManager(Map map)`	Creates an application-managed `EntityManager` with a specified `Map`. The `Map` contains vendor-specific properties to create the manager.
`void close()`	Closes the `EntityManagerFactory`.
`boolean isOpen()`	Checks whether the `EntityManagerFactory` is open.

We have seen the usage of most of the EntityManagerFactory methods in listing 9.2. Perhaps the most interesting aspect of listing 9.2 is the entityManager.joinTransaction() call in the updateItem method. Let's discuss this method in a little more detail.

As we hinted in the beginning of this section, unlike container-managed EntityManagers, application-managed EntityManagers do not automatically participate in an enclosing transaction. Instead, they must be asked to join an enclosing JTA transaction by calling the joinTransaction method. This method is specifically geared to using application-managed EntityManagers inside a container, where JTA transactions are usually available.

Application-managed EntityManagers outside the Java EE container

In Java SE environments, however, JTA is not a possibility. Resource-local transactions must be used in place of JTA for such environments. The EntityTransaction interface is designed with exactly this scenario in mind. We'll explore this interface by reimplementing the code to update an item from listing 9.2 for an SE application. Listing 9.3 also serves the dual purpose of being a good template for using application-managed EntityManagers without any help from the container.

Listing 9.3 Using an application-managed EntityManager outside a container

```
EntityManagerFactory entityManagerFactory =
    Persistence.createEntityManagerFactory("actionBazaar");

                              Gets EntityManagerFactory instance  ❶
EntityManager entityManager =
    entityManagerFactory.createEntityManager();
                                                   ❷ Creates
try                                                   EntityManager
{
    EntityTransaction entityTransaction =          ❸ Creates
    entityManager.getTransaction();                   transaction

    entityTransaction.begin();      ◁─❹ Begins transaction

    entityManager.persist(item);    ◁─❺ Merges Item

    entityTransaction.commit();     ◁─❻ Commits transaction
}
finally
{
    entityManager.close();                ❼ Closes resources
     entityManagerFactory.close();
}
```

The first thing that should strike you about listing 9.3 is the amount of boilerplate code involved to accomplish exactly the same thing as the updateItem method in listing 9.1 (cutting and pasting both code snippets into a visual editor and comparing the code side-by-side might be helpful in seeing the full picture at a glance).

The javax.persistence.Persistence object's createEntityManagerFactory method used in listing 9.3 ❶ is essentially a programmatic substitute for the @PersistenceUnit annotation. The single parameter of the createEntityManagerFactory method is the name of the EntityManagerFactory defined in the persistence.xml deployment descriptor. Since the container is no longer helping us out, it is now important to be sure to close the EntityManagerFactory returned by the createEntityManagerFactory method when we are done, in addition to closing the EntityManager ❼. Just as in listing 9.2, the EntityManagerFactory's createEntityManager method is used to create the application-managed EntityManager ❷.

However, before merging the Item entity to the database ❺, we now create an EntityTransaction by calling the getTransaction method of the EntityManager ❸. The EntityTransaction is essentially a high-level abstraction over a resource-local JDBC transaction, as opposed to the distributed JTA transaction we *joined* in listing 9.2. At first it is natural to think that a joinTransaction call is still necessary to make the EntityManager aware of the enclosing transaction. Remember that since the EntityManager itself is creating the transaction instead of the container, it implicitly keeps track of EntityTransactions, so the join is not necessary. The rest of the transaction code—the begin ❹ and the commit ❻—do exactly what you'd expect. As might be obvious, the EntityTransaction interface also has a rollback method to abort the transaction. Note that application-managed EntityManagers are never transaction scoped. That is, they keep managing attached entities until they are closed. Also the transaction-type must be set to RESOURCE_LOCAL in the persistence.xml file for using the EntityTransaction interface (we'll discuss this further in chapter 11 when we talk about EJB 3 packaging and deployment).

Although there is little doubt that the code in listing 9.3 is pretty verbose and error prone, being able to use application-managed EntityManagers outside the confines of the container accomplishes the vital goal of making standardized ORM accessible to all kinds of applications beyond server-side enterprise solutions, including Java Swing-based desktop applications, as well as enabling integration with web containers such as Tomcat or Jetty.

Using JPA in a web container and the ThreadLocal pattern

If you are using an application-managed entity manager in a web container such as Tomcat or Jetty, some persistence providers such as Hibernate recommend that you use the ThreadLocal pattern. This is widely known as the ThreadLocal session pattern in the Hibernate community. It associates a single instance of the EntityManager with a particular request. You have to bind the EntityManager to a thread-local variable and set the EntityManager instance to the associated thread, as shown here:

```
private static EntityManagerFactory emf;
    public static final ThreadLocal<EntityManager> _
        threadLocal = new ThreadLocal<EntityManager>();

    public static EntityManagerFactory getEntityManagerFactory() {
        if (emf == null) {
            emf =
            Persistence.createEntityManagerFactory("actionBazaar");
        }

        return emf;
    }


    public static EntityManager getEntityManager() {
        EntityManager entityManager = _threadLocal.get();

        if (entityManager == null) {
            entityManager = emf.createEntityManager();
            _threadLocal.set(entityManager);
        }
        return entityManager;
    }
```

Stores **EntityManager** in **ThreadLocal** variable

Creates **EntityManager**

Associates **EntityManager** with a thread

Check your persistence provider's documentation if it requires you to use the ThreadLocal pattern.

Next, we'll tackle the most important part of this chapter: EntityManager operations.

9.3 *Managing persistence operations*

The heart of the JPA API lies in the EntityManager operations, which we'll discuss in upcoming sections. As you might have noted in listing 9.1, although the EntityManager interface is small and simple, it is pretty complete in its ability to provide an effective persistence infrastructure. In addition to the CRUD (Create,

Read, Update, and Delete) functionality we introduced in listing 9.1, we'll cover a few less-commonly used operations like flushing and refreshing.

Let's start our coverage in the most logical place: persisting new entities into the database.

9.3.1 *Persisting entities*

Recall that in listing 9.1, the addItem method persists an Item entity into the database. Since listing 9.1 was quite a few pages back, we'll repeat the addItem method body as reviewed in listing 9.4. Although it is not obvious, the code is especially helpful in understanding how entity relationships are persisted, which we'll look at in greater detail in a minute. For now, let's concentrate on the persist method itself.

Listing 9.4 Persisting entities

```
public Item addItem(String title, String description,
    byte[] picture, double initialPrice, long sellerId) {
    Item item = new Item();
    item.setTitle(title);
    item.setDescription(description);
    item.setPicture(picture);
    item.setInitialPrice(initialPrice);
    Seller seller = entityManager.find(Seller.class, sellerId);
    item.setSeller(seller);
    entityManager.persist(item);        ◁─┐  Persists entity

    return item;
}
```

A new Item entity corresponding to the record being added is first instantiated in the addItem method. All of the relevant Item entity data to be saved into the database, such as the item title and description, is then populated with the data passed in by the user. As you'll recall from chapter 7, the Item entity has a many-to-one relationship with the Seller entity. The related seller is retrieved using the EntityManager's find method and set as a field of the Item entity. The persist method is then invoked to save the entity into the database, as shown in figure 9.6. Note that the persist method is intended to create *new* entity records in the database and not update existing ones. This means that you should make sure the identity or primary key of the entity to be persisted doesn't already exist in the database.

Figure 9.6 Invoking the persist method on the EntityManager interface makes an entity instance managed. When the transaction commits, the entity state is synchronized with the database.

If you try to persist an entity that violates the database's integrity constraint, the persistence provider will throw `javax.persistence.PersistenceException`, which wraps the database exception.

As we noted earlier, the `persist` method also causes the entity to become managed as soon as the method returns. The `INSERT` statement (or statements) that creates the record corresponding to the entity is not necessarily issued immediately. For transaction-scoped `EntityManagers`, the statement is typically issued when the enclosing transaction is about to commit. In our example, this means the SQL statements are issued when the `addItem` method returns. For extended-scoped (or application-managed) `EntityManagers`, the `INSERT` statement is probably issued right before the `EntityManager` is *closed*. The `INSERT` statement can also be issued at any point when the `EntityManager` is *flushed*.

We'll discuss automatic and manual flushing in more detail shortly. For now, you just need to know that under certain circumstances, either you or the `Entity-Manager` can choose to perform pending database operations (such as an `INSERT` to create a record), without waiting for the transaction to end or the `EntityManager` to close. The `INSERT` statement corresponding to listing 9.4 to save the `Item` entity could look something like this:

```
INSERT INTO ITEMS
    (TITLE, DESCRIPTION, SELLER_ID, ...)
VALUES
    ("Toast with the face of Bill Gates on it",
    "This is an auction for...", 1, ...)
```

As you may have noticed, the `ITEM_ID` primary key that is the *identity* for the `Item` entity is not included in the generated `INSERT` statement. This is because the key-generation scheme for the `itemId` identity field of the entity is set to `IDENTITY`. If the scheme were set to `SEQUENCE` or `TABLE` instead, the `EntityManager` would have generated a `SELECT` statement to retrieve the key value first and then include the retrieved key in the `INSERT` statement. As we mentioned earlier, all persistence operations that require database updates must be invoked within the scope of a transaction. If an enclosing transaction is not present when the persist method is invoked, a TransactionRequiredException is thrown for a transaction-scoped entity manager. If you are using an application-managed or extended entity manager, invoking the persist method will attach the entity to persistence context. If a new transaction starts, the entity manager joins the transaction and the changes will be saved to the database when the transaction commits. The same is true for the EntityManager's flush, merge, refresh, and remove methods.

Persisting entity relationships

One of the most interesting aspects of persistence operations is the handling of entity relationships. JPA gives us a number of options to handle this nuance in a way that suits a particular application-specific situation.

Let's explore these options by revisiting listing 9.4. The addItem method is one of the simplest cases of persisting entity relationships. The Seller entity is retrieved using the find method, so it is already managed, and any changes to it are guaranteed to be transparently synchronized. Recall from chapter 7 that there is a bidirectional one-to-many relationship between the Item and Seller entities. This relationship is realized in listing 9.4 by setting the Seller using the item.set-Seller method. Let's assume that the Seller entity is mapped to the SELLERS table. Such a relationship between the Item and Seller entities is likely implemented through a foreign key to the SELLERS.SELLER_ID column in the ITEMS table. Since the Seller entity is already persisted, all the EntityManager has to do is set the SELLER_ID foreign key in the generated INSERT statement. Examining the INSERT statement presented earlier, this is how the SELLER_ID value is set to 1. Note that if the seller property of Item were not set at all, the SELLER_ID column in the INSERT statement would be set to NULL.

Things become a lot more interesting when we consider the case in which the entity related to the one we are persisting does not yet exist in the database. This does not happen very often for one-to-many and many-to-many relationships. In such cases, the related entity is more than likely already saved in the database. However, it does occur a lot more often for one-to-one relationships. For purposes of illustration, we'll stray from our ItemManager example and take a look at saving User entities with associated BillingInfo entities. Recall that we introduced this unidirectional, one-to-one relationship in chapter 7. The method outlined in listing 9.5 receives user information such as username, e-mail, as well as billing information such as credit card type and number, and persists both the User and related BillingInfo entities into the database.

Listing 9.5   Persisting relationships

```
public User addUser(String username, String email,
    String creditCardType, String creditCardNumber,
        Date creditCardExpiration) {
    User user = new User();
    user.setUsername(username);
    user.setEmail(email);

    BillingInfo billing = new BillingInfo();
    billing.setCreditCardType(creditCardType);
    billing.setCreditCardNumber(creditCardNumber);
    billing.setCreditCardExpiration(creditCardExpiration);

    user.setBillingInfo(billing);
    entityManager.persist(user);        ← Persists both User and BillingInfo

    return user;
}
```

As you can see, neither the User entity nor the related BillingInfo entity is managed when the persist method is invoked, since both are newly instantiated. Let's assume for the purpose of this example that the User and BillingInfo entities are saved into the USERS and BILLING_INFO tables, with the one-to-one relationship modeled with a foreign key on the USERS table referencing the BILLING_ID key in the BILLING_INFO table. As you might guess from looking at listing 9.5, two INSERT statements, one for the User and the other for the BillingInfo entity, are issued by JPA. The INSERT statement on the USERS table will contain the appropriate foreign key to the BILLING_INFO table.

Cascading persist operations

Perhaps surprisingly, it is not the default behavior for JPA to persist related entities. By default, the BillingInfo entity would not be persisted and you would not see an INSERT statement generated to persist the BillingInfo entity into the BILLING_ INFO table. The key to understanding why this is not what happens in listing 9.5 lies in the @OneToOne annotation on the billing property of the User entity:

```
public class User {

@OneToOne(cascade=CascadeType.PERSIST)
    public void setBillingInfo(BillingInfo billing) {
```

Notice the value of the cascade element of the @OneToOne annotation. We deferred the discussion of this element in chapter 7 so that we could discuss it in a more relevant context here.

Cascading in ORM-based persistence is similar to the idea of cascading in databases. The `cascade` element essentially tells the `EntityManager` how, or if, to propagate a given persistence operation on a particular entity into entities related to it.

By default, the `cascade` element is empty, which means that *no* persistence operations are propagated to related entities. Alternatively, the `cascade` element can be set to `ALL`, `MERGE`, `PERSIST`, `REFRESH`, or `REMOVE`. Table 9.3 lists the effect of each of these values.

Table 9.3   Effects of various cascade type values.

CascadeType Value	Effect
CascadeType.MERGE	Only `EntityManager.merge` operations are propagated to related entities.
CascadeType.PERSIST	Only `EntityManager.persist` operations are propagated to related entities.
CascadeType.REFRESH	Only `EntityManager.refresh` operations are propagated to related entities.
CascadeType.REMOVE	Only `EntityManager.remove` operations are propagated to related entities.
CascadeType.ALL	All `EntityManager` operations are propagated to related entities.

Since in our case we have set the `cascade` element to `PERSIST`, when we `persist` the `User` entity, the `EntityManager` figures out that a `BillingInfo` entity is associated with the `User` entity and it must be persisted as well. As table 9.3 indicates, the `persist` operation would still be propagated to `BillingInfo` if the `cascade` element were set to `ALL` instead. However, if the element were set to any other value or not specified, the operation would not be propagated and we would have to perform the `persist` operation on the `BillingInfo` entity separately from the `User` entity. For example, let's assume that the `cascade` element on the `@OneToOne` annotation is not specified. To make sure both related entities are persisted, we'd have to change the `addUser` method as shown in listing 9.6.

Listing 9.6   Manually persisting relationships

```
public User addUser(String username, String email,
    String creditCardType, String creditCardNumber,
        Date creditCardExpiration) {
    User user = new User();
```

```
user.setUsername(username);
user.setEmail(email);

BillingInfo billing = new BillingInfo();
billing.setCreditCardType(creditCardType);
billing.setCreditCardNumber(creditCardNumber);
billing.setCreditCardExpiration(creditCardExpiration);

entityManager.persist(billing);        ◁┐  Persists BillingInfo

user.setBillingInfo(billing);
entityManager.persist(user);           ◁┐  Persists User

return user;
}
```

As you can see, the `BillingInfo` entity is persisted first. The persisted `Billing-Info` entity is then set as a field of the `User` entity. When the `User` entity is persisted, the generated key from the `BillingInfo` entity is used in the foreign key for the generated `INSERT` statement.

Having explored the `persist` operation, let's now move on to the next operation in the `EntityManager` CRUD sequence—retrieving entities.

9.3.2 *Retrieving entities by primary key*

JPA supports several ways to retrieve entity instances from the database. By far the simplest way is retrieving an entity by its primary key using the `find` method we introduced in listing 9.1. The other ways all involve using the query API and JPQL, which we'll discuss in chapter 10. Recall that the `find` method was used in the `addItem` method in listing 9.1 to retrieve the `Seller` instance corresponding to the `Item` to add:

```
Seller seller = entityManager.find(Seller.class, sellerId);
```

The first parameter of the `find` method specifies the Java type of the entity to be retrieved. The second parameter specifies the *identity* value for the entity instance to retrieve. Recall from chapter 7 that an entity identity can either be a simple Java type identified by the `@Id` annotation or a composite primary key class specified through the `@EmbeddedId` or `@IdClass` annotation. In the example in listing 9.1, the `find` method is passed a simple `java.lang.Long` value matching the `Seller` entity's `@Id` annotated identity, `sellerId`.

Although this is not the case in listing 9.1, the `find` method is fully capable of supporting composite primary keys. To see how this code might look, assume for the sake of illustration that the identity of the `Seller` entity consists of the seller's first and last name instead of a simple numeric identifier. This identity is encapsulated in a composite primary key class annotated with the `@IdClass` annotation. Listing 9.7 shows how this identity class can be populated and passed to the `find` method.

Listing 9.7   Find by primary key using composite keys

```
SellerPK sellerKey = new SellerPK();

sellerKey.setFirstName(firstName);
sellerKey.setLastName(lastName);

Seller seller = entityManager.find(Seller.class, sellerKey);
```

The `find` method does what it does by inspecting the details of the entity class passed in as the first parameter and generating a `SELECT` statement to retrieve the entity data. This generated `SELECT` statement is populated with the primary key values specified in the second parameter of the `find` method. For example, the `find` method in listing 9.1 could generate a `SELECT` statement that looks something like this:

```
SELECT * FROM SELLERS WHERE seller_id = 1
```

Note that if an entity instance matching the specified key does not exist in the database, the `find` method will not throw any exceptions. Instead, the `Entity-Manager` will return null or an empty entity and your application must handle this situation. It is not strictly necessary to call the `find` method in a transactional context. However, the retrieved entity is *detached* unless a transaction context is available, so it is generally advisable to call the `find` method inside a transaction. One of the most important features of the `find` method is that it utilizes `EntityManager` caching. If your persistence provider supports caching and the entity already exists in the cache, then the `EntityManager` returns a cached instance of the entity instead of retrieving it from the database. Most persistence providers like Hibernate and Oracle TopLink support caching, so you can more or less count on this extremely valuable optimization.

There is one more important JPA feature geared toward application optimization—lazy and eager loading. The generated `SELECT` statement in our example attempts to retrieve all of the entity field data when the `find` method is invoked. In general, this is exactly what will happen for entity retrieval since it is the default behavior for JPA. However, in some cases, this is not desirable behavior.

Fetch modes allow us to change this behavior to optimize application performance when needed.

Entity fetch modes

We briefly mentioned fetch modes in previous chapters but haven't discussed them in great detail. Discussing entity retrieval is an ideal place to fully explore fetch modes.

As we suggested, the `EntityManager` normally loads all entity instance data when an entity is retrieved from the database. In ORM-speak, this is called *eager fetching*, or *eager loading*. If you have ever dealt with application performance problems due to premature or inappropriate caching, you probably already know that eager fetching is not always a good thing. The classic example we used in previous chapters is loading large binary objects (BLOBs), such as pictures. Unless you are developing a heavily graphics-oriented program such as an online photo album, it is unlikely that loading a picture as part of an entity used in a lot of places in the application is a good idea. Because loading BLOB data typically involves long-running, I/O-heavy operations, they should be loaded cautiously and only as needed. In general, this optimization strategy is called *lazy fetching*.

JPA has more than one mechanism to support lazy fetching. Specifying column fetch-mode using the `@Basic` annotation is the easiest one to understand. For example, we can set the fetch mode for the `picture` property on the `Item` entity to be lazy as follows:

```
@Column(name="PICTURE")
@Lob
@Basic(fetch=FetchType.LAZY)
public byte[] getPicture() {
    return picture;
}
```

A `SELECT` statement generated by the `find` method to retrieve `Item` entities would not load data from the `ITEMS.PICTURE` column into the `picture` field. Instead, the `picture` data will be automatically loaded from the database when the property is first accessed through the `getPicture` method.

Be advised, however, that lazy fetching is a double-edged sword. Specifying that a column be lazily fetched means that the `EntityManager` will issue an additional `SELECT` statement just to retrieve the `picture` data when the lazily loaded field is first accessed. In the extreme case, imagine what would happen if all entity data in an application is lazily loaded. This would mean that the database would be flooded with a large number of frivolous `SELECT` statements as entity data is accessed. Also, lazy fetching is an optional EJB 3 feature, which means not every persistence provider is guaranteed to implement it. You should check your provider's documentation before spending too much time figuring out which entity columns should be lazily fetched.

Loading related entities

One of the most intricate uses of fetch modes is to control the retrieval of related entities. Not too surprisingly, the `EntityManager`'s `find` method must retrieve all entities related to the one returned by the method. Let's take the ActionBazaar `Item` entity, an exceptionally good case because it has a many-to-one, a one-to-many, and two many-to-many relationships. The only relationship type not represented is one-to-one. The `Item` entity has a many-to-one relationship with the `Seller` entity (a seller can sell more than one item, but an item can be sold by only one seller), a one-to-many relationship with the `Bid` entity (more than one bid can be put on an item), and a many-to-many relationship with the `Category` entity (an item can belong to more than one category and a category contains multiple items). These relationships are depicted in figure 9.7.

When the `find` method returns an instance of an `Item`, it also automatically retrieves the `Seller`, `Bid`, and `Category` entities associated with the instance and populates them into their respective `Item` entity properties. As we see in listing 9.8, the single `Seller` entity associated with the `Item` is populated into the `seller` property, the `Bid` entities associated with an `Item` are populated into the `bids` `List`, and the `Category` entities the `Item` is listed under are populated into the `categories` property. It might surprise you to know some of these relationships are retrieved lazily.

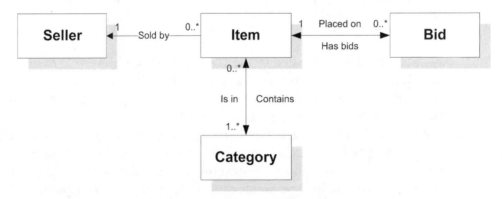

Figure 9.7   The Item entity is related to three other entities: Seller, Bid, and Category. The relationships to Item are many-to-one, one-to-many, and many-to-many, respectively.

All the relationship annotations we saw in chapter 8, including the @ManyToOne, @OneToMany, and @ManyToMany annotations, have a fetch element to control fetch modes just like the @Basic annotation discussed in the previous section. None of the relationship annotations in listing 9.8 specify the fetch element, so the default for each annotation takes effect.

Listing 9.8   Relationships in the Item entity

```
public class Item {
    @ManyToOne        ⊲┘  Many-to-one with Seller
    public Seller getSeller(){
    ...
    @OneToMany        ⊲┘  One-to-many with Bids
    public List<Bid> getBids(){
    ...
                          Many-to-many with Categories
    @ManyToMany       ⊲┘
    public List<Category> getCategories(){
    ...
    }
}
```

By default, some of the relationship types are retrieved lazily while some are loaded eagerly. We'll discuss why each default makes sense as we go through each relationship retrieval case for the Item entity. The Seller associated with an Item is retrieved eagerly, because the fetch mode for the @ManyToOne annotation is defaulted to EAGER. To understand why this make sense, it is helpful to understand how the EntityManager implements eager fetching. In effect, each eagerly fetched relationship turns into an additional JOIN tacked onto the basic SELECT statement to retrieve the entity. To see what we mean, let's see how the SELECT statement for an eagerly fetched Seller record related to an Item looks (listing 9.9).

Listing 9.9   SELECT statement for eagerly fetched Seller related to an Item

```
SELECT
    *
FROM
    ITEMS
INNER JOIN     ⊲┘  Inner join for many-to-one
    SELLERS
ON
    ITEMS.SELLER_ID = SELLERS.SELLER_ID
WHERE ITEMS.ITEM_ID = 100
```

As listing 9.9 shows, an eager fetch means that the most natural way of retrieving the Item entity would be through a single SELECT statement using a JOIN between the ITEMS and SELLERS tables. It is important to note the fact that the JOIN will result in a *single row,* containing columns from both the SELLERS and ITEMS tables. In terms of database performance, this is more efficient than issuing one SELECT to retrieve the Item and issuing a separate SELECT to retrieve the related Seller. This is exactly what would have happened in case of lazy fetching and the second SELECT for retrieving the Seller will be issued when the Item's seller property is first accessed. Pretty much the same thing applies to the @OneToOne annotation, so the default for it is also eager loading. More specifically, the JOIN to implement the relationship would result in a fairly efficient single combined row in all cases.

Lazy vs. eager loading of related entities

In contrast, the @OneToMany and @ManyToMany annotations are defaulted to *lazy loading*. The critical difference is that for both of these relationship types, *more than one* entity is matched to the retrieved entity. Think about Category entities related to a retrieved Item, for example. JOINs implementing eagerly loaded one-to-many and many-to-many relationships usually return more than one row. In particular, a row is returned for every related entity matched.

The problem becomes particularly obvious when you consider what happens when multiple Item entities are retrieved at one time (for example, as the result of a JPQL query, discussed in the next chapter). $(N_1 + N_2 + \ldots + N_x)$ rows would be returned, where N_i is the number of related Category entities for the ith Item record. For nontrivial numbers of N and i, the retrieved result set could be quite large, potentially causing significant database performance issues. This is why JPA makes the conservative assumption of defaulting to lazy loading for @OneToMany and @ManyToMany annotations.

Table 9.4 lists the default fetch behavior for each type of relationship annotation.

Table 9.4 Behavior of loading of associated entity is different for each kind of association by default. We can change the loading behavior by specifying the fetch element with the relationship.

Relationship Type	Default Fetch Behavior	Number of Entities Retrieved
One-to-one	EAGER	Single entity retrieved
One-to-many	LAZY	Collection of entities retrieved
Many-to-one	EAGER	Single entity retrieved
Many-to-many	LAZY	Collection of entities retrieved

The relationship defaults are not right for all circumstances, however. While the eager fetching strategy makes sense for one-to-one and many-to-one relationships under most circumstances, it is a bad idea in some cases. For example, if an entity contains a large number of one-to-one and many-to-one relationships, eagerly loading all of them would result in a large number of JOINs chained together. Executing a relatively large number of JOINs can be just as bad as loading an $(N_1 + N_2 + \ldots + N_x)$ result set. If this proves to be a performance problem, some of the relationships should be loaded lazily. Here's an example of explicitly specifying the fetch mode for a relationship (it happens to be the familiar Seller property of the Item entity):

```
@ManyToOne(fetch=FetchType.LAZY)
public Seller getSeller() {
    return seller;
}
```

You should not take the default lazy loading strategy of the @OneToMany and @ManyToMany annotations for granted. For particularly large data sets, this can result in a huge number of SELECTs being generated against the database. This is known as the N+1 problem, where 1 stands for the SELECT statement for the originating entity and N stands for the SELECT statement that retrieves each related entity. In some cases, you might discover that you are better off using eager loading even for @OneToMany and @ManyToMany annotations. In chapters 10 and 13, we'll discuss how you can eagerly load related entities using JPQL query without having to change the fetch mode on an association on a per-query basis.

Unfortunately, the choice of fetch modes is not cut and dried, and depends on a whole host of factors, including the database vendor's optimization strategy, database design, data volume, and application usage patterns. In the real world, ultimately these choices are often made through trial and error. Luckily, with JPA, performance tuning just means a few configuration changes here and there as opposed to time-consuming code modifications.

Having discussed entity retrieval, we can now move into the third operation of the CRUD sequence: updating entities.

9.3.3 *Updating entities*

Recall that the EntityManager makes sure that changes made to attached entities are always saved into the database behind the scenes. This means that, for the most part, our application does not need to worry about manually calling any methods to update the entity. This is perhaps the most elegant feature of ORM-based persistence since this hides data synchronization behind the scenes and truly allows entities to behave like POJOs. Take the code in listing 9.10, which calculates an ActionBazaar Power Seller's creditworthiness.

Listing 9.10   Transparent management of attached entities

```
public void calculateCreditWorthiness (Long sellerId) {
    PowerSeller seller = entityManager.find        │ Finds Seller
        PowerSeller.class, sellerId);              │ entity

    seller.setCreditWorth(seller.getCreditWorth()
        * CREDIT_FACTOR
            * getRatingFromCreditBureauRobberBarons(seller));
    seller.setCreditWorth(seller.getCreditWorth()
        + (seller.getCreditWorth()                            Saves changes
            * FEEDBACK_FACTOR                                 to entity
                * seller.getBuyerFeedbackRating())));         transparently
    seller.setCreditWorth(seller.getCreditWorth()
        + (seller.getCreditWorth()
            * SELLING_FACTOR
                * getTotalHistoricalSales(seller))));
}
```

Other than looking up the `PowerSeller` entity, little else is done using the `EntityManager` in the `calculateCreditWorthiness` method. As you know, this is because the `PowerSeller` is managed by the `EntityManager` as soon as it is returned by the `find` method. Throughout the relatively long calculation for determining creditworthiness, the `EntityManager` will make sure that the changes to the entity wind up in the database.

Detachment and merge operations

Although managed entities are extremely useful, the problem is that it is difficult to keep entities attached at all times. Often the problem is that the entities will need to be detached and serialized at the web tier, where the entity is changed, outside the scope of the `EntityManager`. In addition, recall that stateless session beans cannot guarantee that calls from the same client will be serviced by the same bean instance. This means that there is no guarantee an entity will be handled by the same `EntityManager` instance across method calls, thus making automated persistence ineffective.

This is exactly the model that the `ItemManager` session bean introduced in listing 9.1 assumes. The `EntityManager` used for the bean has TRANSACTION scope. Since the bean uses CMT, entities become detached when transactions end the method. This means that entities returned by the session bean to its clients are always detached, just like the newly created Item entity returned by the ItemManager's addItem method:

```
public Item addItem(String title, String description,
    byte[] picture, double initialPrice, long sellerId) {
    Item item = new Item();
    item.setTitle(title);
    ...
    entityManager.persist(item);

    return item;
}
```

At some point we'll want to reattach the entity to a persistence context to synchronize it with the database. The EntityManager's merge method is designed to do just that (see figure 9.8).

You should remember that like all attached entities, the entity passed to the merge method is not necessarily synchronized with the database immediately, but it is guaranteed to be synchronized with the database sooner or later. We use the merge method in the ItemManager bean in the most obvious way possible, to update the database with an existing Item:

```
public Item updateItem(Item item) {
    entityManager.merge(item);
    return item;
}
```

As soon as the updateItem method returns, the database is updated with the data from the Item entity. The merge method must only be used for an entity that exists in the database. An attempt to merge a nonexistent entity will result in an IllegalArgumentException. The same is true if the EntityManager detects that the

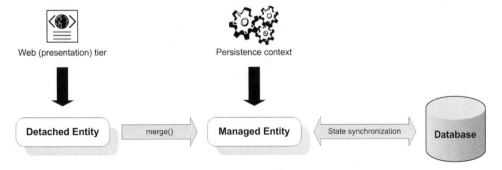

Figure 9.8   An entity instance can be detached and serialized to a separate tier where the client makes changes to the entity and sends it back to the server. The server can use a merge operation to attach the entity to the persistence context.

entity you are trying to merge has already been deleted through the `remove` method, even if the `DELETE` statement has not been issued yet.

Merging relationships

By default, entities associated with the entity being merged are not merged as well. For example, the `Seller`, `Bid` and `Category` entities related to the `Item` are not merged when the `Item` is merged in the previous code snippet. However, as mentioned in section 9.3.1, this behavior can be controlled using the `cascade` element of the `@OneToOne`, `@OneToMany`, `@ManyToOne`, and `@ManyToMany` annotations. If the element is set to either `ALL` or `MERGE`, the related entities are merged. For example, the following code will cause the `Seller` entity related to the `Item` to be merged since the `cascade` element is set to `MERGE`:

```
public class Item {
    @ManyToOne(cascade=CascadeType.MERGE)
    public Seller getSeller() {
```

Note that as in most of the `EntityManager`'s methods, the `merge` method must be called from a transactional context or it will throw a `TransactionRequired-Exception`.

We'll now move on to the final element of the CRUD sequence: *deleting* an entity.

Detached entities and the DTO anti-pattern

If you have spent even a moderate amount of time using EJB 2, you are probably thoroughly familiar with the Data Transfer Object (DTO) anti-pattern. In a sense, the DTO anti-pattern was necessary because of entity beans. The fact that EJB 3 detached entities are nothing but POJOs makes the DTO anti-pattern less of a necessity of life. Instead of having to create separate DTOs from domain data just to pass back and forth between the business and presentation layers, you may simply pass detached entities. This is exactly the model we follow in this chapter.

However, if your entities contain behavior, you might be better off using the DTO pattern anyway, to safeguard business logic from inappropriate usage outside a transactional context. In any case, if you decide to use detached entities as a substitute to DTOs, you should make sure they are marked `java.io.Serializable`.

9.3.4 Deleting entities

The `deleteItem` method in the `ItemManagerBean` in listing 9.1 deletes an `Item` from the database. An important detail to notice about the `deleteItem` method (repeated next) is that the item to be deleted was first attached to the `Entity-Manager` using the `merge` method:

```
public void deleteItem(Item item) {
    entityManager.remove(entityManager.merge(item));
}
```

This is because the `remove` method can only delete *currently attached* entities and the `Item` entity being passed to the `deleteItem` method is not managed. If a detached entity is passed to the `remove` method, it throws an `IllegalArgument-Exception`. Before the `deleteItem` method returns, the `Item` record will be deleted from the database using a `DELETE` statement like this:

```
DELETE FROM ITEMS WHERE item_id = 1
```

Just as with the `persist` and `merge` methods, the `DELETE` statement is not necessarily issued immediately but is guaranteed to be issued at some point. Meanwhile, the `EntityManager` marks the entity as *removed* so that no further changes to it are synchronized (as we noted in the previous section).

Cascading remove operations

Just as with merging and persisting entities, you must set the `cascade` element of a relationship annotation to either `ALL` or `REMOVE` for related entities to be removed with the one passed to the `remove` method. For example, we can specify that the `BillingInfo` entity related to a `Bidder` be removed with the owning `Bidder` entity as follows:

```
@Entity
public class Bidder {
    @OneToOne(cascade=CascadeType.REMOVE)
    public BillingInfo setBillingInfo() {
```

From a common usage perspective, this setup makes perfect sense. There is no reason for a `BillingInfo` entity to hang around if the enclosing `Bidder` entity it is related to is removed. When it comes down to it, the business domain determines if deletes should be cascaded. In general, you might find that the only relationship types where cascading removal makes sense are one-to-one and one-to-many. You should be careful when using the cascade delete because the related entity you are cascading the delete to may be related to other entities you don't know about. For example, let's assume that there is a one-to-many relationship between the `Seller` and `Item` entities and you are using cascade delete to remove a `Seller` and its related `Items`. Remember the fact that other entities such as the `Category` entity also hold references to the `Items` you are deleting and those relationships would become meaningless!

Handling relationships

If your intent was really to cascade delete the `Items` associated with the `Seller`, you should iterate over all instances of `Category` that reference the deleted `Items` and remove the relationships first. The following code does this:

```
List<Category> categories = getAllCategories();
List<Item> items = seller.getItems();
for (Item item: items) {
    for (Category category: categories) {
        category.getItems().remove(item);
    }
}
entityManager.remove(seller);
```

The code gets all instances of `Category` in the system and makes sure that all `Items` related to the `Seller` being deleted are removed from referencing `Lists` first. It then proceeds with removing the `Seller`, cascading the remove to the related `Items`.

Not surprisingly, the `remove` method must be called from a transactional context or it will throw a `TransactionRequiredException`. Also, trying to remove an already removed entity will raise `IllegalStateException`.

Having finished the basic `EntityManager` CRUD operations, let's now move on to the two remaining major persistence operations: flushing data to the database and refreshing from the database.

9.3.5 Controlling updates with flush

We've been talking about `EntityManager` flushing on and off throughout the chapter. It is time we discussed this concept fully. For the most part, you'll probably be able to get away without knowing too much about this `EntityManager` feature. However, there are some situations where not understanding `EntityManager` flushing could be a great disadvantage. Recall that `EntityManager` operations like `persist`, `merge`, and `remove` do not cause immediate database changes. Instead, these operations are postponed until the `EntityManager` is *flushed*. The true motivation for doing things this way is performance optimization. Batching SQL as much as possible instead of flooding the database with a bunch of frivolous requests saves a lot of communication overhead and avoids unnecessarily tying down the database.

By default, the database flush mode is set to `AUTO`. This means that the `EntityManager` performs a flush operation automatically as needed. In general, this occurs at the end of a transaction for `transaction-scoped` `EntityManagers` and when the persistence context is closed for application-managed or `extended-scope` `EntityManagers`. In addition, if entities with pending changes are used in a query, the persistence provider will flush changes to the database before executing the query.

You can set the flush mode to COMMIT if you don't like the idea of autoflushing and want greater control over database synchronization. You can do so using the EntityManager's setFlushMode method as follows:

```
entityManager.setFlushMode(FlushModeType.COMMIT);
```

If the flush mode is set to COMMIT, the persistence provider will only synchronize with the database when the transaction commits. However, you should be careful with this, as it will be your responsibility to synchronize entity state with the database before executing a query. If you don't do this and an EntityManager query returns stale entities from the database, the application can wind up in an inconsistent state.

In reality, resetting flush mode is often overkill. This is because you can explicitly flush the EntityManager when you need to, using the flush method as follows:

```
entityManager.flush();
```

The EntityManager synchronizes the state of every managed entity with the database as soon as this method is invoked. Like everything else, manual flushing should be used in moderation and only when needed. In general, batching database synchronization requests is a good optimization strategy to try to preserve.

We'll now move on to the last persistence operation to be discussed in this chapter: refreshing entities.

9.3.6 Refreshing entities

The refresh operation repopulates entity data from the database. In other words, given an entity instance, the persistence provider matches the entity with a record in the database and resets the entity with retrieved data from the database as shown in figure 9.9.

While this EntityManager method is not used frequently, there are some circumstances where it is extremely useful. In listing 9.1, we use the method to undo changes made by the ItemManager client and return fresh entity data from the database:

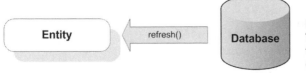

Figure 9.9
The refresh operation repopulates the entity from the database, overriding any changes in the entity.

```
public Item undoItemChanges(Item item) {
    entityManager.refresh(entityManager.merge(item));
    return item;
}
```

The merge operation is performed first in the undoItemChanges method because the refresh method only works on managed entities. It is important to note that just like the find method, the refresh method uses the entity identity to match database records. As a result, you must make sure the entity being refreshed exists in the database.

The refresh method really shines when you consider a subtle but very common scenario. To illustrate this scenario, let's go back to the addItem method in listing 9.1:

```
public Item addItem(String title, String description,
    byte[] picture, double initialPrice, long sellerId) {
    Item item = new Item();
    item.setTitle(title);
    ...
    entityManager.persist(item);

    return item;
}
```

Note a subtle point about the method: it assumes that the Item entity is not altered by the database in any way when the record is inserted into the database. It is easy to forget that this is seldom the case with relational databases. For most INSERT statements issued by the usual application, the database will fill in column values not included in the INSERT statement using table defaults. For example, assume that the Item entity has a postingDate property that is not populated by the application. Instead, this value is set to the current database system time when the ITEMS table record is inserted. This could be implemented in the database by utilizing default column values or even database triggers.

Since the persist method only issues the INSERT statement and does not load the data that was changed by the database as a result of the INSERT, the entity returned by the method would not include the generated postingDate field. This problem could be fixed by using the refresh method as follows:

```
public Item addItem(String title, String description,
    byte[] picture, double initialPrice, long sellerId) {
    Item item = new Item();
    item.setTitle(title);
    ...
    entityManager.persist(item);
    entityManager.flush();
```

```
            entityManager.refresh(item);

            return item;
    }
```

After the `persist` method is invoked, the `EntityManager` is flushed immediately so that the `INSERT` statement is executed and the generated values are set by the database. The entity is then refreshed so that we get the most up-to-date data from the database and populate it into the inserted `Item` instance (including the `posting-Date` field). In most cases you should try to avoid using default or generated values with JPA due to the slightly awkward nature of the code just introduced. Luckily, this awkward code is not necessary while using fields that use the JPA `@Generated-Value` annotation since the `persist` method correctly handles such fields.

Before we wrap up this chapter, we'll introduce entity lifecycle-based listeners.

9.4 Entity lifecycle listeners

You saw in earlier chapters that both session and message-driven beans allow you to listen for lifecycle callbacks like `PostConstruct` and `PreDestroy`. Similarly, entities allow you to receive callbacks for lifecycle events like persist, load, update, and remove. Just as in session and message-driven beans, you can do almost anything you need to in the lifecycle callback methods, including invoking an EJB, or using APIs like JDBC or JMS. In the persistence realm, however, lifecycle callbacks are typically used to accomplish such tasks as logging, validating data, auditing, sending notifications after a database change, or generating data after an entity has been loaded. In a sense, callbacks are the database triggers of JPA. Table 9.5 lists the callbacks supported by the API.

Table 9.5   Callbacks supported by JPA and when they are called

Lifecycle Method	When It Is Performed
PrePersist	Before the `EntityManager` persists an entity instance
PostPersist	After an entity has been persisted
PostLoad	After an entity has been loaded by a query, find, or refresh operation
PreUpdate	Before a database update occurs to synchronize an entity instance
PostUpdate	After a database update occurs to synchronize an entity instance
PreRemove	Before `EntityManager` removes an entity
PostRemove	After an entity has been removed

Entity lifecycle methods need not be defined in the entity itself. Instead, you can choose to define a separate *entity listener* class to receive the lifecycle callbacks. We highly recommend this approach, because defining callback methods in the entities themselves will clutter up the domain model you might have carefully constructed. Moreover, entity callbacks typically contain crosscutting concerns rather than business logic directly pertinent to the entity. For our purposes, we'll explore the use of entity callbacks using separate listener classes, default listeners, and the execution order of entity listeners if you have multiple listeners.

9.4.1 Using an entity listener

Let's see how entity lifecycle callbacks look by coding an entity listener on the Item entity that notifies an ActionBazaar admin if an item's initial bid amount is set higher than a certain threshold. It is ActionBazaar policy to scrutinize items with extremely high initial prices to check against possible fraud, especially for items such as antiques and artwork. Listing 9.11 shows the code.

Listing 9.11 ItemMonitor entity listener

```
public class ItemMonitor {
    ...
    public ItemMonitor() {}
    @PrePersist
    @PreUpdate                   Specifies callbacks
    public void monitorItem(Item item) {
        if (item.getInitialBidAmount() >
            ItemMonitor.MONITORING_THRESHOLD) {
          notificationManager.sendItemPriceEmailAlert(item);
        }
    }
}

@Entity                                                          Registers
@EntityListeners(actionbazaar.persistence.ItemMonitor.class)    listener
public class Item implements Serializable {
```

As you can see in listing 9.11, our listener, ItemMonitor, has a single method, monitorItem, which receives callbacks for both the PrePersist and PreUpdate events. The @EntityListeners annotation on the Item entity specifies ItemMonitor to be the lifecycle callback listener for the Item entity. It's worth noting that the listener callbacks can be defined on an entity class or mapped superclass. All we have to do to receive a callback is to annotate our method with a callback annotation such as @PrePersist, @PostPersist, @PreUpdate, and so on. The monitorItem method checks to see if the initial bid amount set for the item to be inserted or updated is above the threshold specified by the `ItemMonitor.MONITORING_THRESHOLD` variable and sends the ActionBazaar admin an e-mail alert if it is. As you might have guessed by examining listing 9.11, entity listener callback methods follow the form `void <METHOD>(Object)`. The single method parameter of type `Object` specifies the entity instance for which the lifecycle event was generated. In our case, this is the `Item` entity.

If the lifecycle callback method throws a runtime exception, the intercepted persistence operation is aborted. This is an extremely important feature to validate persistence operations. For example, if you have a listener class to validate that all entity data is present before persisting an entity, you could abort the persistence operation if needed by throwing a runtime exception.

Listing 9.12 shows an example listener class that can be used to validate an entity state before an entity is persisted. You can build validation logic in a `PrePersist` callback, and if the callback fails the entity will not be persisted. For example, ActionBazaar sets a minimum price for the `initialPrice` for items being auctioned, and no items are allowed to be listed below that price.

Listing 9.12 ItemVerifier, which validates the price set for an item

```
public class ItemVerifier{

    ...

    public ItemVerifier() {
    }
        @PrePersist
        public  void newItemVerifier(Item item){
            if (item.getInitialPrice()<MIN_INITIAL_PRICE)
                throw new ItemException(
                        "Item Price is lower than "+
                    " Minimum Price Allowed");     }
}
```

All entity listeners are stateless in nature and you cannot assume that there is a one-to-one relationship between an entity instance and a listener instance.

NOTE One great drawback of entity listener classes is that they do not support dependency injection. This is due to the fact that entities may be used outside containers, where DI is not available.

For crosscutting concerns like logging or auditing, it is inconvenient to have to specify listeners for individual entities. Given this problem, JPA enables you to specify default entity listeners that receive callbacks from all entities in a persistence unit. Let's take a look at this mechanism next.

9.4.2 *Default listener classes*

ActionBazaar audits all changes made to entities. You can think of this as an ActionBazaar version of a transaction log. This feature can be implemented using a default listener like the following:

```
public class ActionBazaarAuditor {
    ...
    @PrePersist
    @PostPersist
    ...
    @PostRemove
    public void logOperation(Object object) {
        Logger.log("Performing Persistence Operation on: "
            + object.getName());
```

The `ActionBazaarAuditor` listens for all persistence operations for all entities in the ActionBazaar persistence unit, and logs the name of the entity that the callback was generated on. Unfortunately, there is no way to specify default entity listeners using annotations, and we must resort to using the `persistence.xml` deployment descriptor. Since we have not yet fully described the persistence deployment descriptor, we'll simply note the relevant descriptor snippet here, leaving a detailed analysis to chapter 11:

```
<persistence-unit name="actionBazaar">
    ...
    <default-entity-listeners>
        actionbazaar.persistence.ActionBazaarAuditor.class
    </default-entity-listeners>
    ...
```

In this snippet, the `default-entity-listeners` element lists the default entity listeners for the `actionBazaar` persistence unit. Again, do not worry too much about the specific syntax at the moment, as we'll cover it in greater detail later.

This brings us to the interesting question of what happens if there is both a default listener and an entity-specific listener for a given entity, as in the case of our `Item` entity. The `Item` entity now has two lifecycle listeners: the default `Action-BazaarAuditor` listener and the `ItemMonitor` listener. How do you think they interact? Moreover, since entities are POJOs that can inherit from other entities, both the superclass and subclass may have attached listeners. For example, what if the

User entity has an attached listener named UserMonitor and the Seller subclass also has an attached listener, SellerMonitor? How these listeners relate to each other is determined by the order of execution as well as exclusion rules.

9.4.3 *Listener class execution order and exclusion*

If an entity has default listeners, entity class–specific listeners, and inherited superclass listeners, the default listeners are executed first. Following OO constructor inheritance rules, the superclass listeners are invoked after the default listeners. Subclass listeners are invoked last. Figure 9.10 depicts this execution order.

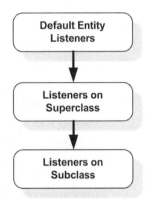

If more than one listener is listed on any level, the execution order is determined by the order in which they are listed in the annotation or deployment descriptor. For example, in the following entity listener annotation, the ItemMonitor listener is called before ItemMonitor2:

```
EntityListeners({actionbazaar.persistence.
    ItemMonitor.class, actionbazaar.persistence.
    ItemMonitor2.class})
```

Figure 9.10   Entity listener execution order. Default entity listeners are executed first, then superclass and subclass listeners.

You cannot programmatically control this order of execution. However, if needed, you can exclude default and superclass listeners from being executed at all. Let's assume that we need to disable both default and superclass listeners for the Seller entity. You can do this with the following code:

```
@Entity
@ExcludeDefaultListeners
@ExcludeSuperClassListeners
@EntityListeners(actionbazaar.persistence.SellerMonitor.class)
public class Seller extends User {
```

As you can see from the code, the @ExcludeDefaultListeners annotation disables any default listeners while the @ExcludeSuperClassListeners annotation stops superclass listeners from being executed. As a result, only the SellerMonitor listener specified by the @EntityListeners annotation will receive lifecycle callbacks for the Seller entity. Unfortunately, neither the @ExcludeDefaultListeners nor the @ExcludeSuperClassListeners annotation currently enables us to block specific listener classes. We hope that this is a feature that will be added in a future version of JPA.

9.5 *Entity operations best practices*

Throughput this chapter, we have provided you with some hints on the best practices of using the `EntityManager` interface. Before we conclude, let's solidify the discussion of best practices by exploring a few of the most important ones in detail.

Use container-managed entity managers. If you're building an enterprise application that will be deployed to a Java EE container, we strongly recommend that you use container-managed entity managers. Furthermore, if you are manipulating entities from the session bean and MDB tier, you should use declarative transactions in conjunction with container-managed `EntityManagers`. Overall, this will let you focus on application logic instead of worrying about the mundane details of managing transactions, managing `EntityManager` lifecycles, and so on.

Avoid injecting entity managers into the web tier. If you're using the `EntityManager` API directly from a component in the web tier, we recommend that you avoid injecting entity managers because the `EntityManager` interface is not thread-safe. Instead, you should use a JNDI lookup to grab an instance of a container-managed `EntityManager`. Better yet, use the session Façade pattern discussed in chapter 12 instead of using the `EntityManager` API directly from the web tier and take advantage of the benefits offered through session beans such as declarative transaction management.

Use the Entity Access Object pattern. Instead of cluttering your business logic with `EntityManager` API calls, use a data access object (we call it entity access object) discussed in chapter 12. This practice allows you to abstract the `EntityManager` API from the business tier.

Separate callbacks into external listeners. Don't pollute your domain model with crosscutting concerns such as auditing and logging code. Use external entity listener classes instead. This way, you could swap listeners in and out as needed.

9.6 *Summary*

In this chapter, we covered the most vital aspect of JPA: persistence operations using entity managers. We also explored persistence contexts, persistence scopes, various types of entity managers, and their usage patterns. We even briefly covered entity lifecycles and listeners. We highly recommend Java EE container-managed persistence contexts with CMT-driven transactions. In general, this strategy minimizes the amount of careful consideration of what is going on behind the scenes and consequent meticulous coding you might have to engage in otherwise. However, there are some valid reasons for using application-managed EntityManagers. In particular, the ability to use the EntityManager outside the confines of a Java EE container is an extremely valuable feature, especially to those of us with lightweight technologies like Apache Tomcat and the Spring Framework or even Java SE Swing-based client/server applications.

We avoided covering a few relatively obscure EntityManager features like lazily obtaining entity references via the getReference method, or using the clear method to force detachment of all entities in a persistence context. We encourage you to research these remaining features on your own. However, a critical feature that we did not discuss yet is robust entity querying using the powerful query API and JPQL. We'll examine this in detail in the next chapter.

10

Using the query API and
JPQL to retrieve entities

This chapter covers

- Creating and executing queries
- The Java Persistence Query Language
- Using SQL queries

Chapters 8 and 9 discussed how the EJB 3 Java Persistence API (JPA) O/R mapping mechanism shields developers from having to write SQL to directly manipulate data. Chapter 8 explained how to map entities to relational tables, and chapter 9 revealed how to manipulate those entities using the `EntityManager` API. The next couple of topics we'll tackle in our quest for JPA mastery are the query API and the Java Persistence Query Language (JPQL). We'll continue to use ActionBazaar to explore these new concepts, incorporating JPQL into our auction system as well as looking at how the various one-to-many and many-to-one mappings work with JPA.

With JPA, you can use the following methods to retrieve entities and related data:

- `EntityManager.find` with the entity's primary key
- Queries written in JPQL
- SQL queries native to the underlying database

We discussed the first option, retrieving entities using a primary key, in chapter 9. In this chapter we'll focus on retrieving entities using the latter two methods: JPQL and SQL queries. First we'll look at the query API and show you how to execute queries; then we'll explore the basics of JPQL. The chapter concludes by exploring the use of SQL queries with EJB 3.

10.1 Introducing the query API

Queries are as important as storing data. Therefore, a flexible query language is an important aspect of ORM. One of the primary problems in EJB 2 was that its query capabilities were limited. EJB 3 greatly improves the query capabilities of entities. In this section we introduce the query API and two types of queries: dynamic and named.

10.1.1 The big picture

In the previous chapter, we used the `EntityManager.find` method to retrieve entities. This method only retrieves entities by their ID or primary key. However, there are many instances when you need more powerful queries. The query API allows developers to write custom queries to retrieve either one or a collection of entities.

The `EntityManager` interface has several methods designed for creating queries to retrieve entities. The `EntityManager` methods are used together with the `javax.persistence.Query` interface methods, which perform the actual query definition, parameter binding, execution, and pagination.

The JPA query API allows you to use either JPQL or SQL to create the queries. We'll cover JPQL in detail in section 10.3. SQL is the standard for querying relational data; we'll discuss how to use SQL to create queries with JPA in section 10.4. If you are not familiar with SQL, refer to appendix B. Most of the time when you use the Query interface, you will likely choose to work with JPQL rather than SQL, since a SQL query returns database records and a JPA query returns entities.

The EntityManager interface methods for creating query instances, the Query interface methods that define and execute the query, and JPQL are referred to as the query API. This is shown in figure 10.1.

As we dive deeper into the query API, you will start to realize that building queries to retrieve entities is often the most challenging task of building any enterprise applications, and almost every aspect of an application requires some data retrieval. The query API supports building and using queries in several ways, as you'll learn in the next few sections. Depending on what you are trying to accomplish, you may devise some interesting ways to utilize queries.

The steps you follow to create a JPA query are similar to those of a traditional JBDC query. Table 10.1 compares using a JDBC query to the basic flow of a JPA query. As you can see, the primary differences lie in the way you obtain the database connection and the way in which you manipulate the query itself. In JDBC it is normal to employ a database connection directly. Conversely, JPA hides the database connection behind the EntityManager.

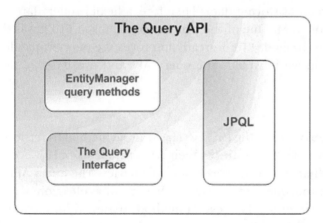

Figure 10.1   The JPA query API includes EntityManager methods to create queries, the methods in the Query interface for executing the query, and the Java Persistence Query Language.

Table 10.1 Comparing a JDBC basic query to a JPA query. The JDBC SQL query returns the data in the database table whereas the JPQL query returns JPA entities.

Basic Steps for JDBC Query Using SQL	Basic Steps for a JPA Query Using JPQL
1. Obtain a database connection.	1. Obtain an instance of an entity manager.
2. Create a query statement.	2. Create a query instance.
3. Execute the statement.	3. Execute the query.
4. Retrieve the results (database records).	4. Retrieve the results (entities).

By now, you must be eager to see what a query looks like. Let's do that next.

10.1.2 *Anatomy of a query*

The query API supports two types of queries: *named* and *dynamic*. Named and dynamic queries have different purposes. Named queries are intended to be stored and reused. For instance, suppose your application requires you to list the most popular item in a specific category. Since this requirement occurs in several places in your application, you know this query will be executed by multiple modules. You'd probably want to create a named query so you wouldn't have to build the query every time you wanted to query the most popular item in that category. On the other hand, say you have a requirement to build a query screen for items and you want to dynamically create the query statement based on user inputs or some conditions in your application logic. In this case, you'd have to use a dynamic query. Dynamic (or ad hoc) queries are different from named queries in that they are created on the fly.

In either case, the format of the queries is similar. For a first taste of how a query works, let's look at an example, starting with a dynamic query. Suppose we want to retrieve all the categories in the system. The following code will perform the desired task:

```
@PersistenceContext em;      ◁─❶ Injects EntityManager        Creates query ❷
...                                                              instance
public List findAllCategories() {
  Query query = em.createQuery("SELECT c FROM Category c"); ...  ◁─┘

  return query.getResultList(); ............  ◁─❸ Retrieves result
}
```

In this example, we first grab an instance of an `EntityManager` provided by dependency injection ❶. Then we create an instance of a `Query` object for querying entities using the `EntityManager.createQuery` method ❷, passing it the query string. (In section 10.2 we discuss the `Query` interface in more detail.) Once we have a query instance, the final step is to return the results list ❸ using its `get-ResultList` method.

Note that in this example we used JPQL to query the entities. You can use either JPQL or native SQL in both named and dynamic queries.

A named query will be almost the same: the only difference is that it uses `createNamedQuery` rather than `createQuery`, and you must pass it a query object that has already been created rather than a query string. In the next section, you'll learn how to create that object for JPQL queries. We'll discuss creating the named query object for SQL queries in section 10.4.

10.1.3 *Defining named queries*

You must create a named (or static) query before you can use it. It is defined either in the entity using annotations, or in the XML file defining O/R mapping metadata. You'll learn about O/R mapping and how to define a named query with XML in chapter 11. A named query is accessed by its name when you create an instance of it. Any query that is used in multiple components of your applications is a candidate for a named query.

Named queries have three primary benefits:

- They improve reusability of queries.
- They improve maintainability of code; queries are not scattered among the business logic.
- They can enhance performance because they are prepared once and can be efficiently reused.

Although a named query can also be stored in the ORM XML file, in this chapter we focus on using it with metadata annotations. Let's look at an example. Say you want to create a named query on the `Category` entity to retrieve all categories by passing a category name. To achieve this, use the `@javax.persistence.Named-Query` annotation:

```
@Entity
@NamedQuery(
  name = "findAllCategories",
  query = "SELECT c FROM Category c WHERE c.categoryName
           LIKE :categoryName ")

public class Category implements Serializable {
..
}
```

For a complex application, you'll probably have multiple named queries. In that case, you can use the `@javax.persistence.NamedQueries` annotation to specify multiple named queries like this:

```
@Entity
@NamedQueries({
  @NamedQuery(
    name = "findCategoryByName",
    query = "SELECT c FROM Category c WHERE c.categoryName
            LIKE :categoryName order by c.categoryId"
  ),
  @NamedQuery(
    name = "findCategoryByUser",
    query = "SELECT c FROM Category c JOIN c.user u
            WHERE u.userId = ?1"
)})
@Table(name = "CATEGORIES")

public class Category implements Serializable {
}
```

NOTE   Keep in mind that a named query is scoped with a persistence unit and therefore must have a unique `name`. We recommend that you devise a naming convention for your applications that will avoid duplicate names for named queries.

So now you know the difference between named and dynamic queries. Next we'll show you how to execute your queries.

10.2 Executing the queries

If you've used Hibernate or TopLink, you'll note many similarities between the query APIs in those frameworks and the EJB 3 Java Persistence API. As you saw in section 10.1.2, there are three steps to running a query in EJB 3:

- Create an instance of the `EntityManager`.
- Create an instance of the query.
- Execute the query.

In chapter 9, you saw how to create an instance of `EntityManager`. (To recap, you can either inject an instance of a container-managed `EntityManager` or create an application-managed `EntityManager` from an `EntityManagerFactory`.) In this section we focus on the last two steps. First we'll look at creating a query instance and then explore the methods in the `Query` interface designed for executing queries.

10.2.1 *Creating a query instance*

As our first example showed, before you can execute a named or dynamic query using JPQL, you must create the query instance to retrieve persistent data. The `EntityManager` interface provides methods for creating a query instance, as well as methods for creating native SQL queries. Table 10.2 lists the methods.

Table 10.2 The EntityManager interface provides several methods to create queries using either JPQL or native SQL statements.

Method	Purpose
`public Query createQuery(String qlString);`	Creates a dynamic query using a JPQL statement.
`public Query createNamedQuery(String name);`	Creates a query instance based on a named query. This method can be used for both JPQL and native SQL queries.
`public Query createNativeQuery(` `   String sqlString);`	Creates a dynamic query using a native SQL statement with UPDATE or DELETE.
`public Query createNativeQuery(` `   String sqlString,Class result-class);`	Creates a dynamic query using a native SQL statement that retrieves a single entity type.
`public Query createNativeQuery(` `   String sqlString,String result-setMapping);`	Creates a dynamic query using a native SQL statement that retrieves a result set with multiple entity types.

In table 10.2, some of the methods for creating query instances use JPQL and others use with native SQL queries. Section 10.3 explores JPQL, and section 10.4 shows you how to work with native SQL queries. In this section, the sample queries are JPQL based. We suggest you use native SQL only as a last resort.

> **NOTE**   You do not need an active transaction to create or execute a query; if one does not exist, the retrieved entities become detached instances.

Creating a named query instance

As we discussed earlier, named queries are globally scoped. You can create a named query instance from any component that has access to the persistence unit to which the entity belongs. You must have an open `EntityManager` instance to create a named query instance. To use a named query stored on the entity, you invoke the `EntityManager.createNamedQuery` method, passing the name of the desired named query as the parameter. In the previous example when we created the stored query, we stored the `findAllCategories` named query in the `Category` entity. Creating a named query from that stored query is as easy as this:

```
Query query = em.createNamedQuery("findAllCategories");
```

The `EntityManager` instance em takes care of all the details of fetching our named query `findAllCategories` and returning a reference, which we assign to the `query` object.

Creating a dynamic query instance

A dynamic query can be created wherever the `EntityManager` is available. This includes using it in session beans, MDBs, web applications, or even outside the container (as long as you can you can access the `EntityManager`). EJB 2 did not support dynamic queries, and many developers found that to be a significant limitation.

We can use the `EntityManager.createQuery` method to create a dynamic query. The only requirement is to pass a valid JPQL statement. It makes no difference whether the `EntityManager` is a container- or application-managed entity manager. The following shows how to create a dynamic query:

```
Query query = em.createQuery("SELECT i FROM Item i");
```

You can see that the JPQL syntax resembles SQL, but JPA recommends that you use JPQL. The differences in notation between SQL and JPQL will be more evident later in section 10.3, when we explore JPQL by itself.

Let's recap where we are now. We've created an instance of the `EntityManager`, and we've created an instance of the query. The next step is the actual execution of the query. The `Query` interface provides the methods we need.

10.2.2 Working with the Query interface

The `Query` interface defines several methods for executing a query. It provides methods to set parameters for a `Query` instance, specify pagination properties for the result, control the flush mode, and so forth. The `Query` interface does not differentiate between JPQL and native SQL, and the same interface can be used for both types of queries. Table 10.3 lists all methods of the Query interface.

You can use these methods on the query instance for setting parameters for the query or for executing the query or iterating through the results after you retrieve them. Here is a quick example of some commonly used Query methods in action:

Table 10.3 The javax.persistence.Query interface enables developers to set parameters for a query, set pagination properties, control the flush mode, and retrieve results for the query.

Method Signature	Purpose
`public List getResultList()`	Retrieves a result set for a query
`public Object getSingleResult()`	Retrieves a single result or object
`public int executeUpdate()`	Executes a JPQL UPDATE or DELETE statement
`public Query setMaxResults(` `    int maxResult)`	Sets the maximum number of objects to be retrieved
`public Query setFirstResult(` `    int startPosition)`	Sets the initial position for the first result being retrieved by the query
`public Query setHint(String hintName,` `    Object value)`	Sets a vendor-specific hint for the query
`public Query setParameter(String name,` `    Object value)`	Sets the value for a named parameter
`public Query setParameter(String name,` `    Date value, TemporalType temporalType)`	Sets the value for a named parameter when the parameter is of the Date type
`public Query setParameter(String name,` `    Calendar value, TemporalType temporalType)`	Sets the value for a named parameter when the parameter is of the Calendar type
`public Query setParameter(int position,` `    Object value)`	Sets the value for a positional parameter
`public Query setParameter(int position,` `    Calendar value, TemporalType temporalType)`	Set the value for a positional parameter when the parameter is of the Calendar type
`public Query setFlushMode(` `    FlushModeType flushMode)`	Sets the flush mode

```
query = em.createNamedQuery("findCategoryByName");
query.setParameter("categoryName", categoryName);   ←❶ Sets parameter
query.setMaxResults(10);
query.setFirstResult(3);
List categories = query.getResultList();   ←❷ Retrieves result
```

In this example, we create a query instance from a named query that was defined earlier. Here we want to retrieve a `List` of `Category` entities by name and hence we set the parameter ❶. We limit the maximum number of items returned to `10`, and we position the first entity to be returned at the third item. Finally we retrieve the result ❷.

In this section we examine all aspects of executing a query: setting parameters, retrieving either a single entity or a list of entities, and setting vendor-specific query hints to improve query performance.

Setting parameters for a query

The number of entities retrieved in a query can be limited by specifying a `WHERE` clause. If we want to retrieve all instances of the `Item` entity with a specific price, the JPQL would look like this:

```
SELECT i FROM Item i WHERE i.initialPrice = ?1
```

In this statement, we've used a parameter (`?1`) for the `WHERE` clause. There are two ways we can specify this parameter: by number or by name. When we have an integer in the parameter, we call it a *positional* (or numbered) parameter. Positional parameters are common in query languages. EJBQL 2 also supported positional parameters.

Before we execute a query, we have to set the parameter for the query:

```
query.setParameter(1, 100.00);
```

In some cases you'll want to specify multiple parameters for a query. Say you want to retrieve all items with an `initialPrice` that falls within a particular range:

```
SELECT i FROM Item i WHERE i.initialPrice > ?1 AND i.initialPrice < ?2
```

The following code should do the trick:

```
query.setParameter(1, 100.00);
query.setParameter(2, 200.00);
```

Here we set the first parameter in position `1` to `100.00`. This is the lower limit of the range in our query. The upper limit is loaded by setting the parameter in position `2` to `200.00`.

NOTE   Always double-check the positions of parameters when using numbered parameters. If you have trouble with your queries using positional parameters, probably one or more of the positions are incorrect, which nearly always forces a data type mismatch. For this reason, we recommend that you use named parameters instead of positional parameters when possible.

When you specify a specific name for a parameter, it's called a *named parameter*. Named parameters improve the readability of code tremendously and make troubleshooting your queries much easier. The previous query can be written using named parameters as follows:

```
SELECT i FROM Item i WHERE i.initialPrice = :price
```

As you can see, the only difference between the positional parameter and the named parameter is the notation of the parameter itself. A positional parameter starts with a ? followed by the parameter's position. A named parameter starts with : and is followed by the name of the parameter. To populate a named parameter, you have to pass the name of the parameter when calling the setParameter method on the query like this:

```
query.setParameter("price", 100.00);
```

This code sets the named price parameter to a value of 100.00. It also makes the developer's intent a little clearer to those reading the code.

Retrieving a single entity

You can retrieve a single entity instance by using the Query.getSingleResult method. Be sure that the query retrieves only one entity when using this method. For example, if we are absolutely sure that no two categories in the ActionBazaar application have exactly the same name and we are retrieving an instance of the Category by its name, we can retrieve it by using

```
query.setParameter(1, "Recycle from Mr. Dumpster");
Category cat = (Category)query.getSingleResult();
```

NOTE   If your query retrieves multiple instances of Category entities with the same name, it will throw NonUniqueResultException. The persistence provider will throw NoResultException when your query does not retrieve any result.

These exceptions will not roll back the active transactions. You must handle these exceptions as follows:

```
try {
  ...
  query.setParameter(1, "Recycle from Mr. Dumpster");
  Category cat = (Category)query.getSingleResult();
  ...
}catch (NonUniqueResultException ex) {
  handleException(ex);
}
catch (NoResultException ex) {
  handleException(ex);
}
```

Retrieving an entity using `getSingleResult` does not require an active transaction. However, if no transactions are available, the retrieved entity will be detached after retrieval. It's worth mentioning that the persistence provider will throw `IllegalStateException` if `Query` contains an `UPDATE` or `DELETE` statement.

Retrieving a collection of entities

Most queries normally retrieve more than one instance of an entity in what is commonly called a result set or result list. You can use the `getResultList` method of the `Query` interface to retrieve the results of a query. For example, to retrieve all instances of `Item` with an initial price between 100 and 200 using named parameters, use the following:

```
query.setParameter("lowPrice", lowPriceValue)
query.setParameter("highPrice", highPriceValue)
  List items = query.getResultList();
```

> **NOTE**   If `getResultList` does not retrieve any results for a query, it returns an empty list. No exceptions are thrown.

Here you see that `lowPrice` is the `name` parameter for the lower range parameter, and the value is provided by `lowPriceValue`. The upper range parameter is named `highPrice` in the query, and its value is specified by `highPriceValue`. The `query.getResultsList` method returns the list of items that fall within this range.

As with retrieving a single entity, retrieving a collection does not require an active transaction, and if one isn't available, the retrieved entities will be detached after retrieval.

Paginating through a result list

A query may retrieve hundreds, or even millions of entities, and processing a retrieved list of entities is not necessarily straightforward. Here's a common way to iterate through a list of items:

```
Iterator l = items.iterator();
while (l.hasNext()) {
    Item item = (Item)l.next();
    System.out.println("Id:" + item.getItemId() +
                    " Initial Price:"+item.getInitialPrice());
}
```

This code does not provide any logic to paginate through a specific set of results. But suppose you need to create a report in which every page is limited to a display of 50 entities, and when the user clicks the Next button, the succeeding 50 entities are displayed. If you used the previous method, you'd have two issues. First, the code would be more complicated than necessary to handle the 50-item page requirement. Second, you'd retrieve all entities from the database at one time, which might consume a lot of memory depending on how many items were returned.

The good news is that JPA provides the ability to paginate through the result set. You can use the following code to specify the pagination property for a query:

```
query.setMaxResults(50);
query.setFirstResult(0);
List items = query.getResultList();
```

The setMaxResults method lets you specify the maximum number of entities being retrieved in the result list, and setFirstResult lets you set the position of the first result in the ResultList. The previous code returns the first 50 entities retrieved by the query. If you want to retrieve the next 50 entities, use the following:

```
query.setMaxResults(50);
query.setFirstResult(50);
List items = query.getResultList();
```

The only difference between the previous two code snippets is the starting offset of the result list.

Instead of hard-coding the offset and page size, you can create a method that takes these settings as a parameter:

```
public List getPagedItems(int pageIndex, int pageSize) {
    ...
    query.setMaxResults(pageSize) ;
    query.setFirstResult(pageIndex) ;
    return query.getResultList();
}
```

You can use this method from your application code to paginate through the entities.

This is starting to look familiar, isn't it? Now let's turn our attention to another topic: controlling the flush mode of the query.

Controlling the query flush mode

You may remember from our discussion in chapter 9 that the flush mode determines how the `EntityManager` performs the database writes. The results of a query can vary depending on the flush mode setting. Chapter 9 discussed setting `Flush-Mode` for the persistence context. `FlushMode` can be changed for a specific query by using the `Query.setFlushMode` method. The default flush mode is `AUTO`, as shown in table 10.4. In `AUTO` mode, when queries are executed within a transaction the persistence provider is responsible for making sure that all entities are updated in the persistence context. This is true whether `FlushModeType.AUTO` is set on the `Query` object or the flush mode is `AUTO` for the persistence context.

Table 10.4   Defined flush modes for persistence providers and how the flush mode affects the results of a query

Flush Mode	Description
`AUTO` (default)	The persistence provider is responsible for updates to entities in the persistence context.
`COMMIT`	Updates made to entities in the persistence context are undefined.

If the `Query` is set to `FlushModeType.COMMIT`, the effect of updates made to entities in the persistence context is not defined by the specification, and the actual behavior is implementation specific. This means your mileage may vary depending on which persistence provider you are using.

The default behavior of the flush mode is acceptable for most cases, and you should not change it unless you absolutely need to tweak this setting.

10.2.3   Specifying query hints

Persistence providers typically include a vendor-specific extension that can be used while executing a query. Such extensions are usually performance optimizations and are passed as query hints. A *query hint* is a tip that is used by the persistence provider while executing queries or retrieving entities. For example, a hint can be a directive to the persistence provider whether to use a cache while executing a query. You can provide a hint for a query by using the `Query.setHint` method. Unfortunately, the hints are implementation specific. If you want to set the timeout for a query to `10` seconds when using Oracle TopLink, you do so with

```
query.setHint("toplink.jdbc.timeout", new Integer(10000));
```

You can do the same with Hibernate by using

```
query.setHint("org.hibernate.timeout", new Integer(10));
```

Notice the difference in how the timeout of 10 seconds is specified for each provider? Be sure to verify the format for the provider you are using by checking the documentation provided by the vendor. Look for hints that may be supported by the container. Table 10.5 lists some commonly used hints for two of the leading JPA providers.

Table 10.5 You can use the setHint method of the Query interface to specify query hints to the persistence provider. Common query hints are supported by two popular ORM frameworks.

TopLink	Hibernate	Purpose
`toplink.jdbc.fetch-size`	`org.hibernate.fetchSize`	Specifies the number of rows fetched by the JDBC driver
`toplink.cache-usage`	`org.hibernate.cacheMode`	Specifies how to use the cache
`toplink.refresh`	`CacheMode.REFRESH`	Specifies whether the cache should be refreshed from the database
`toplink.jdbc.timeout`	`org.hibernate.timeout`	Specifies the query timeout

If you are using named queries, then you can optionally specify the vendor-specific hints using the `hints` element of `@NamedQuery`. This element is specified as a name-value pair using the `@QueryHint` annotation:

```
@NamedQuery(
name = "findUserWithNoItems",
query = "SELECT DISTINCT u FROM User u WHERE u.items is EMPTY",
hints = { @QueryHint(name = "org.hibernate.timeout", value = "10") }
)
```

Whew! How do you feel now that you know all the basics of the JPA query API? Well, there's more where that came from! We'll bet you're ready for an adventurous trek into the winding trails of the Java Persistence Query Language. Lace up your high-tops—those trails are just ahead!

10.3 Introducing JPQL

The meat of this chapter covers the ins and outs of the Java Persistence Query Language. We'll start with a definition of the language, provide numerous examples illustrating almost every aspect, and include some little-known tips along the way. Can you handle a little heavy lifting? Proceed with caution if you think you can; and make sure you have your work gloves on…

Hibernate provides HSQL, while JDO-compliant providers such as BEA's Kodo support JDO QL to query entities. There was not much debate among the EJB 3 Expert Group on which to use as the standard query language for JPA, and it was agreed to use JPQL. JPQL is an extension of EJB QL, the query language of EJB 2. It didn't make sense to invent yet another language for such a well-known domain, so the group voted unanimously to make EJBQL the query language of choice and to address all its previous limitations. It's good news that yet another query language was not forced upon the developer community. The use of JPQL will make the migration of EJB 2 entity beans to EJB 3 persistence easier.

How is JPQL Different from SQL?

JPQL operates on classes and objects (entities) in the Java space. SQL operates on tables, columns, and rows in the database space. While JPQL and SQL look similar to us humans, they operate in two very different worlds.

The JPQL Query Parser or Processor Engine of a persistence provider, as shown in figure 10.2, translates the JPQL query into native SQL for the database being used by the persistence provider.

JPQL looks so much like SQL that it's easy to forget you are looking at JPQL when you're reviewing source code. Just remember that although JPQL may look like SQL, you'll need to be aware of the differences discussed in this chapter to effectively use and troubleshoot JPQL in your programs.

All this talk about JPQL queries has piqued your interest, hasn't it? What do you say we continue this line of thinking by going over the types of statements JPQL supports? Then we'll discuss different elements of a JPQL statement, such as FROM and SELECT clauses, conditional statements, subqueries, and various types of functions. Finally, we'll take a look at updates and delete statements.

Figure 10.2   Each JPQL query is translated to a SQL query by the JPQL query processor and executed by the database. The query processor is supplied by the JPA provider, most likely the application server vendor.

10.3.1 Defining statement types

JPQL supports three types of statements, as shown in table 10.6. You can use JPQL to perform selects, updates, and deletes in your queries.

Table 10.6   Statement types supported by the Java Persistence Query Language

Statement Type	Description
SELECT	Retrieves entities or entity-related data
UPDATE	Updates one or more entities
DELETE	Deletes one or more entities

Let's first focus on retrieving entities using a SELECT statement with JPQL.

Defining and using SELECT

Suppose we get jump-started with a simple JPQL query:

```
SELECT c
FROM Category c
WHERE c.categoryName LIKE :categoryName
ORDER BY c.categoryId
```

This JPQL query has (or can have) the following:

- A SELECT clause that specifies the object type or entity or values being retrieved
- A FROM clause that specifies an entity declaration that is used by other clauses
- An optional WHERE clause to filter the results returned by the query
- An optional ORDER BY clause to order the results retrieved by the query
- An optional GROUP BY clause to perform aggregation
- An optional HAVING clause to perform filtering in conjunction with aggregation

Defining UPDATE and DELETE

In chapter 9, we discussed updating and removing entities using the Entity-Manager API. But these were limited to only one entity instance. What about when you want to remove more than one entity in a single call? Like SQL, JPQL also provides UPDATE and DELETE statements to perform updates and deletions of entities, and we can continue to specify a condition using a WHERE clause. These statements are quite similar to their SQL relatives. They are referred to as bulk updates or deletes because you'll primarily use these to update or delete a set of entities matching a specific condition. In this section we'll limit our discussion to the JPQL syntax for update and delete, and we'll discuss the implications of using bulk updates and deletes in section 10.3.10.

Using UPDATE

Only one entity type can be specified with an UPDATE statement, and we should provide a WHERE clause to limit the number of entities affected by the statement. Here is the syntax for the UPDATE statement:

```
UPDATE entityName indentifierVariable
SET single_value_path_expression1 = value1, ...
    single_value_path_expressionN = valueN
WHERE where_clause
```

You can use any persistence field and single value association field in the SET clause of the UPDATE statement. Assume that we want to provide Gold status and a commissionRate of 10 percent to all Sellers whose lastName starts with Packrat. Start with the following JPQL statement:

```
UPDATE Seller s
SET s.status = 'G', s.commissionRate = 10
WHERE s.lastName like 'PackRat%'
```

It is clear from this statement that the WHERE clause of an UPDATE behaves exactly the same as the one we used in the SELECT statement. We will return to a detailed discussion on the WHERE clause later in this chapter.

Using DELETE

Like UPDATE, DELETE in JPQL resembles its SQL cousin. You can specify only one entity type with a DELETE statement, and again you should specify a WHERE clause to limit the number of entities affected by the statement. Here is the syntax for the DELETE statement:

```
DELETE entityName indentifierVariable
WHERE where_clause
```

For example, if we want to remove all instances of Seller with Silver status we'd use this:

```
DELETE Seller s
WHERE s.status = 'Silver'
```

10.3.2 Using the FROM clause

The FROM clause of JPQL is by far the most important clause. It defines the domain for the query—that is, the names for the entities that will be used in the query. In the previous example we specified the FROM clause as follows:

```
FROM Category c
```

Category is the domain that we want to query, and here we have specified c as an identifier of type Category.

Identifying the query domain: naming an entity

You specify the entity name defined for the entity using the @Entity annotation as the domain type. As you learned in chapter 7, you could define the name for an entity using the name element of the @Entity annotation. If you don't specify the name element, it defaults to the name of the entity class. The name of entity must be unique within a persistence unit. In other words, you cannot have two entities with the same name or the persistence provider will generate a deployment error. This makes sense because the persistence provider would not be able to identify which entity domain to use if duplicate names for entities are allowed.

EJB 2's EJBQL compared to EJB 3's JPQL

If you have used EJBQL with EJB 2, you'll see a significant difference with the new version. Some of the major enhancements in EJB 3 with respect to JPQL are as follows:

- Use of named parameters
- Simplification of syntax
- Support for JOIN operations
- Support for subqueries
- Bulk updates and deletes
- Support for GROUP BY and HAVING

The good news is that these JPQL enhancements may also be available to EJB 2.1 entity beans, because most application servers probably share the same JPQL parser for both EJB 2.1 entity beans and EJB 3 entities.

One of the greatest shortcomings of EJB 2 CMP entity beans is the inability to use dynamic queries and native SQL. Both of these limitations have been addressed by JPQL.

In the previous example, we are assuming the `Category` entity class that we discussed in earlier chapters does not define a name. If we assume that the `Category` class defines an entity name using the `name` element as follows:

```
@Entity(name = "CategoryEntity")
public class Category
```

then we must change the `FROM` clause of the query as follows:

```
FROM CategoryEntity c
```

This change is required in order for JPQL to map the correct entity type as defined by the annotation.

Identifier variables

In our JPQL example, we defined an identifier variable named `c`, and we used that variable in other clauses, such as `SELECT` and `WHERE`. A simple identifier variable is defined using the following general syntax:

```
FROM entityName [AS] identificationVariable
```

The square brackets (`[]`) indicate that the `AS` operator is optional. The identifier variable (which is not case sensitive) must be a valid Java identifier, and it must not be a JPQL reserved identifier. Table 10.7 lists all of the JPQL reserved identifiers for your convenience. Keep in mind that the identifier cannot be another entity name packaged in the same persistence unit.

Table 10.7 JPQL keywords reserved by the specification. You are not allowed to give any of your variables these names.

Types	Reserved Words
Statements and clauses	SELECT, UPDATE, DELETE, FROM, WHERE, GROUP, HAVING, ORDER, BY, ASC, DESC
Joins	JOIN, OUTER, INNER, LEFT, FETCH
Conditions and operators	DISTINCT, OBJECT, NULL, TRUE, FALSE, NOT, AND, OR, BETWEEN, LIKE, IN, AS, UNKNOWN, EMPTY, MEMBER, OF, IS, NEW, EXISTS, ALL, ANY, SOME
Functions	AVG, MAX, MIN, SUM, COUNT, MOD, UPPER, LOWER, TRIM, POSITION, CHARACTER_LENGTH, CHAR_LENGTH, BIT_LENGTH, CURRENT_TIME, CURRENT_DATE, CURRENT_TIMESTAMP

Thus, we cannot define the FROM clause like this:

```
FROM Category User
```

or like this:

```
FROM Category Max
```

because we already have an entity named User in the ActionBazaar application, and MAX is a reserved identifier.

You can define multiple identifiers in the FROM clause, and you'll see how to use them when we discuss joining multiple entities by association or field name later in this chapter.

What is a path expression?

In our JPQL example we used expressions such as c.categoryName and c.categoryId. Such expressions are known as *path expressions*. A path expression is an identifier variable followed by the navigation operator (.), and a persistence or association field. We normally use a path expression to narrow the domain for a query by using it in a WHERE clause, or order the retrieved result by using an ORDER BY clause.

An association field can contain either a single-value object or a collection. The association fields that represent one-to-many and many-to-many associations are collections of types, and such a path expression is a collection-value path expression. For example, if we have a many-to-many relationship between Category and Item, we can utilize a query to find all Category entities that have associated Items as follows:

```
SELECT distinct c
FROM Category c
WHERE c.items is NOT EMPTY
```

Here c.items is a collection type. Such expressions are known as collection-value expressions. If the association is either many-to-one or one-to-one, then the association fields are of a specific object type, and those types are known as single-value path expressions.

You can navigate further to other persistence fields or association fields using a single-value path expression. For example, say we have a many-to-one relationship between Category and User; we can navigate to a persistence field such as firstName using association field user as follows:

```
c.user.firstName
```

We may also want to navigate to the association field `contactDetails` to use its e-mail address:

```
c.user.contactDetails.email
```

While using path expressions, keep in mind that you cannot navigate through the collection-value path expressions to access a persistence or association field as in the following example:

```
c.items.itemName or c.items.seller
```

This is due to the fact you cannot access an element of a `Collection`, and `items` is in fact is a collection of items. Using `c.items.itemName` in JPQL is similar to using `category.getItems().getItemName()`, and this is not allowed.

Next we'll see how you can use path expressions in a `WHERE` clause.

Filtering with WHERE

The `WHERE` clause allows you to filter the results of a query. Only entities that match the query condition specified will be retrieved. Say we want to retrieve all instances of the `Category` entity; we can use a JPQL statement without a `WHERE` clause:

```
SELECT c
FROM Category c
```

Using this code will probably result in thousands of `Category` instances. But say we actually want to retrieve instances of a `Category` by a specific condition. To retrieve the `Category` instances that have a `categoryId` greater than 500, we'd have to rewrite the query like this:

```
SELECT c
FROM Category c
WHERE c.categoryId > 500
```

Almost all types of Java literals such as `boolean`, `float`, `enum`, `String`, `int`, and so forth are supported in the `WHERE` clause. You cannot use numeric types such as octal and hexadecimals, nor can you use array types such as `byte[]` or `char[]` in the `WHERE` clause. Remember that JPQL statements are translated into SQL; SQL is actually imposing the restriction that `BLOB` and `CLOB` types cannot be used in a `WHERE` clause.

Passing parameters: positional and named

Recall from our earlier discussion that JPQL supports two types of parameters: positional and named. Later in this chapter we'll show you how to set values for both named and positional parameters.

The value of the parameter is not limited to numeric or `String` types; the value depends on the type of path expression used in the `WHERE` clause. The parameter can take more complex types, such as another entity type; however, you are limited to using conditional expressions that involve a single-value path expression.

10.3.3 *Conditional expressions and operators*

A condition in the `WHERE` clause that filters results from a query is known as a *conditional expression*. You can build a conditional expression using path expressions and operators supported by the language. JPQL can evaluate a path expression with numeric, string, or boolean values using relational operators. Here's an example of a conditional expression:

```
c.categoryName = 'Dumped Cars'
```

Table 10.8 lists the types of operators supported by JPQL, in order of precedence.

Table 10.8   Operators supported by JPQL

Operator Type	Operator
Navigational	.
Unary sign	+, −
Arithmetic	*, / +, −
Relational	=, >, >=, <, <=, <>, [NOT] BETWEEN, [NOT] LIKE, [NOT] IN, IS [NOT] NULL, IS [NOT] EMPTY, [NOT] MEMBER [OF]
Logical	NOT AND OR

A complex conditional expression may include other expressions that are combined for evaluation using logical operators such as `AND` or `OR`. For instance, we can retrieve a `Category` that meets either of these conditional expressions:

```
WHERE c.categoryName = 'Dumped Cars'
      OR  c.categoryName = 'Furniture from Garbage'
```

We can use all types of relational operators with numeric types of path expressions. `String` and `Boolean` operands can use the relational operators: equality (=) and nonequality (<>).

Using a range with BETWEEN

You can use the BETWEEN operator in an arithmetic expression to compare a variable with a range of values. You can also use the BETWEEN operator in arithmetic, string, or DATETIME expressions to compare a path expression to a lower and upper limit using the following syntax:

```
path_expression [NOT] BETWEEN lowerRange and upperRange
```

Suppose you want to filter the results so that categoryId falls within a specified range. You can use a WHERE clause and named parameters for the range this way:

```
WHERE c.categoryId BETWEEN :lowRange AND :highRange
```

> **NOTE** The lower and upper range used in a BETWEEN operator must be the same data type.

Using the IN operator

The IN operator allows you to create a conditional expression based on whether a path expression exists in a list of values. Here is the syntax for the IN operator:

```
path_expression [NOT] IN (List_of_values)
```

The list of values can be a static list of comma-separated values, or a dynamic list retrieved by a subquery. Suppose you want to retrieve the results for userId that exist in a static list of userIds. This WHERE clause will do the trick:

```
WHERE u.userId IN ('viper', 'drdba', 'dumpster')
```

If you want to retrieve the information from users that do not exist in the same static list, then you can use this WHERE clause:

```
WHERE u.userId NOT IN ('viper', 'drdba', 'dumpster')
```

A subquery is a query within a query. A subquery may return a single or multiple values. You'll learn more about subqueries in section 10.3.8. Let's review an example of a subquery with an IN operator:

```
WHERE c.user IN (SELECT u
                 FROM User u
                 WHERE u.userType = 'A')
```

In this expression you are trying to evaluate the User field with a list of users retrieved by the subquery. When a query contains a subquery, the subquery is executed first, and then the parent query is evaluated against the result retrieved by the subquery.

Using the LIKE operator

The `LIKE` operator allows you to determine whether a single-value path expression matches a string pattern. The syntax for the `LIKE` operator is

```
string_value_path_expression [NOT] LIKE pattern_value_
```

Here `pattern_value` is a string literal or an input parameter. The `pattern_value` may contain an underscore (_) or a percent sign (%). The underscore stands for a single character. Consider the following clause:

```
WHERE c.itemName LIKE '_ike'
```

This expression will return `true` when `c.itemName` has values such as `mike`, `bike`, and so forth. You should be able to extend this technique to embed a space into any search string, effectively making the space a wildcard. If you search for a single space, it will only match a single character.

The percent sign (%) represents any numbers of characters. Whenever you want to search for all `Category` entities with a name that starts with `Recycle`, use this `WHERE` clause:

```
WHERE c.categoryName LIKE 'Recycle%'
```

The expression will return `true` when `c.categoryName` has values such as `Recycle from Garbage`, `Recycle from Mr. Dumpster`, and `RecycleMania — the Hulkster strikes again!`.

Suppose you want to retrieve a result set in which a string expression does not match a literal. You can use the `NOT` operator in conjunction with the `LIKE` operator as in the following example:

```
WHERE c.categoryName NOT LIKE '%Recycle%'
```

The expression will return `false` when `c.categoryName` has any values that includes `Recycle` as any part of the return value, because in this example you used `%` before and after the filter string. Some examples that match this situation are `Dr. T will Recycle your face` and `Recycle from the Garbage, it's the American Way`.

In most applications you probably want to supply a parameter for flexibility rather than use a string literal. You can use positional parameters as shown here to accomplish this:

```
WHERE c.categoryName NOT LIKE ?1
```

Here, the result set will contain all `c.categoryNames` that are not like values bound to the positional parameter `?1`.

Dealing with null values and empty collections

So far we have been able to avoid discussing `null` and how an expression deals with `null` values. Alas, now it is time to deal with this little mystery. You have to remember that `null` is different from an empty string, and JPQL treats them differently. However, not all databases treat an empty string and `null` differently. We already know that JPQL is translated into SQL by the persistence provider. If the database returns `true` when an empty string is compared with `null`, you cannot rely on consistent results from your queries across two different databases. We recommend that you test this situation with your database.

When a conditional expression encounters a `null` value, the expression evaluates to `null` or `unknown`. A complex WHERE clause that combines more than one conditional expression with a boolean operator such as AND may produce a result that is `unknown`. Table 10.9 lists the results of a conditional expression when it is compared with a `null` value.

Table 10.9 Results of boolean operations involving null

Expression 1 Value	Boolean Operator	Expression 2 Value	Result
TRUE	AND	null	UNKNOWN
FALSE	AND	null	FALSE
Null	AND	null	UNKNOWN
TRUE	OR	null	TRUE
Null	OR	null	UNKNOWN
FALSE	OR	null	UNKNOWN
	NOT	null	UNKNOWN

You can use the IS NULL or IS NOT NULL operator to check whether a single-value path expression contains `null` or `not null` values. If a single-value path expression contains `null`, then IS NULL will return `true` and IS NOT NULL will return `false`. If you want to compare whether the single-value path expression is `not null`, use the following WHERE clause:

```
WHERE c.parentCategory IS NOT NULL
```

You cannot use the IS NULL expression to compare a path expression that is of type `collection`; in other words, IS NULL will not detect whether a collection type path expression is an empty collection. JPQL provides the IS [NOT] EMPTY comparison operator to check whether a collection type path expression is empty. The following WHERE clause would work when you want to retrieve all Category entities that do not have any Items:

```
WHERE c.items IS EMPTY
```

As we explained earlier, JPQL statements are translated to SQL statements by the persistence provider. There is no equivalent of the IS EMPTY clause in SQL. So, you must be wondering what SQL statement is generated when IS EMPTY is used. The IS EMPTY clause is used with a collection-valued path expression that is typically an association field, and therefore the generated SQL statement will be determining whether the JOIN for the association retrieves any record in a subquery. To clarify, let's examine this JPQL query:

```
SELECT c
FROM Category c
WHERE c.items IS EMPTY
```

If you recall our discussions from chapters 7 and 8, a many-to-many relationship exists between Category and Item entities, with CATEGORIES_ITEMS as the intersection table. This means the persistence provider will generate the following SQL statement:

```
SELECT
  c.CATEGORY_ID, c.CATEGORY_NAME, c.CREATE_DATE,
  c.CREATED_BY, c.PARENT_ID
FROM CATEGORIES c
WHERE (
  (SELECT COUNT(*)
  FROM CATEGORIES_ITEMS ci, ITEMS i
  WHERE (
    (ci.CATEGORY_ID = c.CATEGORY_ID) AND
    (i.ITEM_ID = ci.ITEM_ID))) = 0)
```

From this generated SQL, you can see that the persistence provider uses a subquery to retrieve the number of associated items for a category by using the COUNT group function, and then compares the result with 0. This means that if no items are found, the collection must be empty, and the IS EMPTY clause is true.

Have you ever had an occasion to detect the presence of a single value in a collection? Sure you have! In JPQL you can use the MEMBER OF operator for just that purpose. Let's take a look at how it works.

Checking for the existence of an entity in a collection

You can use the MEMBER OF operator to test whether an identifier variable, a single-value path expression, or an input parameter exists in a collection-value path expression. Here is the syntax for the MEMBER OF operator:

```
entity_expression [NOT] MEMBER [OF] collection_value_path_expression
```

The OF and NOT keywords are optional and can be omitted. Here is an example of using an input parameter with MEMBER OF:

```
WHERE :item MEMBER OF c.items
```

This condition will return true if the entity instance passed (as :item) in the query exists in the collection of c.items for a particular Category c.

10.3.4 Working with JPQL functions

JPQL provides several built-in functions for performing string or arithmetic operations. These functions can be used either in the WHERE or HAVING clause of a JPQL statement. You'll learn more about the HAVING clause when we cover aggregate functions later in this chapter.

String functions

You can use string functions in the SELECT clause of a JPQL query; table 10.10 lists all string functions supported by JPQL. These functions are only meant to be used to filter the results of the query. You have to use the functions available in the Java language if you want to perform any string manipulations on your data. The primary reason is that in-memory string manipulation in your application will be much faster than doing the manipulation in the database.

Table 10.10 JPQL String functions

String Functions	Description
CONCAT(string1, string2)	Returns the value of concatenating two strings or literals together.
SUBSTRING(string, position, length)	Returns the substring starting at position that is length long.
TRIM([LEADING | TRAILING | BOTH] [trim_character] FROM] string_to_trimmed)	Trims the specified character to a new length. The trimming can either be LEADING, TRAILING, or from BOTH ends. If no trim_character is specified, then a blank space is assumed.

continued on next page

Table 10.10 JPQL String functions *(continued)*

String Functions	Description
`LOWER(string)`	Returns the string after converting to lowercase.
`UPPER(string)`	Returns the string after converting to uppercase.
`LENGTH(string)`	Returns the length of a string.
`LOCATE(searchString,` `    stringToBeSearched[initialPosition])`	Returns the position of a given string within another string. The search starts at position 1 if `initialPosition` is not specified.

Let's look at a couple of common string function examples. Suppose we want to compare the result of concatenating of two string expressions with a string literal. The following WHERE clause will perform the task well:

```
WHERE CONCAT(u.firstName, u.lastName) = 'ViperAdmin'
```

If the concatenation of `u.firstName` and `u.lastName` does not result in `ViperAdmin` then the condition will return `false`.

You can use the SUBSTRING function to determine if the first three letters of `u.lastName` start with `VIP`:

```
WHERE SUBSTRING(u.lastName, 1, 3) = 'VIP'
```

The name of each string function is a good indicator of the functional operation it can perform. The direct analog of string functions is arithmetic functions. We'll look at what JPQL supports in this area next.

Arithmetic functions

Although math is rarely used to perform CRUD operations, it is useful when trying to manipulate data for reports. JPQL only supports a bare minimum set of functions in this regard, and some vendors may choose to add functions to enhance their reporting capabilities. As with all vendor-specific features, be aware that using them will make your code less portable should you decide to change vendors in the future. You can use arithmetic functions in either the WHERE or HAVING clause of JPQL. Table 10.11 lists all arithmetic functions supported by JPQL.

Table 10.11 JPQL arithmetic functions

Arithmetic Functions	Description
`ABS(simple_arithmetic_expression)`	Returns the absolute value of `simple_arithmetic_expression`
`SQRT(simple_arithmetic_expression)`	Returns the square root value of `simple_arithmetic_expression` as a double
`MOD(num, div)`	Returns the result of executing the modulus operation for `num`, `div`
`SIZE(collection_value_path_expression)`	Returns the number of items in a collection

Most of the arithmetic functions are self-explanatory, such as this example of `SIZE`:

```
WHERE SIZE(c.items) = 5
```

This expression will return `true` when the `SIZE` of `c.items` is 5, and `false` otherwise.

Temporal functions

Most languages provide functions that retrieve the current date, time, or timestamp. JPQL offers the temporal functions shown in table 10.12. These functions translate into database-specific SQL functions, and the requested current date, time, or timestamp is retrieved from the database.

Table 10.12 JPQL temporal functions

Temporal Functions	Description
`CURRENT_DATE`	Returns current date
`CURRENT_TIME`	Returns current time
`CURRENT_TIMESTAMP`	Returns current timestamp

Note that because JPQL time values are retrieved from the database, they may vary slightly from the time retrieved from your JVM, if they aren't both running on the same server. This is only an issue if you have a time-sensitive application. You can resolve this issue by running a time service on all servers that are part of your environment.

Next we'll look at the `SELECT` clause of JPQL.

10.3.5 *Using a SELECT clause*

Although you saw some examples of the SELECT clause at the beginning of this chapter, we avoided a detailed discussion of the SELECT clause until now. From the previous examples it is evident that the SELECT clause denotes the result of the query. Here is the JPQL syntax of SELECT clause:

```
SELECT [DISTINCT] expression1, expression2, .... expressionN
```

A SELECT clause may have more than one identifier variable, one or more single-value path expressions, or aggregate functions separated by commas. Earlier we used an identifier in the SELECT clause as follows:

```
SELECT c
FROM Category AS c
```

You can also use one or more path expressions in the SELECT clause:

```
SELECT c.categoryName, c.createdBy
FROM Category c
```

The expressions used in the SELECT clause have to be single value. In other words, you cannot have a collection-value path expression in the clause. The path expressions can be an association field, as in the previous example, where c.createdBy is an association field of the Category entity.

The previous query may return duplicate entities. If you want the result not to contain duplicate data, use the DISTINCT keyword in this way:

```
SELECT DISTINCT c.categoryName, c.createdBy
FROM Category c
```

The following SELECT statement is invalid:

```
SELECT c.categoryName, c.items
FROM Category
```

because c.items is a collection-type association field, and collection-value path expressions are not allowed in a SELECT clause. We'll talk about using aggregate functions in the SELECT clause in the next section.

Using a constructor expression in a SELECT clause

You can use a constructor in a SELECT clause to return one or more Java instances. This is particularly useful when you want to create instances in a query that are initialized with data retrieved from a subquery:

```
SELECT NEW actionbazaar.persistence.ItemReport (c.categoryID, c.createdBy)
FROM Category
WHERE categoryId.createdBy = :userName
```

The specified class does not have to be mapped to the database, nor is it required to be an entity.

Polymorphic queries

You may be surprised to find out that JPA supports polymorphism, and that JPQL queries are polymorphic. This means a JPQL query to retrieve a parent entity in an entity hierarchy is not just limited to the entity, but retrieves all subclasses as well. For example, in ActionBazaar any query to retrieve `User` entities will retrieve its subclasses, such as `Seller`, `Bidder`, and `Admin`.

Suppose we have a query like this:

```
SELECT u
FROM User u
WHERE u.firstName LIKE :firstName
```

The query will retrieve all instances of `Seller`, `Bidder`, `Admin`, and so forth that match this query condition. How do you handle a polymorphic query in your client code? Consider the following:

```
query = em.createNamedQuery("findUserByName");
query.setParameter("firstName", firstName);
List<User> users = query.getResultList();

Iterator i = users.iterator();
while (i.hasNext()) {
    User user = (User) i.next();
    System.out.print("User:"+emp.getUserId());
    if (user instanceof Seller) {
        Seller seller = (Seller) user;
        System.out.println("Seller:" +
            seller.getCommissionRate());
    }
    else if (user instanceof Bidder) {
        Bidder bidder = (Bidder) bidder;
        System.out.println("Bidder:" +
            bidder.getDiscountRate());
    }
}
```

This code snippet uses the `instanceof` keyword to test `user`. Some Java gurus recommend you avoid using `instanceof`, but we use it here as a last resort. You have to ensure that your operations are just as polymorphic as your queries! In our example, you can easily convert the operations to be polymorphic by adding a `getRate` method in all entities. The `getRate` method will return the `commissionRate` for the `Seller` entity, whereas it will return the `discount-Rate` for the `Bidder` entity. The resulting code should look like this:

```
Iterator i = users.iterator();
while (i.hasNext()) {
  User user = (User)i.next();
  System.out.print("User:" + emp.getUserId());
  System.out.println(user.getRate());
}
```

10.3.6 Using aggregations

Aggregations are useful when writing report queries that deal with a collection of entities. In this section we'll discuss support of aggregate functions in JPQL.

Aggregate functions

JPQL provides these aggregate functions: AVG, COUNT, MAX, MIN, and SUM. Each function's name suggests its purpose. The aggregate functions are commonly used in creating report queries. You can only use a persistence field with the AVG, MAX, MIN, and SUM functions, but you can use any type of path expression or identifier with the COUNT function.

Table 10.13 shows all the aggregate functions supported by JPQL.

Table 10.13   JPQL aggregate functions

Aggregate Functions	Description	Return Type
AVG	Returns the average value of all values of the field it is applied to	Double
COUNT	Returns the number of results returned by the query	Long
MAX	Returns the maximum value of the field it is applied to	Depends on the type of the persistence field
MIN	Returns the minimum value of the field it is applied to	Depends on the type of the persistence field
SUM	Returns the sum of all values on the field it is applied to	May return either Long or Double

If we want to find the MAX value for the i.itemPrice field among all Items, use the following query:

```
SELECT MAX(i.itemPrice)
FROM Item i
```

If you want to find out how many `Category` entities exist in the system, use `COUNT` like this:

```
SELECT COUNT(c)
FROM Category c
```

You've just seen some simple examples of aggregate functions. In the next section you'll learn how to aggregate results based on a path expression.

Grouping with GROUP BY and HAVING

In an enterprise business application, you may need to group data by some persistence field. Assuming that there is a one-many relationship between `User` and `Category`, this query will generate a report that lists the number of `Category` entities created by each `c.user`:

```
SELECT c.user, COUNT(c.categoryId)
FROM Category c
GROUP BY c.user
```

As you can see, we have grouped by an associated entity. You can group by a single-value path expression that is either a persistence or an association field. Only aggregate functions are allowed when you perform aggregation using `GROUP BY`. You can also filter the results of an aggregated query with a `HAVING` clause. Suppose you want to retrieve only the `User`s who have created more than five `Category` entities. Simply modify the previous query as follows:

```
SELECT c.user, COUNT(c.categoryId)
FROM Category c
GROUP BY c.user
HAVING COUNT(c.categoryId) > 5
```

In addition, you can have a `WHERE` clause in a query along with a `GROUP BY` clause such as

```
SELECT c.user, COUNT(c.categoryId)
FROM Category c
WHERE c.createDate is BETWEEN :date1 and :date2
GROUP BY c.user
HAVING COUNT(c.categoryId) > 5
```

A `WHERE` clause in a query containing both the `GROUP BY` and `HAVING` clauses results in multistage processing. First, the `WHERE` clause is applied to filter the results. Then, the results are aggregated based on the `GROUP BY` clause. Finally, the `HAVING` clause is applied to filter the aggregated result.

10.3.7 *Ordering the query result*

You can control the order of the values and objects retrieved by a query by using the ORDER BY clause:

```
ORDER BY path_expression1 [ASC | DESC], ... path_expressionN
    [ASC | DESC]
```

Here is an example JPQL query with an ORDER BY clause. In this case we want to retrieve all Category entities and sort them alphabetically by c.categoryName.

```
SELECT c
FROM Category c
ORDER BY c.categoryName ASC
```

By specifying ASC, we've indicated that we want the result set to be ordered in ascending order by c.categoryName. Specifying ASC is optional; if you leave it off, then the persistence provider will assume you want ascending order by default.

If you want results sorted in descending order, then specify DESC for the path expression. You can use compound ordering to further customize the sorting of the query results by using

```
SELECT c.categoryName, c.createDate
FROM Category c
ORDER BY c.categoryName ASC, c.createDate DESC
```

Keep in mind that if you use single-value path expressions instead of an identifier variable, the SELECT clause must contain the path expression that is used in the ORDER BY clause. The previous example used c.categoryName and c.createDate in the ORDER BY clause. Therefore, c.categoryName and c.createDate must also be used in the SELECT clause unless you use the identifier variable in the SELECT statement. This next JPQL snippet is invalid because the ORDER BY clause contains c.createDate but the SELECT clause does not:

```
SELECT c.categoryName, c.createDate
FROM Category c
ORDER BY c.categoryName ASC, c.createDate DESC
```

In a JPQL query that contains both ORDER BY and WHERE clauses, the result is filtered based on the WHERE clause first, and then the filtered result is ordered using the ORDER BY clause.

10.3.8 *Using subqueries*

A *subquery* is a query inside a query. You use a subquery in either a WHERE or HAVING clause to filter the result set. Unlike SQL subqueries, EJB 3 subqueries are not supported in the FROM clause. If you have a subquery in a JPQL query, the subquery will be evaluated first, and then the main query is retrieved based on the result of the subquery.

Here is the syntax for the subquery:

```
[NOT] IN / [NOT] EXISTS / ALL / ANY / SOME (subquery)
```

From the syntax of the language, it is clear that you can use IN, EXISTS, ALL, ANY, or SOME with a subquery. Let's look at some examples of subqueries in more detail.

Using IN with a subquery

We've already discussed using the IN operator where a single-value path expression is evaluated against a list of values. You can use a subquery to produce a list of results:

```
SELECT i
FROM Item i
WHERE i.user IN (SELECT c.user
                 FROM Category c
                 WHERE c.categoryName LIKE :name)
```

In this query, first the subquery (in parentheses) is executed to retrieve a list of users, and then the i.item path expression is evaluated against the list.

EXISTS

EXISTS (or NOT EXISTS) tests whether the subquery contains any result set. It returns true if the subquery contains at least one result and false otherwise. Here is an example illustrating the EXISTS clause:

```
SELECT i
FROM Item i
WHERE EXISTS (SELECT c
             FROM Category c
             WHERE c.user = i.user)
```

If you look carefully at the result of this subquery, you'll notice that it is the same as the query example we used in the previous section with the IN operator. An EXISTS clause is generally preferred over IN, particularly when the underlying tables contain a large number of records. This is because databases typically perform better when using EXISTS. Again, this is due to the work of the query processor translating JPQL queries into SQL by the persistence provider.

ANY, ALL, and SOME

Using the ANY, ALL, and SOME operators is similar to using the IN operator. You can use these operators with any numeric comparison operators, such as =, >, >=, <, <= and <>.

Here is an example of a subquery demonstrating the ALL operator:

```
SELECT c
FROM Category c
WHERE c.createDate >= ALL
            (SELECT i.createDate
             FROM Item i
             WHERE i.user = c.user)
```

If we include the ALL predicate, the subquery returns true if all the results retrieved by the subquery meet the condition; otherwise, the expression returns false. In our example the subquery returns false if any item in the subquery has a createDate later than the createDate for the category in the main query.

As the name suggests, if we use ANY or SOME, the expression returns true if any of the retrieved results meet the query condition. We can use ANY in a query as follows:

```
SELECT c
FROM Category c
WHERE c.createDate >= ANY
            (SELECT i.createDate
             FROM Item i
             WHERE i.seller = c.user)
```

SOME is just an alias (or a synonym) for ANY, and can be used anywhere ANY can be used.

10.3.9 *Joining entities*

If you've used relational databases and SQL, you must have some experience with the JOIN operator. You can use JOIN to create a Cartesian product between two entities. Normally you provide a WHERE clause to specify the JOIN condition between entities instead of just creating a Cartesian product.

You have to specify the entities in the FROM clause to create a JOIN between two or more entities. The two entities are joined based either on their relationships or any arbitrary persistence fields. When two entities are joined, you may decide to retrieve results that match the JOIN conditions. For example, suppose we join Category and Item using the relationships between them and retrieve only entities that match the JOIN condition. Such joins are known as *inner joins*. Conversely, suppose we need to retrieve results that satisfy the JOIN conditions but also include entities from one side of the domain that don't have matching entities on the other side. For example, we may want to retrieve all instances of Category even if there is no matching instance of Item. This type of join is called an *outer join*. Note that an outer join can be left, right, or both.

Let's first look at some examples of different types of inner joins. Then we'll see examples of joins based on arbitrary persistence fields and relationships, and finally we'll look at outer joins and fetch joins.

Theta-joins

Theta-joins are not very common, and are based on arbitrary persistence or association fields in the entities being joined, rather than the relationship defined between them. For example, in the ActionBazaar system we have a persistence field named `rating` that stores the rating for a `Category`. The values for `rating` include DELUXE, GOLD, STANDARD, and PREMIUM. We also have a persistence field named `star` that we use to store a star rating for an `Item`; the values for `star` also include DELUXE, GOLD, STANDARD, and PREMIUM. Assume that both persistence fields store some common values in these fields, such as GOLD, and we want to join these two entities based on the `rating` and `star` fields of `Category` and `Item`, respectively. To accomplish this, we use this query:

```
SELECT i
FROM Item i, Category c
WHERE i.star = c.rating
```

Although this type of join is less common in applications, it cannot be ruled out.

Relationship joins

A more common situation in applications is the need to join two or more entities based on their relationships. Here is the syntax for INNER JOIN:

```
[INNER] JOIN join_association_path_expression [AS]
   identification_variable
```

In ActionBazaar, `Category` and `User` entities have a many-to-one association. To retrieve all users that match a specific criterion we could try this query:

```
SELECT u
FROM User u INNER JOIN u.Category c
WHERE u.userId LIKE ?1

The INNER clause is optional.
```

Remember that when you use the JOIN operator by itself, an inner join is always performed. Now let's move to the other end of the spectrum: outer joins.

Outer joins

Outer joins allow you to retrieve additional entities that do not match the JOIN conditions when associations between entities are optional. Outer joins are particularly useful in reporting. Let's assume that there is an optional relationship between User and Category and we want to generate a report that prints all the Category names for the user. If the user doesn't have any Category, then we want to print NULL. If we specify the User on the left side of the JOIN, we can use either the LEFT JOIN or LEFT OUTER JOIN keyword phrases with a JPQL query as follows:

```
SELECT u
FROM User u LEFT OUTER JOIN u.Category c
WHERE u.userId like ?1
```

This will also retrieve User entities that do not have a matching Category, as well as Users that do. It's worth noting that, if an outer join is not used, the query would only retrieve the users with the matching Category, but would fail to retrieve users that do not have a matching Category.

Are there any other types of JOINs supported by JPQL? We're glad you asked! The final type is called the fetch join.

Fetch joins

In a typical business application, you may want to query for a particular entity but also retrieve its associated entities at the same time. For example, when we retrieve a Bid in the ActionBazaar system, we want to eagerly load and initialize the associated instance of Bidder. We can use a fetch join in JPQL to retrieve an associated entity as a side effect of the retrieval of an entity:

```
SELECT b
FROM Bid b FETCH JOIN b.bidder
WHERE b.bidDate >= :bidDate
```

A fetch join is generally useful when you have lazy loading enabled for your relationship but you want to eagerly load the related entities in a specific query. You can use FETCH JOIN with both inner and outer joins.

Did you have any idea there was so much to JPQL? If you didn't know any better you might think it was a whole other language… Oh wait, it is! And it's just waiting for you to give it a test drive. We hope you were able to get your bearings so that you can get started with JPQL and put it to work in your applications.

We're in the home stretch of this chapter, with only a couple of topics left. We still need to discuss native SQL queries, but first we'll talk about bulk updates and deletes.

10.3.10 *Bulk updates and deletes*

ActionBazaar categorizes its users by Gold, Platinum, and similar terms based on the number of successful trades in a year. At the end of the year, an application module is executed that appropriately set the user status. You could run a query to retrieve the collection of User entities and then iterate through the collection and update the status. An easier way is to use a bulk UPDATE statement to update the collection of entities matching the condition, as in this example:

```
UPDATE User u
SET u.status = 'G'
WHERE u.numTrades >=?1
```

You've seen some examples of DELETE and UPDATE statements in JPQL in previous sections, but we avoided any in-depth discussion until now. Let's assume that ActionBazaar administrators need functionality to remove instances of entities such as Users based on certain conditions. We start with the following code:

```
@PersistenceContext em;
. . .
// start transaction
Query query = em.createQuery("DELETE USER u WHERE u.status = :status ");
query.setParameter("status", 'GOLD');
int results = query.executeUpdate();
//end transaction
```

In this code, the use of UPDATE and DELETE statements is quite similar to using any other JPQL statements, except for two significant differences. First, we use the executeUpdate method of the Query interface to perform bulk updates and deletes instead of getResultList or getSingleResult. Second, we must invoke executeUpdate within an active transaction.

Because bulk updates and deletes involve many pitfalls, we recommend that you isolate any bulk operations to a discrete transaction, because they are directly translated into database operations and may cause inconsistencies between managed entities and the database. Vendors are only required to execute the update or delete operations, and not required to modify any changes to the managed entities according the specification. In other words, the persistence provider won't remove any associated entities when an entity is removed as a result of a bulk operation.

At this point, we've covered a lot of ground: queries, annotations, and JPQL. There's only one topic left to discuss in this arena: using regular SQL queries in EJB 3.

10.4 *Native SQL queries*

Just what is native SQL? It's the SQL understood by the specific database server—Oracle, MySQL, Derby, etc.—that you are using. This section provides what you need to start using native SQL with EJB 3 right now.

> **NOTE**   In EJB 2 CMP entity beans, almost every vendor supported their own way of using SQL to perform queries. The many limitations in EJBQL were the primary driver for the vendor-specific extension for native SQL in EJB 2. Although JPA standardizes use of native SQL queries you should think twice about using native SQL in your applications, unless you are very proficient in SQL and you are trying to take advantage of the proprietary features of your database. Also keep in mind that the use of native SQL will make your applications less portable, if you decide to change your underlying database.

Suppose you want to generate a hierarchical list of categories, each showing its subcategories; it's impossible to do that in JPQL because JPQL does not support recursive joins, similar to databases like Oracle. This means you have to take advantage of native SQL.

Let's assume you're using an Oracle database and you want to retrieve all subcategories of a particular `Category` by using recursive joins in the form of a START WITH ... CONNECT BY ... clause as follows:

```
SELECT CATEGORY_ID, CATEGORY_NAME
FROM CATEGORY
START WITH parent_id = ?
CONNECT BY PRIOR category_id = category_id
```

Ideally, you should limit your use of native SQL to queries that you cannot express using JPQL (as in our Oracle database–specific SQL query). However, for demonstration purposes, in our example in the next section, we've used a simple SQL statement that can be used with most relational databases.

> **NOTE**   A JPA provider just executes SQL statements as JDBC statements and does not track whether the SQL statement updated data related to any entities. You should avoid using SQL INSERT, UPDATE, and DELETE statements in a native query because your persistence provider will have no knowledge of such changes in the database and it may lead to inconsistent/stale data if your JPA provider uses caching.

As in JPQL, you can use both dynamic queries and named queries with SQL. You have to remember the subtle differences between JPQL and SQL. JPQL returns an entity, or set, of scalar values, but a SQL query returns database records. Therefore, a SQL query may return more than entities, because you may join multiple tables in your SQL. Let's see how to use native SQL with both dynamic and native queries.

10.4.1 *Using dynamic queries with native SQL*

You can use the createNativeQuery method of the EntityManager interface to create a dynamic query using SQL as follows:

```
Query q = em.createNativeQuery("SELECT user_id, first_name, last_name "
        + " FROM users WHERE user_id IN (SELECT seller_id FROM "
        + "items GROUP BY seller_id HAVING COUNT(*) > 1)",
        actionbazaar.persistence.User.class);

return q.getResultList();
```

In this statement, the createNativeQuery method takes two parameters: the SQL query and the entity class being returned. This will become an issue if the query returns more than one entity class—which is why JPA allows a @SqlResultSetMapping to be used with the createNativeQuery method instead of passing an entity class. A @SqlResultSetMapping may be mapped to one or more entities.

For example, if we want to create a SqlResultSetMapping for the User entity and use in our native query, then we can use the @SqlResultSetMapping annotation as follows:

```
@SqlResultSetMapping(name = "UserResults",
    entities = @EntityResult(
      entityClass =  actionbazaar.persistence.User.class))
```

Then we can specify the mapping in the Query as follows:

```
Query q = em.createNativeQuery("SELECT user_id, first_name, last_name "
        + " FROM users WHERE user_id IN (SELECT seller_id FROM "
        + "items GROUP BY seller_id HAVING COUNT(*) > 1)",
        "UserResults");

return q.getResultList();
```

This is useful when the SQL query returns more than one entity. The persistence provider will automatically determine the entities being returned based on the SqlResultSetMapping, instantiate the appropriate entities, and initialize those entities with values based on the O/R mapping metadata.

Once you create a query, it makes no difference whether you retrieve the results from a native SQL or a JPQL query.

10.4.2 *Using a named native SQL query*

Using a named native query is quite similar to using a named JPQL query. To use a named native query, you must first create it. You can use the @NamedNativeQuery annotation to define a named query:

```
public @interface NamedNativeQuery {
  String name();
  String query();
  QueryHint[] hints() default {};
  Class resultClass() default void.class;
  String resultSetMapping() default ""; // name of SQLResultSetMapping
}
```

You can either use an entity class or a result set mapping with the @NamedNative-Query annotation. Suppose we want to convert the query that we used earlier to a named native query. The first step is to define the named native query in the User entity:

```
@NamedNativeQuery(
  name = "findUserWithMoreItems",
  query = "SELECT user_id , first_name , last_name,
              birth_date
   FROM   users
   WHERE user_id IN
 ( SELECT seller_id
   FROM items
   GROUP BY seller_id   HAVING COUNT(*) > ?)",
   hints = {@QueryHint(name = "toplink.cache-usage",
       value="DoNotCheckCache")},
   resultClass = actionbazaar.persistence.User.class)
```

Next, if our query returns more than one entity class, we must define SqlResult-SetMapping in the entity class using resultSetMapping as follows:

```
@NamedNativeQuery(
  name = "findUserWithMoreItems",
  query = "SELECT user_id , first_name , last_name,
              birth_date
          FROM users
          WHERE user_id IN
            (SELECT seller_id
             FROM items
             GROUP BY seller_id
             HAVING COUNT(*) > ?)",
   resultSetMapping = "UserResults")
```

You can provide a vendor-specific hint using the queryHint element of the NamedNativeQuery. It is similar to the hints element for NamedQuery discussed in section 10.2.4.

NOTE   There is no difference in executing a named native SQL query and a JPQL named query—except that a named parameter in native SQL query is not required by the JPA spec.

To illustrate how similar the execution of JPQL and native SQL queries is, let's execute the named native query `findUserWithMoreItems` (which we defined earlier in a session bean method):

```
return em.createNamedQuery("findUserWithMoreItems")
            .setParameter(1, 5)
            .getResultList();
```

This statement first creates a query instance for the named native query `find-UserWithMoreItems`. Next, the required positional parameter is set. Finally, we return the result set.

JPA and database stored procedures

If you're a big fan of SQL, you may be willing to exploit the power of database-stored procedures. Unfortunately, JPA doesn't support stored procedures, and you have to depend on a proprietary feature of your persistence provider. However, you can use simple stored functions (without `out` parameters) with a native SQL query.

Well, it appears you made it through the jungle of native SQL queries relatively unscathed. We hope you can see that while it is possible to drop down into the bowels of SQL from JPA, we don't recommend it. Embedding SQL into Java strings can be very time-consuming when it comes to debugging. And you lose all the benefits that JPQL affords you. However, if you really do need to go native, JPA will make it possible.

10.5 *Summary*

Queries are an important piece of the persistence puzzle, and in this chapter we explored the various query capabilities provided by the EJB 3 Java Persistence API. JPA uses the following three methods to query entities:

- `EntityManager.find` with the entity's primary key
- Queries written in JPQL
- SQL queries native to the underlying database

You can either create ad hoc queries dynamically or use named queries that are stored with their associated entities. The `EntityManager` interface provides methods to create JPQL- or SQL-based queries, and the `Query` interface provides methods to execute a query. You can set parameters, pagination properties, and flush mode, and retrieve query results using methods in the `Query` interface. JPQL is the safest bet for writing queries, as it addresses the major limitations of EJBQL and is the only way to build applications that are portable across databases. Avoid using native SQL unless you have to use a vendor-specific feature.

This chapter concludes part 3 of this book. Part 4 assembles everything we've covered thus far, and allows you to apply these new skills in interesting, practical ways. We'll also delve into packaging concerns and explore some EJB design patterns.

Part 4

Putting EJB 3 into action

Part 4 of this book provides guidelines for using EJB 3 effectively in your enterprise Java applications. Chapter 11 offers in-depth coverage of packaging EJB 3 applications and introduces deployment descriptors. Chapter 12 explores design patterns and explains how to use EJB 3 components and JPA from the web tier. In chapter 13, you'll learn best practices for building scalable applications using EJB 3.

Packaging EJB 3 applications

This chapter covers

- Class loading concepts
- Packaging EJB 3 components
- Packaging EJB 3 entities
- O/R mapping with XML
- Deployment issues and best practices

In the previous chapters you learned how to build a business-logic tier with session and message-driven beans, and you used entities to support the persistence tier. The real success of Java EE applications lies in assembly and deployment, as this is the key to delivering on Java's promise of write once, run anywhere (WORA). If you fail to fully grasp this step, your application may not realize this level of portability.

A typical application has a handful of Java classes, and maintenance can be a nightmare if you are shipping your applications from one environment to another. To simplify maintenance you can create a Java archive (JAR) file. Typically, a JAR

Java platform roles: it's all about juggling hats

The Java EE platform defines different roles and responsibilities relating to development, assembly, and deployment of Java EE applications. In this book we are mainly interested in the Developer, Assembler, and Deployer roles, but we introduce you to all the roles so that you can be familiar with them. The roles defined by the specifications are

- Enterprise Bean Provider
- Application Assembler
- Deployer
- EJB Server Provider
- EJB Container Provider
- Persistence Provider
- System Administrator

The database administrator is not one of the defined Java EE roles. The database administrator may not even understand a line of Java code. However, the importance of this role cannot be overlooked, especially in large corporations where relational databases are outside the control of the application developers. Developers, Assemblers, and Deployers may need to work with the DBAs in order to successfully build and release Java EE applications.

It's all about the division of labor. Many believe that the difficulties of earlier EJB practices were a result of the division of the EJB roles. In reality, the previous EJB specifications were not the real culprit—the source of all the confusion is the Java EE specification. While the Java EE and EJB specifications define seven roles, the problem is that many project teams do not even have seven people—how can a two- or three-person team wear that many hats?

file is a file in zip format that contains classes. However, enterprise Java applications are packaged as specialized versions of JAR files—EAR, WAR, and EJB-JAR modules—before they can be deployed to a Java EE–compliant application server.

In this chapter we begin with a discussion of application packaging and deployment. The chapter also provides critical information on class loading, so that you can appreciate why the archives are packaged as they are. This is intended to provide you a better understanding of the packaging requirements for EJBs that include entities. We explain the need for deployment descriptors, and look at how to use them. Finally, we look at a persistence unit and how to perform object-relational (O/R) mapping using XML.

11.1 *Packaging your applications*

A typical enterprise Java application may contain several Java classes of different types, such as EJBs, servlets, JavaServer Faces (JSF) managed beans, and entity classes, as well as static files such as JSPs and HTML files. As we discussed in chapter 1, EJBs run in the EJB container whereas web applications such as servlets and JSF managed beans run in the web container. To run your application you have to make it available to the Java EE application server. This is known as *deployment*. Since EJB is a core part of the Java EE specification, you have to follow the Java EE standard for deployment.

To understand EJB packaging, you must consider how it fits into the bigger picture of Java EE packaging and know what constitutes a complete enterprise Java application. Up to this point we have focused on using EJB components such as session beans and MDBs to build business logic and JPA entities to implement your persistence code. However, your application will not be complete without a presentation tier that accesses the business logic you built with EJBs. For example, the EJBs we built for ActionBazaar do not make sense unless we have a client application accessing them. Most likely, you've used standard technologies such as JSP or JSF to build the web tier of your applications. These web applications, together with EJBs, constitute an enterprise application that you can deploy to an application server.

To deploy and run an application, you have to package the complete application together—the web module and EJBs—and deploy to an application server. Usually you will group similar pieces of the application together in modules. Java EE defines a standard way of packaging these modules in JAR files, and specifies the formats for these JARs. One of the advantages of having these formats defined as part of the specification is that they are portable across application servers.

Table 11.1 lists the archives or modules supported by Java EE 5 and their contents. Note that each archive type is used for packaging a specific type of module, such as EJB or web. For instance, a WAR is used to package a web-tier application module, and the EAR file is intended to be the über archive containing all the other archives so that in the end, you're only deploying one file. The application server will scan the contents of the EAR and deploy it. We discuss how an EAR is loaded by the server in section 11.1.2.

Table 11.1   Enterprise Java applications need to be assembled into specific types of JAR files before they can be deployed to an application server. These are the available module types as specified by Java EE.

Type	Description	Descriptor	Contents
CAR	Client application archives	`application-client.xml`	Thick Java client for EJBs.
EAR	Enterprise application archive	`application.xml`	Other Java EE modules such as EJB-JARs.
EJB-JAR	EJB Java archive	`ejb-jar.xml`	Session beans, message-driven beans, and optionally entities. Needs a `persistence.xml` if entities are packaged.
RAR	Resource adapter archives	`ra.xml`	Resource adapters.
WAR	Web application archives	`web.xml`	Web application artifacts such as servlets, JSPs, JSF, static files, etc. Entities can also be packaged in this module. Needs a `persistence.xml` if entities are packaged.

To create these files, you can use the `jar` utility that comes with JDK. The final step is to assemble all the JAR files into one EAR file for deployment. In 11.3.1 we show you a build script that creates a JAR file. Each of these JAR types contains an optional deployment descriptor that describes the archive. As we have been discussing throughout this book, you can use metadata annotations instead of a deployment descriptor.

In this chapter, we focus primarily on the EAR file and the EJB-JAR file, which contains the session and message-driven beans, as well as entities.

It's worth mentioning that entities can be packaged in most archive types. For example, the ability to package entities in WARs allows you to use the EJB 3 JPA in simple web applications or with lightweight frameworks such as Spring. Note that entities are not supported in RAR modules. This statement, however, begs the question of why Java EE does not have a different archive type to package EJB 3 entities, just as JBoss has the Hibernate Archive (HAR) to package persistence objects with Hibernate's O/R framework.

You may know the answer to this question if you have followed the evolution of the EJB 3 specification. For those who haven't, we now regale you with Tales from the Expert Group (cue spooky music)…

During the evolution of the EJB 3 Public Draft, the PAR (Persistence Archive) was introduced, which mysteriously vanished in the Proposed Final Draft. A huge, emotional battle was fought in the EJB and Java EE expert groups over whether to introduce a module type for a persistence module at the Java EE level, and suggestions were sought from the community at large, as well as from various developer forums. Many developers think a separate persistence module is a bad idea because entities are supported both outside and inside the container. Considering that persistence is inherently a part of any enterprise application, it makes sense to support packaging entities with most module types, instead of introducing a new module type specialized for packaging entities.

Now that you know what modules are supported and a little about how they were arrived at, shall we take a quick peek under the hood of an EAR module?

11.1.1 *Dissecting the EAR file*

To understand how deployment works, let's take a closer look at the EAR file, the top-level archive file that contains other Java EE archives when it is deployed to the application server. For instance, the ActionBazaar application contains an EJB module, a web module, a JAR containing helper classes, and an application client module. The file structure of the EAR file that ActionBazaar uses looks like this:

```
META-INF/application.xml
actionBazaar-ejb.jar
actionBazaar.war
actionBazaar-client.jar
lib/actionBazaar-commons.jar
```

application.xml is the deployment descriptor that describes the standard Java EE modules packaged in each EAR file. The contents of application.xml look something like listing 11.1.

Listing 11.1   Deployment descriptor for the ActionBazaar EAR module

```
<application>
  <module>
    <ejb>actionBazaar-ejb.jar</ejb>        ⊲┘ EJB module
  </module>
  <module>
    <web>
      <web-uri>actionBazaar.war</web-uri>  ⊲┘ Web module
      <context-root>ab</context-root>
    </web>
  </module>
  <module>
    <java>actionBazaar-client.jar</java>   ⊲┘ Application client module
  </module>
</application>
```

If you review the EAR file descriptor in listing 11.1, you'll see that it explicitly identifies each of the artifacts as a specific type of module. When you deploy this EAR to an application server, the application server uses the information in the deployment descriptor to deploy each of the module types.

Java EE 5 made the deployment descriptor optional, even in the EAR. This is a departure from previous versions of Java EE, where it was mandatory. The Java EE 5.0–compliant application servers deploy by performing automatic detection based on a standard naming convention or reading the content of archives; see http://java.sun.com/blueprints/code/namingconventions.html.

Next, let's take a look at how application servers deploy an EAR module.

11.1.2 *Loading the EAR module*

During the deployment process, the application server determines the module types, validates them, and takes appropriate steps so that the application is available to users. Although all application servers have to accomplish these goals, it's up to the individual vendor exactly how to implement it. One area where server implementations stand out is in how fast they can deploy the archives.

While vendors are free to optimize their specific implementation, they all follow the specification's rules when it comes to what is required to be supported and in what order the loading occurs. This means that your application server will use the algorithm from figure 11.1 when attempting to load the EAR file that contains modules or archives from table 1.1.

Before we delve into how EJB components and entities are packaged, let's briefly discuss what class loading is and how it works in the Java EE environment.

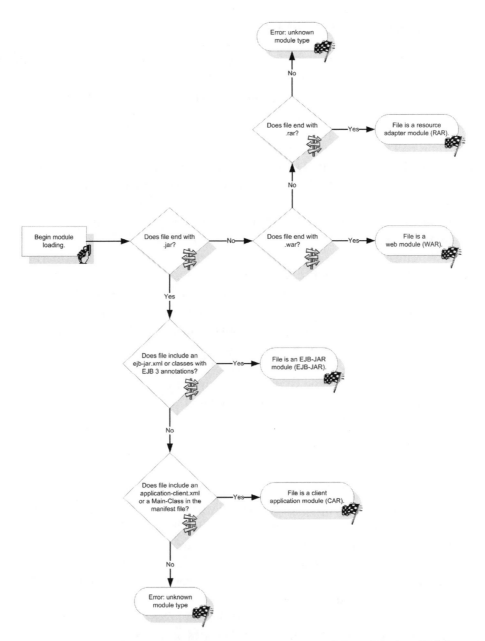

Figure 11.1 Rules followed by application servers to deploy an EAR module. Java EE 5 does not require a deployment descriptor in the EAR module that identifies the type of modules packaged. It is the responsibility of Java EE container to determine the type of module based on its name (extension) and its content. It does so by following this algorithm.

11.2 *Exploring class loading*

There is a misconception among many developers that all classes are loaded into memory when the JVM starts up; *this is not true*. Classes are loaded dynamically as and when they are needed at runtime. This process of locating the byte code for a given class name and converting that code into a Java *class* instance is known as *class loading*. Your application may have hundreds of EJBs and other resources; loading all these classes into the JVM consumes a lot of memory. Most application servers use a sophisticated mechanism to load classes as and when needed. Therefore, your EJB class will be loaded into memory only when a client accesses it. However, it is implementation specific. Application servers support the bean pooling mechanism, so EJB classes would be loaded into memory while some instances would be instantiated and put into the pool during deployment time.

When you build an application using EJB 3, you may use third-party libraries such as Log4J or you may depend on an in-house shared library configured in the application server. You may have web applications that depend on your EJB components and entities. As you can see, a complex application may depend on libraries available at several places. This means that you may run into many deployment errors such as `ClassNotFoundException` or `NoClassDefFoundError`. Understanding the class-loading concepts will educate you on effectively packaging your EJB 3 applications and help you troubleshoot any deployment-related issues.

In this section, we introduce the concept of class loading and look at the class-loader hierarchy in an application server. We then expose the parent delegation model. Finally, we examine class loading in Java EE and explore the dependencies between different modules.

11.2.1 *Class-loading basics*

If you've built simple applications with Java, you must be aware that when you run your application, the classes that make it up (often packaged in a standard JAR file) are made available to the JVM through the `CLASSPATH` environment variable. When a particular class is invoked, the JVM loads that class into memory by locating it from the available byte code files provided either via JAR files in the `CLASS-PATH` or a specified directory structure.

Class loading is initially performed by the JVM when it starts up. It loads the essential classes required, and then subclasses of the `java.lang.ClassLoader` class take the lead. These class loaders allow applications to load classes dynamically that may not be required during the compilation process. By default, the JVM utilizes a few different class loaders. As an illustration, the Sun JVM has a hierarchy of three loaders, as shown in figure 11.2

The boot class loader loads all platform classes that the Java language requires, such as classes in the `java.lang` or `java.util` package. You can optionally use the `bootclasspath` command-line option of the JVM to instruct the boot class loader to load additional classes from other JAR files.

The extension class loader is a child class loader of the boot class loader, and loads classes from any JARs placed in the `$JAVA_HOME/jre/lib/ext` directory, or in a separate directory specified with the `-Djava.ext.dir` system property. By default, it loads the Java cryptography library, as well as the security classes.

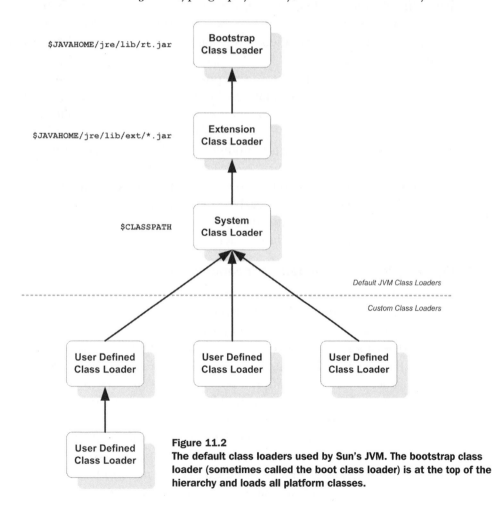

Figure 11.2
The default class loaders used by Sun's JVM. The bootstrap class loader (sometimes called the boot class loader) is at the top of the hierarchy and loads all platform classes.

The system class loader actually loads application classes as specified by an application, and is also known as the application class loader. You can use several mechanisms to specify the location from which the system class loader loads classes. One way is to specify the CLASSPATH environment variable. Another is to specify the manifest Class-Path entry of a JAR file that is being executed or that is in the CLASSPATH.

For example, the JAR file actionBazaar-client.jar has a Manifest.mf file in the META-INF directory that has this entry:

```
Class-Path:  lib/actionBazaar-utility.jar.
```

When the class loader loads the classes, it will search not only for the required class in the actionBazaar-client.jar, but also in the actionBazaar-utility.jar. The location of the JAR specified in the manifest Class-Path is relative to the JAR file that contains it.

For a simple Java application, this process is probably as simple as packaging the classes in a JAR and making the file available in the CLASSPATH. However, in a sophisticated environment such as Java EE, the application servers utilize several mechanisms to load the classes from a variety of locations, such as an application module, a library module, or a shared library configured in the application server environment.

When you start up an application server, a Java process starts loading classes required for the application server. When you deploy and execute an application in a Java application server, the application server loads the classes dynamically by creating new instances of class loaders.

11.2.2 *Exposing the classic parent delegation model*

You must be curious as to why JVM always loads the class from the parent class loader. In this section we will uncover the reason.

Let's review the scenario for ActionBazaar in order to understand the class-loading delegation model. The ActionBazaar website is built with JSP pages that invoke EJBs. When a user visits the ActionBazaar website and browses the items listed for auction, the application server uses class loaders to dynamically load required classes from application modules. All class loaders follow a standard algorithm to load classes, as illustrated in figure 11.3.

A class loader loads a class dynamically on an as-needed basis. It first looks at its local cache to see if it was loaded earlier. If not, it asks its parent to load the class. If its parent cannot load the class, it attempts to load it from its local code sources. Simply put, a code source is a base location, such as a JAR file,

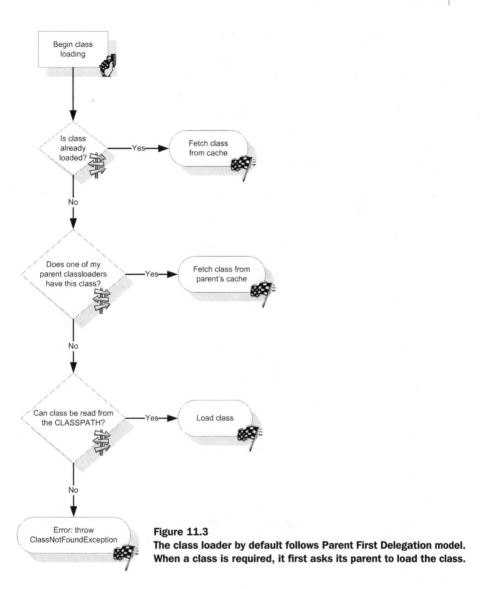

Figure 11.3
The class loader by default follows Parent First Delegation model.
When a class is required, it first asks its parent to load the class.

which the JVM searches for classes. This approach is called the Parent First delegation model.

Now that we've reviewed the basics of Java class loading, let's quickly review how class loading works in a Java EE application.

11.2.3 *Class loading in Java EE applications*

As we discussed earlier, an EJB application may make use of third-party libraries. In order to enable that, most Java EE containers use sophisticated mechanisms to load classes from a variety of places. You may remember from previous discussions that we follow standard practices to package our application components into standard-compliant archives such as EAR, EJB-JAR, WAR, and so forth. Table 11.2 lists the code sources for commonly used Java EE modules. For simplicity we are ignoring resource adapter (RAR) modules.

Table 11.2 A standard archive may load classes either packaged inside it or from any other archives it is dependent on.

Module	Code Sources
EAR	1. All JARs in the `/lib` directory of the EAR 2. Manifest `Class-Path` of any JARs in 1
EJB-JAR	1. EJB-JAR file itself 2. JARs referenced by manifest `Class-Path` of EJB-JAR 3. JARs referenced by manifest `Class-Path` of above JARs (in 2)
WAR	1. `WEB-INF/classes` 2. JARs in `WEB-INF/lib` 3. JARs referenced by manifest `Class-Path` of WAR 4. JARs referenced by manifest `Class-Path` of JARs in 2 and 3

The sooner you develop a good understanding of how the packaging standards work, the easier the whole packaging and deployment process will be.

11.2.4 *Dependencies between Java EE modules*

Unfortunately, no Java EE specification provides a standard for class loading, and each application server implements class loaders in whatever way seems best to the vendor. However, Java EE defines the visibility and sharing of classes between different modules, and we can depict the dependency between different modules as shown in figure 11.4.

As illustrated in figure 11.4, the EAR class loader loads all JARs in the `lib` directory that is shared between multiple modules. Typically a single EJB class loader loads all EJB classes packaged in all EJB-JAR modules. The EJB class loader is often the child of the application class loader, and loads all EJB classes. Because the EJB is a child to the EAR class loader, all classes loaded at the EAR level will be visible to the EJBs.

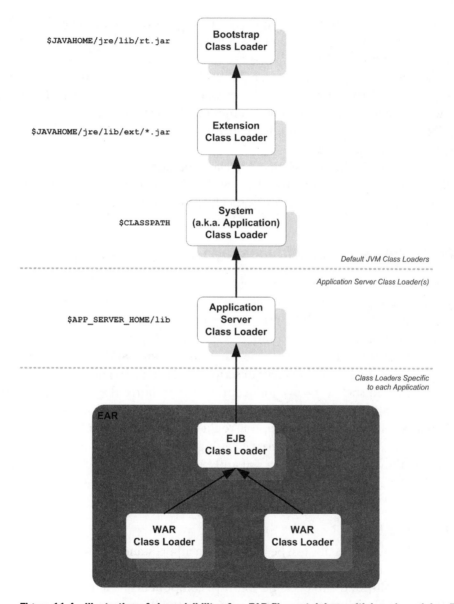

Figure 11.4 Illustration of class visibility of an EAR file containing multiple web modules, EJBs, and shared library modules. The EAR class loader loads the classes in the JARs packaged as library modules, and all classes loaded by the EAR class loader are visible to the EJBs. The classes loaded by EJB class loader are typically visible to the web module in most containers because the WAR class loader is a child of the EJB class loader.

EJBs are accessible from WAR modules. Furthermore, the EJB class loader is the parent of the WAR application class loader, and all EJB classes will be visible to the WAR module by default.

So before we move on to packaging EJBs, let's recap how this is going to help in packaging EJB 3 applications. If you package classes in a specific EJB module, it will probably be visible to only that module. If you want your classes (helper and utility) to be visible to all modules in the EAR file, you can package them as a library module in the EAR.

Armed with this knowledge on class loading, we can now return to the discussion on packaging EJBs. First we'll talk about the packaging of session and message-driven beans, and quickly proceed to the packaging of persistence entities.

11.3 *Packaging session and message-driven beans*

A car manufacturer has to assemble all essential parts of a car before it can run. As an EJB developer you build core classes that make your application, and you have to assemble them as an EJB-JAR and deploy them into your application server before your customers can execute the application.

Throughout this book we have used annotations and avoided deployment descriptors. The EJB deployment descriptor (`ejb-jar.xml`) describes the contents of an EJB-JAR, such as beans, interceptors, the resource they use, security, transaction settings, and so forth. For every annotation we have discussed in this book there is an element in the descriptor. You'll recall from chapter 2 that deployment descriptors can be used to override settings in metadata annotations. Let's now uncover the elements of `ejb-jar.xml` and explain how you can define default interceptors. We'll conclude this section with a discussion on vendor-specific descriptors and annotations.

11.3.1 *Packaging EJB-JAR*

Session beans and MDBs can be packaged in a Java standard JAR file as defined in the Java Archive specification at http://java.sun.com/j2se/1.5.0/docs/guide/jar/. To create an EJB-JAR file to package your EJB components, you have to compile your EJB classes and then create a JAR file using the `jar` tool supplied by JDK. For example, you can use the following command to create the `adventure-ejb.jar`:

```
jar cvf adventure-ejb.jar *
```

This will create a JAR file containing all class files in the current directory, and any subdirectories below the current directory. You can automate building JAR files using several tools. Most modern IDEs support building EJB-JAR modules, and make the creation of JAR modules somewhat transparent to you. A number of specialized utilities in addition to IDEs also support the build process. Today, the most frequently used tool to assist with builds is Apache Ant (http://ant. apache.org/), although there is a strong movement toward Apache Maven (http:// maven.apache.org/). Listing 11.2 shows a sample Ant build script that was created to automate building an EJB-JAR module. Ant build scripts are provided with our code examples and can be downloaded from this book's website (www. manning.com/panda).

Listing 11.2 Sample script for building an EJB-JAR file

```
...
    <target name="compile-ejb-classes" depends="setup">        ◁── Compiles EJB
      <echo message="-----> Compiling EJBs"/>                         classes
      <javac srcdir="${src.ejb.dir}"
        destdir="${bld.ejb.dir}"
        debug="on">
      <classpath>
        <pathelement path="${common.j2ee.class.path}"/>
        <pathelement location="${bld.ejb.dir}"/>
        <pathelement location="${lib.dir}/${ejb.name}.jar"/>
      </classpath>
     </javac>
    </target>

    <target name="ejb-descriptor" depends="setup">        ◁── Copies deployment
      <copy todir="${bld.ejb.dir}/META-INF">                   descriptors
        <fileset dir="${etc.dir}"
                 includes="ejb-jar.xml, persistence.xml"/>
      </copy>
    </target>

    <target name="package-ejb"
            depends="compile-ejb-classes,ejb-descriptor">        ◁── Builds
      <echo message="-----> Create EJB JAR file"/>                   EJB-JAR
      <jar jarfile="${bld.ear.dir}/${ejb.name}.jar">
        <fileset dir="${bld.ejb.dir}" includes="**"/>
      </jar>
    </target>
...
```

The EJB-JAR file must include the interfaces and bean classes. It may also include any helper classes. Optionally the helper classes may be packaged in a separate JAR file in the EAR file. You have two options:

- The JAR containing helper classes may be packaged in the `lib` directory of the EAR file. Using this approach, the packaged classes will be automatically visible to all modules in the EAR module.

- If you want to limit the visibility to only a specific EJB-JAR or WAR module, you can create an entry in the `Manifest.mf` file of the module that contains a `Class-Path` attribute to the JAR file.

Now that you know the structure of EJB-JAR and how to package it, let's look at the elements of `ejb-jar.xml`.

11.3.2 *Deployment descriptors vs. annotations*

An EJB deployment descriptor (`ejb-jar.xml`) describes the contents of an EJB module, any resources used by it, and security transaction settings. The deployment descriptor is written in XML, and because it is external to the Java byte code, it allows you to separate concerns for development and deployment.

The deployment descriptor is optional and you could use annotations instead, but we don't advise using annotations in all cases for several reasons. Annotations are great for development, but may not be well suited for deployments where settings may change frequently. During deployment it is common in large companies for different people to be involved for each environment (development, test, production, etc.). For instance, your application requires such resources as `DataSource` or JMS objects, and the JNDI names for these resources change between these environments. It does not make sense to hard-code these names in the code using annotations. The deployment descriptor allows the deployers to understand the contents and take appropriate action. Keep in mind that even if the deployment descriptor is optional, certain settings such as default interceptors for an EJB-JAR module require a deployment descriptor. An EJB-JAR module may contain

- A deployment descriptor (`ejb-jar.xml`)
- A vendor-specific deployment descriptor, which is required to perform certain configuration settings in a particular EJB container

The good news is that you can mix and match annotations with descriptors by specifying some settings in annotations and others in the deployment descriptor. Be aware that the deployment descriptor is the final source and overrides settings provided through metadata annotations. To clarify, you could set the `TransactionAttribute` for an EJB method as `REQUIRES_NEW` using an annotation, and if you set it to `REQUIRED` in the deployment descriptor, the final effect will be `REQUIRED`.

Annotations vs. XML descriptors: the endless debate

Sugar or sugar substitute? It's a matter of choice. Zero calories versus the risk of cancer? The debate may well be endless, and the same applies to the debate between annotations and deployment descriptors. Some people find annotations elegant, while they see XML as verbose, ugly, and hard to maintain. Others find annotations unsightly, and complain that annotations complicate things by making configurations reside closer to the code. The good thing is that you have a choice, and Java EE allows you to override annotation settings in the code with deployment descriptors if you desire. We suggest you weigh the pros and cons of these options with a clear mind.

Although we won't delve deeply into deployment descriptors, let's look at some quick examples to see what deployment descriptors look like so that you can package a deployment descriptor in your EJB module if you need to. Listing 11.3 shows a simple example of a deployment descriptor for the BazaarAdmin EJB.

Listing 11.3   A simple ejb-jar.xml

```
<ejb-jar version="3.0">          ◁─❶ Specifies version element (must be 3.0)
  <enterprise-beans>
    <session>                              ❷  Identifies EJB
      <ejb-name>BazaarAdmin</ejb-name>    ◁─┘
      <remote>actionbazaar.buslogic.BazaarAdmin</remote>
      <ejb-class>actionbazaar.buslogic.BazaarAdminBean</ejb-class>
      <session-type>stateless</session-type>          ◁─┐ Specifies
      <transaction-type>Container</transaction-type>  ◁─┤ ❸ bean type
    </session>
  </enterprise-beans>                         Specifies
...                                     transaction type ❹
  <assembly-descriptor>
    <container-transaction>     ◁─❺ Contains transaction attribute setting
      <method>
        <ejb-name>BazaarAdmin</ejb-name>
        <method-name>*</method-name>
      </method>
      <trans-attribute>Required</trans-attribute>
    </container-transaction>
    <security-role>
      <role-name>users</role-name>     ◁─❻ Specifies security setting
    </security-role>
  </assembly-descriptor>
</ejb-jar>
```

If you are familiar with EJB 2, you may have noticed that the only notable difference between this deployment descriptor and one in EJB 2 is that the version attribute must be set to 3.0, and the home element is missing because EJB 3 does not require a home interface.

If you are using deployment descriptors for your EJBs, make sure that you set the ejb-jar version to 3.0 ❶ because this will be used by the Java EE server to determine the version of the EJBs being packaged in an archive. The name element ❷ identifies an EJB and is the same as the name element in the @Stateless annotation. These must match if you are overriding any values specified in the annotation with a descriptor. The session-type element ❸ determines the type of session bean. This value can be either stateless or stateful. You can use transaction-type ❹ to specify whether the bean uses CMT (Container) or BMT (Bean). The transaction, security, and other assembly details are set using the assembly-descriptor tag of the deployment descriptor ❺ and ❻.

Table 11.3 lists commonly used annotations and their corresponding descriptor tags. Note that as we mentioned earlier there is an element for every annotation. You will need only those which make sense for your development environment. Some of the descriptor elements you'll probably need are for resource references, interceptor binding, and declarative security. We encourage you to explore these on your own.

Table 11.3   One-to-one mapping between annotations and XML descriptor elements

Annotation	Type	Annotation Element	Corresponding Descriptor Element
@Stateless	EJB type		<session-type>Stateless
		name	ejb-name
@Stateful	EJB type	name	<session-type>Stateful
			ejb-name
@MessageDriven	EJB type		message-driven
		name	ejb-name
@Remote	Interface type		remote
@Local	Interface type		local
@Transaction-Management	Transaction management type at bean level		transaction-type

continued on next page

Table 11.3 One-to-one mapping between annotations and XML descriptor elements *(continued)*

Annotation	Type	Annotation Element	Corresponding Descriptor Element
`@Transaction-Attribute`	Transaction settings method		`container-transaction` `trans-attribute`
`@Interceptors`	Interceptors		`interceptor-binding` `interceptor-class`
`@ExcludeClass-Interceptors`	Interceptors		`exclude-class-interceptors`
`@ExcludeDefault-Interceptors`	Interceptors		`exclude-default-interceptors`
`@AroundInvoke`	Custom interceptor		`around-invoke`
`@PostConstruct`	Lifecycle method		`post-construct`
`@PreDestroy`	Lifecycle method		`pre-destroy`
`@PostActivate`	Lifecycle method		`post-activate`
`@PrePassivate`	Lifecycle method		`pre-passivate`
`@DeclareRoles`	Security setting		`security-role`
`@RolesAllowed`	Security setting		`method-permission`
`@PermitAll`	Security setting		`unchecked`
`@DenyAll`	Security setting		`exclude-list`
`@RunAs`	Security setting		`security-identity` `run-as`

`@Resource`	Resource references (`DataSource`, JMS, Environment, mail, etc.)		`resource-ref`
			`resource-env-ref`
			`message-destination-ref`
			`env-ref`

	Resource injection	Setter/field injection	`injection-target`
`@EJB`	EJB references		`ejb-ref` `ejb-local-ref`
`@Persistence-Context`	Persistence context reference		`persistence-context-ref`
`@PresistenceUnit`	Persistence unit reference		`persistence-unit-ref`

You can find the XML schema for the EJB 3 deployment descriptor at http://
java.sun.com/xml/ns/javaee/ejb-jar_3_0.xsd.

11.3.3 *Overriding annotations with deployment descriptors*

As we explained, you can mix and match deployment descriptors with annotations and use descriptors to override settings originally specified using annotations. Keep in mind that the more you mix the two, the more likely you are
to make mistakes and create a debugging nightmare.

> **NOTE** The basic rule to remember is that the name element in stateless, stateful,
> and message-driven annotations is the same as the ejb-name element in
> the descriptor. If you do not specify the name element with these annota-
> tions, the name of the bean class is understood to be the ejb-name ele-
> ment. This means that when you are overriding an annotation setting
> with your deployment descriptor, the ejb-name element must match the
> bean class name.

Suppose we have a stateless session bean that uses these annotations:

```
@Stateless(name = "BazaarAdmin")
public class BazaarAdminBean implements BazaarAdmin {
...
@TransactionAttribute(TransactionAttributeType.REQUIRES_NEW)
public Item addItem() {
  }
}
```

The value for the name element specified is BazaarAdmin, which is the same as the
value of the ejb-name element specified in the deployment descriptor:

```
<ejb-name>BazaarAdmin</ejb-name>
```

If you do not specify the name element, the container will use the name of
BazaarAdminBean as the name of the bean class, and in order to override annotations you have to use that name in the deployment descriptor:

```
<ejb-name>BazaarAdminBean</ejb-name>
```

We used @TransactionAttribute to specify that the transaction attribute for a
bean method be REQUIRES_NEW. If we want to override it to use REQUIRED,[1] then we
use the following descriptor:

---

[1] Keep in mind the impact of changing a transaction attribute from RequiresNew to Required, as shown
in this example. We investigated this effect in greater detail in chapter 6.

```
<assembly-descriptor>
  <container-transaction>
    <method>                                    ❶ Specifies ejb-name
      <ejb-name>BazaarAdmin</ejb-name>      ◁┘
      <method-name>getUserWithItems</method-name>
      <method-params></method-params>
    </method>
    <trans-attribute>Required</trans-attribute>   ◁┐  Changes transaction
  </container-transaction>                          ❷  attribute setting
</assembly-descriptor>
```

In this example, we used the `assembly-descriptor` element to specify a transaction attribute ❷. In addition, the `ejb-name` element ❶ in the `assembly-descriptor` matches the original `name` specified with the `@Stateless` annotation in the bean class.

11.3.4 *Specifying default interceptor settings*

Interceptors (as you'll recall from chapter 5) allow you to implement cross-cutting code in an elegant manner. An interceptor can be defined at the class or method level, or a default interceptor can be defined at the module level for all EJB classes in the EJB-JAR. We mentioned that default interceptors for an EJB module can only be defined in the deployment descriptor (`ejb-jar.xml`). Listing 11.4 shows how to specify default interceptors for an EJB module.

Listing 11.4   Default interceptor setting in ejb-jar.xml

```
...                          ❶ Defines interceptor binding
<interceptor-binding>    ◁┘
  <ejb-name>*</ejb-name>    ◁─❷ Applies binding to all EJBs
  <interceptor-class>
    actionbazaar.buslogic.CheckPermissionInterceptor
  </interceptor-class>
  <interceptor-class>
    actionbazaar.buslogic.ActionBazaarDefaultInterceptor
  </interceptor-class>
</interceptor-binding>
...
```

The `interceptor-binding` ❶ tag defines the binding of interceptors to a particular EJB with the `ejb-name` element. If we want to define the default interceptor or an interceptor binding for all EJBs in the EJB module, then we can specify * as the value for `ejb-name` ❷. We specify a class to use as the interceptor with the `<interceptor-class>` tag. As evident from the listing, you can specify multiple interceptors in the same binding, and the order in which they are specified in the deployment descriptor determines the order of execution for the interceptor. In our example, `CheckPermissionInterceptor` will be executed prior to `ActionBazaarDefaultInterceptor` when any EJB method is executed.

If you want a refresher on how interceptors work, make a quick detour back to chapter 5 and then rejoin us here. We'll wait...

11.3.5 *Using vendor-specific annotations and descriptors*

We've already explained that stateless session beans and MDBs may be pooled. In addition, you can configure passivation for stateful session beans, and you can set up the handling of poisonous messages for MDBs. However, we have not discussed configuration details for either of these scenarios. Unfortunately, these configurations are left to the vendors as proprietary features, and they can be supported with proprietary annotations, proprietary deployment descriptors, or both. Table 11.4 lists the name of the deployment descriptor file for some popular application servers.

Table 11.4 Vendor-specific deployment descriptors for popular application servers

Application Server	Vendor-Specific Deployment Descriptor
BEA WebLogic	`weblogic-ejb-jar.xml`
IBM WebSphere	`ibm-ejb-jar.xml`
JBoss	`jboss.xml`
Oracle Application Server	`orion-ejb-jar.xml`
Sun GlassFish	`sun-ejb-jar.xml`

Many developers shun deployment descriptors as a matter of inconvenience. Application server vendors will continue to provide support for annotations that match deployment descriptor elements, as developers voice their preference for these features. Chances are that each vendor has a set of proprietary annotations to set configuration information with the code.

For example, you can use the `oracle.j2ee.ejb.StatelessDeployment` proprietary annotation to provide configuration information such as pooling and transaction management for stateless session beans. Look at the following code, which configures pooling with Oracle's proprietary annotation:

```
import oracle.j2ee.ejb.StatelessDeployment;

@StatelessDeployment(
  minInstances = 100, maxInstances = 500, poolCacheTimeout = 120)
@Stateless(name = "BazaarAdmin")
public class BazaarAdminBean implements BazaarAdmin {
}
```

As other Java EE vendors create their implementations of EJB 3, we anticipate that each vendor will devise its own subset of corresponding annotations as well.

You should review these proprietary annotations with caution for a couple of reasons. First, adding configuration information in the code is not a good idea, although application servers provide the ability to override this information with their proprietary deployment descriptors. This is not desirable because in order to make a change to the setting, the code must be edited and compiled, and in most organizations it must go through a significant quality assurance effort before being released to production. Another reason is that as the code is promoted across different environments (Development, Test, Production, etc.), the deployer may change the configuration to accommodate different servers and environmental configurations.

Second, this defeats the goal of portability of applications. Deployment descriptors serve as a guideline to the deployer to understand the contents, the applications, and the suggested configurations. Deployers manage the deployment to each environment by tweaking the configuration. We recommend using the proprietary deployment descriptors instead of using deployment annotations. If you're using Oracle, you could use the following element in Oracle's proprietary descriptor (`orion-ejb-jar.xml`) element as follows:

```
<session-deployment
  name = "BazaarAdmin"
  tx-retry-wait = "60"
  max-instances = "500"
  min-instances = "100"
  pool-cache-timeout = "120"
  location = "BazaarAdmin">
</session-deployment>
```

This concludes our discussion on packaging session beans and message-driven beans. Next we take a peek at packaging entities. Can you feel the anticipation building?

11.4 Packaging entities

Can't you package EJB 3 entities in the same way? Afraid not. We're sure you've noticed that while session and message-driven beans share a lot of characteristics, entities are quite another beast. You may remember from our discussion in chapter 1 that JPA can be used directly from the web container. That means entities will need some additional care and feeding with respect to packaging, so that deployment will work as expected.

This section covers some new deployment files, persistence.xml and orm.xml, and provides a slew of tips and information on how to position your entities for maximum deployment enjoyment. You do want deployment enjoyment, don't you? We know we do. Let's begin by looking at the packaging structure for entities.

11.4.1 Exposing the persistence module

With EJB 3, entities can be used inside either the EJB or web container, or in a Java SE application. Thus, entities may be packaged in a standard Java EE module such as an EJB-JAR, WAR, or JAR file in the root of the EAR module or as a library module in an EAR. When using entities in your applications, you have to package entity classes into a Java EE module such as an EJB-JAR or WAR of simple JAR files, with a simple deployment descriptor named persistence.xml.

If you are using entities within an EJB module, then the EJB (session beans, MDBs) classes and entities need to be packaged together in the same EJB module. Therefore, the EJB-JAR module will contain a persistence.xml file to designate that the module contains one or more persistence units. Recall from our discussion in chapter 9 that a persistence unit is a logical group of entities used together. For example, you may create a persistence unit for all entities in the ActionBazaar application.

Let's look at the structure of a JAR that contains a simple persistence unit, as shown in listing 11.5.

Listing 11.5   Structure of a sample EJB-JAR file containing entities

```
ActionBazaar-ejb.jar:
META-INF/
  persistence.xml
  orm.xml (optional)      ◁─❶  Default O/R mapping file
actionbazaar/
  persistence/
    Category.class
    Item.class
    ...
```

```
      BazaarAdmin.class
...
      secondORMap.xml     ←—❷  Additional O/R mapping file
```

persistence.xml is the deployment descriptor for a persistence module, which is discussed in the next section. The orm.xml ❶ file defines the object-relational mapping (if you use XML mapping). You may package an additional mapping file ❷ that defines O/R mapping for entities that was not defined in orm.xml. We discuss O/R mapping with XML in section 11.5.2. The JAR also contains entity classes—Category.class and Item.class—and another class, BazaarAdmin.class, that is needed in order to make persistence work. Now that you know the structure of a persistence module, let's drill down and learn more about persistence.xml.

11.4.2 *Describing the persistence module with persistence.xml*

In chapter 9 we showed you how to group entities as a persistence unit and how to configure that unit using persistence.xml. Now that you know how to package entities, it's time to learn more about persistence.xml, the descriptor that transforms any JAR module into a persistence module. It's worth mentioning that persistence.xml is the only mandatory deployment descriptor that you have to deal with. We hope the Java EE specification will ease this requirement in future releases of the specification.

At the time of this writing, some EJB containers such as Oracle and JBoss support proprietary extensions of persistence modules without persistence.xml in EJB-JAR modules. Although user-friendly, this feature will not be portable across EJB 3 containers. You can find the schema for persistence.xml online at http:// java.sun.com/xml/ns/persistence/persistence_1_0.xsd.

Listing 11.6 is an example of a simple persistence.xml that we can use with the ActionBazaar application; it should successfully deploy to any Java EE 5 container that supports JPA. The first thing the file does is define a persistence unit and package it to your deployment archive—for example, WAR or EJB-JAR.

> **Listing 11.6 An example persistence.xml**

```
<persistence>
    <persistence-unit name = "actionBazaar"    ←—❶  Persistence unit
                      transaction-type = "JTA">
        <provider>                             ←—❷  Factory class for JPA provider
          oracle.toplink.essentials.PersistenceProvider
        </provider>
```

```
<jta-data-source>jdbc/ActionBazaarDS
    </jta-data-source>
<mapping-file>secondORMap.xml</mapping-file>
<jar-file>entities/ShippingEntities.jar</jar-file>
<class>ejb3inaction.persistence.Category</class>
<class>ejb3inaction.persistence.Bid</class>.
...
    <properties>        <property name = "toplink.ddl-generation"
                value = "drop-and-create-tables"/>
    </properties>
  </persistence-unit>
</persistence>
```

❸ **DataSource used by persistence unit**

❹ **Entity classes included in unit**

❺ **Vendor-specific properties**

Let's run through a quick review of the code before we drill down into the details. We define a persistence unit by using the `persistence-unit` element ❶. We can specify an optional factory class for the persistence provider ❷. The JPA provider connects to the database to store retrieved entities; we specified the data source for the persistence provider ❸. If you have multiple persistence units in a single archive, you may want to identify the entity classes that comprise the persistence unit ❹. Optionally, you can specify vendor-specific configuration using the `properties` element ❺.

We hope you're ready for a detailed exploration on the use of each of the elements in `persistence.xml` from listing 11.6—you'll find it pretty straightforward. After reading the next few pages, you should be fairly comfortable with this new part of the EJB standard.

Naming the persistence unit

Each persistence unit must have a `name`, and that `name` must be unique across the Java EE module. The `name` is important because the container uses it to create an entity manager factory, and then again to create the entity manager instances using the factory to access the entities specified inside the unit. Also, you access the persistence unit by using its `name` when you attempt to perform CRUD operations with the entities packaged in the module. All other elements in a persistence unit can be defaulted.

You can define more than one persistence unit for an application module in `persistence.xml`. All entities identified in a persistence unit are managed by a single set of entity instances. Thus, a `persistence.xml` may have multiple persistence units in a particular JAR module as follows:

```
<persistence>
  <persistence-unit name = "actionBazaar">
...
  </persistence-unit>
  <persistence-unit name = "humanResources">
...
  </persistence-unit>
</persistence>
```

Persistence unit scoping

You can define a persistence unit in a WAR, EJB-JAR, or JAR at the EAR level. If you define a persistence unit in a module, it is only visible to that specific module. However, if you define the unit by placing a JAR file in the `lib` directory of the EAR, the persistence unit will automatically be visible to all modules in the EAR. For this to work, you must remember the restriction that if the same name is used by a persistence unit in the EAR level and at the module level, the persistence unit in the module level will win.

Assume you have an EAR file structure like this:

```
lib/actionBazaar-common.jar
actionBazaar-ejb.jar
actionBazaar-web.war
```

`actionBazaar-common.jar` has a persistence unit with the name `actionBazaar` and `actionBazaar-ejb.jar` has also a persistence unit with the name `actionBazaar`.

The `actionBazaar` persistence unit is automatically visible to the web module, and you can use as follows:

```
@PersistenceUnit(unitName = "actionBazaar")
private EntityManagerFactory emf;
```

However, if you use this code in the EJB module, the local persistence unit will be accessed because the local persistence unit has precedence. If you want to access the persistence unit defined at the EAR level, you have to reference it with the specific name as follows:

```
PersistenceUnit(unitName =
  "lib/actionBazaar-common.jar#actionBazaar")
private EntityManagerFactory emf;
```

Again, the `name` element is important because it is what you use to access the entities. As shown in chapter 9, we use `unitName` to inject a container-managed `Entity-Manager` as follows:

```
@PersistenceContext(unitName = "actionBazaar")
private EntityManager entityManager;
```

Refer to the sidebar "Persistence unit scoping" for more on how a persistence unit is scoped depending on its presence.

Specifying the transaction type

You can specify `transaction-type` in `persistence.xml` (as in listing 11.6) by using the `transaction-type` attribute. `transaction-type` can either be `JTA` or `RESOURCE_LOCAL`. If you do not specify `transaction-type`, the container will assume the default `transaction-type` is `JTA`. You must utilize `JTA` as the transaction-type for a persistence unit packaged in a Java EE module. `RESOURCE_LOCAL` should be specified as a transaction type only when you're exercising JPA outside a Java EE container. As you may recall, we discussed the `javax.persistence.EntityTransaction` interface in chapter 9; we recommend you avail yourself of `EntityTransaction` only when you use EJB 3 persistence outside of a Java EE environment.

Using a specific persistence provider

The `provider` element specifies the factory class of the EJB 3 persistence provider, such as Hibernate or TopLink. You do not have to specify the persistence provider if you're using the default persistence provider integrated with your Java EE 5 container. For example, if you want Hibernate's persistence provider in the JBoss Application Server or TopLink Essentials persistence provider with Sun GlassFish or the Oracle Application Server, you don't have to define the `provider` element in `persistence.xml`. But if you decide to go with the EJB 3 persistence provider from the GlassFish project with either JBoss or Apache Geronimo, then you must specify the `provider` element as follows:

```
<provider>oracle.toplink.essentials.PersistenceProvider</provider>
```

Obviously this example specifies Oracle TopLink as the persistence provider; you can specify the `provider` element for Hibernate as follows:

```
<provider>org.hibernate.ejb.HibernatePersistence</provider>
```

This is helpful when using JPA outside the container.

Setting up a DataSource

Our entities are persistence objects that access databases. Chapters 7 through 10 discussed how O/R mappings are defined with metadata annotations, and how an entity interacts with one or more database tables. We have not, however, broached the subject of how entities interact with a database connection. Back in chapters 3 and 4 we briefly discussed what a DataSource is and how it can be used in an application server by accessing it through JNDI. In addition, you saw examples of session and message-driven beans accessing a DataSource using resource injection. In spite of this, entities cannot use injection, connect to the database themselves, or perform any operation directly; the persistence provider does all that magic behind the scenes. When you persist an instance of an entity, the persistence provider will open or reuse a pooled connection to the database and execute the SQL on your behalf.

To configure a persistence unit to connect to a database, you first have to create a DataSource in your Java EE container. For scalability, each DataSource is commonly associated with a connection pool, and the connection pool contains the information for connecting to the database.

Configuring an application DataSource

Every Java EE application server provides the ability to create and manage Data-Sources and connection pools. Here is an example of a DataSource and a connection pool used by Sun's GlassFish open source project:

```
<jdbc-connection-pool
    connection-validation-method = "auto-commit"
    datasource-classname = "oracle.jdbc.pool.OracleDataSource"
    max-pool-size = "32"
    max-wait-time-in-millis = "60000"
    name = "ActionBazaarDS"
    res-type = "javax.sql.DataSource"
    steady-pool-size = "8">
  <property name = "user" value = "ejb3ina"/>
  <property name = "port" value = "1521"/>
  <property name = "password" value = "ejb3ina"/>
  <property name = "networkProtocol" value = "thin"/>
  <property name = "databaseName" value = "ORCL"/>
  <property name = "serverName" value = "localhost"/>
</jdbc-connection-pool>

<jdbc-resource enabled = "true"
               jndi-name = "jdbc/ActionBazaarDS"
               pool-name = "ActionBazaarDS"/>
```

The DataSource uses the JNDI name and connection pool information for the specified database instance. In this example, the DataSource has a jndi-name of jdbc/ActionBazaarDS. Two common naming techniques are to name the pool either the `DataSource` name without the JNDI reference (`ActionBazaarDS`), or to use the pool in the `DataSource` name (`ActionBazaarPooledDS`). We'll illustrate the first approach here.

Telling the persistence unit about the DataSource

You can specify the `DataSource` for a persistence unit using either the `jta-data-source` or `non-jta-data-source` element in the `persistence.xml` (as we did in listing 11.6). Typically, Java EE containers support two types of `DataSources`: Java Transaction API (JTA) and non-JTA. A JTA (or global) `DataSource` is one that supports JTA or distributed transactions. A non-JTA (or local) `DataSource` only supports local transactions that are limited to the process/server where they begin. For example, we can specify the name of the JTA `DataSource` we created earlier using the `jta-data-source` element as follows:

```
<jta-data-source>jdbc/ActionBazaarDS</jta-data-source>
```

> **NOTE** You have to specify global JNDI names for the data source in the `jta-data-source` and `non-jta-data-source` elements of `persistence.xml`. If you do not specify a `DataSource` for the persistence unit, the persistence unit will try to use the default `DataSource` for the application server. The default `DataSource` for a Java EE application is typically specified using a proprietary mechanism.

Many application servers such as BEA WebLogic Server and Oracle Application Server also allow the packaging of `DataSource` configurations in an EAR.

Identifying entity classes

If you are using JPA within a Java EE container, the persistence provider reads the module and determines which entity classes are annotated with the `@Entity` annotation. You can identify the entity classes that constitute a persistence unit (as we did in listing 11.6). This is useful when you want to divide the packaged entities into more than one persistence unit as follows:

```
<persistence>
  <persistence-unit name = "actionBazaar">
    <class>ejb3inaction.persistence.Category</class>
    <class>ejb3inaction.persistence.Bid</class>
  ...
  </persistence-unit>
  <persistence-unit name = "humanResources">
    <class>ejb3inaction.persistence.Employee</class>
    <class>ejb3inaction.persistence.Department</class>
```

```
...
    </persistence-unit>
</persistence>
```

Packaging at this more granular level may seem like more work at first glance. In reality, it makes sharing the persistence units across applications much easier.

Specifying vendor-specific extensions

Most JPA providers will provide extensions such as caching, logging, and automatic table creation. You can use the `property` element in `persistence.xml` to specify these vendor-specific extensions. The persistence provider will read such configurations while creating the entity manager factory and configure the persistence unit accordingly.

In listing 11.6 we enabled automatic schema generation for the persistence unit when using TopLink:

```
<properties>
    <property name = "toplink.ddl-generation"
              value = "drop-and-create-tables"/>
    <property name =
        "toplink.ddl-generation.output-mode"
        value = "database"/>
</properties>
```

Remember that automatic schema generation is a developer-friendly feature and, when it's turned on, the JPA provider creates the underlying database schema (tables, sequences, etc.) when the persistence unit is deployed. If you want to turn on automatic schema generation for Hibernate, you can do so by adding the following in `persistence.xml`:

```
<property name="hibernate.hbm2ddl.auto" value="create-drop"/>
```

Similarly you can pass configuration parameters for caching, logging, and JDBC configuration when using an outside container as a property. Check your vendor documentation for details.

Specifying additional mapping and JAR files

There may be times when you want to use multiple O/R mapping files for your project. Doing this supports the packaging of smaller functional units into separate JAR files to allow a more granular deployment scheme. Of course, regardless of how many JARs make up your application, they will all need to be in the classpath of the application in order for all the components to be found by the class loader.

For example, if you have mapping information in a separate XML file named secondORMap.xml, you can specify as much by using the mapping-file element that we saw in listing 11.6. It is vital to remember that additional mapping files are not packaged in the META-INF directory of the persistence module, but also that these files may be packaged inside the JAR as a resource (as shown in listing 11.5).

You can include additional JAR files (such as ShippingEntities.jar in listing 11.6). The JAR file location is relative to the persistence module; that is, the JAR file that contains the persistence.xml.

11.4.3 Performing O/R mapping with orm.xml

Chapter 8 discussed how to perform O/R mapping using metadata annotations. Believe it or not, for a large application the use of O/R mapping metadata *within* the code is not a good idea. Using O/R mapping annotations hardwires your relational schema to your object model. Some folks feel it's perfectly okay to hard-code schema information, because they see it as being similar to JDBC. Others consider it a very bad idea. It is also quite possible that for certain projects you may be directed to implement O/R mapping with an XML file. As mentioned earlier (in listing 11.1), you can specify O/R mapping information in a file named orm.xml packaged in the META-INF directory of the persistence module, or in a separate file packaged as a resource and defined in persistence.xml with the mapping-file element.

The source that takes precedence is always the deployment descriptor. EJB 3 persistence specifies that the deployment descriptor can override O/R mapping specified using annotations, the orm.xml file, or any other XML mapping. Listing 11.7 shows an example of an O/R mapping file (orm.xml) used in ActionBazaar.

> **Listing 11.7   An orm.xml that specifies default values for a persistence unit and O/R mapping information**

```
<?xml version="1.0" encoding="UTF-8"?>
<entity-mappings version="1.0"
  xmlns=http://java.sun.com/xml/ns/persistence/orm
  xmlns:xsi=http://www.w3.org/2001/XMLSchema-instance
  xsi:schemaLocation="http://java.sun.com/xml/ns/persistence/orm
  orm_1_0.xsd">

<persistence-unit-metadata>
  <persistence-unit-defaults>        ◁—❶ Defines persistence unit defaults
    <schema>ACTIONBAZAAR</schema>
    <access>PROPERTY</access>
      <entity-listeners>        ◁—❷ Specifies default entity listeners
        <entity-listener
```

```
              class = "actionbazaar.persistence.DefaultListener">
          ...
        </entity-listener>
      </entity-listeners>
    </persistence-unit-defaults>
  </persistence-unit-metadata>

  <package>actionbazaar.persistence</package>
  <access>PROPERTY</access>

  <named-query name = "findAllCategories">
    <query>SELECT c FROM Category AS c</query>
    <hint name = "refresh" value = "true"/>
  </named-query>
```

Specifies entity ❸
mapping

```
<entity name = "Category" class = "Category" metadata-complete = "false">    ◁┘
    <table name = "CATEGORIES" />
    <sequence-generator name = "CATEGORY_SEQ_GEN"
                        sequence-name = "CATEGORY_SEQ"
                        allocation-size = "1"
                        initial-value = "1"/>
    <exclude-default-listeners/>
    <exclude-superclass-listeners/>
    <attributes>
      <id name = "categoryId">
        <column name = "CATEGORY_ID"/>
        <generated-value strategy = "SEQUENCE"
                        generator = "CATEGORY_SEQ_GEN"/>
      </id>
      <basic name = "categoryName">
        <column name = "CATEGORY_NAME"/>
      </basic>
      <basic name = "createDate">
        <column name = "CREATE_DATE"/>
      </basic>
      <many-to-many name = "items" target-entity = "Item">
        <cascade>
          <cascade-all/>
        </cascade>
        <join-table name = "CATEGORY_ITEMS">
          <join-column name = "CATEGORY_ID"
                      referenced-column-name = "CATEGORY_ID"/>
          <inverse-join-column name = "ITEM_ID"
                              referenced-column-name = "ITEM_ID"/>
        </join-table>
      </many-to-many>
    </attributes>
  </entity>
</entity-mappings>
```

The `orm.xml` file defines the actual O/R mapping with XML for the entities packaged in an EAR. Listing 11.7 ❶ shows how to define defaults for a persistence unit using the `persistence-unit-defaults` element. This element defines `schema`, `catalog`, and `access`, default entity listeners, and cascade type. We mentioned schema and catalog types in chapter 8 when we discussed the `@Table` and `@SecondaryTable` annotations. You can define the default values for the schema and catalog type in `persistence-unit-defaults`, and this can be overridden by each entity.

The `access` type may either be `FIELD` or `PROPERTY`.

In chapter 9 you learned that entity listeners can be defined to handle lifecycle callbacks for entities, and that a default listener for all entities in a persistence module can be defined by using the `entity-listeners` subelement in `persistence-unit-defaults` ❷. Use `@ExcludeDefaultListener` on the entity or a mapped superclass if you need to exclude the default entity listener. The `name` element ❸ identifies the name of the entity and is the equivalent of the name in `@Entity`. This value is used in the `from` clause in JPQL queries.

The other O/R mapping elements in `orm.xml` are somewhat self-explanatory, and we won't discuss them in detail.

Table 11.5 lists the one-to-one mapping between the most often used annotations and their associated deployment descriptors. You'll probably notice immediately that the XML element is usually quite similar to its annotation cousin.

Table 11.5 Mapping of persistence annotations to associated deployment descriptor elements

Annotations Grouped by Type	XML Element
Object type	
`@Entity`	`entity`
`@MappedSuperClass`	`mapped-superclass`
`@Embedded`	`embedded`
`@Embeddable`	`embeddable`
Table mapping	
`@Table`	`table`
`@SecondaryTable`	`secondary-table`

continued on next page

Table 11.5 Mapping of persistence annotations to associated deployment descriptor elements *(continued)*

Annotations Grouped by Type	XML Element
Query	
@NamedQuery	named-query
@NamedNativeQuery	named-native-query
@SqlResultsetMapping	sql-result-set-mapping
Primary key and column mapping	
@Id	id
@IdClass	id-class
@EmbeddedId	embedded-id
@TableGenerator	table-generator
@SequenceGenerator	sequence-generator
@Column	column
@PrimaryKeyJoinColumn	primary-key-join-column
@GeneratedValue	generated-value
Relationship mapping	
@ManyToMany	many-to-many
@OneToOne	one-to-one
@OneToMany	one-to-many
@ManyToOne	many-to-one
@JoinTable	join-table
@JoinColumn	join-column
@InverseJoinColumns	inverse-join-column
Listeners	
@ExcludeDefaultListeners	exclude-default-listeners
@ExcludeSuperclassListeners	exclude-superclass-listeners
@PreUpdate	pre-update

continued on next page

Table 11.5   Mapping of persistence annotations to associated deployment descriptor elements *(continued)*

Annotations Grouped by Type	XML Element
Listeners *(continued)*	
`@PostUpdate`	`post-update`
`@PrePersist`	`pre-persist`
`@PostPersist`	`post-persist`
`@PreRemove`	`pre-remove`
`@PostRemove`	`post-remove`
`@PostLoad`	`post-load`

Manually performing O/R mapping using XML can be quite arduous, error-prone, and difficult to troubleshoot. You may want to investigate tools that will assist with this effort.

NOTE   The goal of the Eclipse Dali project (http://wiki.eclipse.org/index.php/ Dali_Project) is to provide developer support for O/R mapping of EJB 3 persistence objects, and help generate O/R mappings with annotations and XML descriptors.

Our trek through packaging EJB 3 is nearing the end. Before we finish, we want to highlight some things you should keep in mind when packaging your shiny new EJB 3 applications.

11.5   Best practices and common deployment issues

After reading this chapter it may appear that a lot of little pieces are required in order to deploy EJB 3 components. That may not be all that far from the truth. The reality, though, is that you don't have to keep track of all the pieces yourself; tools provided by the application servers help, and much of the glue code can be automated. You need to keep in mind some key principles, regardless of which components your application makes use of and which server you plan to deploy it to.

11.5.1   Packaging and deployment best practices

The following list of best practices can make your life easier while you're building and deploying your applications:

- *Understand your application and its dependencies.* Make sure that resources are configured before you deploy the application in your target environment. If an application requires a lot of resources, it is a good idea to use the deployment descriptor to communicate the dependencies for the deployer to resolve before attempting to deploy the application. Improper packaging of classes and libraries causes a lot of class-loading issues. You also need to understand the dependency of your applications on helper classes and third-party libraries and package them accordingly. Avoid duplication of libraries in multiple places. Instead, find a way to package your applications, and configure your application server such that you can share common libraries from multiple modules within the same application.

- *Avoid using proprietary APIs and annotations.* Don't use vendor-specific tags or annotations unless it's the only way to accomplish your task. Weigh doing so against the disadvantages, such as making your code less portable. If you are depending on proprietary behavior, check whether you can take advantage of a proprietary deployment descriptor.

- *Leverage your DBA.* Work with your DBA to automate creation of any database schemas for your application. Avoid depending on the automatic table creation feature for entities, as it may not meet your production deployment requirement. Make sure that the database is configured properly, and that it does not become a bottleneck for your application. Past experience indicates that making friends with the DBA assigned to your project really helps! If your application requires other resources such as a JMS provider or LDAP-compliant security provider, then work with the appropriate administrators to configure them correctly. Again, using O/R mapping with XML and resource dependencies with XML descriptors can help you troubleshoot configuration issues without having to fiddle with the code.

Now that you have some best practices in place, what do you do when that's still not enough? We'll let you in on a few secrets from the trenches that will make solving those packaging problems easier.

11.5.2 Troubleshooting common deployment problems

This section examines some common deployment problems that you may run into. Most can be addressed by properly assembling your application.

- `ClassNotFoundException` occurs when you're attempting to dynamically load a resource that cannot be found. The reason for this exception can be a missing library at the correct loader level; you know, the JAR file containing the class that can't be found. If you're loading a resource or property file in your application, make sure that you use `Thread.currentThread().get-ContextClassLoader().getResourceAsStream()`.

- `NoClassDefFoundError` is thrown when code tries to instantiate an object, or when dependencies of a previously loaded class cannot be resolved. Typically, you run into this issue when all dependent libraries are not at the same class loader level.

- `ClassCastException` normally is the result of duplication of classes at different levels. This occurs in the same-class, different-loader situation; that is, you try to cast a class loaded by class loader (L1) with another class instance loaded by class loader (L2).

- `NamingException` is typically thrown when a JNDI lookup fails, because the container tries to inject a resource for an EJB that does not exist. The stack trace for this exception gives the details about which lookup is failing. Make sure that your dependencies on `DataSources`, EJBs, and other resources resolve properly.

- Your deployment may fail due to an invalid XML deployment descriptor. Make sure that your descriptors comply with the schema. You can do this by using an IDE to build your applications instead of manually editing XML descriptor files.

11.6 Summary

At the heart of Java EE applications lies the art of assembly and packaging enterprise applications. This chapter briefly introduced the concepts of class loading and code sources used by various application archives. We also explained how to package all of the EJB types, including persistence entities. You learned about the deployment descriptor of an EJB-JAR module, and how you can use descriptors to override settings specified in metadata annotations. You saw that `persistence.xml` is the only required deployment descriptor in Java EE 5. We also tackled persistence modules and the various configurations required for a persistence unit, as well as O/R mapping with XML.

Finally, we provided some best practices on packaging, and identified some common deployment issues that you may run into. In the next chapter we discuss how you can use EJBs across tiers.

12

*Effectively integrating
EJB 3 across your
application tiers*

This chapter covers

- Design patterns
- Accessing session beans from the web tier
- Packaging and using JPA from web applications

If you've made it this far, you've come a long way on our journey to the center of EJB 3. So far we've seen how to use session and message-driven beans for business logic, and how to use various facets of JPA to store and retrieve data. So what's next, you ask?

Most enterprise applications are distributed across various tiers: presentation, application (or business logic), persistence. The names and number of tiers varies somewhat depending on the application and its runtime environment, as well as the scalability expectations it is designed to handle. Each of these tiers can utilize a number of possible frameworks, which vary radically due to their purpose and creator's intent. Sprinkle in a few new mechanisms such as dependency injection and the whole thing can leave a developer asking, "Just how can I get all these new toys to work together?"

In this chapter we demonstrate how to integrate EJB 3 into your applications at specific tier boundaries. While drawing the tiers of a distributed application on a diagram is relatively straightforward, making various technologies work to integrate those tiers and coaxing an application to life is usually somewhat more involved. This chapter will expose the core concepts you need to understand regarding multi-tier development with EJB 3, and provide examples of specific combinations you can put to work in your applications.

To start with, we introduce some design patterns to make implementing these concepts easier. Then we discuss various options for invoking EJBs from the presentation tier. And finally, we look at how you can use JPA from web applications and outside of a Java EE container. Let's start by donning our application developer hat and looking at some proven design patterns you can leverage in your applications.

12.1 Design patterns and web technologies

Design patterns are generally accepted solutions that typically work for common problems. They help avoid "Rediscovering the Wheel Syndrome," and offer advice for when and how they should be used. Sun's Java Blueprints Program provides a catalog of core design patterns for building Java EE applications. You can access the catalog of Java patterns online at http://java.sun.com/blueprints/corej2eepatterns/Patterns/index.html.

We'll introduce some important design patterns and technologies in this section by tier:

- For the presentation tier, we'll discuss the Model-View-Controller (MVC) pattern.

- For the persistence tier, we'll introduce the Entity Access Object (EAO) pattern, a version of the Data Access Object pattern, updated for JPA.

- For the application or business logic tier, the Session Façade pattern will be covered. (Sorry, but there's no cool acronym for this pattern…)

Shall we get started? First on deck: the presentation tier.

12.1.1 Presentation tier

While EJB 3 is primarily designed to deal with server-side functionality, it has to be integrated with a front end at some point in order for the whole application to do anything useful as far as an end user is concerned. This section covers a pattern for this tier that focuses primarily on a web point of view, since Java EE functionality is most often accessed from a web tier. Please note that we use the terms *presentation tier* and *web tier* interchangeably. Because EJB 3 is not a presentation-tier technology, this pattern is not demonstrated with EJB 3; we mention it only for completeness and to provide some perspective for how EJB 3 fits into the distributed landscape.

Reviewing the Model-View-Controller pattern

Since you'll need to call all that special business logic you've so cleverly placed in your EJBs from somewhere, there's a good chance it will be from a web application, given the universal drive to "webify" almost everything these days. That means you'll be in the market for a good practice to manage all these EJB calls, and it just so happens there's a great, industry-accepted design pattern for doing this: the Model-View-Controller (MVC) pattern.

Traditionally, the MVC design pattern has been quite popular among Java developers for building web applications, specifically for the presentation tier. This pattern involves three main components, each designed to isolate code into a specific area of responsibility. The Model represents the enterprise data and business logic. You may use session beans and entities for business logic for creating the model of your application. The View is what a user interacts with, and the Controller is the traffic cop in the middle, making sure things work together in an orderly, predictable manner. The MVC pattern commonly has multiple models and multiple views, but usually has only one controller for any specific grouping of models and views at runtime.

You can do all heavy-duty work and implement the MVC pattern in your applications by building your own web framework. However, many frameworks are available to help you do so without your having to reinvent the wheel. Next, we discuss web frameworks and briefly introduce Ajax.

Determining if you need a web framework

Although a web framework isn't required, it's a good place to start when investigating how your web tier will interact with your EJBs in your application tier. Having a solid understanding of design patterns helps during this evaluation; it allows you to not only understand each framework's inner workings, but also to better predict how each may impact design decisions you still need to make.

The market for web frameworks is quite muddled, with more than 50 open source web frameworks from which to choose. By far the most popular framework in this arena is Struts. Other popular frameworks available for your applications are Apache Tapestry, WebWork, Spring MVC, and the heir apparent to Struts: JavaServer Faces (JSF). On the other hand, you may be tempted to build your own web framework, but unless you have very peculiar requirements, we recommend you go with one of the aforementioned frameworks instead of spending your time and energy reproducing others' work.

Manning has published several books on popular web frameworks:

- *WebWork in Action*, by Patrick Lightbody and Jason Carreira
- *JavaServer Faces in Action*, by Kito D. Mann
- *Tapestry in Action*, by Howard M. Lewis Ship
- *Art of Java Web Development*, by Neal Ford
- *Struts in Action*, by Ted Husted, Cedric Dumoulin, George Franciscus, and David Winterfeldt

As far as ActionBazaar goes, we're neutral with respect to which web framework you decide to use. However, we do realize that most web frameworks utilize servlets and possibly JSPs as the respective Controller and View mechanisms of these frameworks, so we'll focus our discussion on servlets. You can easily integrate the web tier with EJBs to provide business logic for your applications by turning these servlets into clients that invoke your EJBs. We'll cover how to invoke EJBs directly from your servlets in this chapter. If you want to see how to invoke EJBs exposed as a web service, drop by chapter 15 when you're done here.

It's worth mentioning that JSF 1.1 is included in Java EE 5 and provides respectable tool support for the majority of Java EE tool vendors. Because it's a part of Java EE 5, JSF integrates well with EJB 3 and we expect to see JSF grow in popularity in the future.

Introducing Ajax and Web 2.0

Since Tim O'Reilly's article (www.oreillynet.com/pub/a/oreilly/tim/news/2005/09/ 30/what-is-web-20.html) pondered the possibility of a Web 2.0 on the horizon, it seems as if the whole Internet has been one big buzz trying to define what Web 2.0 might consist of. While we're not sure anyone has arrived at the definitive answer yet, it does appear that one technology which folks can agree on for building Web 2.0 applications is Ajax (Asynchronous JavaScript and XML). You can use Ajax with practically any web framework, and we believe using EJBs with Java EE–based Ajax applications is not significantly different than using other web frameworks. You can easily expose stateless session beans as web services and access them from Ajax-based applications using some popular APIs such as JavaScript Object Notation (JSON).

More on Ajax

If you are interested in learning more about Ajax, check out the following resources:

- Wikipedia (http://en.wikipedia.org/wiki/Ajax)
- "Ajax: A New Approach to Web Applications," by Jesse James Garrett (www. adaptivepath.com/publications/essays/archives/000385.php)
- *Ajax in Action*, by Dave Crane and Eric Pascarello with Darren James (Manning, 2005)
- Ajax Matters (www.ajaxmatters.com/r/welcome)
- Ajaxian.com (www.ajaxian.com/)
- AjaxPatterns.org (http://ajaxpatterns.org/)
- Mozilla Ajax tutorial (http://developer.mozilla.org/en/docs/Ajax:Getting_Started)

That's a quick overview of MVC design patterns and technologies used in the presentation tier. Let's jump to the persistence tier to see what useful patterns we can find there.

12.1.2 Using the Entity Access Object pattern

Before ORM frameworks like Hibernate gained popularity, many application developers went with straight JDBC to develop data access code. Use of JDBC from business logic led to several maintenance problems, and the Data Access Object (DAO) design pattern was invented to decouple data access code from business logic. The DAO design pattern has been quite popular and has worked not only with JDBC but also with ORM frameworks and CMP entity beans. The Entity Access Object pattern is a new incarnation of the DAO pattern that you can use with JPA.

NOTE While both DAO and EAO are variations of the same pattern, the EAO pattern has been updated to refer to EJB 3 entities. Since EJB 3 entities are POJOs, there is no need to continue the use of the Transfer Object/ Data Transfer Object pattern in conjunction the EAO pattern. Therefore, be aware that no transfer object is required for the EAO pattern.

Introducing the Entity Access Object pattern

Chapter 9 demonstrated how to use the `EntityManager` API directly from the business logic in a session bean. The problem with this approach is that entity access code gets sprinkled throughout the business logic, which is a maintenance nightmare. The Entity Access Object (EAO) pattern decouples the entity access logic from the business logic and improves code maintainability. It allows you to easily change your underlying entity access code without affecting the business logic. If you implement the EAO pattern in your applications, it is significantly easier to change your persistence-tier mechanism from JDBC, EJB 2 CMP, or some proprietary persistence mechanism to JPA.

You can learn more about data access objects from Sun's blueprints website (http://java.sun.com/blueprints/corej2eepatterns/Patterns/DataAccessObject. html). Just replace all references to *DAO* with *EAO*, and references to *transfer objects* with *entities*.

The EAO pattern abstracts data access code, for example, using JPA from the business logic code. Usually you have one EAO object for every domain object (entity) that performs the CRUD operations for the domain objects (entities). Figure 12.1 shows the class diagram of the EAO defined for the `Bid` entity of the ActionBazaar system.

As shown in figure 12.1, `BidEAO` is the entity access object that manipulates the `Bid` entity. A business object such as the `PlaceBid` EJB will persist and retrieve instances of the `Bid` entity by using `BidEAO`. It hides from the `PlaceBid` EJB the actual persistence mechanism used to store the entity.

Now let's explore how to implement an entity access object for the `Bid` entity.

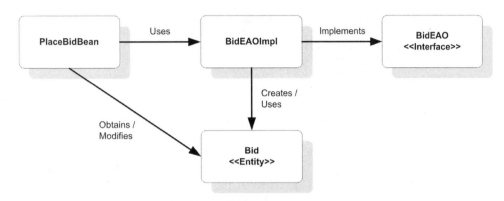

Figure 12.1   **BidEAO is the interface for the EAO object. BidEAOImpl is the EAO class that implements the logic for CRUD operations for the Bid entity.**

Implementing the entity access object

The following code for the `BidEAO` interface exposes the operations that can be performed on a `Bid`:

```
public interface BidEAO {
  public Bid addBid(Item item, String bidderId, double bidPrice);
  public Bid cancelBid(Long bidId);
    ...
}
```

Some developers believe that using an interface for the entity access object is too much trouble. However, you'll learn just how advantageous it is do so when we discuss using the EJB 3 JPA with Spring in chapter 16. An interface allows you to change the underlying persistence provider with no effect on the classes that use the EAO interface.

Listing 12.1 shows the implementation class for the EAO that performs the CRUD operations.

Listing 12.1   JPA-specific implementation class for BidEAO

```
public class BidEAOImpl implements BidEAO {

    private static String EM_NAME = "java:comp/env/actionBazaar";

    public BidEAOImpl() {
    }

    private EntityManager getEntityManager() {
      try {
```

❶ **Looks up container-managed EntityManager**

```
            Context ctx = new InitialContext();
            return (EntityManager)ctx.lookup(EM_NAME);
        } catch (Exception e) {
            e.printStackTrace();
            return null;
        }
    }

    public Bid addBid(Item item, String bidderId, double bidPrice)
                                            throws BidException {
        EntityManager em = getEntityManager();    ◁┐
        if (em != null) {                              ❷ Gets EntityManager
        Bid bid = new Bid();                              instance
        ...
        em.persist(bid);    ◁─❸ Persists Entity
        return bid;
        }
        ...
    }

    public Bid cancelBid(Long bidId) {
        ...
    }
}
```

The code in the implementation class is straightforward. The `getEntityManager` method ❶ uses JNDI lookup to grab an instance of a container-managed `Entity-Manager`. Note that because the EAO is a regular POJO, you cannot use DI, so we have used JNDI to look up and grab an instance of an `EntityManager`. You'll need to make appropriate changes if you want to use an application-managed entity manager. The rest of the code is nothing but moving the entity access code into the EAO instead of embedding it in your business logic. The `addBid` method uses the `getEntityManager` to get an instance of `EntityManager` ❷ and then persist an instance of `Bid` entity ❸.

Let's assume that the client for your EAO code is the `PlaceBid` EJB. Listing 12.2 shows how the code will look.

Listing 12.2   Using BidEAO from the PlaceBid EJB

```
@PersistenceContext(unitName = "actionBazaar",  ◁┐
                    name = "actionBazaar")            ❶ Declares dependency on
@Stateless                                              persistence unit
public class PlaceBidBean implements PlaceBid {
    public Long addBid(String userId, Long itemId, double bidPrice)
        throws BidException {
        ...
```

```
    BidEAO bidEAO = EAOFactory.jpa.getBidEAO();  ◄─②  Creates an instance of EAO
    Bid bid = bidEAO.addBid(item, userId, bidPrice);  ◄─┐
    return bid.getBidId();                                Uses EAO to add
  }                                                 ③   a new Bid
}
```

Listing 12.2 references the persistence unit using the `@PersistenceContext` annotation ❶ because we used JNDI lookup in the EAO to grab an instance of `Entity-Manager`. We then used the `EAOFactory` to create an instance of an EAO ❷. After creating an instance of the EAO, we can use it to perform entity operations ❸.

In the code ❷ we used an `EAOFactory` to create EAO instances. Here is a simple EAO factory that you can use to create instances of EAOs via JPA:

```
public abstract class EAOFactory {
  public static final EAOFactory jpa = new JPAEAOFactory();
  public abstract ItemEAO getItemEAO();
  public abstract BidEAO getBidEAO();
    ...
}

public class JPAEAOFactory extends EAOFactory {
  public JPAEAOFactory(){}
  public BidEAO getBidEAO() {
    return (new BidEAOImpl());
  }
}
```

The advantage of having loose coupling between your business logic and your persistence code should be obvious. If you want to change to a different persistence tier, then you only have to modify your EAO implementation classes. Many tools and utilities such as FireStorm/DAO and Hibernate's `hbm2java` are available that will help generate EAOs for your entities, so adopting EAOs should be relatively painless. This is a good practice to follow, although it may require some additional coding to manage a few extra classes.

Using session beans as EAOs

Since EJB 3 session beans are POJOs, they are clear candidates for EAOs if you are deploying your enterprise applications to a Java EE container. EAOs can simplify things via injection and do not require using an `EAOFactory`. If you decide to implement your EAOs using session beans, then the code will look like this:

```
@Stateless
public class BidEAOImpl implements BidEAO {
  @PersistenceContext(unitName = "actionBazaar")
  private EntityManager em;
```

```
    public BidEAOImpl() {
    }

    public Bid addBid(Item item, String bidderId, double bidPrice) {
      Bid bid = new Bid();
      ...
      em.persist(bid);
      return bid;
    }

    public Bid cancelBid(Long bidId) {
      ...
    }
}
```

This code looks much simpler than the earlier code and is easier to maintain. The code that uses the EAOs is simpler too:

```
@Stateless
public class PlaceBidBean implements PlaceBid {
@EJB
  private BidEAO bidEAO;

  public Long addBid(String userId, Long itemId, Double bidPrice)
      throws BidException {
    ...
    Bid bid = bidEAO.addBid(item, userId, bidPrice);
    return bid.getBidId();
  }
}
```

Implementing EAOs using session beans looks lean and mean. Some purists will resent you considering this approach, but we recommend that you seriously contemplate it because, as a side effect of using session beans for your EAOs, you automatically receive declarative transactions and a container-managed `Entity-Manager`. That's nothing to sneeze at!

We'll discuss how the Spring framework uses the `JpaTemplate` to provide EAO support in chapter 16, when we discuss JPA with Spring applications. But now, let's review the Session Façade pattern.

12.1.3 Visiting the Session Façade pattern

One of the primary reasons the Session Façade pattern was invented was to reduce the number of remote calls for previous EJB incarnations, and this still holds true for EJB 3. In EJB 2 entity beans were remotely accessible by the clients. However, the remoteness comes at a price—namely reduced performance and tight coupling of clients with domain data. With a session bean façade, you can

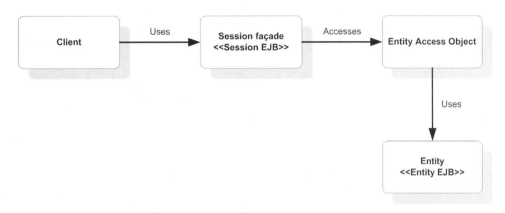

Figure 12.2   The Session Façade design pattern. Client applications may need to access entities or business logic remotely. JPA entities are POJOs and cannot be accessed remotely. You can use a session bean as a façade to the entities and consolidate the logic to manipulate entities in the session façade. Then, using other beans, you can let the clients access the session façade. A coarse-grained session façade also becomes a good candidate for being exposed as a web service.

use entity beans locally and expose the session beans to the clients. This cuts a significant number of RMI calls and encourages loose coupling between client and entity beans, thus improving code maintenance. Figure 12.2 shows the class diagram for the Session Façade design pattern.

Whipping up a session façade amounts to nothing more than designing a coarse-grained session bean and making it available to the client. If you think about it, there are several benefits to making a session bean coarse-grained. One advantage is that it makes managing the transactional and security aspects of your business logic a lot less work than implementing the same functionality for every operation using the fine-grained approach. Let's take a closer look.

Using a session façade for ActionBazaar

Figure 12.3 shows how you might start with the basic Session Façade pattern, and use it for the ActionBazaar application. Instead of using the `EntityManager` API from the client applications, you can create a session façade that manipulates the entities. The client applications access the session façade to manipulate the entities. For example, the ActionBazaar web module uses a stateless session bean (the `PlaceBid` EJB) to manipulate the entities instead of having to manipulate the entities directly from the web applications, such as JSF backing beans. If you have too many fine-grained session beans that you invoke from your web application, you

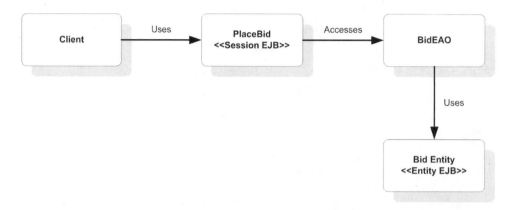

Figure 12.3 Applying the Session Façade pattern to ActionBazaar. Using this pattern improves loose coupling between the client and the business-logic tier. If you access EJBs remotely using the Session Façade pattern, it reduces the number of RMI calls, thus improving application performance.

will be better off creating a coarse-grained session façade that uses the session beans and expose the coarse-grained session façade to the clients.

So how would you actually code this? We'll first show some fine-grained session beans that use entities and illustrate how using the fine-grained session beans creates tight coupling between the web and the application tiers. You'll also see how using these fine-grained session beans will increase the number of remote calls. Then we'll demonstrate how you can create a coarse-grained session façade using the fine-grained session beans, thus improving your application design, achieving better performance, and reducing maintenance costs.

Listing 12.3 shows some examples of fine-grained session beans that can be used by a web client such as a servlet or JSF managed bean.

Listing 12.3 Fine-grained session beans

```
@Stateless
public class ItemManagerBean implements ItemManager {          ItemManager
    ...                                                      ❶ EJB
    Item findByItemId(Long itemId) {
        ...
    }
}


@Stateless
public class BidManagerBean implements BidManager {          BidManager
    Bid findHighestBid(Item item) {                        ❷ EJB
        ...
    }
```

```
  Bid createBid(Item item, Bidder bidder, Double bidPrice) {
    ...
  }
}

@Stateless
public class UserManagerBean implements UserManager {        UserManager
  Bidder findByUserId(String userId) {                    ❸  EJB
  }
}
```

In listing 12.3, we have three fine-grained session beans. UserManagerBean ❸ has a method named findByUserId, ItemManagerBean ❶ has a findByItemId method that helps find items by Id, and BidManagerBean ❷ exposes two methods: findHighestBid and createBid, to find the highest bid item and create a new bid, respectively. You can expose these session beans to the client, and expect the client to perform the business logic as follows:

```
public class ActionBazaarServlet extends GenericServlet {
@EJB private ItemManager itemManager;
@EJB private UserManager userManager;
@EJB private BidManager bidManager;
...

  public void createBid(String userId, Long itemId, Double bidPrice)
      throws BidException {
    Item item = itemManager.findByItemId(itemId);
    Bid highBid = bidManager.findHighestBid(item);
    if (bidPrice <= highBid.getBidPrice()) {
      throw new
        BidException("Bid Price is lower than the current bid price");
    }
    ...
    Bid bid = bidManager.createBid(item, bidder, bidPrice);
  }
}
```

The problem with this approach is that the client is coupled to the persistence and internals of the business logic layer. It quickly becomes a nightmare to manage the security for so many session beans. Also, some of the real business logic gets scattered in multiple places in the code. A better option is to create a session façade like the PlaceBidBean EJB shown here, which uses these operations and exposes PlaceBidBean to the client:

```
@PersistenceContext(unitName = "actionBazaar", name = "actionBazaar")
@Stateless(name = "PlaceBid")
public class PlaceBidBean implements PlaceBid {
```

```
public PlaceBidBean() {
}

public Long addBid(String userId, Long itemId, Double bidPrice)
    throws BidException {
  ...
  Item item = itemEAO.findByItemId(itemId);
  Bid highBid = itemEAO.findHighestBidForItem(item);
  if (bidPrice <= highBid.getBidPrice()) {
    throw new
      BidException("Bid Price is lower than the current bid price");
  }
  ...
  return bidEAO.addBid(item, userId, bidPrice);
}
}
```

There are several merits to the Session Façade pattern. First, it centralizes the real business logic in a single place instead of duplicating it many times. Second, with this pattern the clients don't have to know the internal design of the system. Third, it helps to manage transactions and security centrally instead of managing it for multiple session beans. A final advantage is that it makes the client code much simpler. Take a look at how much the client knowledge is reduced using this approach:

```
@EJB
private PlaceBid placeBid;
...
Bid bid = placeBid.addBid(userId, itemId, bidPrice);
```

If you decide to expose EJBs to remote clients, you will see a dramatic improvement in performance. In addition, such EJBs may be good candidates for being exposed as web services, enhancing reusability and the ability to distribute your enterprise applications.

Stateful vs. stateless session façade

As we saw in the PlaceBid EJB example, most business logic spans only a single method call; therefore, most of your session façades will be stateless in nature. You may choose to make your session façade stateful if your business requires multiple method invocations as a part of some business process and you must maintain conversational state. A stateful session façade also has the benefit of an extended persistence context (discussed in chapter 9) that helps you keep the entities in a managed state that may span across a transaction, and the persistence context is automatically closed when the bean instance is removed. For example, the user registration process is a multistep process. You want to keep the entities managed during the registration process and end the persistence context when the user has completed the registration process. A stateful session façade may be useful in such situations.

This finishes our discussion on EJB design patterns. If you are interested in exploring other design patterns from Sun's blueprints website, please visit http://java.sun.com/reference/blueprints/index.html.

A book about EJB must have an EJB-centric view of the world, mustn't it? In other words, you are probably using a Java EE container with EJBs, or you are using a totally different framework that is incompatible with everything related to EJB 3, right? These statements are true neither of the authors nor of reality. It is useful to know that many aspects of the EJB 3 specification are both available and compatible with alternate approaches to enterprise Java development. The next section delves into some of the options that you may be interested in implementing on your next project.

12.2 *Accessing session beans from the web tier*

You may remember from our discussion in chapter 1 that EJB helps build applications with tiered architecture. You can use session beans to build the business logic of your applications and access the session beans from the presentation or web tier of your enterprise application. Figure 12.4 illustrates where EJBs fit into the architecture of ActionBazaar and how EJBs are accessed from the ActionBazaar web module.

As we discussed in chapter 3, session beans can be accessed using either dependency injection or JNDI lookup. Dependency injection is supported only with managed classes—classes such as servlets, whose lifecycle is managed by the container. While both managed and nonmanaged classes can use JNDI lookup, you'll probably use it only with classes that are not managed. Table 12.1 provides some insight as to types which of classes can access EJBs using dependency injection.

Regardless of which method you use to access your EJBs, you'll interact with them in the same manner after you have obtained an EJB reference.

Your web application may contain a mixture of managed and nonmanaged application components, and in the next sections we'll discuss how you can access session beans from both types of application components. We'll show you how to invoke an EJB 3 session bean from managed classes, such as a servlet, and nonmanaged classes, such as a helper class. We'll also explore what you have to do to demarcate a transaction and the steps required to build a stateful application using stateful session beans.

Table 12.1 An EJB can be accessed from different types of classes in the web tier. Only managed classes can use dependency injection; nonmanaged application components have to use JNDI lookup to obtain a reference to a session bean.

Class Type	Injection
Servlets, filters, event listeners	Yes
JSP tag handlers, library event listeners	Yes
JSF managed beans	Yes
Helper classes, JSPs	No

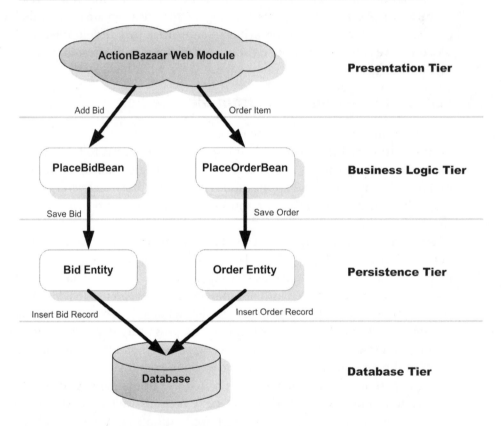

Figure 12.4 ActionBazaar application architecture. The ActionBazaar web module accesses the EJBs that implement the business logic and manipulate entities.

12.2.1 *Accessing session beans using dependency injection*

Dependency injection is by far the easiest way to access an EJB 3 session bean. In this section you'll see how to use dependency injection from the web module to access a session bean. You learned about the `@EJB` annotation in chapter 3, and you probably want to jump into using dependency injection for all your session beans. However, we'll explain why you would want to avoid using dependency injection when accessing a stateful session bean from a multithreaded client.

You can obtain a reference to an EJB in your managed class by using injection in one of two ways:

- By using the `@EJB` annotation
- By using the `ejb-ref` or `ejb-local-ref` element in the `web.xml` deployment descriptor

Assume that ActionBazaar uses a controller servlet. You can use `@EJB` to inject a reference to an EJB as follows:

```
public class ActionBazaarBidControllerServlet extends HttpServlet {
  @EJB private PlaceBid placebid;

  ...
  placeBid.addBid(bidderId, itemId,  bidPrice);
  ...
}
```

This example shows the `PlaceBid` EJB being injected into the `ActionBazaarBidControllerServlet`. The `@EJB` annotation here is clean and straightforward.

If instead we use the `ejb-ref` or `ejb-local-ref` element in the deployment descriptor, we would have a `web.xml` like this:

```
<ejb-ref>
  <ejb-ref-name>PlaceBid</ejb-ref-name>
  <ejb-ref-type>Session</ejb-ref-type>
  <remote>actionbazaar.buslogic.PlaceBid</remote>
  <injection-target>
    <injection-target-name>placeBid</injection-target-name>
    <injection-target-class>
        actionbazaar.web.ActionBazaarBidControllerServlet
    </injection-target-class>
  </injection-target>
</ejb-ref>
```

Compare these two examples. Which one makes more sense to you?

Avoid injecting stateful session beans

If you are using stateful session beans, then you must avoid injecting them into classes that are multithreaded in nature, such as servlets and JSF managed beans.

Let's look at an example. Suppose you inject the `BidderAccountCreator` bean into a servlet that is multithreaded, as shown here:

```
@Stateful(name = "BidderAccountCreator")
public class BidderAccountCreatorBean {

  private LoginInfo loginInfo;
  private BiographicalInfo biographicalInfo;
  private BillingInfo billingInfo;

  @Remove
  public void cancelAccountCreation() {
    ...
  }
}
```

In this case, the single `BidderAccountCreator` instance will be shared by all users of the servlet. This is not the desired behavior since `loginInfo`, `biographicalInfo`, and `billingInfo` are designed to be specific to an individual client.

This becomes trickier when we have a method annotated with the `@Remove` annotation. When a particular user invokes the `cancelAccountCreation` method, the EJB instance will be destroyed. The next time a user tries to access the `Bidder-AccountCreator` EJB, the container will generate a `javax.ejb.NoSuchEJBException`.

If you want to use stateful session beans in your web application, then you need to perform a JNDI lookup and store the returned EJB instance in the `HttpSession` object. This way, the same user reaches the same bean instance for future activity. This also scopes the EJB instance to the user's session, avoiding the possibility of other sessions acquiring or deleting it. We'll explain more about working with stateful session beans in section 12.2.4.

12.2.2 Referencing session beans from helper classes

Sometimes you'll find that you need to access a session bean from a class that is not managed. Dependency injection is not supported in nonmanaged classes. For example, your JSF managed bean may be using some utility classes that are not managed by the container. You cannot inject an instance of an EJB into those classes. Again, in this case you must use JNDI lookup to access your session bean. This method is also used by managed classes when you want to avoid injection. For looking up an EJB from a helper class you have to do the following:

1   Establish the reference to EJB by using the @EJB annotation at the class level or the ejb-ref (ejb-local-ref) descriptor element.

2   Look up the session bean.

Remember from our discussion in part 2 of this book that the @EJB annotation can be used for injecting session bean references to a field or a setter method *or* can be applied at the class level to establish a reference that can be used with JNDI lookup.

The class where you use the @EJB annotation should be the managed class that uses a helper class. For example, say you have a helper class named Bid-Processor that is used by ActionBazaarBidControllerServlet. The BidProcessor class looks up the PlaceBid EJB. You cannot use the @EJB annotation with the Bid-Processor class because it is not a managed class. Here the entry point for the BidProcessor class is ActionBazaarBidControllerServlet, and that's the reason we can use the @EJB annotation as follows:

```
@EJB (name = "ejb/PlaceBid", beanInterface = PlaceBid.class)
public class ActionBazaarBidControllerServlet extends HttpServlet {
}
```

Then look up the EJB in the helper class (BidProcessor) like this:

```
PlaceBid placeBid = (PlaceBid)context.lookup("java:comp/env/ejb/PlaceBid");

placeBid.addBid(bidderId, itemId, bidPrice);
```

In other cases the entry point of your web framework may be a managed class, but you may not be able to modify the code in a way that allows you to use an annotation to establish EJB references. For example, if you are using a framework such as Struts, the entry point for your application is the controller class in the framework, and modifying such frameworks to establish EJB references may not be part of your project. In this case you can use the ejb-ref element in web.xml to establish the EJB references so that the EJBs being used will be bound to the JNDI tree, and thereby visible to your classes via JNDI lookup.

Using the global JNDI name

With some application servers, you may be able to work around specifying references using the @EJB annotation or the web.xml descriptor element by using the global JNDI name. Recall from our discussion earlier that many vendors allow EJB access using global JNDI names, such as the EJB name or by using an EJB class name without having to specify the ejb-ref or ejb-local-ref.

For example, some application servers will allow the lookup of an EJB as follows:

```
PlaceBid placeBid = (PlaceBid)context.lookup("PlaceBid");
```

while others may allow the following type of lookup:

```
PlaceBid placeBid =
    (PlaceBid)context.lookup("actionbazaar.buslogic.PlaceBid");
```

Keep in mind that these approaches are not portable across containers and we recommend you use an EJB reference during lookup.

JNDI and Service Locator design pattern

If you have used EJB 2 or J2EE 1, then you are probably very familiar with service locators. If you haven't used them, take a look at http://java.sun.com/blueprints/corej2eepatterns/Patterns/ServiceLocator.html.

Simply put, the Service Locator design pattern is used to abstract the complexities of JNDI by helping reduce repetitive JNDI code, enforcing a single point of control for lookup, and improving performance of EJB lookups with caching. Many developers believe that the Service Locator pattern will no longer be used with EJB 3 due to dependency injection taking a front-row seat. However, the reality is that EJB 3 dependency injection is not supported in all circumstances and you may still need to rely on good ol' JNDI lookup. Therefore, service locators may not be dead just yet.

There are alternatives to using the Service Locator pattern and JNDI for using resources or EJBs. One such alternative is injecting a bean instance in the managed class and passing it to the helper class as a parameter to its constructor. For example, the `BidManager` EJB uses a helper class, `BidManagerHelper`, that invokes a method in the `ItemManager` EJB. `BidManagerHelper` is a regular POJO, so we cannot inject the `ItemManager` instance. However, we can inject the `Item-Manager` EJB into `BidManagerEJB` and pass it to the helper class as follows:

```
@Stateless
public class BidManagerBean implements BidManager {
@EJB ItemManagerLocal itemManager;

    public Bid placeBid() {
        BidManagerHelper helper = new BidManagerHelper (itemManager);
        ...
    }
}
```

Be sure you evaluate such alternatives before deciding which one best meets your needs.

12.2.3 *Dealing with transactions*

Remember from our discussion in chapter 6 that in your EJB applications you can use either container-managed transactions (CMT) or bean-managed transactions, in which you programmatically manage transactions using the `User-Transaction` API. While CMT is not available in the web container, if your application uses session beans they allow you to use CMTs and avoid `User-Transaction`. We highly recommend you take advantage of CMT. For example, if you want to make multiple EJB method calls from the same transaction, then you may be tempted to do the following:

```
public class ActionBazaarRegistrationControllerServlet
   extends HttpServlet {
...
//--- Do NOT do this!!! This is NOT recommended!!!
@EJB ItemManager itemManager;
@EJB categoryManager categoryManager;
@Resource private UserTransaction ut;
...
public void doPost(HttpServletRequest request,
                HttpServletResponse response)
           throws ServletException, IOException {
...
ut.begin();
...
categoryManager.addCategory(category);
itemManager.addItem();
itemManager.setCategory(category);
...
ut.commit();

}
...
}
```

In this example we are injecting the instances `ItemManager` and `CategoryManager` and then invoking several methods on injected session beans. The first issue here is that you have to write error-prone code to demarcate the transaction. Second, because your EJBs are fine-grained, the business logic gets scattered between the EJBs and the web module. Finally, if the EJBs are remote, these translate to three RMI calls, which can be expensive from a performance perspective. We suggest you avoid this practice. If your application includes such a requirement, we recommend you create a session façade and use that to perform all operations, and then invoke that EJB from the web tier. (We covered the Session Façade design pattern earlier in this chapter.)

12.2.4 *Working with stateful session beans*

If you are building an application that requires maintaining client state end-to-end, you'll most likely use stateful session beans. In section 12.2.1 we listed some reasons why you must avoid injecting instances of stateful session beans into multithreaded classes and use JNDI instead. In this section we'll look at how you can successfully use JNDI and stateful session beans from your web application.

In order to look up a session bean, you have to establish a reference or dependency using the @EJB annotation at the class level and then look up the bean from the environment naming context (discussed in chapter 5) using the reference name specified. If you have worked with EJB 2, using @EJB at the class level is the same as using ejb-ref. The session beans get bound to the environment naming context, or ENC (see chapter 5) as java:comp/env/<name specified with @EJB>.

To begin, you can use the @EJB annotation at the class level to establish an EJB reference or dependency on EJB as follows:

```
@EJB(name = "UserRegistrationBean",
     beanInterface = UserRegistration.class)
public class ActionBazaarRegistrationControllerServlet
   extends HttpServlet {
...
}
```

You must make a JNDI lookup and store the EJB object in the HttpSession object. This will ensure that the same user session gets back the desired bean instance as follows:

```
try {
  InitialContext ctx = new InitialContext();
  userReg = (UserRegistration)ctx.lookup(
              "java:comp/env/UserRegistrationBean");
  session.setAttribute("user_reg", userReg);
} catch (Exception e) {
  handleException(e);
}
```

Now the reference to the session bean can invoke any number of methods. The container ensures that there is a bean instance reserved for a user session and that the bean instance is not shared between multiple user sessions. Be sure to remove the EJB object from the HttpSession when you are invoking a method that is annotated with @Remove. Here's the code that removes the bean instance from the session:

```
userReg.createAccount();
session.removeAttribute("user_reg");
```

Note that the `createAccount` method has been annotated with `@Remove` (see chapter 3), and we must remove the reference to the stateful EJB when the bean instance is destroyed. Otherwise, if we try to use it in the future all we'll get will be the aforementioned `javax.ejb.NoSuchEJBException`. And we wouldn't want that now, would we?

Understanding how clients can best access session beans is great, but what about times when we need to access the persistence mechanism directly?

12.3 *Using JPA from the web tier*

You may not need the power or additional complexity of EJBs for every Java EE application, and therefore decide to forego session beans on occasion. For instance, you may choose to stick with POJOs and servlets to implement business logic, and include the entities directly in the web module (or WAR). In this section, we'll show you how to use entities directly from the web tier.

In chapter 11, we explained that entities can be packaged in the web module, but we skipped over the details of how to do it. You can make your entity classes available to your web module in one of two ways:

- Place entity classes directly in `WEB-INF/classes`. When you package classes in the `WEB-INF/classes` directory of a WAR module, the `persistence.xml` and optional `orm.xml` are placed in the `WEB-INF/classes/META-INF/` directory.

- Alternatively, you can package entity classes in a JAR file and place the file in the `WEB-INF/lib` directory. That way, you can package the `persistence.xml` and optional `orm.xml` descriptors in the `META-INF` directory of the JAR.

This means the structure of your WAR module will look something like this:

```
html/
jsp/
WEB-INF/web.xml
WEB-INF/classes
  actionbazaar/persistence/Bid.class
  ...
  acionbazaar/web/ActionBazaarActionController.class
  META-INF/persistence.xml            ⟻  Required
  META-INF/orm.xml      ⟻  Optional
WEB-INF/lib/entities.jar  ⟻  Optional
```

If you don't package entities in the `WEB-INF/classes`, then you don't have to package `persistence.xml` and the optional `orm.xml` in the WAR file. The `entities.jar` packaged in our example contains entities.

As you can see, packaging the entities with the web module is easy, but you may be wondering how to use them. There are three common scenarios for using EJB 3 JPA from the web container:

- Using a container-managed entity manager in a Java EE 5 container
- Using an application-managed entity manager with a JTA transaction manager in a Java EE 5 container
- Using an application-managed entity manager with local transactions outside the container

The first two cases will be more prevalent because of the power of container-managed entity managers and JTA transactions, but for completeness we'll discuss all three scenarios in this section.

12.3.1 *Using a container-managed entity manager*

Many developers think developing session beans is complex and primarily useful for large applications, and they want to use JPA directly from the web application. If you choose this approach, and if you're using JPA within a Java EE container, a container-managed entity manager is probably the best option, but you still must be careful in the way you use it. For instance, you should avoid dependency injection. Let's look at why this is so.

If you're planning to use JPA from a managed class like a servlet, you may be tempted to inject an instance of an `EntityManager` by using the `@PersistenceContext` annotation like this:

```
//--- Do NOT do this!!! This is NOT recommended!!!
public class ActionBazaarBidControllerServlet extends HttpServlet {
  @PersistenceContext(unitName = "actionBazaar")
  private EntityManager entityManager;
  ...
}
```

If you use this and test your application, it will probably run successfully in your first few attempts. However, you'll likely run into issues when more users try to access the servlet at the same time. You may remember that in chapter 9, we explained that `EntityManager` is not designed to be thread-safe in nature. When you inject an instance of `EntityManager` into a class like a servlet, it is stored in an instance variable at the servlet class level and may be shared by multiple users at the same time. This can result in unexpected errors. Because of this you must avoid injecting an instance of `EntityManager` unless your container vendor (such as Oracle Application Server) guarantees that their `EntityManager` implementation is thread safe. You also have to remember that your code may not be portable when you depend on the thread safety of `EntityManager`.

NOTE You may want to work around this by having your servlets implement `SingleThreadModel`. Although doing so may seem harmless, keep in mind that this is a deprecated feature (since servlet 2.4) and we don't recommend using it because of the many limitations it imposes on applications. This topic is beyond the scope of this book (see www.esus.com/javaindex/j2ee/servlets/servletdiffthread.html).

The right way to use a container-managed `EntityManager` is by avoiding dependency injection and instead performing a JNDI lookup. Bear in mind that the JNDI lookup mechanism can be used in any nonmanaged or managed class.

To use a container-managed `EntityManager`, you must first establish the references to the persistence unit using either the `@PersistenceContext` annotation at the class level or the `persistence-context-ref` element in `web.xml`.

If you're using a managed class such as a servlet or JSF managed bean, then you can establish the reference as follows:

```
@PersistenceContext(name = "actionBazaar/EntityManager",
                    unitName = "actionBazaar")
public class ActionBazaarBidControllerServlet extends HttpServlet {
  private EntityManager entityManager;
...
}
```

If you are using a web framework like Struts where the action classes are not managed, then you can't use annotations to establish references to the persistence context. In this case you will have to use the `persistence-context-ref` element in the `web.xml` as follows:

```
<persistence-context-ref>
  <persistence-context-ref-name>
    actionBazaar/EntityManager
  </persistence-context-ref-name>
  <persistence-unit-name>actionBazaar</persistence-unit-name>
</persistence-context-ref>
```

Regardless of which previous approach you use, your next step is to grab an instance of an `EntityManager` by using JNDI:

```
Context context = new InitialContext();
EntityManager entityManager =
```

```
(EntityManager)context.lookup(
    "java:comp/env/actionBazaar/EntityManager");
```

One thing you need to remember when you don't use session beans to access the
entities is that you have to programmatically manage your transactions since
CMT is not available in the web container. You must use the `UserTransaction` API
in the following way:

```
@Resource private UserTransaction ut;
...
ut.begin();
...
entityManager.persist(item);
...
ut.commit();
```

You'll recall that in chapter 6 we discussed the disadvantages of programmatic
transaction; it's also evident from the previous code that you have to write error-
prone code to manage transactions. If you plan to deploy your web module to a
Java EE container, an EJB container is included as well. We recommend that you
take full advantage of your container by using a session bean to façade your entity
operations. With this approach, you don't have to worry about programmatic
transactions, and you receive extra benefits, such as the ability to inject `Entity-
Manager` and the power of extended persistence context.

Next we'll discuss how you can use an application-managed `EntityManager`
with the JTA transaction manager.

12.3.2 *Using an application-managed EntityManager with JTA transactions*

As you know, we don't typically recommend using an application-managed
`EntityManager`, but in some cases it's your best choice. For instance, you may not
want to use JNDI to grab a container-managed `EntityManager` instance because
you are a fan of dependency injection. In that case, there is another option. You
can consider using the `@PersistenceUnit` annotation to inject an instance of an
`EntityManagerFactory`, and then create an application-managed instance of `Enti-
tyManager` as follows:

```
public class ActionBazaarBidControllerServlet extends HttpServlet {
    @PersistenceUnit(unitName = "actionBazaar")
    private EntityManagerFactory emf;
    ...

}
```

Just remember that you have to manage the lifecycle of an application-managed `EntityManager` (see listing 12.4); the container is not going to do it for you in this situation.

Listing 12.4   Using an application-managed entity manager with a JTA transaction

```
try {
  ...                                              Begins
  ut.begin();           ◀─┘ transaction           Creates
  em = emf.createEntityManager();     ◀─┘         EntityManager
  em.persist(item);
  ...
  ut.commit();
  ...
} catch (Exception e) {
  try {
    ut.rollback();
  } catch (Exception e) {
  } finally {
    em.close();         ◀─┘ Closes EntityManager
  }
}
```

In listing 12.4 we are doing a lot of housekeeping to manage the lifecycle of the `EntityManager` and to manually manage transactions. Unless you have a specific reason to use an application-managed `EntityManager`, we recommend using the Session Façade design pattern (discussed in 12.2.3) with CMT, and a container-managed `EntityManager`. The EJB 3 incarnation of session beans are lightweight POJOs, which make life easier by not requiring the developer to manage the life-cycle of entity managers or transactions.

12.3.3 *Accessing an application-managed EntityManager outside the container*

Developers write all sorts of applications. You might have some applications, such as a Swing or SWT application, for which you'd prefer to use JPA outside the EJB 3 container. Or perhaps you just want to utilize web containers like Tomcat or Jetty that are not Java EE 5 containers, or one of the other lightweight containers that do not have support for a container-managed `EntityManager` or JTA transactions.

Another case in which you might want to use JPA outside the EJB 3 container is when you're testing your entities. You can use the approach we discuss here in conjunction with a test framework such as JUnit and to test entities outside the container.

It's simple to use JPA without an EJB 3 container. All you need to do is create a persistence unit and create an `EntityManager` from the `EntityManagerFactory` obtained from the `Persistence` class. Let's look at an example.

Defining a persistence unit

As you know from chapters 9 and 11, a persistence unit requires a `DataSource` configured in the application server that is used by the persistence provider to connect to the database. Normally, the Java EE container will provide this, but if you are using JPA outside the container, you must provide the JDBC configuration as vendor-specific properties in the `persistence.xml` file.

Listing 12.5 shows a sample `persistence.xml` that illustrates the JDBC configuration for the GlassFish server. The property names will vary depending on which persistence provider you're using.

Listing 12.5   JPA outside a container: an example persistence.xml

```
<persistence
    xmlns = "http://java.sun.com/xml/ns/persistence" version = "1.0">
  <persistence-unit name = "actionBazaar">
    <provider>oracle.toplink.essentials.PersistenceProvider</provider>
    <class>actionbazaar.persistence.Bid</class>
    <class>actionbazaar.persistence.Item</class>
    <properties>
      <property name = "toplink.jdbc.driver"
                value = "oracle.jdbc.OracleDriver"/>
      <property name = "toplink.jdbc.url"
                value = "jdbc:oracle:thin:@//localhost:1521/ORCL"/>
      <property name = "toplink.jdbc.user" value = "scott"/>
      <property name = "toplink.jdbc.password" value = "tiger"/>
    </properties>
  </persistence-unit>                                    JDBC configuration
</persistence>
```

Creating an application-managed EntityManager

To perform CRUD operations on entities, you need to grab an instance of an `EntityManager`. An `EntityManager` may not be available in the JNDI registry or accessible by dependency injection when using JPA outside the Java EE container. In such cases, you have to create an `EntityManager` from the `EntityManagerFactory` that can be created from the `javax.persistence.Persistence` factory class. This is typically the case when you're trying to use JTA in environments such as Java SE or when you're using a web container like Tomcat. (JTA transactions are unavailable outside the Java EE container.)

Listing 12.6 shows an example of how you can use entities outside the container when JTA transactions are not available.

Listing 12.6   Persistence outside the container: a Java SE class using the EJB 3 JPA

```java
public class PlaceBidBeanJavaSE {
  private static EntityManagerFactory emf;
  private static EntityManager em;

  public static void main(String[] args) {
    String userId = "idiot";
    Long itemId = new Long(100);
    Double bidPrice = 2001.50;
try
{
    //Create EntityManagerFactory
    emf = Persistence.createEntityManagerFactory("actionBazaar");

    getEntityManager();
    em.getTransaction().begin();
    addBid(userId, itemId, bidPrice);

    em.getTransaction().commit();
  }
finally
{
closeEntityManager();
emf.close();
}

  private static void getEntityManager() {
    em = emf.createEntityManager();
    }

  private static void closeEntityManager() {
      em.close();
  }
}
```

Creates ❶
EntityManagerFactory

❸ **Begins EntityTransaction**

❹ **Commits EntityTransaction**

❷ **Creates EntityManager**

❺ **Closes EntityManager**

Note that we are using the `javax.persistence.Persistence` class ❶ to create an instance of `EntityManagerFactory`. `Persistence` is the bootstrap class outside the Java EE container that allows us to access the `EntityManagerFactory` by invoking the `createEntityManagerFactory` method. You can create an `EntityManager` instance ❷ after initializing the factory. Keep in mind that you have to use the `EntityTransaction` interface to `begin` and `commit` a transaction ❸ and ❹. Finally we close the `EntityManager` ❺.

When running JPA outside the container, you have to make sure you include all the required files in the CLASSPATH. Check the appropriate documentation for your persistence provider to determine any additional requirements it may have.

12.4 *Summary*

In this chapter you learned how to use EJBs from other tiers. We first looked at how you can use EJB 3 session beans and JPA from the web tier. We described some design patterns that you can use to build better applications. The Model-View-Controller pattern helps separate code based on lines of responsibility. It is most commonly used in frameworks dealing with user interfaces (such as web frameworks). The Entity Access Object design pattern upgrades the trusted DAO pattern to support EJB 3 entities. EAO reduces tight coupling between application tiers, and provides the ability to change persistence code without impacting business logic. Similarly, the Session Façade design pattern reduces the presentation tier's dependencies on the internal workings of the application tier, and improves centralization of transaction management and security. You can access EJB 3 session beans using either dependency injection or JNDI lookup, but you must avoid injecting stateful session beans into multithreaded clients. JPA can be used from web applications without having to depend on session beans. As we showed you in this chapter, you have to use UserTransaction to demarcate transactions when using JPA directly from the web tier.

The next chapter discusses performance and scalability issues around real EJB 3 applications.

Taming wild EJBs: performance and scalability

This chapter covers

- Entity locking
- Performance improvement of JPA entities
- Tuning of session beans and MDB performance
- EJB clustering

When it comes to building software systems, it's the end that matters—not the means. Working, reliable software that is usable is what it all boils down to. In the end, what customers care about is that your product produces consistent results, performs well, and meets scalability and availability requirements. Most developers and users can agree on that. But then there's the part they can't always agree on—the part that's implied and expected by the users, but not always understood by the developers. Surely you've seen it before. You just finish plopping your latest new-fangled application into production and the e-mails start flying and the calls come rolling in. It turns out that the users had some other expectations as well. Something about how they expected the program to perform. Sure, the application has the features they asked for, and everything appeared to work during user acceptance testing (UAT), but now that it's in production everything's so slow. Can anything be done?

In the final assessment, how well your applications perform is important. Users have expectations for performance, even when they don't articulate or just don't communicate them well. In most application development projects, performance goals are ignored during development. While making something work is the first step development should take, some attention must also be paid to performance concerns during development, to avoid the potential rework that will occur if they are completely ignored until the system is deployed. According to some surveys,[1,2] around half of software development projects fail to deliver their performance objectives.

Up to this point we have focused on how to build EJB applications. However, you also need to consider the performance aspects of your application in order to effectively build, configure, and deploy your applications.

In this chapter you'll learn about general performance tuning of all the EJB 3 components and issues surrounding scalability and availability for EJB 3 applications. We'll start by looking at how to handle entity locking. You may remember from our discussion in chapter 6 that consistency is a critical aspect of transactional applications and improper locking mechanisms not only lead to inconsistent data but also may cause performance degradation. An athlete makes sure that he runs within his track before running faster; otherwise he'll be disqualified.

---

[1] According to the Wily Tech 2003 Survey of Java Applications, 60 percent fail to meet performance expectations (http://www.wilytech.com/news/releases/031120.html).

[2] Forrester (2004) reports that 66 percent of the time, developers find out about performance problems from support calls.

Similarly an application is useless if it has consistency issues. We'll begin by discussing entity locking.

13.1 *Handling entity locking issues*

When you build a high-end transactional trading application like ActionBazaar, you need to understand concurrency issues so that you can take appropriate actions during development. Too many users trying to read or update the same piece of data can cause havoc with system performance. Or even worse, one user is working with data that is no longer valid due to the data having been changed or deleted by another user. Dealing with concurrency is a nontrivial problem domain and requires a certain amount of forethought before the coding begins.

When these scenarios have occurred in the past, have they been documented? Are there recommended patterns and terminology on how to discuss and resolve such problems? It turns out that there are some known approaches to handling such problems. Before we discuss them, though, let's get some terminology straight. In a concurrent system, you may run into one or more of the following issues when isolating actions involving multiple users:

- *Dirty read*—Occurs when a user sees some uncommitted transactions from another user. For example, in the ActionBazaar system, suppose a `Seller` reads an `Item` in transaction T1 and makes some changes without committing them, and a `Bidder` gets a copy of the uncommitted changes in a separate transaction T2. Then the `Seller` decides to cancel his change, rolling back the transaction T1. Now we have a situation where the `Bidder` has a copy of an `Item` that never existed.

- *Nonrepeatable read*—Occurs when a user is allowed to change data employed by another user in a separate transaction. Suppose a `Bidder` reads an `Item` in transaction T1 and keeps a copy of the `Item` while at the same time the `Seller` removes the `Item` in transaction T2. The `Bidder` now has a copy of the `Item` that no longer exists and any attempt to create a `Bid` on the `Item` will fail with unexpected (and unexplainable, unrepeatable) errors.

- *Phantom read*—Occurs when a user receives inconsistent results in two different attempts of the same query, in the same transaction. For instance, a `Bidder` runs one query to retrieve a list of `Items` available for bidding on within a specific `Category` in transaction T1, and a `Seller` creates a new `Item` in that `Category` in transaction T2. When the `Bidder` runs the query again, he gets a larger list of `Items` than originally retrieved.

You may recall that we briefly discussed transaction isolation levels in chapter 6, and that we encouraged you to choose the appropriate transactional isolation level supported by the underlying database system(s). Additionally, a highly transactional system must enforce appropriate locking strategies to make sure that users don't step on one another.

Now we're ready to cover the known patterns on how to deal with concurrency. Given how important locking is to multiuser applications, let's discuss the various types of locking next. Then we'll focus on optimistic locking with JPA and show how you can obtain locks on entities using the EntityManager API.

13.1.1 *Understanding locking types*

To avoid concurrency issues, applications must use appropriate locking mechanisms. Locking strategies are generally grouped into two camps: optimistic and pessimistic. Optimistic locking can be viewed as a "cure it" mind-set, whereas pessimistic locking is more of a "prevent it" concept. This section examines the differences between these two locking approaches.

Pessimistic locking

Pessimistic locking is a strategy reflective of a pessimistic state of mind, where you prevent users from doing certain things, assuming that they will go wrong. When using pessimistic locking, you lock all involved database rows for the entire span of time a user shows an interest in modifying an entity.

> **NOTE**   JPA does not have support for pessimistic locking strategies. However, some persistence providers will have vendor-specific extensions to use pessimistic locking.

Figure 13.1 illustrates pessimistic locking. A user may acquire two types of lock on an entity: write or read. A *write* lock prevents users from attempting any kind of operations such as read, update, or delete, on the locked row(s). A *read* lock allows others to read the locked data but they are unable to update or delete it.

A pessimistic lock is relatively easy to implement, since most databases allow you to lock tables, rows, and so forth. You can use the SELECT FOR UPDATE semantics in the database to implement pessimistic locking.

Pessimistic locking has many disadvantages. For instance, it may make your applications slower because all users have to wait for an entity's locks to be released. It may also introduce deadlock conditions into your system. If a system has several users, transactions involve a greater number of objects, or transactions are long-lived, then the chance of having to wait for a lock to be released

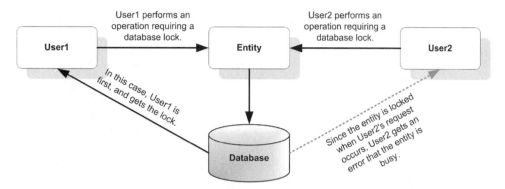

Figure 13.1 In pessimistic locking, when a user wants to update the data the underlying records are locked and no other user can perform any operation on the data. It is typically implemented using SELECT ... FOR UPDATE semantics.

increases. Pessimistic locking therefore limits the practical number of concurrent users that the system can support.

Optimistic locking

By contrast, *optimistic locking* is a strategy that assumes that concurrency problems will occur rarely, and you should detect and resolve each problem when it happens. The optimistic locking mechanism is more difficult to implement, but is a popular approach to enforce control while allowing full data access concurrency. JPA supports the optimistic locking strategy. Although the ActionBazaar system is a high-transaction system, rarely do concurrency problems happen.

In the ActionBazaar system, a Seller (as well as the system administrator) is allowed to update her item. Several Bidders may bid for the same item since they are not allowed to change the item. It is less likely that a Seller and an administrator will be updating the same item at the same time, so an optimistic locking strategy makes sense.

Figure 13.2 depicts how optimistic locking works. When a user retrieves an entity for update, a copy of the object is provided and changes are made to the copy. After the user makes some changes to the entity, he is ready to save it. The application now obtains a write lock on the object and checks whether data has been updated since the user obtained it. If there has been no update to the original data, then the user is allowed to commit the copy of the entity to the database. Otherwise, the application should throw an exception.

The optimistic locking strategy is typically implemented by adding a column to the database table for the entity, and either storing a version number or a

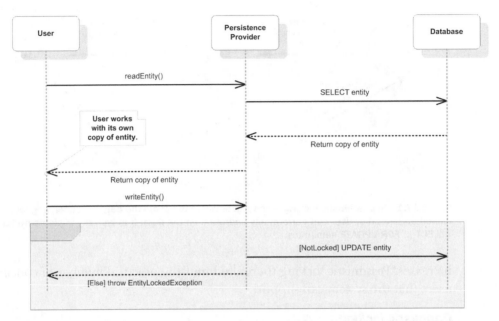

Figure 13.2 How optimistic locking strategy is implemented by a persistence provider. If the locking mode is set to WAIT, the User2 would wait until User1 releases the lock.

timestamp to track changes. The version number approach is preferred and quite reliable, because it could be that two users may be trying to update the same data—at the same instant (timestamp).

Every time a specific database row is updated, the version column is incremented by the application. When a user reads the entity, the version column is retrieved and stored with the entity instance. After making changes in the entity object, as the user tries to save the entity to the database, the application compares the version attribute of the entity object with that of the database. If the version attributes are the same, then the user is allowed to hold a write lock on the object, saves the object to the database, increments the version attribute, and then releases the write lock. If the version attributes are different, then it is assumed the entity has since been updated by someone else and the update is rejected with an OptimisticLockingException.

If you're building an application with JDBC, then you'll have to implement a locking strategy yourself. However, if you're using the EJB 3 JPA, the persistence provider makes your life much simpler. The EJB 3 JPA persistence providers are required to support the optimistic locking strategy using a version number column in the database table. Let's take a closer look at how this is done.

13.1.2 *Optimistic locking and entity versioning*

If any of your entities are accessed concurrently in your applications, or detached entity instances are merged, then you must enable optimistic locking for those entities. For example, in the ActionBazaar application entities such as `Item` and `Category` are accessed concurrently. You must enable optimistic locking for these entities by adding a `version` attribute in these entities.

> **NOTE** The JPA specification does not mandate supporting optimistic locking without a version field on the entity.

We can define a `version` attribute in the `Entity` item as follows:

```
@Entity
@Table(name = "ITEMS")
public class Item implements Serializable {
  @Id
  @Column(name = "ITEM_ID")
  protected Long itemId;
  ...
  @Version        Specifies version property
  @Column(name = "OPT_LOCK")
  private Long version;
  ...
}
```

Stores version in
OPT_LOCK column

As this code shows, you can use `@javax.persistence.Version` on a persistence field or property. The persistence field should be a numeric field of type `long`, `Long`, `int`, or `Integer`, and it should be mapped to a database column on the primary table to which the entity is mapped. In our example, the `version` property is mapped to the `OPT_LOCK` column. You may see some resistance from your DBA to adding an extra column to store the version, but you will have to persuade her that you need this column to support optimistic locking in your applications.

Applications cannot set the `version` attribute, as it is used directly by the persistence provider. The version column is automatically incremented when the persistence provider commits changes to the database. When you merge an entity instance to a persistence context, the persistence provider will check the version column to ensure that the detached entity has not become stale.

If you are using TopLink Essentials, you can enable logging to see SQL statements when a detached entity instance is merged as follows:

```
--Assign return row DatabaseRecord(ITEMS.OPT_LOCK => 2)
... Connection (
... )
```

```
--UPDATE ITEMS SET ITEM_NAME = ?, OPT_LOCK = ?
WHERE ((ITEM_ID = ?) AND (OPT_LOCK = ?))
        bind => [New Title: Vintage Cars from junkyard, 2, 902, 1]
```

In this code, the persistence provider is incrementing the value for the version attribute (ITEMS.OPT_LOCK) and updating the ITEMS table with the new value in the OPT_LOCK column. The WHERE clause includes the OPT_LOCK column and compares it with the old value. If the WHERE clause fails, then the persistence provider will throw an OptimisticLockException.

Some persistence providers may choose to support additional mechanisms to check optimistic locking and, depending on their implementation, may render your applications less portable.

13.1.3 *EntityManager and lock modes*

Although you will very rarely need it, the EntityManager provides a lock method to explicitly acquire a lock on an entity:

```
// begin transaction...
entityManager.lock(item, LockModeType.READ);
  ...
System.out.println(item.getInitialPrice());
```

> **NOTE** The lock mode can be one of two types: READ or WRITE. You must have version attributes on any entity to be locked using the lock method, and the entity must be managed.

As mentioned earlier, some persistence providers may use alternate mechanisms to support an optimistic lock on objects. If you have not created version attributes on your entities and you are attempting to lock them, your persistence provider won't be able to acquire the lock. It will notify the application of this situation by throwing a javax.persistence.PersistenceException. The EntityManager automatically translates these locks to the appropriate database locks.

> **NOTE** If you use LockModeType.READ, then your application acquires a READ lock on an entity. You are ensured that neither of the issues such as dirty reads or nonrepeatable reads will occur in your applications.

One common use of the READ lock is when your application generates reports. You obviously don't want other users updating entities when you are reading them to populate the report.

In addition to this behavior, when you use LockModeType.WRITE, the persistence provider will check for conflicts. When you acquire a WRITE lock on an entity, no

UPDATE or DELETE operation is performed on the entity, even from separate transactions. The persistence provider will generate an OptimisticLockException if another user tries to update the locked entity from a separate transaction. The persistence provider will automatically increment the value for the version column when the transaction successfully commits or roll backs. LockModeType.WRITE is useful when you are trying to manage relationships between two entities that may be updated in different transactions and you want to avoid inconsistencies.

Here is an example of using LockModeType.WRITE:

```
...
Item item = em.find(Item.class, itemId);
em.lock(item, LockModeType.WRITE);
item.addBid(bid);
bid.setItem(item);
...
```

Performance tuning: an iterative approach

Performance tuning is neither an art nor an exact science. There is no silver bullet that you can use to hunt down your application's performance issues. A typical enterprise application that uses EJB components probably has multiple tiers. When you experience performance issues, where do you start? In our experience organizational groups spend more time finger-pointing than trying to investigate and identify the real issues. Sometimes the developers are blamed, sometimes the database group, and sometimes the support personnel. Instead, these groups should spend more time working with one another to find a mutually beneficial resolution.

Performance tuning is a very iterative process. We recommend that you limit changes to a single modification; you should understand the impact of each change by rerunning the whole scenario. Only then can you determine if another change is needed, if further tuning is required, or if the change you made had an unexpected or adverse effect and needs to be reversed. Changing multiple items is uncontrolled and can lead to an unstable, sometimes even unrecoverable, situation. The result of changing one thing at a time is that you can determine if you need to reverse the last change before proceeding to the next. Otherwise, you can accumulate random behavior, which can leave your application in a more unstable state than when it started.

Finding bottlenecks for multitier applications is not an easy task and may involve looking for several things. Several books have been written on tuning the different tiers of distributed applications.

If you get an `OptmisticLockException` in your application, there is no way to recover, and it probably makes sense to retrieve a fresh copy of the entity and try to reapply the changes.

To summarize, if you use the right locking strategy your application won't suffer from consistency issues. If you are trying to implement vendor-specific pessimistic locking, you may have performance issues and we suggest you use optimistic locking instead.

This brings an end to our discussion on locking strategies for entities. It's important that a locking strategy be in place for your applications, and that it be clearly communicated to the development team—especially when there is any turnover within the team. Now that we've put locking strategies in perspective, let's turn our attention to how you can tune the performance of entities in your EJB 3 applications.

13.2 *Improving entity performance*

Many would agree that the persistence tier remains the primary suspect of most performance issues. Sometimes this is due to poor design or a failure to understand the technologies in play and how they interact. Sometimes it can be due to a weak vendor implementation or tool, or insufficient training on how to use the tool properly the way it was intended. Yet another cause can be not getting your database team involved during the design process. Your DBAs should have intimate knowledge of the data and database server(s), and be able to give you some insight on how best to interact with it, as well as be able to make modifications that your application could benefit from.

Our own experience has shown that the response time of applications will improve from 2 to 10 times simply by tuning the data access layer. When you are experiencing unacceptable performance, there might be several reasons to suspect this layer. For instance, the SQL statements are generated by the persistence provider, and unless you know how the persistence provider generates the SQL statement, you put the blame on the JPA provider!

You can take several actions to improve how your applications access the database. In this section we'll offer some advice on these design considerations.

13.2.1 *Remodeling and schema redesign*

Your entity model and the underlying table design may severely impact the performance of your application. This means you must keep performance goals for your applications in mind when designing your entity model and schema.

This section shows how you can align your design with your performance goals. All teams involved in your project should review the design, and you may need to introduce some non-domain-specific data into your domain model in order to achieve your performance goals. This review should take place on a case-by-case basis. Don't hesitate to adjust your domain model to achieve your business objectives.

Merging tables

You may improve performance by merging two small tables and making slight adjustments to the domain model. While building ActionBazaar we found that a one-to-one relationship exists between `BillingInfo` and `Address`. In the original design, `BillingInfo` and `Address` were mapped to two different tables, BILLING_DETAILS and ADDRESSES, as seen here:

```
@Entity
@Table(name = "BILLING_DETAILS")
public class BillingInfo implements java.io.Serializable {

    @Id
    protected long billingId;
    ...

    @OneToOne
    protected Address address;
...
}

@Entity
@Table(name = "ADDRESSES")
public class Address implements java.io.Serializable {

    @Id
    protected long addressId;
    ...

    ...
}
```

We realized that retrieving `BillingInfo` makes no sense without also retrieving the `Address` information. In addition, `Address` is always eagerly loaded and there is always a JOIN performed between the BILLING_DETAILS and ADDRESSES tables. Performance can be improved in this case by merging the ADDRESSES table into the BILLING_DETAILS table and making `Address` an embedded object like so:

```
@Entity
@Table(name = "BILLING_DETAILS")
```

```
public class BillingInfo implements java.io.Serializable {

  @Id
  protected long billingId;
  ...

  @Embedded
  protected Address address;
...
}

@Embeddable
public class Address implements java.io.Serializable {
...
}
```

In this way you can avoid a JOIN between two tables and achieve a little performance boost as a bonus. Another option to consider is to remove secondary tables by merging them into the primary table. This avoids a JOIN between the primary table and secondary table when an entity is loaded.

Dividing a table into multiple tables

In ActionBazaar, a Seller may provide some additional information, such as original purchase date, manufacturing date, warranty information, picture, or video files for an Item. When we originally modeled ActionBazaar, the Item entity had attributes for all these fields, and all the fields were stored in a single table as shown here:

```
@Entity
@Table(name = "ITEMS")
public class Item implements Serializable {
  @Id
  private Long itemId;
  private String title;
  ...
  private String originalPurchaseDate;
  @Lob
  private byte[] itemPicture;
  ...
}
```

Most of this information is not frequently used, so we marked these fields to be lazily loaded. However, what we did not realize is that lazy loading of BLOB fields is not mandatory for EJB 3 persistence providers. In our case, the itemPicture was retrieved when we tried to retrieve an Item instance, and performance was poor. We were able to improve things by dividing ITEMS into two tables: ITEMS and ITEM_DETAILS. Both ITEMS and ITEM_DETAILS share the same primary key, and we remodeled our `Item` entity to carve out two entities: `Item` and `ItemDetails`. We then established a one-to-one relationship between these entities and set the load type for relationship to be `LAZY` as follows:

```
@Entity
@Table(name = "ITEMS")
public class Item implements Serializable {
  @Id
  private Long itemId;
  private String title;
  ...
  @OneToOne(fetch = FetchType.LAZY)
  @PrimaryKeyJoinColumn(name = "ITEM_ID",
                        referencedColumnName = "ITEM_DETAIL_ID")
  private ItemDetails itemDetails;
}

@Entity
@Table(name = "ITEM_DETAILS")
public class ItemDetails implements Serializable {
  @Id
  private Long itemDetailsId;
  private String originalPurchaseDate;
  @Lob
  private byte[] itemPicture;
  ...
}
```

This change gives us the performance we are looking for, and helps us overcome the reality that not all implementations of the EJB 3 specification are done the same way. This way, we remain neutral with respect to application server vendors, and therefore our application is more portable across persistence provider implementations.

Choosing the right inheritance strategy

As you learned in chapter 8, EJB 3 supports three type of inheritance mapping strategies. Each has its own advantages and disadvantages, but the single-table strategy will probably give you the best performance. This is because all entities are stored in a single table and JOINs between tables are avoided. As discussed in chapter 8, we can create a single table named USERS for `User` and all its subclasses such as `Bidder`, `Seller`, `Admin`, etc., and use a discriminator column to track the subtypes. Consider the following:

```
@Table(name = "USERS")
@Inheritance(strategy = InheritanceType.SINGLE_TABLE)
```
❶ **Sets inheritance type strategy**

```
@DiscriminatorColumn(name = "USER_TYPE",
                     discriminatorType = DiscriminatorType.STRING,
                     length = 1)
public class User ...
```
                                                    Configures ❷
                                                    discriminator column

```
@Entity                                  ❸  Specifies Seller
@DiscriminatorValue(value = "S")    ⟵┘   discriminator value
public class Seller extends User ...
```

```
@Entity                                  ❹  Specifies Bidder
@DiscriminatorValue(value ="B")     ⟵┘   discriminator value
public class Bidder extends User
```

Notice ❷ that `discriminatorType` has a data type of `DiscriminatorType.STRING` and a `length` of 1. These are set in conjunction with the inheritance strategy ❶ of `SINGLE_TABLE`. This means that you can assign the actual value as a Java `String` type, but the value will be whatever your application decides to use for the various subtypes supported. In this case `"S"` is used to represent a `Seller` ❸ and `"B"` represents a `Bidder` ❹. But then you already figured that out, didn't you?

13.2.2 *Tuning the JDBC layer*

You remember from our discussion earlier in this book that JPA internally uses JDBC to store and retrieve entities. When you deploy your applications using the EJB 3 JPA in an application server environment, you are taking advantage of the JDBC connection pooling configuration of the application server. Tuning the application server may improve performance of your applications.

Properly sizing the connection pool

Every application server supports pooling connections, and you should not forget to size the connection pool appropriately. In a high-transaction system, if there are more concurrent users than the available number of connections, users have to wait until connections are released in order for their requested functions to be performed. This may degrade performance of your applications. You have to properly size the pool's startup and runtime characteristics (such as both the minimum and maximum number of connections in the pool, and the timeout before an unused connection is automatically returned to the pool) based on your application requirements. Review your vendor's documentation for available options.

Caching SQL statements

The persistence provider executes SQL on your behalf. In a transaction-centric system like ActionBazaar, it is likely that the same SQL statement will be executed by the persistence provider many times. Applications servers such as BEA WebLogic and Oracle Application Server provide the ability to cache SQL statements and reuse them. This lowers the overhead of cursor creation as well as the parsing of SQL statements—both of which can be very time consuming. Typically this is configured in the `data-source` configuration of the application server as follows:

```
<data-source>
  ...
  num-cached-statements = "200"
  ...
</data-source>
```

Check your application server documentation to see whether it supports statement caching and make the appropriate changes.

You must use parameter binding for your queries in order to take advantage of statement caching instead of concatenating the parameters in the query. For example, you may choose to write your query as follows:

```
Query query = em.createQuery(
        "SELECT c FROM Category c" +
        "WHERE c.categoryName = " + categoryName);
```

The problem with this statement is that it does not use parameter binding, and therefore cannot be cached by the persistence provider. Change your query to use a parameter as follows:

```
Query query = em.createQuery(
        "SELECT c FROM Category c" +
        "WHERE c.categoryName = ?1");
query.setParameter(1, categoryName);
```

This allows your query to be a candidate for the cache. This small change to the programming model of the developer can have a huge impact in the overall performance of your application, depending on how many SQL statements your application has, and how often they find their way into the cache at runtime. This is one small change you can make in the early stages of development that can help build better performance into your programs.

Using named queries

Instead of using dynamic queries, make sure that you use named queries in your applications. A named query is prepared once and can be efficiently reused by the persistence provider. Also, the generated SQL can be cached.

You can convert the previous query to a named query like this:

```
@NamedQuery(
  name = "findCategoryByName",
  query = "SELECT c FROM Category c WHERE c.categoryName = ?1")
```

```
public class Category implements Serializable {
}
```

Then you can use the named query in your application as follows:

```
Query query = em.createNamedQuery("findCategoryByName");
query.setParameter(1, categoryName);
```

The named query `findCategoryByName` contains a placeholder for a value to be passed at runtime (?1). This code snippet specifies that parameter 1 should be `categoryName`. You provide the parameters to named queries in the same way you would when using dynamic queries. However, named queries can be optimized, so we recommend you use them whenever possible.

Avoiding transactions for read-only queries

Transaction management is an expensive affair. If the results of your queries won't be updated, then don't use a transaction. By default the `transaction` attribute for a session bean is `REQUIRED`. Change it to `NOT_SUPPORTED` for read-only queries.

13.2.3 Reducing database operations

Reducing database operations directly improves performance of applications. But while using the EJB 3 JPA you don't directly write SQL since the SQL is generated by the persistence provider. At this point you're asking yourself, "Then how you can reduce the database operations?" We're glad you asked…

Choosing the right fetch type

In chapter 9 you learned that a relationship may either be eagerly or lazily loaded. Lazy loading leads to multiple SQL statements, whereas eager loading relates to a SQL `JOIN` statement and translates to unnecessary data. If you're using EJB 3, by default the associated entities are eagerly loaded when you have a one-to-one or many-to-one relationship, or lazily loaded when you have a one-to-many or many-to-many relationship. However, there may be several situations when you don't need a related entity, such as the `BillingInfo` for a given `User`, or a related `Item-Details` for a specific `Item`. In such cases you can disable eager loading.

There may also be situations when you want a related collection of entities to be loaded automatically, where a one-to-many relationship exists that forces you to switch to `EAGER` loading. We warn you to be very careful when turning on eager loading for one-to-many relationships.

If you're not sure whether eager loading is the right strategy for your association, you may want to try setting eager loading in your JPQL query. Suppose you want to eagerly load the `BillingInfo` for a `User` entity. We can use the `FETCH` clause with a `JOIN` like this:

```
SELECT u
FROM User u JOIN FETCH u.billingInfo
WHERE u.firstName like ?1
```

This query will eagerly load the `BillingInfo` object for `User` even if fetch mode is specified as `LAZY` in the association definition.

Deferring database updates until the end of transactions

By default the flush mode for EJB 3 is `AUTO`; that is, the EJB 3 persistence providers execute SQL statements to update the database at the end of the transaction and whenever a query is executed that may retrieve updated data. The persistence providers optimize SQL at the end of the transaction.

You can control the database updates by using the `EntityManager`'s `flush` method. Using `flush` in between a transaction may lead to multiple SQL statements. Excessive use of `flush` may degrade the performance of your application, so we recommend that you not use it unless you have exhausted all other options.

You can optionally set the flush mode to `COMMIT`. This means that all updates are deferred until the end of the transaction. In this situation the `EntityManager` doesn't check for pending changes. You can set `FlushMode` for the `EntityManager` em as follows:

```
em.setFlushMode(FlushModeType.COMMIT)
```

This will set `FlushMode` to `COMMIT` for all queries executed within the active persistence context.

On the other hand, if you want to set `FlushMode` on a per-query basis, you can do this:

```
Query query = em.createNamedQuery("findAllItems");
query.setFlushMode(FlushModeType.COMMIT);
List items = query.getResultList();
```

As you can see, you have the flexibility to manually control flushing by calling the `flush` method, setting `FlushMode` on a persistence context basis (discussed in chapter 9), or setting `FlushMode` on a per-query basis (discussed in chapter 10). The EJB 3 Expert Group wants you to have your `FlushMode` "your way"!

Using the lowest-cost lock in the database

Although the EJB 3 JPA doesn't require persistence providers to support pessimistic locking, your persistence provider may support this lock mode as an extension.

We recommend you avoid pessimistic locking unless you really need it because the database locks the record or page during the transaction. Even if you are using optimistic locking, use the lowest lock (i.e., the READ lock) if it will satisfy your application requirement.

Using DELETE_CASCADE appropriately

In chapter 8, we discussed setting the cascade type to REMOVE for one-to-many or one-to-one relationships. If you set cascade to REMOVE or ALL, when you remove an entity any associated entities are also automatically removed. For example, if we remove a Seller entity, then the associated BillingInfo is also removed. This will lead to at least two DELETE statements in the database.

```
public class Seller {
  ...
  @OneToOne(cascade = CascadeType.REMOVE)
  public BillingInfo getBillingInfo() {
  }
}
```

For a one-to-many relationship, it may lead to removal of multiple rows, which could have a negative impact on performance. Many databases support enforcing a CASCADE DELETE constraint on tables:

```
CREATE TABLE BillingInfo
(
  billing_id number(10) not null,
  ...
  CONSTRAINT fk_user
  FOREIGN KEY (user_id)
  REFERENCES supplier (user_id)
  ON DELETE CASCADE    ←┐  Cascading delete constraint
)
```

We suggest you consider using CASCADE DELETE as a table constraint. This normally yields better performance than a DELETE statement.

Using the cascade property

Remember from our discussions in part 3 that you can set the cascade type of relationships to NONE, PERSIST, MERGE, REFRESH, REMOVE, or ALL, as in this example:

```
public class Seller {
  ...
  @OneToMany(cascade = CascadeType.ALL)
  public Items getItems() {
  }
}
```

Each of these options impacts how the related entities are handled when an entity operation is performed. For example, when set to ALL, the persistence provider will try each operation (persist, merge, refresh, etc.) on the target entity. These may result in unnecessary database operations when you have several associated entities, and each of the operations is cascaded. So when setting the cascade property, take into account the needs of your applications.

Bulk updates

Your application may require changes to multiple entities within one transaction. You may wish to retrieve a collection of entities and iterate through each to make changes. If we want to give Gold status to all Sellers who have been members of ActionBazaar for longer than five years, we can do it like this:

```
Query query = em.createQuery(
  "SELECT s FROM Seller s WHERE s.createDate <= ?1");
...
List sellers = query.getResultList();
Iterator  i = seller.iterator();
while (i.hasNext()) {
  Seller seller = (seller) i.next();
  seller.setStatus("Gold");
}
```

This will lead to many UPDATE statements being generated by the persistence provider. You can reduce this to a single UPDATE statement by using the bulk Update feature of JPQL as follows:

```
Update Seller s
SET s.status = 'Gold' WHERE s.createDate <= ?1
```

This JPQL statement will update all Sellers to a Gold status with the creation date specified—in one fell swoop. If 10,000 sellers meet this criterion, executing this in one SQL statement instead of 10,000 is a huge performance improvement.

Avoiding association tables in one-to-many relationships

Association tables are commonly used to store unidirectional, one-to-many relationships. This is supported in EJB 3 with the @JoinTable annotation. Using an association table will require extra SQL statements to manage the relationship, as well as unnecessary JOINs between the base tables and association tables. You can gain some performance benefit by avoiding association tables.

13.2.4 *Improving query performance*

Even trivial applications can make extensive use of queries. When using EJB 3, you write queries in JPQL and they are translated to SQL. Although you develop in JPQL, you can take certain actions to ensure that the corresponding queries will perform well. DBAs can certainly play a big part in helping improve queries.

You may also be interested in enabling a higher level of logging in your persistence provider to expose and capture the generated SQL statements, and run them through a "tuning utility" provided by your database vendor. This can help you determine whether the SQL can be improved. Certain databases provide an automatic SQL tuning utility that provides suggestions for improving the SQL executed by an application. You can work with your DBA to use such tools and get their recommendations on how to improve query performance.

There is no magic sequence of steps that address all query issues, but we'll discuss some of the more common scenarios.

Avoiding full-table scans

Unless your entity is mapped to a very small table, you must avoid using SELECT statements that perform full-table scans. For example, you can retrieve all items in a query like this:

```
SELECT FROM Item I
```

Next, you retrieve the returned collection, iterate through the collection, and perform one or more operations on the resulting data. The persistence provider will generate the following SQL:

```
SELECT *
FROM ITEMS
```

There are two problems here. First, this code will retrieve and bring in a lot of rows into the middle tier and consume a lot of memory. Second, it will cause a FULL TABLE SCAN in your database and the query will be very slow. Your DBA will advise you to avoid such SQL. Realistically, the number of available items you want is much less than the total number of items in your database. You must utilize the full potential of database filtering by changing your query to limit the number of rows retrieved as follows:

```
SELECT i
FROM Item i
WHERE i.status = "Available"
```

The query will be much faster and you don't have to do any extra filtering work in the middle tier.

Using indexes to make queries faster

Indexes make your query faster. Your DBAs are probably responsible for building the indexes on tables, but there's a good chance that they don't know the details of how your application works. You should work with them so that they understand the queries used by your application. Only then can they build appropriate indexes for your application. Queries that include the primary key always use an indexed scan, meaning that no additional indexes are required. In spite of this, here are some additional cases where you'll want to use an index to improve performance.

Filtering based on a nonidentity field

This is very prevalent in applications. For example, suppose you want to retrieve your Item entities by itemTitle as follows:

```
SELECT i
FROM Item i
WHERE i.itemTitle = ?1
```

This JPQL statement will be translated to SQL as follows:

```
SELECT *
FROM ITEMS
WHERE ITEMS.ITEM_TITLE = ?1
```

If you do not have an index on ITEM_TITLE, the query will include a FULL TABLE SCAN. Therefore, we recommend you create an index in these situations. In this case, the index would be created on ITEM_TITLE.

Using indexes for relationship fields

Relationships are implemented in the database by using foreign key constraints. However, you may not have indexes on the foreign key column(s). When you retrieve an associated entity, a JOIN between the two underlying tables is performed. But this is slow because a FULL TABLE SCAN will be executed on the associated entities. Creating an index on the underlying table will allow the database to use that index while joining the tables, which is must faster than joining two large tables without an index.

In ActionBazaar, Item and Bid have a one-to-many relationship due to eager loading. If you have a JPQL query that uses a JOIN clause, the persistence provider could generate the following SQL statement:

```
SELECT *
FROM BIDS INNER JOIN ITEMS ON ITEMS.ITEM_ID = BIDS.ITEM_ID
WHERE ITEMS.ITEM_ID = ?1
```

If we assume that there is no index on the BIDS.ITEM_ID, the Oracle database handles this SQL statement like so:

```
SELECT STATEMENT ()
NESTED LOOPS ()
  TABLE ACCESS (BY INDEX ROWID ITEMS)
    INDEX (UNIQUE SCAN)        ITEM_PK
  TABLE ACCESS (FULL)          BIDS
```

If you add an index on the ITEM_ID column for the BIDS table, you'll see the query plan for our SQL statement change as follows:

```
SELECT STATEMENT ()
  NESTED LOOPS ()
    TABLE ACCESS (BY INDEX ROWID ITEMS)
      INDEX (UNIQUE SCAN)        ITEMS_PK
    TABLE ACCESS (BY INDEX ROWID BIDS)
      INDEX (RANGE SCAN)         BID_ITEM_IDX
```

Review your queries with your DBAs and they should be able to determine whether adding an index for a column makes sense.

Ordering a collection of entities

You can order the entities retrieved in a collection by using the @OrderBy annotation. In ActionBazaar, if we want to retrieve Bids in descending order of bidPrice, we can do this:

```
@OneToMany
@OrderBy("order by bidPrice DESC")
public List<Bids> getBids() {
  return bids;
}
```

Ordering of rows is an expensive operation in the database, especially when a lot of rows are retrieved. Therefore, it doesn't always make sense to retrieve the entities in an ordered collection. Unless another sort order is required, let's set the default order using a JPQL query as follows:

```
SELECT b
FROM Bid b
WHERE b.item = ?1
ORDER BY b.bidPrice
```

The database will try to order the matching records by BID_PRICE. We expect your DBA will agree that adding an index on BID_PRICE for the BIDS table will improve query performance.

Using functions in the WHERE clause of JPQL

You can use JPQL functions in the `WHERE` clause of a query. For example, you can create a JPQL query as follows:

```
SELECT u
FROM User u
WHERE upper(u.firstName) = ?1
```

This statement will be translated to SQL as follows:

```
SELECT *
FROM USERS
WHERE UPPER(FIRST_NAME) = ?1
```

Remember that when you use a function in the `WHERE` clause, the database won't use an indexed scan, even if an index exists on the `FIRST_NAME` column. Because of this, you should avoid using functions in the `WHERE` clause. Some databases support creating function-based indexes and you can use them if needed. Just be aware that the function-based indexes may not be portable.

For our example, you could consider storing the names in uppercase instead of using the JPQL `Upper` function.

Reducing round-trips to the database

If your query retrieves a lot of entities, that means a lot of rows are retrieved from the database, and this translates into multiple round-trips between your application and the database. Some JDBC drivers provide facilities to reduce the number of round-trips to the database by setting the number of rows to be prefetched in the middle tier while a result set is being populated. This improves performance of queries that retrieve a large number of rows.

You can pass the JDBC fetch size as a vendor-specific `@QueryHint` in either a named query or dynamic query as follows. If you're using TopLink or Hibernate, you can use `toplink.jdbc.fetch-size` or `org.hibernate.fetchSize`, respectively. The following code snippet demonstrates using `@QueryHint` for Hibernate:

```
@NamedQuery(
name = "findUserWithNoItems",
query = "SELECT distinct u FROM User u WHERE u.items is EMPTY",
hints = {@QueryHint(name = "org.hibernate.fetchSize ", value = "50")}
)
```

Check the documentation for your persistence provider to find out whether setting the JDBC fetch size is supported.

13.2.5 *Caching*

The EJB 3 JPA does not require persistence providers to do any type of caching. On the other hand, one of the primary benefits of using most O/R mapping frameworks is that they provide a certain level of caching to reduce trips to the database. Some people think caching is the solution for every performance problem. The reality is that improper use of caching may lead to stale data and a whole different set of performance issues. Before jumping into using a cache, you need to understand how your vendor supports caching.

In most cases, you can improve performance of your applications with the appropriate use of caching. Most persistence providers support caching either entity objects, queries, or both.

Caching probably makes sense for data that is read-only or is not frequently updated (read-mostly). For example, in ActionBazaar some entities such as `Category` rarely change. Knowing this helps us decide that it makes sense to cache `Catalog` entity objects.

Some queries may always result in the same data within a specific time interval. For example, a named query `findFiveMostPopularItems` may always return the same set of entities for a four- to five-hour interval. You may wish to cache the results of that query because almost all users of ActionBazaar would probably wish to see the most popular items.

The caching types you can use with an EJB 3 JPA provider can be broken into three levels, as shown in figure 13.3.

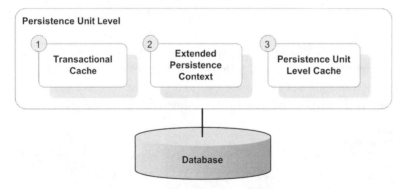

Figure 13.3   You may use caching of objects at three levels: 1) the transactional cache, which is made available by the persistence provider within a transaction to reduce database round-trips; 2) the extended persistence context, which you can use as a caching mechanism with stateful session beans; and 3) the persistence unit level cache (if provided by the persistence provider), which is a shared cache that all clients of the persistence unit can use.

Keep these three levels in mind when evaluating possible options to put in your cache. Try moving items from one cache to another if possible, to determine which configuration works best for your specific application and runtime usage patterns.

Transactional cache

Transactional caching ensures that the object from the cache is returned when the same object is requested again. A typical example is that you run a query that returns an Item entity, and that entity will be cached in the transactional cache. When you use the EntityManager.find method to retrieve the Item again, the persistence provider will return the same Item instance from the transactional cache.

The other benefit of a transactional cache is that all updates to an entity are deferred to the end of the transaction. Imagine what would happen if you did the following in the same transaction:

```
Item item = new Item();
item.setTitle(title);
item.setInitialPrice(initialPrice);
Seller seller = entityManager.find(Seller.class, sellerId);
item.setSeller(seller);
entityManager.persist(item);
item.setInitialPrice(newInitialPrice);
```

If your persistence provider doesn't use a cache and doesn't defer the commit until the end of the transaction, then it probably will perform what translates to at least two SQL statements. First, it will execute a SQL INSERT to persist the Item. This will be followed by a SQL UPDATE to modify the initialPrice. Most persistence providers will make use of a cache and then execute a single INSERT that will take the new price into account.

Hibernate calls this cache its first level or session cache, and TopLink calls it the UnitOfWork cache. Both of these products enable these caches by default. Check whether your persistence provider supports this type of cache. We aren't aware of any reason you'd want to disable the transactional cache.

Using an extended persistence context

The transaction cache will demarcate a single transaction. This could be a problem if your application needs to maintain conversational state between different method calls, since it will require multiple round-trips to the database to retrieve the same entity. You can avoid this situation by using an extended persistence context.

You may remember from our discussions in chapter 9 that only stateful session beans support extended persistence contexts. They allow you to keep entity instances managed beyond single method calls and transaction boundaries. You can use extended persistence context as a cache for your stateful bean instance during the state of conversation, which can reduce the number of round-trips to your database. Additionally, all database updates resulting from persist, merge, remove, and so forth are queued until the end of the persistence context, reducing the number of database operations.

Listing 13.1 shows how you can use an extended persistence context for caching entities between method calls of your application.

Listing 13.1   Using an extended persistence context to cache objects across method calls

```
@Stateful
@TransactionAttribute(TransactionAttributeType.NOT_SUPPORTED)
public class PlaceOrderBean implements PlaceOrder {
@PersistenceContext(unitName = "ActionBazaar",
                    type = PersistenceContextType.EXTENDED)
EntityManager em;

  private Bidder bidder;
  private List<Item> items;                      ❶ Instance variable to
  private ShippingInfo shippingInfo;               hold entities
  private BillingInfo billingInfo;

  public PlaceOrderBean() {
    items = new ArrayList<Item>();
  }

  public void setBidder(String bidderId) {
    this.bidder = em.find(Bidder.class,bidderId);
  }

  public Bidder getBidder(){
    return this.bidder;                          ❷ Methods to set
  }                                                 value of instance
                                                    variables
  public void addItem(Long itemId) {
    Item item = em.find(Item.class,itemId);
    items.add(item);
  }

  public void setShippingInfo(ShippingInfo shippingInfo) {
    this.shippingInfo = shippingInfo;
  }

  public void setBillingInfo(BillingInfo billingInfo) {
    this.billingInfo = billingInfo;
    em.merge(billingInfo);              ❸ Method to merge detached entity
  }
```

```
  @Remove      ⊲—❹  Remove method
  @TransactionAttribute(TransactionAttributeType.REQUIRED)    ⊲┐
  public Long confirmOrder() {                                │
    Order order = new Order();         Transactional          │
    order.setBidder(bidder);               method  ❺          │
    order.setBillingInfo(billingInfo);
    ...
    em.persist(order);
    return order.getOrderId();
  }
}
```

The `PlaceOrderBean` uses an extended `EntityManager` by setting the `Persistence-ContextType` to `EXTENDED`. The persistence context will live during the entire state of conversation and will be destroyed when the bean instance is destroyed or removed ❹. You can store entities as the instance variables of the stateful session bean ❶ and values for the instances are set by different methods ❷, and the entities are managed during the lifespan of the extended `EntityManager` and can be used without having to be detached at the end of the method call. Entity operations such as `merge` ❸ can be performed outside the scope of a transaction since we have set the default transaction attribute for the bean to `NOT_SUPPORTED`. The database updates resulting from these operations are queued up and performed when the persistence context is associated with a transaction ❺. This reduces the number of round-trips to the database.

However, you have to be careful when your stateful session bean invokes another EJB such as a stateless session bean—there are several limitations related to the propagation of extended persistence contexts.

Persistence unit level cache

The transactional and persistence context caching mechanisms can only be used with a single client and cannot be shared. You'll probably see a real performance boost when entity instances in the cache are shared by multiple clients, thus reducing trips to the database for all of them. You can call this an application cache, but we call it a `PersistenceUnit` cache because entities are scoped in a persistence unit. Hibernate calls this a second-level cache, and you need to configure an external cache provider to take advantage of this second level or session factory level cache. TopLink refers to it as a session cache, and it's integrated with the persistence provider. In addition, the TopLink implementation provides several options for configuring this cache. Review your vendor documentation to see whether it provides the ability to cache objects out of the box.

You can either cache entities or queries in the `PersistenceUnit` cache. When you retrieve some entities using a query, those entities will be cached. If you try to retrieve a cached entity by using the `EntityManager`'s `find` method, then the entity instance will be returned from the cache. Typically, persistence providers store the entities in the cache using their identities, so you must use the `find` method to retrieve an entity by its primary key.

If your EJB 3 persistence provider supports caching of entities in a `Persistence-Unit` cache, it is probably done with a vendor-specific name-value pair of properties in a configuration file. In the following example we are trying to cache `5000` instances of the `Category` entity in TopLink Essentials:

```
<persistence>
  <persistence-unit name = "actionBazaar">
    ...
    <properties>
      <property name = "toplink.cache.type.Category"
                value = "CacheType.Softweak"/>
      <property name = "toplink.cache.size.Category"
                value = "5000"/>
    </properties>
  </persistence-unit>
</persistence>
```

If you want to cache a query result, then you probably want to do it on a per-query basis, either stored in an external configuration or as a `QueryHint` for the query. Check your persistence provider documentation to determine how it supports the caching of queries.

Here is an example of how TopLink Essentials can be used for caching in a named query using `@QueryHint`:

```
@NamedQuery(
  name = "findActiveCategory",
  query = "SELECT c FROM Category c WHERE c.status = 'Active",
  hints = {@QueryHint(name = "toplink.cache-usage",
                      value = "CheckCacheOnly")}
  )
```

You can also provide a hint to refresh the cache from the database with a query like this:

```
Set<Category> category = (Category)
  em.createNamedQuery("findActiveCategory")
      .setHint("toplink.refresh", "true")
    .getResultList();
```

Now that you have seen some examples of caching, let's discuss some caching best practices.

Read-only entities

You can significantly improve application performance by using read-only entities. Examine your applications to determine whether any entities may be made read-only. For example, in our ActionBazaar system, office locations change very rarely and we can make the `ShippingType` entity read-only. Unfortunately, like caching features, the read-only feature is a vendor extension and you have to depend on either a vendor-specific API or configuration to mark an entity as read-only. Normally, read-only entity instances will be loaded into the `PersistenceUnit` cache and never discarded.

Read-only entities will significantly improve performance because persistence providers won't calculate the change set for the read-only entity, and no clone or merge operations will be performed against a read-only entity.

Caching best practices

Understanding your applications and checking your caching strategy usually makes sense for your applications. The cache is best used for entities that are not frequently updated or that are read only. Make sure that table data is updated only by the application that is using the cache, because if any external applications update the same cache, someone working with the cache will end up with stale data.

Check your persistence provider for details on how they support caching entities and queries; the caching mechanism varies from provider to provider. For example, one provider may follow this rule: if an entity is updated in a transaction, then the entity will be updated in the cache when the transaction is committed to the database. However, some persistence providers may choose to expire the cache instead.

Stress-test your applications with and without a cache. It's the only way to determine if using the cache, and more specifically the particular cache configuration, will improve or degrade your applications' performance.

That concludes our discussion on improving EJB 3 entity performance. Are you feeling faster yet? Even if you're not, your entities should be. Next, let's look at how you can improve the performance of session and message-driven beans.

13.3 Improving performance of EJB 3 components

Most application servers provide the ability to generate usage and utilization statistics of EJB components such as session beans and MDBs grouped by application. You have to read your vendor documentation about the parameters they provide, and you have to work through some amount of trial and error to utilize these parameters optimally to improve the performance of your EJB components.

This section provides general guidelines, some of which are design practices that you can follow while building your applications. As stated earlier, it's a good idea to factor in performance considerations throughout the development lifecycle of your applications. Don't try to do it all up front, because you'll end up with a more complicated design than you need, and it's going to change anyway at multiple points during the life of the system. Don't try to do it all at the end, because you'll have to make sweeping changes in order to effectively implement the required optimizations. Follow the same strategy you would to fill your car's fuel tank; a little at a time over the life of the vehicle. Sometimes you top the tank off, and sometimes you just get $10 worth. (All right, with today's prices maybe $25.) But you don't calculate how many miles you will ever drive the car and try to carry around that much gas when you buy it. And you certainly don't wait until you want to sell the vehicle before buying any gas; it wouldn't be much use as a form of transportation if you took that approach. Simply think about where you're going in the near future, and buy that much gas. Tackle performance tuning in the same way, and you'll be on your way to a bunch of happy users.

We've already covered performance concerns surrounding entities. Let's see what we can do to make our session and message-driven beans a little snappier.

13.3.1 Session bean performance

Session beans are probably the most frequently used EJB component. Like the teenyboppers vying for a spot on *American Idol*, they're everywhere. It's hard to visit a Java EE application and not hit one. Even with the tremendous pull that alternative inversion-of-control containers like Spring have had, session EJBs live on. Since you're likely to trip over one getting to your Dilbert cube in the morning, this section will focus on how you can improve session bean performance.

Local vs. remote interface

EJB 3 not only provides the ability to invoke components remotely, but also empowers you to build lightweight components that can be deployed and run locally with your presentation modules. If your clients and EJB components are collocated together, then you must make sure you do not mark your interface with the @Remote annotation. @Remote uses an expensive RMI call requiring copy-by-value semantics, even if the clients are in the same JVM. Most containers provide optimizations to change RMI calls to local EJB invocation when possible by setting some attributes in your vendor-specific deployment descriptor. Refer to your application server documentation for details about your specific server.

Use stateful session beans only when necessary

We have observed gross misuse of stateful session beans, which causes developers to become disappointed with their performance. Most enterprise applications are stateless in nature, so you should determine whether you need stateful session beans. Stateless session beans perform much better than stateful session beans since they are not required to manage state. The extended persistence context is supported only with EJB 3 stateful session beans, and there is no way out if you want to use it. Later in this chapter we provide some guidelines to specifically improve performance of stateful session beans.

Refactor multiple method calls to use the Session Façade design pattern

EJB invocation is expensive, particularly when you use it remotely. You should avoid building fine-grained EJBs by following the Session Façade design pattern. Check to see whether you can consolidate several EJB methods into a single coarse-grained EJB method. Reducing multiple method calls to a single call will improve the performance of your EJB applications.

Look at transaction attribute settings

Recall from chapter 6 that transaction management is an expensive affair. Verify that each EJB method really needs a transaction. If you are using CMT (by default), the container will start a transaction for you because the default transaction attribute is `Required`. For methods that don't require a transaction, you should explicitly disable transactions by setting the transaction type to `NOT_SUPPORTED` as follows:

```
@TransactionAttribute(TransactionAttributeType.NOT_SUPPORTED)
public List<Item> findMostPopularItems() {
   ...
}
```

If you are confused about which transaction options are available, refer to chapter 6, or consult your application server's documentation.

Optimize the stateless bean pool

Stateless session bean instances are pooled and shared by clients. You should have sufficient bean instances to serve all your concurrent clients. If you don't have enough bean instances in the pool, the client will block until an instance is available. Most application servers provide the ability to configure the bean pool in a vendor-specific deployment descriptor by specifying a value for the minimum and maximum number of instances to be kept in the bean pool. Keeping it too low will create contention issues, whereas keeping it too high may consume excessive memory. Use the "Goldilocks" principle here, and try to get the minimum/maximum range "just right."

The stateful bean cache and passivation

A stateful bean is associated with a specific client. When a client needs a bean instance, the container creates a bean instance for it. However, the container cannot maintain an infinite number of active bean instances in memory while constantly passivating bean instances that are not actively being used. The container serializes all instance variables stored in a stateful bean and writes the bean's state into secondary storage (an external file) when it decides to passivate the bean instance. The passivated bean instance is activated or brought back into memory when the associated client invokes a method on a bean instance that has been temporarily pushed out of the cache. Unnecessary passivation and activation will slow down the performance of your applications. Investigate your server's configuration options in order to properly set the bean cache or passivation policy so that frequent passivation and activation is avoided.

Use a remove method for stateful beans

You must destroy a stateful bean instance by using the `@Remove` annotation when the conversation ends. As explained in chapter 3, any business method can be annotated with `@Remove` so that upon successful completion of that business method, the bean instance will be destroyed. Take a look at `confirmOrder`:

```
@Remove
public Long confirmOrder() {
}
```

If you do not remove stateful bean instances when they are no longer needed, then the number of inactive (essentially dead) instances will grow, forcing passivation/activation in the container.

In addition to `@Remove`, most containers provide the ability to time out and destroy a bean instance by setting an expiration time in the vendor-specific deployment descriptor. This timeout can be used to help keep the number of bean instances to a manageable number. Its purpose is to set a timer for beans that are not used by clients for longer than the specified expiration time. We recommend you take advantage of this timeout to reduce the time that unused bean instances hang around, soaking up space.

Control serialization by making variables transient

As stated earlier, the container performs serialization and deserialization of instance variables during passivation and activation. Serialization and deserialization are expensive processes. When you store large objects in your instance variables, the server spends a lot of CPU cycles and memory in the serialization and deserialization process. If you don't want to serialize a particular object, mark that object to be a transient object and the container will skip that object during passivation/activation.

```
@Stateful
public class PlaceOrderBean implements PlaceOrder {
  transient private Bidder bidder;
  private List<Item> items;
  private ShippingInfo shippingInfo;
  private BillingInfo billingInfo;
  ..
}
```

Here we have defined `bidder` as a `transient` object and the EJB container will not serialize the `bidder` object when a bean instance gets passivated or when its state is replicated to another server. If after marking several fields as `transient` you observe data missing from your objects, it simply means that you went a little overboard and will need to undo some of the fields you marked as `transient`.

13.3.2 *Improving MDB performance*

The following are some guidelines that you can use to optimize the performance of your MDB applications. We provided some MDB best practices in chapter 5 that you can use as a starting point. After implementing those techniques, you may want to revisit this section for some additional tips.

Tuning the JMS provider

Most of the performance issues surrounding MDBs are generally related to the underlying JMS providers. Some general tips that we provided in chapter 4 include choosing the right messaging models and persistence strategy, using the correctly sized messages, setting the lifetime of messages, and using appropriate filters and handling of poison messages. Check your vendor documentation for the JMS provider you are using for your applications.

Initializing resources

Like stateless session beans, MDB instances are pooled, and initialization tasks are performed only once, for any given MDB instance. You can perform expensive tasks such as initialization of resources (opening database connections, sockets, files, etc.) in any method annotated with `@PostConstruct`. Methods marked with `@PostConstruct` will be invoked only once, immediately after creation. Similarly, close any resources in methods annotated with `@PreDestroy`. This will significantly improve the performance of your classes in general, and your MDBs in particular.

Sizing the pool

MDBs are pooled, and the pool size is usually configured using vendor-specific deployment descriptors. Improper sizing of MDB pools may degrade performance of your applications when large numbers of messages arrive and there is not a sufficient number of bean instances available to process those messages.

Make sure you do some predictive analysis in determining the capacity your system will need to support (including spikes, and growth over the short term). Then run some tests that will show how your hardware, operating system, and application server will perform to meet these expectations. There are almost as many ways to configure hardware and operating systems as there are combinations of the two. Once you are happy with that configuration, make sure your application server pool for MDBs is sized as well.

This concludes the discussion on EJB performance. It's time to focus on scalability and high availability, which are two other important aspects of enterprise applications.

13.4 Clustering EJB applications

High availability and scalability go hand in hand. Every application has some requirement for availability and scalability, and meeting those requirements begins when you start architecting the application. Availability requirements can vary widely. Some applications, say a human resources (HR) application, may have a requirement to be available only during normal business hours. On the other hand, an online bidding system may have a requirement to be available 24/7, year-round. Similarly, the scalability requirements for an HR application may not be as demanding as an online bidding system.

The EJB 3 specification doesn't address clustering aspects for EJB applications. However, most application server vendors allow customers to cluster EJB containers to achieve the desired scalability and availability aspects required by today's demanding enterprise applications. Before we dive into such architectural concerns, let's discuss a couple of concepts that will help you understand the basic aspects of EJB clustering:

- *Load balancing*—This is when multiple application server instances work as a group to balance the incoming request load across all the servers. This allows for scalability of applications. When your user base increases, you can simply add new server instances to the group. This is typically most useful when your application is stateless in nature.

- *Failover*—Adding failover capability to your applications improves the availability of your applications. Clients typically get bound to a specific server instance by stateful applications. In the event of a catastrophic failure of a server, the client requests are routed to a separate server in a seamless manner, transparent to the user.

Clustering of EJB applications adds load balancing and failover capabilities to your applications. Covering all aspects of clustering is beyond the scope of this book. In this section we'll provide architectural primers, and focus on the knowledge you need to effectively build scalable, available EJB applications.

There are several ways to deploy EJB applications. We'll discuss three commonly used approaches. We won't describe any configuration details related to clustering because clustering tends to be vendor specific.

13.4.1 Collocated architecture

This popular architecture is where EJB applications and their clients (web applications) are hosted in the same container, and typically the HTTP requests are load-balanced between multiple instances of application servers. If your application is stateless in nature, then you probably don't have to do anything except deploy the identical application on multiple servers, as illustrated in figure 13.4.

If your application requires statefulness and you want to achieve session failover, then you must enable HTTP and EJB session state replication, which allows you to replicate HTTP session objects between two server instances. This is done so that if one instance fails, the client doesn't lose the session state. If your business logic is stateless in nature, this is something you don't have to worry about. Your application will work as expected when your sessions fail over to another container, assuming the identical application is deployed.

If you are using stateful session beans to store session objects, then things will be a little trickier here. As mentioned in chapter 12, you should store the EJB

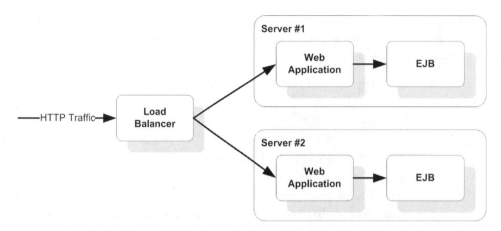

Figure 13.4   EJB(s) and web applications are collocated, and web applications use the local EJB interface to access the nearby EJBs.

object in the `HttpSession` object. Check your vendor documentation before you start developing your applications, because it will avoid frantic refactoring of code the day before you release everything to production.

You have to enable session replication for your application server; that way, when a session failover occurs, the client will be routed to another server instance where the HTTP session was replicated. The `HttpSession` object will be restored and the client can retrieve the EJB object to perform the necessary operations. Some vendors may not allow replication of local EJB stateful session beans, so check your vendor documentation. You may have to use the remote interface, even if the client and bean are collocated in the same Java EE container in order to enable session replication.

What happens when multiple instances of your application are required in order to divide the web and EJB tiers into different containers? Next we'll see how EJB containers support load balancing of stateless EJBs.

13.4.2   *Load-balancing stateless session beans*

Your clients may be located remotely from the EJB container. The clients may be JSF or JSP applications running in a separate container, or Swing/SWT clients running in an application client container. You must realize that when dividing EJBs and their clients into separate JVMs, you are imposing a condition that Remote Method Invocation (RMI) be used to communicate between them. If you plan to use this architecture, you'll have to use remote interfaces for your EJBs.

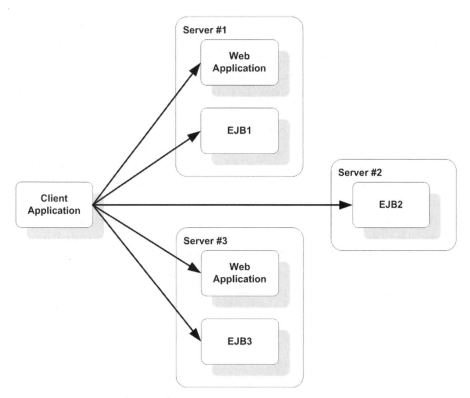

Figure 13.5 **EJB and web applications are in separate JVMs. Clients access EJBs using the remote interface via RMI. The same EJB application can be deployed to multiple servers.**

Most application servers support load balancing of requests between multiple application server instances. When using this architecture, the same application is deployed in all instances. Since the EJBs are stateless, the client can go to any of the servers being load-balanced, as seen in figure 13.5.

If you want to use load balancing of stateless session beans deployed in a cluster, you need a basic understanding of RMI and remote invocation of an EJB. We briefly discussed RMI in chapter 1. Figure 13.6 shows how remote invocation of an EJB works.

Figure 13.6 **The skeleton in the EJB server gives out a stub to the client. This stub is used by the client to communicate with the EJB remotely.**

As evident from figure 13.6, the client stub has the information on how to communicate to the remote EJB server. Most application servers automatically generate the client stub while looking up an EJB remotely.

This information is commonly based on the JNDI environments, which are populated while creating the InitialContext. You typically provide this in a jndi.properties file. If you remember our discussion from chapter 1, you provide the URL for the server that hosts the EJB we are accessing.

Again, because EJB clustering is considered a proprietary enhancement, each application server implements it in its own way. That way, the application server knows the load-balancing algorithm and the servers being load-balanced. An example of this appears in figure 13.7.

A remote EJB lookup requires that you specify a JNDI provider URL for a JNDI server. The client looks up the EJB and downloads the client stub. The stub contains information about all the servers being load-balanced, as well as the load-balancing algorithm being used. Once more, check your vendor documentation for the various JNDI properties that you need for creating the InitialContext. You may have to do some configuration in your EJB applications to enable load balancing between different application server instances.

If you want to use load balancing for stateless session beans, as a developer you'll have to do the following:

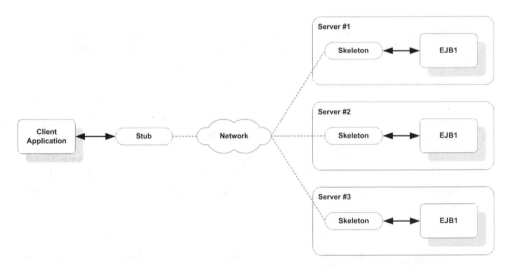

Figure 13.7 The stub that is downloaded by the client is instrumented with the load-balancing algorithm and has knowledge of the load-balancing servers.

- Build a remote interface for your stateless session bean and expose the appropriate methods in the remote interface.

- Reduce the number of method invocations by using a coarse-grained session bean.

- Make appropriate configurations using the vendor-specific deployment descriptors if required.

- Because the client code for the EJB needs to know that you are using clustered application server instances, provide the URL for the clustered JNDI server or application server.

The disadvantage of this approach is that it will only work for stateless applications, not when using stateful session beans. We tackle that situation next!

13.4.3 *Clustering stateful session beans*

As you know, stateful session beans are used to maintain conversation state between the client and server by storing the state in instance variables. If you want end-to-end availability for your applications, then you have to maintain state. You probably also want session state to be replicated to other servers, so that if one server crashes the client state is restored from another server, as shown in figure 13.8. Assume that when a client accesses a stateful session bean in a cluster it gets bound to a stateful EJB in Server 2. It establishes a conversation, and state is stored in the bean instance in Server 2. Because we have session state replication enabled for the EJB, the state is replicated to Server 1 and Server 3. If Server 2 should happen to crash, then the client will be routed to one of the other servers and the conversation state will be restored.

Application servers support several mechanisms to propagate changes in the session state, such as IP multicasting peers and peer-to-peer. The session state change is copied to other servers in the group when one of the following occurs:

- At regular intervals (such as the end of every method call)
- When a JVM is terminated
- At the end of a transaction

Refer to your vendor documentation to learn what propagation mechanisms are supported for session replication. Additionally, you have to make changes in your session bean configuration using either a proprietary annotation or a deployment descriptor to enable session replication. This will set the appropriate propagation mechanism for your session bean. To expedite the configuration process,

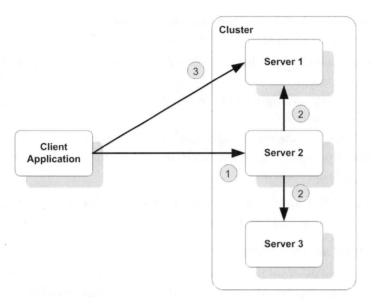

Figure 13.8 Session state is replicated to other servers based on the server: 1) clients establish a session with a stateful bean in Server 2; 2) conversation state is replicated to Server 1 and Server 3 because state replication is enabled; and 3) if Server 2 crashes, the client gets routed to either Server 1 or Server 3 and there will be no loss in its state.

we recommend that you check your vendor's documentation before you implement stateful session bean clustering.

Here are some best practices we recommend to developers for using stateful session bean clustering:

- Check whether you really need stateful session beans and have to replicate the session for them. Stateful session bean replication requires expensive serialization, propagation of the serialization, and deserialization of the session state.

- Make sure any required session state is minimal. Most vendors recommend that you not store stateful objects larger than 4KB. When storing a state, it is better to store a key rather than a large entity object in the session state. Perform some testing on your applications if you think you need more state than this. The common technique to get around the 4KB limit is to store only one or more session keys in the state, and use these to retrieve the larger data on the server where it is used.

- Don't hard-code any vendor-specific annotations to enable session replication. Instead, use vendor-specific deployment descriptors.

- The client code for an EJB needs to know that you are using clustered application server instances and enabling session replication. Therefore, you have to provide the URL for the clustered JNDI server or application server that knows about this information.

13.4.4 *Entities and clustered cache*

Section 13.3 covered how you can enable caching for your persistence unit if you want to enhance the performance of your applications. However, if you are using the same entities in multiple server instances, then each instance has its own cache. It is highly likely that your cache may become stale or out of synch with the actual data when a client writes to the database. If you are using entities in an enterprise application and you want to make the application readily available, then you must have some mechanism to synchronize the cache between different server instances. The approach we'll discuss is depicted in figure 13.9.

Because EJB 3 JPA implementations are new, very few application servers will provide this feature. At the time of this writing, only JBoss's and Oracle's implementations provided support for distributed cache synchronization.

It's a very challenging task to synchronize the cache for a large distributed application, and this becomes nearly impossible when you have a large number of server nodes. You must keep this in perspective when designing the application. The persistence providers typically depend on the clustering configuration of the application servers, which may use IP multicasting, RMI, or JMS to synchronize the caches. Check your vendor documentation for their level of support.

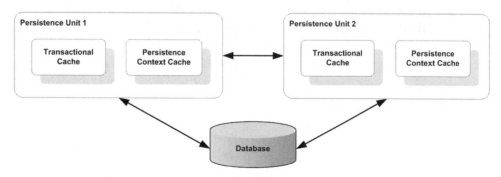

Figure 13.9 Distributed cache synchronization is used to synchronize the entity cache between two different Java EE containers.

Remember to

- Determine whether you really need distributed cache synchronization. Check your vendor documentation to see whether it is supported.

- Analyze your refresh policy. Caching and refreshing queries may not yield the best results in a distributed cache situation.

- Confirm whether the caching solution provides a distributed transactional guarantee. Compare your persistence provider's support against commercial caching solutions such as Tangosol's Coherence. Using a distributed cache is not recommended in a highly transactional system. It is difficult to achieve good performance from a distributed cache.

13.5 *Summary*

In this chapter we provided several guidelines to tame those wild EJBs. First, we discussed various types of locking strategies. The EJB 3 JPA specification requires support for optimistic locking of entities.

We then turned our attention to entity tuning. You can improve performance of your persistence tier by making some modeling and/or schema changes, writing appropriate queries, and working with your DBAs to create appropriate indexes for your database. Persistence providers use caching to reduce roundtrips to the database, and you may benefit from using an appropriate caching strategy to increase your entity performance.

We explored several ways to optimize the performance of session beans and MDBs. We also surveyed the scalability and availability landscape. EJB clustering is not covered in the specification, and we encourage you to evaluate the clustering support in the application server of your choice.

The next chapter considers EJB 3 migration and interoperability issues.

Part 5

Migration and interoperability issues

In the final part of this book, we explore some of the issues you are bound to come across while using EJB 3 in the real world. These advanced topics are primarily geared toward migration, system integration, and interoperability.

If you are already using EJB 2 and are looking at EJB 3, chapter 14 is critically important to you. The chapter discusses migrating from EJB 2 to EJB 3 in great detail. We first see how EJB 2 and EJB 3 can coexist in the short run if necessary. We then look at migrating EJB 2 session beans and MDBs to EJB 3, followed by migrating applications using EJB 2 CMP entity beans, JDBC DAOs, and proprietary O/R frameworks such as Hibernate/TopLink to JPA.

In chapter 15, we move on to the red-hot topic of enabling interoperability through web services. In this chapter we show you how EJB 3 and web services can help integrate Java EE with other disparate technologies such as Microsoft .NET. You'll learn how EJB 3 and web services relate to each other and how stateless session beans can be exposed as web services utilizing Java XML Web Service (JAX-WS) 2.0 support.

Finally, we tackle what very well might be the most intriguing topic of the book: Spring and EJB 3. EJB 3 and the Spring framework are often viewed as competing frameworks. In chapter 16, we present a slightly different take on things. We show you how EJB 3 opens the door to the possibility of integrating with Spring in several ways and combining the power of both of these technologies.

14
Migrating to EJB 3

This chapter covers

- Migrating session beans and MDBs
- Migrating CMP entity beans
- Migrating JDBC DAO and O/R frameworks

In today's IT world, migration has become an integral part of the application development lifecycle. Software products and technology change every few years, requiring the migration of applications from one platform (or one version) to another. From a budget standpoint, migration is certainly less expensive than rebuilding applications, and thus easier to justify to management. IT shops normally migrate their applications to increase their longevity and improve maintainability. Countless applications have been written using EJB 2 and many of these applications will be migrated to use EJB 3. Many customers who have built their persistence tier using JDBC, JDO, or O/R frameworks like Hibernate or TopLink will be migrating to the EJB 3 JPA, since it is the new industry-standard persistence API for the Java platform. Some companies may only be able to justify migrating a portion of their applications to EJB 3, leaving others living in an EJB 2 world. This will introduce a new wave of interoperability issues.

In this chapter we look at the compatibility, interoperability, and migration issues that will surface as you migrate to EJB 3. You may be under the gun to migrate your applications to EJB 3; this may even be the first chapter you're reading in this book. Be advised that you should not consider this chapter the sole reference for all migration issues, although we'll try to address the more common scenarios that you're likely to encounter.

This chapter assumes some familiarity with EJB 2. Once more, we'll use the ActionBazaar application to illustrate migration to EJB 3. Forget for a while that you built ActionBazaar using EJB 3, and pretend that it was originally developed using varieties of EJB 2 technologies such as session beans and CMP entity beans.

14.1 Backward compatibility and interoperability with EJB 2

Up to this point in the book we have focused almost exclusively on EJB 3. If you've used EJB 2 you realize that there have been drastic changes between the two versions. You may be wondering what will happen to your application when you deploy to a container that supports EJB 3. You might also be wondering what will happen if you have two EJB 2 applications that interact with each other when you migrate one of them to EJB 3. Let us put your mind at ease.

The EJB 3 specification requires that all complying containers support EJB 2. This should help relieve any concern as far as upgrading from your existing application server to one that is EJB 3 compliant. However, it seems likely that you will need to do something to make your old apps work in the shiny new EJB 3 app server, and you'll want to make some changes that allow them to talk to newly minted EJB 3 apps. In this section we'll explore what it will take to package applications and invoke components that contain EJBs from both versions.

14.1.1 *Packaging EJB 2 and EJB 3 together*

Unless you're in the enviable situation of conducting green-field development with EJB 3, there is a chance your EJB 3 application will need to peacefully coexist with your EJB 2 applications and components, and vice versa. More than that, you'll probably want them to work together, interoperating with each other.

Now there are several possibilities for using EJB 2 and EJB 3 together. Maybe you have decided to migrate a selected group of application components to EJB 3, while leaving some components in earlier versions as a part of an incremental migration. Another common case is where a newly developed EJB 3 application wants to leverage an existing EJB 2 component. Yet another instance could be that the developers decide to migrate the persistence tier of ActionBazaar built using CMP 2 to use the EJB 3 JPA, leaving all the session beans and MDBs implemented in EJB 2. A less likely but possible case is that you decide to move the business logic tier of your applications to EJB 3, and leave the persistence tier built with CMP 2 untouched. EJB 3 supports all these scenarios and makes the EJB 3 JPA available for use with session beans and MDBs built using EJB 2.

The first EJB 3 migration item to be aware of is that if you want to package both EJB 2–style beans and EJB 3 beans and JPA entities in the same EJB module, then you must set the `version` attribute of the `ejb-jar` module to `3.0` as follows:

```
<?xml version = '1.0' encoding = 'windows-1252'?>
<ejb-jar version="3.0"                                          ⊲──┐ ejb-jar version 3.0
   xmlns:xsi=http://www.w3.org/2001/XMLSchema-instance              required
   xsi:schemaLocation="http://java.sun.com/xml/ns/j2ee
   http://java.sun.com/xml/ns/j2ee/ejb-jar_3_0.xsd">
...
</ejb-jar>
```

If you specify a version other than `3.0` (e.g., `2.1`), then the EJB container will assume the EJB module is an older version and won't scan for annotations. This means it won't detect EJB 3 beans, or detect the persistence unit containing entities packaged in the EJB module. Make sure that `version` is either set to `3.0` or not specified at all.

14.1.2 *Invoking EJB 2 from EJB 3*

You can invoke EJB 2 session or entity beans from EJB 3 session beans or MDBs. You can even use dependency injection to invoke an EJB 2 bean. To illustrate the latter, assume that you have an EJB 2 bean (ChargeCredit) that charges a credit card. Use the @EJB annotation to inject an instance of a home object for ChargeCredit in an EJB 3 POJO like this:

```
@Stateful
public PlaceOrderBean implements PlaceOrder {
..
@EJB
public ChargeCreditHome creditHome;
..
void chargeCreditCard(){
...
ChargeCredit chargeCredit
                  = creditHome.create();
String confirmationNo
        = chargeCredit.add(billingInfo, amount);
..
}
```

ChargeCredit and ChargeCreditHome are the remote and home interfaces, respectively, of ChargeCreditEJB. Use the create method to get a reference to the remote interface, and then invoke the desired business method (in this case add) on the bean. As you can see from this example, EJB 3 supports the EJB 2 concepts, and the programming model is straightforward.

If, instead of calling an EJB 2 session bean you'd like to invoke an EJB 2 CMP entity bean from EJB 3, you'd follow a similar approach to the previous example. Assume that ActionBazaar used EJB 2 CMP entity beans for its persistence tier. The specific case we'll discuss is one in which the PlaceBid EJB persists the Bid bean as follows:

```
@Stateless
public PlaceBidBean implements PlaceBid {
   ...
   @EJB
   public BidLocalHome bidLocalHome;
   ...
   BidLocal bidLocal = bidLocalHome.create(BidDTO);
   ...
}
```

In this example, we create a bean instance (BidDTO) by using a data transfer object (DTO). We'll discuss the DTO design pattern in section 14.3, but essentially the

DTO is used to transfer business object state, not necessarily behavior, across application tiers. Recall that creating an entity bean instance will ask the container to persist the bean instance in the database.

That covers calling EJB 2 from EJB 3, but what about the other way around? Read the next section to solve this mind-numbing mystery… actually, there's nothing mind-numbing about it—it's almost as simple as what we just covered. Go ahead—see for yourself.

14.1.3 Using EJB 3 from EJB 2

You can use both EJB 3 session beans and the EJB 3 JPA from EJB 2 applications. Although there were some discussions in the EJB 3 Expert Group on adding support for dependency injection for EJB 2–style beans, the EJB 3 spec does not require support for injection with EJB 2 (although some vendors may decide to provide it). If your server does not support EJB 2 dependency injection, you must use good old-fashioned JNDI lookup to access EJB 3 session beans and the EJB 3 `EntityManager` from EJB 2 beans. This is shown in figure 14.1.

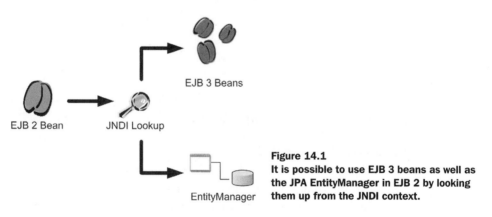

Figure 14.1
It is possible to use EJB 3 beans as well as the JPA EntityManager in EJB 2 by looking them up from the JNDI context.

The method is similar to using EJB 3 beans or JPA using JNDI lookup (which we discussed in chapter 12).

Using EJB 3 session beans from EJB 2

Pretend for a moment that the `PlaceBid` EJB is an EJB 2 session bean that invokes `CheckCredit` in a partner application, KabadiBazaar, but that `CheckCredit` is an EJB 3 session bean. You must have an `ejb-ref` or `ejb-local-ref` element in the `ejb-jar.xml` to establish the reference to the `CheckCredit` EJB as follows:

```
<session>
  <ejb-name>PlaceBidBean</ejb-name>
  <home>actionbazaar.buslogic.PlaceBidHome</home>
  <remote>actionbazaar.buslogic.PlaceBid</remote>
  <ejb-class>actionbazaar.buslogic.PlaceBidBean</ejb-class>
  <session-type>stateless</session-type>
  ...
  <ejb-local-ref>
    <ejb-ref-name>ejb/CheckCredit</ejb-ref-name>
    <ejb-ref-type>Session</ejb-ref-type>
    <local>kabadibazaar.buslogic.CheckCredit</local>
    <ejb-link>kabadibazaar-ejb.jar#CheckCreditBean</ejb-link>
  </ejb-local-ref>
</session>
```

The only difference between the standard deployment descriptor and this one is that the ejb-local-ref element does not have a local-home element. This is because the EJB 3 session bean does not require a home interface. In your application you can use JNDI to look up remote beans with ref-name as follows:

```
public class PlaceBidBean implements SessionBean { //EJB 2 bean
  ...
  public void addBid(Bidder user, double amount) {
    CheckCredit checkCredit = (CheckCredit)
      context.lookup("java:comp/env/ejb/CheckCredit");      ◁⎯ JNDI lookup
        checkCredit.addBid(user, amount);    }


@Stateless
public class CheckCreditBean implements CheckCredit{//EJB 3 bean}
```

The JNDI lookup is identical whether you're using EJB 2 or EJB 3.

Using the EJB 3 JPA from EJB 2

You can use either a container- or an application-managed EntityManager in your EJB 2 beans. Assume that ActionBazaar migrated only the persistence tier to JPA. To use the container-managed EntityManager from an EJB 2 bean, you'd define the persistence-context-ref for the EJB 2 bean as follows:

```
<session>
  <ejb-name>PlaceBidBean</ejb-name>
  ...
  <persistence-context-ref>
    <persistence-context-ref-name>
      ActionBazaarEntityManager
    </persistence-context-ref-name>
    <persistence-unit-name>actionBazaar</persistence-unit-name>
  </persistence-context-ref>
</session>
```

Next, you would look up an instance of a container-managed `EntityManager` via JNDI as follows:

```
Context context = new InitialContext();
EntityManager entityManager = (EntityManager)
  context.lookup("java:comp/env/ActionBazaarEntityManager");
...
entityManager.persist(bid);
```

Notice that this JNDI lookup appears to be like all the others in the book. The only special thing you would have to do is to package a `persistence.xml` that describes the persistence unit and set `version="3.0"` in the `ejb-jar.xml`. It's starting to look familiar, isn't it? Using EJB 3 from EJB 2 boils down to

- Making some modifications to your deployment descriptors
- Working a little JNDI magic to get object references (if your server doesn't support dependency injection for EJB 2)

That's all there is to it! It's so simple that this concludes our discussion on backward compatibility and interoperability of EJB applications.

> **NOTE** The EJB specification requires that an EJB container be interoperable with CORBA applications using RMI-IIOP. While this is possible, we don't think this is commonly used so we won't discuss it in this chapter. If your application requires interoperability with CORBA, we suggest you explore this on your own by referring to the EJB 3 Core Contracts specification.

The new way to achieve interoperability with heterogeneous systems is web services. In chapter 15 we discuss exposing EJB 3 stateless session beans as web services and invoking web services from EJB 3 applications. But that's a whole chapter away, and we're not through talking about migration yet. Let's see; we've talked a bit about swapping bean invocations between EJB 2 and EJB 3—what do you say we explore how to migrate session beans next?

14.2 *Migrating session beans*

If you're using EJB 2 session beans (which will be supported for a while by many major vendors), why you would migrate to EJB 3? Here area few reasons that come to mind:

- You may be releasing a new version of your application and you want to take advantage of new EJB 3 features such as interceptors and dependency injection.

- Migrating beans to use EJB 3 will simplify your code and improve maintainability of your application. Because EJB 3 is POJO based, you can also simplify your unit tests.

- Migrating your applications will renew your applications for a few more years.

Migrating session beans to EJB 3 is quite easy because it is as simple as

- Pruning the existing EJB code to make it a POJO
- Defining at least one business interface
- Using annotations instead of a deployment descriptor
- Replacing redundant JNDI code with dependency injection

The remainder of this section further breaks down the details involved in migrating session beans from EJB 2 to EJB 3.

14.2.1 *Converting interface and bean classes*

An EJB 2 session bean has at least one component interface (local or remote), one home interface, and one bean class. The component and home interfaces extend the EJB-specific interfaces, while the bean class implements the `javax.ejb.SessionBean` interface. After you migrate your bean to EJB 3, it is a POJO and the bean class implements its business interfaces. Table 14.1 summarizes the changes between EJB 2.1 and EJB 3.

Table 14.1 EJB 2 required many interfaces that needed to extend EJB-specific interfaces. EJB 3 makes the home interface optional.

Components of a Session Bean	EJB 2	EJB 3
Remote or local component interface	Extends either `EJBObject` or `EJBLocalObject`	Business interface (POJI).
Home interface	Extends `EJBHome` or `EJBLocalHome`	Optional for maintaining EJB 2 client view. Candidate for removal.
Bean class	Implements `javax.ejb.SessionBean`	Implements business interface.

Given that the home interface is optional, you can consider it deprecated. We recommend you begin the process of making the shift away from the home interface in both your thinking as well as your code. More on removing the home interface in the sections ahead...

Interfaces

If you need to migrate your component interfaces, we've got just the recipe; you'll have to make the following changes:

- Your component interface (remote or local) becomes a regular business interface. In other words, it does not extend one of the EJB interfaces.

- Your business methods don't have to throw unnecessary exceptions such as `RemoteException`.

Figure 14.2 summarizes these differences.

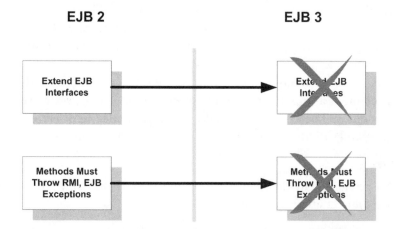

Figure 14.2 The changes necessary to migrate EJB 2 business interfaces to EJB 3. You do not have to extend EJB-specific interfaces or throw RMI or EJB exceptions in the methods.

Let's walk through this modification with an example. Consider the following remote interface of the `PlaceBid` EJB using EJB 2:

```
public interface PlaceBid extends EJBObject {
   public Long addBid(String userId, Long itemId, Double bidPrice)
     throws RemoteException,
     CreateException,
     FinderException,
```

```
        NamingException;
}
```

The `addBid` method throws `CreateException` and `FinderException` because the bean class uses CMP 2 entity beans and throws `NamingException` because it uses JNDI.

After migration to EJB 3, the remote interface will look like this:

```
@Remote
public interface PlaceBid {
  public Long addBid(String userId, Long itemId, Double bidPrice);
}
```

Ah, that's better, isn't it? This code assumes that we have migrated the EJB 2 CMP entity beans to use the EJB 3 JPA and are no longer required to throw `Finder-Exception` and `CreateException`. In addition, we've defined the interface as a remote business interface with the annotation `@Remote`.

Unless you need the home interface (also known as adapted home) for backward compatibility with EJB 2 clients, you probably won't need it, so seriously consider removing it. We'll explain how to use the home interface with the EJB 3 session bean, if for some reason you're unable to migrate a client application that is dependent on your EJB.

If you decide to use a deployment descriptor, then you must remove the `home` or `local-home` element and not have a home interface; otherwise, your EJB module will fail to deploy. The container should generate deployment errors if you forget to do this, and will identify the line number in the deployment descriptor.

The bean class

Migration of a session bean class is just as straightforward as component interfaces. Here are some changes you'll need to make:

- Your bean class doesn't have to implement the `javax.ejb.SessionBean` interface. Just make the bean a POJO and have it implement the business interface.

- You don't have to implement unnecessary lifecycle methods. Furthermore, can use any method name you want for your lifecycle methods, and you can use annotations to mark which methods are lifecycle methods. Table 14.2 provides a list of EJB 2 methods with bean types and corresponding annotations that you can use in EJB 3.

Table 14.2   EJB 2 required implementation of several lifecycle methods. If you implemented any of your application's business logic in any of these methods, then you can use the corresponding methods in EJB 3 to migrate that business logic.

Bean Type	EJB 2 Methods	EJB 3 Methods
Stateless, Stateful	`ejbCreate`	Constructor
Stateless, Stateful	`ejbPostCreate`	Method annotated with `@PostConstruct`
Stateful	`ejbPassivate`	Method annotated with `@PrePassivate`
Stateful	`ejbActivate`	Method annotated with `@PostActivate`
Stateless, Stateful	`ejbRemove`	Method annotated with `@PreDestroy`
Stateful	`remove` method in home interface	Method annotated with `@Remove`
Stateful	`create` method in home interface	Method annotated with `@Init` if the EJB 3 bean has a home interface
Stateless	`ejbTimeout`	Method annotated with `@Timeout`

Figure 14.3 summarizes these migration steps.

The business methods remain unchanged unless you're using other resources or EJBs. The code becomes simplified because you can use injection. This gives you the ability to remove the JNDI code. If you are migrating EJB 2 CMP entity beans and you have a session bean that uses the CMP entity beans, you have to

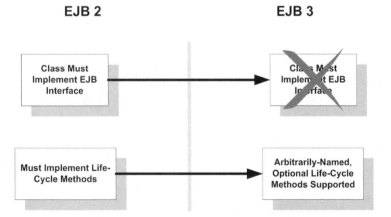

Figure 14.3   The changes necessary to migrate EJB 2.x bean classes to EJB 3. You don't have to implement EJB specific interfaces in EJB 3, and you don't have to implement all required lifecycle methods, as in EJB 2.

migrate your session bean methods to use the `EntityManager` API. We'll discuss migration of entity beans to the EJB 3 JPA in section 14.3.

You can also opt to change the security and transactions settings to use metadata annotations. We'll cover those in a later section.

14.2.2 *Resource usage*

Your EJB applications may be using JNDI lookup to find resources such as `DataSources` or JMS objects, and services such as EJBs or web services. Now that dependency injection is so readily available, you can use it instead of JNDI to find these resources. However, you have to remember the limitations of EJB 3 dependency injection.

If you're using a `DataSource`, the differences between EJB 2 and EJB 3 are shown in table 14.3.

Table 14.3   The use of DataSource in EJB 2 was very complex and has been simplified in EJB 3 by using dependency injection.

EJB 2	EJB 3

Define `resource-ref` in `ejb-jar.xml`
Lookup resource
 	
`Context ctx = new InitialContext();`
`DataSource ds = (DataSource)`
`  ctx.lookup("java:comp/env/`
`  ActionBazaarDS");`
`Connection conn = ds.getConnection();`
	Can use dependency injection
	
	`@Resource(name = "ActionBazaarDS")`
	
	`private DataSource ds;`
	
	`Connection conn =`
	`  ds.getConnection();`

If you're using a JMS resource, the differences between EJB 2 and EJB 3 are shown in table 14.4.

Table 14.4   The use of JMS objects in EJB 2 was also very complex and has been simplified in EJB 3 by using dependency injection.

EJB 2.x	EJB3

Define `resource-ref` in `ejb-jar.xml`
Lookup resource
 	
`Context ctx = new InitialContext();`
`QueueConnectionFactory  qcf =`
`  (QueueConnectionFactory)`
`  ctx.lookup("java:comp/env/jms/Queue`
`  ConnectionFactory");`
`QueueConnection conn =`
`  qcf.createQueueConnection();`
	`@Resource(name =`
	`  "jms/QueueConnectionFactory")`
	`private QueueConnectionFactory qcf;`
	
	`QueueConnection conn = qcf.`
	`createQueueConnection();`

Our comparison on how resources are declared and found between EJB 2 and EJB 3 is intended to underscore how much more straightforward dependency injection is compared to JNDI (no casting required), and how much easier it is for developers to maintain.

14.2.3 *Transactions and security settings*

EJB 2 doesn't define any default transaction and security settings for EJBs. You have to specify the definitions yourself for each and every bean method in a session bean. If you don't, you'll see different behaviors in different EJB containers.

As discussed in chapter 6, EJB 3 defines CMT as the default transaction management type for a bean, and REQUIRED as the default transaction attribute for bean methods. Therefore, you can simplify your transaction settings in your deployment descriptors by only specifying those that need a transaction attribute other than REQUIRED. Optionally, you can use annotations to define transaction settings. The same holds true for security settings. You can leave the security settings as is in the deployment descriptor, or use the security annotations discussed in chapter 6.

14.2.4 *Client applications*

Session beans are server-side components that encapsulate business logic and may be accessed either by remote or local clients. The client for an EJB could be another EJB in the same container, a separate container, a web module, or an application client. When you migrate any session bean to EJB 3, the clients will be impacted. This is mostly due to the fact that home interfaces are no longer needed. All client applications will have to be modified to use the EJB 3 client view. The ejb-ref or ejb-local-ref element in the client application's descriptor will also need to be modified to remove the home element, and the client code will have to be updated to look up the business interface instead of the home interface.

The old EJB 2 client code for the PlaceBid session bean would look like this:

```
Context context = new InitialContext();
PlaceBidHome placeBidHome =
  (PlaceBidHome) PortableRemoteObject.narrow(
    context.lookup("java:comp/env/PlaceBid"), PlaceBidHome.class);

PlaceBid placeBid = placeBidHome.create();
newBidId = placeBid.addBid(userId, itemId, bidPrice);
```

The migrated client code for the PlaceBid EJB will look like this if you continue to use JNDI:

```
Context context = new InitialContext();
PlaceBid placeBid = (PlaceBid)context.lookup("java:comp/env/PlaceBid");
Long newBidId = placeBid.addBid(userId, itemId, bidPrice);
```

If your client is a managed class and uses the Java EE 5 API, you can migrate the client to use dependency injection and further simplify the client code:

```
@EJB private PlaceBid placeBid;

Long newBidId = placeBid.addBid(userId, itemId, bidPrice);
```

So the original EJB 2 lookup took around eight lines of code. The EJB 3 refactoring reduced this to two lines of code, regardless of whether you use JNDI or dependency injection—in this case. Of course, your mileage may vary but we think you'll immediately see some benefits to migrating this code to the new programming model available in EJB 3.

Maintaining backward compatibility with EJB 2 clients

There may be various cases when you cannot afford to migrate your client applications, but you want to move your session beans to EJB 3. This will primarily be an issue when you have a remote interface for a session bean that is used by separate applications, some of which you don't have control over. Or perhaps you're an independent software vendor (ISV) that sells packaged applications and customers may be using your EJB in their EJB 2 applications.

To demonstrate this, imagine that many ActionBazaar `Gold` customers use rich client applications that remotely access EJBs such as `PlaceBid`. Now that `PlaceBid` has been migrated to EJB 3 (POJOs, regular interface, etc.), the rich client applications will break unless you update them. In this release of ActionBazaar you aren't making any client-side changes because you don't want to distribute a newer version of client applications to your customers. At the same time you don't want your client applications to break. Client applications of EJB 2 session beans use the `create` method on the home interface to create an EJB object instance. You can add a home interface and expose a `create` method in the home interface as follows:

```
import javax.rmi.RemoteException;
import javax.ejb.*;

public interface PlaceBidHome extends EJBHome {
  public PlaceBid create() throws CreateException, RemoteException;
}
```

Then use the `@RemoteHome` annotation on the bean class to mark this as a remote home interface as follows:

```
@Stateless(name = "PlaceBid")
@RemoteHome(PlaceBidHome.class)
public class PlaceBidBean implements PlaceBid {
}
```

If you want to maintain backward compatibility with local EJB 2 clients, then you can use the `@LocalHome` annotation. You must remember that you can't use the `@javax.ejb.LocalHome` and `@javax.ejb.RemoteHome` annotations in the home interfaces but only in the bean classes.

This concludes our discussion on migrating session beans. There's not much to it, is there? Let's now move to a discussion on migrating MDBs before we jump into more complex migration tasks involving CMP entity beans.

14.3 *Migrating message-driven beans*

MDBs have been simple Java classes since their introduction in EJB 2, and do not require remote or home interfaces, or unnecessary lifecycle methods. Not many changes to MDBs transpired in EJB 3, so migration of MDBs to EJB 3 is an easy task.

Unlike EJB 2, EJB 3 doesn't require that your MDB class implement the `javax.ejb.MessgeDrivenBean` interface, and the deployment descriptor is now optional. You may prefer to use the `@MessageDriven` and `@ActivationConfig-Property` annotations instead of the complementary deployment descriptors to activate configuration properties. You can migrate your lifecycle methods to custom methods and annotate them with the `@PostConstruct` and `@PreDestroy` annotations. Optionally you can change this such that resources and services use dependency injection instead of JNDI lookup. These migration steps are similar to what we discussed for session beans in section 14.2.2.

This is all that's involved to update your MDBs for EJB 3! Piece of cake! Simple as pie! OK, now we're getting hungry...

The story for entity beans is not so bright; this is one of the areas that was completely overhauled for EJB 3. Are you ready to dive into the EJB 3 migration waters for EJB 2 entity beans? You go right ahead to the next section; we'll meet you there.

14.4 *Migrating CMP 2 entity beans to the EJB 3 JPA*

Migrating CMP entity beans to the EJB 3 JPA is the most complex and involved migration task we'll discuss. It requires careful planning and a thorough understanding of your application.

You now know that there are significant differences between CMP entity beans and EJB 3 entities. CMP entity beans are coarse-grained data objects, whereas EJB 3 entities are lightweight domain objects that represent fine-grained data. EJB 3 entities are regular Java classes and lack some features that CMP 2 entity beans provide, such as remoteness, declarative security, and transactions. We agree with the point of view that imposing those features was a bad idea in the first place. However, you'll have to implement workarounds if you used those features. If you avoided them by using best practices and design patterns, then you are probably in good shape and your overall migration process will be smoother than it would be otherwise.

EJB 2 provided the ability to access an entity bean remotely by using remote interfaces, but design experts recommended against this. As you'll recall from chapter 12, we recommend you use a session façade as a shield to front entity beans, and use DTOs to transfer data between clients and the server. If you've followed these guidelines, it will simplify your migration efforts. Another benefit of using the DAO design pattern is that it may enable you to migrate the persistence tier easily without much impact on the business logic tier.

> ## Signpost up ahead: dead end for BMP entity beans
>
> EJB 2 supported entity beans with bean-managed persistence (BMP), where the code was developed using an API such as JDBC for persisting bean instances. BMP was quite popular initially because CMP implementations from most application servers were not stable. It was also useful when applications required nonrelational data.
>
> However, there are some inherent issues with BMP, such as N+1 problems. Unfortunately, there is no clear migration path for BMP entity beans to EJB 3. This translates into what seems like a dead end for BMP entity beans. As EJB 3 requires support for EJB 2, BMP entity beans will be supported in EJB 3 containers.
>
> If you're using BMP entity beans with a relational database, we recommend you consider migrating these to use the EJB 3 JPA. Otherwise, you may have a huge support issue lurking in your code base!

14.4.1 *Redesign your domain model*

You should seriously consider redesigning your domain model when migrating your CMP applications to EJB 3. CMP entity beans lacked support for OO features such as inheritance and polymorphism. Entity beans were mere representations of fragments of your database schema. Thus, in the OO purist's lingua franca, your domain model was probably anemic; let's see what we can do about that!

During your migration to EJB 3 JPA, you probably want to consider refactoring your entities to take advantage of the object-oriented features supported by the EJB 3 JPA. For example, assume that when ActionBazaar was built using CMP 2 it had an entity bean named `UserBean` that was a representation of the USERS table. Listing 14.1 shows the source code for this `UserBean` entity bean class.

Listing 14.1 User CMP entity bean using EJB 2

```
public abstract class UserBean implements EntityBean {
  private EntityContext context;

  public abstract String getUserId();
  public abstract String getFirstName();
  public abstract void setUserId(String userId);
  public abstract void setFirstName(String firstName);
  public abstract String getLastName();
  public abstract void setLastName(String lastName);
  public abstract String getUserType();
  public abstract void setUserType(String userType);
  public abstract Timestamp getBirthDate();
  public abstract void setBirthDate(Timestamp birthDate);
  public abstract Long getUserBillingId();
  public abstract void setUserBillingId(Long userBillingId);
  public abstract Double getCommRate();
  public abstract void setCommRate(Double commRate);
  public abstract Long getMaxItems();
  public abstract void setMaxItems(Long maxItems);
  public abstract String getUserStatus();
  public abstract void setUserStatus(String userStatus);
  public abstract Long getCreditRating();
  public abstract void setCreditRating(Long creditRating);

  public String ejbCreate() {
    return null;
  }

  public void ejbPostCreate() {
  }

  public void setEntityContext(EntityContext context)
      throws EJBException {
    context = context;
  }

  public void unsetEntityContext() throws EJBException {
    context = null;
  }
```

Annotations in right margin:
- **Abstract persistent properties** (pointing to the abstract getter/setter methods)
- **Lifecycle methods** (pointing to `ejbCreate()`, `ejbPostCreate()`, `setEntityContext(...)`, `unsetEntityContext()`)

```
public void ejbRemove() throws EJBException,
  RemoveException {
}

public void ejbActivate() throws EJBException {      ⊲─┐
}
                                                       │  Lifecycle
public void ejbPassivate() throws EJBException {     ⊲─┤  methods
}                                                      │
                                                       │
public void ejbLoad() throws EJBException {          ⊲─┤
}                                                      │
                                                       │
public void ejbStore() throws EJBException {         ⊲─┘
}
}
```

While migrating the application, we looked at the ActionBazaar system and found that there could be different kind of users, such as `Bidder`, `Seller`, or `Admin`. Therefore, rather than migrating the entity bean to EJB 3, we used inheritance and a single-table-per-entity hierarchy, as shown in listing 14.2.

Figure 14.4 shows the results of the entity refactoring.

Listing 14.2   Remodeled User entity with inheritance

```
@Entity
@Table(name = "USERS")
@Inheritance(strategy = InheritanceType.SINGLE_TABLE)
@DiscriminatorColumn(name = "USER_TYPE",
                     discriminatorType = DiscriminatorType.STRING,
                     length = 1)     ⊲─┐  User superclass
public class User {
}

@Entity                                    Seller, which inherits
@DiscriminatorValue(value = "S")     ⊲─┘  from User
public class Seller extends User {
}

@Entity                                    Bidder, which
@DiscriminatorValue(value = "B")     ⊲─┘  inherits from User
public class Bidder extends User {
}
```

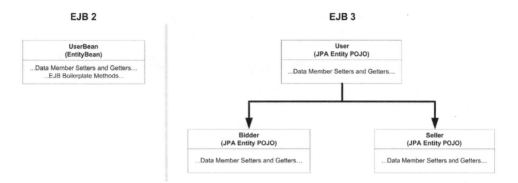

Figure 14.4 While migrating EJB 2 entity beans to EJB 3, it is likely you'll want to refactor to take advantage of features like OO inheritance support. In our example, the UserBean entity bean can be refactored into a User POJO entity superclass and Bidder, Seller, and so forth entity POJO subclasses.

Note that remodeling the entities did not require any changes in the database because we used a single-table-per-entity strategy, and we used the existing USER_TYPE column as the discriminator.

You should carefully plan and execute such a refactoring; it requires more work and testing of your applications than just migrating your CMP entity beans to entity classes as is. But the payoff in maintenance costs can be more than worth that extra work if done correctly.

In the next few sections, we'll focus on strategies that allow you to migrate entity beans to a JPA entity without doing any redesign.

14.4.2 *Using DTOs as entities*

The DTO is a commonly used design pattern. The specific benefit with respect to entity beans is that it allows the transfer of data back and forth between remote clients and entity beans in EJB 2. There are two types of DTOs: fine grained and coarse grained. The *fine-grained* DTO often has a one-to-one mapping between an entity bean and a DTO. The *coarse-grained* DTO represents data from multiple entity beans and is also known as the View object. In reality, a fine-grained DTO looks like a real domain object, just without any behavior; only the state of the object is represented.

Chapter 9 explained that this use of a DTO is no longer required because entities themselves are POJOs that can be transferred between clients and servers. If you used the DTO design pattern and are looking to migrate your entity beans to EJB 3 without spending any effort on remodeling, then you should consider making each DTO a candidate for an EJB 3 entity class.

Assume that ActionBazaar used the DTO design pattern. Listing 14.3 shows a sample of a fine-grained DTO named `UserDTO` that maps to a `UserBean` entity bean.

Listing 14.3   A DTO for the UserBean CMP

```
public class UserDTO implements Serializable {
  private String userId;
  private Date birthDate;
  private String userStatus;              ❶ Field definition
  private Double commRate;
  private Long creditRating;
  private String firstName;
  private String lastName;
  private Long maxItems;
  private Long userBillingId;
  private String userType;

  private Collection bids;     ←❷ Reference to another DTO

  public UserDTO() {    ←❸ Constructor
  }

  public String getUserId() {              ←┐
    return userId;
  }

  public void setUserId(String userId) {   ←┤
    this.userId = userId;
  }                                            ❹ Get/Set methods

  public String getUserType() {            ←┤
    return userType;
  }

  public void setUserType(String userType) { ←┘
    this.userType = userType;
  }
}
```

Reviewing `UserDTO` in listing 14.3, it looks more like an entity. It's a POJO; it has a constructor ❸, fields ❶, and properties ❹ required for the persistent attributes defined. It even has a relationship defined to another DTO ❷ that you can use as a basis for relationships between entities. It's worth considering making this class an entity rather than migrating the abstract entity bean class in listing 14.1 to an entity. You can make the DTO an entity by simply annotating it as an entity with the @Entity annotation, and defining the O/R mapping from your vendor-specific deployment descriptor to either metadata annotations or `orm.xml`. Following is the `UserDTO` (renamed to `User`) converted to an entity with a few JPA annotations:

```
@Entity
@Table(name = "USERS")
public class User implements Serializable {
  @Id
  @Column(name = "USER_ID")
  private String userId;
  private Date birthDate;

  ...
}
```

You have to make sure that you have defined all persistence fields in the entity class by cross-checking the persistence fields defined in the deployment descriptor with your entity bean. You'll also need to migrate the ORM metadata from the vendor-specific deployment descriptor, to either mapping annotations in the entity class or to a mapping file. After you migrate the finder methods and select methods to named queries, you're almost done!

The last step is to recall that your entity beans may have some business logic in the business methods. You have to migrate any business methods from the entity bean to the entity class, or to a session bean façade, as we describe next.

14.4.3 Entity bean classes and interfaces

If your applications have not used DTOs, then we're afraid you're in for a lot of monotonous work as you migrate your entity beans to entities. We hope it's evident from listing 14.1 that since the entity bean class and all methods are abstract, you'll have to convert the bean class to a concrete class with a constructor and define persistence fields as well as the obligatory getter/setter methods. The first step in migration will be similar to creating a DTO for your entity bean and annotating it with `@Entity`.

Persistence fields are actually defined in the EJB deployment descriptor. Migrating all the fields to your bean class and creating the appropriate fields and getter/setter methods in the entity class is required since we're relying on dependency injection to help us out at runtime. You should be able to find some development tools and utilities to help automate these mechanical steps.

Converting interfaces

EJB 2 entity beans required two interfaces: a component (remote or local) interface and a home interface. EJB 3 entities don't require any framework interfaces, so you can entirely eliminate the interfaces from your entities if you like, or convert your component interface to a business interface for the entity.

Optionally, you can use your component interface as the basis for migrating to an entity. Listing 14.4 shows the local interface for the `UserBean` entity bean. A quick glance informs us that it will be easy to migrate this interface to an EJB 3 entity. The interface has all get/set methods for the persistence fields ❶ and the relationships ❷.

Listing 14.4 Local interface for the UserBean CMP

```
public interface User extends EJBLocalObject {

    String getUserId();
    String getFirstName();                          ❶ Get/set methods for
    void setFirstName(String firstName);               persistence fields

    String getLastName();
    void setLastName(String lastName);

    String getUserType();
    void setUserType(String userType);

    Date getBirthDate();
    void setBirthDate(Date birthDate);

    Long getUserBillingId();
    void setUserBillingId(Long userBillingId);

    ...

    Collection getBids();                           ❷ Get/set methods for
    void setBids(Collection bids);                     relationship fields
}
```

If you haven't used a DTO, we recommend you start with the local interface as the basis for creating your entity class.

The home interface in the entity bean serves as the factory method to create, remove, and query bean instances. You can remove the home interface and migrate your finder methods to named queries, as we discuss later in the section. The `create` and `remove` methods are replaced with `EntityManager` operations. Optionally, you can migrate the home interface to be used as a session façade that exposes all factory methods such as `create` and `remove` to minimize the impact on client applications. We'll discuss this in section 14.4.4.

Identifying the primary key

Like the persistence fields, the primary key for CMP 2 is defined in the deployment descriptor. For example, the primary key for the `UserBean` entity bean is defined in the deployment descriptor as follows:

```
...
<prim-key-class>java.lang.String</prim-key-class>
<reentrant>false</reentrant>
<cmp-version>2.x</cmp-version>
<abstract-schema-name>User</abstract-schema-name>
<cmp-field>
  <field-name>userId</field-name>
</cmp-field>
...
<primkey-field>userId</primkey-field>
...
```

You identify the primary key of the entity class in EJB 3 using the `@Id` annotation:

```
@Id
private String userId;
```

CMP 2 did not support the automatic generation of primary key values; this required the use of workarounds such as the Sequence Generator pattern, or vendor-specific extensions to either database sequence or table sequence generators. If you happened to use such features, then you must migrate them to one of the primary key–generation strategies that we discussed in chapter 8.

Creating O/R mapping

The ORM metadata such as table and column mapping for EJB 2 entity beans is defined in the vendor-specific deployment descriptor. Move those mappings to entity classes by using the `@Table` and `@Column` annotations, as discussed in chapter 8. Optionally, you can move them to an OR mapping file, as discussed in chapter 11.

Lifecycle methods

EJB 2 required you to implement a lot of lifecycle methods—a *lot*. These methods are template methods and are rarely used. It's possible that you may have implemented some business logic in these methods. You can migrate the business logic for the lifecycle methods to the entity listener callback methods discussed in chapter 9. Table 14.5 summarizes the methods that you can migrate from EJB 2 lifecycle methods to entity callback methods in EJB 3.

Table 14.5   EJB 2 required implementations of many lifecycle methods. EJB 3 allows you to define lifecycle callback methods. This table lists the corresponding methods for EJB 3 JPA that you can use to migrate an entity bean's lifecycle methods.

EJB 2 Lifecycle Method	Migrated EJB 3 JPA Entity
`ejbCreate`	Constructors in the entity class.
`ejbPostCreate`	A method annotated with `@PostPersist`.
`ejbRemove`	A method annotated with `@PreRemove`.
`setEntityContext,` `unSetEntityContext`	`EntityContext` is not supported in EJB3 JPA. Candidate for removal.
`ejbActivate, ejbLoad`	A method annotated with `@PostLoad` as per the application requirement.
`ejbPassivate`	Candidate for removal.
`ejbStore`	A method annotated with either `@PrePersist` or `@PreUpdate` depending on the application requirement.

If you're like us, you welcome the move away from all these required lifecycle methods. It's long overdue!

Finding an alternative to EntityContext

The EJB 2 entity bean provided environment information with the `javax.ejb.EntityContext` object. EJB 3 entities are no longer components and therefore do not have contexts of their own. This means there is no `EntityContext` equivalent in EJB 3. You have to migrate the use of `EntityContext` to one of the appropriate alternatives. One of the most commonly used methods in the `EntityContext` is the `getPrimaryKey` method. You can create a business method to expose the primary key of the entity to the caller. As outlined in table 14.3, the `setEntityContext` and `unSetEntityContext` methods are now candidates for removal because they are no longer supported.

Business methods

It's quite possible that you may have business methods in your entity classes that are using JNDI to find other entity beans. Perhaps you are using the `ejbSelect` method of another entity bean (e.g., `ItemBean`) in a business method of `UserBean`. You could migrate this code to the entity class by using a named query of the entity class. This would require grabbing an instance of the `EntityManager` using JNDI. However, we recommend against the approach of using JNDI code within your entity classes because it will limit its usability to relying on the container. This boils down to a scenario where you cannot test or use it outside the container. We suggest that you take this opportunity to migrate such code to the service layer (i.e., the session façade).

Finder and select methods

If you've used CMP entity beans in EJB 2, you know that finder and select methods are defined in the home interface for the entity bean as shown here:

```
public interface UserLocalHome extends EJBLocalHome {
  User create() throws CreateException;
  User create(String userId, String firstName, String lastName,
              String userType) throws CreateException;

  User findByPrimaryKey(String primaryKey) throws FinderException;

  Collection findAll() throws FinderException;

  Collection findByFirstName(String name) throws FinderException;
}
```

Notice the two custom finders. The query for the finder methods (`findAll` and `findByFirstName`) are defined in the `ejb-jar.xml` using EJBQL as defined here:

```xml
<query>
  <query-method>
    <method-name>findById</method-name>
    <method-params/>
  </query-method>
  <ejb-ql>select object(o) from User o WHERE o.id = ?1</ejb-ql>
</query>

<query>
  <query-method>
    <method-name>findByFirstName</method-name>
    <method-params>
      <method-param>java.lang.String</method-param>
    </method-params>
  </query-method>
  <ejb-ql>
    SELECT OBJECT(u) FROM User u WHERE u.firstName LIKE ?1
  </ejb-ql>
</query>
```

The finder methods and select methods in the bean class can be converted to named queries in the `User` entity class like so:

```java
@Entity
@NamedQueries({
  @NamedQuery(
```

```
    name = "findUserById",
    query = "SELECT u FROM User u where u.id=?1"
  ),
  @NamedQuery(
    name = "findUserByFirstName",
    query = "SELECT u FROM User u WHERE u.firstName LIKE ?1"
)})

public class User implements Serializable {
...
}
```

While migrating the finder methods to named queries, we have changed the name of the named queries to unique names (findUserById from findById), because named queries are scoped for the persistence units. This is unlike finder methods that can be invoked only on an entity bean instance. You will notice that we have used the simplified syntax of a JPQL query. Optionally, you can migrate your query to an ad hoc or dynamic query in your session façade, but we recommend against that due to the performance reasons we discussed in chapter 13.

Container-managed relationships

In EJB 2.1, relationships are defined in deployment descriptors. Listing 14.5 shows the descriptor elements that define a unidirectional, one-to-one relationship between the User and ContactDetail entity beans, and a one-to-many relationship between the User and Bid entity beans.

Listing 14.5   Container-managed relationship defined in the deployment descriptor

```
<ejb-relation>
  <ejb-relationship-role>
    <ejb-relationship-role-name>
      Users may have one ContactDetail
    </ejb-relationship-role-name>
    <multiplicity>One</multiplicity>             Unidirectional one-to-
    <relationship-role-source>                   one relationship
      <ejb-name>User</ejb-name>
    </relationship-role-source>
    <cmr-field>
      <cmr-field-name>contact_contactUserId</cmr-field-name>
    </cmr-field>
  </ejb-relationship-role>
</ejb-relation>

<ejb-relation>
  <ejb-relation-name>Bids - Users</ejb-relation-name>
  <ejb-relationship-role>
    <ejb-relationship-role-name>
      Bids may have one User
```

```
        </ejb-relationship-role-name>
        <multiplicity>Many</multiplicity>
        <relationship-role-source>
          <ejb-name>Bids</ejb-name>              Bidirectional one-to-
        </relationship-role-source>              many relationship
        <cmr-field>
          <cmr-field-name>bidder</cmr-field-name>
        </cmr-field>
      </ejb-relationship-role>
      <ejb-relationship-role>
        <ejb-relationship-role-name>
          User may have many Bids
        </ejb-relationship-role-name>
        <multiplicity>One</multiplicity>
        <relationship-role-source>
          <ejb-name>User</ejb-name>
        </relationship-role-source>
        <cmr-field>
          <cmr-field-name>bids</cmr-field-name>
          <cmr-field-type>java.util.Collection</cmr-field-type>
        </cmr-field>
      </ejb-relationship-role>
    </ejb-relation>
```

The relationships need to be migrated to the entity class using the appropriate association annotations such as @OneToOne or @OneToMany. Note that we have used Java Generics and changed the association field to a Set from Collection type and such change will require appropriate changes in the client code. The simplified code looks like this:

```
@Entity
public class User {
  @Id
  protected String userId;
  protected String email;
  @OneToOne
  protected ContactDetail contactDetail;
  @OneToMany(mappedBy = "bidder")
  protected Set<Bid> bids;
  ...
}

@Entity
public class ContactDetail {
  @Id
  protected Long contactId;
  ...
}
```

```
@Entity
public class Bid implements Serializable {
  @ManyToOne
  protected User bidder;
  ...
}
```

In EJB 2, entity beans supported the concept of container-managed relationships. The container was automatically updating the reverse side of relationships when one side was updated. When migrating your relationships to EJB 3, you have to be aware that you are now responsible for managing both sides of your relationships. For example, if you had the following method in the User entity to update a relationship:

```
public addBid(Bid bid) {
  getBids.add(bid);
}
```

you'd have to change this code to add the back pointer (i.e., set the relationship from Bid to User) as follows:

```
public void addBid(Bid bid) {
  getBids().add(bid);
  bid.setUser(this);
}
```

As you can see, there's not a lot of code involved, but the burden of keeping things bidirectional falls squarely on your shoulders now.

Transactions and security settings

CMP entity beans provided the ability to specify transactions and security settings for bean methods. In practice, these were rarely used in favor of the more popular session façade approach. EJB 3 entities don't provide such facilities, which means that you need to move security and transaction settings to your session façades.

14.4.4 *Client applications*

In EJB 3, we use the EntityManager API to perform entity operations such as persisting, finding, and removing entities. In EJB 2 the home interface acted as a factory interface to provide methods to create, remove, and find entity bean instances. Clients used these methods to persist, remove, and query bean instances. In the new EJB 3 world, client applications should be modified to use the EntityManager API.

Let's say we have an EJB 2 newUser method in the BazaarAdminBean that is a session façade used to create an instance of a User entity bean as follows:

```
public void newUser(UserDTO user) throws
    CreateException,
    FinderException,
    NamingException {

  User userLocal = getUserLocalHome().create(
                      user.getUserId(),
                      user.getFirstName(),
                      user.getLastName(),
                      user.getUserType());
  ...
}
```

Our example code uses a DTO named `UserDTO`. After migration, the client code (where `User` is an entity) will look much simpler:

```
public void newUser(User user) {
  getEntityManager().persist(user);
}
```

Similarly, you can migrate other operations, such as removal, or queries to use the `EntityManager` API. You have to remove the client code to handle exceptions such as `CreateException` and `FinderException` that were previously required to be handled in CMP entity beans but are no longer imposed.

Translating entity home to a session façade

It's fairly effortless to migrate the home interface to a session façade by moving all factory methods such as `create`, `remove`, and `find` to this façade. We first create a `UserLocalHome` interface:

```
public interface UserLocalHome {
    User create(String userId, String firstName, String lastName,
                String userType) throws CreateException;

    User findByPrimaryKey(String primaryKey) throws FinderException;

    Collection findAll() throws FinderException;

    Collection findByFirstName(String name) throws FinderException;
}
```

This interface is exactly the same as before except it does not extend `EJBLocal-Home`. The session bean implements the `UserLocalHome` interface and implements all factory methods using the `EntityManager` API as follows:

```
@Stateless
public class UserLocalHomeBean implements UserLocalHome {
@PersistenceContext EntityManager em;
```

```
    User create(String userId, String firstName, String lastName,
            String userType) throws CreateException
{
    User user = new User(userId, firstName, lastName, userType);

    try
    {
        em.persist(user);
    }
    catch (Exception e)
    {
        throw new CreateException(e.getMessage());
    }

    returnuser;
}

User findByPrimaryKey(String primaryKey) throws FinderException
{
    try
    {
        return (User)em.find(User.class, primaryKey);
    }
    catch (Exception e)
    {
        throw new FinderException(e.getMessage());
    }
}
}
```

This code throws the EJB 2–specific exceptions that may be expected by clients. You can use this session bean façade to mimic the home interface, thereby reducing the number of changes required on the client side.

This concludes our discussion on migrating applications using CMP entity beans to the EJB 3 JPA. As we told you at the start of this section, migrating your CMP beans to JPA is the most involved of the tasks you're likely to undertake when upgrading to EJB 3. Revising your domain model, using DTOs and session facades, and the required API changes will all help you achieve your migration goal. Your EJB 2 applications may already use DTOs and session facades, in which case much of this is familiar to you. Either way, we've provided a roadmap that will lead you down the migration trail.

At this point, we know *exactly* what you're thinking—OK, what you're *probably* thinking. What about all that JDBC code? You guys got any tips for converting it to JPA? It just so happens we do, and if you mosey on over to the next section you can see what these tips are.

14.5 Migrating JDBC DAOs to use the EJB 3 JPA

Almost every Java developer in the universe has used JDBC to persist data to a database. If your code also uses the DAO pattern, then migrating to the EJB 3 JPA may be a relatively painless process.

Migration from JDBC requires three major tasks:

1   Identify your entities.

2   Change the DAO implementation classes to use the `EntityManager` API to perform entity operations instead of using JDBC.

3   Migrate your SQL queries to use JPQL and the `EntityManager` API.

These steps are summarized in figure 14.5.

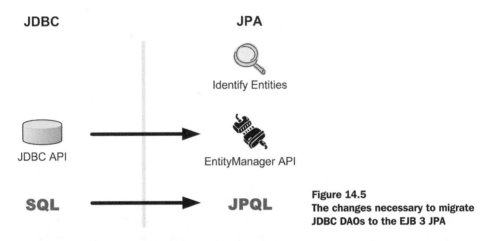

JDBC   **JPA**

Identify Entities

JDBC API   EntityManager API

SQL ⟶ **JPQL**

Figure 14.5
The changes necessary to migrate
JDBC DAOs to the EJB 3 JPA

The next three sections break down each of these steps, and we provide examples to illustrate exactly what you need to do.

14.5.1 Identifying entities

This is the most challenging task in the migration process and requires a good understanding of your application. The good news is that applications using DAOs don't have any impact on the business logic tier of the application, and the migration effort is limited only in the persistence tier. If you followed the DAO design pattern religiously, you most likely created value or transfer objects (similar to DTOs) that are used by the business tier to retrieve or update data from the database. A careful look reveals that these transfer objects resemble entities. A little analysis is all that is required to understand the relationship between these transfer objects, allowing them to safely be converted to entities.

Suppose that ActionBazaar initially used JDBC DAOs for persistence and the transfer object `BidTO` looked similar to listing 14.6.

Listing 14.6   Bid transfer object used with a DAO

```
public class BidTO implements Serializable {
  private Timestamp bidDate;       │ Instance
  private Long bidId;              │ fields
  private Double bidPrice;
  private String bidStatus;

  private ItemTO item;            │ Pointer to other
  private UserTO bidder;          │ transfer objects

  public BidTO() {        ◁┐ Constructor
  }

  public Timestamp getBidDate() {                    ◁
    return bidDate;
  }                                                     Get/set
                                                        methods
  public void setBidDate(Timestamp bidDate) {   ◁
    this.bidDate = bidDate;
  }
}
```

If you look at the code for `BidTO` carefully, it looks surprisingly similar to the `Bid` entity that we discussed in chapter 2. It even has references to the associated transfer objects. The only difference is that it does not have JPA annotations. You can use JPA annotations to convert your transfer objects to entities. The steps are similar to those we listed in section 14.4.2 when we discussed considering DTOs to be entities. Next you'll see how to make the switch to the `EntityManager`.

14.5.2   Reworking a DAO implementation class to use the EntityManager API

The database-specific implementation class has JDBC code to persist the value or transfer object to the database. Assume that the `BidDAOImpl` class uses JDBC to persist and retrieve data. The next step in the process is for you to migrate the JDBC code to use the `EntityManager` API.

1   Replace the code that opens and closes JDBC connections to obtain an instance of an `EntityManager`. For example, your `BidDAOImpl` class has a method that returns a database connection. You can change that method to return an `EntityManager` instance.

2   Replace your SQL INSERT/UPDATE/DELETE statements to use the `Entity-Manager` API. For instance, one of `BidDAOImpl`'s methods has an INSERT statement that creates an instance of `Bid` in the database, as seen here:

```
private final static String INSERT_BID_QUERY_STR =
  "INSERT INTO BIDS " +
  "(BID_ID,BIDDER_ID,ITEM_ID,BID_STATUS,BID_PRICE) " +
  "VALUES (?, ?, ?, ?, ?)";

private void insertBid(BidTO bid) {
  ...
  stmt = dbConnection.prepareStatement(INSERT_BID_QUERY_STR);

  stmt.setLong(1, bid.getBidId());
  stmt.setString(2, bid.getBidder().getUserId().trim());
  stmt.setLong(3, bid.getItem().getId());
  stmt.setString(4, bid.getStatus().trim());
  stmt.setDouble(5, bid.getBidPrice());
}
```

After migrating the JDBC code to use the `EntityManager` API, the migrated code will look like this:

```
private void insertBid(Bid bid) {
  ...
  em.persist(bid);
}
```

Wow! Can you believe that? Similarly, you can use the `em.remove` and `em.merge` methods to migrate the JDBC code for remove or update operations. Next we'll explain how you can migrate your SQL SELECT statements to use JPQL.

14.5.3 *Swapping SQL queries for JPQL*

Although it may be a little difficult to let go, you have to remember that there are no equivalents for `ResultSet` and `Rowset` in the EJB 3 JPA. Most typical applications use SQL statements to retrieve data and construct transfer objects, which are returned to the client instead of returning a `ResultSet`. Not following the DAO and Transfer Object design patterns will mean additional work for you.

Listing 14.7 shows a method in the `BidDAOImpl` class that returns a list of `BidTO`s by retrieving a `ResultSet` from the database.

Listing 14.7 Method that returns a list of transfer objects to the client

```java
public ArrayList getBids(Long itemId) throws BidDAOException {

  PreparedStatement stmt = null;
  ResultSet result = null;
  Connection dbConnection = null;

  ArrayList bids = new ArrayList();
  try {
    dbConnection = DAOUtils.getDBConnection("jdbc/ActionBazaarDS");
    stmt = dbConnection.prepareStatement("SELECT " +
      "BID_ID,BID_STATUS, BID_PRICE FROM BIDS WHERE ITEM_ID = ?");
    stmt.setLong(1, itemId);
    result = stmt.executeQuery();              Contains JDBC   ❶
    if (!result.next()) {                       statements
      throw new BidDAOException("No Bid found for item:" + itemId);
    } //

    do {
      int i = 1;
      Long bidId = result.getLong(i++);
      String bidStatus = result.getString(i++);    ❷ Constructs
      Double bidPrice = result.getDouble(i++);       collection of
      bids.add(new BidTO(BidId, bidStatus, bidPrice));  BidTOs
    } while(result.next());
                      ❸ Returns collection of TOs
    return(bids);
  } catch (SQLException se) {
    ...
  } finally {
    DAOUtils.closeResultSet(result);
    DAOUtils.closeStatement(stmt);
    DAOUtils.closeConnection(dbConnection);
  }
}
```

The method in listing 14.7 constructs a list of transfer objects of type `BidTO` ❷ by executing a JDBC SQL statement ❶ and returns ❸ them to the client. Assuming you have created an entity named `Bid` that corresponds to the `BidTO` transfer object, you can easily migrate this method to use JPQL and the `EntityManager` API. You can use a dynamic query in the `getBids` method as follows:

```java
public List getBids(Long itemId) {
  Item item = (Item)em.find(Item.class, itemId);
  Query query =
    em.createQuery("SELECT b FROM Bid b WHERE b.item = ?1");
  Query.setParameter(1, item);
```

```
    return query.getResultList();
  }
```

However, we recommend using a named query instead of a dynamic query, and moving the JPQL statement to the `Bid` entity as a named query like this:

```
@Entity
@NamedQuery(
  name = "findBidsByItem",
  query = "SELECT b FROM Bid b WHERE b.item = ?1")

public class Bid implements Serializable {
...
}
```

Use the named query in the `getBids` method of the `BidDAOImpl` class:

```
public List getBids(Long itemId) {
  Item item = (Item)em.find(Item.class, itemId);
  Query query = em.createNamedQuery("findBidsByItem");
  Query.setParameter(1, item);

  return query.getResultList();
}
```

If you look at the migrated methods (`insertBid` in section 14.5.2 and `getBids`) and compare them with the original methods in `BidDAOImpl`, they should look much simpler. You can follow our guidelines to migrate all your JDBC DAO code to use the EJB 3 Persistence API with very little impact on the business tier of your applications. Don't you just love it?

Next we tackle migrating applications that currently use O/R frameworks over to our new friend, the EJB 3 JPA.

14.6 *Helping O/R frameworks to use the EJB 3 JPA*

EJB 3 persistence is the result of a lot of hard work between individuals; vendors of major O/R mapping solutions such as Hibernate, TopLink, and JDO, and countless others. If you've ever used any of these frameworks, you know that the EJB 3 JPA looks an awful lot like your favorite O/R framework, which will make it easier for you to migrate to EJB 3 from an existing O/R solution. Covering detailed migration steps from each of these persistence solutions is out of the scope of this book. However, we will provide some generic steps for migrating applications that utilize O/R frameworks to convert to the EJB 3 JPA.

The EJB 3 JPA is now the standard API to build the persistence tier for applications. Each of the persistence providers will provide some mechanisms to facilitate migration to EJB 3. Check your vendor documentation for tools or utilities to ease the migration process.

If you are using an O/R framework, it is assumed that you'll migrate an existing domain model to the EJB 3 JPA. Migration of applications using proprietary O/R solutions will involve three or four major steps:

1 Migrate proprietary mapping metadata to use the EJB 3 JPA O/R mapping annotations or `orm.xml`. Check your vendor's documentation to see if they provide any tools to assist in this effort.

2 Migrate vendor-specific APIs (e.g., Hibernate's Session API to perform CRUD operations) to use the `EntityManager` API. Table 14.6 shows what the migrated code will look like when you migrate from two popular frameworks.

Table 14.6   Comparison of application code to persist an instance of an entity with two popular O/R frameworks

Hibernate (from this)	```Session sess = sessions.openSession();```
	```Transaction tx = sess.beginTransaction();```
	```sess.save(category);```
	```tx.commit();```
	```sess.close();```

TopLink (or from this)	```UnitOfWork uow = session.acquireUnitOfWork();```
	```uow.registerObject(category);```
	```uow.commit();```

EJB 3 (to this)	```ut.begin();```
	```em.persist(category);```
	```ut.commit();```

3 You have to migrate both dynamic and named queries from any vendor-specific query language to use JPQL. For instance, if you are using JDO for O/R mapping and you have the following code using JDO QL:

```
Query query = pm.newQuery("SELECT FROM " +
  "actionbazaar.buslogic.User WHERE firstName == :firstName");

List<User> people = (List<User>)
query.execute(firstName);
```

you will need to revise it to this:

```
Query query = em.createQuery(
  "SELECT u FROM User u WHERE u.firstName = :firstName");
query.setParameter("firstName", firstName);

List<User> = (List<User>)query.getResultList();
```

4   This is an optional step depending on how many advanced features you are already using. If you've used any vendor-specific features such as caching, you'll need to configure those features as properties in `persistence.xml`, or potentially as `queryHints` in your JPQL.

Your conversion efforts should take into account the fact that many persistence providers have been around for years and provide numerous features not supported in the EJB 3 JPA. Your application may be working with some features from a persistence provider that may not have an equivalent in the EJB 3 JPA. It is anticipated that most EJB 3 persistence providers will allow mixing such features with the EJB 3 JPA. You'll have to decide whether continuing to use these vendor-specific features is worth more than remaining in compliance with the specification.

This brings to a close our discussion on migrating O/R frameworks to EJB 3 JPA. Next we'll take a quick look at some overall project-level approaches targeted at easing the course of migration.

14.7 Approaches to migration

Like any software development project, migrating your applications to use EJB 3 may be quite challenging. A thorough understanding of your applications and knowledge of EJB 3 is required. If you're migrating EJB 2 applications to EJB 3, you have to understand that *other* applications may have a dependency on *your* application. Making the jump to EJB 3 may break the dependent applications, because the client view of EJBs has changed.

14.7.1 Strategies

Depending on the size of your applications, and the number of applications you plan on upgrading, the strategy you choose could have a big impact on your success. You may go for either a *phased* approach or an *all-at-once* approach, depending on your comfort level with your code base and the availability of resources. An incremental approach may be better suited for most applications if you aren't comfortable with the technology. It allows you to validate the technology, gives you firsthand experience through trial and error, and has minimal impact on the complete application.

Our advice is that you consider an agile approach to migration, and properly test your application after migrating only a small portion. Testing as you go along will give you confidence that you are on the right track, and let you know fairly quickly if you've gone off the rails. Of course, there are situations where it may not be practical to follow an incremental migration strategy. Only you know the capabilities of your team, your corporate culture, and the unique pressure associated with keeping your applications in a production-ready state.

14.7.2 *Manual vs. automated*

It is evident from our earlier discussions in this chapter that migration is mostly a mechanical and boring chore, and finding the right resources for such a task may be challenging. We certainly expect that many development tools will emerge promising to automate 100 percent of the migration workload. However, we recommend that you not rely completely on such tools. Tools can certainly simplify the migration process, but will require some degree of guidance so that your knowledge of your applications is taken into consideration during the process.

Tools can ease your task in converting classes to use EJB 3, but the resulting application may not be foolproof due to the scores of changes in the programming model between EJB 2 CMP entity beans and the EJB 3 JPA. We suggest you try migrating a part of your application with the tool and then examine the entire application to determine whether it behaves as expected. In many cases, you'll want to change your domain model. In such situations your intervention will most likely be required because you are the only one who can make these decisions.

14.8 *Summary*

This chapter examined the major issues related to interoperability, compatibility, and migration to EJB 3. The EJB 3 specification requires backward compatibility with EJB 2. You learned how you can mix-and-match EJB 2 and EJB 3 components in the same applications, as well as convert applications completely over to EJB 3. We provided guidelines for migrating each EJB 2 component to EJB 3.

Migration of session beans and MDBs to EJB 3 is easy but still requires you to carefully plan the process because client applications may break due to changes in the client view of EJBs between EJB 2 and EJB 3. Migration of CMP entity beans is the most difficult task, but you can simplify the migration if you use design patterns such as DTO, Session Façade, and DAO.

This chapter also explained how to convert JDBC DAOs to use the EJB 3 JPA. Finally, you saw that the migration from using existing O/R mapping frameworks to using the EJB 3 JPA is a very straightforward task. With these guidelines and a good knowledge of your applications, you will have no problem migrating your applications to use EJB 3.

In the next chapter, you'll learn how to expose EJBs as web services, and how to invoke web services from EJB applications.

15

Exposing EJBs as
web services

This chapter covers

- Web service primer
- Java-XML web services
- Developing EJB web services

Service-oriented architecture (SOA) and web services are no longer buzzwords. These technologies have become a reality in the past few years. Web services are definitely the new industry standard for application-to-application (A2A) and business-to-business (B2B) integration.

What do web services have to do with EJB 3? Exposing your business logic component as web service is a snap with EJB 3. Stick with us through this chapter and we'll demonstrate how EJB 3 can be combined with web service metadata to provide compelling solutions for exposing business logic as web services.

Let's illustrate this with another scenario from the ActionBazaar application. The promoters of ActionBazaar are being forced to expose some components as web services because their competitors now offer competing services. Action-Bazaar wants to stay competitive, and needs to quickly enable their business functionality in a way that users of the system can easily consume.

At first, they thought they might have to move to the Microsoft .NET platform to create the web services. When you consider that J2EE 1.4 was criticized by many for its complexities in building service-oriented applications, it's easy to see why the caretakers of ActionBazaar were considering that move. They heard rumors that the developers of KabadiBazaar,[1] a sister web auction site similar to Action-Bazaar that specializes in miscellaneous household items, had demonstrated how it was easy to build web services with .NET. The promoters of ActionBazaar are hesitant, though, because they are enthusiastic about the simplification of web service development brought to Java by using metadata annotations and the Java API for XML-Based Web Services (JAX-WS) 2.0 specification. In the end, they have decided to create their web services using EJB.

This chapter assumes that you are familiar with web services, and in-depth coverage of web service development with the Java EE platform is not within the scope of this book. Other books are available on that topic; it would be difficult to cover all aspects of web service development in a single chapter.

In this chapter we first offer a quick review of a web service and its components, and discuss high-level approaches to web service development. We follow this with the details of building EJB web services, and conclude with some best practices to get your web services up and working quickly with EJB 3.

---

[1] In Hindi, KabadiBazaar is a marketplace where household junk/scraps are sold.

15.1 *What is a web service?*

It's very difficult to arrive at a single definition of web service that all camps will agree on. Simply put, a web service is a standard platform that provides interoperability between networked applications out of the box. For example, if you build a web service using Java EE and deploy it to an application server, you can invoke that service from any of a number of possible client applications interested in the service. This even includes client applications built using the Windows Communication Foundation[2] (WCF, formerly code-named Indigo), Microsoft's latest web service platform.

SOA is a new way of building loosely coupled applications. With SOA, you focus on building *services*. Thus, services are somewhat analogous to Java objects and components such as EJBs. Unlike objects, however, services are self-contained, maintain their own state, and provide a loosely coupled interface. Simply put, a service is a self-contained software module that performs a predetermined task: validating a credit card, for example. Many developers think SOA and web services are the same, but in reality SOA is an architecture principle whereas a web service is a platform to build loosely coupled applications. You can implement a service-oriented application with many other technologies such RMI but web services has been the most popular technology to implement service-oriented applications.

The most important aspect of a service is the service description. When using web services as the implementation technology for SOA, Web Services Description Language (WSDL) describes the messages, types, and operations of the web service, and is the contract to which the web service guarantees it will conform.

Let's start with an example. Assume that ActionBazaar built a web service and provides a WSDL that describes the service. The service is registered in the UDDI (Universal Description, Discovery, and Integration) registry. A client application (KabadiBazaar) finds the WSDL describing how to call the service from the registry, generates the endpoint interface and proxy classes, and then invokes the web service as shown in figure 15.1.

Beside interoperability and application integration, the primary benefit that a web service provides is reusability of discrete business functionality. How this functionality might be used is rarely known in its entirety when the service is created (sometimes known as *publishing* the web service). Client applications can even search for multiple similar services and determine which one to use on the fly at

---

[2] http://msdn.microsoft.com/winfx/technologies/communication/default.aspx

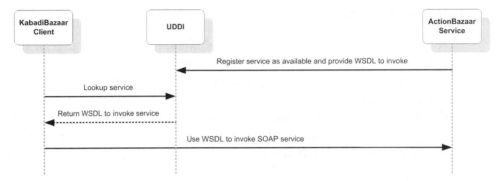

Figure 15.1 ActionBazaar built a web service and registered it in the UDDI registry. A client application searches the registry to find the service. The registry returns the WSDL registered by the service, and uses the WSDL to invoke the web service.

runtime, depending on known data, user preferences, user locale, or any number of other circumstances unique to the client application at that moment in time. The ActionBazaar developers build a few loosely coupled services such as Credit-VerificationService and CreditCardChargeService. These are exposed as web services and are seamlessly found and consumed by the KabadiBazaar application, even though it was built using a completely different technology. Of course, 100 percent compatibility between different platforms is still eluding the masses. Most developers are more than willing to accept 95 to 98 percent compatibility out of the box and make the final adjustments themselves. The alternative is to do a lot more work, for a lot less reward.

Web Services-Interoperability (WS-I)

WS-I (www.ws-i.org) is an open industry consortium, with members from diverse industries. It consists of large vendors such as Microsoft, Oracle, IBM, BEA, and Sun Microsystems. WS-I's primary goal is to promote interoperability of web services across middleware platforms, operating systems, and programming languages.

WS-I provides a specification known as Basic Profile that lists a set of recommendations to achieve maximum interoperability of web services between heterogeneous platforms. Java EE 5 requires support for the Basic Profile 1.1 specification in order for any implementation to claim compatibility.

We recommend you check out Eric Pulier and Hugh Taylor's *Understanding Enterprise SOA* (Manning, 2005) for more in-depth coverage of this topic. Also, here are some web sites to visit:

- http://www.w3c.org/2002/ws (W3C Consortium on web services)
- http://www.ws-i.org (The WS-I [Web Services-Interoperability] Organization)
- http://msdn.microsoft.com/webservices/ (Microsoft Developer Network)
- http://www-128.ibm.com/developerworks/webservices (IBM's "SOA and Web Services" page)
- http://ws.apache.org/ (Apache)

In this section we'll first look at core components of a web service. Then we'll discuss the various styles of web services and their differences. Finally, we'll examine some approaches to web service development.

15.1.1 *Identifying web service components*

The web service landscape is comprised of an alphabet soup of standards, protocols, and technologies. At its core, a web service is published by a service producer and accessed by a service consumer. This almost always ends up with an XML document being sent over an HTTP transport. As a general rule the data protocol shared between service consumer and producer is based on some flavor of XML,

---

REST web services

Representational State Transfer (popularly known as REST) is a popular architectural style of building web services. It doesn't depend on a SOAP envelope, but it does leverage XML and the HTTP protocol. Statistics revealed by large web-based companies like Amazon and Yahoo! shows that a majority of their consumers use a REST interface.

Unfortunately, Java EE 5 doesn't require support for REST web services and each vendor supports its own approach. GlassFish supports RESTful web services by creating an implementation of the `javax.ws.Provider` interface. Vendors such as Oracle allow you to convert a Java object into a web service by using proprietary configuration or a proprietary annotation. Check your vendor's documentation to see if they provide REST support, and see how that support is implemented. For more information on REST, hop over to http://en.wikipedia.org/wiki/Representational_State_Transfer.

but the transport can be any network protocol. Implementations exist for several standard transport protocols besides HTTP, including JMS, SMTP, and FTP.

Several approaches are available for implementing a web service. The three most widely used are REST (Representational State Transfer), XML-RPC (Extensible Markup Language–Remote Procedure Call), and SOAP. Although there are valid reasons to use REST and XML-RPC, the majority of enterprise applications use some form of a SOAP stack for their web services. This is primarily due to the fact that most standards for sharing industry-specific data (such as travel, health care, financial) via web services are based on the SOAP architectures. This chapter will focus on the SOAP stack because it is the most prominent of the three architectures.

That's enough talk about the general SOA landscape. We'll start with some basics of the SOAP architecture. Let's begin by defining what a typical SOAP stack includes:

- *Service messaging*—Messages are sent between the client and service in XML, the universal format for metadata. For a SOAP stack, this means that the messages follow the SOAP standard for message structure and definition (www.w3.org/TR/soap/).

- *Service description*—Each web service has a corresponding XML document that describes the web service, the parameters that it expects to be passed, which ones are optional and which are required, what their data types are, what will be returned, and so forth. A web service client "consumes" the WSDL file in order to communicate with a web service (www.w3.org/TR/wsdl).

- *Service discovery*—Think of this as the Yellow Pages for web services. When a web service wants to make itself known, it registers itself to a UDDI registry by providing the WSDL required to access the service. Clients can browse registries looking for services that meet their requirements (www.uddi.org/specification.html).

- *Service transport*—This is the network mechanism responsible for transporting messages between the client and the service. The Hypertext Transfer Protocol (HTTP) is most commonly used, but any transport should work.

Stick with us as we take a closer look at these web service building blocks.

Defining a message: SOAP

The Simple Object Access Protocol (SOAP) is a distributed protocol similar to CORBA and Java RMI. It lets applications talk to each other by exchanging messages over a network protocol, most commonly HTTP. SOAP is heavily dependent on XML, and every SOAP message is an XML document that contains several elements (such as `Envelope`, `Header`, and `Body`). The SOAP header contains application-specific infrastructure data, such as security information. The SOAP body contains the message being exchanged between applications. While the SOAP header is optional for a SOAP message, the SOAP envelope and body are mandatory.

Here is an example of a SOAP message with an empty header. The body includes an XML representation of ActionBazaar's `addBid` method with its parameters:

```
<SOAP-ENV:Envelope
  xmlns:SOAP-ENV="http://schemas.xmlsoap.org/soap/envelope/"
  SOAP-ENV:encodingStyle="http://schemas.xmlsoap.org/soap/encoding/">
  <SOAP-ENV:Header/>
  <SOAP-ENV:Body>
    <addBid xmlns="http://actionbazaar.com/Bidding">
      <user-id>viper</user-id>
      <item-id>100</user-id>
      <bid-price>2000.24</bid-price>
    </addBid>
  </SOAP-ENV:Body>
</SOAP-ENV:Envelope>
```

This snippet shows the skeleton of each and every SOAP message. The message starts off with an `Envelope`, which typically declares a namespace and may include encoding. Immediately inside the `Envelope` is the `Header`, which is optional. This contains meta-information about the message, such as security, network routing, and other data required to get the message to its destination. The last piece of the SOAP message is the `Body`, which in the case of our example, defines the `addBid` method and its associated parameters.

Describing a web service: WSDL

The Web Services Description Language (WSDL) is central to a web service because it describes the service to possible consumers. It specifies the message type, port, supported operations, data types, and all other details about how the web service works, where it can be found, and what the client should expect in return. Listing 15.1 shows a sample WSDL for ActionBazaar's `PlaceBidService`.

Listing 15.1 WSDL for the PlaceBid service

```
<?xml version = '1.0' encoding = 'UTF-8'?>
<definitions xmlns="http://schemas.xmlsoap.org/wsdl/"
xmlns:soap12="http://schemas.xmlsoap.org/wsdl/soap12/" xmlns:soap
  ="http://schemas.xmlsoap.org/wsdl/soap/" xmlns:xsd
```

```
   ="http://www.w3.org/2001/XMLSchema" xmlns:mime
   ="http://schemas.xmlsoap.org/wsdl/mime/" xmlns:tns
   ="http://ejb3inaction.example.buslogic/" name="PlaceBidBeanService"
    targetNamespace="http://ejb3inaction.example.buslogic/">
     <types>                                              ⊲──❶ Data types
         <schema xmlns="http://www.w3.org/2001/XMLSchema"
 xmlns:wsdl="http://schemas.xmlsoap.org/wsdl/" xmlns:xsi=
 "http://www.w3.org/2001/XMLSchema-instance" xmlns:soap11-enc=
 "http://schemas.xmlsoap.org/soap/encoding/" targetNamespace=
 "http://ejb3inaction.example.buslogic/" elementFormDefault="qualified">
            <element name="addBid" type="tns:addBid"/>
            <complexType name="addBid">
                <sequence>
                   <element name="userId" type="string" nillable="true"/>
                   <element name="itemId" type="long" nillable="true"/>
                   <element name="bidPrice" type="double" nillable
                     ="true"/>
                </sequence>
            </complexType>
       <element name="addBidResponse" type="tns:addBidResponse"/>
            <complexType name="addBidResponse">
                <sequence>
                   <element name="return" type="long" nillable="true"/>
                </sequence>
            </complexType>
        </schema>
    </types>
    <message name="PlaceBidBeanPortType_addBid">     ⊲──❷ Messages
    <part name="parameters" element="tns:addBid"/>
    </message>
    <message name="PlaceBidBeanPortType_addBidResponse">
      <part name="parameters" element="tns:addBidResponse"/>
    </message>
    <portType name="PlaceBidBean">        ⊲──❸ Port types
        <operation name="addBid">
            <input message="tns:PlaceBidBeanPortType_addBid"/>
            <output message="tns:PlaceBidBeanPortType_
                            addBidResponse"/>
        </operation>
    </portType>
    <binding name="PlaceBidBeanSoapHttp"
                 type="tns:PlaceBidBean">   ⊲──❹ SOAP binding
        <soap:binding style="document"
        transport="http://schemas.xmlsoap.org/soap/http"/>
        <operation name="addBid">                    ⊲─┐
            <soap:operation soapAction=""/>     ❺   Operations
            <input>
                <soap:body use="literal"/>
            </input>
            <output>
                <soap:body use="literal"/>
```

```
            </output>
        </operation>
    </binding>
    <service name="PlaceBidBeanService">   ⬅─❻ Service
        <port name="PlaceBid"                     ❼ Port
                binding="tns:PlaceBidBeanSoapHttp">   ⬅┘
            <soap:address location="${oracle.scheme.host.port.
                and.context}/PlaceBid"/>
        </port>
    </service>
</definitions>
```

Let's briefly look at some important parts of a WSDL. In listing 15.1, the `types` element ❶ defines the data types exchanged when the web service is invoked. The parameters passed to and returned from a method are considered data types. The code ❷ defines the messages the service supports. A message may contain more than a message part. Each *message part* is actually part of the SOAP message being sent, and is either a parameter or result being passed. The code ❸ then defines the `portType`. A `portType` is the most important part of a WSDL; it defines operations that can be performed and the messages involved. The message, operations ❺, and protocol details of a service are defined using a binding ❹. This example defines the service to be a `document` style service. Finally, the code ❻ defines a top-level service that uses the binding we defined, using the port definition ❼.

Java to WSDL mapping

There is no one-to-one mapping between XML data types and Java; there never has been. This presents a problem because the data types expected by a service are defined in the WSDL. If a service is implemented in a non-Java language, that language must provide support for binding XML to it. But when a service is implemented in Java, the binding is accomplished through the Java Architecture for XML Binding (JAXB) 2.0 specification. JAXB allows web services to use the complete XML schema, which results in improved interoperability and ease of use.

While the details of binding Java to WSDL are beyond the scope of this book, you can find out more from the Java API for XML-Based Web Services (JAX-WS) specification at http://jcp.org/en/jsr/detail?id=224, and check out the JAXB specification at http://www.jcp.org/en/jsr/detail?id=222. You'll find an easy-to-use reference for mapping Java data types to XML and WSDL types at http://download-west.oracle.com/docs/cd/B25221_04/web.1013/b25603/apptypemapping.htm#BABCCAHA.

XML-RPC

When the forerunner of web services was in the lab of UserLand, Microsoft thought it might be something of value. Distributed remote procedure calls could be one way to solve certain technical problems they were looking at, and XML was just coming on the scene and gaining a lot of industry acceptance as a general-purpose metadata language. The team dubbed this new beast *XML-RPC* and the specification was less than seven pages long!

All of this was going along swimmingly until Microsoft decided they would rather go a different direction. Microsoft leaving the party wasn't a problem until about a year or so later, when they wanted back in. Their return to the idea of web services was different this time and they wanted more control of the XML-RPC direction. Users of XML-RPC were now concerned about the future of their successful little protocol, and what would happen if Microsoft took the reigns. UserLand and others in the community opted to make XML-RPC open source to avoid a Microsoft power play, and of course the Redmond Giant opposed this move. After wrestling for months, Microsoft eventually decided to go in a different direction, and began promoting what we now know as SOAP. As Paul Harvey is fond of saying, here's the rest of the story...

According to rumors, the original web service protocol was named SOAP. As you know, SOAP stands for Simple Object Access Protocol. A specification that can be defined in only seven pages definitely meets the "Simple" criterion. But when Microsoft wanted to part ways the second time, they wanted to take their name with them. The community of SOAP users at that time renamed their protocol XML-RPC, and Microsoft dubbed their new web service protocol SOAP. This explains how the SOAP protocol, which is neither simple, nor an object access protocol, got its name. At least that's how the rumor goes!

You can find out more about XML-RPC at http://en.wikipedia.org/wiki/XML-RPC.

Discovering a service: UDDI

If you plan on having a lot of services to share, you're going to need a way to find them. That's the whole reason that UDDI was invented. UDDI is a platform-independent, XML-based registry that enables clients to find available services.

The basic process is that a service can publish information about itself to a known UDDI registry, including the WSDL required for a client to communicate with the service. A client can search the registry looking for a particular type of service, vendor name, and similar information. Once a service catches the eye of the client, the client requests the WSDL for the service. The client will then consume the WSDL, bind to the service, and invoke the service using the published service description.

It is possible for mere humans to browse UDDI registries and manually sift through available services. This might be something interesting for you to do if you have never experienced a UDDI registry, or you aren't familiar with how they work. You can check out one such UDDI browser at http://soapclient.com/uddisearch.html and take a peek at the services hosted at this site while you're there.

For more details about the UDDI specification, hop over to www.oasis-open.org/committees/uddi-spec/doc/tcspecs.htm. Just be careful when you get there and make sure you can find your way out; we wouldn't want to lose you in the registry…

Transporting messages

For a service consumer and producer to communicate, they need a way to send messages to each other. These messages are sent over a network using a protocol that both parties can support. Given that the Web is ubiquitous, HTTP is everywhere. It makes sense that it would be the most widely used transport for web service messages. HTTP also has the advantage that it is one of the few protocols allowed through firewalls, as long as well-known ports like 80 and 8080 are used.

But as we stated, web services just need to operate over a network. That means almost any network protocol could be used to transport messages. Where HTTP is not an option, some protocols that are in use include SMTP, FTP, and JMS. What? Your favorite gopher protocol not in the list? Why not grab the SOAP spec and implement it yourself? That ought to be a fun weekend project.

15.1.2 Web services styles

There are two primary types of web services styles: RPC-oriented and document-oriented. The RPC style of web services was popular initially, but more recently the pendulum has swung in the direction of document-oriented web services. One reason for this shift is that you can make better use of an XML schema with document-oriented web service. To learn some of the differences between RPC and document-oriented web services, visit http://expertanswercenter.techtarget.com/eac/knowledgebaseAnswer/0,295199,sid63_gci984152,00.html.

The messaging style for a web service may be either literal or encoded. When you use literal, the messages are exchanged with plain XML. However, an encoded message includes an external rule about how to decode the message. The receiver of the message has to decode the message by using the decoding attribute. The WS-I Basic Profile 1.1 doesn't support encoded messages.

The most popular combination of web service style and messaging style is document/literal. This is because the WSI Basic Profile only supports the document/literal combination for maximum interoperability between platforms. Document/literal-style messages are constrained by an XML schema. The schema can reside in the WSDL or can be referred to with an URI. The end result is that you can manage the structure of your message in the same way that DBAs manage table definitions with versioning. The RPC/encoded combination puts the schema in the actual message itself, which makes it much more tightly coupled to the message. Stick with what the WSI Basic Profile supports (document/literal), and your web services will enjoy maximum interoperability and acceptance by the widest possible audience.

15.1.3 Approaches to developing web services

Only a few standard approaches exist for building a web service. These approaches are independent of whatever tools you may be using but are somewhat specific to the SOAP style of building web services.

Bottom up

The *bottom-up strategy* is the most popular approach to developing a web service. It allows you to reuse your investments by exposing your existing applications. For example, ActionBazaar is an existing application with proven business value. Competitive pressure is moving ActionBazaar to expose some of this business functionality as web services. The implementation class already exists. All that is needed is to create a WSDL and expose the implementation class as a web service. Java EE 5 allows either POJOs or stateless EJBs to be exposed as web services. Most application servers provide tools and utilities to generate WSDL from existing Java classes.

Top down

Top down is the correct way to build any new web service, and is often termed the "pure approach" to building a web service. Also known as *contract first web services*, this approach starts with the WSDL (the *contract*) by defining operations, messages, and so forth. Then you build the endpoint interface, and finally the implementation class. If you are building a web service from scratch, we recommend that you follow this approach. Most application servers provide development tools to create WSDL and then provide the ability to generate a Java class from the WSDL. Just add your business logic to the generated class, stir in a little water, bake at 350 degrees for 5 minutes, and your new web service should be ready to pop out of the oven!

Meet in the middle

In the meet-in-the-middle approach, you start with both the WSDL and implementation class and wire the WSDL with the implementation class. This is harder to implement and can be difficult to maintain since you have to pay a lot more attention to keeping things in synch. We recommend you avoid this approach if at all possible.

The movement from the bottom-up to the top-down approach of building SOAP-based web services is still in progress. Many IT shops are still using bottom up as the tool support is by far the best for this approach, and because web services have been limited to use within the enterprise for many industries. As interoperability between companies and technologies increases in value, we expect top down, specifically contract first web services, to become the widest adopted approach to defining and building web services.

Now that you are aware of the approaches to building SOAP-based web services, what protocols and standards exist to assist you in such an endeavor? The next section points you down the path that so many have helped to build: the path to the Java web services platform.

15.2 JAX-WS: Java EE 5 web services platform

Java EE 5 provides a robust platform on which you can build and deploy web services. Java EE 5 allows you to build web services with either regular Java class (POJO) or EJB 3 stateless session beans. In this section we'll briefly introduce the web services platform and then explain why you would choose EJB 3 session beans over POJOs.

15.2.1 Introducing the web services platform

The Java API for XML-Based Web Services (JAX-WS[3]) 2.0 is the core specification that defines the web services standard for Java EE 5. JAX-WS 2.0 is an extension of the Java API for XML-RPC (JAX-RPC) 1.0. The goal for JAX-WS 2.0 is to simplify development of web services applications. It depends on several other specifications, listed in table 15.1. You can expect that several books will be written

---

[3] http://www.jcp.org/en/jsr/detail?id=224

Table 15.1   Specifications Java EE 5.0 builds on to support web services

Specification	Purpose
Java API for XML Web Services 2.0	Platform specification
Java API for XML Binding 2.0	Binding for WSDL to Java
WS Basic Profile 1.1	Interoperability with .NET
Web Services Metadata 2.0	Metadata approach to define web service
Java API for XML RPC 1.1	Backward compatibility with J2EE 1.4 web services

about these specifications, and we encourage you to become familiar with them as they are made available.

As you can see on table 15.1, a lot of time and sweat has been spent by various industry groups in thinking about and defining web services. Folks who tell you web services are still in their infancy are just not up to speed with what's going on in this arena. This chapter is littered with references pointing you to just a fraction of the overwhelming amount of information available on web services. If you want more in-depth coverage of a specific topic, you're only a browser page or two away from opening the mother lode!

Of course, this begs the question: why consider using EJB 3 as your web service implementation instead of POJOs? There are some distinct advantages to the EJB 3 option, which we discuss in the next section.

15.2.2 *Why choose EJB over a POJO for a web service?*

JAX-WS 2.0 allows both regular Java classes and stateless EJBs to be exposed as web services. If you were using J2EE 1.4, you're probably wondering why you'd use a stateless EJB as a web service. A look at the code for a POJO and for EJB 3 web services reveals that there are hardly any differences, with the exception that the EJB 3 web service will have a few extra annotations. A Java class web service is packaged in a web module, whereas an EJB web service is packaged in an EJB-JAR.

Both a Java web service and an EJB web service support dependency injection and lifecycle methods such as `@PostConstruct` and `@PreDestroy`, but you gain a few extra benefits from using EJB 3 web services.

First, you automatically get the benefits of declarative transaction and security available only to EJB 3 components. You can use interceptors and the timer service if your applications need them, without depending on extra layering.

Second, a web service that uses EJB 3 can easily expose your business applications using additional protocols, such as RMI, by adding a remote interface. As you saw in the previous section, exposing an EJB 3 stateless session bean is easy and can be done by simply adding the @WebService annotation.

Table 15.2 compares the features supported by EJB 3 web services with a regular Java web service.

Table 15.2 Feature comparison of Java web services to EJB 3 web services

Feature	Java Web Service	EJB 3 Web Service
POJO	Yes	Yes
Dependency injection of resources, persistence units, etc.	Yes	Yes
Lifecycle methods	Yes	Yes
Declarative transaction	No	Yes
Declarative security	No	Yes
Requires annotation processing in an external Annotation Processing Tool (APT)	Yes	Most EJB containers do not require this.
Can be run in a web container like Tomcat	Yes	No

When this chapter was written, most Java EE containers required regular Java classes using web services metadata to run through an annotation processor before deployment. This is in contrast to EJB 3 annotations, which are dynamically processed during deployment, thus greatly simplifying the development process. This optimization is yet another reason to consider using EJB 3 for your web service implementations.

Next we'll see how to expose a stateless EJB as a web service, as defined in the Web Services Metadata 2.0 specification. This isn't the only way to expose an EJB as a web service (you could use deployment descriptors), but you'll go this route if you're using the JAX-WS 2.0 approach. If you like annotations, this one's for you!

15.3 Developing EJB web services with JAX-WS 2.0

Using JAX-RPC web services with EJB 2.1 makes exposing a simple EJB as a web service a lot more difficult than it should be. You have to perform the following steps, typically by hand:

- Generate the WSDL describing the service.
- Build a service endpoint interface (SEI)—the actual service portion of the web service.
- Identify the endpoint interface in `ejb-jar.xml`.
- Package all of these with `webservices.xml`.

If you prefer that approach, you can certainly use it—every time you want to publish a new service! The good news is that EJB 3 and JAX-WS 2.0 tremendously simplify the whole process. You don't piddle around with WSDL, mapping files, or descriptors, as these are automatically generated for you during deployment. Web service metadata makes bottom-up development much simpler.

Let's first see a straightforward EJB 3 example exposed as a web service, and then dive into the details of some commonly used annotations that can make defining web services even easier. Listing 15.2 shows the `PlaceBid` bean exposed as a web service.

Listing 15.2 PlaceBid EJB as a web service

```
@WebService(targetNamespace                          ❶ Exposes web service
  = "urn:ActionBazaarPlaceBidService")
@SOAPBinding(style = SOAPBinding.Style.DOCUMENT)
@Stateless(name = "PlaceBid")                        ❷ Defines binding style
public class PlaceBidBean implements PlaceBid {
@PersistenceContext private EntityManager em;
  public PlaceBidBean() {
  }
                    ❸ Exposes method in web service
  @WebMethod
  @WebResult(name = "bidNumber")       ❹ Customizes name for
  public Long addBid(                      return parameter
    @WebParam(name = "User") String userId,          ❺ Customizes name for
    @WebParam(name = "Item") Long itemId,               passed parameter
    @WebParam(name = "Price") Double bidPrice) {
      return persistBid(userId, itemId, bidPrice);
  }

  private Long persistBid(String userId, Long itemId, Double bidPrice)
  {
  }
}
```

In listing 15.2, we used the `@javax.jws.WebService` annotation ❶ to expose `Place-BidBean` as a web service. You can use the annotation with an endpoint interface or the bean class itself. As in our example, if you use the @WebService annotation in the bean class the endpoint interface will be generated automatically. We'll elaborate on the details of this annotation in the next section. We specified that the web service is a document-style web service by using the @javax.jws.SOAPBinding annotation ❷. We used the @javax.jws.WebMethod annotation to expose the addBid method in the web service ❸. You can use the @javax.jws.WebResult ❹ and @javax.jws.WebParam ❺ annotations to control the parameter names generated in the WSDL.

> **NOTE** Using the @WebService annotation creates a stateless EJB to a web service. The rest of the annotations are optional.

In this section you'll learn how to use web services metadata annotations. We'll start with using the @WebService annotation to convert an EJB to a web service. You'll then see how to use the @SOAPBinding annotation to specify the web service style. You'll also learn about other annotations, such as @WebMethod, @WebParam, and @WebResult.

15.3.1 *Using the @WebService annotation*

The @WebService annotation is used on a bean or an interface class. If you use this annotation on the bean class, the annotation processor or the EJB container will generate the interface for you. If you already have a bean interface, then you can mark the @WebService annotation on the interface and the bean class will look like this:

```
@WebService
public interface PlaceBidWS {
  public Long addBid(String bidderId, Long itemId, Double bidPrice);
}

@Stateless(name = "PlaceBid")
public class PlaceBidBean implements PlaceBidWS, PlaceBid {
  ...
}
```

If you use the @WebService annotation on the interface, then all public methods on the web service endpoint will be exposed in the web service. In our example we have only one method (addBid), and it will be exposed in the web service.

A careful look at the code reveals that the @WebService endpoint interface looks similar to the remote interface. You might be tempted to mark the same interface as both a web service and a remote interface, like this:

```
@WebService
@Remote
public interface PlaceBid {
    public Long addBid(String bidderId, Long itemId, Double bidPrice);
}
```

Unfortunately, although some vendors allow this as an extension, this is not part of the specification, and code that uses this particular attribute combination won't be portable.

Next, let's take a peek at how you can use different elements of the @Web-Service annotation to customize different elements in your WSDL. Listing 15.3 shows the details of the @WebService endpoint interface.

Listing 15.3   Elements of the @WebService annotation

```
@Target({TYPE})
public @interface WebService {
    String name() default "";
    String targetNamespace() default "";
    String serviceName() default "";
    String wsdlLocation() default "";        ⊲──┐ Location of WSDL
    String endpointInterface() default "";   ⊲─┐ Fully qualified interface
    String portName() default "";            │ name for SEI
};
```

All elements on the @WebService annotation besides wsdlLocation and endpoint-Interface are used to customize the WSDL generation. wsdlLocation is useful when you are following a meet-in-the-middle approach and you want to use a pre-existing WSDL. It defines the URL for the WSDL; for example:

```
@WebService(wsdlLocation = "META-INF/myPlaceBidService.wsdl")
public interface PlaceBidWS {
    public Long addBid(String bidderId, Long itemId, Double bidPrice);
}
```

When you specify wsdlLocation, the server will use the WSDL specified. If there are any inconsistencies between the existing WSDL and the implementation class, the container will generate the corresponding deployment errors.

As stated earlier, the server automatically generates the service endpoint interface (SEI) if the @WebService annotation is used in the bean class. This generated name is vendor specific, and most of the time that works just fine. If you find yourself needing to specify the endpointInterface element to use a specific name, try this:

```
@WebService(endPointInterface = "actionbazaar.buslogic.PlaceBidSEI")
@Stateless(name = "PlaceBid")
public class PlaceBidBean implements placeBid{}
```

Use the `name` element in the `@WebService` annotation to specify the name of the web service. If you don't specify the `name` element, the name of the bean class or interface will be used by default. This is the same as the `name` attribute in the `portType` tag in the WSDL. In our example, the server will use the name `PlaceBidBean` because of the following setting:

```
<portType name = "PlaceBidBean">
   ...
</portType>
```

You can use the `targetNamespace` element to specify the target namespace for the WSDL elements generated by the web service. If you don't specify this element, the EJB container will use the Java package name to generate a default XML namespace.

You can use the `serviceName` element to specify the service name. Specifying the `serviceName` is only allowed when you annotate the bean class. The name specified using `serviceName` is used for generating the `name` attribute in the service element in the WSDL. If you don't specify the `serviceName` element, the server will generate it using the default, which is the bean class name appended with `Service`.

```
<service name = "PlaceBidBeanService">
   ...
</service>
```

This code snippet shows what happens if the `serviceName` isn't specified for the `PlaceBidBean` EJB. The bean name `PlaceBidBean` is concatenated with `Service` by the WSDL generator, and `PlaceBidBeanService` is specified as the name of the web service in the WSDL.

Similarly, you use the `portName` element to set the name of the `port` specified in the WSDL.

15.3.2 *Specifying the web service style with @SOAPBinding*

As discussed earlier, the two types of services supported are document-oriented or RPC-oriented web services. You can use the `@javax.jws.SOAPBinding` annotation to control the style of the web service. This example shows the `@SOAPBinding` annotation in action:

```
@WebService(targetNamespace = "urn:ActionBazaarPlaceBidService")
@SOAPBinding(style = SOAPBinding.Style.RPC,
```

```
            use = SOAPBinding.Use.ENCODED,
            parameterStyle = SOAPBinding.ParameterStyle.BARE)
@Stateless(name = "PlaceBid")
public class PlaceBidBean implements PlaceBid {
}
```

Now let's consider the various elements of the @SOAPBinding annotation and how they work. These elements are defined in listing 15.4.

Listing 15.4   Elements of the @SOAPBinding annotation

```
@Retention(value = RetentionPolicy.RUNTIME)
@Target({TYPE})
public @interface SOAPBinding {
  public enum Style {
    DOCUMENT,
    RPC                                           ❶ Web service style
  };
  Style style() default Style.DOCUMENT;

  public enum Use {
    LITERAL,
    ENCODED                                       ❷ Messaging style
  };
  Use use() default Use.LITERAL;

  public enum ParameterStyle {
    BARE,
    WRAPPED
  };                                                   Parameter style ❸

  ParameterStyle parameterStyle() default ParameterStyle.WRAPPED;
}
```

You can use the style element to define the web service style. Valid values are DOCUMENT and RPC ❶ in listing 15.4. The default style is DOCUMENT. You can specify the use element to configure the messaging style with one of the valid values, LITERAL or ENCODED ❷. You must use the LITERAL style of messaging if you expect your services to work with clients not developed by you, because SOAP encoding can cause problems with interoperability of web services and therefore is not allowed by the WS-I Basic Profile 1.1. You can specify parameterStyle to configure how message parameters are specified. The valid values for parameterStyle are BARE and the default, WRAPPED ❸.

15.3.3 *Using @WebMethod*

You can apply the `@javax.jws.WebMethod` annotation on a method to expose it as part of the web service. If you have multiple methods in the bean implementation class and you use a generated endpoint interface, you must annotate `@WebMethod` on the methods you want to expose in the web service. The following listing shows the details of the `@WebMethod` annotation:

```
@Target({METHOD})
public @interface WebMethod {
  String operationName() default "";
  String action() default "" ;
  boolean exclude() default false;
};
```

If you don't use the `@WebMethod` annotation, all public methods in the bean class that use a generated interface will be exposed in the web service. There are several reasons why this may not be a good idea. First, it is inefficient to have fine-grained web service methods. Like EJBs, web services should be coarse-grained. Second, it might create a tight coupling between your server and potential clients.

> **NOTE** If you use the `@WebMethod` annotation on an endpoint interface, your server will ignore it and expose all methods of the endpoint interface in the web service.

If you have multiple methods in the bean class and there are methods that you don't want to expose in the web service, you can set the `exclude` element to `true` as follows:

```
@WebService(endPointInterface = "PlaceBidSEI")
@Stateless
public class PlaceBidBean {
  public Long addBid(..) {
  }

  @WebMethod(exclude = "true")
  public Long persistBid(..) {
  }
}
```

Using this technique, the `persistBid` method will not be exposed in the web service when the `PlaceBid` EJB web service is deployed.

   You can use the `operationName` and `action` elements in the `@WebMethod` annotation to specify the operation and SOAP action, respectively, as in the following example.

```
@WebMethod(operationName = "addNewBid",
           action = "http://actionbazaar.com/NewBid")
public Long addBid(...) {
}
```

The `operationName`, as defined above the `addBid` method, will generate the following WSDL:

```
<portType name = "PlaceBidBean">
  <operation name = "addNewBid">
    ...
  </operation>
</portType>
```

Notice how the actual method name is `addBid` but the method named exposed in the web service is `addNewBid`. You can use this to help map the service contract to the actual implementation. Even if that implementation changes over time, the contract can remain intact. If the `operationName` isn't specified, it will default to the implementation name of the method.

Similarly, the `action` element we defined earlier will be used for generating the `SOAPAction` in the WSDL as follows:

```
<operation name = "addNewBid">
  <soap:operation soapAction = "http://actionbazaar.com/NewBid"/>
...
</operation>
```

The `SOAPAction` element determines the `header` element in the HTTP request message. It is used by the web service client when communicating with the web service using SOAP over HTTP. The content of the `SOAPAction` header field is used by the endpoint to determine the true intended destination rather than having to parse the SOAP message body to find this information.

This section gave you a tour of the `@WebMethod` annotation so you know how to define the method name for a web service. Next we'll look at how to define parameters for our new web methods with the `@WebParam` annotation.

15.3.4 *Using the @WebParam annotation*

You can utilize the `@javax.jws.WebParam` annotation in conjunction with `@Web-Method` to customize a parameter for the web service message part generated in the WSDL. You saw a simple use of `@WebParam` in the `PlaceBid` EJB web service in section 15.3; here is a more comprehensive example:

```
@WebMethod
public Long addBid(
```

```
@WebParam(name = "user",
          mode = WebParam.Mode.IN) String userId, ...) {
...
}
```

Let's break this example down by looking at this annotation's details. The specification for the @WebParam annotation looks like this:

```
@Target({PARAMETER})
public @interface WebParam {
  public enum Mode { IN, OUT, INOUT };
  String name() default "";
  String targetNamespace() default "";
  Mode mode() default Mode.IN;
  boolean header() default false;
  String partName() default "";
};
```

The name element can specify the name parameter for the message in the WSDL. If you do not specify name, the default value generated will be the same as the name of the argument.

You can use the targetNamespace element for customizing the XML namespace for the message part. If you do not specify targetNamespace, the server will use the namespace used for the web service.

The mode element will work to specify the type of the parameter. Valid options are IN, OUT, or INOUT (both). This mode determines how the parameter is flowing. If you specify a parameter as OUT or INOUT, the argument must be of type javax.xml.ws.Holder as follows:

```
@WebParam(name = "user", mode = WebParam.Mode.INOUT)
  Holder<String> userId, ...) {
  ...
}
```

The holder class provides a reference to immutable object references. You can use a Java generic holder type, javax.xml.ws.Holder<String>, which is defined by the Java XML web services specification. The details of Holder types are not within the scope of this book; for more details, refer to the Java XML WS 2.0 specification.

You can set the header element to true if the message is pulled from the header of the message and not from the message body.

As we discussed earlier, you can pass any optional information (such as security) that isn't part of the actual message in the SOAP header. When a SOAP message is exchanged between parties, it may go through several intermediaries, such as an authentication system. These intermediaries are not supposed to read the actual payload or message body, but are allowed to read the SOAP header. Setting header to `true` will generate the WSDL with the SOAP header as follows:

```
<operation name = "addNewBid">
  <soap:operation soapAction = "urn:NewBid"/>
  <input>
    <soap:header message = "tns:PlaceBid_addNewBid"
                 part = "user"
                 use = "literal"/>
    <soap:body use = "literal" parts = "parameters"/>
  </input>
...
</operation>
```

You can use the `partName` element to control the generated `name` element of the `wsdl:part` or XML schema element of the parameter, if the web service binding style is RPC, or if the binding style is `document` and the parameter style is BARE. If you don't specify the name for an RPC-style web service and `partName` is specified, the server will use `partName` to generate the name of the element.

15.3.5 *Using the @WebResult annotation*

The `@WebResult` annotation is very similar to `@WebParam`. It operates in conjunction with `@WebMethod` to control the generated name for the message return value in the WSDL, as illustrated here:

```
@WebMethod
@WebResult(name = "bidNumber")
public Long addBid(...){}
```

The `@WebResult` annotation specification resembles the specification for `@WebParam`. You'll notice it's a bit smaller, though, because you have less control over return values than you do over parameters.

```
public @interface WebResult {
  String name() default "return";
  String targetNamespace() default "";
  boolean header() default false;
  String partName() default "";
};
```

The `name` element specifies the name of the value returned in the WSDL.

Use the `targetNamespace` element for customizing the XML namespace for the returned value. This works for document-style web services where the return value binds to an XML namespace. If you don't specify `targetNamespace`, the server will use the namespace allocated for the web service.

You can set the header element to true if the return value is returned as a part of the message header.

As with the @WebParam annotation, you have to use the partName argument to customize the name of value returned from an operation.

15.3.6 *Using @OneWay and @HandlerChain*

The web services metadata annotation specification defines two more annotations: @OneWay and @HandlerChain. We'll briefly introduce them, and we encourage you to explore them if you think you need to. The @OneWay annotation is used with a web service operation that does not have a corresponding output (return value). It can be used on a method as follows:

```
@WebMethod
@OneWay
public void pingServer() {
}
```

In this case, pingServer doesn't return anything and @OneWay optimizes the message to reflect this.

The @HandlerChain annotation is used to define a set of handlers that are invoked in response to a SOAP message. Logically, handlers are similar to EJB interceptors that were discussed earlier in part 2 of this book. Handlers are defined in an XML file. It probably makes sense to align interceptor annotations and web services handlers in a future release of Java EE, and use the interceptor programming model for JAX-WS handlers. Also, it's worth mentioning that in an EJB web service, both EJB 3 interceptors and message handlers will fit the bill.

> **TIP** If you are using both JAX-WS handlers and interceptors in the same web service, invoking InvocationContext.getContextData() in the interceptor or WebServiceContext.getMessageContext() in the JAX-WS handler will return the same Map instance.

This concludes our discussion of web service metadata. The metadata makes development of EJB 3 web services very easy. You can essentially just annotate the bean class with @WebService and it automagically converts it to an EJB web service. Is this a huge improvement over the previous approach, or what?

Exposing a web service is one thing. What about consuming a web service? Is being on the client end of the web service connection easier with EJB 3? The next section walks you through using an EJB 3 session bean as a client to a web service. We think after you've read it you just may answer the previous question with a resounding yes!

15.4 Accessing a web service from an EJB

The first step to building a web service is to publish some standalone services that can be used by interested parties. But there's a whole lot more to building an SOA than that. You'll need to move to level 2 (to borrow terminology used in the gaming world). The next level of web services involves building aggregate services. This is where two or more services are combined to provide an even more coarse-grained functionality.

Of course, there is the simpler case where the service you expose simply needs to leverage a service not built by you. Either way, you're the client in this scenario, so let's see what's involved in invoking web services from EJB 3. First we'll examine a standalone Java client for testing the `PlaceBid` web service that we built in an earlier section; then we'll explore how you can access a web service from an EJB such as a session bean or MDB.

15.4.1 Accessing the PlaceBid web service

An EJB web service doesn't differ from any other web service and can be invoked by a client written in Java, .NET, or any other programming language. The client for the EJB web service can be any of the following types:

- Java application client
- Dynamic proxy
- Dynamic Invocation Interface (DII)

Details about each of these clients are beyond the scope of this book. In this section, we'll see an example of Java EE application client that uses the `@WebService-Ref` annotation to invoke the web service. Listing 15.5 shows an example of an application client invoking the `PlaceBid` web service that we built earlier.

Listing 15.5 Java application client accessing the PlaceBid web service

```
import javax.xml.ws.WebServiceRef ;                    ❶ Generated service
import actionbazaarplacebidservice.PlaceBidService;       interface

@WebServiceRef(wsdlLocation=             Injects web service reference ❷
        "http://localhost:8080/PlaceBidService/PlaceBidBean?WSDL")
  private static PlaceBidService placeBidService;

    public static void main(String [] args) {    Gets a proxy to ❸
        try {                                      web servicee
            actionbazaarplacebidservice.PlaceBidBean placeBid =
                    placeBidService.getPlaceBidBeanPort();
```

```
                System.out.println("Bid Successful, BidId Received is:"
                +placeBid.addBid("dpanda",
                                 Long.valueOf(9001),   2000005.50 ));    ◄─┐
            } catch (Exception ex) {
                ex.printStackTrace();                        Invokes method  ❹
            }
        }
    }

    }
```

In listing 15.5, the client uses `actionbazaarplacebidservice.PlaceBidService`, which is the generated service interface ❶. We use the `@WebServiceRef` annotation to inject a reference to the `PlaceBid` service by specifying the WSDL location ❷. We retrieve the web service port from the injected web service by invoking the `getPlaceBidBeanPort` method ❸. After we retrieve the port, we can invoke the operations allowed on the port ❹. We'll discuss `@WebServiceRef` in more depth in the next section. For now, all you need to know is that it is used to inject web service references.

If you use an application, as we did in our example, you must use the web services utility provided by your vendor to generate the client-side artifacts for accessing the web service. The tool reads the WSDL document and generates the endpoint interface and the `proxy` classes that can be used to invoke methods on the web service as a local object.

For example, the GlassFish/Java EE SDK provides utilities named `wscompile` or `wsimport` to generate the client-side proxy classes. Check out the build script (`build.xml`) of the online code samples for chapter 15 (www.manning.com/panda); in the sample provided for the Java EE 5 SDK (GlassFish) and you'll see a task named gen-proxy:

```
<target name="gen-proxy" depends="setup">

    <exec executable="${J2EE_HOME}/bin/${wsimport}" failonerror="true">
      <arg line="-keep -d ${cli.proxy.dir} http://${admin.host}:
        ${http.port}/PlaceBidService/PlaceBidBean?WSDL"/>
    </exec>
  </target>
```

As you can see, `wsimport` takes the WSDL as input and generates the client-side artifacts, which includes the service interface and proxy classes. After compiling the client and other artifacts, you should be able to run the client to test the web service.

Now that you've seen an example web service client, let's expand on the topic and see how you can access a web service.

15.4.2 EJB as a web service client

You can use either a session bean or an MDB to invoke a web service. For example, customers can track the status of items ordered from ActionBazaar. Internally, ActionBazaar uses the `TrackOrder` EJB to track this status. An external company, the Turtle and Snail Trucking Company, is used to ship the orders. The trucking company happens to be a heavy user of Microsoft technologies, and they provided a web service to track the status of orders. The `TrackOrder` EJB invokes this web service to check the delivery status of orders. The following code snippet of the `TrackOrder` EJB invokes a web service:

```
@Stateless
public class TrackOrderBean implements TrackOrder {

  @WebServiceRef(TrackDeliveryService.class)      ◁─❶ Injects web service
  private TrackDeliverySEI deliveryService;

  public String checkOrderDeliverStatus(String shipId) {
    ...

    String deliveryStatus =
      deliveryService.checkDeliveryStatus(shipId);   ◁─❷ Invokes web service
    ...
  }
}
```

You learned from an earlier example that you can use `@javax.xml.ws.WebServiceRef` to reference and inject an instance of either the service class or endpoint interface. As you'll recall, in listing 15.5 we used a generated service interface.

Injection of `@WebServiceRef` is supported only in managed classes. In our example we are injecting an endpoint ❶, and then invoking a method on the endpoint interface ❷. Optionally you can use `@WebServiceRef` to inject a service interface as follows:

```
@WebServiceRef
private TrackingService service;
```

If you're using a service interface (`TrackingService`), then it must extend `javax.xml.ws.Service`. The service interface or endpoint interfaces and the client-side proxy classes can typically be generated either on the fly by tools or utilities provided with the SOAP stack. These vary by vendor.

Although the Turtle and Snail Trucking Company uses the .NET platform for developing the tracking web service, you can't use that interface with the Java EE platform. Therefore, you have to generate the endpoint interface by using tools supplied by your vendor. You do this by pointing the tool at the WSDL of `Track-DeliveryService`.

The `@WebServiceRef` annotation is similar to `@javax.annotation.Resource` (which we discussed in chapter 5). You can use the `@WebServiceRef` annotation to establish a reference at the class level or use field/setter injection. Table 15.3 describes the various elements of the `@WebServiceRef` annotation.

Table 15.3   Elements of @WebServiceRef

Element	Description
`name`	The JNDI name for the web service. It gets bound to `java:comp/env/<name>` in the ENC.
`wsdlLocation`	The WSDL location for the service. If not specified, then it is derived from the referenced service class.
`type`	The Java type of the resource.
`value`	The service class; always a type extending `javax.xml.ws.Service`.
`mappedName`	Vendor-specific global JNDI name for the service.

This concludes our discussion of invoking a web service from an EJB. You've now seen how to expose your web service for potential clients to consume, as well as how to access other web services on the network regardless of what technology was used to develop them. The new JAX-WS 2.0 annotations make defining and working with web services significantly easier than previous web service standards.

Next we'll discuss some best practices you can use to build web services that maximize their interoperability opportunities.

15.5 *Best practices for web service development*

In this section we outline some of the best practices for building web services.

Determine whether you really need your application to be exposed as a web service and that your application requires interoperability. If not, then consider using alternative technologies and protocols because you will most likely find better performance in using alternative protocols such as RMI. Regardless of the technology used, at this point in the SOAP web service paradigm, messing around with all that XML can put a real strain on your network. Options for sending binary web service messages are just now emerging, but they are still a few years away from being widely available.

So the first recommendation is for you not to expose all your EJBs as web services. In addition, whenever considering methods to expose, only expose coarse-grained EJBs as web services. Either build a service endpoint interface for your EJB, or use the `@WebMethod` annotation to limit the methods exposed in the web service.

Analyze whether you need RPC-oriented or document-oriented web services. You can use the `@SOAPBinding` annotation to control the style for your EJB web service. RPC-style web services may perform better than document style web services. However, document style web services provide more flexibility because you can use XML schemas to define the messages. Similarly, avoid using message encoding because it makes your services less interoperable, as well as less portable between SOAP implementations. Document/literal is the recommended combination for an interoperable web service.

Design your EJB web service so that it creates very minimal network traffic. Avoid sending large objects over the wire. It's better to send an `Id` or reference to an object instead of sending the entire object. All objects sent via SOAP are serialized into XML. The XML representation of data can be quite large, making SOAP messages much more expensive than retrieving the object in the target location. In addition, if your EJB involves a long-running transaction, avoid exposing it as a web service, or mark it as not returning a value so that it can be invoked in a more asynchronous manner.

Use JAX-WS data types as the method parameters for your web service to give it interoperability with heterogeneous web services. Suppose you have an object graph involving `Collections`, `HashMaps`, and `Lists` as web service parameters. Using these data types in the WSDL makes your application less interoperable. Test your applications to make sure they comply with the WS-I Basic Profile if interoperability is important for your application.

There are several mechanisms to secure your web services. You must weigh your security requirements against performance, because security comes with a high cost. The performance costs of end-to-end security are commonly higher than the initial perceived costs. This is true in general of system/application security, but even more so with regard to web services that are designed to be shared with unknown client applications.

15.6 *Summary*

In this chapter you learned how to expose a stateless session bean as a web service. First, we walked through a brief review of web service components and approaches to web service development. You saw that web service metadata greatly simplifies the development of EJB 3 web services by turning an EJB into a web service using one annotation: @WebService. JAX-WS 2.0–compliant containers dynamically generate endpoint interfaces, WSDL, and mapping files, and don't require that you perform the mundane task of packaging several deployment descriptors and mapping files. You saw that different annotations supported by web services metadata can be used for controlling specific elements of the WSDL. It's also possible to use an existing WSDL with an EJB 3 web service.

EJB 3 web services provide several benefits compared with regular Java class web services, although there is hardly any difference in coding style.

Your EJB application may require invoking a web service, and you can use either a SEI or service interface via the @WebServiceRef annotation.

Finally, we reviewed some best practices in using EJB 3 with web services. Following these guidelines can make your web services more interoperable and better performing.

EJB 3 and Spring

This chapter covers

- Spring-enabled session beans
- Injecting session beans into Spring POJOs
- Using JPA with Spring

When the EJB portion of J2EE first came along, the industry flocked toward it. Imagine, an industry-wide specification for building distributed applications with layers and tiers and business logic! Prior to EJB 1's attempt to do this, developers were constantly wrestling with two options, neither of which was ideal: use a proprietary vendor product or write your own. Both amounted to the same option; it's just that in the second case the development team was the vendor with the one-of-a-kind solution. No matter how you looked at the domain, it meant vendor lock-in.

The road to EJB acceptance was not without challenges. The specification was vast and rigid, and placed a lot of constraints on developers and impacted how they built their applications. The industry wasn't quite thrilled. EJB 2 went into development in an attempt to plug all the holes in EJB 1. Although EJB 2 did address many of the issues that plagued developers (such as defining more consistency in how vendors implemented the specification in order to make EJB applications more portable between vendor platforms), the programming model was still too verbose. It had become an all-or-nothing proposition for EJB 2. You either bought into the whole EJB 2/J2EE programming paradigm, or you didn't buy into any of it. Architects found it difficult to design applications that only used parts of the specification. Enter the dawn of the lightweight Java application framework. (Cue eerie music…)

Sure, various pockets of the open source software (OSS) community had been working on these issues for a while—almost as soon as EJB 1 was released. Developers have a way of wanting to explore new avenues and solve hard problems; the application container crowd is no different. Apache did have some success with their Avalon[1] framework, which may be the most well known, but others wading into these waters discovered some useful principles for building lightweight containers. A couple of these are the Keel framework (www.keelframework.org) and the DNA framework (http://dna.codehaus.org). While there was interest in such lofty-minded goals, most of the industry viewed this commotion as fringe activity and ignored it until sometime around the middle of 2004, when Rod Johnson and a talented set of developers from Interface 21 began energetically promoting the Spring Framework (www.springframework.org).

By now you may be looking up from this book and staring off into space, contemplating the question "What does Spring have to do with EJB 3?" Well, we're glad you're perceptive enough to ponder such matters, and we'll see if we can answer that question by continuing with our little story.

---

[1] This project is now closed; it's no longer an active Apache project.

Spring and EJB proponents haven't always seen eye to eye. Spring adopters have more likely than not been burned by the weight of previous EJB specifications. In contrast, the EJB faithful have felt that the Spring folks have gone too far by moving away from an industry standard. This has created some fracturing in the Java community. Yet we still have to deal with the developer's insatiable desire to explore, understand, and solve hard problems. Hmmm... where might this lead us?

We propose that this leads us to the reality that some in the Spring camp are interested in EJB 3. They would like to experiment with it, but they don't want to leave their newfound comfort zone of the Spring container. The staunch EJB camp may also be intrigued by the whole Spring movement. After all, this movement is still growing; there has to be something to it, doesn't there? Then there's the third group: those who haven't used Spring or EJB. Which way should they go?

In the spirit of OSS, we hope the reader views this chapter as the extension of an olive branch. Given the popularity of the Spring framework, we want to demonstrate that it is possible to peacefully coexist—to find the power in both options and use them effectively. We want to emphasize that EJB 3 is a specification and Spring is a framework. Although they are often characterized as two sides of the same coin, these two are not the same thing.

In this chapter you'll learn how to use JPA entities and EJBs with Spring. We'll also throw in some tips for using both EJB 3 and Spring in your applications, with examples that show both Spring 1.2 and 2.0 features. This chapter does not cover how to use Spring itself. For a thorough beginner-to-advanced treatment of Spring, be sure to check out *Spring in Action* (2nd edition) by Craig Walls and Ryan Breidenbach (Manning, 2007).

So what do you think? Are you ready to get EJB 3 and Spring working together?

16.1 *Introducing the Spring framework*

Simply put, Spring is an inversion of control (IoC) and AOP framework. While it is also a container, it is widely popular for its framework benefits. The Spring framework built on many of the lessons learned from the other projects, either directly or indirectly, by understanding the importance of certain principles now known as IoC and separation of concerns (SoC). The primary goal for the Spring framework is to simplify development of enterprise Java applications. In this section we'll briefly introduce the Spring framework and then explore the IoC principle behind it.

16.1.1 *Benefits of the Spring framework*

Spring is one of the driving forces behind popularizing the POJO programming model and dependency injection. Enterprise application development with J2EE 1.4 and EJB 2 was very complex, and Spring gained popularity because it addressed many complexities and limitations of J2EE 1.4 and EJB 2. It provided a simple programming model for using resources such as JDBC or JMS or using popular persistence frameworks like Hibernate or TopLink by abstracting low-level API and configuration from developers without limiting developers' choices.

Many developers want to choose a persistence, web, or messaging framework without having to do the integration work. The developers of the Spring framework realized that no matter which persistence, web, messaging, or "whatever" framework they selected to support, someone would want to use something else, and a better alternative would eventually come along. Also, this type of integration is typically expensive. By following the IoC and SoC principles, Spring was able to be both lightweight enough to let developers decide how much of the framework they needed, and flexible enough to support many permutations of competing component frameworks.

Spring provides several modules, such as the following:

- AOP module
- JDBC abstraction and DAO module
- ORM integration module
- Web module
- MVC framework

Although the Spring framework supports almost as many features as a Java EE container, it is not positioned as an alternative to Java EE but as a framework that facilitates the development of applications with Java EE. That's one of the primary reasons for Spring being successful as a framework. You can use the Spring framework on its own or inside a Java EE container. Most application servers, such as Oracle and WebLogic, provide additional support to use Spring.

Now let's turn our focus to the IoC principle driving the Spring framework.

16.1.2 *The inversion of control principle*

Sometimes explained as the "Don't Call Us, We'll Call You" principle. It's the idea that a component or service should do one thing, and do it well, and not have to know too much—if anything—about the other matters in the context of doing its job.

Let's say you have a ThingAmaJig component that needs a WhatchaMaCallIt and a DooHickey in order to do its job. Now the ThingAmaJig can try to find the other two components when it's invoked—*or* it could expect its caller to provide them. This second approach is the IoC principle.

Humans instinctively use IoC all the time and are not even aware of it. If you are at a client location and someone walks up to you and tells you that you have a call waiting from your coworker, they also hand you the phone that is already connected to your office, or tell you where the phone is. They don't expect you to just "know" where your coworker was calling from, nor do they expect you to figure it out. They provide the needed information for you to complete the conversation.

The same is true for someone invited to speak at a conference. The speaker isn't expected to provide the conference room, audience, refreshments, and so forth. Those are provided by someone else. However, these other components are critical to the speaker being able to perform the requested tasks—especially consuming the refreshments!

An article by Martin Fowler (www.martinfowler.com/articles/injection.html) proposed that while the IoC principle was good, its name could use a slight adjustment. He proposed *dependency injection* as a name that more accurately described what IoC did. It appears that most of the industry has agreed, and this is why you will see DI referenced more than IoC in newer literature, especially EJB 3 documentation.

16.1.3 *The separation of concerns principle*

For a component architecture to succeed in being both easy to use and flexible to extend, the ideas of interface and implementation need to be considered. The interface is the functional aspect describing what is to be done. The implementation is the specific *how* and *what* is to be accomplished.

This means that if you write a logging component and you would like to have the flexibility to log to a number of locations (database, file, socket, unknown, etc.) and support various protocols (HTTP, RMI, JINI, unknown, etc.), you have a design decision to make. You can try to guess which locations and protocols are the most popular, or you can write the log functionality in an interface, write a few implementations that use that interface, and encourage others to write any implementations that they may need.

The SoC idea is also sometimes referred to as the plug-in principle, which is more often how it is described. Spring allows separation of concerns with its rich support for aspect-oriented programming (AOP). It helps developers to focus on writing business logic without having to worry about system-level concerns such as performing transactions or logging in their code.

After looking more deeply into the principles Spring was built on, and with their new list of priorities for EJB 3 in hand, the EJB 3 Expert Group did several things to bring EJB 3 more in line with the goals being realized by Spring. These goals include POJO programming model, dependency injection, and use of interceptors.

> **NOTE** At the time of this writing, the Spring framework developers released Spring 2.0 with support for the EJB 3 JPA. It shipped TopLink Essentials as the default persistence provider. It is worth mentioning that Spring is adding partial support directly for EJB 3 as a part of Pitchfork project (www.interface21.com/pitchfork). This will enable you to use EJB 3 annotations such as @Stateless, @Interceptors, and @Resource in Spring beans.

Now that you have an idea what the Spring framework is, let's explore how you can use Spring with JPA.

16.2 *Using JPA with Spring*

Spring has wide support for ORM technologies, including Hibernate, TopLink, and JDO. The approach Spring takes in how you use their framework makes coding to these ORM options and swapping between them very easy. Spring 2.0 extended this rich support for ORM technologies to include JPA. Table 16.1 shows the Java classes that developers are interested in for using EJB 3 JPA in Spring.

Table 16.1   Spring classes available for using JPA

Spring Class	Description
JpaTemplate	Simplifies JPA access code
JpaDaoSupport	Superclass for Spring DAOs for JPA data access
JpaTransactionManager	Used for transactional access of JPA
LocalEntityManagerFactoryBean	Factory that creates local entity manager when JPA is used outside Java EE
JpaDialect	Intended to use with a persistence provider outside Java EE

We'll outline the steps for using the EJB 3 JPA from your web applications. We'll assume you have some basic familiarity with Spring and that you are comfortable with entity packaging and EAOs.

We'll primarily focus on using `JpaDaoSupport` and `JpaTemplate`, because they are intended to simplify the use of the EJB 3 JPA by shielding you from the details of the `EntityManager` API. We'll assume you have experience with the general usage of the `EntityManager` API (which means you'll appreciate even more how Spring is trying to simplify the EJB 3 JPA programming model).

Suppose that the ActionBazaar developers thought it would be cool to use Spring in their systems. They started creating a prototype to use Spring with JPA, and decided to implement a part of ActionBazaar in Spring as shown in figure 16.1.

We'll work with the ActionBazaar bidding module shown in figure 16.1, in which a simple Spring EAO (`BidSpringEAO`) is used for accessing the ActionBazaar persistence unit using Spring's `JpaTemplate`. We'll create a Spring bean (`BidService`) and configure it to use the EAO. We'll build an EAO that uses Spring's `JpaTemplate` to manipulate entities and use the EAO in a Spring service bean. Finally, we'll explore the Spring configuration that magically glues the `EntityManager`, EAO, and the Spring bean together.

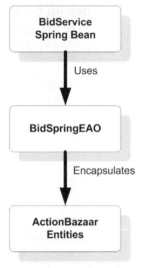

Figure 16.1 This ActionBazaar bidding module uses Spring with JPA. The Spring bean employs an entity access object to access the entities using JpaTemplate.

16.2.1 Building JPA EAOs for Spring

In chapter 12 you learned that the Entity Access Object design pattern improves code maintainability by decoupling the persistence logic from the business logic. Spring provides EAO (Spring still calls it DAO) for JPA and many O/R mapping frameworks such as Hibernate and TopLink.

Spring provides two ways to access and manipulate entities in building Spring EAOs: using the JPA API directly or using `JpaTemplate`. In chapter 12 we used EAOs to call the `EntityManager` API directly. We'll now demonstrate how to change the implementation classes to use JPA from Spring applications with the Spring `JpaTemplate`. Listing 16.1 shows the ActionBazaar EAO implementation classes you need when using JPA from Spring applications. Note that the Spring classnames continue to use the DAO naming convention instead of the revised EAO naming that we're featuring in this book.

Listing 16.1   EAO implementation when using JPA from Spring applications

```
package actionbazaar.persistence.eao;

import org.springframework.orm.jpa.support.JpaDaoSupport;

public abstract class BasicSpringEAO extends JpaDaoSupport {      ◁─┐
}                                                    Extends JpaDaoSupport  ❶
public class BidSpringEAO extends BasicSpringEAO implements BidEAO {
  public Bid addBid(Item item, String bidderId, double bidPrice) {
    Bid bid = new Bid();
    ...
    getJpaTemplate().persist(bid);    ◁─❷  Uses JpaTemplate to persist
    return bid;
  }

  public Bid cancelBid(Long bidId) {
    Bid bid = (Bid)getJpaTemplate().find(Bid.class, bidId);
    bid.setBidStatus(BidStatus.CANCELLED);
    getJpaTemplate().merge(bid);    ◁─┐
    return bid;                   ❸   Uses JpaTemplate to merge
  }
}
```

The class that implements the EAO interface must extend `JpaDaoSupport` ❶. Instead of using the `EntityManager` API, you use `JpaTemplate`. In listing 16.1, we've used the `persist` and `merge` methods ❷ and ❸ to persist or merge entity instances.

Using JpaTemplate

How are exceptions handled with regard to `JpaTemplate`? We're glad you asked. You need to be aware that `JpaTemplate` does not throw any persistence API exceptions. Instead, it throws Spring's `DataAccessException`. The primary benefit of this to developers is that by translating exceptions into those provided by the Spring framework, the persistence mechanism is neutral. This means you can swap out persistence mechanisms and your application code won't have to change to support the new framework's error handling. This makes it easier to migrate from one persistence toolkit to another, or to support multiple toolkits if you are a tool vendor. Table 16.2 describes some of the important methods in `JpaTemplate`.

Table 16.2   Important JpaTemplate methods provided by Spring

JpaTemplate Methods	Description
`persist(Object entity)`	Persists an entity instance
`remove(Object entity)`	Removes an entity instance
`merge(T entity)`	Merges a detached entity instance
`refresh(Object entity)`	Refreshes an entity instance from the database
`<T> T find(Class<T> entityClass, Object Id)`	Retrieves an entity instance by primary key
`List find(String queryString)`	Retrieves a list of entities using a dynamic query
`List find(String queryString, Object values)`	Restricts a list of entities using a dynamic query with positional parameters
`findByNamedQuery(String queryName)`	Retrieves a list of entities using a named query
`findByNamedQuery(String queryName, Map<String,Object> params)`	Retrieves a list of entities using a named query with named parameters

You can use the `JpaTemplate` methods to access entities. Spring limits some of the repetitive use of the EJB 3 JPA. For example, if you want to you use a dynamic query to retrieve all `Bidders` with `Gold` status, then `JpaTemplate` will yield the following:

```
List bidders = getJpaTemplate().find(
           "SELECT b FROM Bidder b WHERE status = ?1", "Gold");
```

The equivalent code with the `EntityManager` API will look like this:

```
List bidders = em.createQuery(
            "SELECT b FROM Bidder b WHERE status = ?1")
          .setParameter(1, "Gold")
          .getResultList();
```

This code makes it evident that Spring makes using the EJB 3 JPA simpler. We encourage you to explore other `JpaTemplate` methods.

The only problem we see with `JpaTemplate` is that it does not provide fine-grained access to the `EntityManager` API's methods.

JPA EAO in your service beans

Spring's service beans are similar to the EJB 3 session beans that you work with to implement business logic. In our example the `BidServiceBean` is used to place a bid on an item, and it uses the EAOs to manipulate the entities. You can use the EAOs in your service classes, and the EAOs can be injected into the POJOs with Spring's setter injection as follows:

```
public class BidServiceBean implements BidService {

  protected ItemEAO itemEAO;
  protected BidEAO bidEAO ;

  public BidServiceBean() {
  }

  //Inject Instances of Item and BidEAO
  public void setItemEAO(ItemEAO itemEAO) {
    this.itemEAO = itemEAO;
  }

  public void setBidEAO(BidEAO ) {
    this.bidEAO = bidEAO;
  }

  public Long addBid(String userId, Long itemId, Double bidPrice) {
  ...
  }
}
```

The `BidServiceBean` class looks similar to the `PlaceBidBean` class—the only remarkable difference is that it is a POJO with no annotations, JNDI lookup, or use of EAO factory code of any kind.

If you are new to Spring, you must be wondering, "If all classes are POJOs, then how does the framework know about the `EntityManager`, and how does it inject instances of `EntityManager`?" It's all based on a little Spring configuration magic, which we dive into next.

16.2.2 *Configuring Spring to use the JPA*

The real power of Spring comes from how it configures services via dependency injection. For our example this means you need to configure the `EntityManager-Factory`. To coax ActionBazaar to work with Spring, you'll need the configuration shown in listing 16.2.

Listing 16.2   Spring configuration to use JPA

```
<bean id = "entityManager"          ←┘ Configures EntityManager
      class = "org.springframework.jndi.JndiObjectFactoryBean">
    <property name = "jndiName"
              value = "java:comp/env/actionBazaar"/>
```

```
</bean>

<bean id = "bidEAO"          ◁⎤ Defines Spring EAO
      class = "actionbazaar.persistence.eao.BidSpringEAO"
      autowire = "byType">
   <property name = "entityManager"
                 ref = "entityManager"/>
</bean>

<bean id = "bidService"                              ⎪ Specifies
      class = "actionbazaar.buslogic.BidServiceBean">  ◁⎤ bidService bean
  <property name = "bidEAO">
    <ref bean = "bidEAO"/>
  </property>
</bean>
```

Even if you're not familiar with Spring, you can probably figure out what's going on in this configuration file (actionBazaar-service.xml). The first bean instance, entityManager, injects an instance of the EntityManager by retrieving it from the JNDI namespace when it is referenced from another bean instance. The next bean, bidEAO, asks Spring to automatically wire it to use the previous entity-Manager. The final bean, bidService, requests that Spring inject the bidEAO bean as the implementation for it to use at runtime.

Configuring Spring to use the EntityManager

Because Spring is a lightweight container, it can work either inside a Java EE container or independently. Spring can use a container- or an application-managed EntityManager either inside or outside the container. While you're using Spring within a Java EE container, it acts as a proxy between the container and the application and injects an EntityManager or EntityManagerFactory when your application needs it. That way, you don't have to worry about including extra JPA code.

In this chapter we primarily focus on Spring as a framework within the Java EE container. This means you have to configure Spring so it can retrieve an EntityManager from the Java EE container and inject an instance of an Entity-Manager whenever you use a JpaTemplate. If you're using Spring within a Java EE 5 container, you must use either the JndiObjectFactoryBean or Spring 2.0's new jee:jndi-lookup mechanism to wire an instance of EntityManager (as we did in listing 16.2). If you want the new Spring 2.0 configuration instead of Jndi-ObjectFactoryBean, then use this configuration:

```
<jee:jndi-lookup id = "entityManager"
                 jndi-name = "actionBazaar"
                 resource-ref = "true"/>
```

Remember, this notation works only if you've upgraded to version 2 of Spring.

Using Spring outside Java EE container with JPA

As we discussed earlier, Spring 2.0 acts as a container and supports the container-managed `EntityManager` with JPA. The Spring container manages the persistence unit. You have to use `LocalContainerEntityManagerFactoryBean` to wire an `entityManagerFactory`. The `LocalContainerEntityManagerFactoryBean` reads the `persistence.xml` packaged in the application to configure the persistence unit by using the data source supplied. It can also perform load-time weaving to search for annotated entity classes. Here is an example configuration of the container-managed `EntityManager`:

```
<beans>
  <bean id = "entityManagerFactory"
        class = "org.springframework.orm.jpa.
LocalContainerEntityManagerFactoryBean">
    ...
    <property name = "loadTimeWeaver">
      <bean class = "org.springframework.instrument.classloading.
SimpleLoadTimeWeaver"/>
    </property>
  </bean>
  <bean id = "bidEAO"
        class = "actionbazaar.persistence.eao.BidSpringEAO"
        autowire = "byType">
    <property name = "entityManagerFactory"
              ref = "entityManagerFactory"/>
  </bean>
</beans>
```

For more information, refer to the Spring documentation.

If you're using Spring outside a Java EE container, you can use a `LocalEntityManagerFactory` and your configuration will look like this:

```
<bean id = "entityManagerFactory"
      class = "org.springframework.orm.jpa.LocalEntityManagerFactoryBean">
  ...
</bean>
```

This, of course, demonstrates that JPA can work independently of both a Java EE container and EJB 3.

Wiring entity access objects

The EAOs use `JpaTemplate`, so we need to wire the EAOs to use `JpaTemplate`'s methods. The EAOs are wired in the Spring configuration as in listing 16.2. If you recall, the EAOs extend the `org.springframework.orm.jpa.support.JpaDao-Support` and it has a dependency on `EntityManager`; therefore, we need to inject an instance of `EntityManager`. Spring's autowire-by-type mechanism indicates to the Spring container that it should find a single instance of a Spring bean that matches the property being wired. In this case, the EAO class uses the `entityManager` property to obtain an instance of `EntityManager` that we defined earlier in listing 16.2. You must pass `EntityManager` as a property to the EAO as follows:

```
<property name = "entityManager" ref = "entityManager"/>
```

At runtime Spring will take care of creating the `entityManager` and injecting it into the EAO.

If you're using an application-managed entity manager or using Spring with JPA outside the container, you have to wire the `entityManageFactory` property instead of an `entityManager` as follows:

```
<bean id = "bidEAO"
      class = "actionbazaar.persistence.eao.BidSpringEAO"
      autowire = "byType">
   <property name = "entityManagerFactory"
             ref = "entityManagerFactory"/>
</bean>
```

Wiring service beans

Your web applications use service beans to access entities from the presentation tier. You simply wire your service beans (as in listing 16.2) in the Spring configuration file to have them injected. Some steps can be quite mechanical, and are required for every EAO and service bean.

Appropriately configuring Spring for your server allows you to deploy the application using Spring, proving again that you can use JPA outside of a Java EE container.

Let's now examine how you unite the power of Spring and EJB 3 components (session beans and MDBs).

16.3 Combining the power of EJB 3 and Spring

In addition to using JPA with Spring, you may combine the flexibility of Spring beans with the power of EJB 3 in your applications. You have two options. You can use the power of Spring—POJO injection, AOP features, etc.—by developing Spring-enabled EJB applications, or you can invoke an EJB from a Spring bean. At the time of this writing, Spring 2.0 has no documented support for EJB 3 session beans, but we found some ways to make EJB 3 beans work with Spring beans and in this section we'll reveal our discoveries.

In this section you'll see two ways you can combine power of EJB 3 components and Spring beans. First you'll learn about using Spring from EJB 3 components; then we'll show you how to access an EJB 3 session bean from a Spring bean.

16.3.1 Developing Spring-enabled EJBs

Let's say you want to use declarative transactions, timers, security, and the web services features of EJB in your applications, but you also want to leverage the POJO injection, AOP, and `JpaTemplate` features of Spring 2.0. Spring provides several support classes, listed in table 16.3, that you can use to integrate EJBs. Note that these are the classes provided for use with EJB 2, and we expect there will be several changes in these classes to be used with EJB 3. However, you can still use these abstract classes with EJB 3 beans.

The abstract classes provide access to the Spring bean factory, and you have to implement the `onEjbCreate` method in your EJB class to retrieve a Spring bean.

Table 16.3 Spring support classes for building Spring-enabled EJBs

Support Class	Purpose
AbstractStatelessSessionBean	Used for Spring-enabled stateless session beans
AbstractStatefulSessionBean	Used for Spring-enabled stateful session beans
AbstractJMSMessageDrivenBean	Used for Spring-enabled JMS message-driven beans
AbstractMessageDrivenBean	Used for Spring-enabled connector-based MDBs

In ActionBazaar we want to use Spring with session beans. This means that the BidServiceBean we developed in section 16.1 is used by the PlaceBid EJB, as shown in figure 16.2.

The BidServiceBean is defined as a Spring bean using a Spring configuration file named actionBazaar-service.xml as follows:

```
<beans>
...
  <bean id = "bidService" class =
      "actionbazaar.buslogic.BidServiceBean">
  </bean>
...
</beans>
```

When an EJB instance is created, a Spring bean factory is automatically created and is made available to the EJB. While using this approach, you typically use the EJB as a façade and delegate the task to Spring beans.

Listing 16.3 shows the PlaceBid EJB developed as a Spring-enabled stateless session bean. In this example, the PlaceBid EJB acts as a façade and delegates the actual business logic to the BidServiceBean.

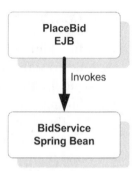

Figure 16.2 You can combine the power of Spring and EJB 3 by developing a Spring-enabled session bean. You can use the declarative transaction, security, and web services features of EJB 3 with the POJO injection and JpaTemplate features of Spring.

Listing 16.3 Spring-enabled stateless PlaceBid EJB

```
@Stateless(name = "PlaceBid")
public class PlaceBidBean
  extends AbstractStatelessSessionBean        ←❶ Extends Spring class
  implements PlaceBid {

    private BidServiceBean bidService;         ←❷ Defines POJO

    public PlaceBidBean() {
    }

    protected void onEjbCreate() {
     bidService =                                      Retrieves bean ❸
       (BidServiceBean) getBeanFactory().getBean("bidService");  ←┘

    }

    public Long addBid(String userId, Long itemId, Double bidPrice) {
       return bidService.addBid(userId, itemId, bidPrice);  ←┐
    }                                                    ❹ Uses bean

}
```

In listing 16.3 the bean class extends the Spring support class in the (`org.spring-framework.ejb.support.AbstractStatelessSessionBean`) package **❶**. Note that the EJB bean cannot inherit from another bean or class because Java does not support multiple inheritances.

The `BidServiceBean` POJO is defined as an instance variable **❷**. When a `Place-Bid` EJB instance is created, the `onEjbCreate` method is invoked and an instance of `BidServiceBean` is retrieved **❸** and stored in the POJO that we defined **❷**. The business method delegates the task to the `BidServiceBean` when it is invoked **❹**.

Now you must be wondering how the Spring bean factory is created and how the Spring configuration is provided. Under the covers, when an EJB instance is created it performs a JNDI lookup to locate the path (`java:comp/env/ejb/Bean-FactoryPath`) for the bean factory. Therefore, you have to define the following environment variable in the EJB deployment descriptor for the EJB:

```
<session>
  <display-name>PlaceBid</display-name>
  <ejb-name>PlaceBid</ejb-name>
  <env-entry>
    <env-entry-name>ejb/BeanFactoryPath</env-entry-name>
    <env-entry-type>java.lang.String</env-entry-type>
    <env-entry-value>/actionBazaar-service.xml</env-entry-value>
  </env-entry>
</session>
```

The `env-entry-value` for the `ejb/BeanFactoryPath` environment variable is set to `/actionBazaar-service.xml`.

After you package the EJB and Spring configuration file, you should be able to invoke the EJB, and internally it will use Spring beans to perform the intended task.

16.3.2 *Using session beans from Spring beans*

Perhaps by now you've grown fond of EJB 3 and worked with it in your application. Some of your other application modules happen to use Spring. What you'd like to do is reuse the business logic you've developed in your EJBs by incorporating it into your Spring component, as shown in figure 16.3. In this section we'll show you how to inject instances of session beans into your Spring beans.

Suupose you have a session bean named `ItemManager`:

```
@Stateless(name = "ItemManager")
public class ItemManagerBean implements ItemManager {
```

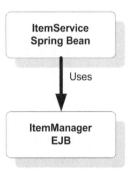

Figure 16.3 You can access a session bean from a Spring bean and reuse the business logic.

```
    public Item addItem(String title, String description,
                        Double initialPrice, String sellerId) {
      ...
      return item;
    }
  }
```

You want to use the `ItemManager` session bean in the `ItemServiceBean`, which is a Spring POJO (see listing 16.4).

Listing 16.4 A Spring POJO that uses an injected stateless session bean

```
public class ItemServiceBean implements ItemService {

  private ItemManager itemManager;        ◁──┐  Specifies instance
                                           ❶  variable for EJB
  public ItemServiceBean() {
  }

  // Setter injection of ItemManagerEJB
  public void setItemManager(ItemManager itemManager) {  ◁─❷  Injects setter
    this.itemManager = itemManager;
  }

  public Long addItem(String title, String description,
                      Double initialPrice, String sellerId) {
    Item item = itemManager.addItem(title, description,
                                    initialPrice, sellerId);    ◁──┐
    return item.getItemId();
  }                                                  Invokes EJB
}                                                    method  ❸
```

In listing 16.4 you will see no difference in using a POJO because EJB 3 session beans are also POJOs. In the Spring bean, we've defined an instance variable for the EJB interface `ItemManager` ❶ and we use setter injection to inject an instance of the EJB object ❷ and invoke a method on the EJB ❸.

You must be wondering where the actual magic happens. We aren't doing a JNDI lookup, and we're not using the `@EJB` annotation to inject an EJB object. The real magic occurs in wiring the EJB in the Spring configuration, as shown in listing 16.5. Spring has factory classes for wiring invocation of EJB 2.1 session beans. Fortunately, you don't need those and you can use the `JndiObject-FactoryBean`.

Listing 16.5 A Spring POJO that uses an injected stateless session bean

```
<bean id = "itemManager"
      class = "org.springframework.jndi.JndiObjectFactoryBean">
  <property name = "jndiName"
            value = "java:comp/env/ejb/ItemManager"/>
</bean>                                              Defines bean ❶
                                                    to access EJB
<bean id = "itemService"
      class = "actionbazaar.buslogic.ItemServiceBean">
  <property name = "itemManager" ref = "itemManager"/>    ◁─❷ References EJB
</bean>
```

In listing 16.5 we define a bean instance that injects an EJB instance by looking it up in the JNDI ❶ when referenced by another bean instance ❷.

If you are a big fan of the new Spring 2.0 configuration, then you'll be tempted to use the following instead of `JndiObjectFactoryBean`. Go ahead; indulge your temptation.

```
<jee:jndi-lookup id = "itemManager"
                 jndi-name = "ejb/ItemManager"
                 resource-ref = "true"/>
```

Unlike in EJB 2, there is no difference between invoking remote or local EJBs in EJB 3, and the configuration will be identical for both local and remote session beans.

We encourage you to explore the latest Spring 2.0 documentation at www.springframework.org/documentation to learn about the latest support of EJB 3 features in the Spring framework.

16.4 Summary

This chapter explained that even though EJB 3 is a specification and Spring is a framework, you can use them together successfully to build flexible, powerful applications. You can use parts of the EJB 3 implementation, or all of it, within your Spring applications. Spring can simplify the use of both EJB 3 and JPA, but at the price of foraging through Spring's XML configuration files. You learned how to develop a Spring-enabled EJB (session bean or MDB) and leverage the power of Spring within your EJB components. Similarly, you can access an EJB 3 session bean from your Spring bean and reuse your business logic.

EJB 3 is a great framework for building enterprise Java applications, and it significantly improves developer productivity. It has some minor limitations, such as support for POJO injection, and we hope that these limitations will be addressed in the next version of the specification. Throughout this book we provided many best practices and tuning tips, and we trust you can use this information to effectively build your next application.

RMI and JNDI

Java Remote Method Invocation (RMI) and the Java Naming and Directory Interface (JNDI) are two central Java technologies that EJB 3 uses extensively under the hood. RMI is the technology that enables transparent Java native remote communication between EJB clients and beans. JNDI, on the other hand, enables a whole host of EJB functionality by acting as the central service registry for a Java EE container. One of the major enhancements in EJB 3, dependency injection (DI), is simply a wrapper over JNDI lookups.

In this appendix we offer a brief primer on both of these technologies, especially as they relate to EJB 3.

A.1 *Distributed communication with RMI*

Java RMI made its debut very early in Java's history. (also known Java Remote Method Protocol (JRMP)). It became clear that, as a platform that touts the distributed computing mantra "The network is the computer," Java must provide a simple and robust mechanism for communication across JVM instances. Ideally, method calls on an object running in one JVM should be executed transparently in another remote JVM. With the help of a small amount of boilerplate setup code combined with a few code-generation tools, RMI delivers on this promise. To invoke an object method remotely using RMI, you must

- Register the remote object implementing the method with an *RMI registry*.
- Look up the remote object reference from the registry (the remote reference is accessed through an interface).
- Invoke the remote method through the reference obtained from the registry.

The idea of a *registry* to store remote object references is central to RMI. All objects that need to be invoked remotely must be registered with an RMI registry. In order to be registered with an RMI server and be invoked remotely, an object must extend a few RMI classes as well as implement a *remote interface*. A remote interface defines the object methods that can be invoked remotely. Like the target remote object itself, a remote interface must extend a few RMI interfaces.

Once a remote object is registered with a registry, any client that can access the registry can obtain a reference to it. To get a reference to a remote object, the client must retrieve it from the registry by name and then invoke it through the remote interface. Each time a client invokes a method through the remote interface, the method invocation request is carried transparently across the wire to the remote object. The remote object method is then executed inside its own JVM.

The result of the method invocation (such as a return value) is transported back across the network to be delivered to the client by RMI.

To better understand what is happening in the remote interface scenario, let's draw an analogy with something familiar to all of us: a television. Think of a television as the remote object to be called. The remote control for our television is the remote interface. The infrared protocol sent by the remote control and picked up by the television is like the RMI protocol. While using the remote control, we don't have to know all of the details of how the infrared signal works; all we need to know is what each of the buttons on the remote does (the interface methods). Figure A.1 shows how a typical RMI invocation scenario works.

The parallels between EJB and RMI are obvious. Like the EJB object discussed in chapter 5, RMI works through proxies on both the client and remote object endpoints to transparently provide distributed computing as a service. In the EJB world, the business interface plays the same role as the "remote" interface, while the EJB bean itself is the "remote object." Just as RMI handles the communication details between the remote client and the object, the container handles the communication details between the EJB client and the managed bean. Before EJB 3, the linkages between RMI and EJB were even more obvious—for example, remote business interfaces had to put `java.rmi.RemoteException` in their `throws` clause. In EJB 3, the fact that EJB uses RMI for remoting is rightfully hidden far behind the API as an implementation detail you can safely ignore.

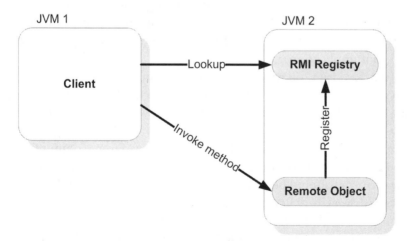

Figure A.1 Communication between the RMI client and server (remote object). The RMI server binds an object in the RMI registry. The client performs a lookup in the RMI registry to get a reference to the remote object and then invokes the method on the remote object through the remote interface.

When you annotate a session bean business interface using the `@Remote` annotation as we did in chapters 2 and 3, the container automatically makes the bean callable via RMI as a remote object. Similarly, when you inject a remote bean using the `@EJB` annotation, the container talks to the bean through RMI under the hood.

The greatest benefit for RMI is that it provides location transparency. The client invokes methods on a remote object as if the object were located in the same virtual machine, without having to worry about the underlying plumbing. This also means that RMI is generally a lot easier to use and flexible compared to writing TCP/IP sockets by hand for remote communication.

As compelling as RMI might seem from our very high-level discussion, like all technologies it has its own set of problems.

Remote object invocation uses *pass-by-value* semantics. When the client passes a parameter to the remote method, RMI sends the data held by the object across the network as a byte stream. The byte stream is received by RMI on the other end of the communication tunnel, copied into an object of the same type as passed in by the client, and weaved in as a parameter to the remote object. Objects returned by the remote method go through the same translation-transport-translation steps. The process of turning an object into a byte stream is called *marshaling*, and the process of turning a byte stream into an object is called *unmarshaling*. This is exactly why all objects transported across the network by RMI must implement the `java.io.Serializable` interface. For large objects, the cost of marshaling and unmarshaling can be pretty high, making RMI a performance bottleneck compared to local invocation. This is why you want to make sure that objects passed over RMI are not large, because they can slow down your application.

Like EJB 2, RMI isn't too easy to use. You often find yourself performing functions such as extending obscure interfaces or classes, and following a strange programming model. Luckily, EJB 3 does all the hard work of generating RMI code behind the scenes.

Last but not least, RMI is great for Java-to-Java transparent communication but is not good for interoperability with Microsoft .NET and the like. If interoperability is a concern, you should be using web services instead of RMI. Note, however, web services is overkill if not absolutely needed, primarily because text-based, parsing-intensive XML performs much worse than binary-based protocols like RMI. Moreover, it is possible to use RMI-IIOP to interoperate between Java and CORBA components written in languages like C++. Every EJB container must support RMI-IIOP and enabling RMI-IIOP is simply a matter of configuration.

If you want to learn more about RMI, check out http://java.sun.com/products/jdk/rmi/.

A.2 *JNDI as a component registry*

JNDI is the JDBC of naming and directory services. Just as JDBC provides a standard Java EE API to access all kinds of databases, JNDI standardizes naming and directory service access. If you've ever used a Lightweight Directory Access Protocol (LDAP) such as a Microsoft Active Directory server, you already know what a naming and directory service is.

In simple terms, a naming service provides the ability to locate a component or service by name. You give a naming service the complete name for a resource and it figures out how to get you a handle to the resource that you can use. Domain Name Service (DNS) is a relatively well-known example of a naming service. When we point our web browser to http://yahoo.com, the DNS server conducts a lookup and directs us to the right IP address for Yahoo. The RMI registry is another example of a naming service. In a sense, even an operating system file manager is a naming service. You give the file manager the complete path to a file and it gives you a handle to the file you are looking for.

As figure A.2 shows, JNDI provides a uniform abstraction over a number of different naming services such as LDAP, DNS, Network Information Service (NIS), Novell Directory Services (NDS), RMI, Common Object Request Broker Architecture (CORBA), and so on. Once you have an instance of a JNDI context, you can use it to locate resources in any underlying naming service available to the context. Under the hood, JNDI negotiates with each available naming service given the name of a resource to figure out where to look up the service's actual location.

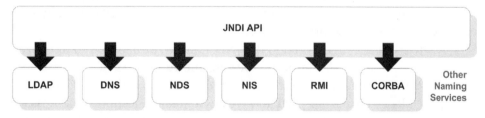

Figure A.2   JNDI provides a single unified API to access various naming services such as LDAP, NDS, NDS, NIS, RMI, and CORBA. Any naming service with a JNDI Service Provider Interface (SPI) provider can be plugged into the API seamlessly.

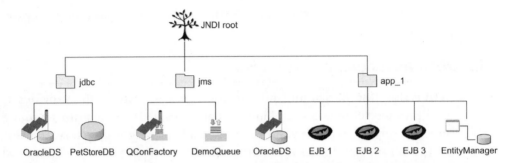

Figure A.3 An example JNDI tree for an application server. All global resources such as jdbc and jms are bound to the root context of JNDI tree. Each application has its own application context, and EJBs and other resources in the application are bound under the application context.

Like RMI, JNDI plays a vital role in EJB 3, although it is by and large hidden behind the scenes (also like RMI, JNDI used to be a lot more visible and made EJB much more cumbersome as of EJB 2). In a very real sense, JNDI is to EJB what the RMI registry is to RMI. JNDI is used as the central repository for resources managed by the container.

As a result, every bean managed by the container is automatically registered with JNDI. In addition, a typical container JNDI registry will store JDBC data sources, JMS queues, JMS connection factories, JPA entity managers, JPA entity manager factories, and so on. Whenever a client (such as an EJB) needs to use a managed resource, they use JNDI to look up the resource by its unique name. Figure A.3 shows how a typical JNDI tree for a Java EE application server might look.

As you can see in figure A.3, resources are stored in a JNDI tree in a hierarchical manner. This means that JNDI resource names look much like Unix file pathnames (they also sometimes start with a protocol specification such as java:, much like a URL address you would enter in a browser navigation bar). As with RMI, once you procure a handle to a resource from a JNDI context, you can use it as though it were a local resource.

To use a resource stored in the JNDI context, a client has to initialize the context and look up the resource. Despite the robustness of the JNDI mechanism itself, the code to do so isn't that intimidating. The code in listing A.1 looks up a JDBC data source from JNDI and creates a new connection from it. As you might imagine, the JDBC connection then might be used to issue SQL to the underlying database pointed to by the retrieved data source.

Listing A.1   Looking up a JDBC data source using JNDI

```
Context context = new InitialContext();
DataSource dataSource =
    (DataSource)context.lookup("java:comp/env/jdbc/ActionBazaarDS");
Connection connection = dataSource.getConnection();
Statement statement = connection.createStatement();
```

In listing A.1, the JNDI lookup takes place in the first two lines. First, an `Initial-Context` object is instantiated. The `InitialContext` object connects to any given JNDI tree. In the case of the parameter-less version of the constructor used in listing A.1, the `InitialContext` object connects to the "default" JNDI tree. The JNDI defaults are determined by the contents of a file named `jndi.properties` that can be stored anywhere in the JVM's `CLASSPATH`. The Java EE application server usually provides this properties file, and the settings in the file typically point to the JNDI tree of the local application server. As a result, the default `InitialContext` constructor is most useful while looking up resources within the same JVM. If you are looking up a resource (such as an EJB) on a remote application server, then you must feed environment properties to the `InitialContext` constructor. This can be done as follows:

```
Properties properties = new Properties();
properties.put(Context.INITIAL_CONTEXT_FACTORY,
    "oracle.j2ee.rmi.RMIInitialContextFactory");
properties.put(Context.PROVIDER_URL,
    "ormi://192.168.0.6:23791/appendixa");
properties.put(Context.SECURITY_PRINCIPAL, "oc4jadmin");
properties.put(Context.SECURITY_CREDENTIALS, "welcome1");
Context context = new InitialContext(properties);
```

In the example, the custom `Properties` entries specify that we are trying to connect to a remote Oracle application server JNDI tree. Note JNDI connection properties are vendor (application server) specific and our example cannot be used universally, so you should consult with your application server's documentation to see how you can connect to it remotely. In general, you might find that most application servers require a common set of JNDI properties defined as constants in the `Context` interface. Table A.1 summarizes the most common environment properties that are used for Java EE application servers.

Note that instead of providing environment properties programmatically, you can also simply modify the `jndi.properties` file in your runtime `CLASSPATH`. If you are using EJB 3 DI, this is the only way of connecting to a remote server.

Table A.1 Common JNDI environment properties required for creating an initial context to connect to a remote JNDI service provider in a Java EE environment. These are specified either as system properties in the jndi.properties file in the JVM at the client side or as Property object entries passed to the constructor in your Java code. Of these options, a properties file is recommended as it improves maintainability of your application code.

Property Name	Description	Example Value
`java.naming.factory.initial`	The name of the factory class that will be used to create the context	`oracle.j2ee.rmi.RMIInitialContextFactory`
`java.naming.provider.url`	The URL for the JNDI service provider	`ormi://localhost:23791/chapter1`
`java.naming.security.principal`	The username or identity for authenticating the caller in the JNDI service provider	`oc4jadmin`
`java.naming.security.credentials`	The password for the username/principal being used for authentication	`welcome1`

In the second line of listing A.1, the lookup is performed using the context instantiated in the first line. The single parameter of the `lookup` method is the full name of the resource you are seeking. In our case, the JNDI name of the JDBC data source we are looking for happens to be `jdbc/ActionBazaarDS`. Note that because the `lookup` method returns the `Object` type, we must *cast* the retrieved resource to the correct type. In the case of EJBs, references returned by JNDI must be cast to a valid business interface implemented by the EJB.

While the code in listing A.1 looks harmless, don't be taken in by appearances. JNDI lookups were one of the primary causes for EJB 2's complexity. First of all, you had to do lookups to access any resource managed by the container, even if you were only accessing data sources and EJBs from other EJBs located in the same JVM. Given that most EJBs in an application depend on other EJBs and resources, imagine the lines of repetitive JNDI lookup code littered across an average business application! To make matters worse, JNDI names of resources aren't always that obvious to figure out, especially for resources that are bound to the environment naming context (which must use the arcane `java:comp/env/` prefix for portability of applications instead of using a global JNDI name).

The good news is that except for certain corner cases, you won't have to deal with the evils of JNDI in EJB 3. EJB 3 puts the mechanical details of JNDI lookups well hidden behind metadata-based DI. DI does such a great job in abstraction that you won't even know that JNDI lookups are happening behind the scenes, even for remote lookups. DI is discussed in chapters 2, 3, 4, and 5.

You can find more about JNDI from Sun's website at http://java.sun.com/ products/jndi/.

Reviewing relational databases

Relational databases have been an integral part of enterprise development for a few decades now. The fact that these business data storage mainstays are backed by their own body of mathematical theory (relational algebra) speaks to the elegance and robustness of this mature technology. E. F. Codd first introduced the theory of relational databases in 1970 while working at IBM. This groundbreaking research eventually led to the creation of today's database products, including IBM's own highly successful DB2 database. Oracle is the most popular database in existence today, in vibrant competition with products like Microsoft SQL Server, Sybase, MySQL, and many others, in addition to IBM's DB2. Fundamentally, relational databases store and organize related data into a hierarchy of *schemas*, *tables*, *columns*, and *rows*.

Other types of databases exist, including flat-file, hierarchical, network, and object-oriented databases. Each of these is worthy of study on its own merits. However, the EJB 3 specification only supports relational databases, and that will be where we draw the line with regard to the database discussions in this book. The focus of this appendix is to briefly discuss each of the relational concepts.

B.1 *Database tables, columns, rows, and schema*

Tables are the most basic logical unit in a relational database. A table stores conceptually related data into *rows* and *columns*. Essentially, tables are the object-oriented (OO) counterparts of objects. Hence, we might imagine that the ActionBazaar database contains tables like CATEGORIES, ITEMS, ORDERS, and so forth. A *column* is a particular domain of data, and a table is a set of related columns. If tables are the equivalent of objects, columns are the equivalent of object attributes. Consequently, the CATEGORIES table probably has columns such as CATEGORY_ID, CATEGORY_NAME, MODIFICATION_DATE, and CREATION_DATE, as seen in figure B.1.

As with object attributes in Java, each relational table column has a data type. Table B.1 lists some column data types commonly used across various databases and their Java equivalents.

Table B.1 Common column data types and their Java equivalents

Relational Database Type	Java Type
CHAR, VARCHAR2, VARCHAR, LONG	`java.lang.String`
Char	`char, Char`

continued on next page

Table B.1 Common column data types and their Java equivalents *(continued)*

Relational Database Type	Java Type
INTEGER, NUMBER	`int, Integer, BigInteger`
NUMBER	`double, float, BigDecimal, Double, Float`
Raw, BLOB	`java.sql.Blob, byte[]`
CLOB	`java.sql.Clob, char[],java.lang.String`

A *row* is a record saved in the database composed of related data in each column of a table. A row, in effect, is equivalent to an *instance* of a particular object, in contrast to the class definition. For most OO developers it's not a big leap to imagine an instance of the Category object being saved into a row of the CATEGORIES table.

A *schema* can be compared to a Java package. In other words, a schema is a collection of related tables, similar to how a Java package contains a set of related classes. Usually, all of the tables used in a particular application are organized under a single schema. All the tables used in our example application might be stored under a schema called ACTIONBAZAAR.

Typically, a schema stores much more than just tables. It might also have views, triggers, and stored procedures. A detailed discussion of these database features is beyond the scope of this appendix. For coverage of these and other database topics, feel free to investigate a good reference book such as *An Introduction to Database Systems,* 7th edition, by C. J. Date (Addison Wesley Longman, 1999).

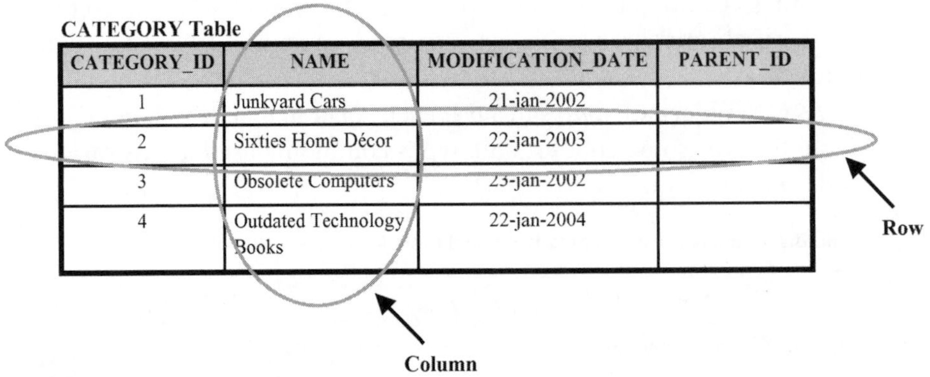

CATEGORY Table

CATEGORY_ID	NAME	MODIFICATION_DATE	PARENT_ID
1	Junkyard Cars	21-jan-2002	
2	Sixties Home Décor	22-jan-2003	
3	Obsolete Computers	23-jan-2002	
4	Outdated Technology Books	22-jan-2004	

Row

Column

Figure B.1 Rows and columns in the CATEGORIES table. While columns store a domain of data, rows contain a record composed of a set of related columns in a table.

We will, however, cover a few more database concepts essential in understanding EJB 3 Persistence next, namely database constraints such as primary and foreign keys.

B.2 Database constraints

Constraints are the concept that is closest to business rules in a basic relational database schema. In effect, constraints maintain data integrity by enforcing rules on how data may be modified. Since most database vendors try to differentiate their products by offering unique constraint features, coming up with a list of constraints to discuss is not easy. We have chosen to cover the bare minimum set necessary to understand EJB 3 persistence features, namely primary/foreign keys, uniqueness constraints, NULL constraints, and sequence columns.

B.2.1 Primary keys and unique columns

Just as a set of fields or properties uniquely identifies an entity, a set of columns uniquely identifies a given database record. The column or set of columns identifying a distinct record is called a *primary key*. For example, the CATEGORY_ID column is the primary key for the CATEGORIES table. When you identify a column or set of columns as the *primary key*, you essentially ask the database to enforce uniqueness. If the primary key consists of more than one column, it is called a *compound* or *composite key*. For example, instead of CATEGORY_ID, the combination of CATEGORY_NAME and CREATION_DATE could be the primary key for the CATEGORIES table.

Primary keys that consist of business data are called *natural keys*. A classic example is using some business data such as a Social Security number (represented by an SSN column) as the primary key for an EMPLOYEES table. CATEGORY_ID or EMPLOYEE_ID, on the other hand, are examples of *surrogate keys*. Essentially, surrogate keys are columns created explicitly to function as primary keys. Surrogate keys are popular and we highly recommend using them, especially as opposed to compound keys. Other than naming, primary key and *uniqueness constraints* do exactly the same thing, and the constraint is usually applied to columns that can function as alternate natural keys.

B.2.2 Foreign key

The interaction of primary and foreign keys is what makes relational databases shine. *Foreign keys* are essentially primary key values of one table stored in another table. Foreign keys are the database equivalents of object references, and

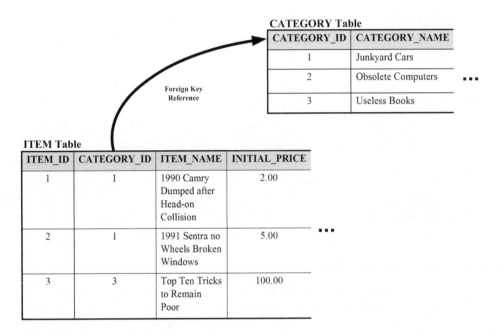

CATEGORY Table

CATEGORY_ID	CATEGORY_NAME
1	Junkyard Cars
2	Obsolete Computers
3	Useless Books

Foreign Key
Reference

ITEM Table

ITEM_ID	CATEGORY_ID	ITEM_NAME	INITIAL_PRICE
1	1	1990 Camry Dumped after Head-on Collision	2.00
2	1	1991 Sentra no Wheels Broken Windows	5.00
3	3	Top Ten Tricks to Remain Poor	100.00

Figure B.2   The CATEGORY_ID foreign key in the ITEMS table points to the primary key of the CATEGORIES table.

signify relationships between tables. As shown in figure B.2 (from our Action-Bazaar example), a column named CATEGORY_ID in the ITEMS table pointing to the CATEGORY_ID column in the CATEGORIES table signifies the fact that an item belongs in a category.

A database foreign key constraint means that the database will ensure every value that is put into the foreign key column exists in the primary key column it points to.

B.2.3 *NOT NULL*

The NOT NULL constraint is essentially a data integrity mechanism that ensures some table columns always have valid, nonempty values. For example, if the business rules dictate that a Category record must always have a name, we can specify a NOT NULL constraint on the CATEGORY_NAME column, and the database will only allow rows to be inserted where a CATEGORY_NAME is specified. If no CATEGORY_NAME is provided, the database will not allow the row to be inserted.

B.2.4 Sequences

An easy way to ensure uniqueness for surrogate primary keys is to set the key for a new record to a number greater than the last created record. Although you could manage this kind of column yourself, databases provide various mechanisms for managing key sequences. The easiest and most transparent of these mechanisms is an *identity column* constraint (such as the identity column constraints supported by DB2, Sybase, and SQL Server). When you designate a column as an identity, the database automatically generates a value for you when you create a new record. For example, if the ITEM_ID primary key for the ITEMS table is an identity, when we create a new record we do not specify a primary key value ourselves. Instead, during record creation the database looks at the last row inserted, generates a new value by incrementing the last key, and sets the ITEM_ID value on our behalf.

Some other databases like Oracle don't support incrementing keys as an internal function of the column, but help you generate keys using an external mechanism called *sequences* (DB2 supports sequences in addition to identities). Each time you insert a new record, you can ask the sequence to generate a key that you can use in the INSERT statement. A few databases don't support sequence generation at all, in which case you must implement similar functionality yourself. Fortunately, EJB 3 transparently handles all these situations on your behalf, using the table generator.

B.3 Structured Query Language (SQL)

If relational theory is the bedrock of the relational database, SQL is the crown jewels. Java developers with strong OO roots may find SQL's verbose syntax and unmistakably relational feel less than ideal. The truth is that even O/R solutions such as the EJB 3 Persistence API generate SQL under the hood. The fact that you use O/R is no excuse not to have a solid understanding of SQL, particularly during debugging and fine-tuning.

SQL (which stands for Structured Query Language) arose as a result of the initial relational research conducted at IBM. The American National Standards Institute (ANSI) has since standardized SQL. Almost all major databases comply with the SQL-92 standard for the most part. Even then, writing portable SQL is a tricky business at best. Luckily, O/R relieves us from this meticulous work to some degree by automatically generating SQL suited to a particular database.

SQL statements include the familiar CREATE, INSERT, DELETE, UPDATE, and, of course, everyone's favorite, SELECT. As a testament to the power of the SELECT statement, some elements of it have been ported over into the O/R world through EJB-QL (which we cover in chapter 10).

Database normalization

In the relational world, it is extremely important that the same conceptual data not be replicated throughout the database. The importance of avoiding redundancy stems from two facts. First, most databases hold a huge amount of data. For example, it is easy to think that storing department name and location in a table with employee information is no big deal. The problem is that if a thousand employees work in the same department, the department information would be duplicated across a thousand employee table rows! If a department location changes, you would have to accurately update each of the records for the thousand employees who work for the department. Second, this redundancy can easily lead to inconsistency. Both of these problems can be solved by storing a foreign key to the department table (say department ID) in the employee table instead.

Relational theory has formalized the process of checking the database design for redundancy. This process is called *database normalization*. IBM researchers initially proposed three different levels of normalization: first, second, and third normal form, each consisting of a well-defined, incrementally strict set of rules to check for database fitness. Later, more levels were introduced: BCNF (Boyce-Codd Normal Form), fourth, and fifth normal form. Relational theory recognizes the fact that normalization can lead to trading off speed for space efficiency. Most DBAs go through the process of selective *denormalization* when faced with tricky performance issues.

Coverage of SQL syntax is well beyond the scope of this appendix. However, at least a basic grasp of SQL is essential to understand chapters 8, 9, and 10. If you don't already have a working knowledge of SQL, we highly recommend that you investigate it on your own.

Annotations reference

In this appendix, we list all the EJB 3 annotations we talked about throughout the book. This appendix is designed to be a quick reference you can use while developing your enterprise application. See the individual chapters for the full details of each annotation.

The annotations are organized by topic, roughly following the same sequence as the chapters.

C.1 Session and message-driven beans

The following are all the annotations that are used in session and message-driven beans.

C.1.1 Session beans

These annotations are used for stateless and stateful session beans.

javax.ejb.Stateless

Marks a POJO as a stateless session bean.

```
@Target(TYPE) @Retention(RUNTIME)
public @interface Stateless {
    String name() default "";
    String mappedName() default "";      ⟵┘ Vendor-specific bean name
    String description() default "";
}
```

javax.ejb.Stateful

Marks a POJO as a stateful session bean.

```
@Target(TYPE) @Retention(RUNTIME)
public @interface Stateful {
    String name() default "";
    String mappedName() default "";      ⟵┘ Vendor-specific bean name
    String description() default "";
}
```

javax.ejb.Remove

Denotes a business method as the remove method of a stateful session bean.

```
@Target(METHOD) @Retention(RUNTIME)
public @interface Remove {
    boolean retainIfException() default false;
}
```

The @Remove annotation has one element: retainIfException. If it is set to true and an exception is thrown from designated method, the bean will not be removed.

javax.ejb.Remote

Marks a POJI as a session bean remote business interface.

```
@Target(TYPE) @Retention(RUNTIME)
public @interface Remote {
    Class[] value() default {};
}
```

The @Remote annotation can be applied on both on a bean class or on a business interface. The class element is used to specify the name of the interface when @Remote is applied on the bean class.

javax.ejb.Local

Marks a POJI as a session bean local business interface.

```
@Target(TYPE) @Retention(RUNTIME)
public @interface Local {
    Class[] value() default {};
}
```

The @Local annotation can be applied on a bean class or on a business interface. The class element is used to specify the name of the interface when @Local is applied on the bean class.

javax.ejb.RemoteHome and javax.ejb.LocalHome

The RemoteHome and LocalHome annotations are used for backward compatibility with EJB 2 session bean clients. You can use these annotations with EJB 3 session beans that provide an EJB 2 client view.

```
@Target(TYPE) @Retention(RUNTIME)
public @interface RemoteHome {
Class value();        ◁─┐ Home interface
```

```
@Target(TYPE) @Retention(RUNTIME)
public @interface LocalHome {
Class value();        ◁─┐ Local home interface
```

javax.ejb.Init

The @Init annotation is used primarily for backward compatibility with EJB 2 session beans. It can be used on a method and will have behavior similar to that of the create<METHOD> method of an EJB 2 session bean.

```
@Target(METHOD) @Retention(RUNTIME)
public @interface Init{
String value() default "";
}
```

C.1.2 Message-driven beans

These annotations apply to message-driven beans.

javax.ejb.MessageDriven

Marks a POJO as an MDB.

```
@Target(TYPE) @Retention(RUNTIME)
public @interface MessageDriven {
    String name() default "";
    Class messageListenerInterface() default      | Specifies listener
        java.lang.Object.class;                     | interface
    ActivationConfigProperty[] activationConfig() default {};  ← Configures
    String mappedName() default "";    ←─ Contains vendor-specific    properties
    String description() default "";      bean name
}
```

javax.ejb.ActivationConfigProperty

Specifies a name-value pair of configuration properties that may be used for an MDB to receive messages from a message source.

```
@Target({}) @Retention(RUNTIME)
public @interface ActivationConfigProperty {
    String propertyName();
    String propertyValue();
}
```

C.1.3 Dependency injection

These annotations are used to inject both EJBs and resources.

javax.ejb.EJB

Injects an EJB reference into a field or method.

```
@Target({TYPE, METHOD, FIELD}) @Retention(RUNTIME)
public @interface EJB {
    String name() default "";
    Class beanInterface() default Object.class;
    String beanName() default "";
    String mappedName() default "";    ←─┘ Vendor-specific JNDI bean name
    String description() default "";
}
```

javax.ejb.EJBs

Denotes references to multiple EJBs. Used at the class level. This annotation is not discussed in this book. We encourage you to explore it on your own.

```
@Target(TYPE) @Retention(RUNTIME)
public @interface EJBs {
    EJB[] value();
}
```

javax.annotation.Resource

Injects a container resource into a field or method.

```
@Target({TYPE, METHOD, FIELD}) @Retention(RUNTIME)
public @interface Resource {
    public enum AuthenticationType {
        CONTAINER,
        APPLICATION
    }
    String name() default "";
    Class type() default Object.class;
    AuthenticationType authenticationType()
        default AuthenticationType.CONTAINER;
    boolean shareable() default true;
    String mappedName() default "";        ←┘ Vendor-specific resource name
    String description() default "";
}
```

javax.annotation.Resources

Denotes references to multiple resources. Used at the class level. This annotation is not discussed in this book. We encourage you to explore it on your own.

```
@Target(TYPE) @Retention(RUNTIME)
public @interface Resources {
    Resource[] value();
}
```

C.1.4 Transaction management

These annotations are used for declarative transaction management.

javax.ejb.TransactionManagement

Specifies transaction type, such as BMT or CMT, for an EJB.

```
@Target(TYPE) @Retention(RUNTIME)
public @interface TransactionManagement {
    TransactionManagementType value()
        default TransactionManagementType.CONTAINER;
}
```

```
public enum TransactionManagementType {
    CONTAINER,
    BEAN
}
```

javax.ejb.TransactionAttribute

Specifies the transaction attribute for an EJB method.

```
@Target({METHOD, TYPE}) @Retention(RUNTIME)
public @interface TransactionAttribute {
    TransactionAttributeType value()
        default TransactionAttributeType.REQUIRED;
}

public enum TransactionAttributeType {
    MANDATORY,
    REQUIRED,
    REQUIRES_NEW,
    SUPPORTS,
    NOT_SUPPORTED,
    NEVER
}
```

javax.ejb.ApplicationException

Denotes a checked or unchecked exception as an application exception.

```
@Target(TYPE) @Retention(RUNTIME)
public @interface ApplicationException {
    boolean rollback() default false;
}
```

C.1.5 Security management

These annotations are used for declarative security management.

javax.annotation.security.DeclareRoles

Defines the roles used in an application.

```
@Target({TYPE}) @Retention(RUNTIME)
public @interface DeclareRoles {
    String[] value();
}
```

javax.annotation.security.RolesAllowed

Specifies the roles allowed to invoke a bean method.

```
@Target({TYPE, METHOD}) @Retention(RUNTIME)
public @interface RolesAllowed {
    String[] value();
}
```

javax.annotation.security.PermitAll

Specifies business methods that are accessible to any role.

```
@Target ({TYPE, METHOD}) @Retention(RUNTIME)
public @interface PermitAll {}
```

javax.annotation.security.DenyAll

Specifies that no roles be allowed to invoke a business method.

```
@Target (METHOD) @Retention(RUNTIME)
public @interface DenyAll {}
```

javax.annotation.security.RunAs

Specifies that a business method should run under a given role when it is invoked.

```
@Target(TYPE) @Retention(RUNTIME)
public @interface RunAs {
    String value();
}
```

C.1.6 EJB lifecycle management

These annotations are used for EJB lifecycle callbacks.

javax.annotation.PostConstruct

Marks a method in the bean class or an interceptor class as a postconstruct lifecycle callback method.

```
@Target({METHOD}) @Retention(RUNTIME)
public @interface PostConstruct {}
```

javax.annotation.PreDestroy

Marks a method in the bean class or an interceptor class as a predestroy lifecycle callback method.

```
@Target({METHOD}) @Retention(RUNTIME)
public @interface PreDestroy {}
```

javax.ejb.PostActivate

Marks a stateful EJB method as a postactivate lifecycle callback method.

```
@Target({METHOD}) @Retention(RUNTIME)
public @interface PostActivate {}
```

javax.ejb.PrePassivate

Marks a stateful EJB method as a prepassivate lifecycle callback method.

```
@Target({METHOD}) @Retention(RUNTIME)
public @interface PrePassivate {}
```

C.1.7 Interceptors

These annotations are used for interceptors.

javax.interceptor.Interceptors

Designates interceptors for an entire EJB or a bean method.

```
@Target({TYPE, METHOD}) @Retention(RUNTIME)
public @interface Interceptors {
    Class[] value();
}
```

javax.interceptor.AroundInvoke

Designates a method in an interceptor class as the around-invoke method.

```
@Target({METHOD}) @Retention(RUNTIME)
public @interface AroundInvoke {}
```

javax.interceptor.ExcludeClassInterceptors

Marks a bean method to exclude interceptors defined at the class level.

```
@Target({METHOD}) @Retention(RUNTIME)
public @interface ExcludeClassInterceptors {}
```

javax.interceptor.ExcludeDefaultInterceptors

Marks a bean class or bean method to exclude interceptors defined at the module (default) level.

```
@Target({TYPE, METHOD}) @Retention(RUNTIME)
public @interface ExcludeDefaultInterceptors {}
```

C.1.8 Timers

The following annotation is used for EJB timers.

javax.ejb.Timeout

Marks a bean method as the timeout method that is triggered when an EJB timer expires.

```
@Target({METHOD}) @Retention(RUNTIME)
public @interface Timeout {}
```

C.2 *Java Persistence API annotations*

These are the annotations used for the Java Persistence API.

C.2.1 *Defining domain objects*

The following annotations are used to define domain objects such as entities, embedded objects, and entity identity.

javax.persistence.Entity

Marks a POJO as a JPA entity.

```
@Target(TYPE) @Retention(RUNTIME)
public @interface Entity {
    String name() default "";
}
```

javax.persistence.Embeddable

Marks a POJO as an embeddable object (stored as a part of another entity).

```
@Target({TYPE}) @Retention(RUNTIME)
public @interface Embeddable {}
```

javax.persistence.Embedded

Specifies that a persistence field or property is an embeddable class.

```
@Target({METHOD, FIELD}) @Retention(RUNTIME)
public @interface Embedded {}
```

javax.persistence.Id

Denotes a persistence field or property that is the unique identifier for an entity.

```
@Target({METHOD, FIELD}) @Retention(RUNTIME)
public @interface Id {}
```

javax.persistence.IdClass

Used to define a composite primary key.

```
@Target({TYPE}) @Retention(RUNTIME)
public @interface IdClass {
    Class value();
}
```

javax.persistence.EmbeddedId

Denotes an embeddable object as the unique identifier for an entity.

```
@Target({TYPE}) @Retention(RUNTIME)
public @interface EmbeddedId {}
```

C.2.2 *Defining domain object data*

These annotations are used to define entity data.

javax.persistence.Transient

Marks a field or property as transient (not persisted).

```
@Target({METHOD, FIELD}) @Retention(RUNTIME)
public @interface Transient {}
```

javax.persistence.Lob

Specifies that a persistence field or property be mapped to a large object type (BLOB or CLOB) in the database.

```
@Target({METHOD, FIELD}) @Retention(RUNTIME)
public @interface Lob {}
```

javax.persistence.Temporal

Specifies the mapping data type of a persistence field or property as `java.util.Date` or `java.util.Calendar`.

```
@Target({METHOD, FIELD}) @Retention(RUNTIME)
public @interface Temporal {
    TemporalType value();
}

public enum TemporalType {
    DATE,                           ←┘ java.sql.Date
    TIME,      ←┘ java.sql.Time
    TIMESTAMP    ←┐ java.sql.Timestamp
}
```

javax.persistence.Enumerated

Denotes options for a persistence field or property of type `enumerated`.

```
@Target({METHOD, FIELD}) @Retention(RUNTIME)
public @interface Enumerated {
    EnumType value() default ORDINAL;
}

public enum EnumType {
    ORDINAL,
    STRING
}
```

C.2.3 *Mapping entity data*

The annotations in this section are used to map entity data to the database.

javax.persistence.Table

Defines the primary table an entity is mapped to.

```
@Target({TYPE}) @Retention(RUNTIME)
public @interface Table {
    String name() default "";
    String catalog() default "";        ←⌐ Table catalog
    String schema() default "";                        ←⌐ Table schema
    UniqueConstraint[] uniqueConstraints() default {};
}
```

javax.persistence.SecondaryTable

Defines secondary table an entity is mapped to.

```
@Target({TYPE}) @Retention(RUNTIME)
public @interface SecondaryTable {
    String name();
    String catalog() default "";        ←⌐ Table catalog
    String schema() default "";                        ←⌐ Table schema
    PrimaryKeyJoinColumn[] pkJoinColumns() default {};
    UniqueConstraint[] uniqueConstraints() default {};
}
```

javax.persistence.UniqueConstraint

Defines a unique constraint for a table used for entity mapping.

```
@Target({}) @Retention(RUNTIME)
public @interface UniqueConstraint {
    String[] columnNames();
}
```

javax.persistence.Column

Maps an entity field or property to a table column.

```
@Target({METHOD, FIELD}) @Retention(RUNTIME)
public @interface Column {
    String name() default "";
    boolean unique() default false;
    boolean nullable() default true;
    boolean insertable() default true;
    boolean updatable() default true;
    String columnDefinition() default "";      ←⌐ Column DDL
    String table() default "";
    int length() default 255;
    int precision() default 0;      ←⌐ Decimal precision
    int scale() default 0;      ←⌐ Decimal scale
}
```

javax.persistence.Basic

Specifies some simple mapping attributes. Can be used with any association mapping or specify the fetch type for a field or property.

```
@Target({METHOD, FIELD}) @Retention(RUNTIME)
public @interface Basic {
    FetchType fetch() default EAGER;
    boolean optional() default true;
}
```

javax.persistence.AttributeOverride

Overrides the mapping of an entity property or field. This annotation is not discussed in this book. We encourage you to explore it on your own.

```
@Target({TYPE, METHOD, FIELD}) @Retention(RUNTIME)
public @interface AttributeOverride {
    String name();
    Column column();
}
```

javax.persistence.AttributeOverrides

Specifies multiple mapping overrides. This annotation is not discussed in this book. We encourage you to explore it on your own.

```
@Target({TYPE, METHOD, FIELD}) @Retention(RUNTIME)
public @interface AttributeOverrides {
    AttributeOverride[] value();
}
```

javax.persistence.GeneratedValue

Used for automatic generation of values; typically used for primary keys.

```
@Target({METHOD, FIELD}) @Retention(RUNTIME)
public @interface GeneratedValue {
    GenerationType strategy() default AUTO;
    String generator() default "";
}

public enum GenerationType { TABLE, SEQUENCE, IDENTITY, AUTO }
```

javax.persistence.TableGenerator

Denotes a generator that may be used for automatic key generation using a sequence table.

```
@Target({TYPE, METHOD, FIELD}) @Retention(RUNTIME)
public @interface TableGenerator {
    String name();                    ⟵ Unique generator name
    String table() default "";
```

```
        String catalog() default "";        ◁┘  Table catalog
        String schema() default "";          ◁┐  Table schema
        String pkColumnName() default "";
        String valueColumnName() default "";
        String pkColumnValue() default "";
        int initialValue() default 0;
        int allocationSize() default 50;    ◁┘  Amount to increment by
        UniqueConstraint[] uniqueConstraints() default {};
    }
```

javax.persistence.SequenceGenerator

Denotes a generator that may be used for automatic key generation using a database sequence.

```
    @Target({TYPE, METHOD, FIELD}) @Retention(RUNTIME)
    public @interface SequenceGenerator {
        String name();                       ◁┘  Unique generator name
        String sequenceName() default "";    ◁┐  Name of database sequence
        int initialValue() default 1;
        int allocationSize() default 50;     ◁┐  Amount to increment by
    }
```

C.2.4 *Defining domain relationships*

These annotations are used to define one-to-one, one-to-many and many-to-many relationships between entities.

javax.persistence.OneToOne

Specifies a one-to-one entity association.

```
    @Target({METHOD, FIELD}) @Retention(RUNTIME)
    public @interface OneToOne {               Entity class if not
        Class targetEntity() default void.class;  ◁┘  Java generics
        CascadeType[] cascade() default {};
        FetchType fetch() default EAGER;
        boolean optional() default true;       Relationship
        String mappedBy() default "";        ◁┘  owner
    }

    public enum CascadeType { ALL, PERSIST, MERGE, REMOVE, REFRESH };
    public enum FetchType { LAZY, EAGER };
```

javax.persistence.ManyToOne

Specifies a many-to-one entity association.

```
    @Target({METHOD, FIELD}) @Retention(RUNTIME)
    public @interface ManyToOne {
        Class targetEntity() default void.class;  ◁┘  Entity class if not Java generic
        CascadeType[] cascade() default {};
```

```
        FetchType fetch() default EAGER;
        boolean optional() default true;
    }
```

javax.persistence.OneToMany

Specifies a one-to-many entity association.

```
    @Target({METHOD, FIELD}) @Retention(RUNTIME)
    public @interface OneToMany {                          Entity class if not
        Class targetEntity() default void.class;    ◁┘   Java generic
        CascadeType[] cascade() default {};
        FetchType fetch() default LAZY;
        String mappedBy() default "";    ◁┘  Relationship owner
    }
```

javax.persistence.ManyToMany

Denotes a many-to-many association with another entity.

```
    @Target({METHOD, FIELD}) @Retention(RUNTIME)
    public @interface ManyToMany {                         Entity class if not
        Class targetEntity() default void.class;    ◁┘   Java generic
        CascadeType[] cascade() default {};
        FetchType fetch() default LAZY;
        String mappedBy() default "";    ◁┘  Relationship owner
    }
```

C.2.5 *Mapping domain relationships*

These annotations are used to map entity relations to the database.

javax.persistence.JoinColumn

Denotes a mapping column for an entity association.

```
    @Target({METHOD, FIELD}) @Retention(RUNTIME)
    public @interface JoinColumn {
        String name() default "";
        String referencedColumnName() default "";
        boolean unique() default false;
        boolean nullable() default true;
        boolean insertable() default true;
        boolean updatable() default true;
        String columnDefinition() default "";    ◁┘  Column DDL
        String table() default "";
    }
```

javax.persistence.JoinColumns

Denotes a mapping column for an entity association when a composite key is used.

```
    @Target({METHOD, FIELD}) @Retention(RUNTIME)
    public @interface JoinColumns {
```

```
    JoinColumn[] value();
}
```

javax.persistence.PrimaryKeyJoinColumn

Denotes the primary key column that is used as a foreign key to join to another table. It is used in one-to-one relationships and the joined subclass inheritance strategy.

```
@Target({TYPE, METHOD, FIELD}) @Retention(RUNTIME)
public @interface PrimaryKeyJoinColumn {
    String name() default "";                          Key in current table   Key in
    String referencedColumnName() default "";                                 joined table
    String columnDefinition() default "";     Column DDL
}
```

javax.persistence.PrimaryKeyJoinColumns

Specifies composite primary keys used as foreign key to join to another table.

```
@Target({TYPE, METHOD, FIELD}) @Retention(RUNTIME)
public @interface PrimaryKeyJoinColumns {
    PrimaryKeyJoinColumn[] value();
}
```

javax.persistence.JoinTable

Specifies a join table used in a one-to-many or many-to-many association.

```
@Target({METHOD, FIELD}) @Retention(RUNTIME)
public @interface JoinTable {
    String name() default "";
    String catalog default "";      Table catalog
    String schema default "";          Table schema     Join column(s) in
    JoinColumn[] joinColumns default {};                 owning side
    JoinColumn[] inverseJoinColumns default {};       Join column(s) in
    UniqueConstraint[] uniqueConstraints default {};  inverse side
}
```

javax.persistence.AssociationOverride

Overrides a many-to-one or one-to-one mapping of property or field for an entity relationship.

```
@Target({TYPE, METHOD, FIELD}) @Retention(RUNTIME)
public @interface AssociationOverride {
    String name default "";
    JoinColumn[] joinColumns default {};
}
```

javax.persistence.AssociationOverrides

Overrides mappings of multiple many-to-one or one-to-one relationship properties or fields.

```
@Target({TYPE, METHOD, FIELD}) @Retention(RUNTIME)
public @interface AssociationOverrides {
    AssociationOverride[] value();
}
```

javax.persistence.OrderBy

Specifies ordering of a collection-valued association such as one-to-many and
many-to-many when it is retrieved.

```
@Target({METHOD, FIELD}) @Retention(RUNTIME)
public @interface OrderBy {
    String value() default "";
}
```

javax.persistence.MapKey

Specifies the mapping keys for an entity association of type `java.util.Map`.
This annotation is not discussed in this book. We encourage you to explore it
on your own.

```
@Target({METHOD, FIELD}) @Retention(RUNTIME)
public @interface MapKey {
    String name() default "";
}
```

C.2.6 *Mapping object-oriented inheritance*

The following annotations are used to map OO inheritance to relational database tables.

javax.persistence.Inheritance

Defines the inheritance mapping strategy for entities in the entity hierarchy.

```
@Target({TYPE}) @Retention(RUNTIME)
public @interface Inheritance {
    InheritanceType strategy() default SINGLE_TABLE;
}

public enum InheritanceType { SINGLE_TABLE, JOINED, TABLE_PER_CLASS };
```

javax.persistence.DiscriminatorColumn

Defines the discriminator column used when the single-table or joined inheritance strategy is used.

```
@Target({TYPE}) @Retention(RUNTIME)
public @interface DiscriminatorColumn {
    String name() default "DTYPE";
    DiscriminatorType discriminatorType() default STRING;
    String columnDefinition() default "";    ⟵ Column DDL
    int length() default 31;
}

public enum DiscriminatorType { STRING, CHAR, INTEGER };
```

javax.persistence.DiscriminatorValue

Specifies the value for a discriminator column for storing the entity type when the single-table or joined inheritance strategy is used.

```
@Target({TYPE}) @Retention(RUNTIME)
public @interface DiscriminatorValue {
    String value();
}
```

C.2.7 *Java Persistence Query Language annotations*

These annotations are used in conjunction with JPQL.

javax.persistence.NamedQuery

Defines a named query. A named query uses JPQL.

```
@Target({TYPE}) @Retention(RUNTIME)
public @interface NamedQuery {
    String name();
    String query();
    QueryHint[] hints() default {};    ⟵ Vendor-specific hints
}

@Target({}) @Retention(RUNTIME)
public @interface QueryHint {
    String name();
    String value();
}
```

javax.persistence.NamedQueries

Defines a number of named queries.

```
@Target({TYPE}) @Retention(RUNTIME)
public @interface NamedQueries {
    NamedQuery[] value ();
}
```

javax.persistence.NamedNativeQuery

Defines a named query. A named native query uses SQL.

```
@Target({TYPE}) @Retention(RUNTIME)
public @interface NamedNativeQuery {
    String name();
    String query();
    QueryHint[] hints() default {};      ⟵┘ Vendor-specific hints
    Class resultClass() default void.class;
    String resultSetMapping() default "";
}
```

javax.persistence.SqlResultSetMapping

Specifies the mapping for the result of a SQL query.

```
@Target({TYPE}) @Retention(RUNTIME)
public @interface SqlResultSetMapping {
    String name();
    EntityResult[] entities() default {};      ⟵┘ Mapping to entities
    ColumnResult[] columns() default {};       ⟵┐ Mapping to scalar value
}
```

javax.persistence.SqlResultSetMappings

Denotes more than one mapping.

```
@Target({TYPE}) @Retention(RUNTIME)
public @interface SqlResultSetMappings {
    SqlResultSetMapping[] value();
}
```

javax.persistence.Version

Specifies the version column used for optimistic record locking.

```
@Target({METHOD, FIELD}) @Retention(RUNTIME)
public @interface Version {}
```

C.2.8   Entity lifecycle annotations

The annotations in this section are used for entity lifecycle management.

javax.persistence.EntityListeners

Specifies entity listener classes for an entity.

```
@Target({TYPE}) @Retention(RUNTIME)
public @interface EntityListeners {
    Class[] value();
}
```

javax.persistence.ExcludeSuperclassListeners

Disables any entity listeners defined in the superclass of an entity.

```
@Target({TYPE}) @Retention(RUNTIME)
public @interface ExcludeSuperclassListeners {}
```

javax.persistence.ExcludeDefaultListeners

Disables default entity listeners defined in the persistence module.

```
@Target({TYPE}) @Retention(RUNTIME)
public @interface ExcludeDefaultListeners {}
```

javax.persistence.PrePersist

Marks a method in the entity or listener class as a pre-persist callback (executed before an entity is persisted).

```
@Target({METHOD}) @Retention(RUNTIME)
public @interface PrePersist {}
```

javax.persistence.PostPersist

Marks a method in the entity or listener class as a postpersist callback (executed after an entity is persisted).

```
@Target({METHOD}) @Retention(RUNTIME)
public @interface PostPersist {}
```

javax.persistence.PreUpdate

Marks a method in the entity or listener class as a preupdate callback (executed before entity data is updated in the database).

```
@Target({METHOD}) @Retention(RUNTIME)
public @interface PreUpdate {}
```

javax.persistence.PostUpdate

Marks a method in the entity or listener class as a postupdate callback (executed after entity data is updated in the database).

```
@Target({METHOD}) @Retention(RUNTIME)
public @interface PostUpdate {}
```

javax.persistence.PreRemove

Marks a method in the entity or listener class as a preremove callback (executed before an entity is removed from the database).

```
@Target({METHOD}) @Retention(RUNTIME)
public @interface PreRemove {}
```

javax.persistence.PostRemove

Marks a method in the entity or listener class as a postremove callback (executed after an entity is removed from the database).

```
@Target({METHOD}) @Retention(RUNTIME)
public @interface PostRemove {}
```

javax.persistence.PostLoad

Marks a method in the entity or listener class as a postload callback (executed before an entity is loaded from the database).

```
@Target({METHOD}) @Retention(RUNTIME)
public @interface PostLoad {}
```

C.2.9 *JPA dependency injection*

The annotations in this section are used for injecting JPA resources.

javax.persistence.PersistenceContext

Injects an instance of a container-managed entity manager.

```
@Target({TYPE, METHOD, FIELD}) @Retention(RUNTIME)
public @interface PersistenceContext {
    String name() default "";          ⟵  Name if used at class level
    String unitName() default "";
    PersistenceContextType type default TRANSACTION;
    PersistenceProperty[] properties() default {};  ⟵  Vendor-specific
}                                                       properties

public enum PersistenceContextType {
    TRANSACTION,
    EXTENDED
}
```

javax.persistence.PersistenceUnit

Injects an instance of an entity manager factory that you can use to create an application-managed entity manager.

```
@Target({TYPE, METHOD, FIELD}) @Retention(RUNTIME)
public @interface PersistenceUnit {
    String name() default "";          ⟵  Name if used at class level
    String unitName() default "";
}
```

javax.persistence.PersistenceUnits

Denotes multiple persistence units. Used at the class level.

```
@Target(TYPE) @Retention(RUNTIME)
public @interface PersistenceUnits {
    PersistenceUnit[] value();
}
```

Deployment descriptors reference

In this appendix we list all the elements of EJB 3 descriptors. The appendix is designed to be a quick reference you can consult when you plan to use a descriptor in your enterprise application. Each descriptor is defined by an XML schema, and we describe the elements of the schema.

As we have explained throughout the book, you have a choice of using annotations, XML descriptors, or both, to define these elements. We have mainly used annotations throughout this book, so here we also list what annotation is overridden by the descriptor, when applicable.

This appendix has three sections. The first section (D.1) provides a reference to ejb-jar.xml, which is the descriptor for session beans and MDBs. The second section (D.2) provides a reference to persistence.xml, the descriptor that makes a module a persistence module. The third section (D.3) describes the O/R mapping metadata used by JPA.

The schemas are referenced at http://java.sun.com/xml/ns/javaee/#2.

D.1 Reference for ejb-jar.xml

ejb-jar.xml is the optional deployment descriptor that is packaged in an EJB module. ejb-jar.xml has two primary elements: enterprise-beans is used to define beans, resources, and services used by the beans, and assembly-descriptor is used to declare security roles, method permissions, declarative transaction settings, and interceptors. In this section we provide references only to the elements relevant to EJB 3, and we don't discuss any elements in the schema that are for the sole purpose of backward compatibility with EJB 2. You can refer to the schema of ejb-jar.xml at http://java.sun.com/xml/ns/javaee/ejb-jar_3_0.xsd.

D.1.1 enterprise-beans

The enterprise-beans element is used to define EJBs in an EJB-JAR module. You can use session or message-driven tags to define session beans or MDBs.

session

Corresponding annotations: @javax.ejb.Stateless and @javax.ejb.Stateful

The session tag is used to define a session bean.

Element/Attribute Name	Description
ejb-name	A logical name for the session bean. This is the same as the name element of the @Stateless or @Stateful annotation.

continued on next page

Element/Attribute Name	Description
mapped-name	A vendor-specific name for the bean.
remote	Remote interface for the EJB.
local	Local interface of the EJB.
service-endpoint	Web service endpoint interface for the EJB. Only applies to stateless beans.
ejb-class	Name of the bean class.
session-type	Type of session bean, i.e., stateless or stateful.
transaction-type	Transaction type used with the EJB, i.e., BEAN or CONTAINER.
timeout-method	Timeout method for the EJB. Applies only to stateless beans.
remove-method	Remove method for stateful EJBs.
init-method	EJB 2-style create method for EJB 3 stateful EJBs.

message-driven-bean

Corresponding annotation: `@javax.ejb.MessageDriven`

The `message-driven-bean` tag is used to define an MDB.

Element/Attribute Name	Description
ejb-name	A logical name for the MDB. This is the same as the `name` element of `@MessageDriven` annotation.
mapped-name	A vendor-specific name for the bean.
message-driven-destination	Name of the destination that MDB listens to. Primarily used for EJB 2 MDBs.
messaging-type	Messaging type supported, i.e., message listener interface supported by the MDB.
service-endpoint	Web service endpoint interface for the EJB. Only applies to stateless beans.
ejb-class	Name of the bean class.
transaction-type	Transaction type used with the EJB, i.e., Bean or `Container`.

activation-config-property	Configuration property for an MDB. Specified using a name-value pair using
	`activation-config-property-name`
	`activation-config-property-value`
	Similar to the `@ActivationConfigProperty` annotation.

Common elements for session and message-driven beans

The following elements are commonly used with session and message-driven beans.

ejb-local-ref

Corresponding annotation: @javax.ejb.EJB

Used to specify dependencies on local EJBs.

Element/Attribute Name	Description
ejb-ref-name	The name used to bind the referenced EJB to the ENC. Same as the name element in the @EJB annotation. ejb-ref-name must be specified.
ejb-link	The name of the target enterprise bean. This optional setting is used to link an EJB reference to a target enterprise bean.
local	The EJB 3 local business interface.
ref-type	The EJB reference type, i.e., session.
injection-target	Target where the EJB reference is injected when dependency injection is used.

ejb-ref

Corresponding annotation: @javax.ejb.EJB

Used to specify remote EJB references.

Element/Attribute Name	Description
ejb-ref-name	The name used to bind the referenced EJB to the ENC. Same as the name element in the @EJB annotation. ejb-ref-name must be specified.
ejb-link	The name of the target enterprise bean. This optional setting is used to link an EJB reference to a target enterprise bean.
remote	The EJB 3 remote business interface type.
ref-type	The EJB reference type, i.e., "session".
injection-target	Target where the EJB reference is injected when dependency injection is used.

resource-ref

Corresponding annotation: @javax.annotation.Resource

Used to specify resource references, e.g., data source, JMS connection factories, etc.

Element/Attribute Name	Description
res-ref-name	The name used to bind the referenced resource into the ENC. Same as the `name` element in the `@Resource` annotation.
mapped-name	A vendor-specific global JNDI name for the referenced resource.
res-type	Fully qualified class of the type of resource referenced, e.g., `javax.sql.DataSource`.
res-auth	Authentication type for the resource. Valid values are `Container` or `Application`.
res-sharing-scope	Specifies whether multiple beans can share the resource. Valid values are `Shareable` and `Unshareable`.
injection-target	Target where the referenced resource is injected when dependency injection is used.

resource-env-ref

Corresponding annotation: `@javax.annotation.Resource`

Used to specify resource JMS destination references, such as a `Queue` or `Topic`.

Element/Attribute Name	Description
resource-env-ref-name	The name used to bind the referenced JMS destination to the ENC. Same as the `name` element in the `@Resource` annotation.
mapped-name	A vendor-specific global JNDI name for the referenced JMS destination.
resource-env-type	Type of JMS destination referenced, such as `javax.jms.Queue` or `javax.jms.Topic`.
injection-target	Target where the referenced destination is injected when dependency injection is used.

env-entry

Corresponding annotation: `@javax.annotation.Resource`

Defines environment entries for an EJB.

Element/Attribute Name	Description
env-entry-name	The name used in the environment entry in the ENC. Same as the `name` element in the `@Resource` annotation.

continued on next page

Element/Attribute Name	Description
env-entry-type	Type of the `env` entry used. Legal types are `java.lang.Boolean`, `java.lang.Byte`, `java.lang.Character`, `java.lang.String`, `java.lang.Short`, `java.lang.Integer`, `java.lang.Long`, `java.lang.Float`, and `java.lang.Double`.
env-entry-value	Value specified for the environment entry.
injection-target	Target where the referenced destination is injected when dependency injection is used.

service-ref

Corresponding annotation: `@javax.xml.ws.WebServiceRef`

Used to specify dependency on a web service.

The referenced schema is `javaee_web_services_client_1_2.xsd`, and we have discussed only elements that are useful for EJBs.

Element/Attribute Name	Description
service-ref-name	The name used to bind the referenced web service into the ENC. Same as the `name` element in the `@WebServiceRef` annotation.
service-interface	Fully qualified class for the JAX-WS service interface the client depends on, i.e., `javax.xml.rpc.Service`.
service-ref-type	Type of service that will be returned.
wsdl-file	The URL location of the WSDL.
handler-chains	Defines handler chain.
injection-target	Target where the web service reference is injected when dependency injection is used.

persistence-context-ref

Corresponding annotation: `@javax.persistence.PersistenceContext`

Defines references to a container-managed entity manager.

Element/Attribute Name	Description
persistence-context-ref-name	The name used to bind the referenced persistence context to the ENC. Same as the `name` element in the `@PersistenceContext` annotation.

continued on next page

Element/Attribute Name	Description
persistence-unit-name	Name of the persistence unit referenced.
persistence-context-type	Type of persistence context, i.e., Transaction or Extended. Extended is supported only in stateful session beans.
persistence-property	A name value-pair of vendor-specific persistence properties.
injection-target	Target where the EntityManager is injected when dependency injection is used.

persistence-unit-ref

Corresponding annotation: @javax.persistence.PersistenceUnit

Defines references to a persistence unit (i.e., entity manager factory).

Element/Attribute Name	Description
persistence-unit-ref-name	The name used to bind the referenced persistence unit (EntityManagerFactory) to the ENC. Same as the name element in the @PersistenceUnit annotation.
persistence-unit-name	Name of the persistence unit referenced.
persistence-context-type	Type of persistence context, i.e., Transaction or Extended. Extended is supported only in stateful session beans.
persistence-property	A name value-pair of vendor-specific persistence properties.
injection-target	Target where the EntityManagerFactory is injected when dependency injection is used.

injection-target

This defines the name of a class and a name (field or property) within that class into which a resource, EJB, entity manager, etc. should be injected.

Element/Attribute Name	Description
injection-target-class	The fully qualified name of the class into which a resource, EJB, entity manager, etc. should be injected.
injection-target-name	Name of the injection target, i.e., the name of the property or field in the injection target class.

post-construct, pre-destroy, pre-passivate, post-activate

Corresponding annotations: `@javax.annotation.PostConstruct`, `@javax.annotation.PreDestroy`, `@javax.ejb.PrePassivate`, `@javax.ejb.PostActivate`

Used to define lifecycle methods.

Element/Attribute Name	Description
`lifecycle-callback-class`	The fully qualified name of the class in which the lifecycle callback is defined. Leave empty if the callback is in the same bean class.
`lifecycle-callback-method`	Name of the method defined as the lifecycle callback method.

security-role-ref

Corresponding annotation: `@javax.annotation.security.DeclareRoles`

Used to specify security role references.

Element/Attribute Name	Description
`role-name`	Name of the role referenced. The referenced role is used as a parameter in `EJBContext.isCallerInRole(String roleName)`. See chapter 6.
`role-link`	A pointer to the role name defined in the module using the `security-role` element.

D.1.2 assembly-descriptor

You can use the `assembly-descriptor` element to specify declarative transactions, security role and method permissions, and interceptor binding.

security-role

Corresponding annotation: `@javax.annotation.security.DeclareRoles`

Used to define the security roles used in the application. This is similar to the `@DeclareRoles` annotation.

Element/Attribute Name	Description
`role-name`	Name of the security role.

method-permission

Corresponding annotation: `@javax.annotation.security.RolesAllowed`

Defines the security for EJB methods and signifies which roles are allowed to execute which methods.

Element/Attribute Name	Description
ejb-name	Name of the EJB. Must match the `ejb-name` defined for an EJB or the `name` element of the `@Stateless` and `@Stateful` annotations.
method	Name of the EJB method for which security is defined.
role-name	Name of the role allowed executing the method.
unchecked	Specifies that all roles be allowed to execute the method.

container-transaction

Defines the transaction settings for different EJB methods. Equivalent of the `@TransactionAttribute` annotation.

Element/Attribute Name	Description
ejb-name	Name of the EJB. Must match the `ejb-name` defined for an EJB or the `name` element of the `@Stateless` and `@Stateful` annotations.
method	Name of the EJB method.
trans-attribute	Specifies the `Transaction` attribute of the method. Valid values are `Required`, `RequiresNew`, `NotSupported`, `Supports`, `Never`, and `Mandatory`.

interceptor-binding

Defines interceptors either at the module (default interceptor), class, or method level. Similar to the `@javax.interceptor.Interceptors` annotation.

Element/Attribute Name	Description
ejb-name	Name of the EJB. Must match the `ejb-name` defined for an EJB or the `name` element of the `@Stateless` and `@Stateful` annotations. It can have the wildcard value `*`, which is used to define interceptors that are bound to all beans in the EJB-JAR.
method	Name of the EJB method.

continued on next page

Element/Attribute Name	Description
interceptor-class	Name of the interceptor class.
exclude-default-interceptors	Specifies that default interceptors are not to be applied to a bean-class and/or business method.
exclude-class-interceptors	Specifies that default interceptors are not to be applied to a bean-class and/or business method.

exclude-list

Corresponding annotation: @javax.annotation.security.DenyAll

Lists the names of the methods customers are not allowed to execute.

Element/Attribute Name	Description
ejb-name	Name of the EJB. Must match the ejb-name defined for an EJB or the name element of the @Stateless and @Stateful annotations.
Method	Name of the EJB method being marked as uncallable.

application-exception

Corresponding annotation: @javax.ejb.ApplicationException

Defines an application exception.

Element/Attribute Name	Description
exception-class	Fully qualified name of the exception class.
Rollback	Specifies whether the container should roll back the transaction before forwarding the exception to the client.

D.2 persistence.xml reference

The persistence.xml file defines a persistence unit. It can be packaged in an EJB-JAR module, web module, or a standard JAR file. This is the only descriptor that is required by Java EE 5. There are no corresponding annotations for persistence.xml.

You can refer to the schema of persistence.xml at http://java.sun.com/xml/ns/persistence/persistence_1_0.xsd.

persistence-unit elements

The following table describes two different elements in `persistence.xml` for the `persistence-unit` element.

Element/Attribute Name	Description
name	Name of the persistence unit. This name is used in applications to either inject or establish a reference to a persistence unit by using the `@PersistenceContext` and `@PersistenceUnit` annotations or the `persistence-context-ref` or `persistence-unit-ref` descriptor element in a client application.
transaction-type	Transaction type used for the persistence unit. Possible values are `JTA` or `RESOURCE_LOCAL`.

persistence-unit subelements

The following table describes all subelements of the `persistence-unit` element.

Element/Attribute Name	Description
provider	Name of the factory class of the JPA provider.
jta-data-source	JTA `DataSource` that points to the database that contains underlying tables for the entities configured in the persistence unit.
non-jta-data-source	Non-JTA `DataSource` that points to the database that contains underlying tables for the entities configured in the persistence unit. A `non-jta-resource` will be used when `transaction-type` is `RESOURCE_LOCAL`.
mapping-file	Name of the mapping file that contains O/R mapping info.
jar-file	Lists the additional JAR file that contains entities.
class	Identifies entity classes. Entity classes must be annotated with the `@Entity` annotation.
exclude-unlisted-classes	When set to `true` it will include entities included in the class element.
properties	A name-value pair of vendor-specific properties. Vendor-specific properties may include caching, automatic table creation directives, etc.

D.3 *orm.xml (O/R mapping metadata)reference*

This file defines the O/R mapping metadata for entities. It overrides any mapping metadata defined using annotations.

You can reference the XML schema for O/R mapping at http://java.sun.com/xml/ns/persistence/orm_1_0.xsd.

persistence-unit-metadata

You can use `persistence-unit-metadata` to specify metadata for the persistence unit. Note that it is not just for mapping a file where it is specified. It has two elements: `persistence-unit-defaults` and `metadata-complete`. When the `metadata-complete` element is set to `true`, any mappings using annotations will be ignored.

This table lists all elements in the `persistence-unit-defaults` element.

Element/Attribute Name	Description
schema	Database schema that contains the tables to which entities in the persistence unit are mapped.
catalog	Database catalog that contains the tables to which entities in the persistence unit are mapped.
access	Access type for all entities in the persistence unit, i.e., field or property.
cascade-persist	Specifies cascade persist for relationships for all entities.
entity-listeners	Default entity listeners for the persistence unit.

named-query

Corresponding annotation: `@javax.persistence.NamedQuery`

A named query element is used to define a named query using JPQL. The named query is global to the persistence unit.

Element/Attribute Name	Description
name	Name of the named query. Must be unique in the persistence unit.
query	Query in JPQL.
hint	One or more vendor-specific query hints.

named-native-query

Corresponding annotation: the @javax.persistence.NamedNativeQuery

A named native query element is used to define a named query using native SQL.

Element/Attribute Name	Description
name	Name of the named query. Must be unique in the persistence unit.
query	Query in native SQL.
hint	One or more vendor-specific query hints.
result-class	Name of the entity class returned as a result of the native query.
result-set-mapping	Name of ResultSetMapping returned by the query.

sql-result-set-mapping

Corresponding annotation: @javax.persistence.SqlResultSetMapping

A native query may return a result set mapping that is defined using multiple entity classes.

Element/Attribute Name	Description
name	Name of the sql-result-set-mapping.
entity-result	Name of the entity class.
column-result	Columns returned in the query.

sequence-generator

Corresponding annotation: @javax.persistence.SequenceGenerator

A sequence generator is used for automatic generation of numbers using a database sequence. It is defined globally and may be used with one or more entities in the persistence unit.

Element/Attribute Name	Description
name	Name of the sequence generator.
sequence-name	Name of the database sequence.
initial-value	Initial value generated when the sequence generator is used.

continued on next page

Element/Attribute Name	Description
allocation-size	The amount the JPA provider will increase while allocating sequence numbers.

table-generator

Corresponding annotation: @javax.persistence.TableGenerator

A table generator is used for automatic generation of numbers using a sequence table. It is defined globally and may be used with one or more entities in the persistence unit.

Element/Attribute Name	Description
name	Name of the table generator.
table	Name of the sequence table.
catalog	Catalog containing the table.
schema	Schema containing the table.
pk-column-name	Name of the primary key column in the table.
value-column-name	Name of the column that stores the primary key value.
pk-column-value	Column that stores a value to distinguish table generators from one another.
initial-value	Initial value.
allocation-size	The amount the JPA provider will increase while allocating primary key values.

mapped-superclass

Corresponding annotation: @javax.persistence.MappedSuperClass. Most subelements correspond to an annotation.

The mapped-superclass element has three attributes and several subelements. The attributes class, access-type, and meta-data-complete are used to specify the name of the mapped superclass, access type (i.e., field or property), and whether the XML metadata specified is complete.

Element/Attribute Name	Description
id-class	Name of the primary key class if used.
exclude-default-listeners	Set to TRUE if you want to exclude firing of the default listener for the entity.
exclude-superclass-listeners	Set to TRUE if you want to exclude firing of the superclass listener for the entity.
entity-listeners	Defines the entity listeners for the superclass.
pre-persist	Name of the prepersist method in the entity class.
post-persist	Name of the postpersist method in the entity class.
pre-remove	Name of the preremove method in the entity class.
post-remove	Name of the postremove method in the entity class.
pre-update	Name of the preupdate method in the entity class.
post-update	Name of the postupdate method in the entity class.
post-load	Name of the postload method in the entity class.
attributes	Defines the attributes/persistence fields of the mapped class.

attributes

The attributes element is used to define mapping of persistence and association fields.

There is no equivalent annotation for the attributes element; each element of attributes corresponds to an annotation.

Element/Attribute Name	Description
id-class	Designates the primary key class.
id	Designates the id field of the entity.
basic	Designates a field to be a direct-to-field mapping.
version	Defines the attribute to the version field used for optimistic locking.
many-to-one	Defines the field to be many-to-one association.
one-to-many	Defines the field to be one-to-many association.
one-to-one	Defines the field to be one-to-one association.

continued on next page

Element/Attribute Name	Description
many-to-many	Defines the field to be many-to-many association.
embedded	Defines the attribute to be an embedded field.
transient	Designates the field to be transient.

basic

The basic element is used to define direct-to-field mapping, and the following table lists subelements of the basic element. It is equivalent to the @Basic annotation, and most elements have corresponding annotations.

Element/Attribute Name	Description
name	Name of the persistence field.
fetch	Specifies the fetch type, i.e., LAZY or EAGER.
optional	Set to true if the field is optional.
column	Name of the column.
lob	Field is LOB type.
temporal	Time or Date type.
enumerated	Enumerated type.

many-to-one

Used to map a many-to-one relationship between two entities. The following table lists elements and attributes of the basic element. It is equivalent to the @ManyToOne annotation. The join-column and join-table elements correspond to the @JoinColumn and @JoinTable annotations, respectively.

Element/Attribute Name	Description
name	Name of the association field.
target-entity	Entity class being joined.
cascade	Specifies the cascade type for the associated entities.
fetch	Specifies the fetch type, i.e., LAZY or EAGER.

continued on next page

Element/Attribute Name	Description
optional	Specifies whether relationship is optional.
join-column	Defines join column.
join-table	Specifies the association table if any.

one-to-one

Used to map a one-to-one relationship between two entities. It is equivalent to the @OneToOne annotation. The join-column and the primary-key-join-column elements correspond to the @JoinColumn and @PrimaryKeyJoinColumn annotations, respectively.

Element/Attribute Name	Description
name	Name of the association field.
target-entity	Entity class being joined.
cascade	Specifies the cascade type for the associated entities.
fetch	Specifies the fetch type, i.e., LAZY or EAGER.
optional	Specifies whether the relationship is optional.
mapped-by	Designates the owner of the relationship.
join-column	Defines join column.
join-table	Specifies the association table if any.
primary-key-join-column	Defines join column if joined by the primary key.

one-to-many

Used to map a one-to-many relationship between two entities. It is equivalent to @OneToMany annotation. The join-column, join-table, order-by, and map-key elements correspond to the @JoinColumn, @JoinTable, @OrderBy, and @MapKey annotations, respectively.

Element/Attribute Name	Description
name	Name of the association field.
target-entity	Entity class being joined.

continued on next page

Element/Attribute Name	Description
cascade	Specifies the cascade type for the associated entities.
fetch	Specifies the fetch type, i.e., LAZY or EAGER.
mapped-by	Designates the nonowning side of the relationship.
join-column	Defines join column.
join-table	Specifies the association table if any.
order-by	Specifies the order in which the collection of entities is retrieved.
map-key	Specifies the map key.

many-to-many

Used to map a one-to-many relationship between two entities. It is equivalent to @ManyToMany annotation. The join-column, join-table, order-by, and map-key elements correspond to the @JoinColumn, @JoinTable, @OrderBy, and @MapKey annotations, respectively.

Element/Attribute Name	Description
name	Name of the association field.
target-entity	Entity class being joined.
cascade	Specifies the cascade type for the associated entities.
fetch	Specifies the fetch type, i.e., LAZY or EAGER.
mapped-by	Designates the nonowning side of the relationship.
join-column	Defines join column.
join-table	Specifies the association table if any.
order-by	Specifies the order in which the collection of entities is retrieved.
map-key	Specifies the mapping keys for an entity association of type java.util.Map.

column

Used to define column mapping for a persistence field. It is equivalent to the @Column annotation.

Element/Attribute Name	Description
name	Name of the column.
unique	True if the column value is unique.
nullable	Designates whether the column is a nullable or mandatory column. Useful for automatic table generation.
insertable	Set to `true` if the column is included in the `INSERT` statement generated by the provider. Useful when the column is populated by triggers, default values, etc.
updatable	Set to `true` if the column is included in the `UPDATE` statement generated by the provider. Typically useful for primary keys.
column-definition	Definition of column. Useful for automatic table generation.
table	Name of the table to which the column belongs. Typically useful for an entity that is mapped to multiple tables.
length	Length of column for `char`/`varchar2` types.
precision	Precision of numeric type columns.
scale	Scale of numeric type columns.

join-column

Used to show the relationship between two persisted entities. It is equivalent to the `@JoinColumn` annotation.

Element/Attribute Name	Description
name	Name of the column.
referenced-column-name	Name of the column in the referenced table.
unique	Specifies whether the join column stores unique values.
nullable	Specifies whether the relationship column is nullable or mandatory.
insertable	Set to `true` if the column is included in the `INSERT` statement generated by the provider.
updatable	Set to `true` if the column is included in the `UPDATE` statement generated by the provider.
column-definition	Definition of column. Useful for automatic table generation.
table	Name of the target table name being joined.

primary-key-join-column

Used either for a one-to-one relationship or for joining secondary tables for an entity. It is equivalent to @PrimaryKeyJoinColumn annotation.

Element/Attribute Name	Description
name	Name of the primary key column.
referenced-column-name	Name of the referenced primary key column in the join table.
column-definition	Defines primary key column. Used for table creation.

join-table

Defines the association table for a many-to-many or one-to-many relationship.

Element/Attribute Name	Description
join-column	Defines join column for the owning side of the relationship.
inverse-join-column	Defines join column for the inverse side of the relationship.
unique-constraint	Unique constraint of the join table. Used for automatic table creation.
name	Name of the join table.
catalog	Name of catalog where the table is stored.
schema	Name of the schema where the table is stored.

generator-value

Used to define the generator used with a persistence field. It is equivalent to the @GeneratedValue annotation.

Element/Attribute Name	Description
strategy	The strategy used to generate values. Valid values are AUTO, SEQUENCE, TABLE, and IDENTITY.
generator	Name of the generator used.

discriminator-column

Used to define the discriminator column used for defining entity inheritance strategies. It is equivalent to the @DiscriminatorColumn annotation.

Element/Attribute Name	Description
name	Name of the discriminator column.
discriminator-type	Type of discriminator (STRING, CHAR, INTEGER).
column-definition	Defines column. Used for automatic table creation.
length	Length of discriminator column.

embedded

Defines an embedded object defined in an entity. It is equivalent to the @Embedded annotation.

Element/Attribute Name	Description
name	Name of embedded object.
attribute-override	Specified if the entity overrides any attribute defined in the original embeddable object.

entity

Equivalent to the @Entity annotation. This is the most important element and defines a persistence object, i.e., an entity. Most subelements such as name, class, access, and metadata-complete all correspond to a specific annotation.

Element/Attribute Name	Description
name	Name of the entity. This name is used in the queries.
class	Name of the entity class.
access	Access type for the entity.
table	Name of the primary table the entity is mapped to.
secondary-table	Secondary table for the entity.
id-class	Name of the primary key class.
primary-key-join-column	Primary key join mapping for the joined entities.
inheritance	Inheritance type.
discriminator-value	Discriminator value if a subclass of entity inheritance.

continued on next page

Element/Attribute Name	Description
discriminator-column	Discriminator column.
sequence-generator	Name of the sequence generator if values are automatically generated.
table-generator	Name of the table generator if values are automatically generated.
named-query	Named query definition for the entities.
named-native-query	Named native query definition for the entities.
sql-result-set-mapping	SQL result set mapping defined for the entity.
exclude-default-listeners	Set to TRUE if you want to exclude firing of the default listener for the entity.
exclude-superclass-listeners	Set to TRUE if you want to exclude firing of the superclass listener for the entity.
entity-listeners	Defines the callback listeners for the entity.
pre-persist	Name of the prepersist method in the entity class.
post-persist	Name of the postpersist method in the entity class.
pre-remove	Name of the preremove method in the entity class.
post-remove	Name of the postremove method in the entity class.
pre-update	Name of the preupdate method in the entity class.
post-update	Name of the postupdate method in the entity class.
post-load	Name of the postload method in the entity class.
attribute-override	Defines any column mapping being overridden from the mapped superclass or embeddable class.
association-override	Defines any association mapping being overridden from the mapped superclass or embeddable class.
attributes	Defines the mapping of persistence fields of the entity.
metadata-complete	Designates whether XML has complete metadata mapping.

embeddable

Defines an embeddable object. It is equivalent to the `@Embeddable` annotation.

Element/Attribute Name	Description
attributes	Defines the mapping of persistence fields of the embeddable object.
class	Name of the embeddable class.
access	Access type of embeddable class.
metadata-complete	Designates whether XML has complete metadata mapping.

E

Installing and configuring the Java EE 5 SDK

Throughout the book, we evaded the topic of installing application servers and configuring our sample application inside an installed server. We avoided this subject for two reasons. First, this book is about the EJB 3 standard and we didn't want to slant this book toward a specific application-server implementation. Second, providing application-server-specific instructions is a tricky business at best. This is because application-server implementations change quite often, making instructions out of date. This is especially true for a potentially long-lived technology like EJB 3.

However, we don't want to leave you completely high and dry, even if it means providing instructions that may not be up-to-date when you read this. You should treat the material in this appendix as a general guideline more than anything else. We'll provide the basic instructions for installing and configuring the Action-Bazaar application using the Java EE SDK based on the GlassFish application server, which seems like an obvious choice since it's the "official" reference implementation for Java EE 5. Note that in no sense do we endorse GlassFish as something you should be using for anything other than the purposes of learning EJB 3 with this book.

Also note that the website for this book, www.manning.com/panda, contains up-to-date instructions for installing and configuring all popular application servers that support EJB 3. The instructions in this appendix are for a Windows machine, but they can be easily adapted for any other operating system, such as Linux.

The installation and configuration instructions can be broken down into three distinct steps:

1   Installing the Java EE 5 SDK
2   Configuring and running the application server and database
3   Installing and running the ActionBazaar application

E.1   *Installing the Java EE 5 SDK*

Sun bundles a GlassFish distribution with the Java EE 5 SDK. The first logical step is to download and install the SDK from the Sun site.

1   You can download the Java EE 5 SDK from http://java.sun.com/javaee/ technologies/index.jsp. You want the Java EE 5 SDK Update 2 (or the latest available for download). You can download the SDK with or without a JDK. Java EE 5 requires Java SE 5 or higher. The safest bet is to use the version that comes bundled with a JDK. This version of the downloaded file is named something like java_ee_sdk-5*-windows.exe.

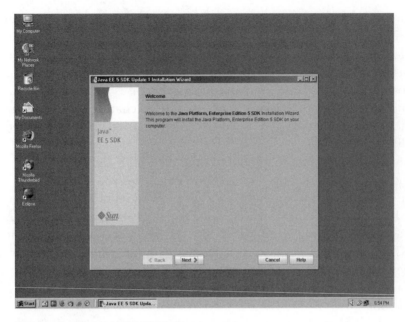

Figure E.1   The Java EE 5 SDK welcome screen

2   Double-click on the downloaded executable and you will see the screen in figure E.1.

3   Click Next on this screen to start the installation process.

4   The next screen shows the licensing agreement (figure E.2). Click Yes to accept the agreement and click Next.

5   As shown in figure E.3, the next screen prompts you to enter an installation directory for the application server. Unless there is a specific reason not to do so, accept the default.

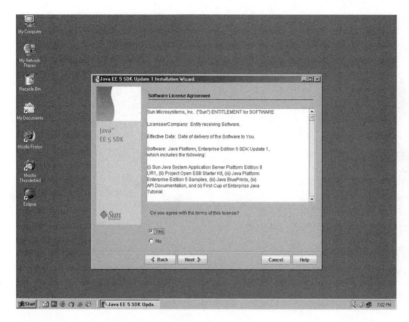

Figure E.2   The Java EE 5 SDK license screen

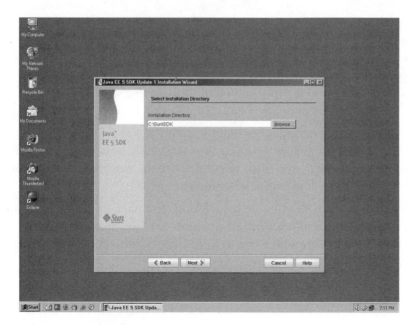

Figure E.3   The Select Installation Directory screen. Unless there is a reason not to do so, accept the defaults here.

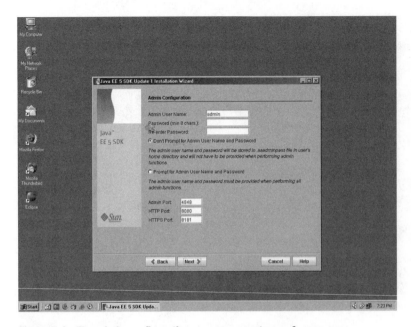

Figure E.4 **The admin configuration screen prompts you for server administration details.**

6   The next screen (figure E.4) prompts you for some administrative details for the application server such as Admin User Name, Password, and the ports the server should use. Accept the default username, enter a password (twice), and accept the default port settings.

7   The next screen (figure E.5) prompts you with some installation options. You'll need to change a few defaults here. You should deselect the Register Application Server option unless you really want to go through a few more tedious screens. Also, select the Create Windows Service option to make server startup happen behind the scenes.

8   The next screen displays an installation summary, as shown in figure E.6. Click Next to start the install process. The installation is not short, so you'll have to wait a bit for it to finish. Feel free to go water the plants!

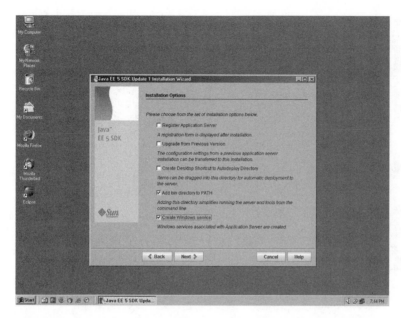

Figure E.5   Some of the defaults on the Installations Options screen need to be changed.

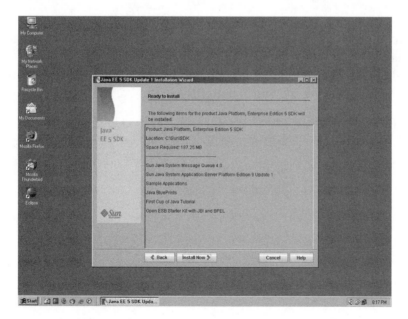

Figure E.6   The Ready to Install screen summarizes all of the options you've selected so far.

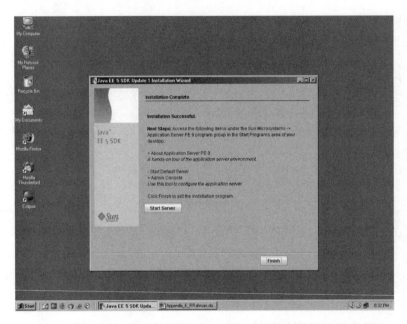

Figure E.7   You will need to start the server from this screen before closing it.

9   After the installation finishes, you'll see the Installation Complete screen
     in figure E.7. Don't be too quick to dismiss this screen. You must actually
     start the server by clicking the Start Server button on this screen. It will
     take a moment for the server to start. Once it does, you can close this
     screen by clicking the Finish button.

This completes the installation of the Java EE 5 SDK. The next major step is to
configure GlassFish in preparation for deploying the ActionBazaar application.

E.2 *Running the application server and database*

At this point, you should verify that the application server is running. You can do this by accessing the built-in web-based administrative interface.

1 The administrative interface runs on port 4848 of your local machine. To access it, go to Start > Programs > Sun Microsystems > Application Server PE 9 > Admin Console. The first screen you see is the login interface (figure E.8). Enter the admin username and password you specified during installation here.

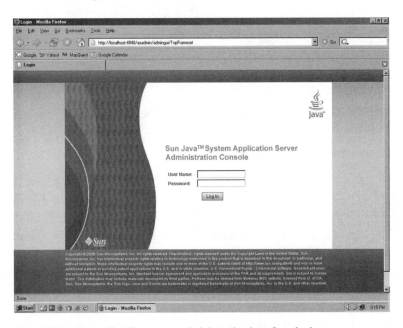

Figure E.8   The application server administrative interface login screen

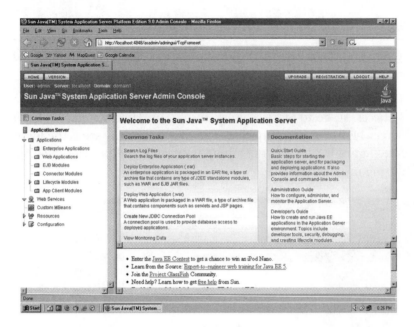

Figure E.9   Spend some time exploring the admin console.

2   The Server Admin Console home page shown in figure E.9 appears. Take a moment to explore the administration console before moving on.

3   The Java EE 5 SDK comes with the default Apache Derby database. To simplify matters, you can use this database for the ActionBazaar application. You must start the database to install and configure the sample code. To start the database, navigate to Start > Programs > Sun Microsystems > Application Server PE 9 > Start Java DB, as shown in figure E.10.

4   The Derby database will start in a command-line window. After the database starts, you'll see a screen similar to the one in figure E.11. By default, the Derby database is started in the background. You can safely close the command window by pressing the Enter key at the prompt.

Now that both GlassFish and the Derby database are up and running, you are ready to install and run the ActionBazaar application.

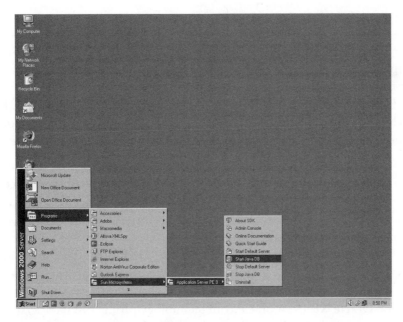

Figure E.10 Select Start > Programs > Sun Microsystems > Application Server
PE 9 > Start Java DB.

Figure E.11 The Derby DB startup command-line interface

E.3 *Installing and running ActionBazaar*

As you've seen, you can install and configure an application from the console. To make things a little easier on you, we are going to take a slightly simpler route. The ActionBazaar source code comes with Ant build scripts to deploy the application. If you are unfamiliar with Apache Ant, you may read up on it at http://ant.apache.org. Ant is a way of automating common project configuration and deployment tasks that you would typically perform manually. Feel free to explore the XML Ant scripts we have supplied.

1   The first step to installing the application is to download the source code bundle from http://manning.com/panda/. The source file bundle is named codeexamples-javaeesdk.zip. Unzip the source into any directory, such as c:\ejb_3_in_action\code_examples.

We assume that you will be using the Derby database shipped with GlassFish, so the data sources in the Ant setup script are for Derby. However, you could use any other database, such as MySQL, PostgreSQL, or the free Oracle XE (www.oracle.com/technology/products/database/xe/index.html) database. You'll simply need to make the appropriate changes to the Ant tasks.

If you plan to use a database other than Derby, don't forget to copy the JDBC driver to the %RI_HOME%\lib directory and restart RI server. For example, if you want to use the Oracle XE database, then copy the ojdbc14.jar JDBC driver to the server library directory.

2   Edit the common.xml file in the code examples directory root and change the admin password for GlassFish. If you are using a database other than Derby, you'll need to change the jdbc.url and other database information in the build.xml file in the code examples root.

3   Open a command window. Type in the following:

```
set J2EE_HOME=C:\Sun\SDK                             Where GlassFish is installed
set JAVA_HOME=C:\Program Files\java\jdk1.5           Where JDK is installed
cd C:\ejb_3_in_action\code_examples
ant
```

This will prepare data sources and JMS resources necessary for the database. The output of the Ant task is shown in figure E.12.

If you're using another database, such as Oracle XE, then you can configure the Java EE SDK (or reference implementation) server by typing

```
ant configure-xe
```

Figure E.12   The output from the command-line Ant task that sets up the data sources and JMS resources necessary for the ActionBazaar application

4   You are now ready to start deploying the examples for each chapter. Each chapter example is packaged into a separate application. To deploy an example application, move into the directory for the chapter and run the Ant task. For example, to deploy the application for chapter 1, run

```
cd chapter1
ant
```

This Ant task will compile the classes, package them as an EJB-JAR/EAR, and then deploy the application into the GlassFish server.

5   You can run the deployed application by typing

```
ant run
```

The output printed by the EJB will be printed to the log file of the application server. In our case, the contents of the C:\Sun\SDK\domains\ domain1\logs\server.log will have the entry shown in figure E.13.

A very interesting thing to consider is how the deployed application— including the data sources and the JMS resources—looks in the admin console. If you go back to the admin console, you'll see something similar to figure E.14.

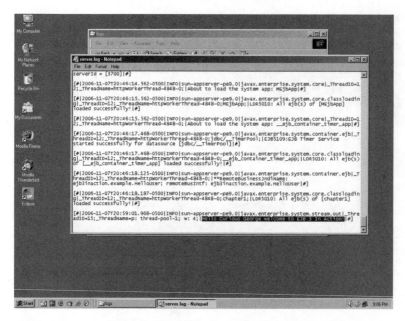

Figure E.13   The output of running the deployed application for chapter 1

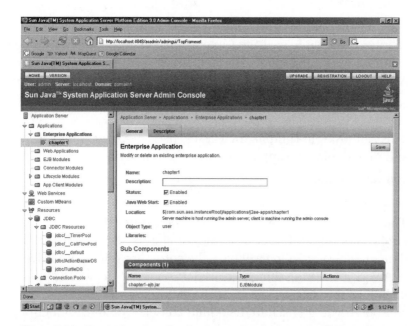

Figure E.14   The deployed application for chapter 1 in the admin console

You can explore the code further by opening it up in an IDE. At the time of this writing, NetBeans and Oracle JDeveloper had good support for EJB 3 and Java EE 5 in general. However, it is very likely that other popular IDEs such as Eclipse will catch up very soon.

Resources

Print resources

Bauer, Christian and Gavin King. (2004) *Hibernate in Action*. New York: Manning Publications.

Crane, Dave and Eric Pascarello with Darren James. (2005) *Ajax in Action*. New York: Manning.

Evans, Eric. (2003) *Domain-Driven Design: Tackling Complexity in the Heart of Software*. Boston: Addison-Wesley.

Fowler, Martin. (2002) *Patterns of Enterprise Applications Architecture*. Boston: Addison-Wesley.

Laddad, Ramnivas. (2003) *AspectJ in Action*. New York: Manning Publications

Richardson, Chris. (2006) *POJOs in Action*. New York: Manning Publications.

Walls, Craig and Ryan Breidenbach. (2005) *Spring in Action*. New York: Manning Publications.

Online resources

"Ajax: A New Approach to Web Applications," by Jesse James Garrett: www.adaptivepath.com/publications/essays/archives/000385.php

Apache Ant Project: http://ant.apache.org

Apache Maven Project: http://maven.apache.org/

Apache Web Services Project: http://ws.apache.org/

Catalog of Java patterns: http://java.sun.com/blueprints/corej2eepatterns/Patterns/index.html

"Classloading in Oracle9*i*AS Containers for J2EE," by Bryan Atsatt and Debu Panda: www.oracle.com/technology/tech/java/oc4j/pdf/ClassLoadingInOC4J_WP.pdf

Core J2EE Patterns – Data Access Objects: http://java.sun.com/blueprints/corej2eepatterns/Patterns/DataAccessObject.html

Eclipse Dali Project: www.eclipse.org/dali/

Essays on O/R mapping by Scott W. Ambler: www.ambysoft.com/essays/mappingObjects.html

IBM's "SOA and Web Services" page: www-128.ibm.com/developerworks/webservices

"Inversion of Control Containers and the Dependency Injection Pattern," by Martin Fowler: www.martinfowler.com/articles/injection.html

Java BluePrints: http://java.sun.com/reference/blueprints/index.html

Java 5 Metadata Annotations: http://java.sun.com/j2se/1.5.0/docs/guide/language/annotations.html

"Making the Most of Java's Metadata," by Jason Hunter: www.oracle.com/technology/pub/articles/hunter_meta.html

"Migrate J2EE Applications for EJB 3.0," by Debu Panda: www.ftponline.com/javapro/2005_07/magazine/features/dpanda/

"Migrating JDBC Data Access Objects to Use EJB3," by Debu Panda: www.theserverside.com/tt/articles/article.tss?l=MigratingJDBC

Representational State Transfer: http://en.wikipedia.org/wiki/Representational_State_Transfer

"Standardizing Java Persistence with the EJB3 Java Persistence API," by Debu Panda: www.onjava.com/pub/a/onjava/2006/05/17/standardizing-with-ejb3-java-persistence-api.html

W3C Consortium on web services: www.w3c.org/2002/ws

Web Services and Other Distributed Technologies, Microsoft Developer Network: http://msdn.microsoft.com/webservices/

Windows Communication Foundation: http://msdn.microsoft.com/winfx/technologies/communication/default.aspx

WS-I (Web Services Interoperability) Organization: www.ws-i.org

XDoclet: Attribute-Oriented Programming: http://xdoclet.sourceforge.net/xdoclet/index.html

Specifications and Sun websites for Java technologies

Guidelines, Patterns, and Code for End-to-End Java Applications: http://java.sun.com/blueprints/code/namingconventions.html

Hierarchy for Package javax.persistence: http://java.sun.com/products/persistence/java-doc-1_0-fr/javax/persistence/package-tree.html

Java API for XML Messaging (JAXM): http://java.sun.com/webservices/jaxm/

Java Archive (JAR) Files: http://java.sun.com/j2se/1.5.0/docs/guide/jar/

Java Authentication and Authorization Service (JAAS): http://java.sun.com/products/jaas/

Java Message Service Specification API: http://java.sun.com/products/jms/docs.html

Java Naming and Directory Interface (JNDI): http://java.sun.com/products/jndi/

Java Servlet Technology: http://java.sun.com/products/servlet/

Java Transaction API (JTA): http://java.sun.com/products/jta/

JSR 220: Enterprise JavaBeans 3.0: www.jcp.org/en/jsr/detail?id=220

JSR 222: Java Architecture for XML Binding (JAXB) 2.0: www.jcp.org/en/jsr/detail?id=222

JSR 224: Java API for XML-Based Web Services (JAX-WS) 2.0: http://jcp.org/en/jsr/detail?id=224

JSR 250: Common Annotations for the Java Platform: http://www.jcp.org/en/jsr/detail?id=250

Remote Method Invocation (RMI): http://java.sun.com/products/jdk/rmi/

Schema for `ejb-jar.xml`: http://java.sun.com/xml/ns/javaee/ejb-jar_3_0.xsd

Schema for `persistence.xml`: http://java.sun.com/xml/ns/persistence/persistence_1_0.xsd

index

MORE TITLES FROM MANNING

ANT in Action: Second Edition of
Java Development with ANT
    by Steve Loughran and Erik Hatcher
    ISBN: 1-932394-80-X
    670 pages
    $49.99
    June 2007

Spring in Action: Second Edition
    by Craig Walls
        with Ryan Breidenbach
    ISBN: 1-933988-13-4
    600 pages
    $49.99
    July 2007

For ordering information go to www.manning.com

Groovy in Action
   by Dierk König
   with Andrew Glover, Paul King,
      Guillaume Laforge and Jon Skeet
   foreword by James Gosling
   ISBN: 1-932394-84-2
   696 pages
   $49.99
   January 2007

Windows PowerShell in Action
   by Bruce Payette
   foreword by Jeffrey Snover
   ISBN: 1932394-90-7
   576 pages
   $44.99
   February 2007

For ordering information go to www.manning.com

MORE TITLES FROM MANNING

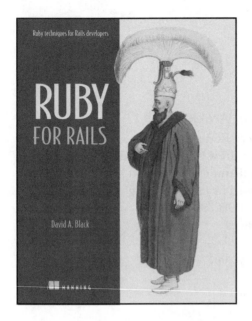

Ruby for Rails: Ruby Techniques for Rails Developers
    by David A. Black
    ISBN: 1-932394-69-9
    532 pages
    $44.95
    May 2006

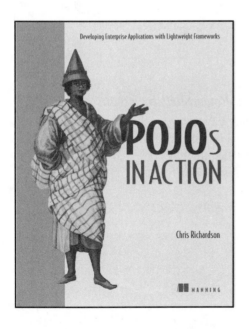

POJOs in Action
    by Chris Richardson
    ISBN: 1-932394-58-3
    592 pages
    $44.95
    January 2006

For ordering information go to www.manning.com

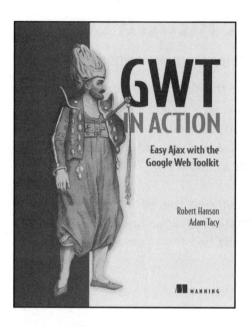

GWT in Action
  Easy Ajax with the Google Web Toolkit
  by Robert Hanson and Adam Tacy
  ISBN: 1-933988-23-1
  600 pages
  $49.99
  June 2007

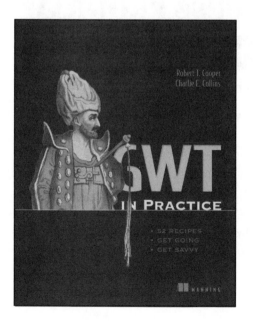

GWT in Practice
  by Robert Cooper and Charles Collins
  ISBN: 1-933988-29-0
  450 pages
  $44.99
  August 2007

MANNING EBOOK PROGRAM

All ebooks are 50% off the price of the print edition!

In the spring of 2000 Manning became the first publisher to offer ebook versions of all our new titles as a way to get customers the information they need quickly and easily. We continue to publish ebook versions of all our new releases, and every ebook is priced at 50% off the print version!

Go to www.manning.com/panda to download the ebook version of this book and have the information at your fingertips wherever you might be.

MANNING EARLY ACCESS PROGRAM

Get Early Chapters Now!

In 2003 we launched MEAP, our groundbreaking Early Access Program, to give customers who can't wait the opportunity to read chapters as they are written and receive the book when it is released. Because these are "early" chapters, your feedback will also help shape the final manuscript.

Our entire MEAP title list is always changing and you can find the current titles at www.manning.com